Oxford Anthology
of Western Music

Oxford Anthology *of* Western Music

Volume Two
The Mid-Eighteenth Century
to the Late Nineteenth Century

Klára Móricz & David E. Schneider

New York   Oxford
OXFORD UNIVERSITY PRESS

Oxford University Press, Inc., publishes works that further Oxford University's objective of excellence in research, scholarship, and education.

Oxford New York
Auckland Cape Town Dar es Salaam Hong Kong Karachi
Kuala Lumpur Madrid Melbourne Mexico City Nairobi
New Delhi Shanghai Taipei Toronto

With offices in
Argentina Austria Brazil Chile Czech Republic France Greece
Guatemala Hungary Italy Japan Poland Portugal Singapore
South Korea Switzerland Thailand Turkey Ukraine Vietnam

For titles covered by Section 112 of the US Higher Education
Opportunity Act, please visit www.oup.com/us/he for the latest
information about pricing and alternate formats

Published by Oxford University Press, Inc.
198 Madison Avenue, New York, New York 10016
http://www.oup.com

ISBN 978-0-19-976826-4 (paper)

Printing number: 9 8 7 6 5 4 3 2 1

Printed in the United States of America
on acid-free paper

Contents

Preface

This volume serves as a companion anthology to the late-eighteenth- and nineteenth-century portion of the textbook *Oxford History of Western Music*, College Edition, by Richard Taruskin and Christopher H. Gibbs. With the essays that introduce each of the scores, we have also aimed to make it possible for the anthology to stand on its own as a text for courses, both historical and analytical, on what is commonly referred to as music of the "Classical" and "Romantic" periods. A few of the essays are edited excerpts from Richard Taruskin's six-volume *Oxford History of Western Music*; a larger number are newly written for this anthology. Although mainly analytical, in content, the essays also provide historical context for the works discussed. Because many of the works in this volume will be the students' first encounter with important formal concepts such as "sonata form," some of the essays are extensive in analytical detail.

In addition to a number of landmark works likely to be found in many historical surveys, we have included important pieces that are rarely anthologized—Piccinni's *La buona figliuola*, Strauss's "Blue Danube" Waltz, Smetana's *The Moldau*, and Glinka's *Kamarinskaya*, to name only a few. Our selection begins with Wilhelm Friedemann Bach and ends with Puccini; it features forty-four different composers from seven different countries. In keeping with Taruskin's original text, we have included a large selection of Russian music, an extended excerpt of a French grand opera, and several examples of "Orientalist" compositions.

To save space and to enable students to analyze works more easily, the scores provided are sometimes piano reductions, although most pieces are given in their original full scoring. For those unfamiliar with reading full scores, we provide a table of foreign names of instruments (and their abbreviations) that occur in the volume as well as a note about reading transposing instruments (see "Note on Score Reading," immediately following this Preface). We have added measure numbers to each score, starting with measure 1 at the beginning of the portion we provide. References to specific pitches in the analytical text are given according to the system in which middle C is designated as c^1 (the octave below is c, the octave above is c^2). For works including sung texts in languages other than English, we provide our own literal translation after the introductory essay. When translations are included in the score, they are singing translations and not necessarily reliable for conveying the precise meaning of the original.

Since it has become easy to look up the exact meaning of terms in this age of Internet dictionaries, we have not included a glossary of terms. We do, however, provide an Index of Names and an Index of Terms, which enable students to look up the terms in the context of the essays in the anthology.

We are happy to acknowledge the many individuals who have helped this volume to come to life. First and foremost we are indebted to Richard Taruskin, whose six-volume *Oxford History of Western Music* has served as a basis and inspiration for the present anthology. Christopher Gibbs, coauthor of the textbook version of Taruskin's work, has been an ideal collaborator. We are particularly thankful to Beth Levy (UC Davis), who read through our entire manuscript and made many insightful comments. We are also much indebted to the following musicological colleagues who have fielded questions large and small, helped us with translations, and provided feedback on our work: Stephen Arthur Allen (Rider University), Laura Basini (Sacramento State), Matthew Baumer (Indiana University of Pennsylvania), David Breckbill (Doane College), Mary Hunter (Bowdoin College), Philip Gossett (University of Chicago), Gregory Harwood (Georgia Southern University), Kevin Karnes (Emory University), Ben Korstvedt (Clark University), Jim Leve (Northern Arizona University), Stephen Meyer (Syracuse University), Anna Nisnevich (University of Pittsburgh), Seow-Chin Ong (University of Louisville), Heather Platt (Ball State University), Jay Rosenblatt (University of Arizona), David Schulenberg (Wagner College), László Somfai (Institute for Musicology, Budapest, Hungary), and Michael Zwiebach (San Francisco Conservatory of Music). Our colleagues Jay Kaplan and Laure Katsaros of the Department of French and Christian Rogowski of the Department of German at Amherst College have also provided invaluable assistance in checking our translations. Any mistakes that may remain are our own.

At Amherst College we are blessed with two exceptionally fine music librarians, Jane Beebe and Ann Maggs, both of whom have helped us locate hard-to-find scores and provided all manner of practical support. We are also grateful to Janet Spongberg of the Smith College Josten Arts Library for accommodating a number of our special requests. A project like this would also not have been possible without the work of Amherst College's extraordinarily patient interlibrary loan staff: Douglas Black, Molly-Beth Brown, Susan Lisk, and Winnifred Manning. Don Giller expertly set excerpts by Pergolesi, Gluck, and Rossini. Jan Beatty, Executive Editor at Oxford University Press, has been a skilled coordinator and mentor of the entire project. Cory Schneider and Lauren Mine, Associate Editors, and Nichole LeFebvre, Editorial Assistant, in Higher Education at Oxford, and Jay Crowley of Jay's Publishers Services have all been models of efficiency and good cheer in helping us sort out the numerous logistical details of production.

Thank you to the many reviewers for Oxford University Press:

Stephen Allen, Rider University
Pedro Aponte, James Madison University
Candace Bailey, North Carolina Central University
Paul T. Barte, Ohio State University
Laura Basini, Sacramento State University
Glen Bauer, Webster University
Matthew Baumer, Indiana University of Pennsylvania

Jonathan Bellman, University of Northern Colorado
John Brobeck, University of Arizona
Tom Brothers, Duke University
Lance Brunner, University of Kentucky
Gordon Callon, Acadia University
Charles Carson, University of Delaware
Alice Clark, Loyola University, New Orleans
Mel Comberiati, Manhattanville College

Jane Dahlenburg, University of Central Arkansas

Terry Dean, Indiana State

Silvio dos Santos, University of Florida

Ralph Dudgeon, State University of New York, Cortland

Robert Eisenstein, Mt. Holyoke College and University of Massachusetts, Amherst

Sarah Eyerly, Butler University

Howard Goldstein, Auburn University

David Grayson, University of Minnesota, Twin Cities

Richard Greene, Georgia College & State University

Daniel Grimley, University of Nottingham

Olga Haldey, University of Maryland

L. Curtis Hammond, Morehead State University

Gregory Harwood, Georgia Southern University

Karl Hinterbichler, University of New Mexico

Julie Hubbert, University of South Carolina

Kevin Karnes, Emory University

Derek Katz, University of California, Santa Barbara

Ben Korstvedt, Clark University

Jonathan Kregor, University of Cincinnati

Jonathan Kulp, University of Louisiana, Lafayette

Zoe Lang, University of South Florida

James Leve, Northern Arizona University

David Levy, Wake Forest University

Nora Lewis, Kansas State

Melanie Lowe, Vanderbilt University

Gayle Sherwood Magee, University of Illinois, Urbana–Champaign

James Maiello, Vanderbilt

Peter Marsh, California State University, East Bay

Kerry McCarthy, Duke University

Bruce D. McClung, University of Cincinnatti

Alyson McLamore, California Polytechnic State University, San Luis Obispo

Honey Meconi, Eastman School of Music

Steve Meyer, Syracuse University

Vera Micznik, University of British Columbia

Michael Miranda, Loyola Marymount University

Sharon Mirchandani, Rider University

Simon Morrison, Princeton University

Caroline Polk O'Meara, University of Texas at Austin

Mathew Peattie, University of Cincinnati College Conservatory of Music

Thomas Peattie, Boston University

Elaine Peterson, Mississippi State University

Mark Radice, Ithaca College

Christina Reitz, Western Carolina University

Eric Rice, University of Connecticut

Jerry Rife, Rider University

David Rothenberg, Case Western Reserve University

Kailan Rubinoff, University of North Carolina, Greensboro

Peter Schimpf, Metropolitan State College

David Schulenberg, Wagner College

Douglass Seaton, Florida State University

Jennifer Thomas, University of Florida

Nina Treadwell, University of California, Santa Cruz

Robin Wallace, Baylor University

Sarah F. Williams, University of South Carolina

Stephen A. Willier, Temple University

Note on Score Reading

The full scores used in the anthology list instruments in Italian or German. The following table lists the English, German, and Italian names of the instruments that occur in these scores, along with their abbreviations.

Instrument Name	Designations in Italian and German	Plurals
piccolo(s) (Picc.)	flauto piccolo (Fl. Picc.), Kleine Flöte (Kl. Fl.)	flauti piccoli
flute(s) (Fl.)	flauto (Fl.), Flöte (Fl.)	flauti, Flöten
oboe(s) (Ob.)	oboe (Ob.), Hoboe (Hb.)	oboi, Hoboen
clarinet(s) (Cl., Clt., Clar.)	clarinetto (Cl., Clar.), Klarinette (Kl.)	clarinetti, Klarienetten
bassoon(s) (Bsn., Bssn.)	fagotto (Fag., Fg.), Fagott (Fag., Fg.)	fagotti, Fagotte
contrabassoon (C. Bsn.)	contrafagotto (Cfg., C. Fag.), Kontrafagott (Kfg.)	contrafagotti, Kontrafagotte
French horn(s) (Hr., Hn.)	corno (Cor., C.), Horn [Hr.])	corni, Hörner
trumpet(s) (Trp., Trpt.)	tromba (Tr.), Trompete (Tr., Trp.)	trombe, Trompeten
cornet	cornetta, Kornett	cornetti, Kornette
trombone(s) (Tr., Tbe., Trb., Trm., Trbe.)	trombone (Tbni., Trni.), Posaune (Ps., Pos.)	tromboni, Posaunen
tuba (Tb.)	tuba (Tb., Tba.), Tuba (Tb.)	
bass tuba	tuba basso, Basstuba (Btb.)	
kettledrums (K.D.)		timpani (Timp., Tp.), Pauken (Pk.)
bass drum (B. drum)	gran tamburo/Gran cassa (Gr. Cassa) Grosse Trommel (Gr. Tr.)	
bells		campane (Cmp.), Glocken
violin(s) (V., Vl., Vln., Vi.)	violino (V., Vl., Vln.)	violine (V., Vl., Vln.)
viola (Va., Vl.)	viola (Va., Vla.), Bratsche (Br.)	
violoncello, cello (Vcl., Vc.)	viloncello (Vc., Vlc.), Violoncell (Vc., Vlc.)	
double bass (D. Bs.)	contrabasso (Cb., C.B.), Kontrabass (Kb.)	contrabassi or bassi (C. Bassi)

Some instruments in the orchestra are "transposing" instruments, which means that they sound higher or lower than written in the score. Some are designated as such in the score (e.g., "Clarinet in E♭") some are not (e.g., the piccolo, which sounds an octave higher than written). The simplest way to read transposing instruments is to decide how much higher or lower one should read them. For instance, a "Clarinet in E♭" will sound the written C as E♭; hence all its written notes should be read a minor third higher than written. The following table gives a concordance of written note and sound for the most typical transposing instruments.

Piccolo	sounds an octave higher than written
Clarinet in E♭	sounds a minor third higher than written
Clarinet in B♭	sounds a major second lower than written
Clarinet in A	sounds a minor third lower than written
Contrabassoon	sounds an octave lower than written
Trumpet in F	sounds a perfect fourth higher than written
Trumpet in E	sounds a major third higher than written
Trumpet in E♭	sounds a minor third higher than written
Cornet in B♭	sounds a major second higher than written
Horn in F	sounds a perfect fifth lower than written
Horn in E	sounds a minor sixth lower than written
Horn in E	sounds a major sixth lower than written
Horn in D	sounds a minor seventh lower than written
Contrabass	sounds an octave lower than written

In scores in which names of instruments are listed in Italian or German, the letter names of pitches differ from English usage: in Italian C = ut, D = re, E = mi, F = fa, G = sol, A = la, B = si. Flats are designated with ♭ (E♭ = Mi♭), sharps with ♯ (G♯ = Sol♯); in German the letter names are the same, except B natural is designated as H, while B♭ is named B. Sharps add an "is" to the name of the note (C♯ = Cis), and flats add an "es" (D♭ = Des) (except the B♭).

1

Wilhelm Friedemann Bach (1710–84)

[handwritten: martin Falck – 1st dissertion of WF / organized.]

Sonata in F Major (Falck 6a, ca. 1735–40, revised ca. 1740 and after 1750?)

Wilhelm Friedemann Bach (WF) composed the first version of his keyboard Sonata in F Major some fifteen years before the death of his father, Johann Sebastian Bach (JS). Although it is easy to find surface similarities between the works of father and son, WF's compositional style differs significantly from that of JS. Indeed, the word "sonata" meant something different to father and son. For JS the primary meaning of the word was trio sonata, or sonata for solo instrument and basso continuo in which the right hand of the keyboard acts as a melody instrument. JS's most common approach in these works, especially in the fast movements, was to spin them out in a highly contrapuntal style. In contrast, WF used "sonata" most frequently to designate a three-movement work for solo keyboard, the movements of which were in binary (two-part) form and the texture of which was not contrapuntal but either two-part or based on harmonic figuration.

The three movements of WF's sonata are all cast in binary form, which follows a harmonic plan that moves from tonic to dominant in the first section and from dominant to tonic, by way of a section in a distant key (a "far out point"), in the second. Our analysis focuses on the first movement in detail and briefly summarizes the second and third movements.

At a glance WF's busy first movement does not look all that different from his father's music. Indeed, it even begins with a canon. This canon, however, lasts only two measures. Imitative counterpoint à la JS, though clearly a technique WF had at his disposal, was not his primary mode of composition.

WF's melodic design, in contrast to JS's continuous counterpoint, features short-range contrast and balance. The first four measures of the sonata tell the whole story. Both melodically and harmonically, they divide in the middle. The first pair of measures continually circles around the tonic. The second pair puts more emphasis on the dominant harmony and underscores the harmonic contrast with a motivic one.

In what follows, melodic contrasts and balanced phrase lengths continue. The fifth, sixth, and seventh measures all have a new motive. Measure 8 continues with the motive introduced in m. 7, which once again creates a symmetrical divide—measures 5–8 thus break down into

(1 + 1) + 2. These motives are cast in rhythms that carry definite associations with the fashionable galant style. The fast triplets alternating freely with duple divisions are one specifically galant rhythm. The "lombard" rhythms (quick short-long pairs) are even more distinctly galant and are rare in JS's work.

All the surface variety and decorative dazzle obscures the tonal plan of the binary form, and WF takes his time while completing this meticulously laid-out back-and-forth harmonic trajectory. The first part of the movement consists of sixteen measures, which is balanced by the second part. The process of modulating to the dominant begins with the B naturals in m. 6. The dominant is firmly established as local tonic on the downbeat of m. 9 and is repeatedly confirmed thereafter. The ideal, far from the "Baroque" aim of generating great motivic and tonal momentum, seems to be to provide a maximum of ingratiating detail over a satisfyingly stable ground plan. *[handwritten: as much detail while still being appealing to listener]*

The second part begins as did the first. Its first four measures (mm. 17–20) consist of a simple transposition to the dominant of the first four measures. In m. 21, however, we hit a big jolt, expressed at once through harmony, texture, and melody. The harmony is a diminished-seventh chord, the most dissonant chord in the vocabulary of the time. Texturally, this is the first full chord in the movement. Melodically, too, there is disruption, in which obsessive syncopated repetition of single tones and dissonant leaps replace the earlier smoother melodic flow.

This is not unexpected, since this is the point in the form when we would expect movement to a distant key, but here the movement is especially dramatized. After a good deal of harmonic wandering, one last, extraordinarily chromatic modulatory passage lets us off in m. 38 within hailing distance of the tonic—on IV, which proceeds to V and then home to I. The return of stable harmonic functions is accompanied by the return of stable thematic material. The return to tonic in m. 39 dramatically coincides with a return to the original theme, making this a "double return" (a simultaneous return of tonic key and opening theme). Two measures later, in m. 41, the whole section originally appearing in the dominant (mm. 7–16) returns in the tonic and finishes the movement with a sense of elegantly restored balance.

The second movement is a minuet paired with a trio in the relative minor. This is an example of a light, "modern" dance characterized by simple texture, periodic structure, and short melodic motives. WF's minuet is simpler than those of his father, who would never have settled for such an uncomplicated texture or for so much straightforward alternation of tonics and dominants, measure by measure, such as one finds especially in the second half of the "trio." WF is using the simplicity and "naturalness" of the unaffected dance to provide repose between the more sophisticated outer movements.

The third movement of the sonata, a rollicking Presto, contrasts with the first movement in mood and texture. But it also follows the same form and achieves the very same sense of roundedness and stability. Practically the entire first section of the piece is recapitulated in the second half. The first six measures are actually restated twice: at the very beginning of the second half (mm. 33–38), where they are transposed to the dominant, and toward the end, where they provide a "double return" to both the main theme and the tonic key (mm. 75–80).

[handwritten vertical margin note: poor 3rd movement]

[handwritten bottom notes: Xornamentation does not take away from melody ; galant – melodically dominated / less harmonically dense (stable harmony to support appealing melody) ; lightness of style]

Measure Nos.	Formal Designation	Sections	Keys	Comments
First Momemment				
1–16	1st Part			Establishes tonic, modulates to dominant, and confirms dominant
1–5		Tonic presentation	F	
6–8		Transition (bridge)	F to C (I to V)	
9–16		Modulation confirmed	C	
17–50	2nd Part			Begins in dominant and returns to tonic after a period of modulation
17–38		Modulatory section (quasi-development)	C, d, e, a, g, a	
39–50		Recapitulation	F	Begins with "double return" of key and initial thematic material (mm. 1-2)

Un poco Allegro

Minuetto da Capo

2

Carl Philipp Emanuel Bach (1714–88)

– alfred Wotquenne

FULL CD III: TRACK 2

Fantasia in C Minor, Wq. 63/6/iii (1753)

Carl Philipp Emanuel Bach (CPE) wrote his Fantasia in C Minor as a lesson piece to accompany the first volume of his influential treatise *An Essay on the True Art of Playing Keyboard Instruments* (*Versuch über die wahre Art das Clavier zu spielen*) (1753). The Fantasy exhibits many of the traits of the highly expressive mid-eighteenth-century North German style known as the *empfindsamer Stil* (translated as "sensitive, sentimental, or ultra-sensitive style"). Composers associated with this style used abundant appoggiaturas (often associated with sighs), nuanced dynamics, and chromaticism in service of intimate and often-volatile expression. In his *Essay* CPE described the genre of fantasy as "consisting not of previously memorized passages or borrowed ideas," but as music "arising spontaneously from a good and musical soul," that is, as notated improvisation. In CPE's day, direct expression of feelings in the form of improvisation was considered proof of true musicianship. CPE regarded the fantasy as a piece in which "the keyboard player, more than any other musician, can achieve the effect of speech, the abrupt surprise of changes in mood."

As the irregular phrase structure and abrupt mood changes in the C-minor Fantasy illustrate, CPE did have speech in mind, more precisely musical speech or recitative—although his imaginary singer has superhuman range and vocal technique. The recitative invoked here does not imitate the most common type of recitative, designated as "simple" or "dry" (*secco*) recitative, in which large amounts of text were declaimed over sparse continuo accompaniment. Instead, CPE's instrumental recitative recalls the more dramatically powerful and musically rich accompanied recitative (*recitativo accompagnato*), in which the orchestra takes part and the singer's gestures tend to be especially impassioned. Using the idiom of theatrical vocal music in an instrumental work indicates a dedication to emotional expression that results in a willingness to break the conventions of instrumental music, among them balanced phrase structures and formal designs and metrical uniformity.

The highly emotional quality of the Fantasy stems, in part, from CPE's flexible treatment of rhythm, meter, and tempo. As CPE pointed out, although common time is indicated at the beginning of the piece, it is not followed throughout. Bar lines are omitted, as was customary in the genre. "Regular meter," CPE wrote, "carries with it a certain constraint." In contrast, in

improvisation

expressive, idiomatic for keyboard specifically

accompanied recitative in opera, CPE observed, "the tempo and meter need to be changed frequently in order to arouse and to calm many different emotions in rapid succession." CPE relies on regular meter ($\frac{3}{4}$) only in the *Largo* middle section of his Fantasy, which switches from recitative to another operatic model, the more metrically and melodically regular arioso.

While the more regular meter and melody of the *Largo* contrast with the rhapsodic freedom of the first part, it continues and intensifies the harmonic instability and dynamic contrasts. Although it starts in clearly delineated E♭ major, it soon runs into quickly rising sequential progressions (mm. 10–13). An arpeggiated dominant-seventh chord brings us back to E♭ major (m. 13, beat 3), only to start a new sequential adventure (mm. 15–17), now spiced with augmented-sixth chords (mm. 15–16). The *Allegro moderato* (m. 22) returns to the texture of the opening, but it does not return immediately to C minor. Intensely expressive diminished-seventh chords dominate until the end. Only the final cadence arrives at a tonality-defining, root-position chord in C minor. The tonal wandering of the Fantasy plays a large role in communicating hyper-expressivity associated with the *empfindsamer Stil*.

Despite the rhapsodic structure created by the juxtaposition of contrasting textures, harmonies, phrases, dynamics, keys, and rhythmic gestures, the Fantasy is not entirely without equilibrium. Virtuoso flourishes are answered by more declamatory phrases (cf. mm. 1f and 1g), rising lines balance with descents, and the sparse harmonic accompaniment of the recitative-like passages is balanced by the more continuous bass line of the *Largo*. The melodic phrases indicate not only passionate speech but also dialogue, in which questions are asked and answered not by words but by musical gestures. The best instrument for such an intimate "conversation" was the clavichord, a quiet instrument for the drawing room. This was the preferred keyboard instrument of composers writing in the *empfindsamer Stil*, both for its sensitivity and for being the only instrument capable of the *Bebung*, a plaintive vibrato produced by varying pressure on the key (indicated by dots under a slur above the note—mm. 1g, 19–21, 22b).

Note on Fingerings

The prescriptive fingerings in the present score, which reflect the pedagogical intent of the work, are the composer's own. CPE's fingerings represent the eighteenth-century trend toward increased use of crossing over the thumb, a fundamental principle of modern keyboard technique.

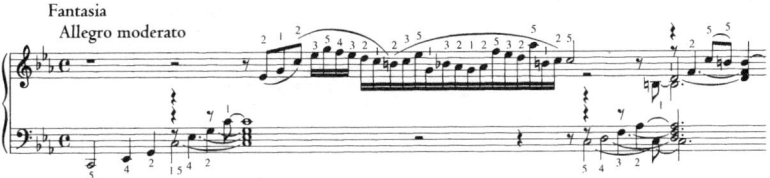

*Rhythmic notation of inner voice ambiguous; see p. xxi.   †Descending arpeggio

3

Johann Christian Bach
(1735–82)

Sonata in D Major, Op. 5, No. 2 (1768)

Johann Christian (JC) Bach's Sonata in D Major exemplifies a different relationship to eighteenth-century opera than does the previous work in this anthology, the C-minor Fantasy of JC's half-brother and teacher, CPE Bach. Whereas CPE's Fantasy made use of the gestures of impassioned operatic recitative, JC's Sonata is closely related to the Italian opera overture, forerunner of the early symphony. CPE's Fantasy is intimate and dark—emotionally "deep"; JC's sonata is public and bright—emotionally "light." Like WF Bach's Sonata in this anthology, all three movements of JC's Sonata are binary structures.

Movement 1: *Allegro di molto*

The first movement contains highly contrasting sections that break up and dramatize the form in a manner that in the nineteenth century would come to be known as *sonata form*. In sonata form the standard modulatory plans of binary structures (from the tonic to a new key, then back to the tonic after a period of harmonic exploration) are realized in three sections: exposition, development, and recapitulation. The exposition extends from the beginning of the movement until the repeat sign and always contains a modulation (to the dominant in movements in a major key, to the relative major in movements in minor). The development, a section of harmonic wandering, begins directly after the repeat sign and extends to the "double return" (of tonic key and opening material), which marks the beginning of the recapitulation. The recapitulation replays the material of the exposition modified to remain in the tonic key throughout. A coda sometimes follows the recapitulation.

Exposition

The exposition of the first movement of JC's Sonata in D Major, like most movements that exhibit the characteristics of sonata form, consists of four main sections: presentation of a primary theme (or group of themes); a "bridge" or modulatory section; presentation of a secondary theme (or group of themes) in a new key; and a closing (or cadential) section. In JC's Sonata

the sections are articulated with great clarity; modulations and the appearance of new themes are dramatized, as is befitting in a genre so closely related to opera.

1. Primary Theme (mm. 1–8). This section establishes the main key by alternation of tonic and dominant. It provides the harmonic launching pad for the movement. Also characteristic is the balance created by the two *forte* and two *piano* measures of the two four-measure phrases making up this primary theme.

2. Bridge or Modulatory Section (mm. 9–18). The next ten measures (asymmetrically divided 7 + 3) accomplish a "bridging" or modulatory function starting on the tonic and ending on V of the dominant key. The fact that the function of this section is primarily connective is equally apparent from its harmonic instability and from its melodic asymmetry—the two factors are frequently interdependent. The noisy sixteenth-note figures in the right hand (mm. 9–15) approximate the effect of stormy violin tremolos. The active texture of this section dramatizes the modulatory action of the bridge.

3. Secondary Theme Group (mm. 19–34). The next sixteen measures reestablish harmonic stability (in A major, the key of the dominant) and melodic symmetry: The first eight measures end on a half cadence (a cadence on the dominant), which is balanced by the following eight measures ending on a full cadence. A common feature of sonata form found here is the light and tuneful nature of the secondary material in comparison with the heavier tone of the primary theme.

4. Closing or Cadential Section (mm. 35–42). The last eight measures (beginning with the pickup to m. 35) function as a thematically distinct cadence that confirms arrival and effects closure. Like the other thematic areas in this sonata, the closing section is symmetrically balanced, consisting of a 2 + 2 phrase, which is repeated for greater emphasis.

Development and Recapitulation

Composers use a great variety of approaches to the development section (here mm. 43–72). It is not uncommon for motives and themes already heard in the exposition to reappear here, nor is it uncommon for this section to contain new material. In this movement both new and familiar thematic material appear. First comes a new melody (mm. 43–47) over an Alberti bass, an accompanimental figure consisting of broken triads. The new tune begins by continuing in the dominant, but after a telltale asymmetrical five-measure unit it elides with a modulatory phrase (mm. 48–51). The harmonic goal of the modulatory phrase is B minor (vi), which holds for nine measures (mm. 52–60) and serves as the key area of farthest remove from the tonic in this movement. The return from this "far out point" occurs in two stages: a 2 + 2-measure modulatory phrase (mm. 61–64) and a 4 + 4-measure melody (mm. 65–72). Note particularly how A, the dominant pitch, acts as a pedal throughout the entire eight measures of the melody that immediately precedes the return (m. 73), creating a harmonic tension that demands release, which comes dramatically at the double return.

Measure Nos.	Formal Designation	Sections	Keys	Comments
1–42	Exposition			
1–8		Primary theme	D	Fanfare (4 + 4)
9–18		Bridge	Ends on V/V	
19–34		Secondary themes	A	4 + 4 and 4 + 4
35–42		Closing material	A	4 + 4
43–72	Development			
43–47		New theme	A	Alberti bass
48–51		Modulation	e, b	Thematic material from bridge
52–60		"Far out point"	b	
61–72		Retransition	Dominant pedal, mm. 64–72	
73–111	Recapitulation			
73–81		Primary theme	D	
81–87		Bridge	D	Shorter than in Exposition, stays in I
88–103		Secondary themes	D	4 + 4 and 4 + 4
104–111		Closing material	D	4 + 4

The section, from the double return to the end of the movement, is commonly referred to as the *recapitulation* because it almost literally replays the exposition, now with the secondary theme group and closing material transposed to the tonic key. The tonal stability of the recapitulation balances the modulation of the exposition and provides a sense of tonal closure.

Movement 2: *Andante di molto*

The remaining movements of the sonata (the name now referring to the whole multimovement piece, not to be confused with sonata form), like most sonata movements of the generation of Bach's sons, are also cast in binary form—but not in the highly dramatized sonata-form version of the first movement. The second movement makes use of a procedure much closer to that of Bach the father: the two halves closely mirror one another melodically as they trace the customary tonal progression (tonic to dominant and dominant back to tonic). The two parts differ chiefly after the first double bar, where the second half makes its customary tonal exploration—here represented by a single chord, an augmented-sixth harmony over ♭VI (E♭, m. 32).

Movement 3: *Minuetto*

The last movement, while also cast in a seemingly familiar traditional form (a pair of minuets), displays an interestingly novel feature: Like the first movement, both minuets sport "double returns" in their second halves. Also worth noting is the tonal trajectory of the second minuet from D minor to its relative major (F major) and back. The use of III, the relative major, as the goal of modulation in pieces in the minor mode was becoming a standard practice at this time.

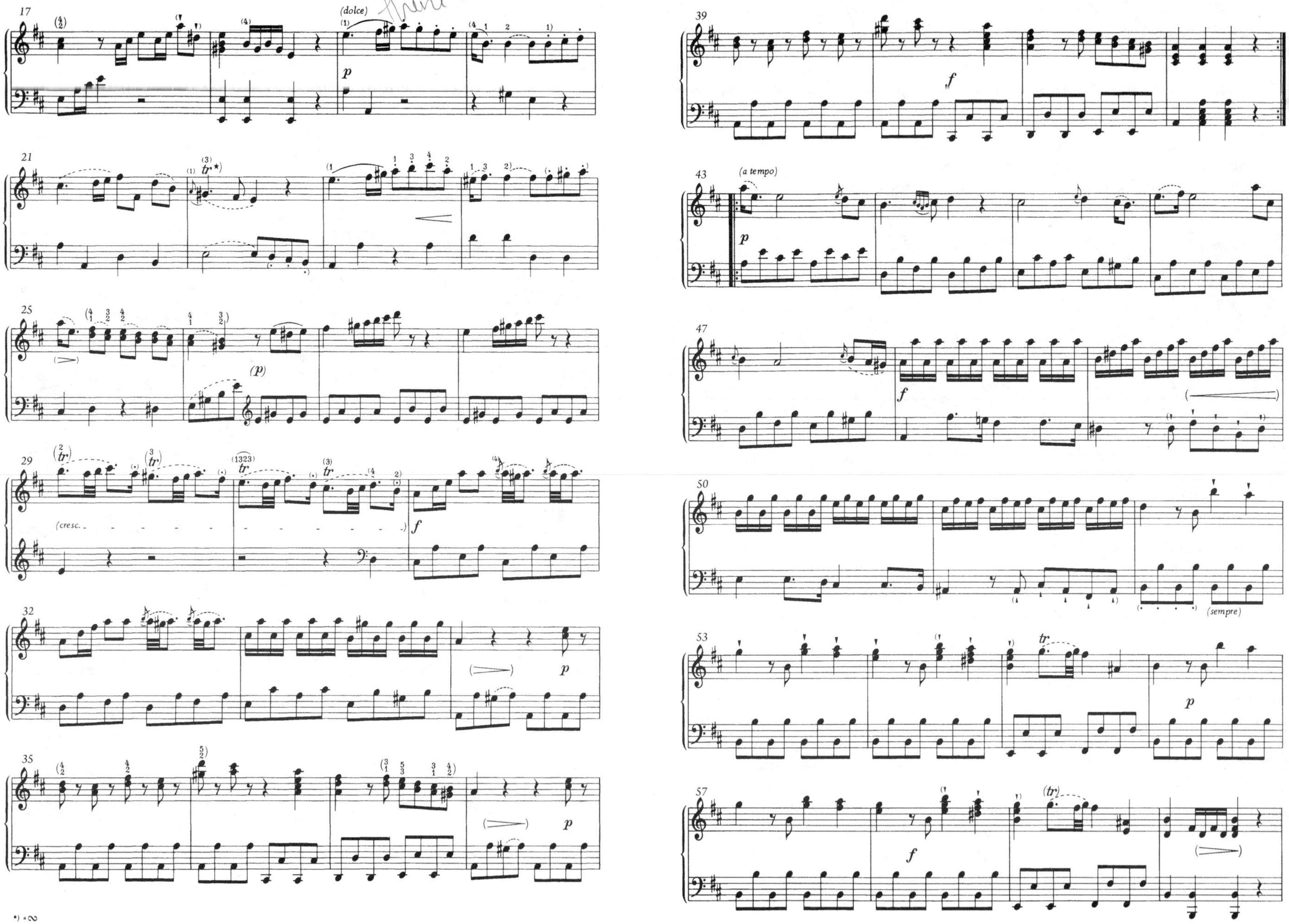
(dolce)
(cresc.
(a tempo)
(sempre)

*) = ∞

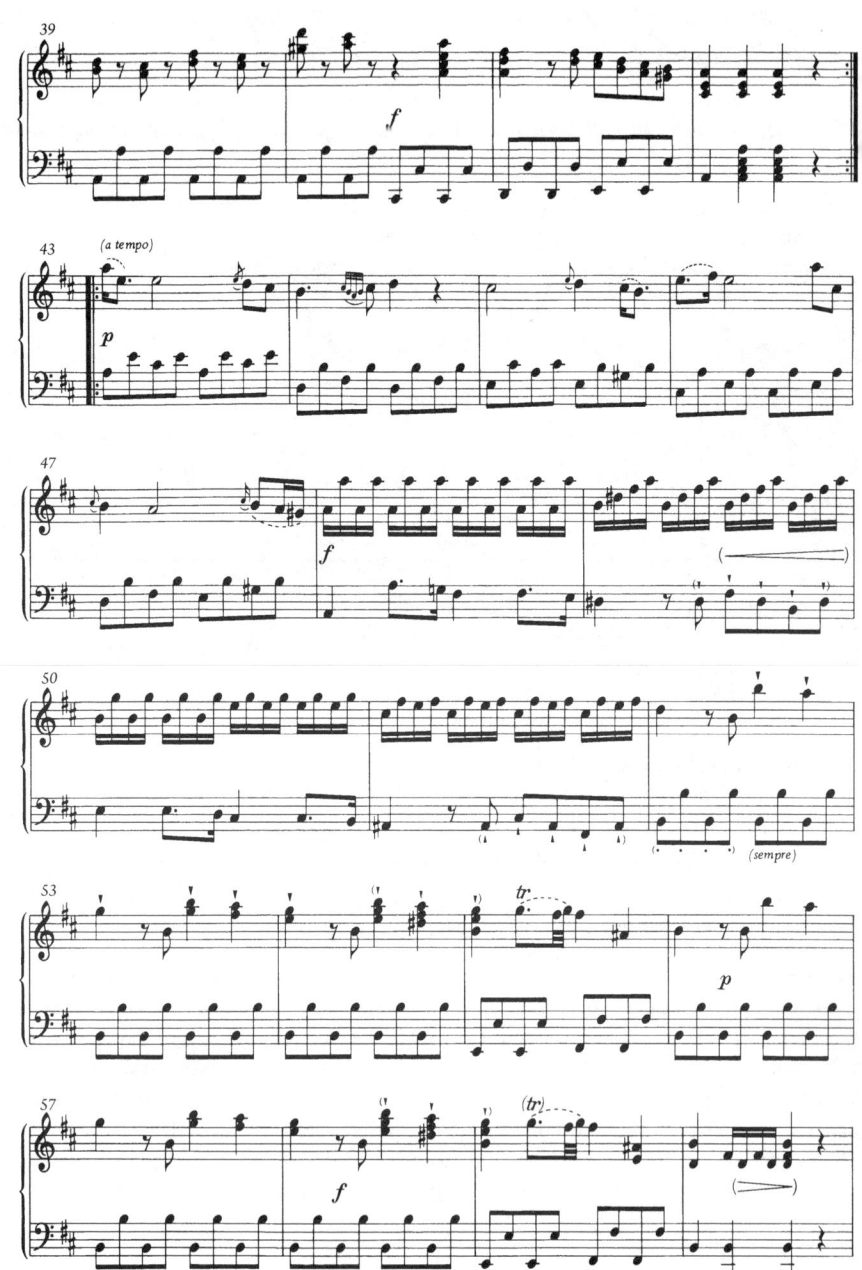

(Da Capo il Maggiore)

4

Giovanni Battista Pergolesi (1710–36)

FULL CD III: TRACKS 4–5
CONCISE CD II: TRACK 8

La serva padrona (The Maid as Mistress) (1733)

La serva padrona is an *intermezzo*, a short comic opera intended for performance between the acts of *opera seria* (serious opera). First performed with Pergolesi's opera seria *Il prigioniero superbo* (The Proud Prisoner) in Naples in 1733, *La serva padrona* took Europe by storm in the middle of the eighteenth century. Its comic style had a major influence on later eighteenth-century music. The plot is a simple farce involving two singing characters—the cunning maid, Serpina (soprano), and her master, Uberto (bass)—and one mute role for a manservant. By the end of the *intermezzo*, Serpina succeeds in tricking the grumbling Uberto into agreeing to marry her. Thus she, the maid (*la serva*), becomes mistress (*padrona*) of the house. A wedding, or the prospect of one, was the typical ending for comedies in the eighteenth century.

a. "A Serpina penserete" ("You'll think of Serpina")

In Serpina's coaxing aria, "A Serpina penserete" ("You'll think of Serpina"), we see how irony—the very essence of comedy—engenders musical contrast. Pretending to be on the verge of leaving Uberto to marry a gruff soldier, Serpina addresses Uberto to the strains of a melting *Largo* designed to elicit sympathy and lead him to propose. As she senses Uberto falling for her ploy, Serpina addresses us, the spectators, through ironic asides, set as perky little jigs of joy (*Allegro*). Serpina thus uses two styles, which alternate to comic effect: The *Allegro* sections, with numerous playful accents on beats 2 and 3, express her true, spirited self; while the *Largo* sections convey a sentimental pose. The contrasting sections complicate the otherwise straightforward da capo form (ABA, with the B section [mm. 61–78] distinguishable from A only by its minor key). They divide the A section into four subsections (a, b, a^var, b^var), first modulating from tonic B♭ to dominant F, then back from F to B♭. The alternating styles in the A section of an aria was a new musical device for opera, created to satisfy a new dramatic situation in which abrupt changes replace the uniform mood ("unity of affect") characteristic of opera seria. Here we see the psychological, dramatic, and representational impetus for the contrast and balance that would come to characterize late-eighteenth-century music.

Intermezzi were known for their simplicity of expression and texture—Pergolesi's viola part generally doubles the bass at the octave, and the two violin parts often play in unison or double the voice, frequently leaving a spare two-part texture. In the *Largo* sections of this aria, however, Pergolesi mimics the tone of opera seria by occasionally employing somewhat more complex textures (e.g., the violas have an independent part in mm. 1-2, and second violins are frequently independent thereafter). Accordingly, Serpina's vocal part in the *Largo* sections is full of little grace notes and sigh motives, as if the servant girl had obtained a higher musical style than her social status would normally allow. Pergolesi also resorts to fancy harmonies (e.g., the augmented-sixth chord at "Ah poverina" ["Oh, poor thing"], m. 6) and to pompous dotted figures in the *Largo* to underscore her pretend tragic tone. There is ironic contrast even within this mock-seria section: The high repeated thirty-second notes in m. 2, which can be heard as imitations of weeping, laughing, or Serpina's sharp tongue, throw the sincerity of her sentiment into question even before she begins to sing.

Serpina

A Serpina penserete,	You'll think of Serpina,
qualche volta, e qualche dì;	once in a while, someday,
e direte: Ah! poverina!	and you'll say: Oh! poor thing!
Cara un tempo ella mi fù.	She was once dear to me.
(S'incomincia, sì, già pian piano	(Already it seems to me that little by little
s'incomincia a intenerir.)	he's beginning to soften.)
S'io poi fui impertinente,	If I was a little impertinent,
mi perdoni:	forgive me!
Malamente mi guidai:	I behaved badly,
lo vedo, sì.	I admit it, yes.
(Ei mi stringe per la mano,	(He's squeezing my hand,
meglio il fatto non può gir!)	it couldn't be going better!)

b. "Son imbrogliato io già" ("I'm really in a fix")

Uberto, who cares deeply for Serpina despite her insolence, finds himself torn when it seems she will leave him to marry a soldier—should he marry her in spite of her low social status? Like Serpina's aria "A Serpina penserete," which precedes it, Uberto's aria "Son imbrogliato io già" ("I'm really in a fix") is full of contrast born of irony. There is only one meter and tempo this time; the joke of the piece lies in the contrast between Uberto's opening "fretting motive" in eighth notes at a breakneck speed and his periodic attempts to take himself sternly in hand, intoning in stately whole notes: "Uberto, pensa a te" (Uberto, think of yourself!). To prepare for these "serious" moments the music slips into rather distant minor tonalities (first to B♭ minor, mm. 26–27, then to F minor, mm. 28–39)—another humorous contrast that became standard operating procedure by the end of the century. The passage in whole notes again borrows its style from opera seria. Here Uberto sings with a deep, profound tone—a standard method for invoking the supernatural in serious opera. (What Uberto in his confusion hears as a deep voice coming from beyond is in reality Serpina's soprano chattering.)

It is probably no accident that the middle part of this da capo aria (mm. 83–101) ends in G minor (mm. 91–99), the key Serpina used most shamelessly to elicit sympathy in the previous number. There may also be some dramatic significance in the fact that the repetitive cadential bass line opening Uberto's aria (mm. 1–3 and 12–15) is the same as the one that underlay Serpina's blandishments in the preceding aria (mm. 1–4). Or was this bass line just a cliché of the buffa style—one of the alluring gestures that made it so popular and, for all its levity, so important to the history of music?

Uberto

Son imbrogliato io già!	I'm really in a fix!
Ho un certo che nel core	my heart is saying something,
che dir per me non so,	but I don't know
s'è amore o s'è pieta?	is it love or pity?
Sent' un che, poi mi dice:	I hear something telling me:
Uberto pensa a te!	Uberto, think of yourself!
Io sto fra il sì e il no,	I'm torn between yes and no,
fra il voglio, e fra il non voglio,	between wanting and not wanting,
e sempre più m'imbroglio.	and I'm ever more confused.
Ah! misero infelice,	Oh, miserable unhappy me,
che mai sarà di me?	what will become of me?

5

Niccolò Piccinni (1728–1800)

FULL CD III: TRACK 6

La buona figliuola (The Virtuous Maiden), Act 2, Finale (1760)

Piccinni's *La buona figliuola*, also known as *La Cecchina* (after its heroine), is an *opera buffa* (comic opera) in three acts to a libretto by Carlo Goldoni (1707–93). In contrast to an *intermezzo*, an opera buffa constituted a full evening's entertainment. It involved more characters than an *intermezzo*—including those of high social status who sing in the elevated style of opera seria—and a more complicated plot. Based on Samuel Richardson's 1740 novel *Pamela*, Piccinni's opera is a "rags-to-riches" story about the love between an Italian nobleman (Il Marchese [Marquis]) and Cecchina, a poor but virtuous young woman he employs as a gardener. The Marquis's sister and her lover oppose the match because of Cecchina's low social status, but a German soldier brings news that proves she is in fact the long lost daughter of an exiled baron. The couple may therefore wed without breaking social convention.

The shape of comic libretti depended on plots that are first hopelessly tangled, then sorted out. Both the tangle (*imbroglio*) and the sorting out were enacted in ensemble finales in which many characters participated. In an *intermezzo* like *La serva padrona* these were mere duets. In full-length opera buffa, finales could be scenes of great length and intricacy, in which the changing dramatic situation unfolds quickly in numbers strung together without any intervening recitative.

The finale to the second act of *La buona figliuola* represents the height of the opera's imbroglio. Tagliaferro, the German soldier (whose name means "chisel"), has just persuaded the Marquis that Cecchina is the lost baroness Mariandel on account of a distinctive blue birthmark on her breast. The Marquis immediately rushes off to order preparations for their wedding, leaving Tagliaferro alone with the sleeping Cecchina. She calls tenderly in her sleep to her lost father. Tagliaferro, moved, responds in kind. Sandrina and Paoluccia, two maidservants jealous of Cecchina, witness this curious exchange. The finale then begins.

At first the comic characters dominate: Sandrina and Paoluccia, sharp-tongued gossips, and Tagliaferro, a bumbling bass who comically mixes German and French into his garbled Italian. The women accuse Tagliaferro of trying to seduce Cecchina. When the Marquis returns (his entry underscored with a modulation to the subdominant and a marching bass line, mm. 70–76), Sandrina and Paoluccia denounce Tagliaferro. The Marquis, however, does not believe

them and rejects their malicious tale in a melting aria (mm. 123–161). Written in $\frac{3}{8}$, the Marquis's aria is a *siciliano*, a slow aria type (or instrumental piece) usually associated with pastoral scenes and melancholy emotions. (The *siciliano* is frequently notated in $\frac{6}{8}$ or $\frac{12}{8}$ with simple melodies and harmonies.) Here the *siciliano* expresses the purity of the Marquis's love (note the flights of coloratura in mm. 150–161 that define him as a character of high social position). A quick change of tempo (m. 162) turns the *siciliano* into a madcap jig as the two girls argue with the two men, finally reaching a peak of frenzied raving that is captured musically in a breathless *prestissimo* that returns to the opening patter tune of the finale (mm. 250ff), thus tying the whole imbroglio into a tidy musical package.

Sandrina and Paoluccia (together)	**Sandrina and Paoluccia** (*together*)
Sì, signora, di lassù	Yes, miss, from up there
Si è veduto che quaggiù	We saw that down here
Col soldato fortunato	You were entertaining the attentions
Si badava a divertir.	Of this fortunate soldier.
Cecchina	**Cecchina**
Sventurata, io mi sognai . . .	Miserable me, I dreamt . . .
Cosa dite? Come mai?	What are you saying? What on earth?
Ah, mi fate tramortir!	Oh, you're making me faint!
Tagliaferro	**Tagliaferro**
Questa ciofane* star mia,	This girl is mine,
E foi altre passa fia:	And you two, move along:
Star patron de qua fenir.	I am the master of who comes here.
Cecchina	**Cecchina**
Ma chi siete? (to Tagliaferro)	But who are you?
Tagliaferro	**Tagliaferro**
Star soldato.	I'm a soldier.
Sandrina and Paoluccia	**Sandrina and Paoluccia**
È un amante.	He's a lover.
Tagliaferro	**Tagliaferro**
Star mandato . . .	I have been sent . . .
Sandrina and Paoluccia	**Sandrina and Paoluccia**
Si è veduto.	He's for sale.

*This is the first of many instances of Tagliaferro's bungled Italian ("ciofane" instead of "giovene").

Tagliaferro
Lasiar dir! Colonnello . . .

Tagliaferro
Let me explain! The Colonel . . .

Sandrina and Paoluccia
Non lo credo.

Sandrina and Paoluccia
I don't believe it.

Tagliaferro
Mi mandato . . .

Tagliaferro
Has sent me . . .

Sandrina and Paoluccia
Non è vero.

Sandrina and Paoluccia
It's not true.

Tagliaferro
Per trofar . . .

Tagliaferro
To find . . .

Sandrina and Paoluccia
Non sa che dir.

Sandrina and Paoluccia
He doesn't know what to say.

Tagliaferro
Maledette, lasciar dir!

Tagliaferro
You scoundrels, let me speak!

Cecchina
Io non so . . .

Cecchina
I don't know . . .

Sandrina and Paoluccia
Sappiamo noi!

Sandrina and Paoluccia
We know!

Cecchina
Io dormia . . .

Cecchina
I was sleeping . . .

Sandrina and Paoluccia
Celar non puoi.

Sandrina and Paoluccia
You can't deny it.

Cecchina
Non so niente.

Cecchina
I don't know anything.

Sandrina and Paoluccia
A che mentir?

Sandrina and Paoluccia
Why lie?

Tagliaferro
Maledette, lasciar dir!

Tagliaferro
Scoundrels, let me speak!

Sandrina and Paoluccia
Oh che ardita! Che briccone!
Il padrone lo saprà.

Sandrina and Paoluccia
How bold you are! What a rascal!
We'll tell the master.

Cecchina and Tagliaferro
Non paventa, l'innocenza;

Cecchina and Tagliaferro
Innocence has nothing to be afraid of;

L'insolenza finirà.

This insolence will cease.

Il Marchese (*arriving unexpected*)
Ah, Cecchina è risvegliata!
Sarà tutta consolata,
Più timor non averà.

Il Marchese (*arriving unexpected*)
Oh, Cecchina has awoken!
She will be completely consoled,
She will fear no more.

Cecchina
Ah, signor . . .

Cecchina
Oh, Sir . . .

Sandrina and Paoluccia
La sfacciatella . . .

Sandrina and Paoluccia
The impudent girl . . .

Tagliaferro
Je star qui . . .

Tagliaferro
Je [I] am here . . .

Sandrina and Paoluccia
Colla sua bella . . .

Sandrina and Paoluccia
With his sweetheart . . .

Cecchina
Non so niente!

Cecchina
I don't know anything!

Sandrina and Paoluccia
E' innamorata . . .

Sandrina and Paoluccia
She's in love . . .

Tagliaferro
Poferina! [Poverina]

Tagliaferro
Poor thing!

Sandrina and Paoluccia
Era abbracciata!

Sandrina and Paoluccia
She was embracing him!

Cecchina and Tagliaferro
Non è vero.

Cecchina and Tagliaferro
That's not true.

Sandrina and Paoluccia
Signor sì! E l'amico è questo qui.

Sandrina and Paoluccia
Yes, it is! And here's her boyfriend.

Il Marchese (*to Sandrina*)
Abbracciata?

Il Marchese (*to Sandrina*)
Embracing him?

Sandrina
Sì, signore.

Sandrina
Yes sir.

Il Marchese (*to Paoluccia*)
Coll' amico?

Il Marchese (*to Paoluccia*)
With her boyfriend?

Paoluccia
Ella è così.

Paoluccia
Exactly.

Il Marchese (to Sandrina)
Coll' amico?

Il Marchese (*to Sandrina*)
With her boyfriend?

Sandrina
Castigatela!

Sandrina
Punish her!

Il Marchese (to Paoluccia)
Abbracciata?

Il Marchese (*to Paoluccia*)
Embracing him?

Paoluccia
Via cacciatela.
(The Marquis looks uncertain)

Paoluccia
Chase her away.

**Cecchina, Tagliaferro, Sandrina
   and Paoluccia**
(Cosa pensa? Che dirà?)

**Cecchina, Tagliaferro, Sandrina
   and Paoluccia**
(What's he thinking? What will he say?)

Il Marchese (to Sandrina and
   Paoluccia)
Donne mie, non me ne importa,
il soldato so chi è:
E se non importa a me,
Non vi avete da scaldar.

Il Marchese (*to Sandrina and
   Paoluccia*)
My dear women, it's not important to me.
I know who the soldier is:
And if it's not important to me,
You shouldn't get worked up over it.

Sandrina and Paoluccia
Bravo! Bravo!

Sandrina and Paoluccia
Very good! Very good!

Tagliaferro
Viva! Viva!

Tagliaferro
Hurrah! Hurrah!

Cecchina (to the Marquis)
Il soldato vada via.

Cecchina (*to the Marquis*)
The soldier was going.

Il Marchese (to Cecchina)
Anzi voglio che ci stia,
E di qua non ha d'andar.

Il Marchese (*to Cecchina*)
On the contrary, I want him to stay,
And he does not have to leave.

Sandrina and Paoluccia
   (to the Marquis)
Buon pro faccia, padron mio!
(to Tagliaferro)
Buon pro faccia al corazzier!

Sandrina and Paoluccia (*to the Marquis*)

Good luck, my master!

Good luck to the grenadier!

Il Marchese and Tagliaferro
Insolenti, temerarie!

Il Marchese and Tagliaferro
Insolent, audacious women!

Sandrina and Paoluccia
Quesa qui la vo' goder!

Sandrina and Paoluccia
This girl just wants pleasure!

Il Marchese
Mano a me.
(takes Cecchina's hand)

Il Marchese
Give me your hand.

Cecchina
Signor no.

Cecchina
Sir, no.

Il Marchese
Io comando, e così vo'!
(Tagliaferro takes Cecchina's hand.)

Il Marchese
I command it, and so it will be!

Sandrina and Paoluccia
   (to the Marquis)
Bravo, bravo! Dividete.

Sandrina and Paoluccia
   (*to the Marquis*)
Very good, you can share . . .

Il Marchese and Tagliaferro
Via, tacete, disgraziate!
Rispettate questa qui.

Il Marchese and Tagliaferro
Go away, be quiet, you wretches!
Show this girl some respect.

Sandrina and Paoluccia
Bravo, bravo, signor sì!

Sandrina and Paoluccia
Very good, yes Sir!

Il Marchese and Tagliaferro
Consolata, fortunata,
La Cecchina goderà.

Il Marchese and Tagliaferro
Consoled and fortunate,
Cecchina will be pleased.

Sandrina, Paoluccia, and Cecchina
Oh, che rabbia ch' ho nel petto!
Che dispetto che mi fa!

Sandrina, Paoluccia, and Cecchina
Oh, what rage I have in my breast!
How vexing!

Fine dell'Atto II.

6

Christoph Willibald Gluck (1714–87)

FULL CD III: TRACKS 7–8
CONCISE CD II: TRACK 9

Orfeo ed Euridice (Orpheus and Eurydice) (1762)

Orfeo ed Euridice was the first opera Christoph Willibald Gluck wrote in collaboration with the librettist Ranieri Calzabigi (1714–95) and also the first example of their operatic reform. Gluck and Calzabigi aimed to reestablish the dramatic integrity—in the eighteenth-century German art historian Johann Winckelmann's terms, the "noble simplicity"—of opera lost in the over-complicated plots and vocal pyrotechnics of opera seria. Calzabigi reduces the plot of his *Orfeo* to its essentials and involves only three characters: Orpheus, Eurydice, and Cupid (Amore). In this version of the tale Cupid helps Orpheus on his trip to the Underworld to regain his wife, Eurydice, who died on the day of their wedding. Orpheus loses Eurydice for a second time when he disobeys the gods by looking at her before they emerge from the Underworld. All ends well, however, since Cupid, moved by Orpheus's love, brings Eurydice back to life once again.

Calzabigi's reduction of characters was matched by Gluck's purposeful elimination of da capo arias and reduction of virtuoso passages associated with opera seria. In place of an emphasis on da capo arias, the opera is packed with choruses; their prominent role is one of several aspects of the work that reflect the influence of French opera on Calzabigi and Gluck's work. Ironically, the success of *Orfeo,* an opera that intended to counter the artificiality of opera seria, was partly due to the fine interpretation of Orpheus's role by the alto castrato Gaetano Guadagni, for whom Handel had revised *Messiah* for showy operatic effect a dozen years before. Since that time Guadagni had transformed himself into a paragon of nobly simple and realistic acting under the influence of the great Shakespearean actor David Garrick.

a. Opening Chorus and Recitative

The opera begins after the death of Eurydice. The scene takes place on the field surrounding Eurydice's tomb. Shepherds and nymphs bring offerings while Orpheus lies prostrate on a rock. The shepherds and nymphs sing a solemn chorus that evokes a feeling of somber ritual. Orpheus's role in the first chorus is reduced to three cries of "Eurydice," which Gluck once urged the French tenor Joseph Legros to "scream with as much pain as if someone were sawing your leg off." There is nothing showy about this elegy. Besides short sigh motives, the vocal parts avoid embellishment and move along with the continuous quarter-note pulse in the

bass. Contrast and variety are achieved through occasional syncopation in the rhythm; through alternating blocks of short, *piano* three-part soli passages (mm. 32–33; mm. 42–47) with *forte tutti* responses; and through orchestration, which, in addition to the usual strings and continuo, includes independent parts for trombones and cornetto—instruments used at the time more in church than in the theater.

The recitative that follows the first chorus, in which Orpheus sends away his mourning friends, is set as an accompanied recitative in which all parts of the orchestral strings are written out. This form of recitative, formerly reserved for dramatic high points in opera seria, is the only type of recitative that Gluck employs in *Orfeo.*

Chorus	**Chorus**
Ah! se intorno a quest' urna funesta	Ah! If around this funeral urn,
Euridice, ombra bella, t'aggiri;	Eurydice, sweet spirit, you wander;
Orpheus	**Orpheus**
Euridice!	Eurydice!
Chorus	**Chorus**
Odi i pianti, i lamenti, i sospiri,	Hear the crying, the laments, the sighs,
che dolente si spargon per te.	which are sadly scattered for you.
Orpheus	**Orpheus**
Euridice!	Eurydice!
Chorus	**Chorus**
Ed ascolta il tuo sposo infelice,	And listen to your unhappy husband,
che piangendo ti chiama, e si lagna.	who, weeping, calls you and moans.
Orpheus	**Orpheus**
Euridice!	Eurydice!
Chorus	**Chorus**
Come quando, la dolce compagna,	As when the amorous dove
tortorella amorosa perdè.	has lost her sweet companion.
Orpheus (recitativo)	**Orpheus (recitativo)**
Basta, basta, o compagni!	Enough, enough, my friends!
Il vostro duolo aggrava il mio!	Your grief increases my own!
Spargete purpurei fiori,	Scatter purple flowers,
inghirlandate il marmo,	And place garlands on the marble tomb,
partitevi da me!	leave me!
Restar vogl'io solo fra quest' ombre	I want to remain alone among these
funebri e oscure coll'empia compagnia	mournful and dark shadows,
di mie sventure.	in the company of my misfortunes.

gl'i - o   so - lo fra quest' om - bre fu - ne - bri e o - scu - re   coll' em - pia com - pa - gnia   di mie sven - tu - re.

b. "Che farò senza Euridice!" ("What am I to do without Eurydice!"), Act III, Scene 1

The most striking example of "noble simplicity" in Gluck's opera is Orpheus's signature aria, "Che farò senza Euridice?" which he sings after losing Eurydice for the second time. Frustrated that Orpheus was unwilling to look at her while he was leading her out of the Underworld, Eurydice pretends to die. Losing his composure, Orpheus turns around, thus breaking his vow to the gods not to look at his wife until they leave the Underworld behind. In contrast to the dark key of C minor in the opening chorus, this aria, despite the tragic content of its text, is set in the bright key of C major—the beauty of this lament, not its tragic feeling, moves the gods to intervene on Orpheus's behalf. Although written for Guadagni, a virtuoso castrato, it lacks long melismas and has few of the embellishments typical of opera seria. The paired eighth notes that characterize the vocal line give a plain and simple quality to the aria, inspiring Gluck's contemporary, the music historian Charles Burney (1726–1814), to compare it to English ballads.

Gluck's decision to set Orpheus's aria of noble mourning as a two-episode rondo (ABACAA′), a form favored by composers of French opera, again points to French influence on Gluck and Calzabigi's operatic reforms. In Orpheus's aria the vocal refrain or rondo theme (A) appears three times in the tonic key (see chart), framing two episodes (B and C), the first in G major (the dominant of the tonic key), the second in C minor (the parallel minor of the tonic key). The episodes contrast with the rondo theme not only in their key but also in their slower tempo and short, fragmentary motivic structure. While the A section of the rondo unfolds in a balanced antecedent-consequent pair (4 + 4 with a two-measure extension), the episodes lack symmetrical structure and break into shorter phrases, often only one measure in length. The short, threefold descending phrase over a dominant pedal (mm. 42–45) that follows Orpheus's cries of "Euridice!" captures the tragic monotony of Orpheus's hopeless situation. As a gentle nod towards word painting, the range of the melodic line illustrates the difference between the world of the humans ("né dal mondo," medium range, mm. 45–46) and the world of the gods ("né dal ciel," higher range, mm. 47–48), both incapable of easing Orpheus's despair.

Note on Editions

Our piano reduction of "Che farò senza Euridice" follows the original Viennese version of the score (1762). For the 1774 French version of the opera Gluck rewrote Orpheus's part for tenor, transposed this aria to F major, and increased the range by a half step to achieve a higher climax

Measure Nos.	Section	Text	Key	Comments
1–16	A	"Che farò senza Euridice!"	C	6-measure orchestral intro precedes 1st full statement of A
17–29	B	"Euridice, Euridice!"	G	
30–39	A	"Che farò senza Euridice!"	C	
40–48	C	"Euridice, Ah! non m'avanza più soccorso"	c	
49–66	A	"Che farò senza Euridice!"	C	A lengthened by 2 mm. and followed by 6-measure orchestral conclusion

in the final strophe. This change to the end of the aria is sometimes used even when the aria is performed in its original C major.

Orfeo

Che farò senza Euridice!
Dove andrò senza il mio ben!
Euridice, Euridice,
Oh Dio! Rispondi!
Io son pure il tuo fedele.

Che farò senza Euridice . . .

Euridice! Euridice!
Ah! non m'avanza,
più soccorso più speranza,
nè dal mondo, nè dal ciel!

Che farò senza Euridice . . .

Orfeo

What will I do without Eurydice?
Where will I go without my love?
Eurydice, Eurydice,
O Gods! Answer!
I am still faithful to you.

What am I to do without Eurydice . . .

Eurydice! Eurydice!
Ah! There is no relief,
and no hope to offer me,
neither on earth nor in heaven!

What am I to do without Eurydice . . .

Andante espressivo

CHRISTOPH WILLIBALD GLUCK: *Orfeo ed Euridice* (Orpheus and Eurydice)

7

Giovanni Battista Sammartini (1700/01–75)

Symphony No. 13 in G Major (before ca. 1744)

Giovanni Battista Sammartini's Sinfonia in G, likely written in the 1730s, is one of the earliest freestanding concert symphonies—that is, it does not appear to have been written to serve as the introduction or overture to a larger work. As we have come to expect in eighteenth-century instrumental music, movements 1, 3, and 4 are all in binary form. Movement 2, hardly a movement at all, consists of a six-measure chordal progression that provides an introduction to movement 3. Sammartini originally planned movement 3 as the last of a three-movement plan (fast-slow-fast), the most common arrangement for early symphonies. Movement 4 is a later addition. Like most of Sammartini's early symphonies, this one is scored simply for string orchestra with basso continuo.

Movement 1: *Allegro ma non tanto*

The first movement, a "dramatized binary" form (or "sonata form") also called "symphonic binary" in acknowledgment of its origin in the early symphony, is the most forward-looking and most distinctively symphonic of the set. In this movement, as we have already seen in the first movement of JC Bach's Sonata in D, each section of the form has a specific musical texture that dramatizes its formal function. In the exposition: mm. 1–2 display vigorous, "curtain-raising" quadruple-stop strokes of the bow that correspond to their "opening" function; mm. 9–11 contain agitated "action music" dramatizing the modulation that provides the "bridge" to the lighter "second theme" in the dominant key (mm. 12–15); and mm. 16–17 feature rapid descending scales that bring the exposition to a close. (Note that mm. 16–17 repeat the material of mm. 1–2, the music initially in the bass and viola now moved to the first violin, thus adding a sense of rounding to these closing measures.)

The development section of the first movement (mm. 18–33) begins as if it were going to parallel the thematic structure of the first part, but it soon begins the modulations typical of development, with a three-measure sequence beginning in m. 22. The harmonic journey vividly contrasts a passage of sharpward-leaning chromaticism (introducing D♯ as leading tone to E minor, the "far out point," in m. 24) with a flatward-leaning cascade (mm. 27ff) that gets as far as E♭

in m. 31. (E♭ is the enharmonic equivalent of D♯, the goal of the sharpward-leaning motion.) The recapitulation begins with the "double return" of tonic key and opening theme in m. 34.

Movement 2: *Grave*, and Movement 3: *Allegro assai*

In place of a lyrical second movement, Sammartini inserts a slow-moving harmonic progression on a descending bass that begins on the flat sixth (E♭) and ends on the dominant of the home key. These measures thus serve as a slow introduction to the following movement.

The third movement is a lively gigue, which, like a rondo, has a main theme that returns several times but also exhibits some of the characteristics of symphonic binary or sonata form, albeit without the high drama exhibited in the first movement. When first heard, the twelve-measure theme remains open on the dominant. A contrasting episode follows (mm. 13–24) that serves as a modulating bridge touching on the parallel minor before, with a bold chromatic movement in the outer voices, it leads us to A, the dominant of the dominant key, D major (mm. 22–24). In place of a contrasting "second theme," the main theme transposed to the dominant key returns to close the first part of the binary form.

The second part of the binary form starts with the repetition of the theme in the dominant key. After six measures the theme assumes developmental features and loses itself in modulatory sequences (the "far out point" is the B-minor section, mm. 53–70) before the double return of the original key and the main theme in m. 89. More in the spirit of a rondo than sonata form, the double return leads only to the opening theme and a brief concluding section rather than to a replay of all the music of the first part.

Movement 4: *Minuetto*

The last movement is a transposition of a minuet from an early Sammartini trio sonata. This borrowing and the dance topics of movements 3 and 4 signal the early symphony's debt to the sonata da camera and the dance suite. The movement is a clearly articulated minuet, without a trio and without the customary double return. Unlike in the other movements, the viola has no independent part but doubles the bass line at the octave. The top staff contains a variation of the melody staff below. It appears to provide a clue as to how performers were expected to embellish simple melodies on repetition.

* m. 14: Quarter rest in the manuscript.

* mm. 23, 24: ♪♪ ?

II

Transition

passus dec

III

gigue
Allegro assai

IV

no trio

Minuetto

* m. 16: ♩ ♪ in all sources, which is appropriate for the variation, but not for the minuet proper.

8

Johann Christian Bach (1735–82)

FULL CD III: TRACK 13

Symphony in B♭ Major, Op. 18, No. 2, First movement (*Allegro assai*) (1774)

Johann Christian (JC) Bach's Symphony in B♭ Major, Op. 18, No. 2, was originally composed as the *sinfonia avanti l'opera* ("symphony before the opera" or overture) to his opera seria *Lucio Silla*. (The same libretto had already been set three years earlier by Mozart for the opera house in Milan.) Publication followed seven years later in London, in a set entitled "Six Grand Overtures," of which two others were opera overtures and the remaining three were symphonies composed for concert use. The use of the word "overture" to refer to what we now call symphonies persisted in London to the end of the eighteenth century.

JC's *Lucio Silla* was first performed in November 1775, at the court of Mannheim, which by then boasted a major opera house. The real claim to fame of the Mannheim court was, however, its magnificent orchestra—JC's symphony contains many details that show that he was writing for the particular strengths of this famous ensemble of virtuoso musicians. Already the unusually rich orchestration of the symphony displays the composer's reliance on the special Mannheim forces. In addition to the usual strings, oboes, and horns (typical for symphonies from ca. 1740 through the 1770s), JC includes two flutes, two bassoons, and, the most important novelty of the Mannheim orchestra, two clarinets, the last member of the woodwind family to become a standard member of the orchestra. The woodwinds not only double and reinforce the strings as in most orchestral music of the time but also have their own independent thematic material that provides textural and dynamic contrast (e.g., the woodwind solos in mm. 50–62). The tempo marking of the first movement, *Allegro assai* (very fast), shows JC's confidence in the orchestra's virtuoso abilities.

The Mannheim orchestra was especially known for its precision of ensemble and dramatic use of dynamics. The movement begins with a loud *tutti* on the tonic triad, a dramatic effect that in late-eighteenth-century parlance was called *premier coup d'archet* (literally: "first stroke of the bow"). The abruptly reduced texture and dynamic in m. 2 followed by a crescendo coupled with a rising line (mm. 4–5), a so-called "Mannheim rocket," show that JC was intimately familiar with techniques used by composers writing for the Mannheim orchestra.

Like the first movement of JC's keyboard sonata in D major and, to a somewhat lesser degree, Sammartini's symphony discussed earlier in this anthology, the first movement of this symphony displays an abundance of different thematic materials, which are presented in a highly dramatized, contrasting manner. While clearly organized around the binary (tonic/dominant) axis (first theme group in B♭ major [mm. 1–11], "bridge" [mm. 11–19], second theme group in F major [mm. 20–42]), the form of the movement does not entirely conform to sonata principles: it lacks the repeat of the exposition, a common variation of binary form in overtures and Mannheim symphonies, and, in place of a development section leading to a distant key, it has two new themes in the tonic key (mm. 43–50, mm. 50–64), another common feature of opera overtures. Both of these themes have a dominant pedal, and thus together they function as a "re-transition" to the first theme. The "double return" (m. 65) arrives with all the rhetorical bravado that is its due, which almost makes us forget that in the section that replaced the "development" we have not left the tonic key.

This is not the end of the surprises JC has in store for us. In the "recapitulation" the "bridge" does not return; instead, we encounter what in the exposition served as the secondary theme (cf. mm. 20–25 and mm. 75–86), but now it is made to modulate—as if JC had placed a development section after the "double return." At the end of this modulatory passage another unusual thing happens: the two new themes from the first developmental section reappear (cf. mm. 43–64 and mm. 98–110). The movement ends with closing gestures featuring dotted rhythms borrowed from the end of the exposition (cf. mm. 36–39 and mm. 114–117). With its brilliant orchestration and multitude of pleasing themes, JC's symphony is music aimed at pleasing a wide public.

Note on Performance Practice

The marking *"attacca"* at the end of the movement in the modern edition indicates that the second movement (not included here) of the three-movement symphony should follow immediately. When used as an overture to a stage work, all the movements of a symphony would have been played together. When played in concert, however, it was common to treat movements as separate units and to perform other works between them.

Measure Nos.	Formal Designation	Sections	Keys	Comments
1–42	Exposition			
1–11		Primary theme	B♭	*Premiere coup d'archet* and "Mannheim rocket"
11–19		Bridge	Ends on F	
20–42		Secondary themes 1–3	F	Three themes in dominant: mm. 20–25, 26–30, 31–40
43–64	Quasi- Development		Dominant pedal in viola and violins is typical of retransition	
43–50		new theme 1	B♭	
50–64		new theme 2	B♭	Soloistic wind parts = Mannheim innovation
65–123	Quasi- Recapitulation		Begins with return of primary theme, but becomes developmental	
65–74		Primary theme	B♭	Not followed by bridge material
75–87		Secondary theme 1	c, B♭, E♭, B♭	Modulation normally associated with development
87–97		New material	E♭, B♭	Texture typical of bridge
98–114		"New themes" 1 and 2 from quasi-development	E♭, B♭	Restatement of themes from quasi-development gives them function similar to secondary themes
114–123		Closing section		cf. theme in m. 31

Allegro assai

Flöten
Oboen
Klarinetten in B
Fagotte
Hörner in B
Violine I
Violine II
Viola
Violoncello u. Kontrabaß

[Handwritten annotations:] wind band · rocket power · string orch. · rocket!! · cello · bass · playing in octaves, doubled · 4 bar phrases · foreshadowing/development of modern sonata-allegro form

9

Franz Joseph Haydn
(1734–1807)

FULL CD III: TRACK 14
CONCISE CD II: TRACK 10

Symphony No. 45 in F♯ Minor ("Farewell"),
First movement (*Allegro assai*) (1772)

Joseph Haydn's Symphony No. 45 was first performed at the summer palace of Prince Esterházy in November 1772. It is an exceptional work both because of its key (there is no other symphony in F♯ minor among the roughly 16,000 entries in Jan LaRue's *Union Thematic Catalogue*, a directory of symphonies written between 1720 and 1810) and because of the program suggested by the finale, a highly unusual *Adagio* section that calls for the musicians to leave the stage one by one or two by two after playing solo turns (an ingenious way for Haydn to communicate to his employer that he had kept the musicians of his entourage away from their families for too long).

The form of the first movement is famously enigmatic. With its uniquely "remote" key and its consequently anomalous timbre (at least when played on the winds and horns of Haydn's time), this strange and stormy movement is the most extreme representative of a special group of symphonic compositions by Haydn in the early 1770s that are often associated with a German literary movement known as *Sturm und Drang* ("Storm and Stress"). The emotional turmoil that characterized this literary movement can also be seen in the unremitting, agitated syncopations in the accompaniment to the movement's opening and one of its secondary themes (mm. 56–59). A more significant symptom of the eccentric *Sturm und Drang* style, however, is Haydn's peculiar treatment of the sonata form. After a straightforward presentation of the first theme and modulation to the relative major, a sudden introduction of C natural pushes the music into A minor (m. 38) and additional modulations. Where we would expect the secondary theme with contrasting character, we find a continuation of the stormy, agitated music now in C♯ minor (mm. 56–74). This key is the "minor dominant," a rare choice at a time when an opening theme in the minor mode was conventionally counterbalanced by a theme in the relative major. Even C♯ minor is contradicted on the other side of the double bar by another sudden move: a switch to A major, the key originally expected and deferred.

The development starts dutifully in A major, with the recasting of the first theme in its new key, but soon modulates to B minor (m. 98), stopping on a half cadence (m. 109). Here we finally hear a contrasting second theme (an important precedent for Beethoven's introduction of a new, E-minor theme in the development of his "Eroica" Symphony [see Anthology Vol 2-19]). Structurally misplaced, it is cast in neither the dominant nor the relative major— the "normal" alternate keys in a minor-mode movement. The key of the lyrical "second theme" in this movement is actually that of the "far out point," the submediant D major (mm. 110–143). This is perhaps the most serious departure from the conventions of sonata form as established and practiced by Haydn himself, according to which the "far out point" is to be reached through *thematische Arbeit* (thematic working out), not suddenly introduced with new thematic material.

As if that were not enough, this placid D-major theme is approached and left not by transitions but by pauses on either side. It has the air of an insertion, not a development, set off further from its surroundings by its scoring, which initially lacks bass instruments and winds. Furthermore, it comes to no final cadence; rather, it seems (by the use of an arpeggiated diminished-seventh chord) to dissolve into thin air (like a mirage, as the Haydn specialist James Webster has suggested). Clearly this music is deliberately enigmatic.

This is not the last surprise Haydn has in store. After the double return (m. 144) he produces what might be considered a second development by introducing a section of modulation (mm. 150ff.) that briefly touches on G♯ minor (mm. 154–156), tonally the point of furthest remove in the entire movement. Haydn notates the dominant chord as D♯-G-A♯-C♯ (mm. 152–153). Here Haydn added a footnote to his manuscript: "*sapienti pauca*" (to the wise, little is sufficient), which jokingly indicates that good musicians should recognize that the notated G natural should be understood and played as F double sharp, the leading tone of G♯ minor.

In its peculiar features this symphony thus departs from what had become accepted norms of composition by the time it was written—especially at the Esterházy court. Haydn was violating the conventions he had created, and he could only have been expecting his audience to notice the fact. From this example we can generalize about compositional "norms," many of which Haydn established in the realms of the symphony and string quartet. Norms are not laws that must be strictly adhered to. Indeed, absolutely unchallenged "normality" is perhaps the most boring mode of discourse. Rather, the existence of norms allows departures to become meaningful—and thereby expressive.

57

Measure Nos.	Formal Designation	Sections	Keys	Comments
1–74	**Exposition**			
1–16		1st theme	f♯	
17–55		Bridge		Extended by excursion to a, m. 38
56–74		2nd theme	c♯	Key of minor dominant is an unusual choice for 2nd theme
75–143	**Development**			Begins in A, the key expected for the 2nd theme
75–109				Working of 1st theme
104–109			b	Working of 2nd theme
110–143		New theme	D	Lyrical in the manner of a 2nd theme. Derived from the bridge (m. 23); D functions as "far out point" of development
144–211	**Recapitulation**			
144–197		1st theme and bridge	f♯	After 4 mm. the 1st theme begins to modulate, thus merging with the bridge, which feels much like a second development
197–211		2nd theme	f♯	

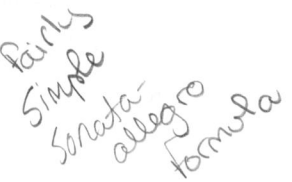

Fairly simple sonata-allegro formula

Rhetorical pause

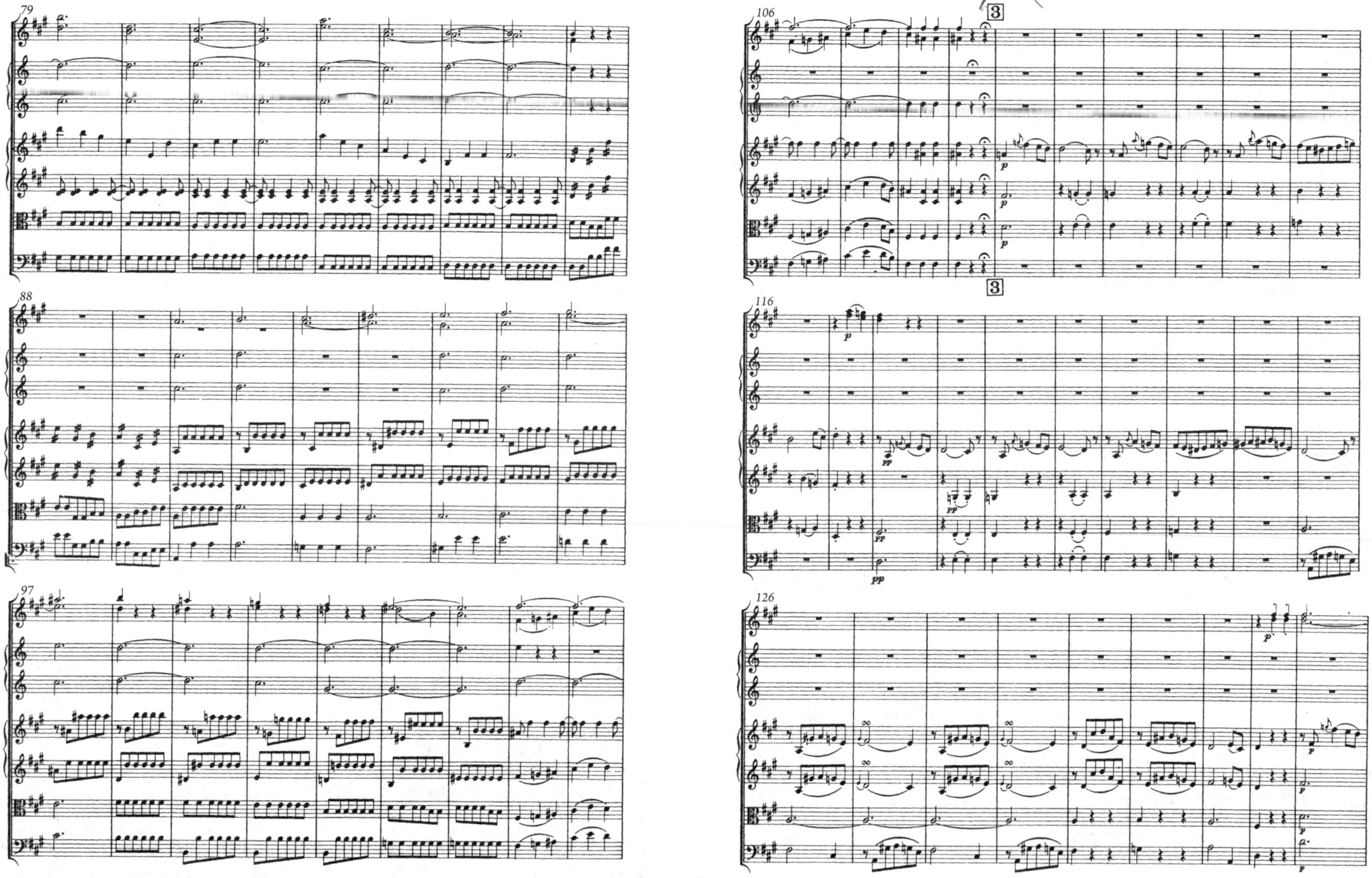

10

Franz Joseph Haydn (1734–1807)

String Quartet in E♭ Major ("The Joke"), Op. 33, No. 2 (Pub. 1782)

The six string quartets by Haydn issued as Op. 33 in 1782 constitute his first set of quartets published by the Viennese firm Artaria, from then on Haydn's main publisher. They were the first quartets by Haydn not alternatively billed as divertimentos, and the second, after the pioneering Op. 20 series, in which the lower three instruments are frequently given material that matches in interest that of the first violin. The witty second quartet of the set ("The Joke") shows that Haydn was able to play with newly established conventions and musical procedures to gain meaning generated by the interplay between the expected and the unexpected. (The Op. 33 quartets are subtitled "Gli scherzi" because they include movements labeled "scherzo"—literally "joke" or "jest"—instead of "minuet.")

Movement 1: *Allegro moderato, cantabile*

As the chart outlines, the first movement is in sonata form. The movement exhibits Haydn's penchant for working with motives. In this case the opening three notes (two sixteenth notes followed by a longer note) constitute the rhythmic motive that provides the bulk of the material for the movement. Haydn playfully contrasts this anapestic (short-short-long) figuration with its dactylic counterpart (long-short-short). The contrast between the two is clearest in mm. 51–56, in which the anapestic figurations in the second violin, viola, and cello are directly juxtaposed with the dactylic rhythm in the first violin.

A particular specialty of Haydn's is inventing material that can work as gestures of both opening and closing. Observe that, in addition to initiating the bridge (pickup to m. 13) and the second theme group (pickup to m. 21), the motive closes the first phrase of the first theme (m. 4), the exposition (m. 32), and finally the entire movement. This type of playing with the function of the motive and therefore with our expectations helps give Haydn's music its wit.

One aspect of Haydn's approach to sonata form in this movement worth noting is that the second theme group is not strongly articulated. After several iterations of the main motive

Measure Nos.	Formal Designation	Sections	Keys	Comments
1–32	**Exposition**			
1–12		Primary theme	E♭	4 + 4 + 4 (aba)
13–20		Bridge		
21–28		Secondary theme	B♭	Beginning of theme not clearly articulated
29–32		Closing material	B♭	Related to theme 1 "b"
33–62	**Development**			
33–34		Closing material	B♭, E♭	
35–42		Theme 1	A♭, f, E♭	Contrapuntal elaboration
43–48		Further modulation "far out point"	e♭	Using rhythm of primary theme head motive; circle-of-fifths sequence
49–58		Closing material	f, c	
59–62		Theme 1	C	False recapitulation
63–90	**Recapitulation**			
63–70		Primary theme	E♭	4 + 4
71–77		Bridge	Ends on V/E♭	
78–86		Secondary theme	E♭	
87–90		Closing material	E♭	Ends with opening gesture

(mm. 21–22) above a tonic pedal, it gives way to an elaborated cadence on the dominant (mm. 23–28). This cadential music is not particularly distinctive as thematic material; it functions to provide some neutral space to support a harmonic close.

Movement 2: *Scherzo, Allegro*

Haydn's second movement is a dance in the form of a minuet and trio. Placement of the dance movement second rather than third among the four movements of a quartet was frequent in Haydn's early string quartets, which may be explained in part by the history of the genre. Haydn's string quartets were closely related to the divertimento, a genre in which it was common to have five movements, including two minuets, one before and one after a central slow movement. For Haydn it was just a choice, so to speak, of which minuet to "omit" in the composition of a quartet. More unusual was Haydn's use of the word "Scherzo" to designate this movement. Here the designation seems to indicate that the minuet should be played a little faster than usual. The humor of the movement stems in part from the fact that it does not adhere to the standard tonal trajectory of a minuet. The expected modulation to the dominant takes place only after the double bar. The traditional "double return" thus becomes a literal restatement of the first strain since there is no need to "correct" the modulation (mm. 25–34).

Haydn reproduces this scheme—no modulation before the double bar and full literal restatement of the first strain at the double return—in the Trio. As was the norm, the texture of the Trio is simpler than that of most of the rest of the work. A novel aspect of the Trio is Haydn's placement of glissandi between the large leaps in the first violin at mm. 51 and 53 (not marked in our edition of the score), which contributes to the rough-hewn sound of the music. This is an example of Haydn's mock-primitive style—a highly sophisticated composer imitating the efforts of uncouth village musicians.

Measure Nos.	Formal Designation	Sections	Keys	Comments
1–37	Rondo theme	A: 8 + 20 + 8 (aba)	B♭	"b" with extended dominant pedal
38–71	Episode 1	B	A♭, c, E♭	Developmental, with dominant pedals
72–107	Rondo theme	A: 8 + 20 + 8 (aba)	E♭	
108–140	Episode 2	C	E♭ V	Starts like episode 1, stays in E♭
141–148	Rondo theme	A: 8 (a)	E♭	
149–152	"Episode 3"	D	E♭	*Adagio* interruption
153–172	Rondo theme	A (a)	E♭	With interruptions; ends after restarting the theme

Movement 3: *Largo sostenuto*

The quartet's slow movement—as is frequently the case with Haydn—is cast in the most "original," least classifiable form, although it is based on familiar procedures, such as variation and rondo. The opening eight-measure duet, in which the viola enunciates the movement's lyrical main theme (thus reasserting its "emancipated" role after its rustic subordination in the Trio), is repeated four more times in different instrumental pairings, with textural elaboration in the form of countermelodies. The intervening episodes (mm. 21–31, preceded by a four-measure transition, mm. 17–20; mm. 40–51; mm. 60–63) provide thematic contrast and tonal balance.

Movement 4: *Presto*

The last movement gave the "Joke" Quartet its nickname. The form is that of a rondo. The theme is shaped exactly like those of the Scherzo and Trio: a repeated eight-measure strain that cadences in the tonic key, followed by a second strain that moves to the dominant and ends with a literal repeat of the first strain.

The "joke" comes at the end of the movement, when Haydn interrupts the fast flow of the *Presto* with a sudden *Adagio* section. When the theme resumes, he inserts general pauses between each two-measure unit of the eight-measure theme. Instead of allowing the piece to end with the *last* two measures of the theme, however, Haydn closes, after an exaggerated extended pause, with the *first* two measures of the theme, ingeniously demonstrating the interchangeability of opening and closing gestures. What takes the audience by surprise is not the music they hear but that the movement is over.

Finale
Presto

IV

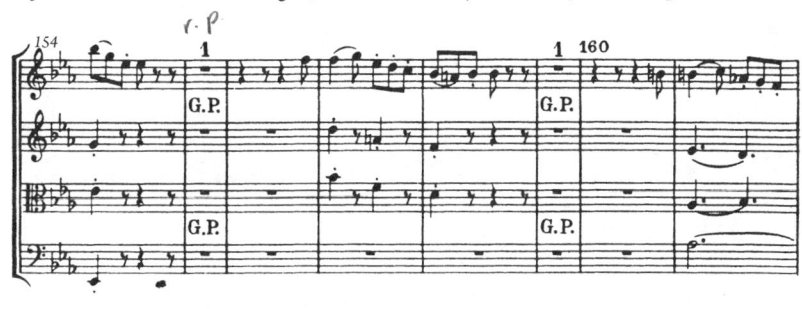

11

Franz Joseph Haydn (1734–1807)

FULL CD III: TRACKS 19–22
CONCISE CD II: TRACKS 12–13

Symphony No. 104 in D Major ("London") (1795)

Haydn's Symphony No. 104, written for performance at a series of subscription concerts in London, is his last work in the genre and only his fifth symphony to include clarinets. It has never left the repertory of major orchestras since its first performance in May 1795.

Movement 1: *Adagio–Allegro*

The slow introduction to the first movement, which had become standard in Haydn symphonies, begins with an audience-summoning fanfare typical of symphonies intended for a large paying public (as opposed to performance in court). In its brief sixteen measures the slow introduction encompasses the complete tonal trajectory of a typical binary form: from tonic (D minor) to relative major (F major) and back (compare the tonalities of the fanfares mm. 1–2, 7–8, and 14–15). The progression to F major is very direct. The progression back (mm. 9–13) is, as always, more tortuous. The modulations are achieved through manipulation of a motive derived from the theme, the rhythm of which is applied to stepwise melodic motion. On regaining the tonic in mm. 14–15, Haydn modifies the theme to use a falling fifth in place of the original falling fourth, reaching G, harmonized not as the root of a G-minor chord but as the bass of E♭⁶, a "Neapolitan sixth," that prepares a half cadence on V so that the slow introduction leads directly to the tonic at the *Allegro*.

The *Allegro* section of the first movement is in the full-blown sonata, or symphonic binary, form that had become a requirement for the first movement of a symphony. Typically for Haydn, the tune beginning the first theme group (mm. 1–15)* is also used to begin the second theme group (mm. 49–64), now transposed to the dominant. The exposition is thus "monothematic." Although nineteenth-century theorists regarded the lack of melodic contrast between the "primary" and "secondary" themes as unusual, for Haydn and his audience symphonic binary form was defined by tonal contrast, not thematic contrast, and by development

---

*The score in this anthology begins counting the measures from "1" again at the beginning of the *Allegro*.

Measure Nos.	Formal Designation	Sections	Keys	Comments
1–17	Slow Intro	*Adagio*	d, F, d	Tonal trajectory of binary form
1–107	Exposition	*Allegro*		NB: mm. begin at 1 again
1–16		1st theme	D	8 + 8 (aa′)
16–48		Bridge	Ends on V/V	New theme, *forte*, related to 1st theme
49–83		2nd theme area	A	Same material as 1st theme
84–107		Closing section	A	
108–176	Development			Motivic work
108–129			b, e, c♯	From mm. 3–4 of 1st theme
130–142		"far out point" (mm. 130–139)	c♯, g♯, f♯, E, e	From beginning of 1st theme
143–176			E, b, ends on V/D	From mm. 3–4 of 1st theme, ends w/dominant pedal
177–278	Recapitulation			
177–192		1st theme	D	Ends with counterpoint
192–231		Bridge		Bridge theme
231–250		2nd theme area	D	Fragments of theme come first, section truncated
251–278		Closing section	D	

of the musical material not only in the development section but also throughout the movement. This is precisely what Haydn provides.

The opening theme of the *Allegro* consists of a sixteen-measure period, eight measures ending on a half cadence and then a repetition coming to a full cadence. The dramatic *tutti* that marks the elision of the full cadence (i.e., the overlap of the theme's cadence with the arrival of new thematic material in m. 16) also signals the "bridge" (mm. 16–48): thirty-three measures without a pause, ending on the V of V to prepare for the arrival of the tonicized dominant.

The modulatory passage, or bridge, has a close rhythmic relationship to the first theme. It begins with the rhythm of the first measure of the first theme (mm. 16, 18; see also the timpani mm. 22–23) and recalls that rhythm again in the first violins at mm. 38–39. The rhythm of the first violins, flutes, and especially first oboe at mm. 34–35 is distinctly related to both the rhythm and the pitch repetitions of the first theme at mm. 3–4.

At m. 49 the first theme returns wholesale to mark the secondary key. This time the transitional passage that interrupts the theme with an elided cadence in m. 64 makes reference to the theme's syncopated inner voice (cf. mm. 4–6, second violins, and mm. 64–66, lower strings). The only "new" thematic material in the exposition comes in the closing section (mm. 84–107), though even here there are subtle, motivic correspondences with the main theme.

In the development Haydn harvests great bounty from the two-measure repeated-note idea first heard in the third and fourth measures of the first theme. The first restatements of it after the double bar (mm. 108–113) are nearly literal. Thereafter the idea is altered melodically in various ways over the invariant original rhythm. Even where the principal melodic line stems not from mm. 3–4 but from mm. 1–2 of the theme (e.g., mm. 130–139), the repeated quarter notes in the bass are still related to mm. 3–4 (the way they are highlighted by the bassoon in mm. 134–139 leaves no doubt as to the purposefulness of the reference).

The reassertion of the original key at the double return is more dramatic than usual in this movement, since the development section had been confined to minor tonalities. Indeed, thanks to some particularly ingenious deceptive cadences, it is a wider range of minor tonalities than we have yet encountered before in this anthology, including two (C♯ minor, mm. 130–133, and G♯ minor, mm. 134–136) very distant from the home key, making the passage mm. 130–139 an extreme example of a "far out point." The economy of thematic content is thus combined with the generous expansion of the tonal trajectory.

Movement 2: *Andante*

As we have already seen in connection with his string quartets, the forms of the slow movements of Haydn's symphonies often diverge from standard patterns. This *Andante* is a ternary form—ABA′ much like a minuet–trio–minuet—although close inspection reveals at least two unusual features: The B section is developmental in nature, and A′ does not simply vary the material of A but also includes developmental excursions.

A (mm. 1–37) is itself a binary structure, complete with a cadence on the dominant at the first double bar and a return to tonic by the second double bar by way of harmonic excursion. Oddly, however, there are two returns to tonic G major in this section (m. 17 and m. 33), each preceded by a section of tonal wandering. The return to G in m. 17 is a double return, which remains true to the opening theme for four measures before setting off in a new direction.

B (mm. 38–73) resembles the development section of a sonata form. It begins with a four-measure statement of the main theme in G minor before a tonally unstable storm breaks out (mm. 42–55). After the storm, the first part of the theme returns in B♭ major in m. 57—its first cadence in m. 60 elides with a second stormy section, in which the first measure of the theme is developed in sequence. This storm now gives way to a retransition over a dominant pedal (mm. 67–73).

A mm.	A′ mm.
1–8	74–81
1–8	82–89 (variation)
9–16	90–97 (variation)
17–22	98–103 (variation)
23–25	104–121 (much developed and expanded)
17–25	122–133 (variation, mm. 131–133 = written-out fermata of m. 25)
26–37	134–145 (varied)
	146 to the end (coda)

A′ (m. 74 to the end) brings back the material of A in the original key. This time, however, Haydn adds variations, repetitions, and harmonic excursions that increase the length by some thirty-five measures. The following table gives a comparison of A and A′.

Movement 3: *Allegro*

As was typical, the minuet movement in fact consists of two minuets—the second dubbed "trio" in honor of its frequently reduced texture. A "da capo" repetition of the first minuet follows the trio and results in an ABA form (minuet-trio-minuet). Typically the minuet and trio are both in binary form and in closely related keys. In this minuet Haydn does not modulate until after the first double bar, and, having already repeated the material of the first eight measures with a reduced dynamic and scoring, he foregoes the customary repeat of the first strain of the minuet. As was the case in the minuet of the "Joke" Quartet, lack of modulation in the first strain goes together with a mock peasant style—note the "crude" tonic D pedal in the bass in the first four measures of the theme and the "uncouth" *sforzandi* on the third beats of mm. 1–3 and 6.

In contrast, the trio is all smoothness and sophistication, with elegant writing for the winds (a common feature in orchestral trio sections). Haydn slips into B♭ major, the key of the trio and the flat-sixth degree of the key of the minuet, via the common tone D. The closing cadence on B♭ (m. 94), however, needs a more extensive transition to prepare for the da capo return of the D-major minuet. Haydn adds this transitional section (mm. 95–104) after the second double bar.

Movement 4: *Allegro spiritoso*

The main theme of the finale is a simple eight-measure tune with rustic character. Some have related the tune to a folk song Haydn may have known from childhood; others have associated the melody with London street cries. Neither of these theories can be proved, but they both

Measure Nos.	Formal Designation	Sections	Keys	Comments
1–118	**Exposition**			
1–18		1st theme	D	Rustic, with tonic pedal
19–83		Bridge		mm. 19–22, cf. m. 5
				mm. 31–39, cf. theme 1
				mm. 44–52, cf. mm. 5–6
				mm. 55–65, cf. theme 1
				mm. 65–81, cf. m. 13 (violin 2)
84–101		2nd theme	A (affirmed in m. 90)	Deceptive resolution of preceding V of A
102–118		Closing section		
119–192	**Development**			
155–165		"Far out point"	b	
167–192		Development of secondary theme	Used as retransition	
193–334	**Recapitulation**		1st statement of 1st theme omitted	
193–202		1st theme	D	
203–246		Bridge		Order of sections rearranged
247–264		2nd theme	D (affirmed in m. 253)	Deceptive resolution of preceding V
265–334		Closing/coda	D	Much working of main motive

signal that audiences have recognized the melody as borrowed from some popular source. The D pedal that begins the movement imitates the sound of a bagpipe and thus highlights the pastoral quality of the theme.

Although the movement is clearly in sonata form, there is (as is often the case with Haydn) some ambiguity as to the beginning of the second key area and the coda. We interpret the movement as containing an extended bridge made up of several sections. Despite the movement's rustic theme, the finale, as typical of Haydn's late works, does not lack contrapuntal intricacies (see, for instance, Haydn's combination of the motive at the end of the exposition with the main theme at the beginning of the development in mm. 119ff). The movement is also notable for the substantial length and weight of its coda, which has elements that suggest a second development. Within a decade of this work, the finales of symphonies (often with extended codas) would regularly come to rival and sometimes surpass the length and weight of their first movements.

how he
(gets there)

II

*Fehlt im Autograph

III

Menuetto Allegro

* Fehlt im Autograph

Men. D.C.

IV

Finale: Spiritoso

* Fehlt im Autograph

12

Franz Joseph Haydn (1734–1807)

FULL CD III: TRACKS 23–24
CONCISE CD II: TRACK 14

Die Schöpfung (*The Creation*), No. 1, Overture,
"Die Vorstellung des Chaos" ("The Representation of Chaos"),
and No. 2, Recitative and chorus

In 1795 Haydn returned from his second and last trip to London with a libretto for an oratorio, reputedly originally written for Handel. The text, entitled *The Creation of the World*, was based on the Bible and Milton's *Paradise Lost*. In Vienna Haydn had the libretto adapted and translated into German by his friend the Baron van Swieten (1733–1803). Haydn set it as an oratorio for orchestra, chorus, and vocal soloists. With its 1798 premiere in Vienna, *The Creation* became Haydn's most beloved work.

In place of a traditional overture, which at the time would have been an *allegro* movement in sonata form, Haydn opens the work with a slow movement representing the chaos preceding the biblical Beginning. Haydn's depiction of Chaos and the formation of the cosmos is likely to have been influenced by what was then the most advanced scientific theory of the origin of the universe: the so-called nebular hypothesis, first proposed by Immanuel Kant in 1755. According to the nebular hypothesis, the solar system originated as an immense body of rarefied gas and dust swirling in space that gradually cooled, contracted, and condensed to form the sun and the planets. Or, as the Bible put it, in the beginning "the earth was without form and void" until God gave the Word, whereupon the processes described in the nebular hypothesis commenced. Haydn's "Representation of Chaos," then, was a representation of a process in which something without form took shape.

As inchoate matter strives, according to the nebular hypothesis, toward shape and differentiation, so the music of Haydn's introduction strives toward articulation of the key. Haydn expertly prolongs and delays the process of tonal clarification by avoiding straightforward resolution of chords. A cadence identifying the tonic and dominant, normally given at the outset of a composition, is withheld until the end of the introduction. The unharmonized Cs of m. 1 imply the key of C, but they do not confirm it, nor do they suggest whether the key is major or minor. The C–E♭ dyad in m. 2 suggests C minor, but the A♭ in the second half of the measure points in a different direction. A dominant chord appears briefly on beat 3 of m. 3 but resolves deceptively to an A♭-major chord in first inversion (m. 5). Deceptive resolutions, chromatic motion, and the absence of melody all work against a coherent sense of order (at least by eighteenth-century

standards) until Haydn finally allows a full cadence on C minor to occur, *pianissimo*, in m. 50 and again more decisively in m. 58. Here there is an added dimension made explicit by the entry of a bass singer impersonating the angel Raphael intoning the opening words of the Book of Genesis: "In the Beginning God created the heavens and the earth." The imminence of Creation has been announced. But its first forecast was not the Angel's speech; it came wordlessly in the earlier C-minor chords played by the strings, finally fulfilling, in a whisper, the promise of form. In effect, Haydn turned the techniques of keyboard improvisation and fantasia writing (as we have observed them in CPE Bach) into a metaphor for Biblical creation.

Orchestration plays an important role throughout the "Representation of Chaos" as a "nebular" metaphor. Swirling figures in the woodwinds, including a couple of spectacular runs for the flute and for the still-novel clarinet, and unusual crescendos on single notes in the strings (mm. 26–30) contribute tellingly to the uncanny effect of the whole.

The Biblical account continues in a remarkable recitative in which the chorus, which may impersonally represent the voice of God, takes part. Haydn's suddenly radiant passage that follows the first act of Creation (". . . and there was LIGHT") so astounded the audience at the premiere that the performance had to be stopped for some minutes. The entrance of the woodwinds and brass en masse after a long silence contributes decisively to the sublimity of the moment, but there is nothing technically astonishing about the passage. It is an ordinary (if unusually assertive) authentic cadence on C, of a kind that every composer of Haydn's time wrote every single day. The very special context creates its overwhelmingly fraught significance, reminding us that what lends any utterance meaning is never confined to its mere "content" but is the product of an interaction between sender, context, and receiver(s). The tonal trajectory of the astounding introduction to *The Creation*—from a dark and murky "unformed" C minor to a radiantly triumphant C major— became a favorite narrative archetype for composers of succeeding generations.

Raphael
*Im Anfangen schuf Gott
Himmel und Erde;
und die Erde war ohne Form und leer;
und Finsternis war auf der Fläche
   der Tiefe.*

Chorus
*Und der Geist Gottes schwebte
auf der Fläche der Wasser;
und Gott Sprach: Es werde Licht,
und es ward Licht.*

Uriel
*Und Gott sah das Licht, dass es gut war;
und Gott schied das Licht von
   der Finsternis.*

Raphael
In the beginning God created
the heavens and the earth;
and the earth was without form and void;
And darkness was upon the face of the deep.

Chorus
And the Spirit of God moved
upon the face of the waters;
and God said: Let there be Light,
and there was Light.

Uriel
And God saw the Light, that it was good;
and God divided Light from the darkness.

"Handel on drugs" - really?

contra

piccolo

tenor

bass trombone

piano - in between harpsichord & modern piano

Scene 1

No. 2   Recitative (Raphael/Uriel) and Chorus

Im Anfange schuf Gott Himmel und Erde · *In the beginning God created the heaven and the earth.*
Und der Geist Gottes schwebte auf der Fläche der Wasser · *And the Spirit of God moved upon the face of the waters.*

13

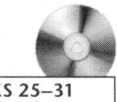

FULL CD III: TRACKS 25–31
CONCISE CD II: TRACKS 15–16

Wolfgang Amadè Mozart
(1756–91)

Don Giovanni (Don Juan), K. 527, Acts I and II (1787)

Don Giovanni, the second of Mozart and the librettist Lorenzo Da Ponte's three famous operatic collaborations, was first performed in Prague in 1787. On the libretto's title page was the designation "drama giocoso" (jocular drama), a term coined by Venetian playwright Carlo Goldoni (1707–93) to describe an opera inhabited by character types from serious opera, stock buffa types, as well as so-called *mezzo carattere* (in the middle), characters that combine elements of buffa and seria. The opera depicts the adventures and eventual downfall of the infamous Spanish libertine Don Juan (Don Giovanni), first given literary treatment in Tirso de Molina's *El burlador de Seville* (The Trickster of Seville, 1630) and subsequently the subject of many literary and dramatic works. In Da Ponte and Mozart's opera, the climax occurs in the second-act finale, when Don Giovanni is dragged to hell by the stone statue of the Commendatore (commander), a high-ranking nobleman whom Don Giovanni had killed in the opening scene after trying to seduce his daughter.

a. Overture

By Mozart's day the sinfonia, or overture, was no longer in three movements but in a single (*Allegro*) movement in a sonata form that omits the repeat of the exposition. Mozart precedes the *Allegro* with a dramatic *Andante* that forecasts the plot's grisly resolution with music that reappears when the statue of the Commendatore confronts Don Giovanni. The forecast is one not only of musical theme and mood but also of key (D minor). It was a convention that the second-act finale end in the key in which the overture begins, thus matching musically the resolution of the plot. There were in practice only three tonics that could be used in this way: C, D, and E♭, the keys of the natural trumpets and horns that would normally figure at the opera's loudest moments.

Measure Nos.	Formal Designation	Sections	Keys	Comments
1–30	Slow introduction	*Andante*	d	Taken from climactic entrance of the Commendatore at the end of the opera
31–120	Exposition			Repeat of Exposition omitted in overtures
31–46		Primary theme	D	*Allegro*
46–55		Bridge	ends on V	
56–76		Secondary theme 1	A	In three sections: mm. 56–61, 62–66, 67–76
77–99		Secondary theme 2	A	
99–120		Closing theme	A	
121–192	Development			
121–140		Secondary theme 2		Sequentially developed
141–156		Primary theme	G, B♭	
157–192		Secondary theme 2	B♭, g, d, ends on V/D	
193–274	Recapitulation			
193–207		Primary theme	D	
207–216		Bridge		Ends on V/d
217–237		Secondary theme 1	D	
238–247		Secondary theme 2	D	
248–260		Further modulation	d, F, d	Developmental
260–272		Closing theme		
272–292		Transition to scene 1	G, V/F	Secondary theme 2

b. Introduction

There were usually three main sections in a late-eighteenth-century opera buffa in which action was uninterrupted by recitatives: the *introduzione,* or beginning of the first act, in which the plot was set in motion; the first-act finale, in which the *imbroglio* reached its peak, and the second act finale, in which the action was driven home to closure.

In the *introduzione* of *Don Giovanni,* the first vocal entrance belongs to the noble title character's grumpy manservant, Leporello, a stock opera buffa type, always sung by a bass. The scene's opening march-like ritornello sketches Leporello's impatient pacing as he stands guard and awaits the return of his master. (His about-faces are painted in the short scale runs that give emphasis to the first beats of every second measure.) Mozart sets Leporello's line of envy, "I'd like to live like a gentleman" ("Voglio far il gentiluomo"), with a flowing melody such as a gentleman might sing that contrasts with the less elevated music of his opening complaint. The last cadence of the vocal melody initiates a modulation (mm. 70–73). This modulation from F major to B♭ major, casts Leporello's whole song in retrospect as a sort of upbeat in the dominant to the first bit of fast-paced action, the entrance of Don Giovanni, who rushes onstage pursued by the enraged Donna Anna, the lady with whom he has been keeping company while his servant had been outside keeping watch.

The three characters now onstage sing a tense trio in B♭ major, Donna Anna accusing the Don of attempted rape and calling for help, the Don attempting to flee, and Leporello cowering off to one side. The end of this section also segues into modulation: Tremolando violins intrude on its final cadence (m. 134), and an incongruous F♯ is introduced to coincide with the entrance of the Commendatore (m. 138), Donna Anna's father. This F♯ wrenches the tonality into an unstable G minor for another, much shorter trio, in which the two noblemen exchange threats while Leporello, hiding, continues his frightened commentary.

The final cadence of the male trio is on D minor (m. 166), a key the significance of which has already been signaled by the menacing slow introduction to the overture. The Don and the Commendatore draw swords and fight to a modulating orchestral passage ending on a diminished-seventh chord that coincides with Don Giovanni's fatal thrust. The tempo now changes radically as the Commendatore, mortally wounded, falters and dies, while Don Giovanni gloats and Leporello panics, all in the remote key of F minor—remote, that is, in terms of the immediately preceding music, but coming full circle with respect to the opening of the *introduzione,* which had begun with Leporello's F-major complaint.

Not even this ending section of the *introduzione,* though, makes a full cadence. The last dominant chord peters out into *its* dominant, the continuo group (harpsichord/fortepiano and cello) takes over, and we begin to hear the "normal" succession of recitatives and musical numbers continues for most of the opera. In the space of less than 200 measures, lasting only a few minutes, we have met four characters, witnessed an attempted arrest and a murder, and been through a veritable tonal whirlwind. This kind of uninterrupted action music seemed to eighteenth-century listeners to reproduce the rhythms and the passions of life itself. Its sustained dramatic pressure was unprecedented.

SCENE 1

Leporello, in a cloak, pacing in front of Donna Anna's house.

Leporello	**Leporello**
Notte e giorno faticar,	Slaving night and day,
per chi nulla sa gradir;	for one whom nothing pleases:
piova e vento sopportar,	enduring rain and wind,
mangiar male e mal dormir . . .	ill fed and short of sleep . . .
Voglio far il gentiluomo,	I'd like to play the gentleman
e non voglio più servir.	and serve no more.
Oh che caro galantuomo!	Oh what a fine gallant!
Voi star dentro colla bella,	He likes to be indoors with a beauty
ed io far la sentinella!	while I keep watch outside!
Ma mi par, che venga gente;	But it seems, people are coming;
Non mi voglio far sentir.	I don't want to be seen.
(He hides.)	

(Donna Anna enters holding tightly to the arm of Don Giovanni, who is still trying to conceal himself.)

Donna Anna	**Donna Anna**
Non sperar, se non m'uccidi,	Do not hope, unless you kill me,
ch'io ti lasci fuggir mai.	that I'll ever let you flee.
Don Giovanni	**Don Giovanni**
Donna folle! indarno gridi,	Crazy woman! You scream in vain,
chi son io tu non saprai.	you will not discover who I am.
Leporello (*aside*)	**Leporello** (*aside*)
(Che tumulto! oh ciel, che gridi!	(What a racket! Heavens, what screaming!
Il padron in nuovi guai!)	My master's in trouble again!)
Donna Anna	**Donna Anna**
Gente! servi! al traditore!	People! Servants! Seize the traitor!
Don Giovanni	**Don Giovanni**
Taci e trema al mio furore!	Be quiet and tremble at my fury!
Donna Anna	**Donna Anna**
Scellerato!	Evil man!
Don Giovanni	**Don Giovanni**
Sconsigliata!	Impudent woman!

Leporello
(Sta' a veder che il libertino
mi farà precipitar.)

Leporello
(We will see if this libertine
will be my downfall.)

Donna Anna
Come furia disperata
ti saprò perseguitar.

Donna Anna
Like a desperate fury
I will pursue you.

Don Giovanni
(Questa furia disperata
mi vuol far precipitar.)

Don Giovanni
(This desperate fury
wants to be my downfall.)

(Hearing the Commendatore, Donna Anna releases Don Giovanni and runs into the house.)

Il Commendatore
Lasciala, indegno, batiti meco!

Let her go, villain, fight with me!

Don Giovanni
Va, non mi degno di pugnar teco.

Don Giovanni
Go, I won't deign to fight you.

Il Commendatore
Così pretendi da me fuggir?

Is this how you think you will escape me?

Leporello
(Potessi almeno di quà partir!)

Leporello
(If I could only get away!)

Don Giovanni
Misero! attendi
se vuoi morir!

Don Giovanni
Miserable man! En garde
since you want to die!

Il Commendatore
Batiti!

Fight!

(They fight.)

Il Commendatore *(mortally wounded)*
Ah ... soccorso! ... son tradito! ...
l'assassino ... m'ha ferito ...
e dal seno palpitante
veggo l'anima partir.

Ah ... Help! ... I am betrayed!
the assassin ... has wounded me ...
and from my throbbing breast
I feel my life departing.

Don Giovanni
(Ah! già cade lo scaiagurato
affannosa e agonizzante
già dal seno palpitante
veggo l'anima partir.)

Don Giovanni
(Oh the scoundrel has fallen already
in agony and distress;
already I see life is parting
from his beating breast.)

Leporello
(Qual misfatto! Qual eccesso!
Entro il sen, dallo spavento,
palpitar il cor mi sento!
Io non sò che far, che dir.)

Leporello
(What a crime! What excess!
In my breast I feel my heart
pounding in terror!
I don't know what to do or say.)

SCENE 2
recitative

Don Giovanni
Leporello, ove sei?

Don Giovanni
Leporello, where are you?

Leporello
Son qui per mia disgrazia; e voi?

Leporello
I'm here, to my disgrace; and you, Sir?

Don Giovanni
Son qui.

Don Giovanni
I'm here.

Leporello
Chi è morto, voi, o il vecchio?

Leporello
Who's dead, you, or the old man?

Don Giovanni
Che domanda da bestia! il vecchio.

Don Giovanni
What a stupid question, the old man!

Leporello
Bravo!
due imprese leggiadre!
Sforzar la figlia, ed ammazzar il padre!

Leporello
Well done
two impressive exploits!
Force the girl and murder the father!

Don Giovanni
L'ha voluto, suo danno!

Don Giovanni
He asked for it, it's his fault!

Leporello
Ma donn'Anna,
cosa ha voluto?

Leporello
And Donna Anna ,
did she ask for it?

Don Giovanni
Taci,
non mi seccar, vien meco, se non vuoi
qualche cosa ancor tu!

Don Giovanni
Silence!
don't provoke me, come along, unless you
want me to give something to you, too!

(threatening to strike him)

Leporello
Non vo' nulla, Signor, non parlo più.

Leporello
I don't want anything, sir, I won't say another
word.

(They leave.)

Overture.

W. A. MOZART.

Act I.

Nº 1. Introduction.

Scene — A Garden, Night.

Leporello, in a cloak, discovered watching before the house of Donna Anna; then Donna Anna and Don Giovanni, afterwards the Commandant.

(wrapt in a dark mantle, impatiently pacing to and fro before the steps to the palace).

Not-te e gior-no fa-ti - car, per chi nul-la sa gra-dir; pio-va e
Rest I've none by night or day, Scant-y fare and doubtful pay, Ev-'ry

ven - to sop-por-tar, mangiar ma-le e mal dor — mir!_____
whim I must ful - fil; Take my place who-ev - er will!_____

Vo - glio far il gen-til - uo - mo, e non
I my-self will go a-court-ing, I the

c. Act II, Finale

The conventions of opera buffa dictate that the second and final act culminate in a finale consisting of an extended section of continuous ensemble music (uninterrupted by arias or recitatives) and continuous action in which all the singers take part and the plot is resolved. In the second-act finale of *Don Giovanni,* which occupies approximately the last third of the act, we witness the Don's downfall. The beginning of the act found him as brazen as ever, wooing the maid of his former conquest Donna Elvira with a serenade. In the second scene, Donna Elvira was shown softening toward the irresistible Don. The third scene was the turning point. Don Giovanni, having escaped another scrape by leaping a wall into a graveyard, was brought up short by the voice of the Commendatore emanating from his statue. With his usual bravado, the Don had Leporello invite the statue to dinner. To Leporello's horror and Don Giovanni's bewilderment, the statue nodded assent.

The second-act finale is a party scene: Don Giovanni is getting ready for the repast to which he had mockingly invited the Commander's statue. The scene features stage music: a wind band (*Harmonie* in German) such as actually did furnish music at aristocratic gatherings. The band plays three excerpts from comic operas well known in Vienna in 1787: first (mm. 47ff), an excerpt from Da Ponte and Martìn y Soler's *Una cosa rara* (A Rare Thing); next (mm. 118ff), a tune from Giuseppe Sarti's *Fra i due litiganti il terzo gode* ("While two dispute, a third rejoices"), the most popular opera in Vienna at the time; and, finally (mm. 162ff), a hit tune from Mozart and Da Ponte's own *The Marriage of Figaro* (1786).

These jolly excerpts not only entertain the pair on stage and the audience in the opera house; they also establish the finale's fluid tonal scheme and its tonal boundaries: the first excerpt in D major, the key both of the overture and of the final cadence; the second in F major, which shares its key signature of one flat with the parallel minor key, in which the statue's music will be played; and the third in B♭ major. These keys also recapitulate the tonalities from the opening of the opera: the overture (D), Leporello's pacing (F), and the Don's entrance (B♭).

The final cadence of the excerpt from *Figaro* (m. 199) is bizarrely elided into loud chords signaling the sudden arrival of Don Giovanni's abandoned lover, Donna Elvira, in a state of feverish anxiety. She has had a premonition of the Don's impending doom and has come to warn him. In an agitated trio, Giovanni derides her concern and insultingly invites her to dine with him (mm. 291–294), just as he had previously addressed the statue of the Commander. Even Leporello is appalled at his master's coarse behavior.

Elvira rushes off in despair but rushes right back in again in horror, her scream matched in the orchestra by a bellowing diminished-seventh chord, horror-harmony par excellence (mm. 352–353). She flies out at the opposite end of the stage, and Don Giovanni sends Leporello to investigate. Leporello, too, recoils. In a breathless duet, with the voice parts interrupted by panting rests, Leporello explains that he has seen "the man of stone, the white man" (L'uom di sasso, l'uomo bianco) and imitates his crushing steps (and knocking on the door), "ta! ta! ta! ta!"

With undiminished bravado, Don Giovanni flings open the door. His gesture is greeted by what was surely at the time the most awful noise that had ever sounded in an opera house: another diminished-seventh chord, blasted in his face by the full orchestra, augmented by three trombones, announces the statue's arrival (mm. 433–434). The harmony is the very one that accompanied Don Giovanni's fatal thrust in the *introduzione*; its recurrence seems to bracket the whole intervening action and to cast the whole opera in terms of Giovanni's murder of the Commendatore and the price he will soon pay for it.

The stone guest now enters, accompanied by the grim music that had launched the overture, thus providing a musical recapitulation. A hideous trio of three basses develops as the statue advances, the Don scoffs, and Leporello trembles. Things get worse. The statue's command that Don Giovanni repent is sung to another gruesomely portentous recapitulation: the duel music from the *introduzione* that had accompanied Don Giovanni's horrible crime (cf. mm. 167ff of the *introduzione* and mm. 525ff of the finale). The Don remains proudly unrepentant, but at the icy touch of the statue's hand, his demeanor crumbles into one of rack and ruin. A unison chorus of hellish spirits replaces the statue's music (mm. 578ff), and searing dissonances riddle the harmony as the orchestra's noisiest resources are summoned: trombone *sforzandi*, timpani rolls, string tremolos. As the Don disappears, screaming in agony, the orchestra settles in on a chord of D major. (Here Mozart came as close as he would ever come to violating his own belief that "music, even in the most terrible situations, must never offend the ear, but must please the hearer.")

And now the resolution: D major resolves to G major as dominant to tonic (m. 603), the stage brightens, and (according to the standard formula) the librettist assembles all the remaining characters on stage: Donna Anna, Donna Elvira (who has presumably summoned the rest), Don Ottavio (Donna Anna's fiancé), and Zerlina and Masetto (a peasant couple wronged by the Don) all rush on stage to join the dazed Leporello. The five pursuers, singing in a sort of chorus, interrogate Leporello about Don Giovanni's fate.

When all are satisfied that the Don has truly perished, they react by turning their attention to the Don Giovanni–free future and providing the action with its long-awaited closure. In a tender *Larghetto*, Don Ottavio and Donna Anna make their plans to marry. Elvira announces that she is bound for a convent. Zerlina and Masetto agree to patch things up and resume their domesticity. Leporello vows to find himself a better master.

Meanwhile, the harmony has been quietly veering back to D major through its dominant, on which the *Larghetto* makes its (half) cadence (mm. 750–754). It is time to wrap things up in D major with a moral, launched *Presto* by the women's voices in what sounds like the beginning of a fugue. Instead of a fugue, all six characters continue in chorus to the final cadence, to the accompaniment of exuberant scales and fanfares in the orchestra, in a fully restored buffa style.

NO. 24, FINALE

A large, well-lighted hall. A table has been prepared with a supper.

Don Giovanni
Già la mensa è preparata.

(to the musicians)

Voi suonate, amici cari:
Giàcche spendo i miei danari,

Don Giovanni
The table is already prepared.

Play, dear friends!
Since I'm spending my money

io me voglio divertir.
Leporello, presto in tavola!

Leporello
Son prontissimo a servir . . .

Don Giovanni
Già la mensa è preparata, etc.

I'd like to be entertained at once.
Leporello, serve quickly!

Leporello
Immediately, at your service . . .

Don Giovanni
The table is already prepared, etc.

(The wind band play a selection from Martín y Soler's opera Una cosa rara.*)*

Leporello
Bravi! "Cosa rara!"

Leporello
Hooray! "Cosa rara!"

Don Giovanni
Che ti par del bel concerto?

Don Giovanni
What do you think of the pretty concert?

Leporello
È conforme al vostro merto.

Leporello
It's consistent with your worth.

Don Giovanni
Ah, che piatto saporito!

Don Giovanni
This is a tasty dish!

Leporello
(Ah, che barbaro appetito!
Che bocconi da gigante!
mi par proprio di svenir.)

Leporello
(What a ravenous appetite!
What giant mouthfuls,
and I'm faint with hunger!)

Don Giovanni
(Nel veder i miei bocconi
gli par proprio di svenir!)
Piatto!

Don Giovanni
(While watching me eat
he's faint with hunger!)
Next course!

Leporello
Servo!

Leporello
I'm serving it!

(The wind band plays an excerpt from Sarti's opera Fra i due litiganti il terzo gode.*)*

Leporello
Evvivano i "litiganti"!

Leporello
Three cheers for the "Litiganti"!

Don Giovanni
Versa il vino!
Eccellente marzimino!

Don Giovanni
Pour the wine!
Excellent *marzimino* [type of wine]!

Leporello
(Questo pezzo di fagiano,
piano piano vo' inghiottir.)

Leporello
(This piece of pheasant
I'll swallow very quietly.)

Don Giovanni
(Sta mangiando quel marrano!
fingerò di non capir.)

(The wind band plays an excerpt from Mozart's The Marriage of Figaro.*)*

Leporello
Questa poi la conosco pur troppo . . .

Don Giovanni (*calling without looking at Leporello*)
Leporello!

Leporello (*replying with his mouth full*)
Padron mio!

Don Giovanni
Parla schietto, mascalzone!

Leporello
Non mi lasia una flussione
le parole proferir.

Don Giovanni
Mentre io mangio, fishia un poco.

Leporello
Non sò far.

Don Giovanni
Cos'è?
(He "notices" that Leporello is eating.)

Leporello
Scusate!
sì eccellente è il vostro cuoco,
che lo volli anchi'io provar.

Don Giovanni
Sì eccellente è il cuoco mio,
che lo volli anchi'ei provar.

Donna Elvira (*rushes in distractedly*)
L'ultima prova
dell'amor mio
ancor vogl'io
fare con te.

Don Giovanni
(The rascal's eating!
I'll pretend not to know.)

Leporello
This I know all too well . . .

Don Giovanni (*calling without looking at Leporello*)
Leporello!

Leporello (*replying with his mouth full*)
My master!

Don Giovanni
Speak clearly, scoundrel!

Leporello
I've something in my throat
that prevents me from speaking.

Don Giovanni
Whistle a bit while I'm eating.

Leporello
I can't.

Don Giovanni
Why not?

Leporello
Excuse me!
your cook is so excellent
that I thought I'd try him too.

Don Giovanni
My cook is so excellent
that he thought he'd try him too.

Donna Elvira (*rushes in distractedly*)
I want to give
you one last
proof of
my love.

Più non rammento
gl'inganni tuoi,
pietade io sento . . .

Don Giovanni (*rising*) **and Leporello**
Cos'è? cos'è?

Donna Elvira (*kneeling*)
Da te non chiede
quest'alma oppressa
della sua fede
qualche mercé.

Don Giovanni
Mi maraviglio!
cosa volete?
Se non sorgete
non resto in piè!
(He kneels beside her.)

Donna Elvira
Ah! non deridere
gli affanni miei!

Leporello
Quasi da piangere
mi fa costei.

Don Giovanni (*He stands up and helps up Donna Elvira.*)
Io ti deridere!
Cielo! perché?
Che vuoi, mio bene?

Donna Elvira
Che vita cangi.

Don Giovanni
Brava!

Donna Elvira and Leporello
Cor perfido!

Don Giovanni
Lascia chi'io mangi;

I no longer remember
your deceptions,
I feel pity for you . . .

Don Giovanni (*rising*) **and Leporello**
What's this? What's this?

Donna Elvira (*kneeling*)
This oppressed soul
seeks no mercy from you
for its
faithfulness.

Don Giovanni
I'm astonished!
what do you want?
If you won't stand up,
I won't remain on my feet!

Donna Elvira
Ah! do not mock
my sorrows!

Leporello
She almost makes
me cry.

Don Giovanni (*He stands up and helps up Donna Elvira.*)
I, mock you?
Heavens! why?
What do you want, my dear?

Donna Elvira
That you change your way of life.

Don Giovanni
Wonderful!

Donna Elvira and Leporello
Treacherous heart!

Don Giovanni
Let me eat;

(He returns to his seat and resumes eating.)
e se ti piace,
mangia con me!

and if you like,
eat with me!

Donna Elvira
Restati, barbaro!
nel lezzo immondo,
esempio orribile
d'iniquità!

Donna Elvira
Remain, barbarous one,
in your filthy stench,
a horrible example of
wickedness!

Leporello
Se non si muove
del suo dolore,
di sasso ha il core,
o cor non ha!

Leporello
If he's not moved
by her pain,
he has a heart of stone,
or he hasn't got a heart at all!

Don Giovanni *(raising his glass)*
Vivan le femmine,
Viva il buon vino,
sostegno e gloria
d'umanità!

Don Giovanni *(raising his glass)*
Long live women,
Long live good wine,
the sustenance and glory
of mankind!

(exit Donna Elvira)

Donna Elvira *(rushes back in screaming and then out another door)*
Ah!

Donna Elvira *(rushes back in screaming and then out another door)*
Ah!

Don Giovanni and Leporello
Che grido è questo mai?

Don Giovanni and Leporello
What on earth is that scream?

Don Giovanni
Va' a veder che cosa è stato.

Don Giovanni
Go and see what's going on.

Leporello *(leaves and then screams)*
Ah!

Leporello *(leaves and then screams)*
Ah!

Don Giovanni
Che grido indiavolato!
Leporello, che cos'è?

Don Giovanni
What a devilish cry!
Leporello, what is it?

Leporello
Ah, signor! per carità!
non andate fuor di qua!
L'uom di sasso, l'uomo bianco,
ah! padrone! io gelo, io manco.

Leporello
Oh, master! for pity's sake! . . .
don't go out of here! . . .
The man of stone, the white man,
oh, master! I'm freezing, I'm fainting.

Se vedeste che figura,
se sentiste come fa:
ta ta ta ta!

If you had seen him,
if you had heard how he walks:
ta ta ta ta!

Don Giovanni
Non capisco niente affatto.

Don Giovanni
I don't understand anything of this.

Leporello
Ta ta ta ta!

Leporello
Ta ta ta ta!

Don Giovanni
Tu sei matto in verita!

Don Giovanni
You're a madman indeed!

(There is knocking at the door.)

Leporello
Ah, sentite!

Leporello
Oh listen!

Don Giovanni
Qualcun batte!
Apri!

Don Giovanni
Someone's knocking.
Open it!

Leporello
Io tremo!

Leporello
I'm trembling!

Don Giovanni
Apri, dico!

Don Giovanni
Open it, I say!

Leporello
Ah!

Leporello
Oh!

Don Giovanni
Matto! Per togliermi d'intrico
ad aprir io stesso andrò.

Don Giovanni
You lunatic! To clear up this intrigue
I'll open it myself.

(He takes a candle and goes to open the door.)

Leporello
*(Non vo' più veder l'amico
pian pianin m'asconderò.)*

Leporello
(I don't want to see my friend again;
I'll hide very quietly.)

(He hides under the table; Don Giovanni opens the door.)

The Statue
Don Giovanni, a cenar teco
m'invitasti e son venuto!

Don Giovanni, you invited me
to dine and I have come!

Don Giovanni
Non l'avrei giammai creduto;

Don Giovanni
I never would have believed it,

ma farò quel che potrò.
Leporello! un altra cena
fa che subito si porti!

but I'll do what I can!
Leporello! another dinner,
have it brought immediately!

Leporello (*from under the table*
Ah padron! siam tutti morti.

Leporello (*from under the table*)
Oh master we are all dead!

Don Giovanni
Vanne dico!
(Leporello begins to crawl out.)

Don Giovanni
Go, I say!

The Statue
Ferma un po'!
Non si pasce di cibo mortale
chi si pasce di cibo celeste;
altre cure più gravi di queste,
altra brama quaggiù mi guidò!
(Leporello crawls back under the table.)

The Statue
No, stay a bit!
He has no need for mortal food
who has fed on the food of heaven;
other concerns graver than these,
another desire led me down here!

Leporello
(La terzana d'avere mi sembra,
e le membra fermar più non sò.)

Leporello
(It's as if I had a fever
and my limbs can't stop shaking.)

Don Giovanni
Parla dunque: che chiedi, che vuoi?

Don Giovanni
Speak, then: what do you want?

The Statue
Parlo; ascolta!
più tempo non ho!

The Statue
I'm speaking; listen!
I have no more time!

Don Giovanni
Parla, parla, ascoltando ti sto.

Don Giovanni
Speak, speak, I'm listening to you.

The Statue
Tu m'invitasti a cena,
il tuo dover or sai.
Rispondimi: verrai
tu a cenar meco?

The Statue
You invited me to dinner,
you know your obligation now.
Answer me: will you
come and dine with me?

Leporello (*from further away,*
trembling)
Oibò; tempo non ha, scusate.

Leporello (*from further away,*
trembling)
Oh no; he doesn't have time, sorry.

Don Giovanni
A torto di viltate tacciato mai sarò.

Don Giovanni
Of cowardice I will never be accused.

The Statue
Risolvi!

The Statue
Resolve!

Don Giovanni
Ho già risolto!

Don Giovanni
I have already resolved!

The Statue
Verrai?

The Statue
Will you come?

Leporello
Dite di no!

Leporello
Say no!

Don Giovanni
Ho fermo il cuore in petto:
Non ho timor: verrò!

Don Giovanni
My heart is firm in my breast:
I am not afraid: I will come!

The Statue
Dammi la mano in pegno!

The Statue
Give my your hand as a pledge!

Don Giovanni
Eccola! Ohimè!

Don Giovanni
Here it is! Alas!

The Statue
Cos'hai?

The Statue
What's the matter?

Don Giovanni
Che gelo è questo mai?

Don Giovanni
What is this iciness?

The Statue
Pentiti, cangia vita:
è l'ultimo momento!

The Statue
Repent, change your life:
this is your last chance!

Don Giovanni (*vainly trying to*
free himself)
No, no, ch'io non mi pento,
vanne lontan da me!

Don Giovanni (*vainly trying to*
free himself)
No, no, I do not repent,
Get away from me!

The Statue
Pentiti, scellerato!

The Statue
Repent, scoundrel!

Don Giovanni
No, vecchio infatuato!

Don Giovanni
No, you pompous old man!

The Statue
Pentiti!

The Statue
Repent!

Don Giovanni
No!

Don Giovanni
No!

The Statue
Sì!

Don Giovanni
No!

The Statue
Ah tempo più non v'è!

(Exit. Flames appear all around, the earth trembles.)

Don Giovanni
Da qual tremore insolito
sento assalir gli spiriti!
dond'escono quei vortici
di foco pien d'orror?

Chorus [of demons] *(from below)*
Tutto a tue colpe è poco!
Vieni, c'è un mal peggior!

Don Giovanni
Chi l'anima mi lacera?
Chi m'agita le viscere?
che strazio, ohimè, che smania!
Ah! che inferno, che terror!

Leporello
Che ceffo disperato!
Che gesti da dannato!
che gridi, che lamenti!
come mi fa terror!

Don Giovanni
Ah!

(Don Giovanni is engulfed in flames.)

Leporello
Ah!

Donna Elvira, Zerlina,
 Don Ottavio, Masetto
Ah, dov'è il perfido?
Dov'è l'indegno?
tutto il mio sdegno

The Statue
Yes!

Don Giovanni
No!

The Statue
Ah, there is no more time!

(Exit. Flames appear all around, the earth trembles.)

Don Giovanni
I feel my spirits attacked
by an unusual trembling!
from whence come these horrific
whirlpools of fire?

Chorus [of demons] *(from below)*
All this is nothing compared to your sins!
Come, worse things await you!

Don Giovanni
Who lacerates my soul?
Who shakes my viscera?
What torture, alas, what delirium!
Oh! what an inferno, what terror!

Leporello
What a brutally deformed face!
What gestures from the damned!
what screams, what wails!
how it terrifies me!

Don Giovanni
Ah!

(Don Giovanni is engulfed in flames.)

Leporello
Ah!

Donna Elvira, Zerlina,
 Don Ottavio, Masetto
Ah, where is the scoundrel?
Where is the shameful one?
I want to vent

sfogar io vo'!

Donna Anna
Solo mirandolo
stretto in catene,
alle mie pene
calma darò.

Leporello *(emerging from hiding)*
Più non sperate
di ritrovarlo,
più non cercate.
Lontano andò.

All
Cos'è? favella!
Via presto, sbrigati!

Leporello
Venne un colosso . . .
Ma se non posso . . .
Tra fumo e fuoco . . .
badate un poco . . .
l'uomo di sasso . . .
fermate il passo . . .
giusto là sotto . . .
diede il gran botto . . .
giusto là il diavolo
se'l trangugiò.

All
Stelle, che sento!

Leporello
Vero è l'evento!

Donna Elvira
Ah, certo è l'ombra
che m'incontrò.

Donna Elvira, Zerlina,
 Don Ottavio, Masetto
Ah, certo è l'ombra
che l'incontrò.

all my indignation!

Donna Anna
Only seeing him
bound in chains
will ease
my pain.

Leporello *(emerging from hiding)*
Do not hope
ever to find him,
don't look for him any more.
He went far away.

All
What? tell us about it!
Be quick, hurry!

Leporello
A giant statue came along . . .
But I can't go on . . .
Amid smoke and flames . . .
pay attention . . .
the man of stone . . .
halted his steps . . .
right down there . . .
gave the great blow . . .
right there the devil
swallowed him up.

All
Heavens, what do I hear!

Leporello
It's true, it really happened!

Ah, that must be the ghost
that I met.

Donna Elvira, Zerlina,
 Don Ottavio, Masetto
Ah, that must be the ghost
that she met.

Don Ottavio

Or che tutti, o mio tesoro,
vendicati siam dal cielo,
porgi, porgi a me un ristoro,
non mi far languire ancor.

Don Ottavio

Now that all of us, o my treasure,
have been avenged by heaven,
give, give me some relief,
do not make me continue to languish.

Donna Anna

Lascia, o caro! un anno ancora
allo sfogo del mio cor.

Donna Anna

Give me, my dear, one more year
for the relief of my heart.

Don Ottavio

Al desio di chi m'adora
ceder deve un fido amor.

Don Ottavio

To the wish of she who loves me
a faithful love must yield.

Donna Anna

Al desio di chi t'adora
ceder deve un fido amor.

Donna Anna

To the wish of her who loves you
a faithful love must yield.

Donna Elvira

Io men vado in un ritiro
a finir la vita mia!

Donna Elvira

I will go to a cloister
for the rest of my life!

Zerlina

Noi, Masetto, a casa andiamo!
a cenar in compagnia!

Zerlina

We, Masetto, are going home!
to dine together!

Masetto

Noi, Zerlina, a casa andiamo!
a cenar in compagnia!

Masetto

We, Zerlina, are going home!
to dine together!

Leporello

Ed io vado all'osteria
a trovar padron miglior.

Leporello

And I'm going to the inn
to find a better master.

Zerlina, Masetto, Leporello

Resti dunque quel birbon,
con Proserpina e Pluton.
E noi tutti, o buona gente,
ripetiam allegramente
l'antichissima canzon:

Zerlina, Masetto, Leporello

May the wretched man remain
with Proserpina and Pluto.
And all of us, good people,
will joyfully repeat
the ancient song:

All

Questo è il fin di chi fa mal.
E de' perfidi la morte
alla vita è sempre ugual.

All

This is the fate of evil doers.
The wicked die
as they have lived.

15147

gual,   è   sem - pre u - gual,   sem - pre u -
friend, with - out   a   friend.   Thus   they

gual,   è   sem - pre u - gual,   sem - pre u -
friend, with - out   a   friend.   Thus   they

gual,   è   sem - pre u - gual,   sem - pre u -
friend, with - out   a   friend.   Thus   they

gual,   è   sem - pre u - gual,   sem - pre u -
friend, with - out   a   friend.   Thus   they

gual,   è   sem - pre u - gual,   sem - pre u -
friend, with - out   a   friend.   Thus   they

gual.
end.

gual.
end.

gual.
end.

gual.
end.

gual.
end.

End of the Opera.

14

Wolfgang Amadè Mozart (1756–91)

FULL CD III: TRACK 32

Symphony No. 40 in G Minor, K. 550, First movement (*Allegro molto*) (1788)

Mozart composed his last three symphonies, including the Symphony in G Minor, in the summer of 1788. The reason for their composition remains unclear, and there is no record of their performance in Mozart's lifetime. Nevertheless, the fact that Mozart revised the Symphony in G Minor to include clarinets suggests that he did so with a particular occasion in mind and implies that this symphony was likely performed while Mozart was alive. Aside from an early symphony in G minor (K. 183), this is Mozart's only symphony in a minor key.

As was expected, the form of the first movement of this symphony is in symphonic binary, or sonata, form, highly dramatized by the presentation of contrasting and clearly articulated themes. Because the tonic is G minor, the first goal of the movement's tonal trajectory is B♭ major, the relative major, as opposed to the dominant, as it would be were the symphony in a major key.

A Mozartean characteristic of the symphonic treatment of sonata form is the striking contrast between the themes, which is aided by Mozart's colorful orchestration. The first theme (mm. 1–20), which features the violins with an agitated accompaniment in the violas, has a restless quality. The bridge starts as if repeating the first theme at m. 21 but then presents its own theme (mm. 28–42), which uses the full force of the orchestra and features biting arpeggios and ascending scales in pompous, rigid declamation reminiscent of opera seria. The second theme (mm. 44–72) contrasts sharply with both of the preceding themes in its languid, descending chromatic lines and initial abandonment of eighth notes in the accompaniment. Mozart's treatment of the winds in alternation with the strings lends a pastoral air to this theme. The reintroduction of eighth notes in the second violins and violas (m. 58) coincides with increased agitation that provides a transition to the closing theme (mm. 72–100), which juxtaposes snippets of the main motive of the first theme with vigorous descending scales that can be heard as inversions of the ascending scales of the bridge theme.

Melodically, the opening of the symphony begins in a straightforward manner with an eight-measure, 4 + 4, antecedent–consequent phrase (mm. 2–9). The relationship of the melody to its accompaniment is, however, subtler than the simple balance of the melodic phrases implies. In the opening statement of the theme Mozart lays down an agitated accompaniment before the entrance of the melody. Thus, the pickup of the melody is to m. 2 rather than to m. 1. In later iterations of the theme, however, Mozart brings in this accompaniment a full two measures later in relation to the melody, which makes the first two beats of the theme sound like an upbeat. Additionally, Mozart's choice of pitches for the first two beats of the melody, E♭–D ($\hat{6}$–$\hat{5}$ in G minor) allows the opening to be accompanied by either a tonic or dominant harmony. Mozart uses this property to great effect several times, most notably to slip smoothly into the recapitulation, which begins melodically with the pickup to m. 165 but harmonically only at m. 166, where the dominant pedal resolves to tonic.

The entire movement, is built to an unusual degree on iterations of the short-short-long (anapestic) rhythmic pattern of the first three notes of the first theme. This rhythmic motive also features prominently at two points in the closing theme: its first section (mm. 72–85, wind solos alternating with first violins), and its last (mm. 95–98, winds and second violins).

Virtually the entire development is taken up with the first theme—after two transitional measures (101–102) every measure of the development contains at least the first two eighth notes of its main motive. Although references to the first theme frequently include longer portions of it, toward the end of the development they are confined to fragmented repetitions of the theme's three-note opening motive (beginning at m. 148 in the winds). An interesting feature of the development section is that, after a three-measure transition, it begins already at the tonal "far out point" of the movement (F♯ minor, m. 104). Thus, the entire development is concerned with wending its way back to the sphere of G minor.

Some commentators have found numerous connections between the themes. For example, the half step of the opening E♭–D may be seen as thematically connecting numerous gestures: mm. 16–20, woodwinds; mm. 35–37, bass line; and the descending chromatic lines of the second theme, to name just a few. But more than motivic connections, what continues to captivate audiences is the astounding range of expression and invention that Mozart achieves in this symphony.

Measure Nos.	Formal Designation	Sections	Keys	Comments
1–100	**Exposition**			
1–20		1st theme	g (ends on V/g)	
21–43		Bridge	Ends on V/B♭	Starts with 1st theme, new theme at m. 28
44–72		2nd theme	B♭	
72–100		Closing	B♭	With motives of 1st theme
101–164	**Development**			After m. 102 every measure in the development contains main anapestic (da-da-dum) motive from pickup to 1st theme
101–138		1st theme	f♯, e, d, F, g, d, V/g	
139–164		Retransition	Dominant pedal (m. 153)	Fragmentation of 1st theme, gestures in winds from bridge (cf. mm. 153–158 and mm. 30–33)
165–284	**Recapitulation**			
165–183		1st theme	g (ends on V)	
184–226		Bridge	B♭, ends on V/g	1st theme, bridge theme
227–260		2nd theme	g	
260–284		Closing	g	
285–299	**Coda**			Beginning of coda overlaps with end of closing theme

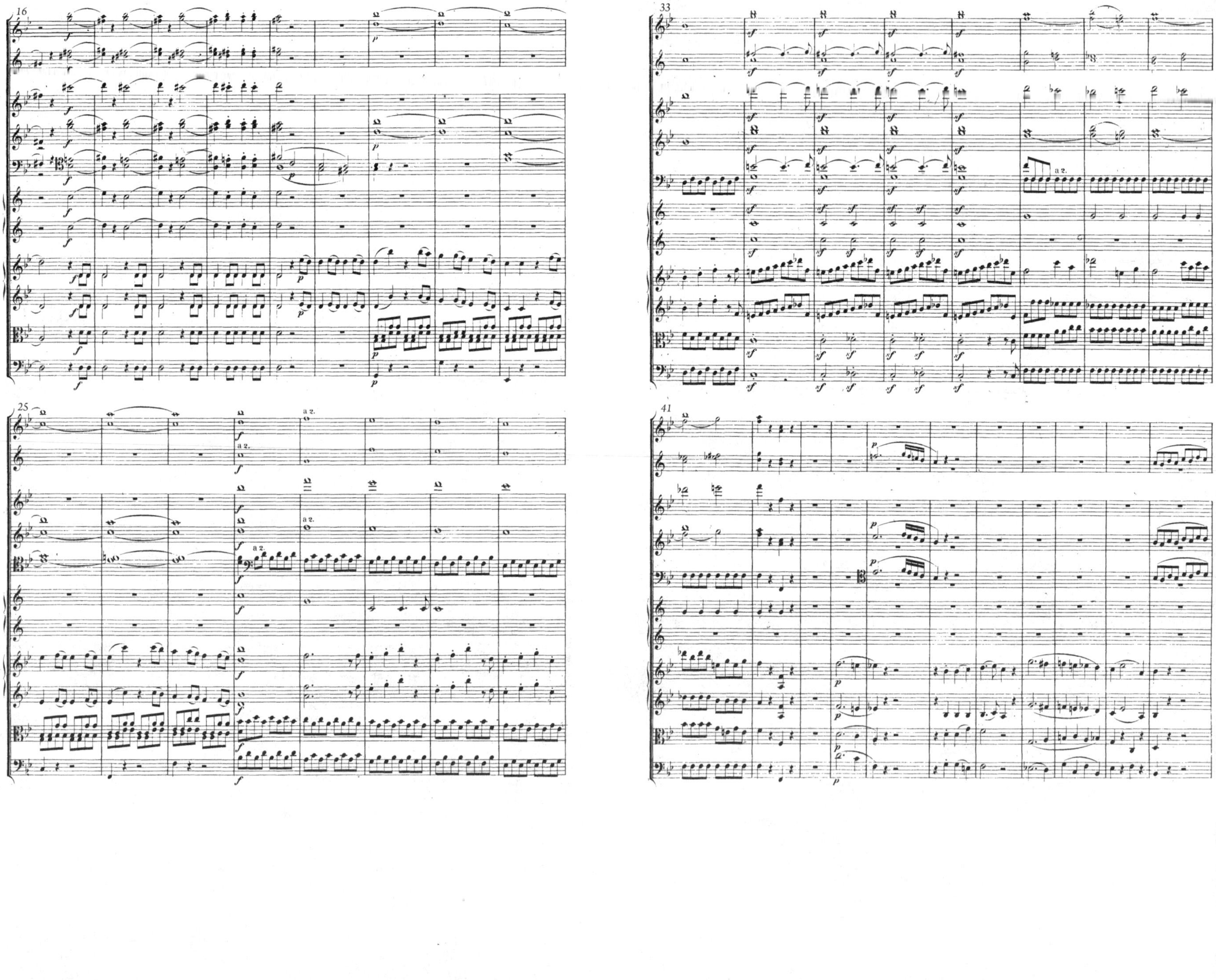
16
25
a 2.
33
a 2.
41

W. A. M. 550

15

Wolfgang Amadè Mozart (1756–91)

FULL CD III: TRACK 33
CONCISE CD II: TRACK 17

Symphony No. 41 in C Major ("Jupiter"), K. 551, Fourth movement (*Molto Allegro*) (1788)

Mozart finished his "Jupiter" Symphony on 10 August 1788, shortly after the completion of the in G Minor Symphony discussed in the previous entry. Mozart might have chosen C major as the key for his last symphony in order to write a grand symphony with trumpets, drums, fanfares, and other military gestures in recognition of Austria's war with the Turks, which had begun earlier that year. The origin of the symphony's subtitle, "Jupiter," does not come from the composer. It may stem from Haydn's associate, the London impresario Johann Peter Salomon (1745–1815), who appears to have appended it to the symphony in the beginning of the nineteenth century. The nickname was probably inspired by the stately fanfares of the first movement, but it also fits the bright, contrapuntally intricate finale.

As the first symphony in which the finale carries more weight than any of the previous movements, Mozart's "Jupiter" is a landmark in the history of music. In this finale Mozart achieves grandeur not with pompous themes but with a dazzling display of contrapuntal technique, which reaches its apex in the coda with five-part counterpoint that combines all the important themes of the movement in an elevated, "learned" style. The effect of the coda on an attentive listener is literally overwhelming—it is nearly impossible to absorb all of the thematic threads at once despite their individual clarity.

In addition to its military associations, C major was a key connected with church music, which often featured intricate counterpoint. C major was also a common key for opera buffa finales. In the fourth movement of the "Jupiter" symphony, Mozart's use of counterpoint in the context of a sparkling finale evokes both of these traditions. The movement combines the elevated "learned" style with a free *galant* idiom. As musicologist Elaine Sisman has pointed out, what distinguishes Mozart's finale from other contrapuntally intricate finales of the time is that it does not begin with the fugue and that its primary and secondary themes both have *galant* (homophonic) and "learned" (highly contrapuntal) versions (cf. mm. 1–8 with mm. 36ff; and mm. 74–77 with mm. 95ff). In the coda Mozart reverses the procedure of moving from *galant* to "learned" styles by beginning with the most intricate counterpoint of the entire work (mm. 361–402) and ending with ebullient homophony (mm. 403ff).

In terms of its proportions and tonal layout, the movement adheres to sonata form. In the following chart we attempt to capture Mozart's ingenuity by tracking the intricate course of the relevant thematic units in the context of the form. The first four notes played by the first violins (C–D–F–E in whole notes, labeled "A" in the chart) are the beginning of a melody widely used for teaching polyphonic composition in the eighteenth century. Thus, though homophonic in texture, the opening serves to signal the contrapuntal focus of the movement.

Measure Nos.	Formal Designation	Sections	Keys	Comments
1–157	**Exposition**			
1–35		1st theme group, part 1	C	3 main units: **A** (whole notes, mm. 1–4); **B** (repeated-note answer, mm. 5–8); **C** (dotted figure and scale, mm. 19–22)
36–55		1st theme group, part 2		Thematic unit **A** treated in imitation; ends with 3-measure statement of **A** in full orchestra
56–73		Bridge	C–G	1 new unit: **D** (rest followed by rising scale) treated in overlapping imitation (stretto) and sequence. Also **C** (treated in imitation, mm. 64–67)
74–94		2nd theme group, part 1	G	1 new unit: **E** (half notes followed by descending scale and rising gesture, mm. 74–77ff, 1st violins). Also **C** (mm. 77–78ff, bassoon) and **B** (mm. 77–79ff, flute)
94–115		2nd theme group, part 2		Continues **E** in stretto
115–157		Closing		**B** (mm. 115–128) and **C** (mm. 135–145), in stretto and inverted
158–224	**Development**		c, a, d, g, C, F, e	**A** (in original rhythm in violins, mm. 158–168) and in altered rhythms (in oboe and flute, mm. 189–206) and **C** (often in stretto and inversion, mm. 161–224)

(continued)

(*continued*)

Measure Nos.	Formal Designation	Sections	Keys	Comments
225–356	**Recapitulation**			
225–232		1st theme group, part 1	C	**A** and **B**
233–252		1st theme group, part 2		**A** sequenced by step (mock "learned" style)
253–271		Bridge		**D** in imitation and sequence (mm. 253–260), **C** in stretto (mm. 262–271)
272–291		2nd theme group, part 1		**E, D,** and **C**
292–312		2nd theme group, part 2		**E** in stretto
313–356		Closing		**B** and **C** in stretto and inversion (mm. 334ff)
357–424	**Coda**			
357–360				Repetition of closing gesture and **C** (inverted and original)
361–372				**A** (inverted) in stretto
372–402		Climactic counterpoint		All units except **B** played in canon, often creating 5-part texture: **E** (viola in m. 372), **A** (cello in m. 373), **D** (cello in m. 377), **C** (cello in m. 385)
403–424		Closing flourishes		**B** (mm. 403–405) and **C** (mm. 409ff)

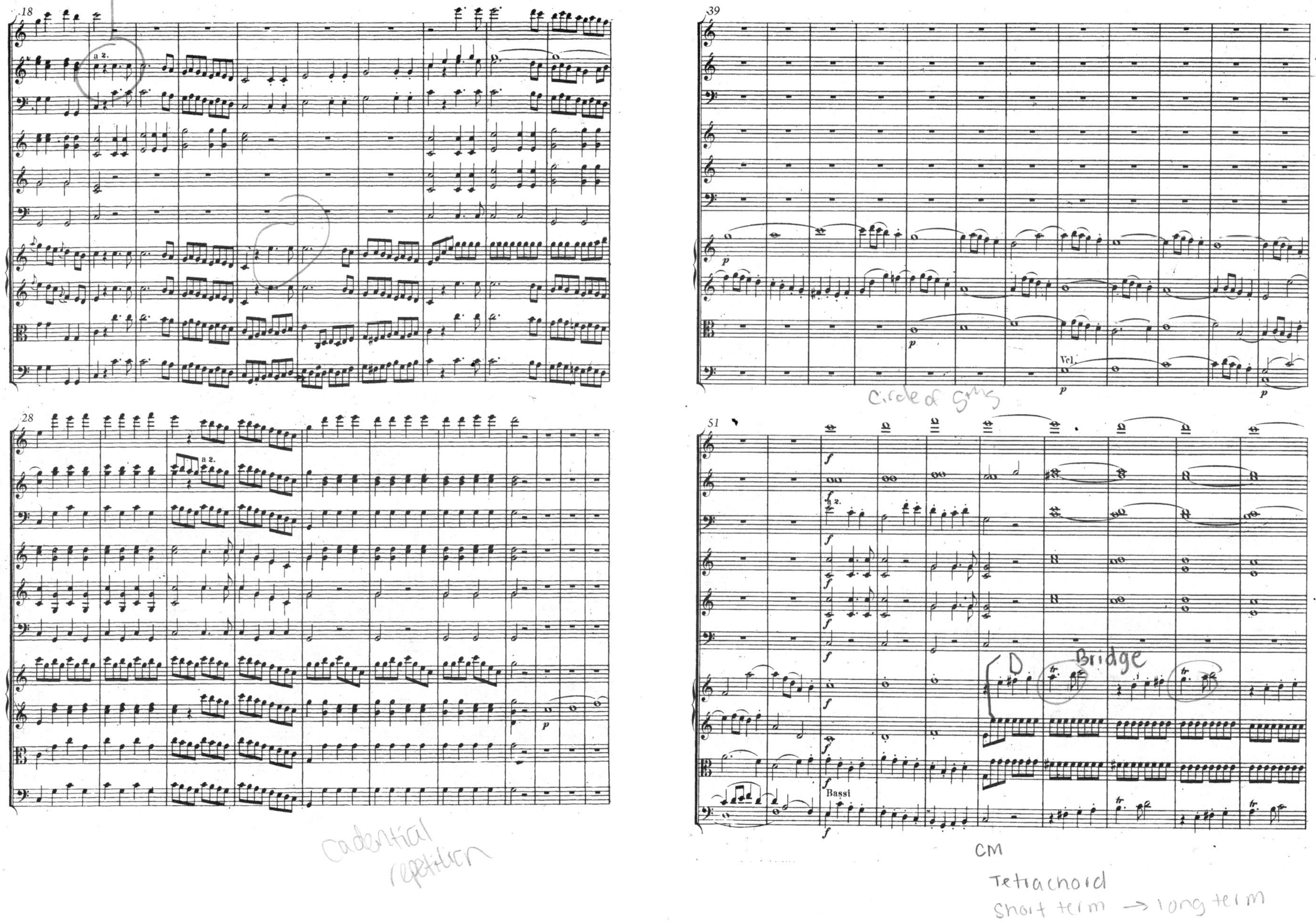
fanfare
18
a 2.
28
a 2.
39
p
Vcl.
circle of 5ths
51
f
a 2.
D
Bridge
tr
Bassi
cadential repetition
CM
Tetrachord
short term → long term

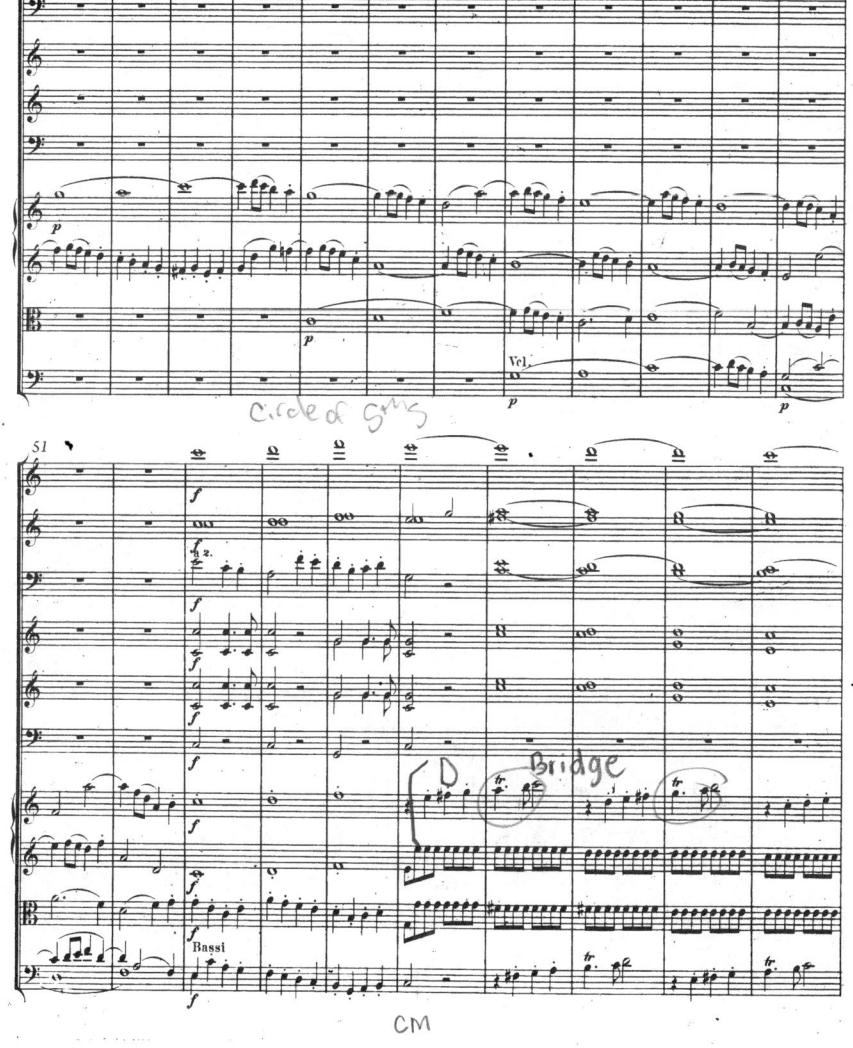

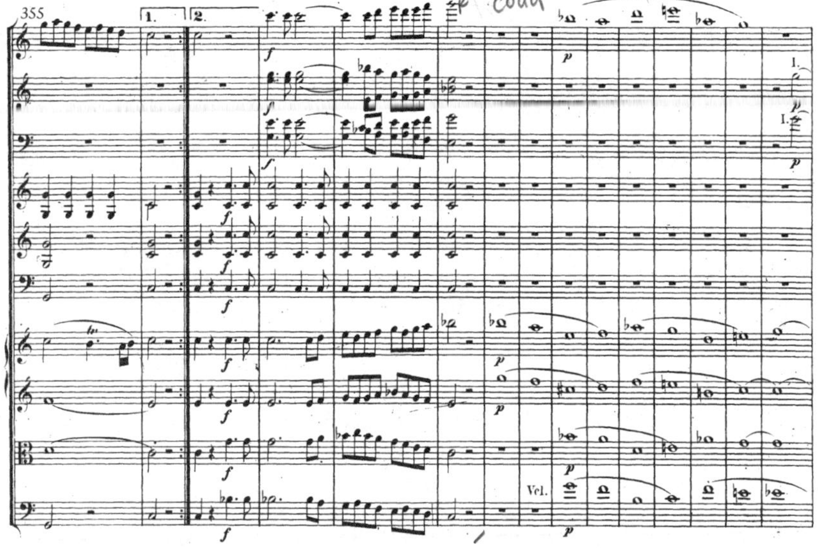
355
1.
2.
I.
Vcl.

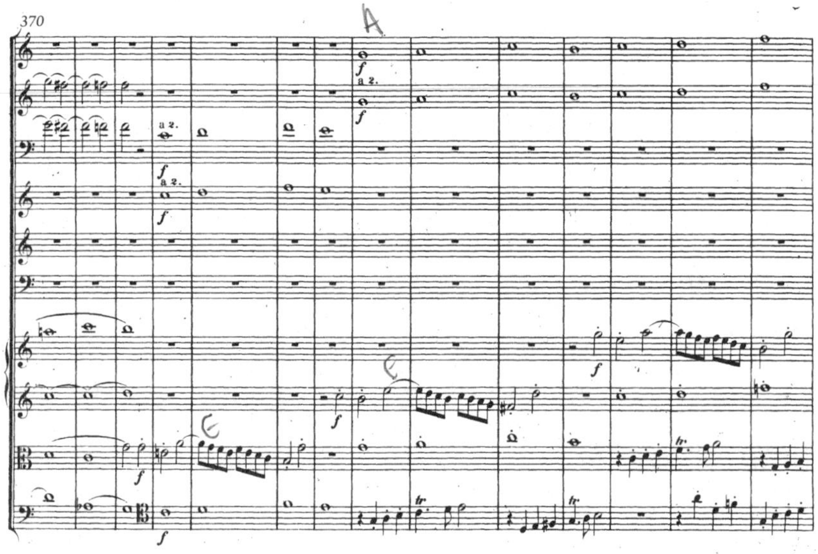
370
a 2.

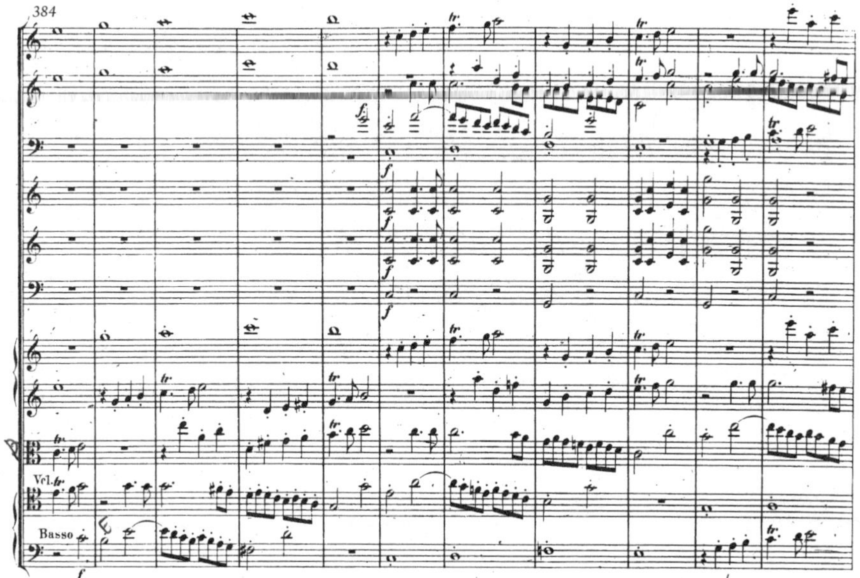
384
Vcl.
Basso

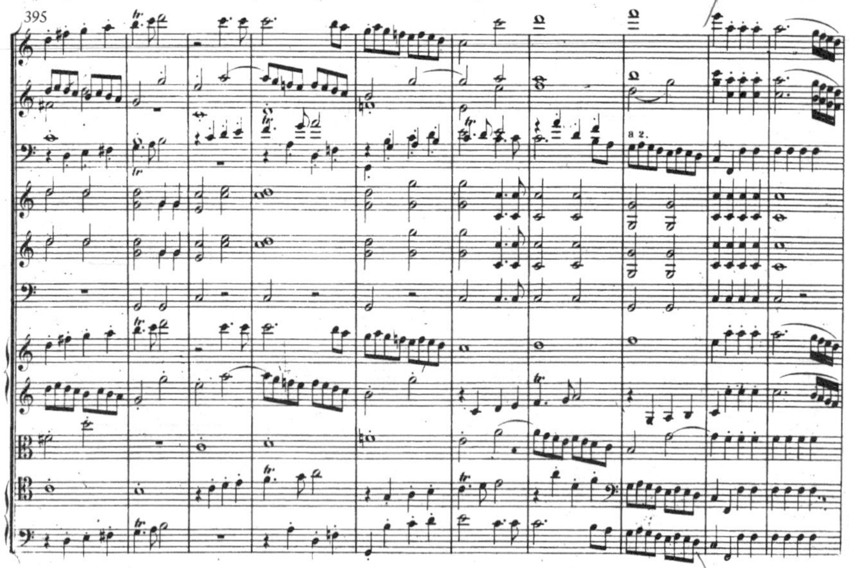
395
a 2.

16

FULL CD III: TRACKS 34–36
CONCISE CD II: TRACK 18

Wolfgang Amadè Mozart (1756–91)

Piano Concerto No. 17 in G Major, K. 453 (1784)

Mozart completed this Piano Concerto in G Major, K. 453, on 12 April 1784. It was written for his pupil Barbara Ployer, and perhaps for this reason the notated score is more detailed than the scores of concertos intended for his own performance.

Movement 1: *Allegro*

Measure Nos.	Formal Designation	Sections	Keys
1–73	**Tutti (1st exposition)**		
1–16		Primary theme	G
16–35		Bridge (new theme)	G
35–49		Secondary theme 1	G
49–57		Flat 6 excursion	(E♭)
58–69		Closing theme and . . .	G
69–74		Cadential flourish	
74–183	**Solo (2nd exposition)**		
74		*Eingang* for piano	G
75–94		Primary theme	G
94–109		Bridge	G, V/D
110–126		Secondary theme 2 ("piano theme")	D
126–139		Bridge	
139–153		Secondary theme 1 and . . .	D
153–171		Passagework	
171–178		Closing theme and . . .	D
178–183		Cadential flourish interrupted by . . .	
184–226		**Central passagework (development)**	
184–207		Modulation to "far out point"	B♭, ã, B♭, ẽ
207–226		Retransition (to V) (motive from "piano theme")	
226–349		**Recapitulation**	
226		*Eingang* in violins	G
227–242		Primary theme	G
242–257		Bridge	
257–277		Secondary theme 2 (preceded by 4-measure transition in piano)	G
277–290		Bridge	
290–304		Secondary theme 1 (piano and orchestra)	G
304–327		Passagework, leading to I $^6_4$	
327		Cadenza	Ends on V
328–340		Closing theme and . . .	G
340–349		Cadential flourish	G

Like virtually all solo concertos, this one is cast in three movements, the first of which is in a ritornello form that has been adapted to accommodate highly dramatized symphonic-binary/sonata strategies. As in other concertos, both the opening orchestral ritornello and the first solo episode function as expositions, but with a significant difference: While the orchestral ritornello, even its secondary theme, remains in the tonic key, the solo section modulates to the dominant key. Mozart starts his orchestral exposition with an elegant violin phrase marked *piano*, the soft dynamic of the opening possible only because public concerts never started with a solo concerto. Although it does not modulate to the dominant, the orchestral exposition has all the equivalent parts of the symphonic binary form: a first theme that runs into a rambunctious bridge section that reaches the dominant (although not the dominant key); a typically Mozartean lyrical second theme displayed in alternating strings and woodwinds (mm. 35–49); and a closing section of repeated cadential gestures (mm. 58–74). A leap into E♭ major following the deceptive cadence at the end of the second theme in m. 49 brings some tonal variety to tonic-centered orchestral exposition and makes the reaffirmation of the tonic in the closing theme necessary.

After the piano's little introductory figure (*Eingang*) (m. 74), the events of the first exposition are repeated, with the piano now replacing the strings in dialogue with the woodwinds. The bridge section (mm. 94–109), which now has a real modulatory function, is less noisy and gives the pianist an opportunity to display virtuoso sixteenth-note flourishes. Instead of the orchestral second theme, however, the dominant is marked by the piano's unaccompanied solo theme (mm. 110ff), which remains the soloist's own property throughout the movement. A second bridge starts with a sudden plunge into the dark parallel minor before the final cadence of the second theme and, moving through a circle of fifths (mm. 126–138), leads to the orchestra's second theme, in the dominant key, with the piano playing in dialogue with the woodwinds (mm. 139–171).

The moment equivalent to the final cadence of the ritornello is replaced by a move to a B♭-major harmony that launches a long modulatory development section that reaches a surprising "far out point" on B natural (m. 207). The double return of tonic key and first theme occurs in m. 227. The section that follows is similar to a sonata recapitulation, in that it stays in the tonic, but it actually owes a greater historical debt to the older precedent of the da capo aria. This final major section of the movement has all the thematic material from the modulating exposition, including the pianist's unaccompanied theme, and culminates in the solo cadenza.

The cadenza, an extended, usually improvised solo section preceding the last ritornello, can also be related to the da capo aria. Originally an embellishment of the soloist's final cadence or trill, by the end of the eighteenth century it had become a significant section in its own right.

Movement 2: *Andante*

The form of the slow movement is unusual on two counts. First, it has a true symphonic binary shape, rarely found in a slow movement; and second, it also includes a recurring "motto."

The movement may be broken down into four large sections plus a coda, each large section introduced by a motto consisting of a slightly unbalanced five-measure phrase that ends inconclusively with a half cadence (mm. 1–5, 30–34, 64–68, 90–94). The phrase is almost literally a question—to which the ensuing music responds.

The four sections this motto phrase introduces could be described as corresponding, respectively, to an opening ritornello (or nonmodulating exposition, mm. 6–29), an opening solo (or modulating exposition, mm. 35–63), a developmental section (mm. 69–89), and a recapitulation (mm. 95–122). The coda, or closing segment following the cadenza, begins with what sounds like another repetition of the motto (mm. 123–127); but it differs very tellingly from the others, as we shall see.

Precisely because it does not come to a full stop but demands continuation, the prefatory motto lends the material that follows it a heightened air of expressive importance. That sense of poetic gravity is reinforced by the emotionally demonstrative behavior of the solo part. Following the nonmodulating first section, the first solo starts right off with an impetuous turn to G minor (mm. 35ff), reinforced by a sudden increase in volume and a thickening of the piano texture beyond anything heard in the first movement. Although the skies have lightened by the time the final cadence on the dominant is made and the next incantation of the motto begins, as soon as the soloist returns (mm. 69ff), the mood turns restless again.

Now the harmony wanders wildly—all the way to the radical "far out point" of G♯ major (mm. 84–86), from which Mozart returns to the motto in the tonic C major in an ingeniously

rapid yet smooth transition (mm. 87–90). From this "double return" to the end the emphasis is on progressive reconciliation and accommodation. At m. 95 the piano gets one more outburst to parallel the one in m. 35; but although it still invokes a dark, minor coloration, it is C minor, the tonic minor, that is invoked, and the cloud is easily dispelled. The cadence embellished by the cadenza prepares the ultimate reconciliation of harmonic conflicts. The final orchestral statement of the motto (mm. 123ff) beautifully symbolizes the concluding mutual adjustment and cooperation between orchestra and soloist. This time the motto lacks its embellished half cadence and suspenseful fermata; rather, it hooks up with a balancing phrase in the solo part to bring things back, peacefully, to the tonic. There are a few chromatic twinges in the closing measures to recall old aches, but the end comes quietly, with gracious resignation. Even more than in the first movement, in this *Andante* we experience the tensions created by the dual medium of solo piano and orchestra in highly emotional terms.

Movement 3: *Allegretto—Presto*

The third and last movement of a concerto is traditionally the lightest. This one—a jolly theme with five variations (*Allegretto*) and a madcap coda (*Presto*)—is no exception. Mozart's orchestration of the theme in the flute and first violins, replete with plentiful grace notes, gives this rustic theme a distinctive "chirpy" quality—little wonder Mozart taught it to his pet starling!

As is typical of themes used as the basis for variations, this one has a clear symmetrical construction. Forming a sixteen-measure period, the theme is divided into two eight-measure phrases (each of which is repeated): an antecedent (mm. 1–8) that modulates to the dominant and a consequent (mm. 9–16) that begins in the dominant and returns to the tonic. Each of these phrases also divides into two four-measure units. All the four-measure units begin with a pickup, and the first, second, and fourth units end with the same rhythmic figure. Thus the four four-measure sections of the theme could each be seen as analogous to a line in a four-line poem with the rhyme scheme AABA. B, the third four-measure unit (mm. 9–12), is exceptional in several ways: It is the only unit to begin away from the tonic, the only unit to break away from the overall homophonic texture (note the imitative counterpoint in the lower strings at mm. 10 and 12), the only unit to be divided 2 + 2, and the only unit to end with a different rhythmic figure ("rhyme"). It thus functions as a mini "far out point."

The variations are arranged to contrast highly with what precedes and follows them. Unlike the theme played by the orchestra without the soloist, Variation 1 (mm. 17–32) begins with the unaccompanied piano playing nearly continuous eighth notes that circle around the notes of the theme. Beginning with Variation 2 (mm. 33–64), Mozart abandons repeat signs and writes out what had been literal repetitions in the theme. In Variation 2 he puts the theme back in the orchestra. In the next variation (mm. 65–96), the melodic relationship to the theme becomes more difficult to follow, although the phrase lengths continue to match exactly those of the theme, and the main notes of the melody and the general harmonic outline are maintained. In this variation the principal winds, the soloists of the orchestra, sing in dialogue with the solo piano. Variation 4 (mm. 97–128), with longer note values and syncopations in the tonic minor, is melodically and tonally the most abstract of the variations. It provides an eerie, dreamy contrast to the rest of the movement. Variation 5 (mm. 129ff) returns to G major, with a march-like rhythm in the orchestra, which plays the first and third phrases. After the piano plays the last eight-measure unit of the thirty-two-measure variation, the music breaks from the variation pattern in mm. 160ff with a series of chromatic runs in the piano that come to rest on a fermata that implies embellishment with an improvised flourish or brief cadenza.

Having broken free of the yoke of the variation form, an extended coda marked *Presto* brings the movement to sparkling end in the manner of an opera buffa finale. Particularly noteworthy are the hunting calls in horns and bassoons that first appear in the third and fourth measures of the *Presto* section. The topic of the hunt appears to be quite apt when, after an energetic chase, the solo piano finally "catches up" with the first half of the long-lost theme (mm. 249ff).

end of bridge
Second theme
"excursion" - key area
29
a 2.
a 2.
38
I.
I.
47
55
I.
I.
descending 3-notes
dramatic manner
3 note descent
Circle progression
Divided violas
ex. bass line to support melody not an continuo
chromatic
diminution
pedal

ur motives - spinning out of ideas
↓
igin

development

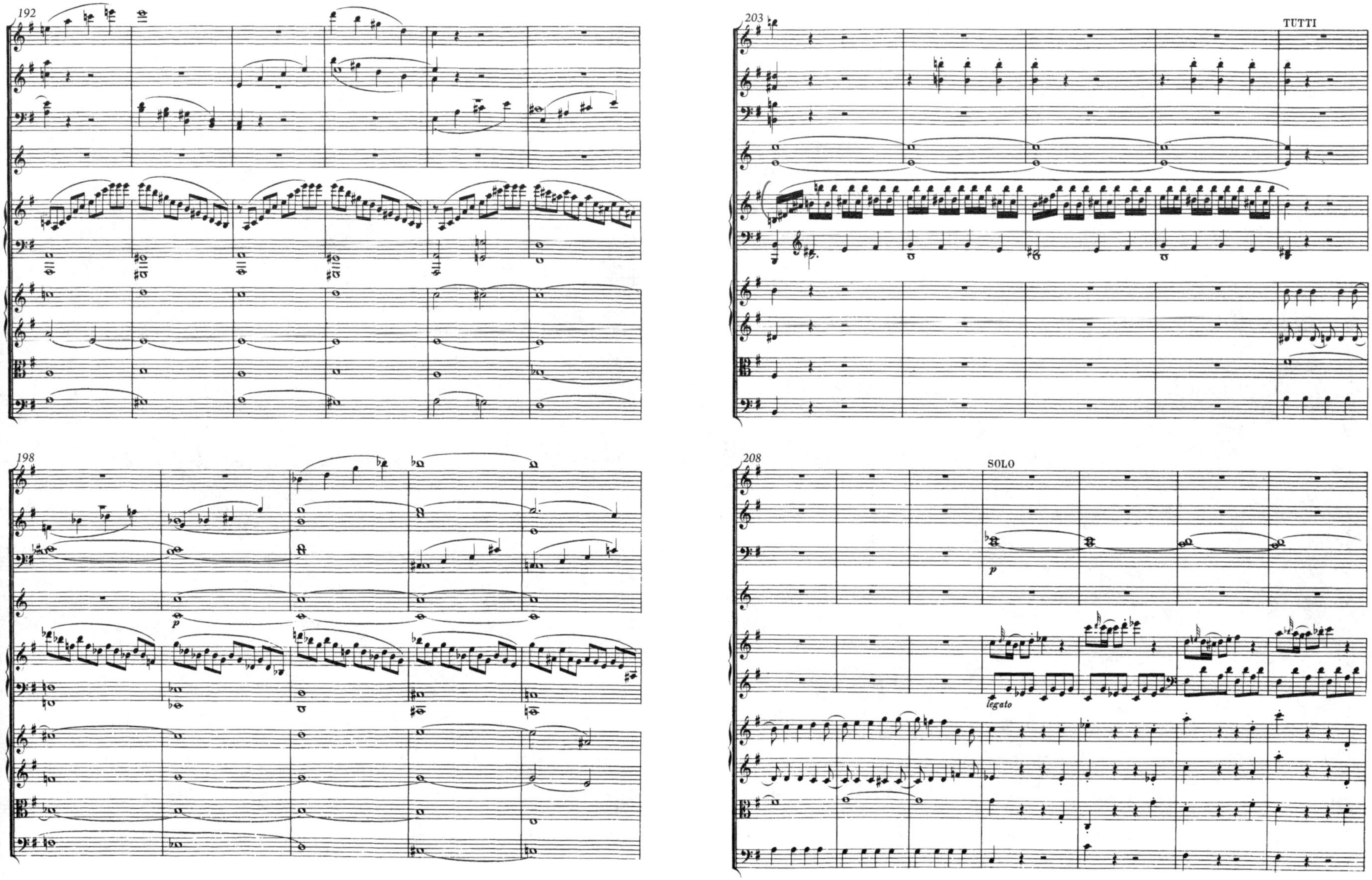
192
198
203
TUTTI
208
SOLO
p
legato

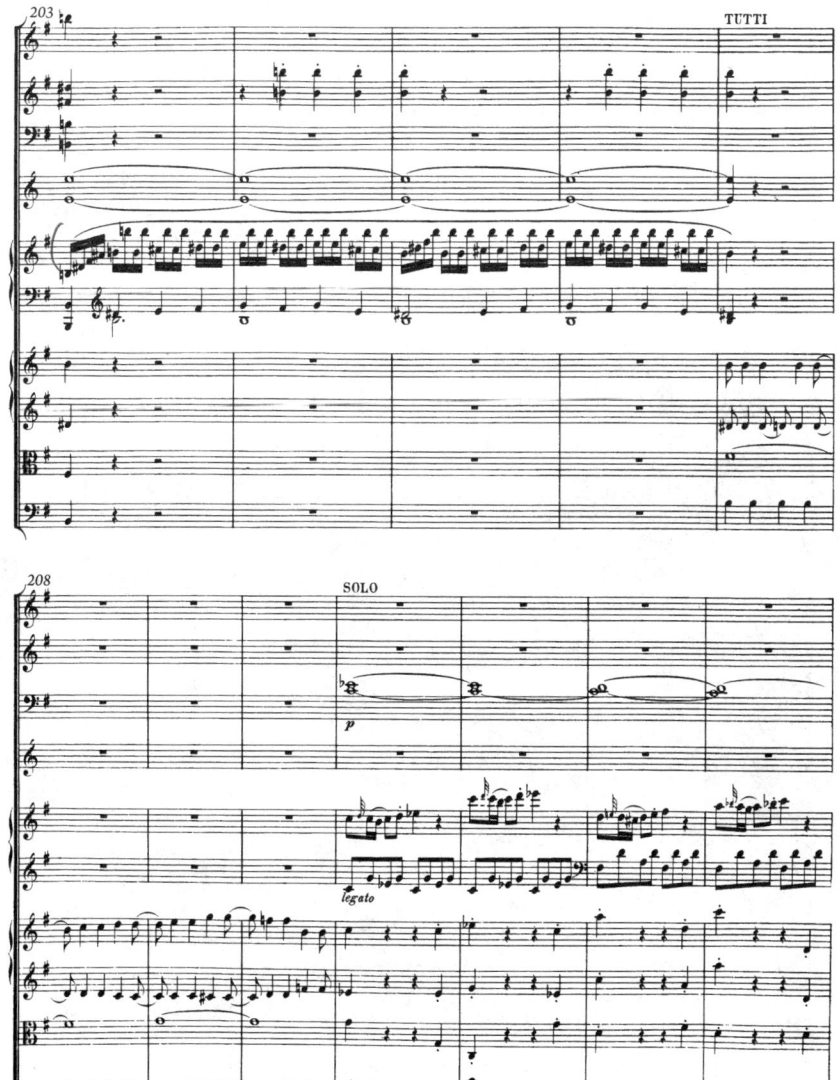

v. 3

v.S

17

Ludwig van Beethoven
(1770–1827)

FULL CD III: TRACK 37
CONCISE CD II: TRACK 19

Sonata No. 8 in C Minor ("Pathétique"), Op. 13,
First movement (Grave—*Allegro con molto e con brio*) (1798)

Beethoven completed his C-Minor Sonata, Op. 13, in 1798 and dedicated it to Prince Carl von Lichnowsky, his most important Viennese patron. The subtitle "Pathétique" originated from Beethoven's publisher and suggests the contemporaneous response to the work's emotional intensity. The expression stems from the Greek word *pathos*, which refers to an appeal to the audience's emotions. The irregularities in the form and the dark minor colors of the first movement may all be seen as characteristic of the heightened expressivity of Beethoven's style in this wok.

The "Pathétique" was the first of Beethoven's sonatas to open with a slow introduction. The remainder of the movement is cast in sonata form, but with several unusual aspects. Most strikingly, truncated versions of the slow introduction reappear at two structurally important moments: the beginning of the development (m. 135) and the beginning of the coda (m. 297). Also unusual is that the first theme recurs as a retransition at the end of the exposition and recapitulation (mm. 121 and 287) and as a seemingly new beginning in the coda (m. 301).

Characteristic of the "heroic style" of his middle period (also represented in this volume by the "Eroica" Symphony), in this sonata Beethoven maintains tonal tension by systematically evading cadences. He eludes tonic closure in the first theme of the *Allegro* by leaving it suspended on the dominant (m. 27). The second theme defies expectations by appearing in E♭ minor as opposed to the expected E♭ major as well as by mimicking developmental procedures by moving through several keys. Indeed, the second theme does not come to a satisfactory cadence. Instead of resolving normally, the B♭ dominant pedal slips down to A♭, which supports a sequential replay of the theme in D♭ major the Neapolitan key of C minor. After further modulation Beethoven ends the section on the dominant of E♭ (m. 88). Only the closing theme provides a standard cadence, ending with a melodically fluid codetta on a I–vi–ii–V–I progression.

Beethoven unifies the movement with two rhythmic gestures: a long-short figure, in both front-accented (m. 11) and syncopated versions (m. 13); and a four-note gesture of three

pickups leading to a downbeat (mm. 35–36). One can argue that both rhythmic gestures are already implied in the first measure of the slow introduction: the long-short figure in the concluding sigh figure (E♭–D), the four-note gesture in the three-note dotted upbeat leading to the F♯ diminished-seventh chord. The closing theme (mm. 89–90) starts with an augmented version of the long-short figure; both the second theme and the bridge rely heavily on the four-note rhythmic motive.

Beethoven further unifies the movement with motivic connections between thematic areas with different character. The first motive of the second theme can be seen as derived from the first rising gesture of the slow introduction (cf. mm. 1 and 51), and the sigh figure in measure 1 provides the building block for much of the thematic material in the movement. The sigh's inversion (a rising half step) seems to express aspiration, as it does in the pleading figures of the slow introduction (m. 8). Rising pairs of half steps supply the first theme with its explosive energy (E–F, G–A♭, B–C in mm. 11–12). The bridge section combines the rising and the falling half-step figures in quick succession (mm. 43–44) and in augmentation (mm. 45–49).

Beethoven's emphasis on minor seconds provides more than motivic unification. In the eighteenth century chromatic minor seconds were considered one of the musical-rhetorical figures expressing pathos. The transitional emotional states associated with pathos in the eighteenth century also find a parallel in Beethoven's restless tonal plan that presents the sonata as being constantly on the move, in search of new tonal areas and new expressions.

Beethoven's style in the "Pathètique" shares some characteristics with the style designated as "*Sturm und Drang*" (storm and stress) in the 1770s (see Haydn's "Farewell" Symphony in this anthology). Both styles are characterized by irregularities in form, interrupted processes, and dark minor colors. Both styles build on sharp contrasts: between sections (compare the intimate tone of the *Grave* to the brilliance of the *Allegro*), in texture (heavy chordal texture directly juxtaposed with ornamental right-hand figures, m. 4), in register (both in terms of juxtaposition of high and low ranges, suggesting dialogue, as in m. 5; and extreme registrar separation between the hands, as in m. 98), in dynamics, and keys (G minor juxtaposed with E minor in mm. 136–138). Beethoven builds the first and second themes and the bridge on long pedal tones. The very low range of the dominant pedal under the retransition (mm. 169ff) evokes drum rolls in symphonic depictions of thunder. These orchestral effects, including the magisterial dotted rhythms of the introduction recalling the old French-overture style, signal Beethoven's penchant for evoking the awe-inspiring sublime.

Grave introduction – comes back

C minor = somber

215

Measure Nos.	Formal Designation	Sections	Keys	Comments
1–10	Slow introduction (*Grave*)		c	Moves to E♭, m. 5, ends on V of c
11–134	Exposition (*Allegro*)			
11–27		Theme 1	c	Ends on dominant pedal
27–50		Bridge		Ends on V of E♭
51–88		Theme 2	e♭	Theme in minor. Modulates to D♭, m. 62, and to f, m. 80
89–121		Closing group	E♭	
89–113		Closing theme 1		
113–121		Closing theme 2		
121–134		Retransition, with theme 1	E♭, to V of c	
135–196	Development			
135–138		Return of *Grave*	g, V of e	
139–169		New theme, similar to theme 1 (with pedal)	e/D/g/d/V of c	
169–196		Retransition with dominant pedal	V of c	
197–296	Recapitulation			
197–223		Theme 1	c	
223–254		Theme 2	f/c	
255–287		Closing group	c	
287–296		Transition to coda, with theme 1		Ends on F♯ diminished-seventh chord
297–312	Coda			
297–300		Return of *Grave*	c	
301–312		Return of theme 1		

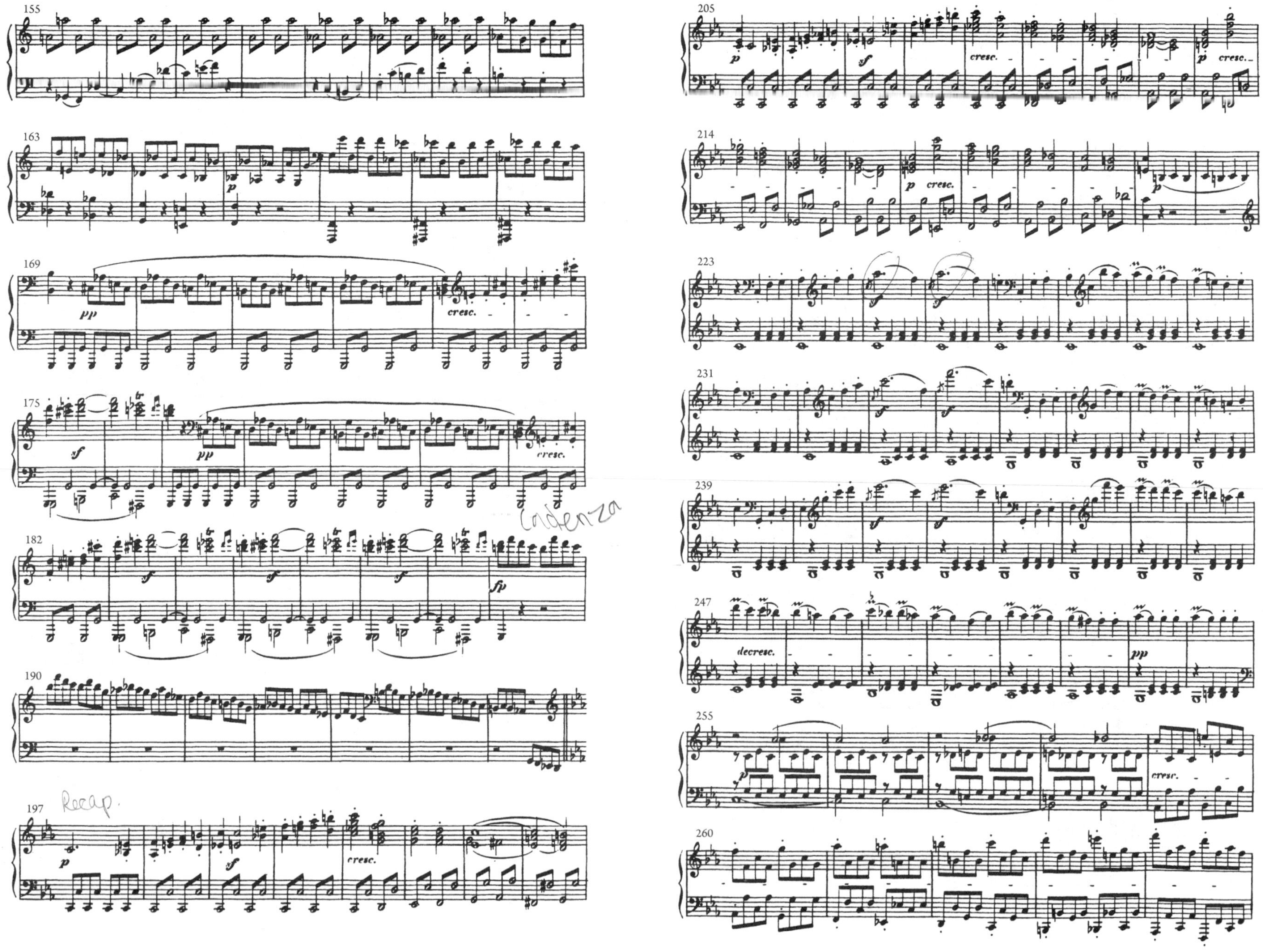

155
163
169
175
182
Cadenza
190
197
Recap.
205
214
223
231
239
247
255
260
pp
cresc.
sf
fp
p
decresc.

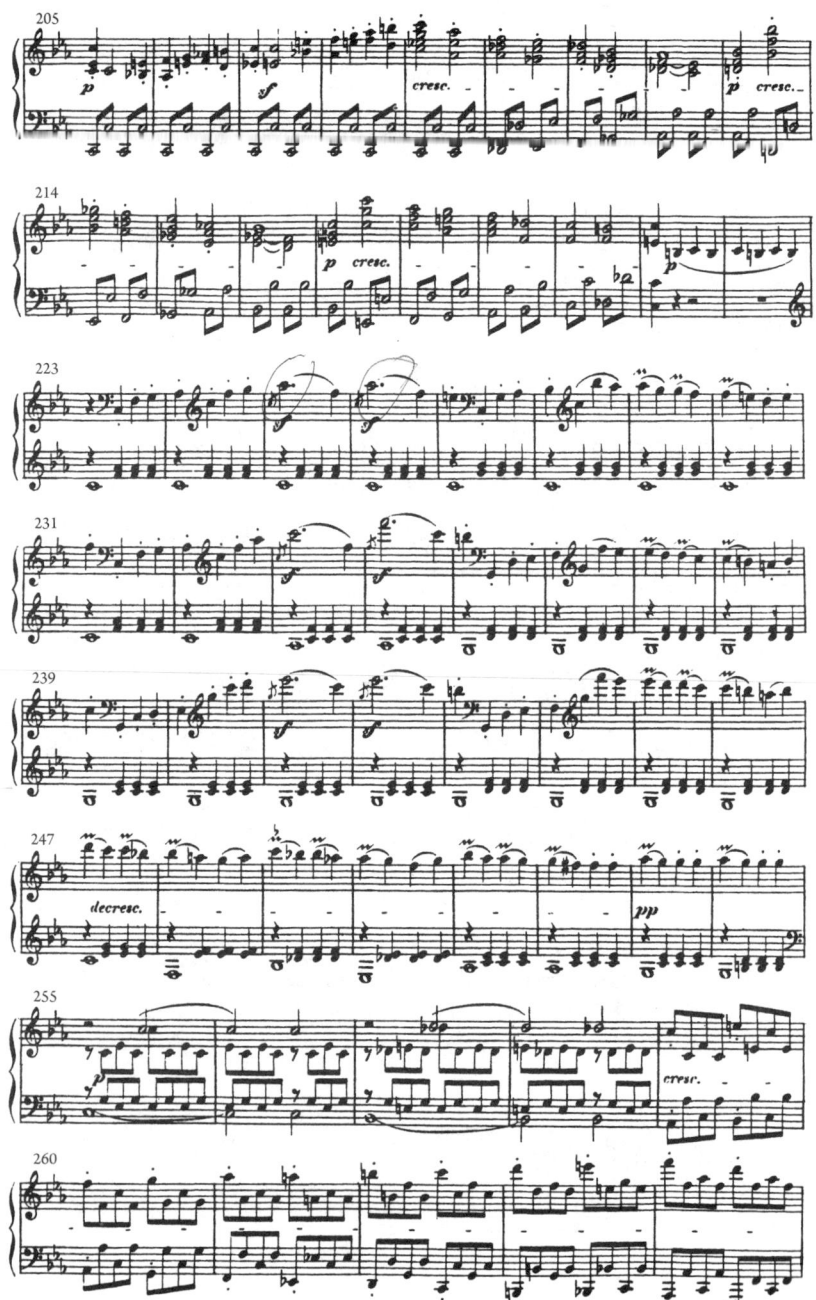

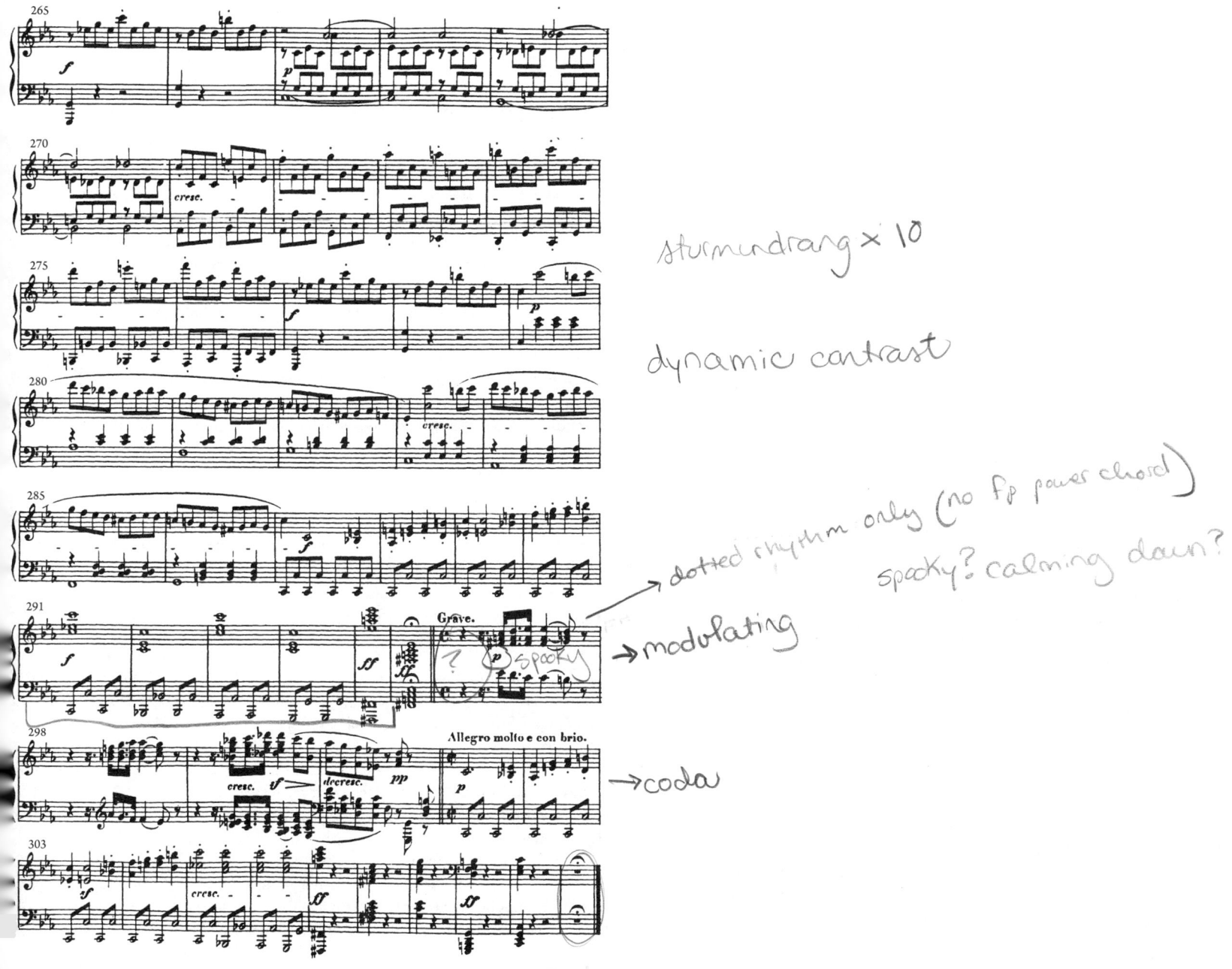

18

Ludwig van Beethoven (1770–1827)

FULL CD III: TRACKS 38–39

Septet in E♭ Major, Op. 20, Fourth movement, Tema con Variazione (*Andante*) and Fifth movement, Scherzo (*Allegro molto e vivace*) (1800)

Beethoven's Septet for clarinet, bassoon, horn, violin, viola, cello, and double bass is representative of what is usually referred to as Beethoven's first creative period. It demonstrates a style more akin to Haydn and Mozart than to that of the mature Beethoven bent on deviating from tradition in his effort to create highly original compositions. It is indeed hard to find the later, famously defiant composer in this pleasing, lightweight piece, dedicated to the music-loving Empress Maria Theresa. The first performance took place at a private gathering, followed shortly by a public concert at Vienna's Burgtheater featuring, along with selected numbers from Haydn's *Creation* and a Mozart symphony, Beethoven's own First Symphony. During Beethoven's lifetime the Septet was his most popular piece; It was issued in several transcriptions and was his most frequently performed work abroad. The Septet was also the last piece that Haydn, Beethoven's former teacher and later rival, admired without reservation.

In view of the composer's later development, the Septet seems insignificant (later critics described it as "amiable but rather mindless"). Even Beethoven is reported to have regretted its success in later life when he famously proclaimed that he wished he had burned it and judged it bitterly as having "rather too much sentimentality and rather too little skill." Yet the work is crucial for understanding the taste of early-nineteenth-century audiences.

Although Beethoven calls the work simply Septet, it displays stylistic features characteristic of divertimenti or serenades, light pieces written for various combinations of strings or winds and used frequently for outdoor entertainment. Divertimenti have various numbers of movements, from one to as many as thirteen. Beethoven's Septet has six, including two slow movements (an *Adagio* and a Theme and Variations) and two dance movements (a Minuet and a Scherzo). Only a few aspects of the piece point beyond the unpretentious nature of divertimenti: the slow introduction to the first and last movements, and the cadenza that Beethoven boldly inserted in the final movement, potentially to display the virtuoso technique of Ignaz Schuppanzigh (1776–1830), the first violinist who played the work.

We include two movements of the Septet in the anthology, the fourth (Theme and Variations) and the fifth (Scherzo); both show Beethoven to be a master of the light, unpretentious style much beloved by the Viennese.

Tema con Variazioni, *Andante*

The theme of the B♭-major variation movement is a simple four-line melody (aa'ba"), with a first line ending on the dominant, the second (a varied form of the first line) on the tonic, the third briefly tonicizing the submediant and the dominant, and the fourth returning to the tonic key. As in most movements of the Septet, the violin and clarinet alternate taking the leading role in the presentation of the theme. The five variations bring variety in instrumental color and in rhythmic density. The fourth variation provides emotional variety and tonal contrast with its turn to B♭ minor. The last variation, which returns in a slightly varied version to the original key and form of the melody, presents the "a" line of the theme with a steady dominant pedal that reinforces the serene mood of the movement.

Beethoven attaches a coda after the fifth variation, which introduces a seemingly new theme (but which follows the melodic, formal, and harmonic outline of the first two lines of the original theme). The coda liberates Beethoven from the formal constraints of the theme and enables him to end the movement with something like a Haydnesque joke. First the original theme appears in unison in the low strings with an accented, flat third degree (mm. 127–128). Measure 128 is then sequentially repeated, and the two notes initiated by the "correction" become a stumbling block in the cadential process that Beethoven suspends for eight measures. By alternating this two-note motive between different registers at increasing pace and decreasing volume, Beethoven frustrates the audience's expectation for a final cadence. After such preparation, the *fortissimo* final chords produce a closure at once humorous and crude.

Scherzo, *Allegro molto e vivace*

This Scherzo has none of the uneasy agitation typical of Beethoven's later scherzos. Its tone remains light throughout the movement. Apart from short tonicizations of C minor (mm. 17–20) and B♭ major (mm. 21–26), the Scherzo stays in the tonic key of E♭ major. Likewise the Trio never strays from E♭ for long. Instead of tonal tension, Beethoven uses orchestration to provide the movement with color and energy. The horn begins the Scherzo with a descending tonic triad, which will be balanced with the violin and bassoon's descending dominant triad in the second phrase. Following convention, Beethoven reduces the texture of the Trio—except for the bassoon, which doubles the bass in lieu of the cello that plays the melody—Beethoven uses no wind instruments here.

Some places in the movement convey a sense of jest. For example, Beethoven adds an overly zealous violin line to the return of the theme in the horn (mm. 47–54). The violin parodies the horn's descending movement by climbing more than three octaves. Beethoven continues to have fun with contrasting melodic movement in the second part of the Trio (mm. 97ff).

in which the descending motion in the bass parodies the cello's unrefined ascending scalar melody. The humor is not as gentle Haydn's; its bluntness shows a composer with a flair for strong effect.

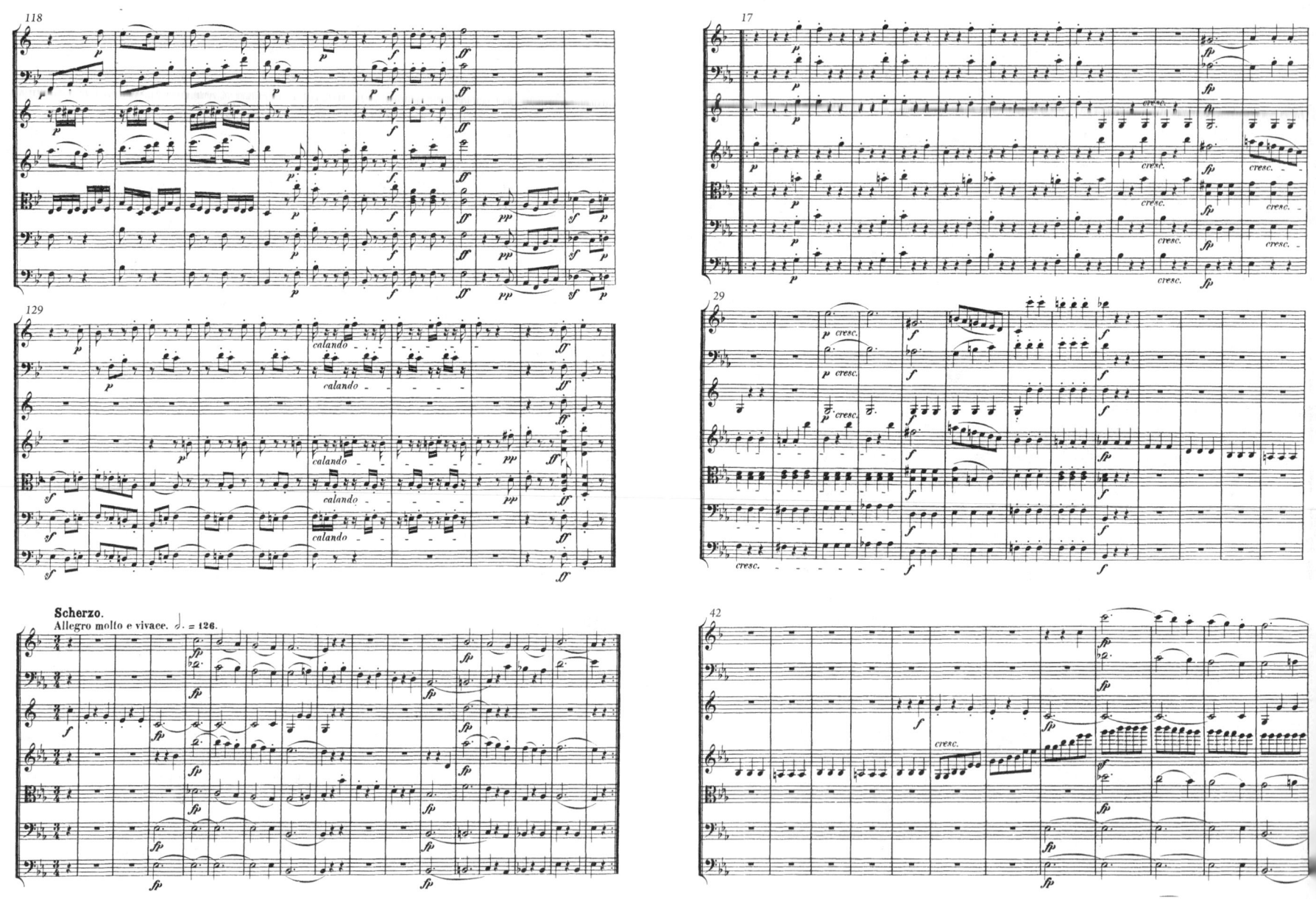

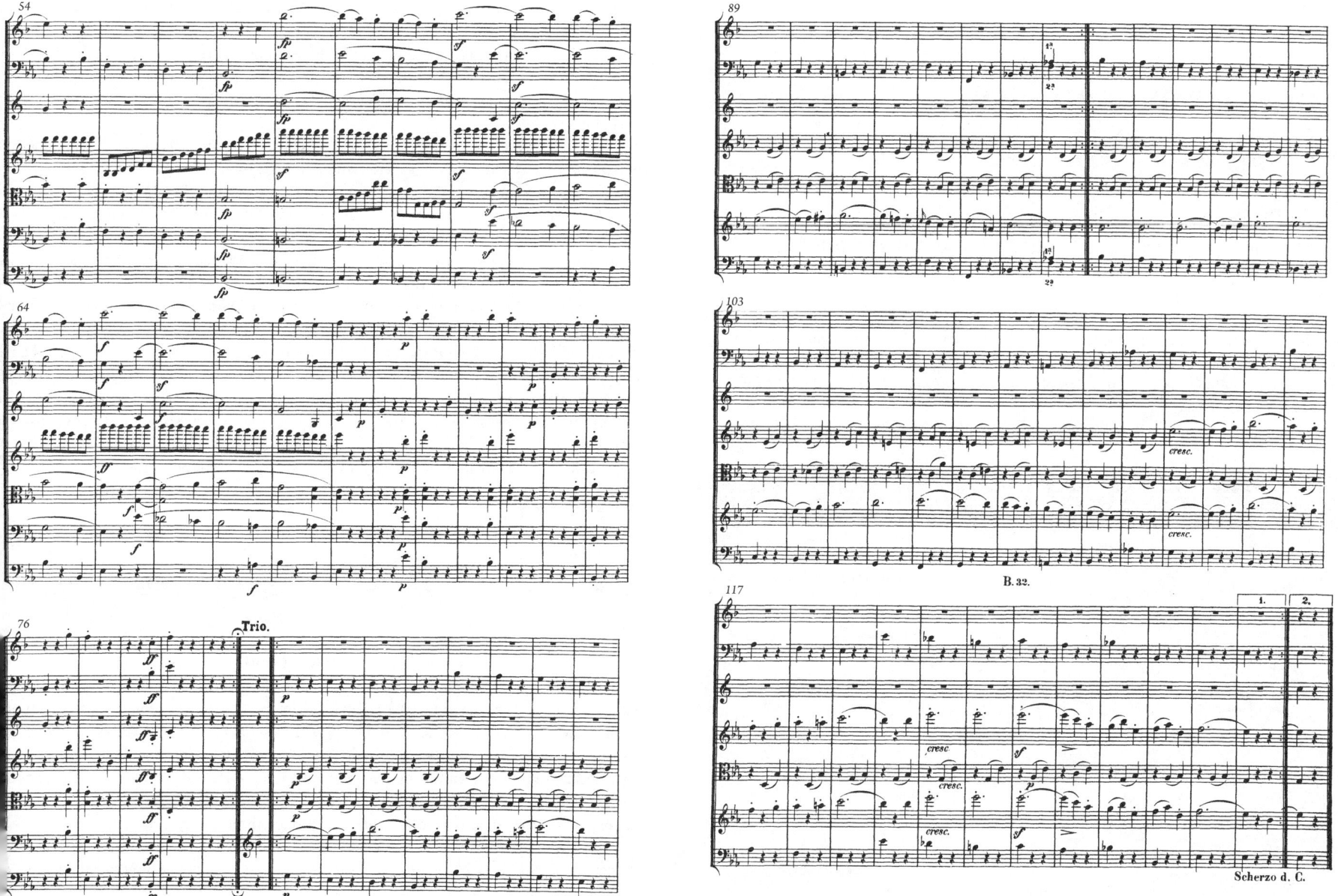

19

Ludwig van Beethoven (1770–1827)

FULL CD III: TRACK 40

Symphony No. 3 in E♭ Major, *Sinfonia Eroica* (Heroic Symphony), Op. 55, First movement (*Allegro con brio*) (1804)

Beethoven completed his third symphony in the summer of 1804. He originally dedicated it to "Bonaparte" but, enraged at Napoleon's crowning himself Emperor of the French, replaced the dedication with the title "Heroic Symphony [*Sinfonia Eroica*] Composed to Celebrate the Memory of a Great Man."

The first movement of the *Eroica* fits the broad outlines of sonata form:

Measure Nos.	Formal Designation	Sections	Keys
1–155	**Exposition**		
1–45		1st theme group	E♭
45–83		Bridge	
83–108		2nd theme group	B♭
109–155		Closing material	B♭
155–401	**Development**		
288–303		New theme	E
402–551	**Recapitulation**		
402–452		1st theme group	E♭
452–490		Bridge	
490–516		2nd theme group	
516–561		Closing material	E♭
561–695	**Coda**		

This chart, however, does not capture the intense "heroic" drama of the movement. In music terms, the most important aspects of Beethoven's "heroic style" exhibited by the moveme include: themes not simply presented but achieved through struggle; extended developmen with extreme "far out points"; and enormous codas that resolve the tension accumulated in t movement. These characteristics are the result of extraordinary processes that are worth follov ing in detail.

The first theme is a veritable bugle call, which bears resemblance to the beginning of t overture the twelve-year-old Mozart wrote for his little singspiel *Bastien und Bastienne* (Ex. 19–1 But while Mozart's theme is entirely conventional in its symmetry, Beethoven's treatment of t same four-measure fanfare idea is altogether unprecedented. The C♯ that immediately follov the E♭-major arpeggio on the downbeat of m. 7 is possibly the most famous single note in t entire symphonic literature for the way it contradicts the fanfare's implications. Rather th initiating a balancing phrase, it violently unbalances and extends it. Relative harmonic stabil: is restored in m. 9 by the move of the uncanny chromatic note back to a normal scale degr (the leading tone), marked with the first of countless *sforzandi*. But the two-measure "time ou in mm. 7–8 has stopped all possibility of phrase symmetry—all possibility, that is, of "them hood," at least for the moment. Not counting the two-measure chordal preparation at the or set, the first appearance of the theme has lasted an entirely indivisible thirteen measures— extraordinarily off-balance opening. A cadence in mm. 14–15 provisionally restores the balar and elides with the winds' restatement of the opening four-measure fanfare. The dominant reached at m. 23, whereupon harmonic motion is stalled, preventing closure.

Example 19–1

The long series of syncopated *sforzandi* that follows (mm. 25–34) seems to push ha against an implied harmonic barrier, until an exhilarating breakthrough to the tonic (m. 3 initiates a climactic statement of the original fanfare motif, replete with martial trumpets a drums. Even this statement, however, dissipates in a sequence without achieving closure. far this thematic exposition has furnished no stable point of departure; instead it has involv us from the beginning in turbulent dynamic growth: not state, but process; not being, but l coming. The theme is not so much presented as it is achieved through struggle, and closure deliberately withheld. This process continues through the ensuing bridge section (mm. 45f carrying the listener through a great wealth of new melodic ideas before reaching the seco theme—and when it finally arrives (m. 83) it provides no more than a brief touching-down the way to the main cadence of the exposition.

Although the overall harmonic plan of the development section is the same as in earlier symphonies, the degree of drama is so extreme that the plan is hardly recognizable. Consider the move to the "far out point" in the development section from m. 240. This is the F-minor beginning of a fugato, a common device for speeding up harmonic rhythm toward an implied goal. After only thirteen measures, however, the harmony once again stalls and strains against an invisible barrier suggested by syncopated *sforzandi*. This time (m. 252) it stalls on a diminished-seventh chord built on G♯, implying resolution to A, a note outside the tonic scale. The stall therefore arrests the harmonic motion at a far more threatening point than did a similar stall earlier in the movement; for even when resolution takes place (m. 258), there is no sense of achievement—just another delay. Seven measures later (m. 264) the A-minor harmony gives way to an even more remote sonority, a dominant seventh on B natural, implying resolution to E natural.

Resolution to the unlikely goal of E natural does come eventually, but not before one last detour through another set of wrenching harmonic stalls that finally reapproaches the dominant seventh of E through the Neapolitan of E (F⁶₅ at mm. 280–283). This Neapolitan chord is expressed with a fiercely dissonant E that the flute retains as a suspension from the preceding C-major chord. The suspended E rubs painfully against F, the chord's root, in the other flute part. The grating semitone between the flutes resolves only in another register, played on other instruments (the E resolving to the first violins' D♯ in m. 284, the F, most unconventionally, to the viola F♯). The resolution chord (m. 284), B⁹, still throbs tensely, owing to the second violins' C natural, suspended from the preceding chord. Tension then reduces by degrees until the smoke metaphorically clears in m. 288, and we are left in E minor.

So far from home no symphonic development had ever seemed to stray before. Having dramatized the disruption, Beethoven now dramatizes the sense of distance by unexpectedly introducing a new theme in the unearthly new key (mm. 288ff). By far the most placid, most symmetrically presented melody in the movement, it expresses not "process" but "state" for a change—the state of being tonally adrift. Understood enharmonically, E natural is equivalent to F♭, the "Neapolitan," or "flatted"-second, degree of the tonic E♭-major scale; thus Beethoven could quickly achieve the "double return" if he so desired. Instead he strategically delays the moment of recapitulation, enhancing the emotional payoff when the long-awaited event is finally allowed to occur in m. 402. By this time suspense has been deliberately jacked up to an unbearable degree—so literally unbearable, in fact, that at m. 398 the first horn goes figuratively berserk with a premature entry on the first theme in the tonic while the violins still dissonantly protract the dominant function in a seemingly endless tremolo.

Full redemption of the movement's disruptive forces and full discharge of its tonal tensions come only after the end of the recapitulation, in a mammoth coda that begins at m. 561 with a shockingly sudden intrusion of D♭, the enharmonic equivalent of the C♯ that sounded the first disruptive note in m. 7. The coda takes up and resolves two pieces of unfinished business. First it recapitulates the E-minor theme within the normal purview of the tonic by having it appear in F minor, the ordinary diatonic ("unflatted") second degree of E♭ major (mm. 585–599). The coda's main business, however, is to provide at last the fully articulated, cadentially closed version of the opening theme. It arrives at m. 635 in the form of a quietly confident horn solo that makes up, as it were, for the horn's harried "false entrance" 237 measures earlier. Its symmetrical

eight-measure phrase finally juxtaposes tonic and dominant versions of the opening arpeggio, thus for the first time closing the harmonic circle at close range.

The phrase occurs four times in rapid succession together with a rushing countersubject, in a massive crescendo that ultimately engulfs the whole orchestra, the trumpets and drums entering on the third go-round with a military tattoo (pickup to m. 651) and, on the fourth, finally breaking the melodic surface in a final thematic peroration (mm. 659–666). Yet even this crest is immediately trumped by one final disruption, the diminished-seventh chord in mm. 667–668, with D♭/C♯ as the climactic note in the bass. From here there is nothing left to do but retake the goal in one last eight-measure phrase, after which only a clinching I–V–I remains (the V extended through one more characteristic "stall," mm. 685ff) to bring home the final pair of tonic chords (mirroring the pair in the first two measures of the movement) as one last victory through struggle. This long-deferred resolution creates in the listener what E. T. A. Hoffmann called the "unutterable portentous longing" that is the hallmark of Romantic art.

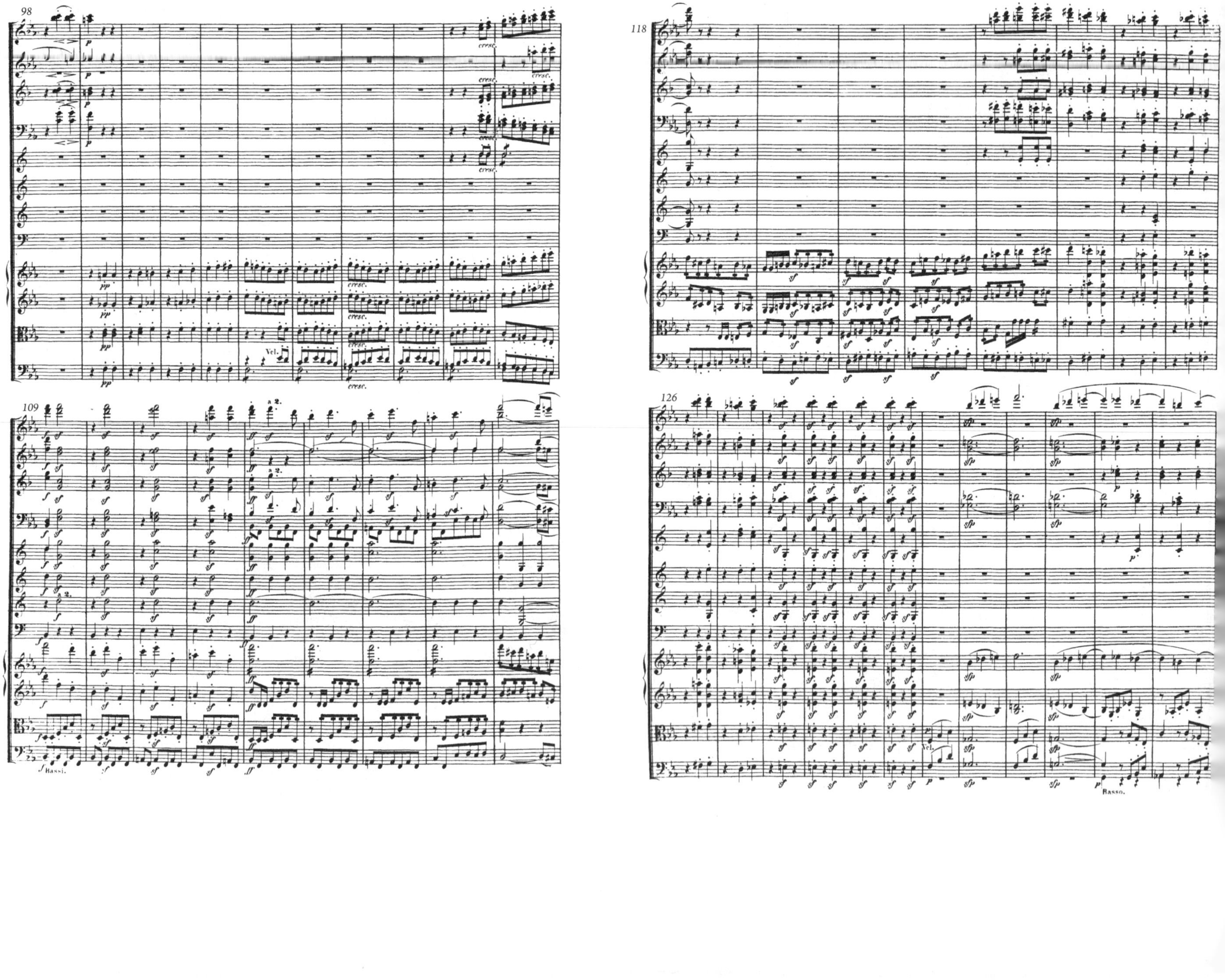
98
cresc.
pp
Vel.
109
a 2.
Bassi.
118
126
Basso.

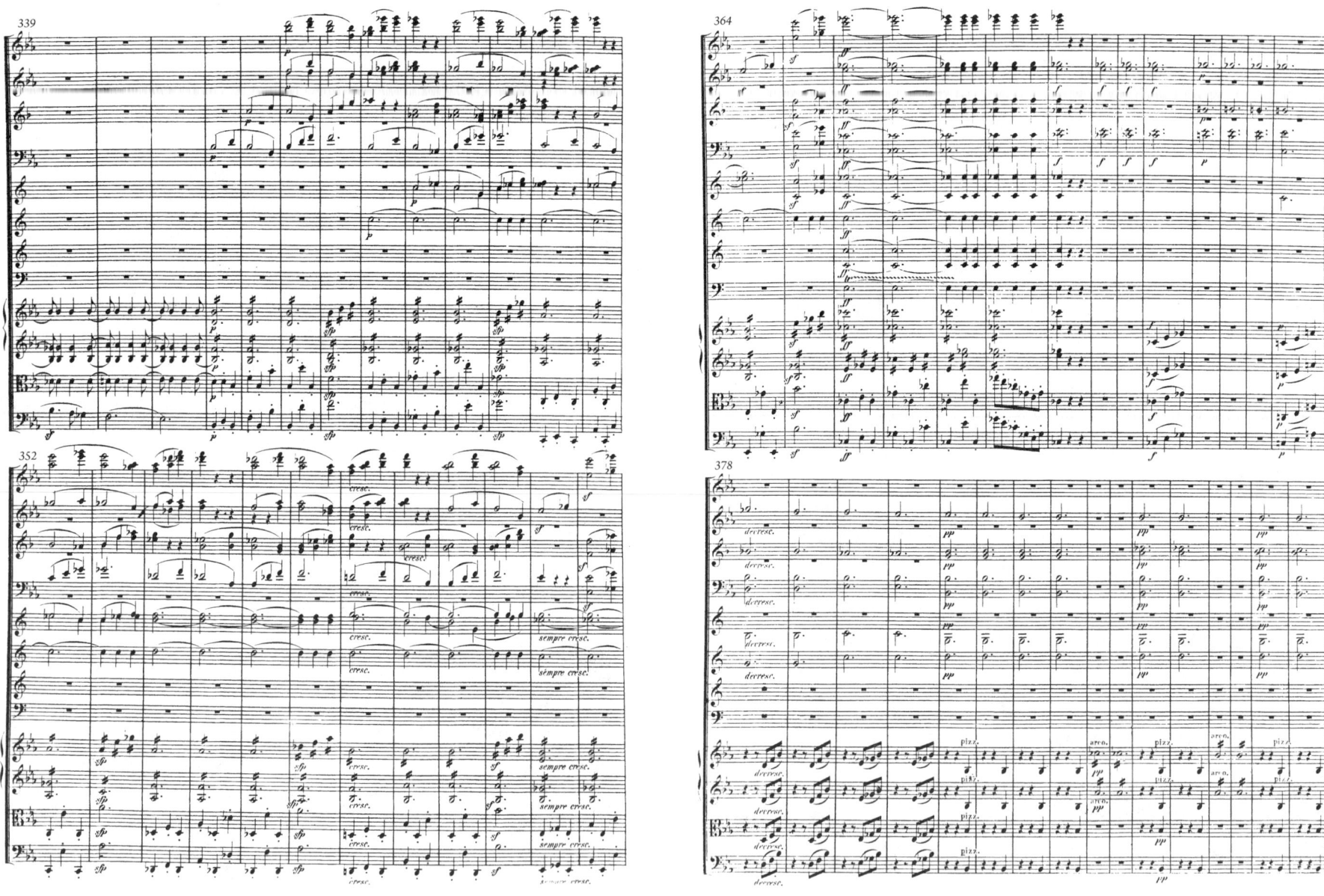

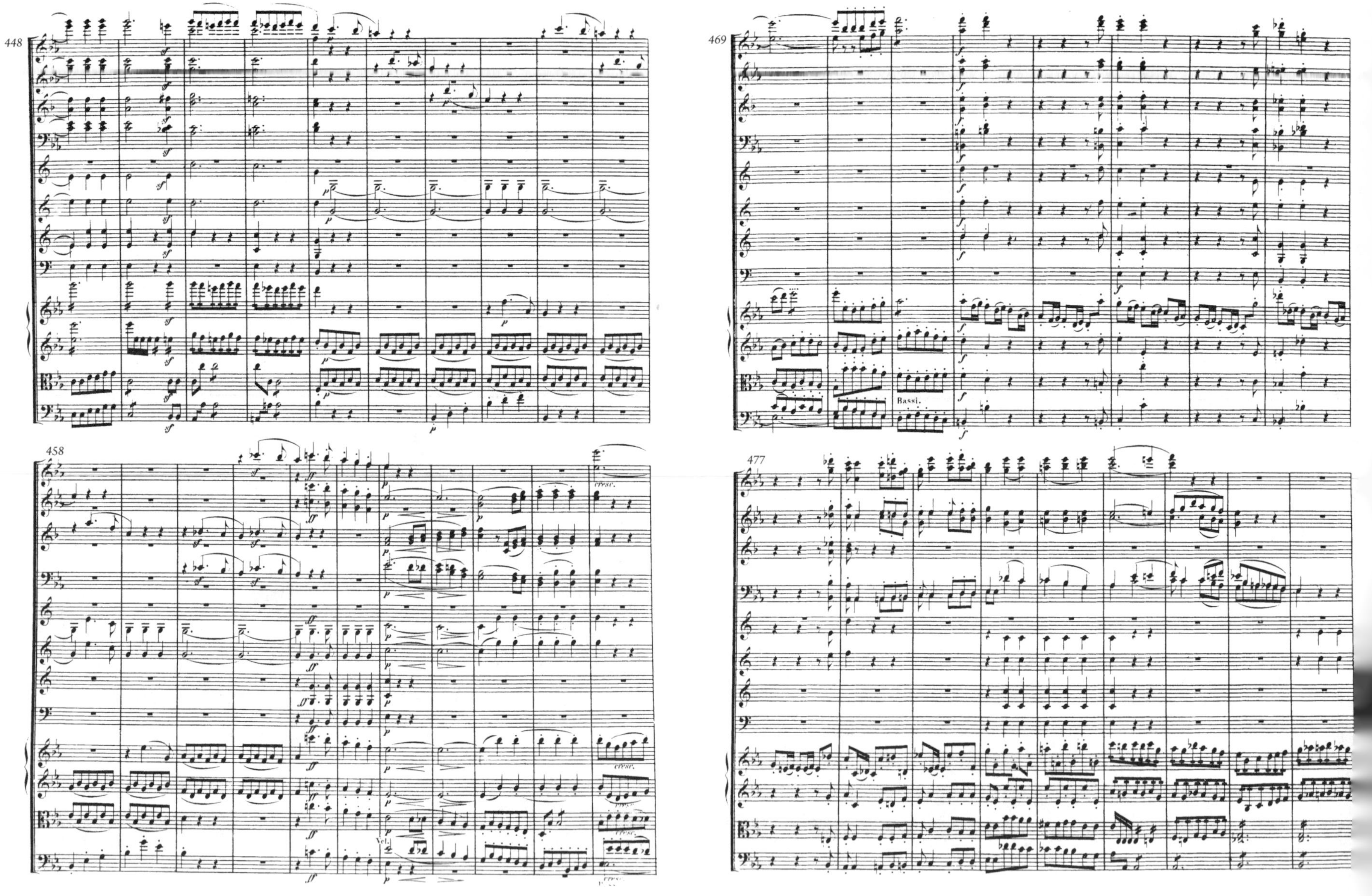
448
458
469
477
Bassi.
cresc.

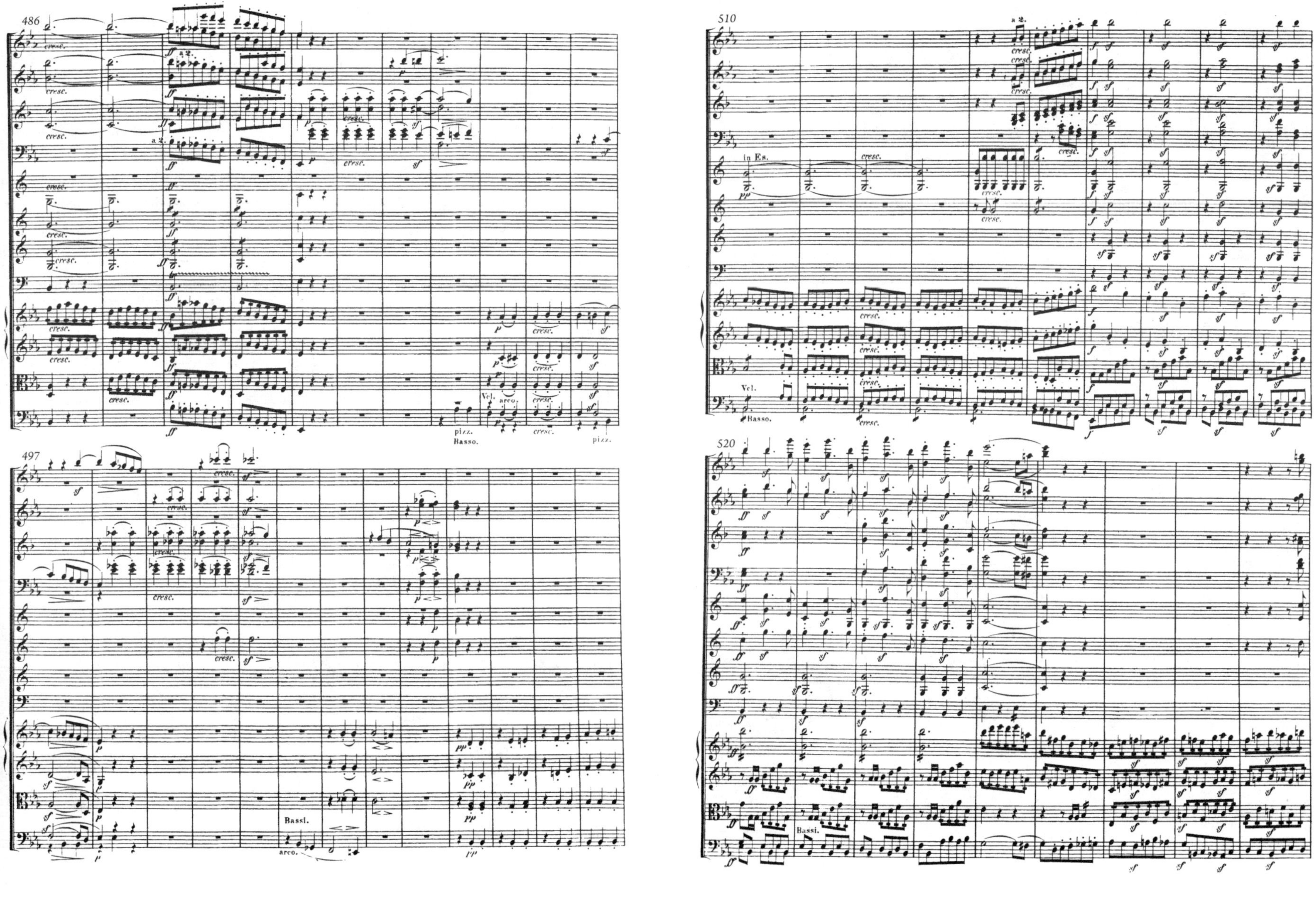
486
a 2.
cresc.
Vel.
arco.
pizz.
Basso.
497
Bassi.
510
in Es.
520

20

Ludwig van Beethoven (1770–1827)

Symphony No. 5 in C Minor, Op. 67 (1808)

FULL CD III:
TRACKS 41–44
CONCISE CD II:
TRACKS 20–21

Beethoven began composing his Fifth Symphony soon after completing the *Eroica* in 1804. After many disruptions, he completed the symphony four years later. Its first performance took place on 22 December 1808 in a gargantuan four-hour concert consisting entirely of Beethoven premieres, including the Sixth Symphony, Choral Fantasy, Fourth Piano Concerto, several movements of the Mass in C, a concert aria, and Beethoven's improvisation at the piano. Like the *Eroica*, the Fifth typifies the new Beethovenian symphonic model, in which conventional sonata procedures are presented as a psychological journey, a goal-oriented process at the end of which triumph is achieved through struggle and pain. Beethoven attains this effect by relying on themes caught in a developmental process from the moment they appear, by avoiding tonal resolutions, and by linking the movements through motivic and thematic references.

Since E. T. A. Hoffmann's famous review of the Fifth Symphony in 1810, it has been considered the paragon of "organic" construction, that is, a whole that develops from a single cell. Indeed, the famous first motive (short-short-short-long), which listeners, allegedly based on Beethoven's own statement, heard as "fate knocking at the door," appears in almost every measure of the first movement. It shapes the character of the first theme, drives the bridge section (mm. 34–58), announces the second subject at mm. 59–62, shadows the steady quarter notes of the Eb-major second theme in the bass (mm. 65ff), marks the end of the closing subject (mm. 110ff), and provides fodder for the entire development (mm. 125–248) and coda (mm. 374ff). In the spirit of organicism, one can hear the little triplet turns in the second movement as derivative from the main motive of the symphony (see mm. 14, 18–20). The rhythm of the second, triumphant theme in the second movement (first introduced *dolce* in the winds, m. 23) is unmistakably related to it. Similarly unambiguous is Beethoven's reference to the motive in the third movement, in which it grows into another triumphant theme (mm. 19ff). In the finale, the clearest manifestation of the motive is in the triplet figures leading to quarter notes in the second theme, first heard at m. 45.

Measure Nos.	Formal Designation	Sections	Keys	Comments
1–124	Exposition			
1–21		Primary theme	c, ending on V	"Fate motive"
22–58		Bridge	Ends on V/Eb	Starts with "fate motive"
59–94		Secondary theme	Eb	Starts with "fate motive," continues with "fate motive" in the bass
94–124		Closing theme	Eb	"Fate motive" in figuration
124–248	Development		Works with "fate motive"	
124–179			Eb, f, c, g	
179–239			G, C, f , Bb, Gb, f♯	Works with beginning of theme 2, fragmentation mm. 195ff to single chords mm. 210ff, "far out point" mm. 216–228
240–248		Retransition		"Fate motive"
248–374	Recapitulation			
248–268		Primary theme	c, V/c	Oboe cadenza (m. 268) embellishes fermata in exposition (m. 21)
269–302		Bridge		
303–346		Secondary theme	C	
346–374		Closing theme	C	
374–512	Coda			
374–438				Developmental
439–469		New theme (march)		
478–512		Primary theme reappears	C	

First Movement: *Allegro con brio* (C minor)

Beethoven's emphasis on motivic work and forward-moving processes define the character of the first movement. Although it begins with a *fortissimo*, assertive unison, the first theme initially seems to be hesitant and uncertain of its proper key and proper length. After the first three notes it stops on a fermata, then stops again on an even longer note, as if looking for a new direction. Indeed something is strangely off with the theme: instead of starting in the tonic key of C minor, it begins with what can be heard as part of a tonic and a dominant chord in E♭ major. C appears first in the cellos and bassoons in m. 7, yet the imitative passage initiated by the second violins a measure before cannot reach a tonic cadence until the whole process of assertive beginning and hesitant continuation is repeated after a fermata on the dominant chord at m. 21. The first tonic cadences duly arrive at mm. 29 and 32, but are almost imperceptible—the cadential gesture needs to be extended to achieve a more emphatic ending in m. 51. Yet here again the forceful cadential gesture is immediately contradicted by the harmony on the next downbeat, a diminished seventh on A that leads to a B♭ dominant at m. 58 in an abrupt preparation for the second-subject area in the relative major. The new theme (with ominous reminders of the main motive in the bass) soon begins to modulate (m. 76) and runs directly into the closing theme at m. 94.

The contrast between forward drive (embodied in the rhythmic urgency of the main motive) and hesitancy (manifested in the fermatas of the first theme) comes to the fore in the development. The theme that in the exposition introduced the second subject (mm. 59–62) at m. 179 initiates a process that leads to its fragmentation, first reduced to alternating two chords in the winds against two in the strings (mm. 196–209), then alternating single chords (mm. 210–227) over eerie harmonies (m. 209–210, B♭ minor is the "far out point"). A forceful reintroduction of the short-short-short-long motive (m. 240) leads to the recapitulation at m. 248. One of the most unusual moments of the movement, the oboe "cadenza" that unexpectedly grows out of the prolonged dominant chord at m. 268, can also be heard as an emphatic moment of hesitation, an extension of the metric freedom first introduced by the fermata in m. 2.

Like many of Beethoven's symphonic binary movements, this one ends with a long coda (mm. 374ff), the first chord of which anticipates the triumphant C-major ending of the symphony. The coda reiterates the most emphatic statements of the main motive, leading to a section of military assertiveness (mm. 423ff), which again foretells events to come in the remaining movements of the symphony. Beethoven compensates for the avoided cadence of the first theme at the beginning by finishing the theme in the coda with aggressively pounding tonic and dominant chords in the original C minor (mm. 491ff).

Second Movement: *Andante con moto* (A♭ major)

The second movement presents two contrasting themes in a series of variations, presumably modeled on Haydn's similar forms. Theme 1 is a flowing melody in A♭ major. Theme 2, while first introduced quietly in A♭, is best characterized by its *fortissimo* outbursts in C major,

Measure Nos.	Formal Designation	Sections	Keys	Comments
1–23	Theme 1		A♭	
23–38	Theme 2		A♭, C	*Piano dolce* statement in A♭, followed by *fortissimo* statement in C major with military character, short-short-short-long (mm. 32–33) from main motive of movement 1
38–49		Retransition		
49–71	Theme 1, Var. 1		A♭	
72–87	Theme 2, Var. 1		A♭, C	Again *piano dolce* statement in A♭, followed by *fortissimo* statement in C
87–98		Retransition		
99–123	Theme 1, Var. 2		A♭	
124–147		Codetta		First eight measures over dominant pedal
147–158	Theme 2, Var. 2		C	Truncated
158–166		Retransition		
167–176	Theme 1, Var. 3		a♭	Variation in minor
177–184	Transition			
185–204	Theme 1, Var. 4		A♭	
205–247	Coda		A♭	From themes 1 and 2

which break in with increasing aggressiveness three times in the course of the movement—trumpeting the short-short-short-long motive from the first movement. The form of the second movement may be summarized as follows:

In the first theme Beethoven preserves something of the minor inflection and the hesitant opening of the first movement by briefly shifting the tonal center to F minor (mm. 3–4) and by adding "afterthoughts" to the final cadence (mm. 16–22). Even the assertive second theme starts with some indecision in A♭ major at m. 23, being incapable of moving beyond a diminished-seventh chord on A that stops its forward motion in m. 27. The theme regains its forward motion with a *fortissimo* augmented-sixth chord on A♭ (m. 29), which leads into the subsequent C major. It is probably because of such sudden shifts in mood that E. T. A. Hoffmann heard in the movement "the awful phantom that seized our hearts in the Allegro [threatening] at every moment to emerge from the storm-cloud into which it disappeared." This first military outburst quickly dies away, dissipating into a mysterious, chromatic passage at mm. 41–48 (notice the chromatically ascending and descending lines in the first violins and the celli), which accomplishes the modulation back to A♭ major.

The last appearance of the second theme (mm. 148ff) is even more violent than the first; without preparation it bursts into the quiet codetta following the bass rendition of the first theme at mm. 115ff. Its full-blown, triumphant tone is balanced by the first and only *fortissimo* utterance of the first theme at m. 185, reinforced with brass and timpani. The military tone of the second theme thus finally penetrates the simple, serene character of the first theme. Strangely the minor variant of this first theme, in which the steady eighth notes in the strings highlight the dotted figures in the melody, gives us a first glimpse of its potentially martial character. The coda, in a faster tempo (mm. 205ff), reiterates fragmentary statements from the first theme. The ascending arpeggiated triads starting at m. 213 might be heard as anticipating the beginning of the scherzo.

Third Movement: *Allegro* (C minor)

The third movement is a scherzo with a regular ABA structure. Because of the highly evocative character of its themes, this movement has elicited highly programmatic explanations. The musicologist Donald Francis Tovey (1875–1940) called it a "dream of terror," and the novelist E. M. Forster compared the first theme to "a goblin walking quietly over the universe" and called the middle section the "interlude of elephants dancing."

The upward-rushing, whispering arpeggiated triads in the first theme indeed suggest mysteries (if not goblins) to come. As in the first movement, the opening statement is presented in octaves and the progression is arrested by fermatas, here stopping twice on the dominant (mm. 8 and 18). The contrasting second theme (mm. 19ff) exchanges the whispering of the opening with full-throated shouting. Its rhythm calls to mind the main motive of the first movement ("fate" knocking even more insistently). Like the first theme, the second gets halted on a dominant chord, now in the key of E♭ minor (mm. 38–44). In fact no full cadence occurs until the end of the A section (m. 140), which remains throughout in minor keys. The last part of the A section (mm. 101ff) combines the rhythmic drive of the second theme and the trochaic (long-short) rhythm from the first theme into a swelling crescendo climaxing in mm. 133–136.

The B section, or Trio, usually the locus of simplified texture and bucolic charm, here presents contrapuntal complexity. The theme of this C-major fugato is clumsy and moves awkwardly in the low register of the double bass and the cello (hence Forster's analogy to "elephants dancing").

Shortly into the return of the A section at m. 237, Beethoven switches to *pizzicato* in the strings (mm. 246ff), which obscures the difference between the section's two themes and gradually dissipates the movement into barely audible whispering. At the very end, the dominant chord, instead of moving to the tonic, shifts to the submediant (m. 325), initiating an eerie transition that ends with a lengthy dominant pedal that erupts without pause into the triumphant C-major finale, which appears, as Hoffmann put it, as "a brilliant shaft of blinding sunlight suddenly penetrating the darkness of night." The relief the listener feels at the arrival of the finale is even greater after the seven measures of extreme dissonance, created by the insistent tonic pedal in the violas, bassoons, and timpani that grates against a dominant-seventh chord (mm. 368–374).

Fourth Movement: *Allegro* (C major)

As if to compensate for the lack of major keys in the previous movements, the finale revels in C major and the ecstatic restatements of authentic cadences. It is one of the first movements in the history of symphony to employ trombones (formerly used mainly in sacred music, the theater, and military bands) and the first symphonic work to use trombones in combination with the piccolo and the double bassoon. The movement follows unambiguously the outline of sonata form, with two characteristic tonic themes in the exposition (mm. 1ff and mm. 26ff), the second initiating a bridge to the dominant key, G major, where the second theme duly appears (m. 45ff). The dominant area also has two themes, the closing theme arriving at m. 64. These dominant themes, played mainly by the strings, are less bombastic than the tonic themes. The first recalls the short-short-short-long rhythm of the "fate motive"—expressed as a triplet followed by a quarter note—and features in its accompaniment a motive (see mm. 47–48 in the cello) that will play a central role in the contrapuntal texture of the development.

The most unusual feature of the finale is the sudden change of meter, which brings back the second theme from the scherzo right before the recapitulation (mm. 155–208). This theme from the third movement appears in its ghostly pizzicato guise, providing Beethoven with the opportunity to reprise the thrilling sense of victorious arrival when the recapitulation arrives after fifty-three measures of tension-producing suspense.

The coda, which by the time of the Fifth had become a mandatory ingredient of Beethoven symphonic binary forms, is built on three themes: the dominant theme, a rapid version of the second tonic theme that in the exposition initiated the bridge, and the closing theme, which appears here in a new tempo (*Presto*). At the end Beethoven brings back the first theme of the movement, leading it sequentially to a long series of aggressively pounding dominant and tonic chords. The brutal force of this enormous coda, and the reminiscence from the scherzo that appeared previously suggest that this coda resolves not only conflicts in the last movement but also tensions that run through the entire symphony. Contemporary listeners heard the progression through pain, suffering, and striving (in Hoffmann's words, "infinite yearning") in the first three movements to the mighty, awe-inspiring triumph of the finale as the epitome of the sublime.

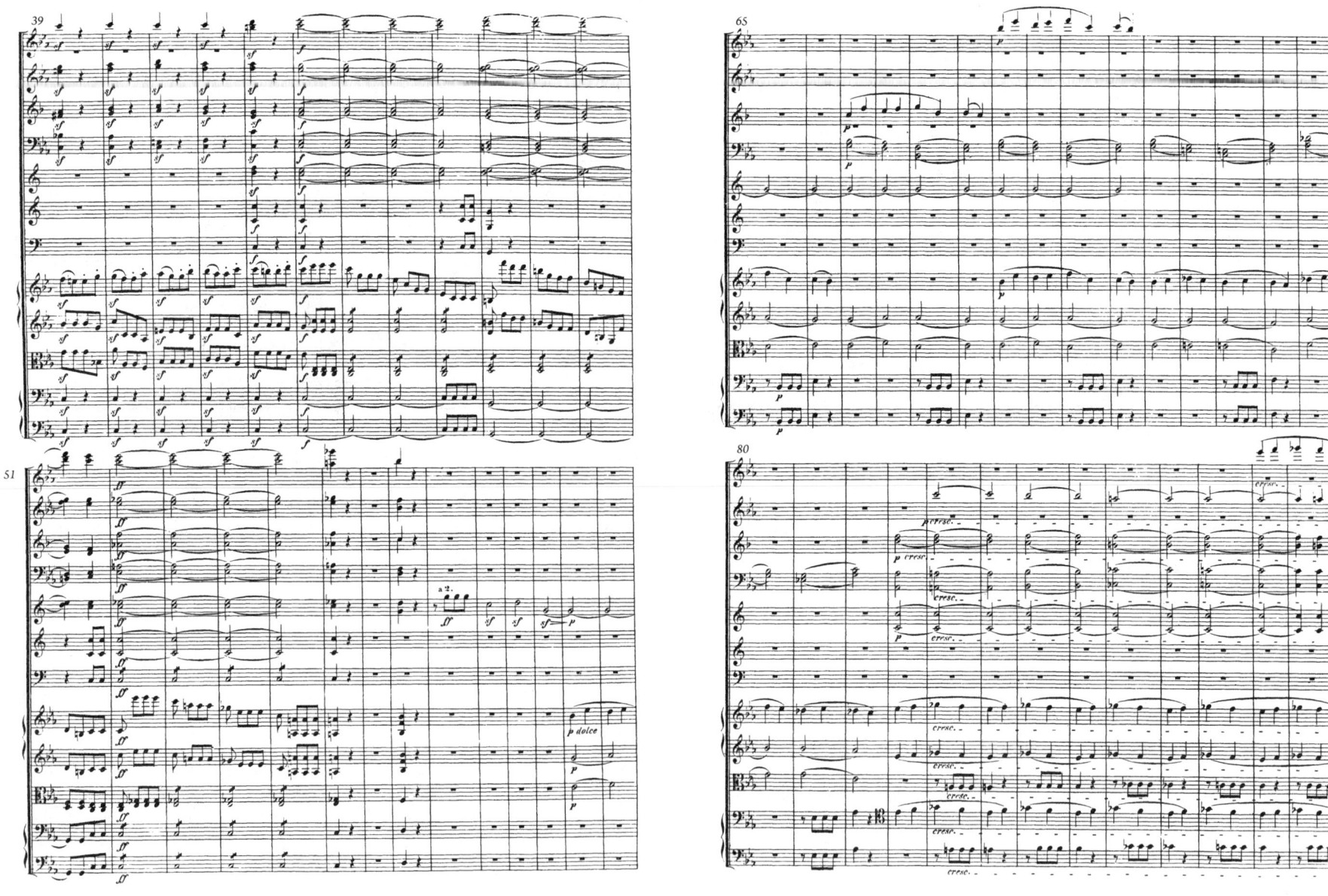

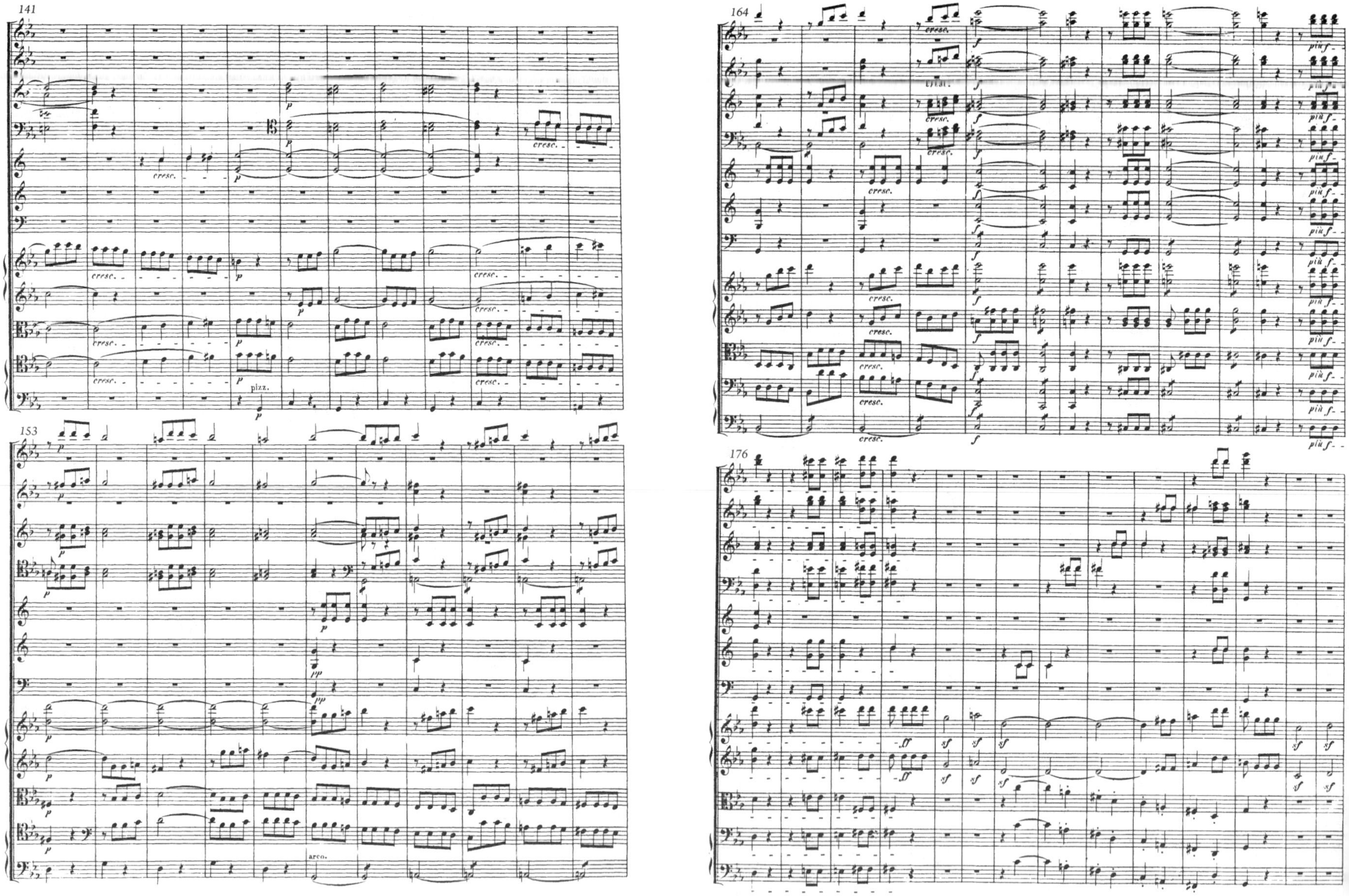
141
cresc.
pizz.
153
arco.
164
cresc.
più f.
176

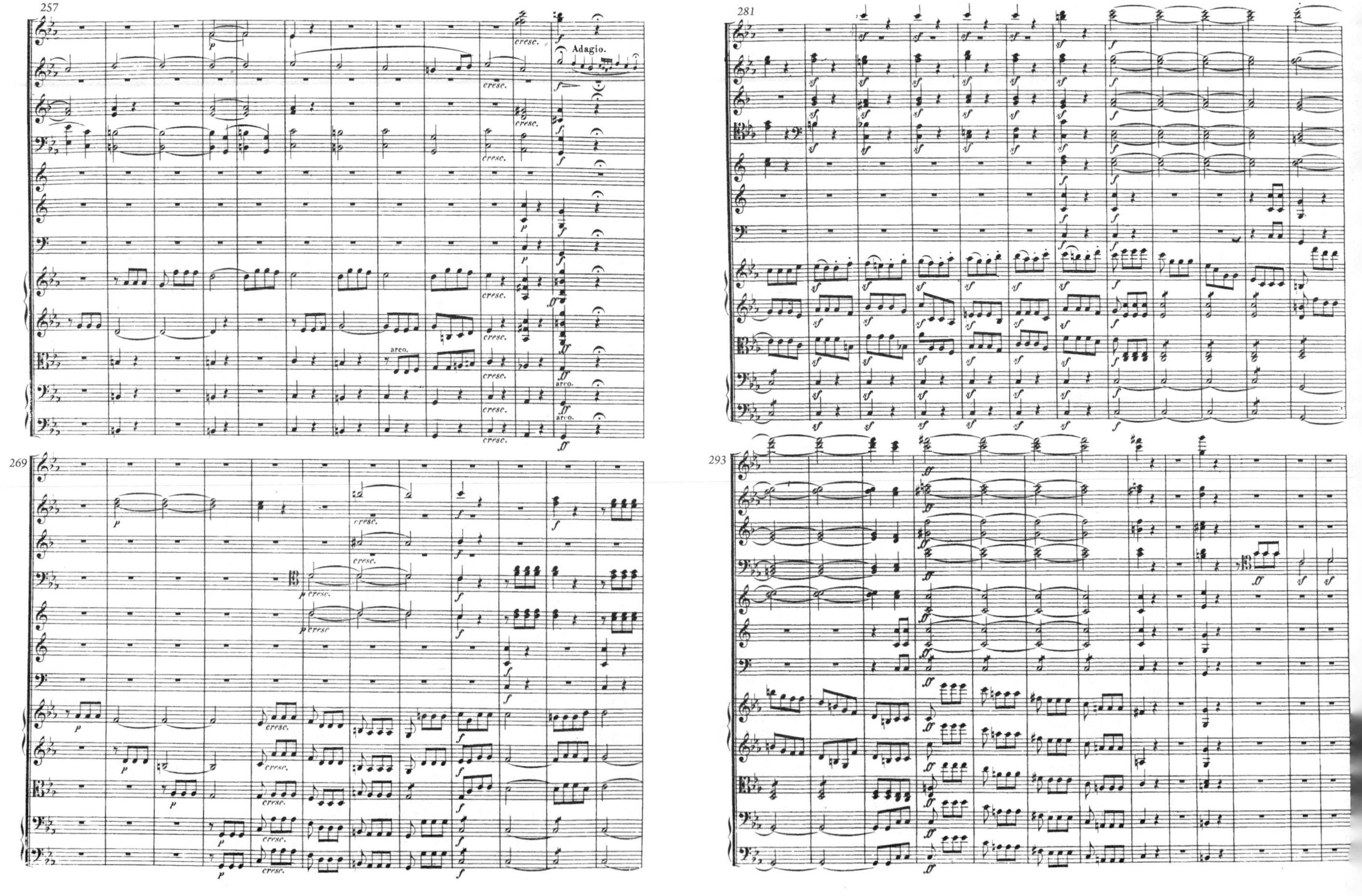
257
Adagio.
cresc.
arco.
269
cresc.
281
293

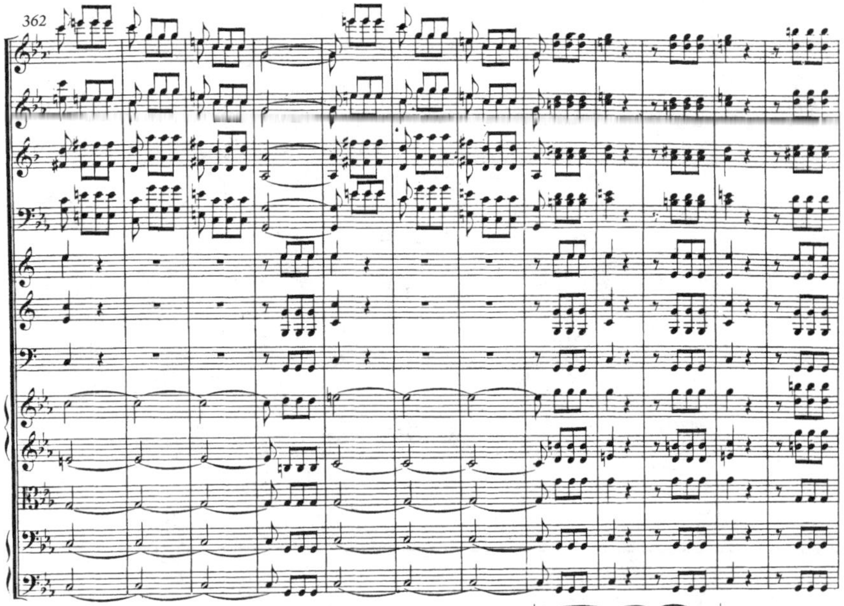
362

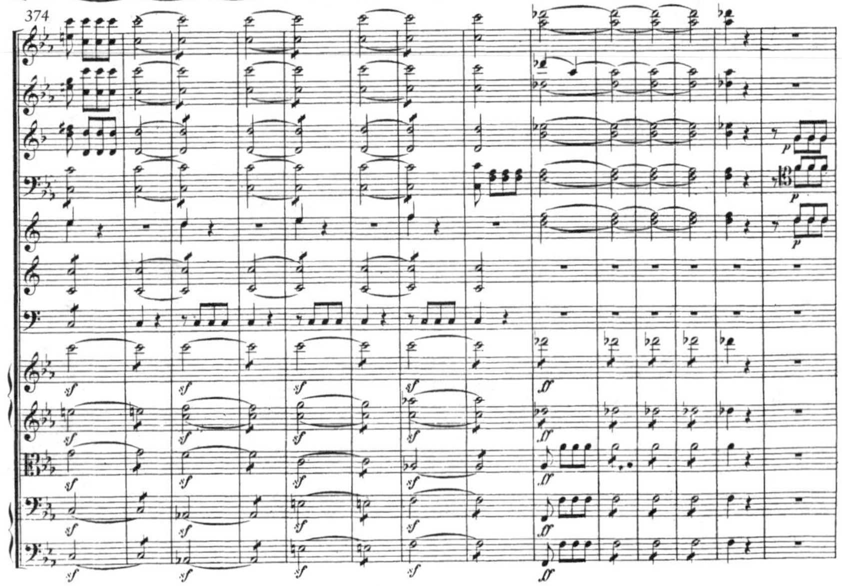
374

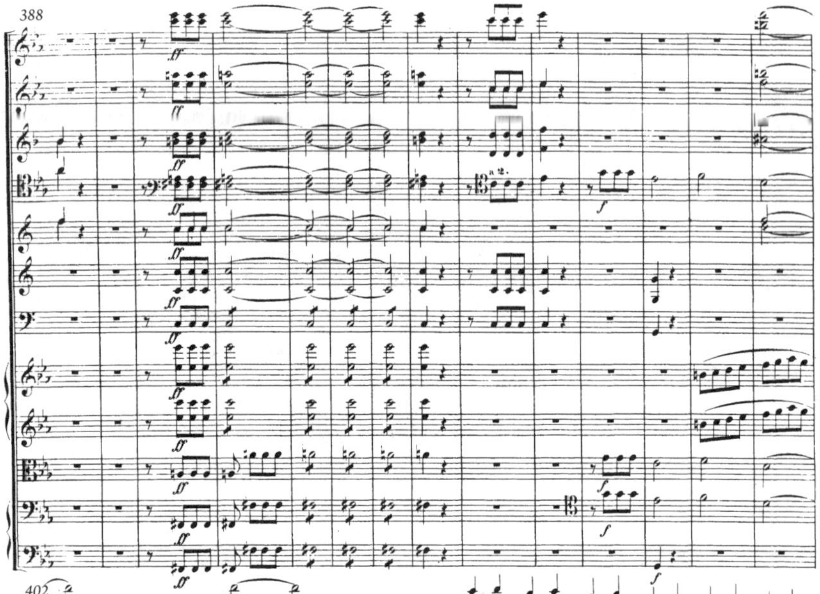
388

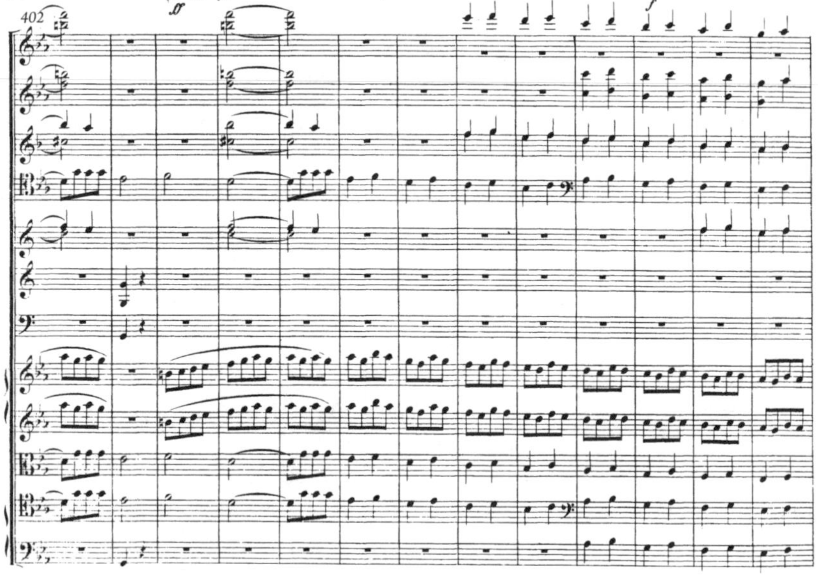
402

476
490

Andante con moto. ♪ = 92.
Flauti.
Oboi.
Clarinetti in B.
Fagotti.
Corni in C.
Trombe in C.
Timpani in C.G.
Violino I.
Violino II.
Viola.
Violoncello.
Basso.
p dolce
pizz.
arco.
11
cresc.

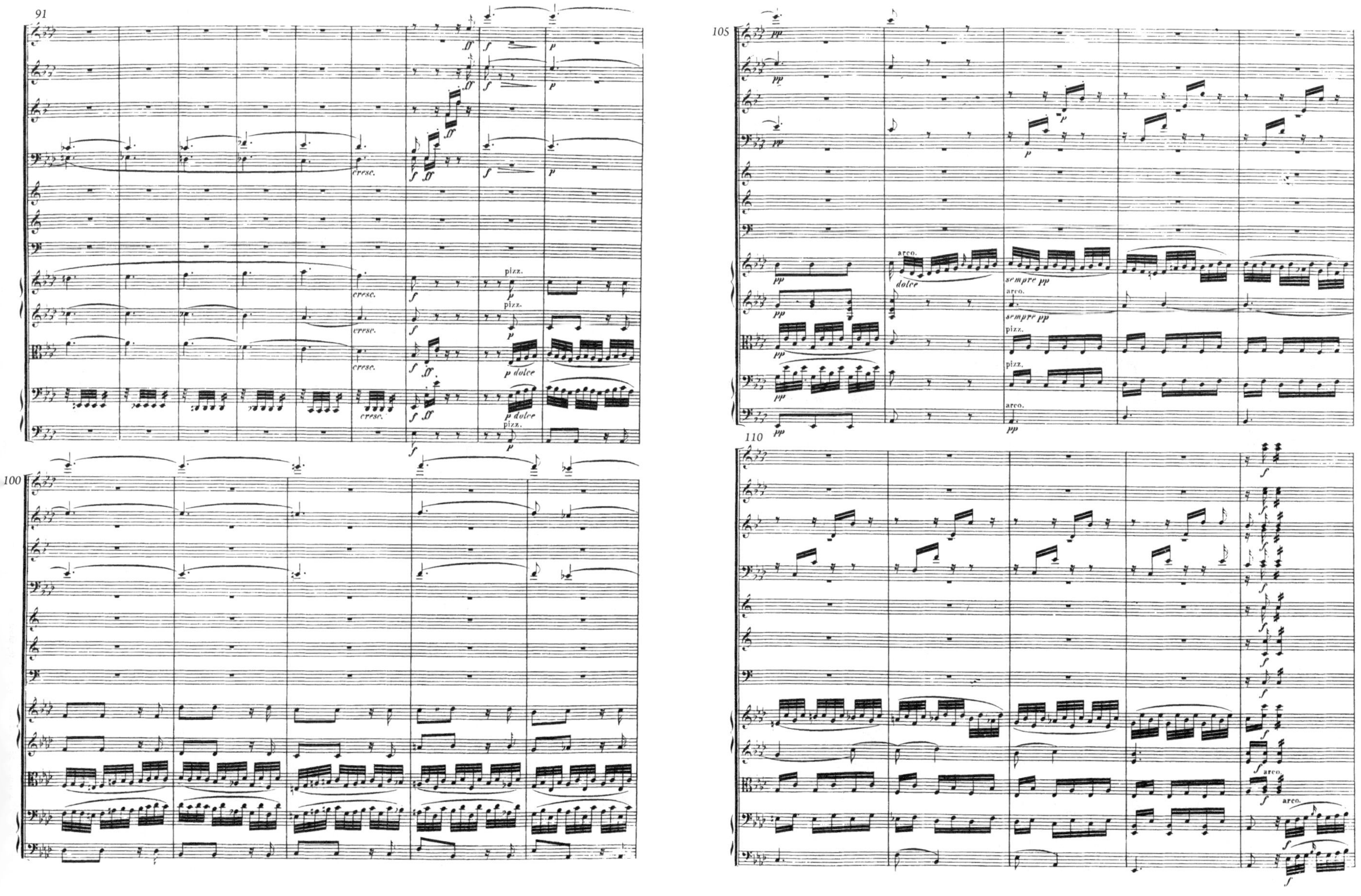
91
cresc.
pizz.
p dolce
100
105
arco.
dolce
sempre pp
110

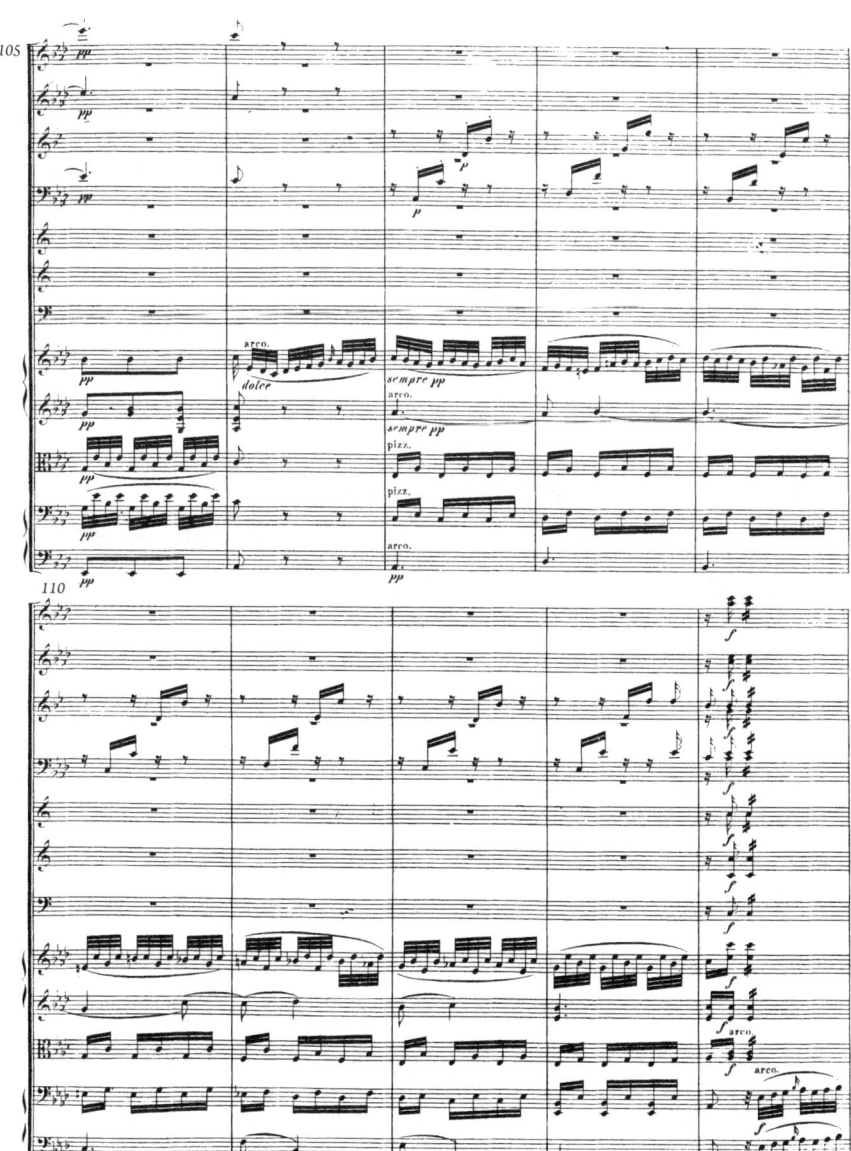

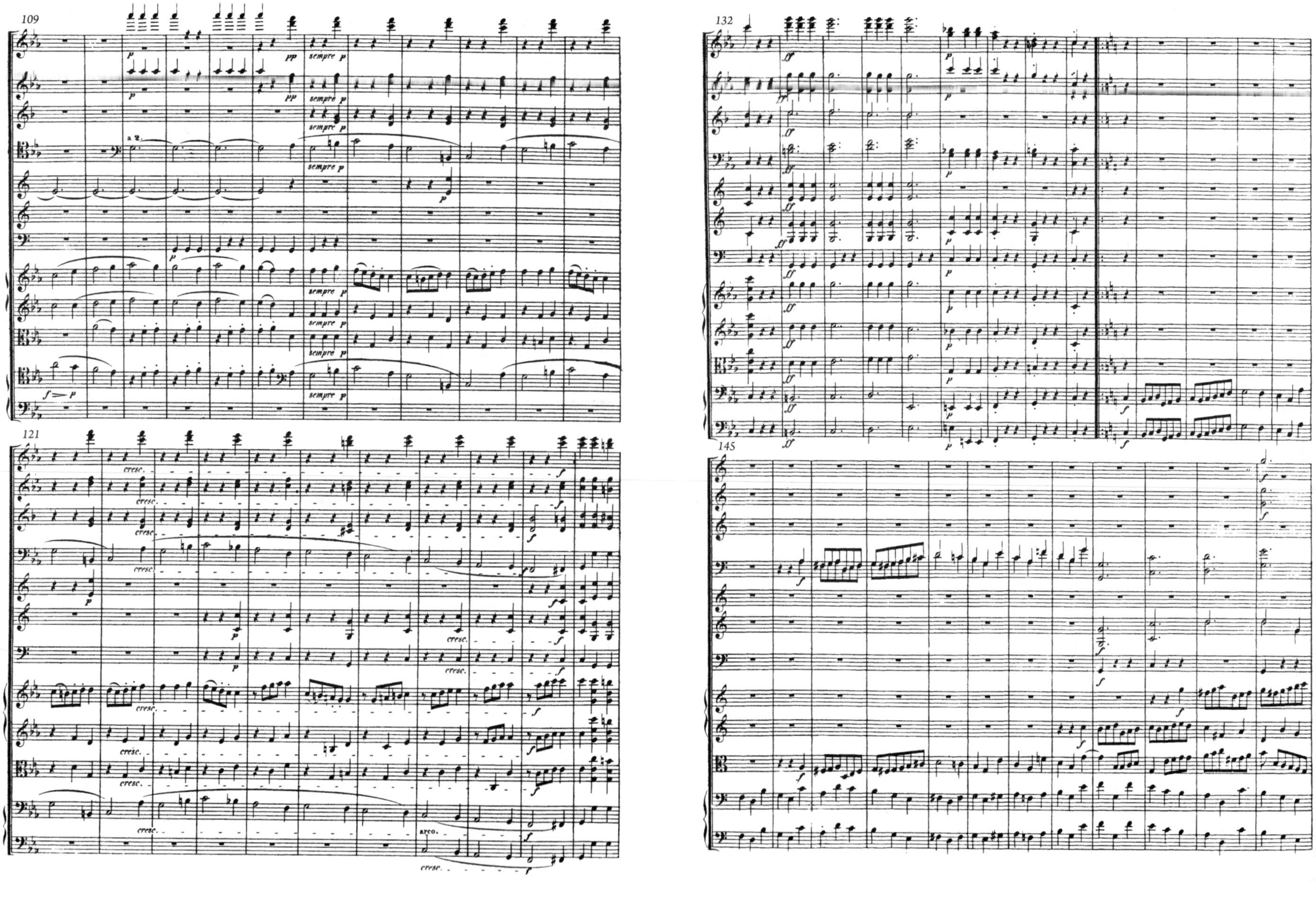
109
a 2.
sempre p
pp
121
cresc.
arco.
132
ff
145

197
dimin.
dimin.
207
sempre più p
sempre più p
sempre più p
sempre più p
218
sempre pp
sempre pp
sempre pp
sempre pp
230
pizz.
arco.
pizz.
arco.

244
poco ritard.
a tempo.
poco ritard.
a tempo.
pizz.
arco.
sempre pp
pp
p

257
pizz.
arco.
sempre pp
pp

269
sempre pp

281
sempre pp
pp
p

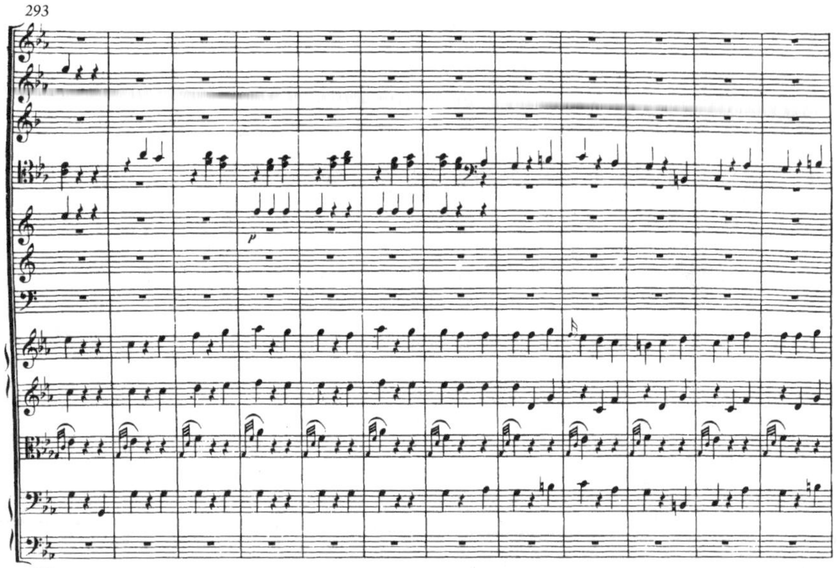
293
p

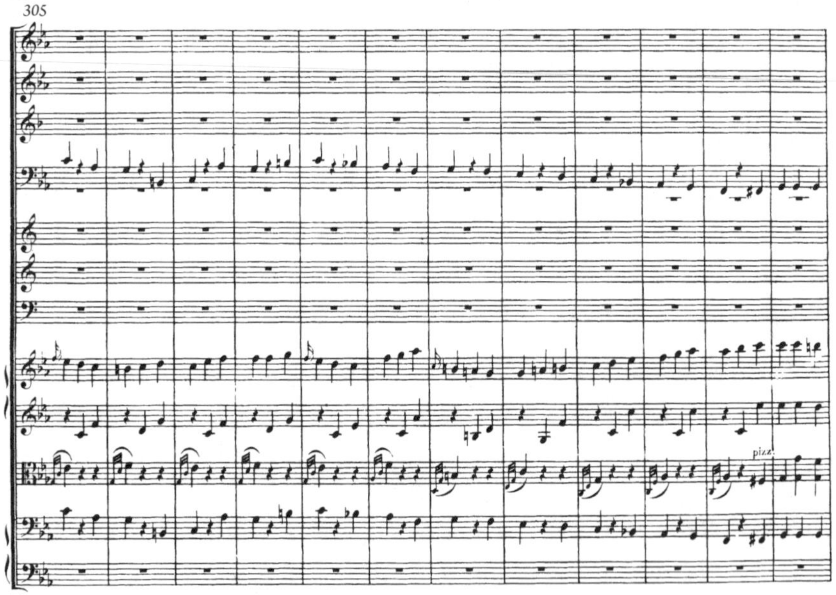
305
pizz.

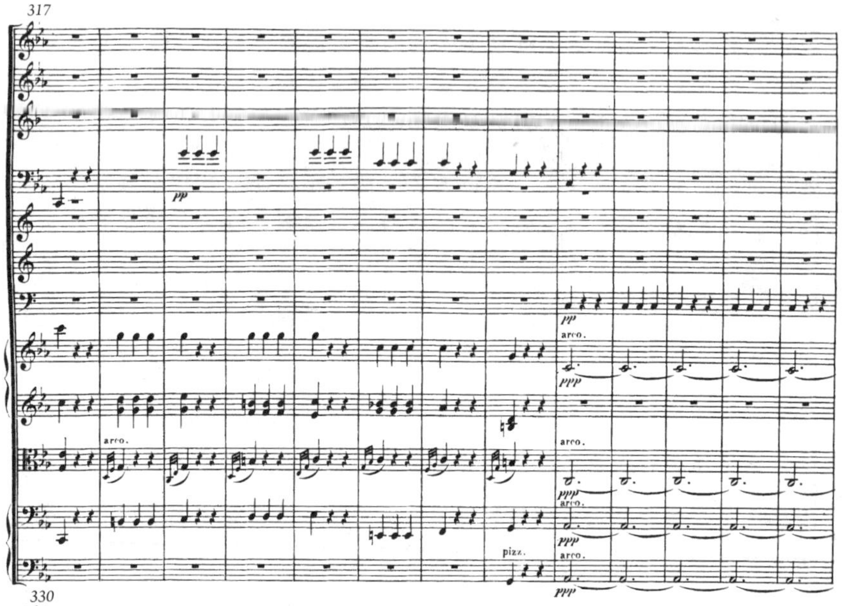
317
pp
arco.
ppp
pizz.

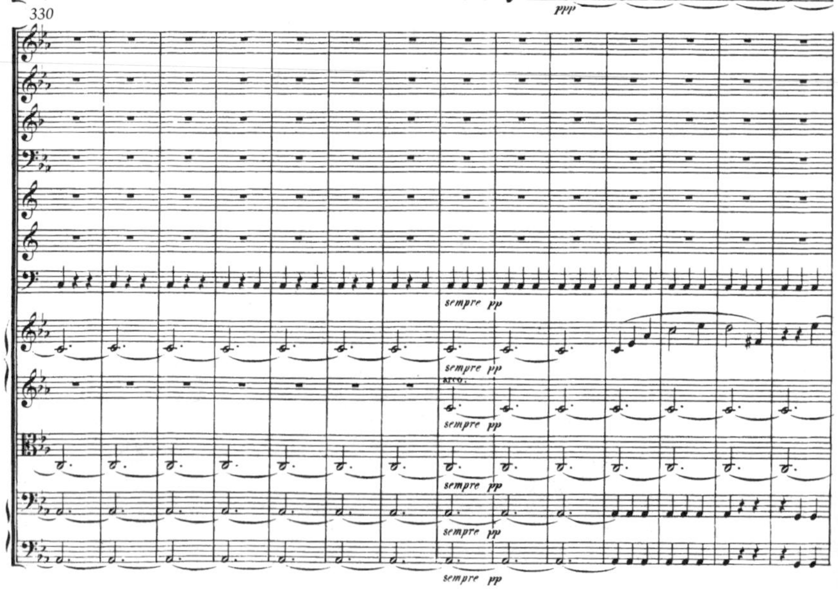
330
sempre pp
arco.

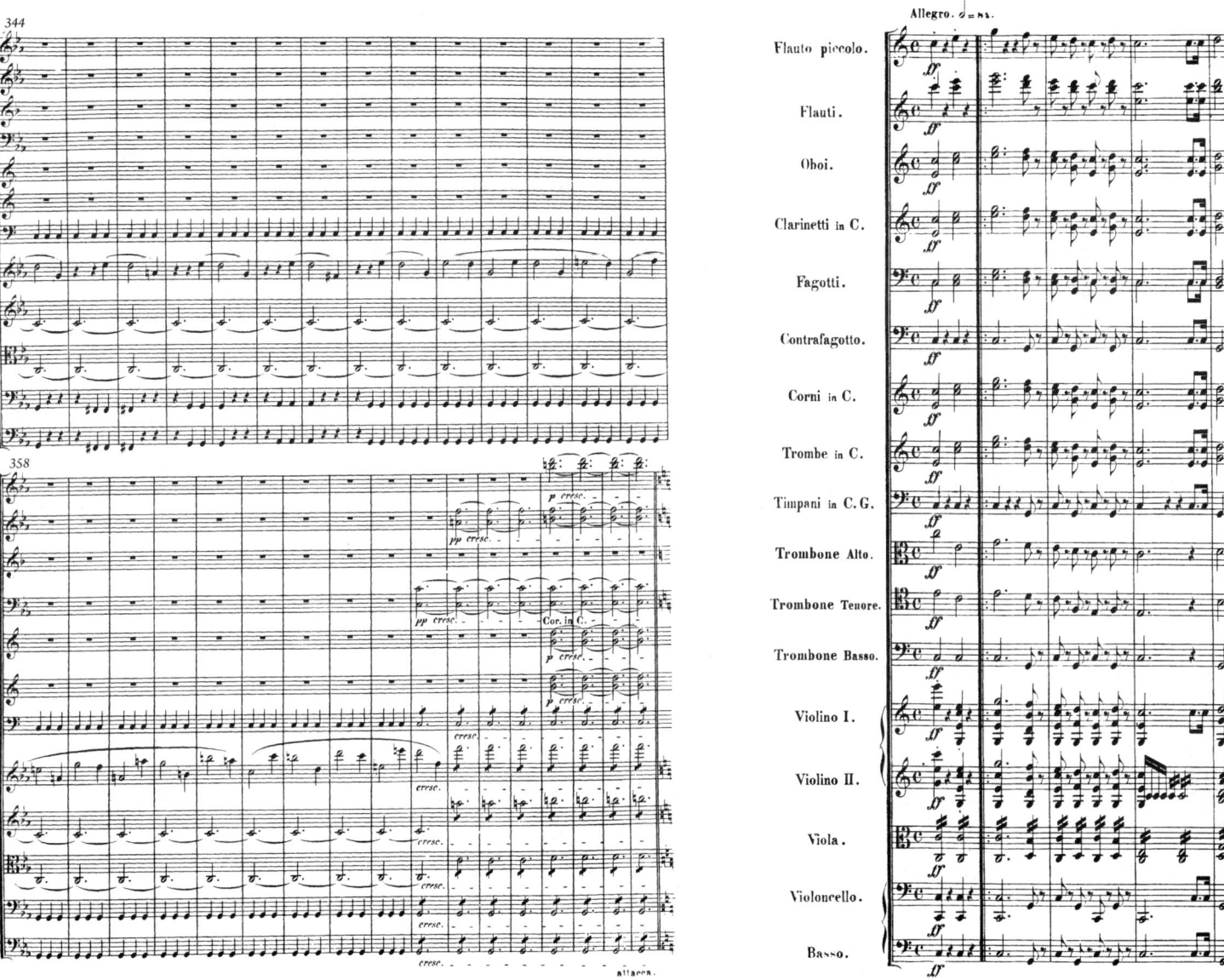

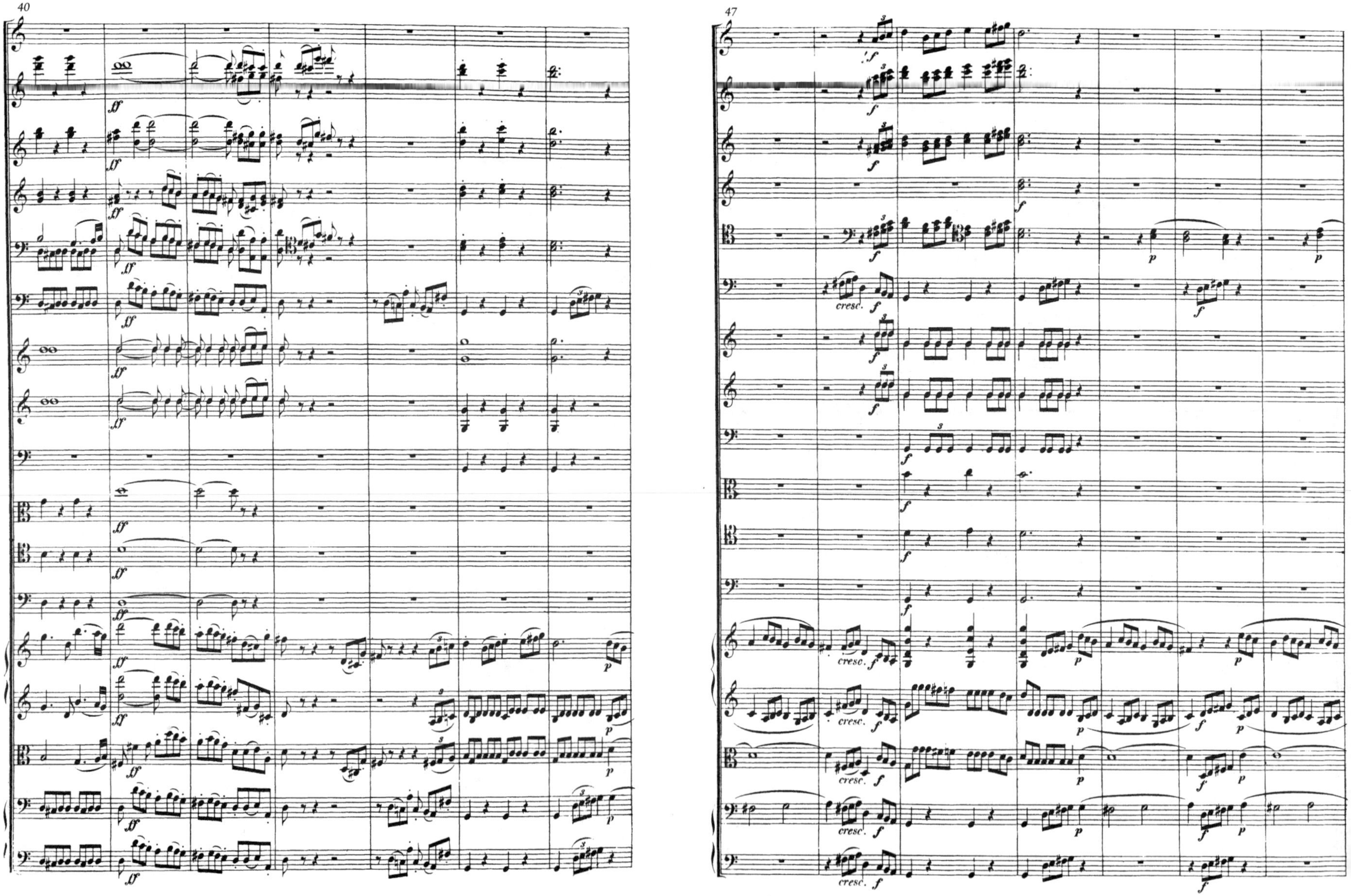
40
47
cresc.

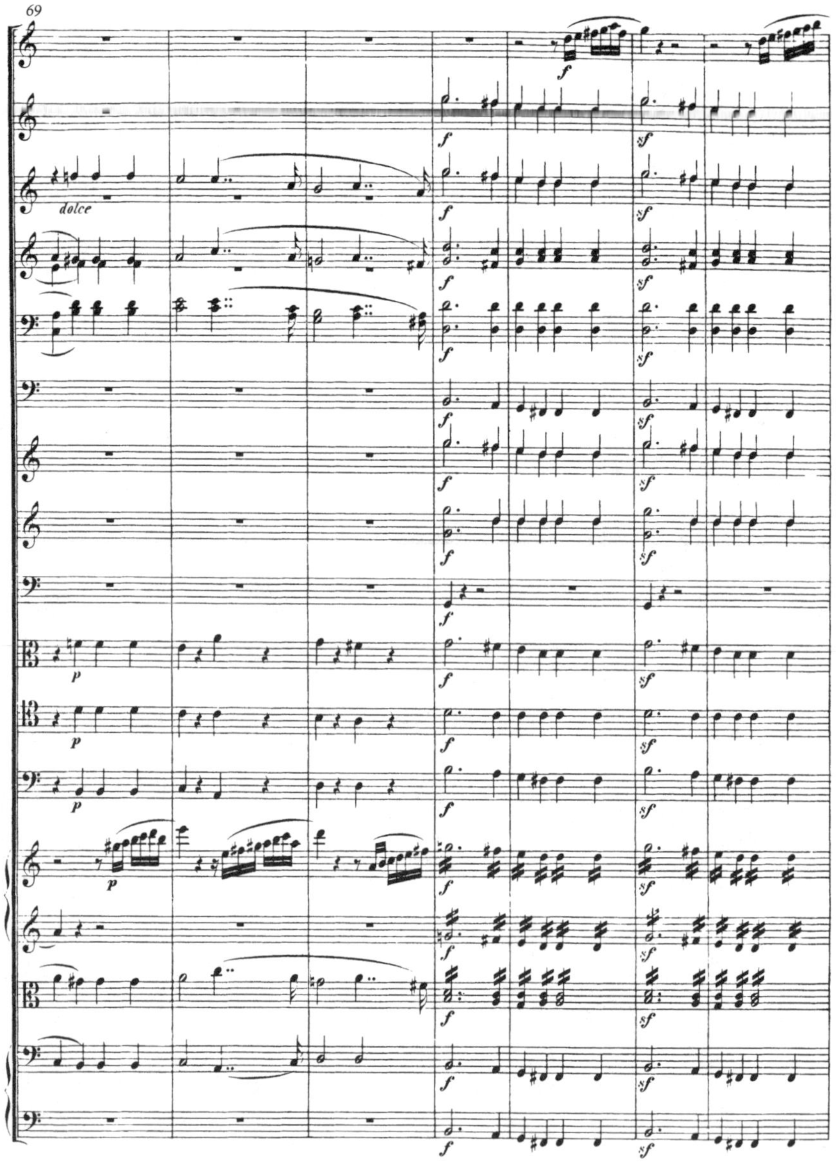
69
dolce

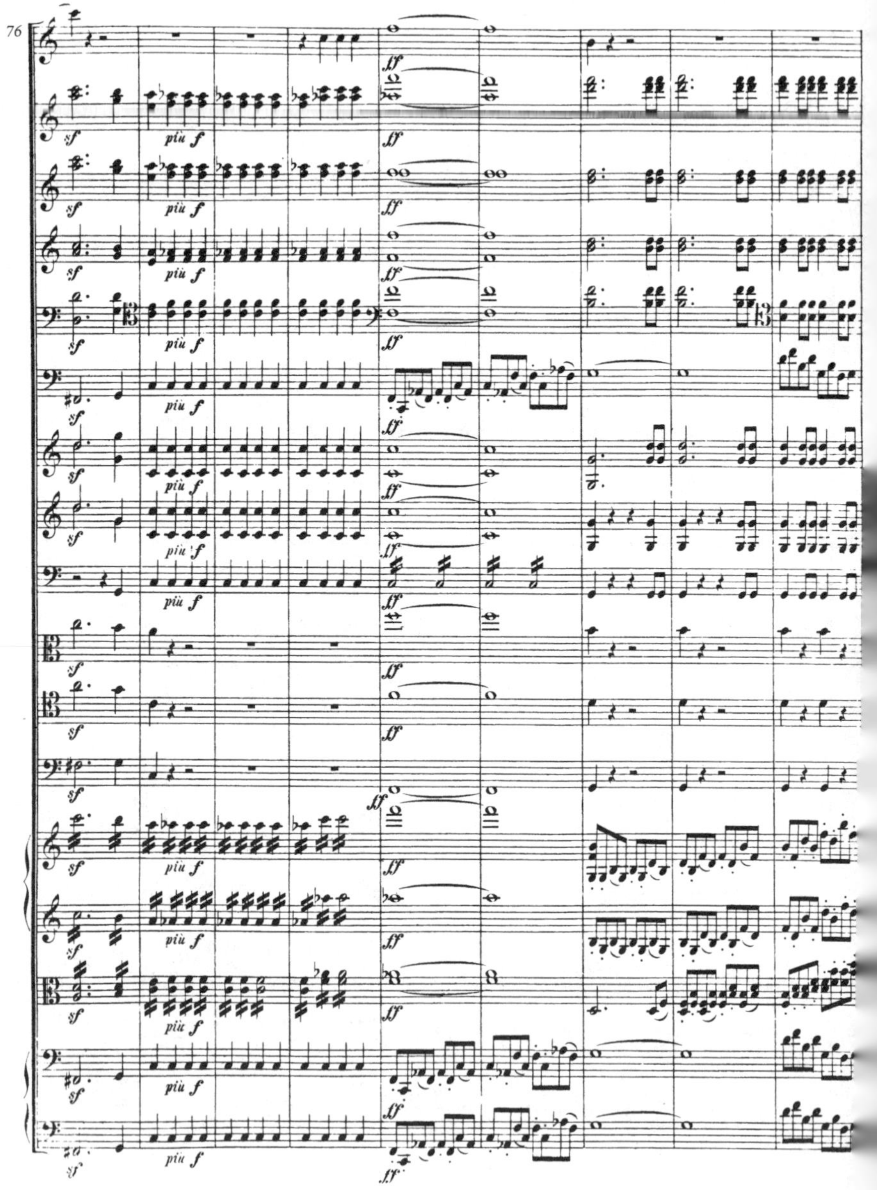
76
piu f

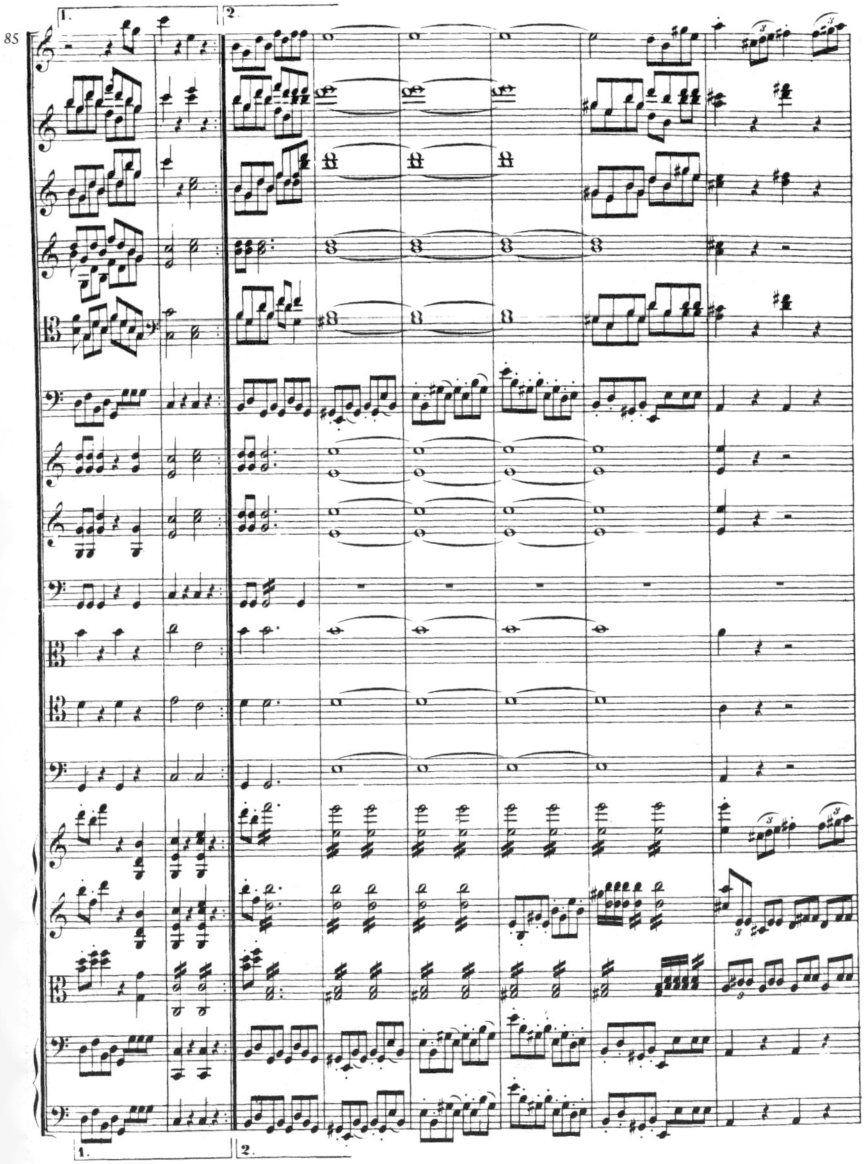
85
1.
2.

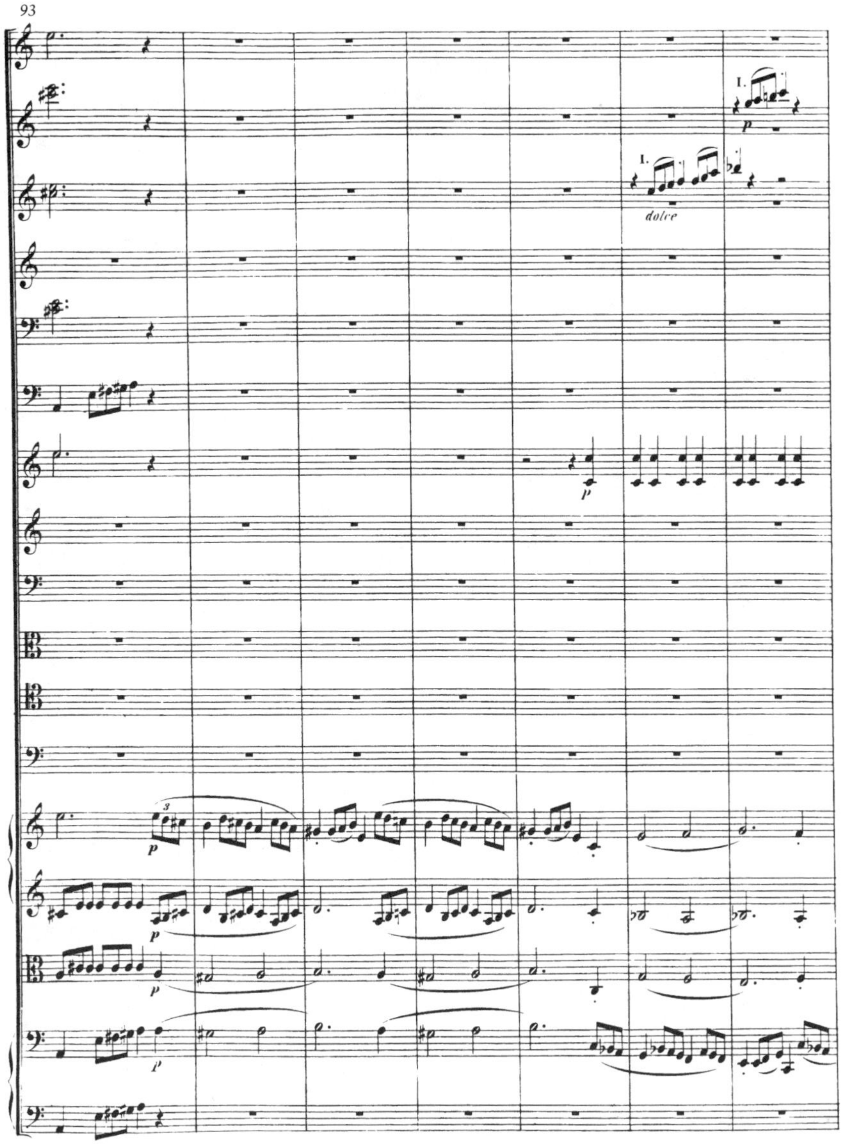
93
1.
dolce
p

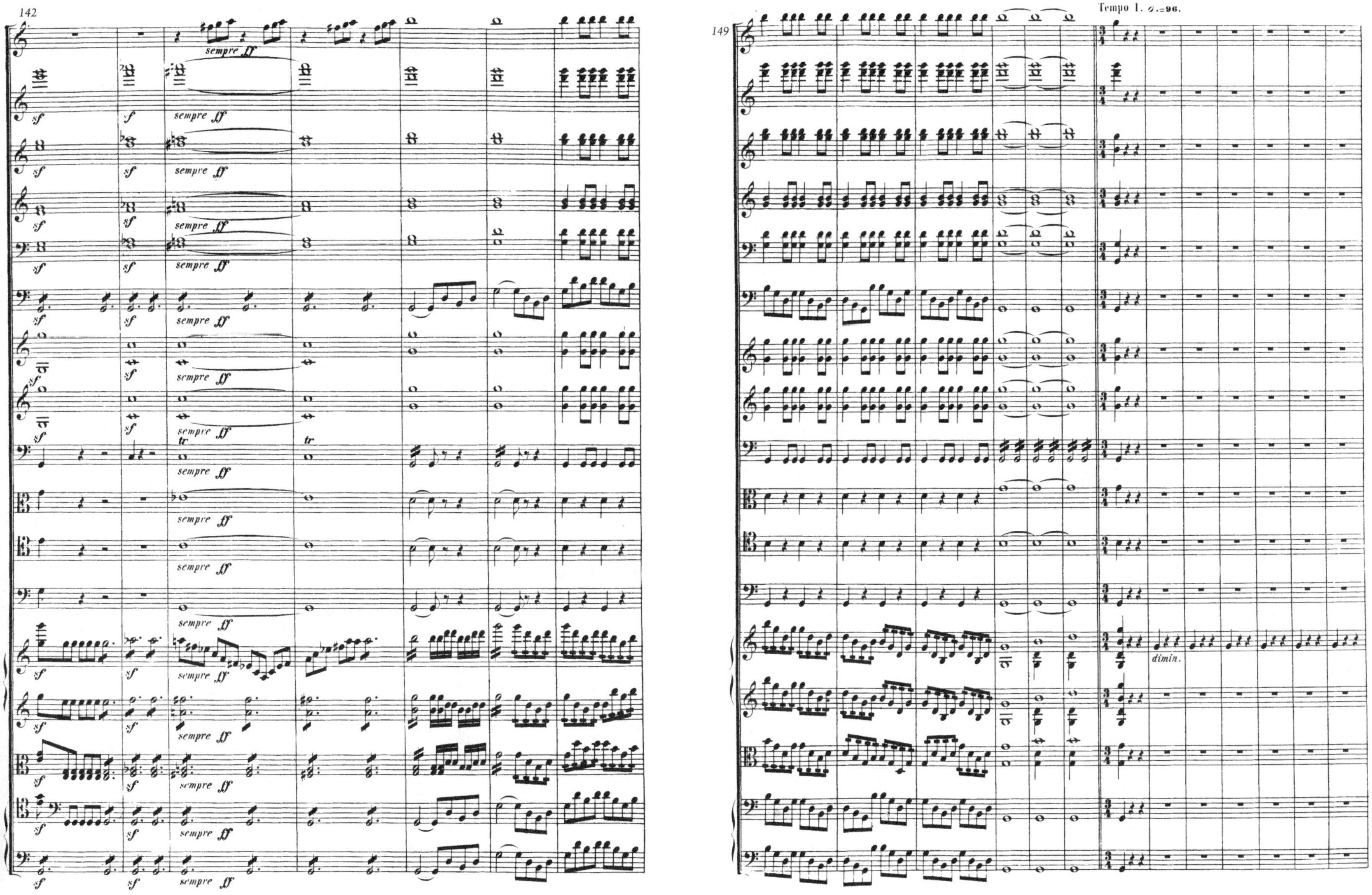
142
sempre ff
sf
tr
149
Tempo I.
dimin.

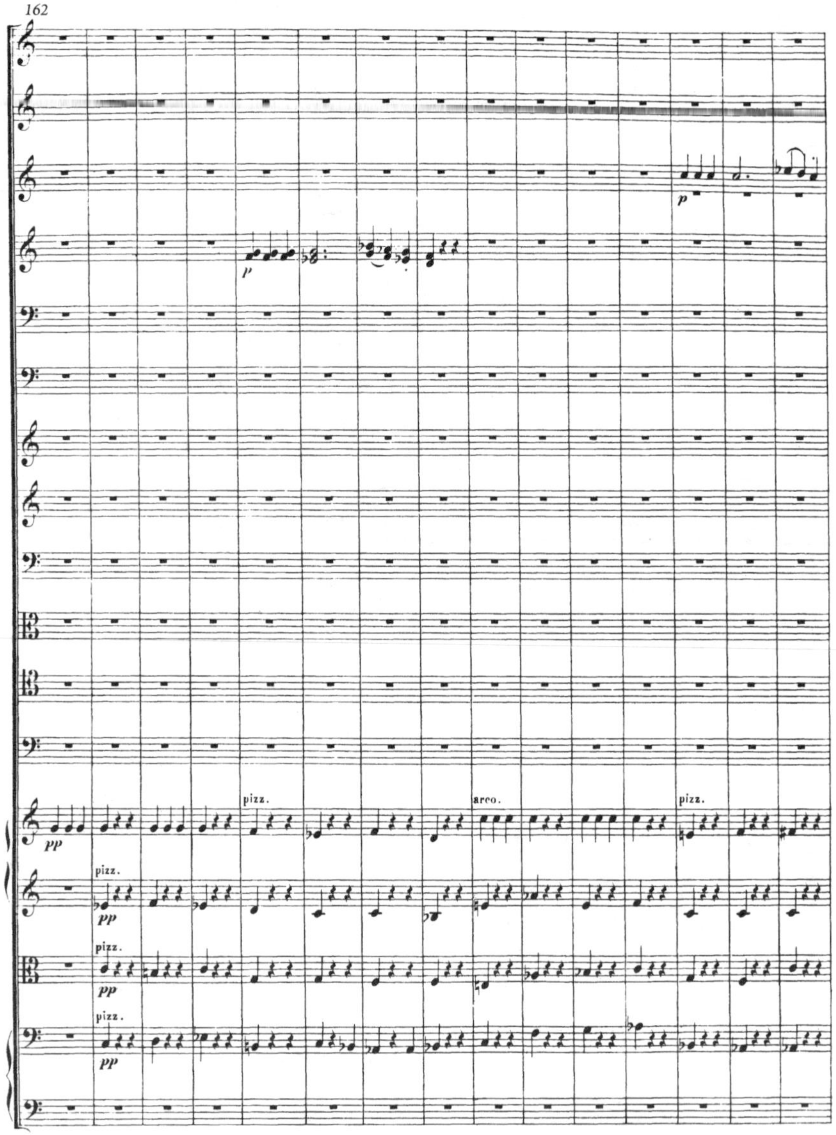
162
p
p
pizz.
arco.
pizz.
pp
pizz.
pp
pizz.
pp
pizz.
pp

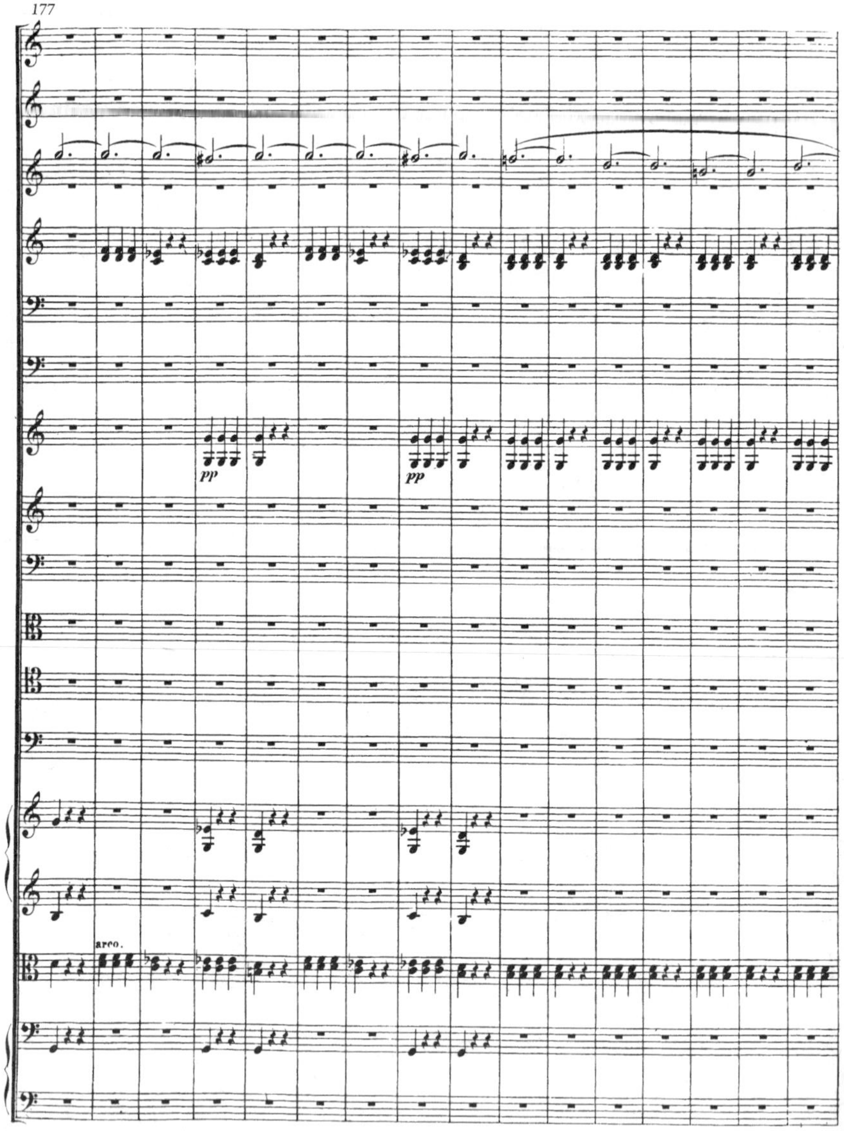
177
pp
pp
arco.

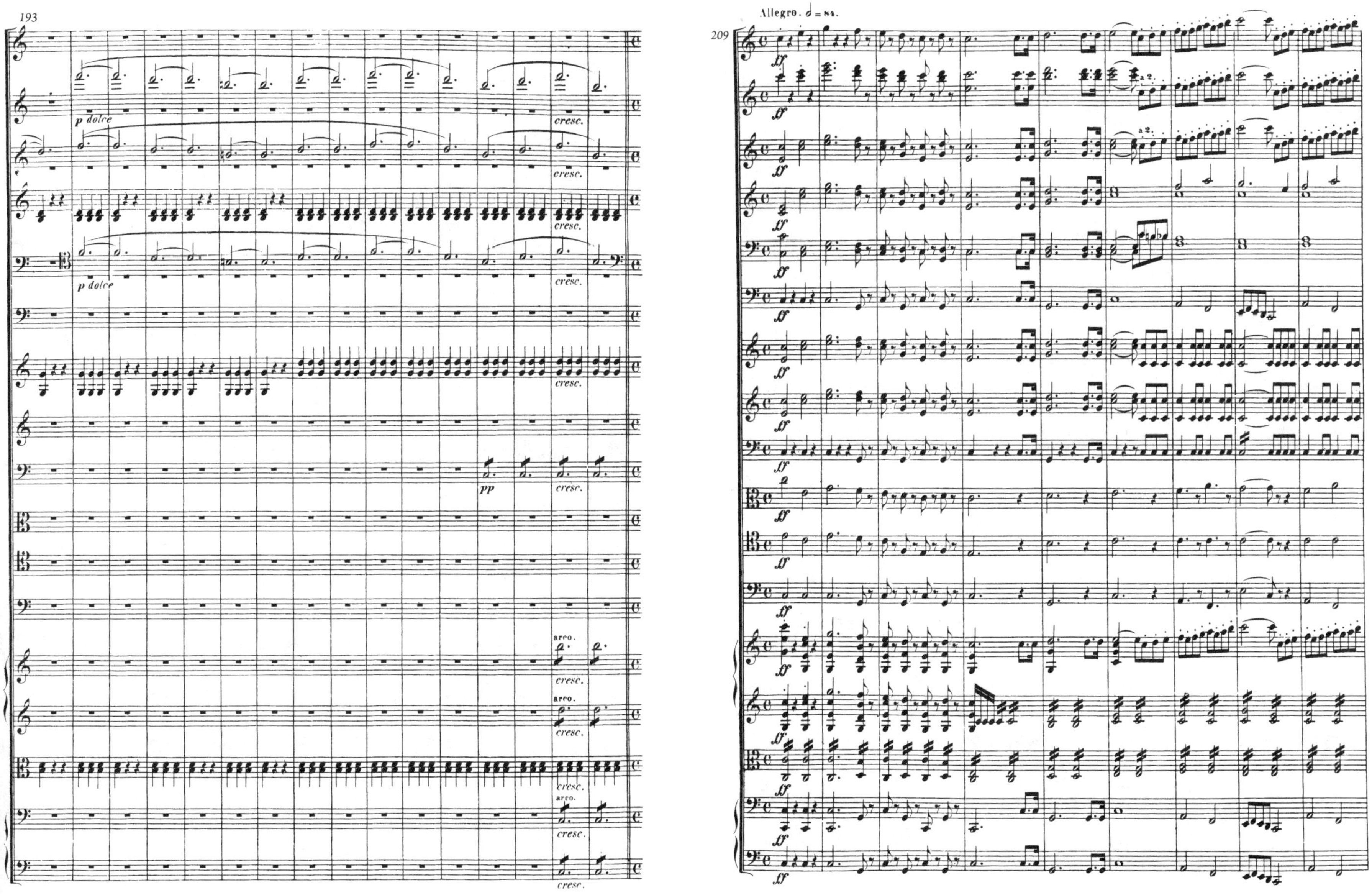
193
p dolce
cresc.
pp
arco.
209
Allegro. 𝅗𝅥 = 84.
ff
a 2.

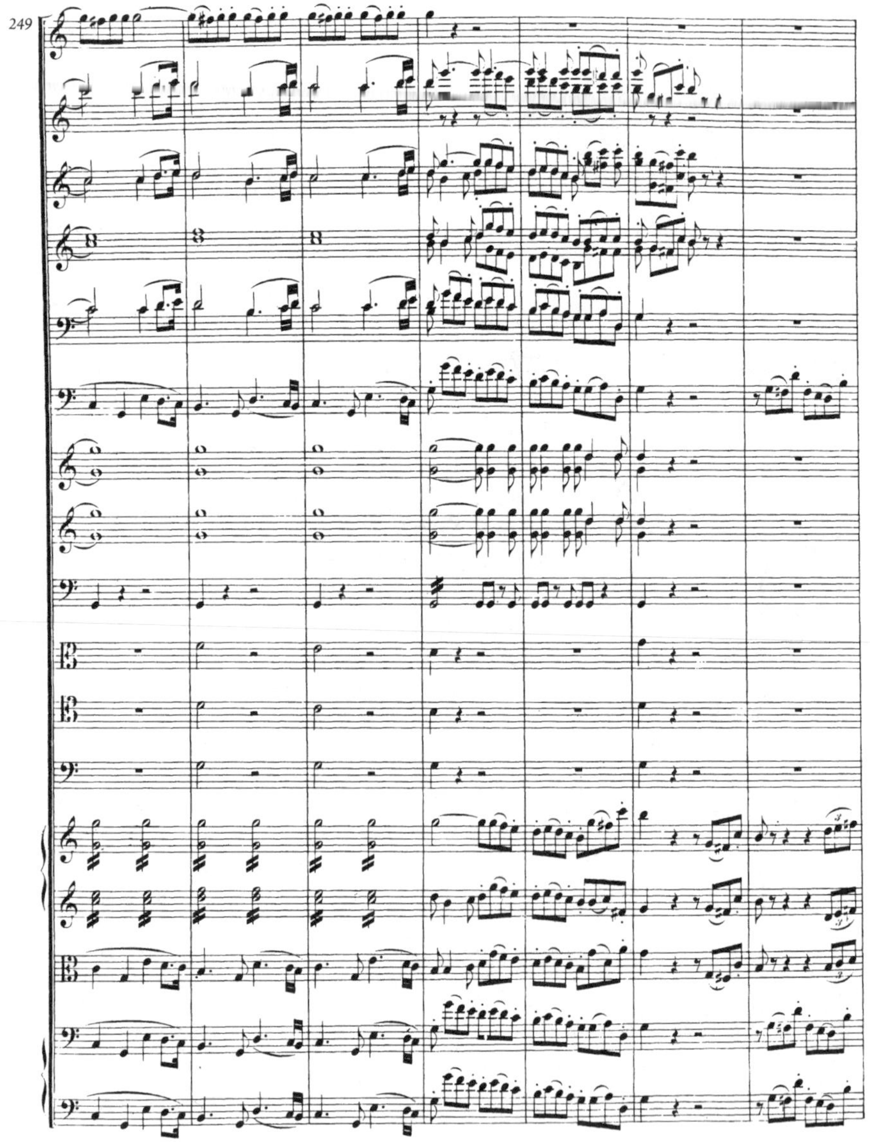
249

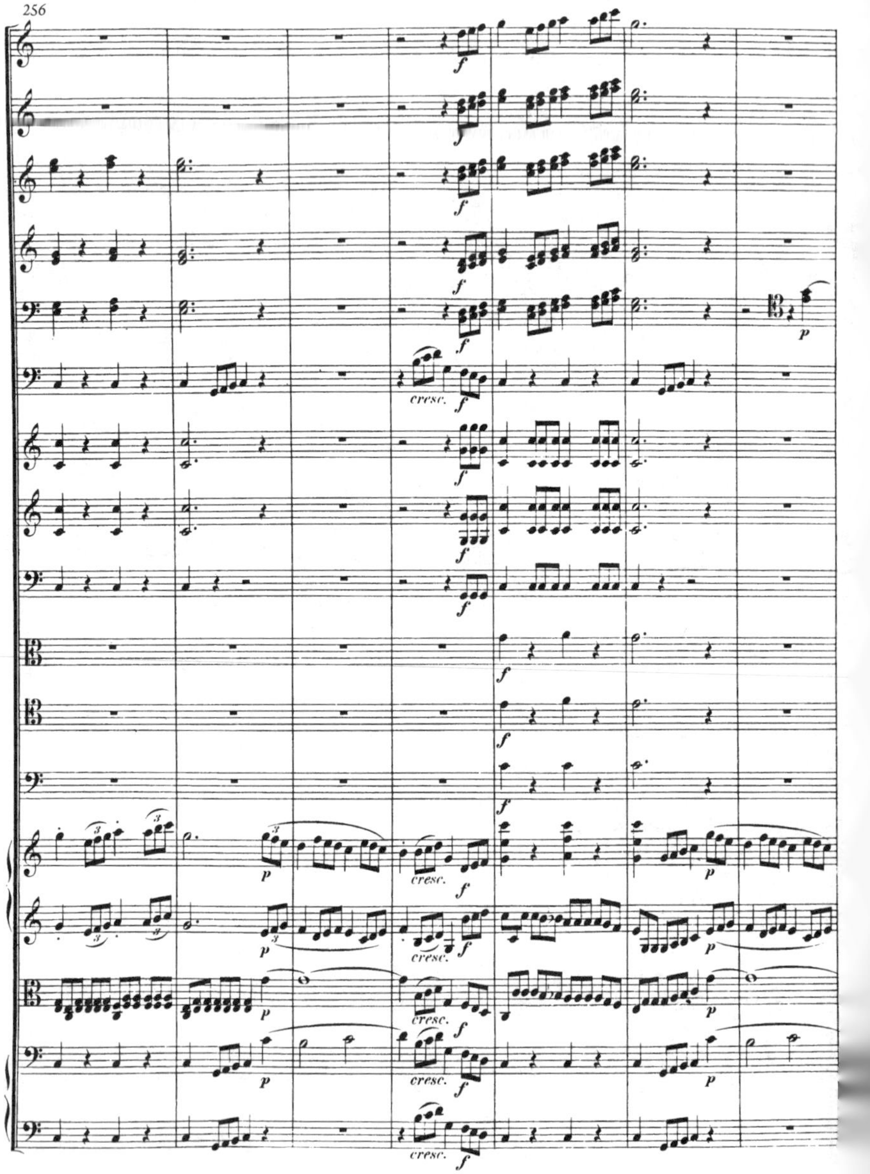
256
f
p
cresc.

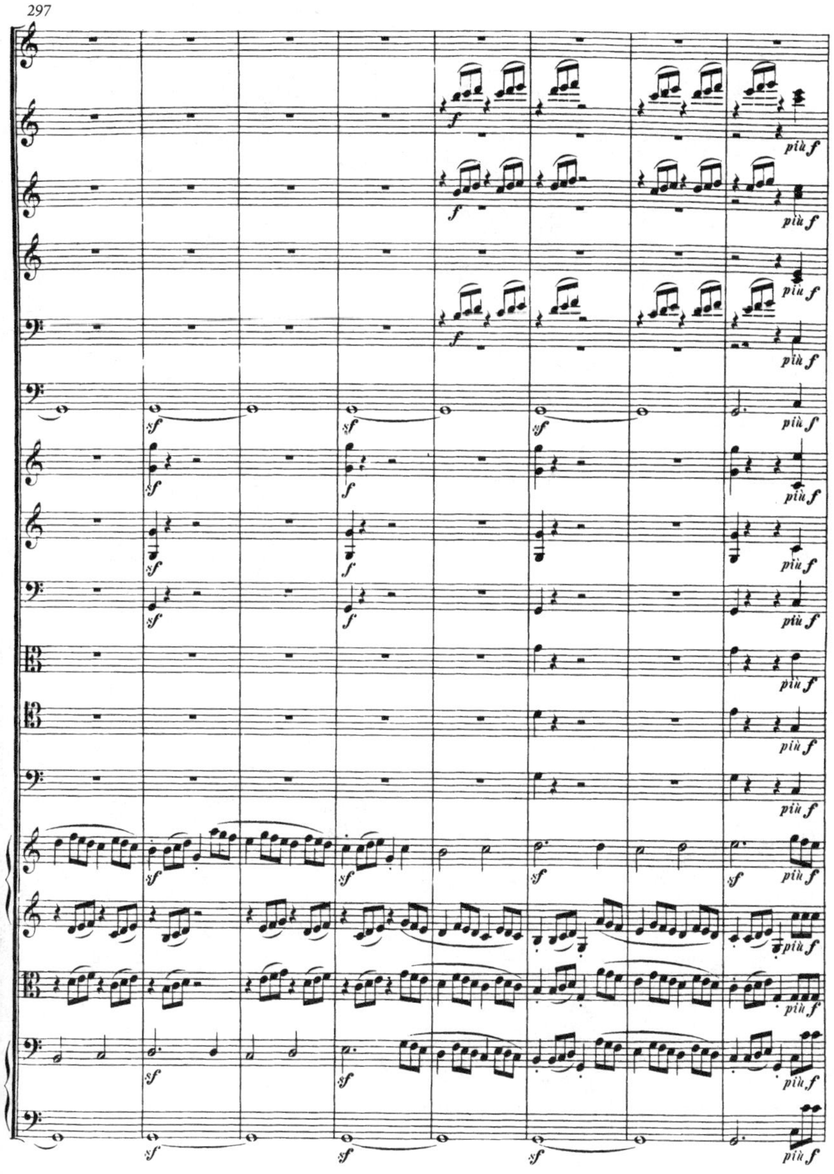
297
f
sf
più f

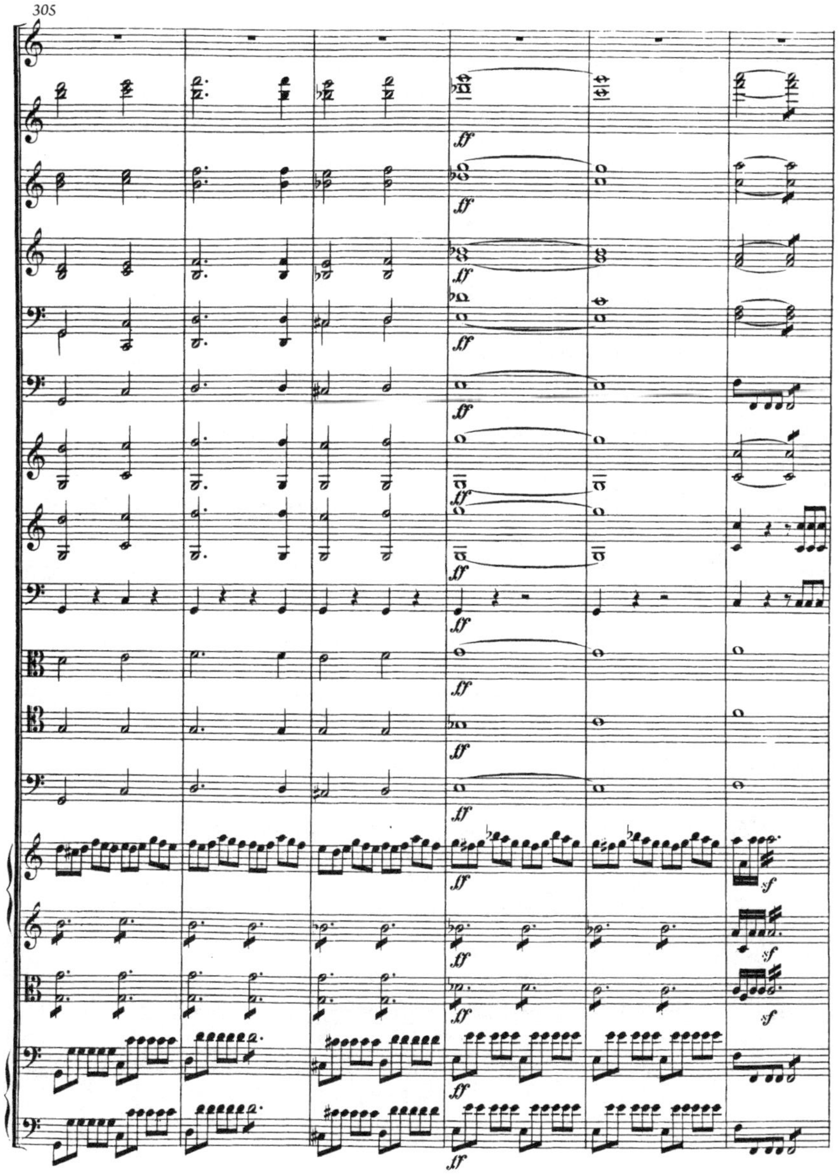
305
ff
sf

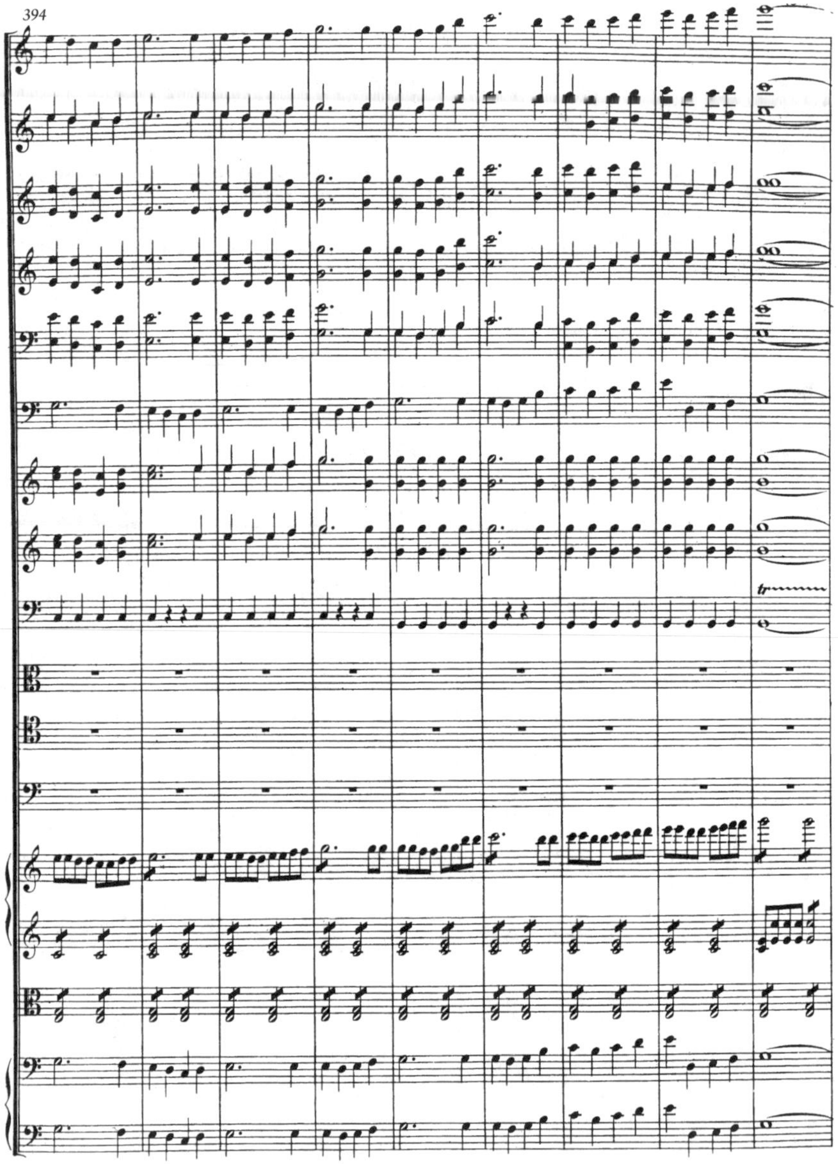
394
tr

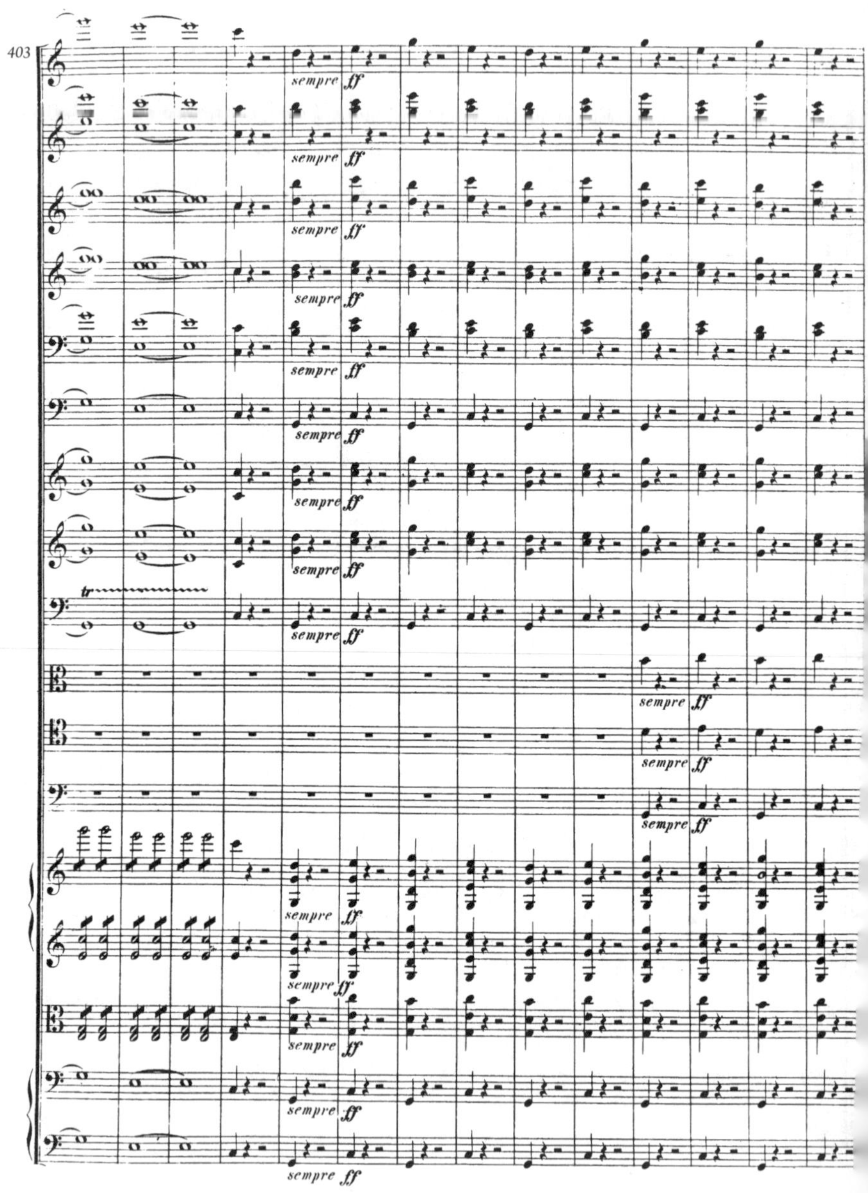
403
tr
sempre ff

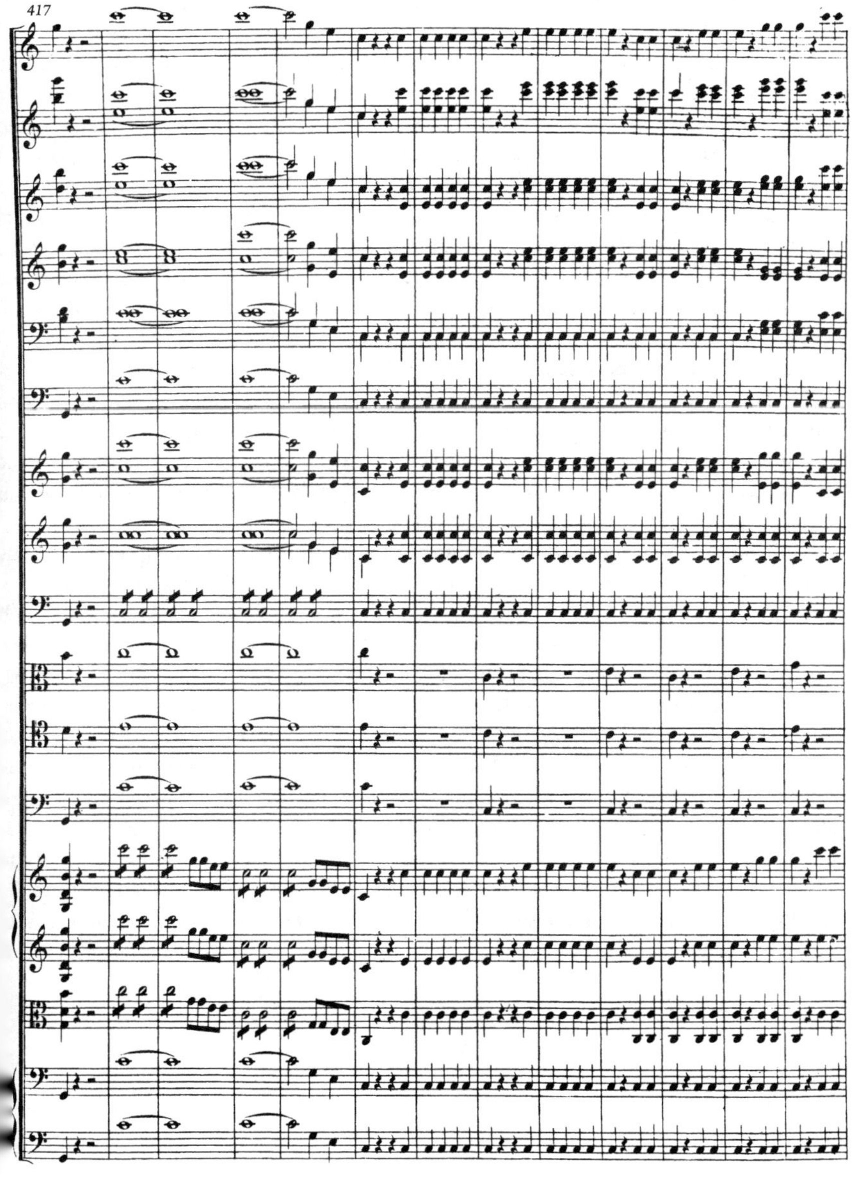
417

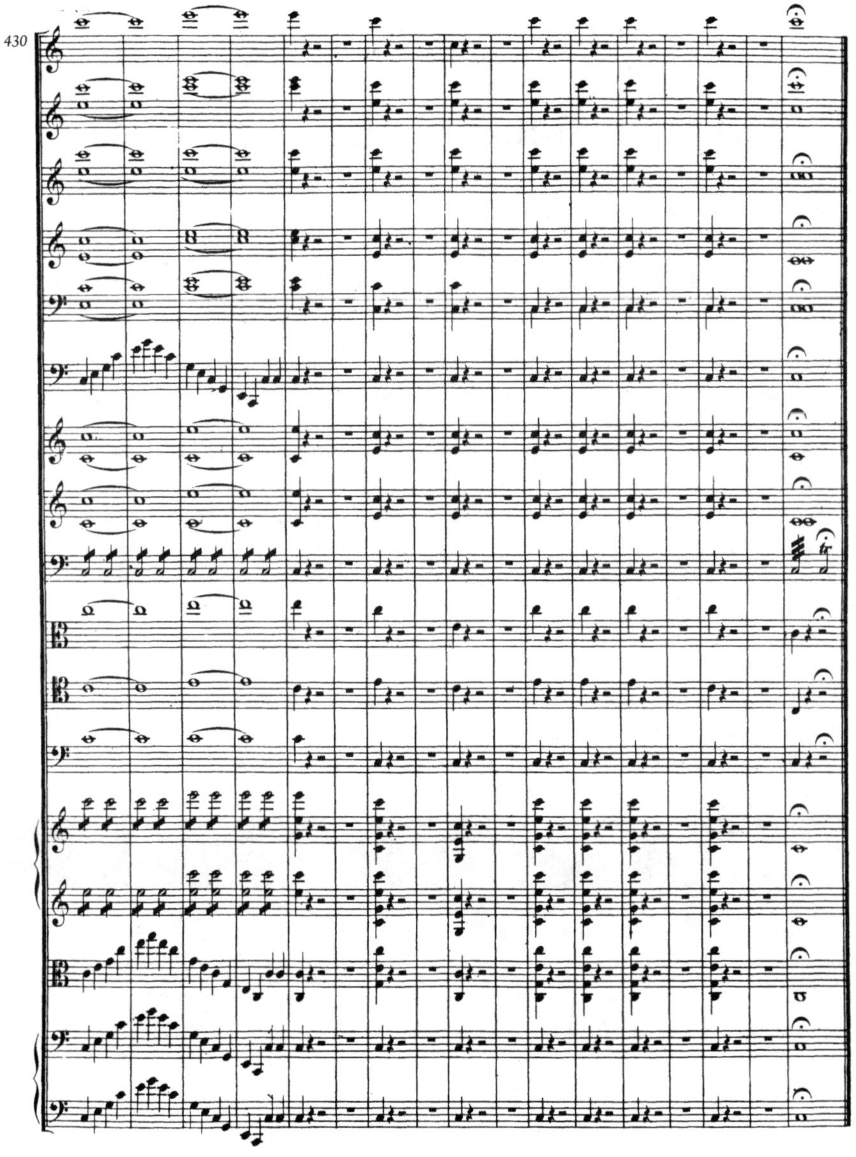
430

21

Ludwig van Beethoven (1770–1827)

String Quartet in B♭ Major, Op. 130, "Cavatina" (1825–26)

As if feeling the urge to turn inward after the great public appeal expressed in the Ninth Symphony, Beethoven spent the last two-and-a-half years of his life composing string quartets. Many believe that these last five string quartets are Beethoven's greatest works, showing the composer's originality and intense expression at its most radical. The Quartet in B♭ Major, Op. 130, which Beethoven composed between 1825 and 1826, consists of six movements, the last a replacement for a grand fugue that Beethoven originally intended for the finale of the quartet (the original fugue became a separate piece, the Great Fugue, Op. 133). The quartet has two slow movements, the second of which Beethoven entitled "Cavatina," a term used here to mean short aria.

In this "Cavatina" the vocal role is given to the first violin, which sings its hymn-like song with heartbreaking sincerity but without the specificity of words. Beethoven's desire to reach for more direct modes of communication was thus combined with the need to hide the exact meaning of such expression.

The form of the "Cavatina" is fairly straightforward:

Measure Nos.	Formal Designation	Sections	Keys	Comments
1–9	A		B♭	
10–17	A′		B♭, c	Ends on V in c
17–22	B			Sequential, modulatory, ends on V/B♭
23–30	C		B♭	
31–39	C′		B♭	
40–48	D	"Beklemmt"/Anguished	C♭, a♭	Disruption
49–57	A″		B♭	
58–66	Coda		B♭	

Like much of Beethoven's music, the "Cavatina" is tightly constructed, presenting in its first measure many of the elements that will prove to be important in the course of the movement: The second violin's *sotto voce* melody begins on G, the third degree on which the piece will end, and its eighth notes in the first measure provide a central motive in the movement. This motive drives the modulatory sequence in the B section (mm. 17–21) and serves as a farewell gesture in the coda (mm. 58–59, 61–62). The leading role of the second violin in the opening signals that the instrument will be a compassionate partner in the first violin's song. The opening cello line also contains a little expressive gesture—a three-note chromatic ascent—that appears several times in the course of the movement, as does its inversion (mm. 14–15 and 35 in the cello, m. 44 in the first violin). The most expressive gesture, the first violin's leaping sixth, is also contained in the first measure. Its inversion, first heard at m. 6, lends a sense of urgency to the B section (see mm. 18, 21, and 22).

Just as the opening measure prefigures many things to come, the coda sums up many previously heard gestures: the ascending sixth leading to a climax on G (mm. 58–59 and its echo in the cello at mm. 61–62), the first motive of the second violin moving from instrument to instrument, the appearance of C minor (here in the form of a deceptive cadence at m. 60), the theme of section C in m. 63, a brief reference to the flat sixth (C♭) in m. 63, which was the key of the middle section, and last but not least the ending on G.

More important to the expressive content of the movement than its impressive motivic tightness is the outpouring of emotions in the disruptive D section that creates the sense of overhearing an intimate, personal confession. Here the first violin stammers its agonized melody, clearly unaware of the metric regularity of the accompanying triplets. Beethoven marked the section "beklemmt" (anguished). The key of ♭VI, here C♭ major, is the romantic key par excellence for indicating excursion to the inner regions of the soul, and the melody line, with its frequent pauses, suggests the labored breathing of a an operatic character in emotional upheaval. The passage has the feeling of dramatic recitative. Instrumental recitative was not Beethoven's invention. We have already encountered similar passages earlier in this volume, in the C-minor Fantasia of CPE Bach. The desire to confess private emotions in instrumental music was similar in the two composers. In Beethoven's music, however, it did not represent a short-lived period of heightened expressive fashion such as that associated with *Empfindsamkeit*; rather, it was the beginning of a long-lived musical aesthetic that placed value on inner feelings. This emphasis on what the Germans called "Innigkeit" (inwardness) became the core of German Romantic music in the nineteenth century.

Cavatina.
Adagio molto espressivo.

22

Gioachino Rossini
(1792–1868)

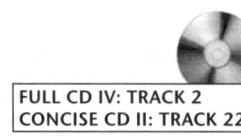

Il Barbiere di Siviglia (The Barber of Seville), Overture (1816)

Rossini's overture to *Il Barbiere di Siviglia,* a two-act opera buffa (comic opera) based on Pierre Beaumarchais's comedy of the same title, is one of his most popular works. Originally written for his opera seria *Aureliano in Palmira* (1813), the overture was attached to the newer opera as part of an attempt to rescue *Il Barbiere* after its disastrous first performance. The substitution could be made because of the formulaic nature of Rossini overtures, which served simply to introduce operas and were not required to relate in mood or in thematic content to the drama that followed.

Like all Rossini overtures, this one starts with an extended slow introduction of the kind we have encountered in Haydn's London Symphony and Mozart's *Don Giovanni,* but it is more elaborate than either (see chart). It makes the customary functional progression from a strong tonic opening (in E) to an expectant dominant finish (on B), but it is cast very decoratively in a miniature ternary (ABA) form of its own: The midsection, consisting of a flowery *cantabile* melody reminiscent of an aria (mm. 11–17), appears between two segments that feature a harmonically malleable motive (four repeated thirty-second notes as upbeat to an eighth note).

The *Allegro* section of the overture is cast in a form similar to sonata, or "symphonic binary," form but without a repeat of the exposition and with a four-measure transition in place of a development section.

Also unlike the usual symphonic binary movement, especially in Beethoven's hands, is the full-blown structure of both themes. Particularly striking is the second, cast in the form of elaborate wind solos (including a juicy solo turn for the horn in mm. 104–109, the instrument of Rossini's father).

The closing section is Rossini's special trademark: a long passage that over a tonic–dominant pendulum swells in dynamics until it reaches its climax in a *fortissimo tutti* outburst in which the formulaic melody shifts to the bass instruments. This inexorable orchestral upsurge—commonly referred to as the "Rossini crescendo"—was the moment people waited for.

The exposition having come to its brilliant conclusion, a perfunctory four-measure transition (mm. 151–154) leads into a truncated recapitulation, with both themes in the tonic key (the first in minor, the second in major) and the transition between them virtually eliminated. In the tonic the "Rossini crescendo" of the closing section makes a bigger splash than ever (mm. 201–225). In

Measure Nos.	Formal Designation	Sections	Keys	Comments
1–24	**Introduction**		E	
1–11		A		Features 32nd-note–8th-note motive
11–17		B		Aria-like
17–24		A		Ends on V
25–150	**Exposition**			
25–48		1st theme	e	Theme mainly in violins, typical of Rossini's 1st themes
48–91		Bridge		Soloistic use of woodwinds, typical of Rossini's 2nd themes
92–115		2nd theme	G	
115–150		Closing section	G	"Rossini crescendo"
151–154	**Transition**			Modulates back to e
154–225	**Recapitulation**			
154–177		1st theme	e	Leads directly to 2nd theme without bridge
177–201		2nd theme	E	In tonic major with varied orchestration
201–225		Closing section		"Rossini crescendo"
225–264	**Coda**		E	*Più mosso* (even faster)

fact, the way the recapitulation is abbreviated to speed its arrival makes the repetition of the rollicking crescendo seem like the overture's very raison d'être. To cap off the overture, Rossini runs the crescendo headlong into an even more energetic coda (mm. 225–264).

Virtually all Rossini overtures have the same structure: tripartite slow introduction, bithematic exposition with a noisy bridge between the themes, closing section/codetta with a Rossini crescendo, and recapitulation without a preceding development section. Yet they all differ in their details, most specifically in their rich melodic invention and orchestration. Rossini's overtures not only lack development sections, they also have no real "far out point" in their tonal design, and have little rigorous motivic unfolding. In other words, they do not display the harmonic drama that was considered to be the most important aspect of Beethovenian symphonic binary form. Rossini likely found development unnecessary for his purposes. His special appeal, encapsulated by the "Rossini crescendo," was the result of brilliant control of volume, color, and texture, all belonging to music's sensuous surface, which has sometimes been considered secondary in importance by adherents of Beethovenian aesthetics.

23

Gioachino Rossini
(1792–1868)

FULL CD IV: TRACKS 3–8

L'Italiana in Algeri (The Italian Woman in Algiers), Act I, Finale (1813)

Rossini wrote the opera buffa *L'Italiana in Algeri* in 1813, shortly after the successful premiere of his opera seria *Tancredi*. For *L'Italiana* Rossini used a libretto by Angelo Anelli (1761–1820). The fact that Rossini completed the opera in twenty-seven days shows him to be a master of the genre already at the age of twenty-one.

The story of the opera treats the popular topic of Europeans trapped in an "exotic" country. The best-known eighteenth-century precedent is Mozart's *Die Entführung aus dem Serail* (The Abduction from the Seraglio, 1782), which takes place in the harem of a Turkish ruler. Rossini's opera also takes place in an "exotic" land, but there is an important difference in the representation of foreign rulers in Mozart's and Rossini's operas. In *Entführung*, Pasha Selim is an enlightened ruler who shows mercy and thus stands as a model for European sovereigns. In contrast, Rossini's Bey of Algiers, Mustafà, is a stock comic figure: brutal, barbarian, and easily fooled.

At the beginning of the first act, Mustafà, tired of his wife, Elvira, decides to have her married to his recently captured Italian slave, Lindoro. He sends out his pirates to seek a new Italian wife for him. The pirates return with the shipwrecked Isabella, who has traveled to Algiers in search of her lost lover, Lindoro. According to buffa convention, the height of confusion (imbroglio) is reached in the finale of the first act. Rossini's first-act finale takes place in Mustafà's harem, where the eunuchs praise their master for his unmatched skills at taming women. The opening C-major march, usually indicative of nobility and heroism, mocks Mustafà, whose main achievement, according to his eunuchs, is that he can turn "tigers into lambs"—fierce women into compliant wives. The arrival of Mustafà's head pirate, Ali, interrupts the mock majestic scene. He brings the captured Isabella to the harem. As the eunuchs remark on her beauty in hushed tones, the music turns to minor.

The extensive use of coloratura in Isabella's entrance music indicates her volatile temperament and shows her to be more than a match for Mustafà. While her vocal technique is familiar from opera seria, here the effect is comic rather than ennobling—Isabella, in continuous asides, muses about the ugliness of her captor. Mustafà's first reaction to Isabella is animal hunger

("Che pezzo da Sultano!" [A choice morsel fit for a Sultan]), but he suppresses his feelings and imitates her elaborate musical style in order to present himself as a "civilized" suitor. Isabella, however, wins the prize for cleverness: As opposed to the comic, accented sixteenth notes of her asides, she addresses Mustafà in lyrical, legato phrases, presenting herself as a weak creature in desperate need of male protection. By the end of this section they are happily singing together—Mustafà, totally taken in, and Isabella, rejoicing in her success.

The entrance of Taddeo, Isabella's male companion, who was captured with her, interrupts the idyll. Desperately in love with Isabella (though pretending to be her uncle), Taddeo is appalled to find his beloved in a tête-à-tête with the barbaric Mustafà. He is even more shocked when he realizes that his life is in danger. Isabella turns the tables on the Mustafà by demanding and securing Taddeo's release. The scene culminates in a quartet in which Isabella flatters Mustafà, Mustafà tries to woo Isabella, Ali enjoys Taddeo's fear, and Taddeo laments the hazardous nature of Mustafà's rule. Another imbroglio is thus straightened out, but there are more surprises in store.

After the temporary calm, an *Andantino* section ensues in a slow minuet tempo (in G major). Mustafà's wife, Elvira, her husband-to-be, Lindoro, and her confidante, Zulma, enter to say goodbye to Mustafà before departing for Italy. Lindoro and Isabella recognize each other; their asides disrupt the calm flow of the trio. The music marks their astonishment with a more agitated accompaniment and then by modulation. The section is on the verge of turning into a love duet between Isabella and Lindoro when Mustafà, sensing that something has gone wrong, interrupts the lovers. Instead of a love duet, the scene culminates in a septet, led by Mustafà and Lindoro, who repeats Mustafà's phrase in different keys. The loss of direction is expressed by constant modulation.

Isabella interrupts with a forceful inquiry about the identity of Elvira. Hearing that she is Mustafà's wife, Isabella insists that Mustafà restore Elvira's former status. Isabella also requests that Mustafà assign Lindoro to herself as a personal slave. Isabella's anger at hearing that Elvira is to be sent away is first indicated by a sudden harmonic shift (from C major to A♭ major, the key of the flat sixth scale degree) and then by furious coloratura outbursts that culminate with her sending Mustafà and his barbarian customs "to the devil."

The concluding *Allegro vivace* section—the indispensable ensemble at the end of buffa finales in which everyone sings at the same time—returns the music to C major. The sinking feeling of the characters is expressed by the simile of the shipwreck, an operatic favorite. This *Più mosso* section, an example of a "Rossini crescendo," starts with Elvira's announcement that she hears a bell in her head ("din, din"). The other characters join in, all bringing different onomatopoetic sounds into the tizzy of the ensemble. In Lindoro's head a clock is ticking ("tac, tac"), in Taddeo's a raven crows ("crà, crà"), in Ali's a hammer is hammering ("tac, tac"), and in Mustafà's a cannon is roaring ("bum, bum"). This section was entirely Rossini's invention; there are no such sound effects in the original libretto. When the section is repeated it is customary to sing it even faster, leaving the audience with a genuine feeling of confusion.

NB: In the interest of saving space we omit the score of this excerpt, which can be followed easily by ear.

SCENE 10

(*A magnificent room. On the right, a sofa for Mustafà, the Bey of Algiers. In the background an accessible balcony, on which the women of the seraglio can be seen. Mustafà is surrounded by eunuchs, who sing in chorus.*)

Chorus of Eunuchs

Viva, viva il flagel delle donne,
che di tigri le cangia in agnelle.
Chi non sa soggiogar queste belle

venga a scuola dal gran Mustafà.

Ali

Sta qui fuori la bella Italiana . . .

Mustafà

Venga . . . venga . . .

Chorus

Oh! Che rara beltà.

SCENE 11

Isabella

(*Oh! Che muso, che figura!*
quali occhiate! . . . ho inteso tutto.
Del mio colpo or son sicura.
Sta a veder quell ch'io so far.)

Mustafà

(*Oh! Che pezzo da Sultano!*
Bella taglia! . . . viso strano . . .
Ah! M'incanta . . . m'innamora.
Ma convien dissimilar.)

Isabella

Maltrattata dalla sorte,
condannata alle ritorte . . .
Ah, voi solo, o mio diletto.
mi potete consolar.

Mustafà

(*Mi saltella il cor nel petto.*
Che dolcezza di parlar!)

Chorus of Eunuchs

Long live the scourge of women,
who transforms them from tigresses to lambs,
whoever does not know how to subjugate these
    beauties
should take lessons from the great Mustafà.

Ali

The lovely Italian girl awaits outside . . .

Mustafà

Bring her in, bring her in!

Chorus

Oh! What rare beauty.

Isabella

(Oh, what a face, what a figure!
how he ogles me! . . . I understand everything.
I am sure now of my effect.
We'll see what I can do.)

Mustafà

(Oh, a choice morsel fit for a Sultan!
Lovely figure . . . unusual face . . .
Ah! I'm enchanted . . . I'm in love.
But I'd better conceal it.)

Isabella

Ill-treated by fate,
condemned to chains . . .
Ah, you alone, my beloved,
can comfort me.

Mustafà

(My heart leaps in my breast.
How sweet is her speech!)

Isabella

(*In gabbia è già il merlotto,*
nè più mi può scappar!
Del mio colpo or son sicura.
Oh! Che muso, che figura! . . .
Sta a veder quell ch'io so far.)

Mustafà

(*Io son giù caldo e cotto,*

nè più mi so frenar.
Ah! M'incanta . . . m'innamora.
Che taglia! . . . Ma bisogna simular.
Oh! che pezzo! . . . ma bisogna simular.)

SCENE 12

Taddeo pushing past Ali, who is trying to hold him back.

Taddeo

Vo' star con mia nopote,
io sono il signor zio.
M'intendi? Sì, son io.
Va' via: non mi seccar.
Signor . . . Monsieur . . . Eccellenza . . .
(*Ohimè! . . . Qual confidenza! . . .*
Il turco un cicisbeo
comincia a diventar.
Ah, chi sa mai, Taddeo,
quel ch'or ti tocca a far?)

Ali

Signor, quello sguaiato . . .

Mustafà

Sia subito impalato.

Taddeo

Nipote . . . ohimè . . . Isabella . . .
Senti, che bagatella?

Isabella

Egli è mio zio.

Isabella

(The poor fool's already entrapped;
he can't escape me now!
I'm sure now of my effect.
Oh, what a face, what a figure!
We'll see what I can do.)

Mustafà

(I'm already on fire and head-over-heels in
    love,
I can no longer restrain myself.
Ah! I'm enchanted . . . I've fallen in love.
What a figure! . . . But I must pretend.
Oh, what a prize! . . . but I must pretend.)

Taddeo

I want to be with my niece;
I'm her uncle.
Do you understand me? Yes, that's me.
Go away: don't annoy me.
Sir . . . Monsieur . . . Your Excellency . . .
(O dear! . . . What self-assurance she has! . . .
The Turk has already started
to become a dainty lady's man.
Ah, who knows, Taddeo,
what you should do now?)

Ali

My lord, this blockhead . . .

Mustafà

Have him impaled at once.

Taddeo

Niece . . . alas! . . . Isabella . . .
Did you hear that little trifle?

Isabella

He's my uncle.

Mustafà
Cospetto!
Haly, lascialo star.

Isabella
Caro, capisco adesso
che voi sapete amar.

Mustafà
Non so che dir, me stesso,
cara, mi fai scordar.

Taddeo
(Un palo a dirittura?
Taddeo, che brutto affar!)

Ali
(Costui dalla paura
non osa più parlar.)

FINAL SCENE
Elvira, Zulma, Lindoro
Pria di dividerci da voi, Signore,
veniamo a esprimervi il nostro core,
che sempre memore di voi sarà.

Isabella
(O ciel!)

Lindoro
(Che miro!)

Isabella
(Sogno?)

Lindoro
(Deliro? Quest'è Isabella!)

Isabella
(Questi è Lindoro!)

Lindoro
(Io gelo.)

Isabella
(Io palpito.)

Mustafà
Good heavens!
Ali, let go of him.

Isabella
My dear, now I realize
that you know how to make love.

Mustafà
I don't know what to say,
my dear, you make me forget myself.

Taddeo
(Impaled at once?
Taddeo, what a terrible affair!)

Ali
(That fellow won't dare, out of fear,
to speak up again.)

Elvira, Zulma, Lindoro
My lord, before parting from you
we have come to show you our hearts,
which will always retain memories of you.

Isabella
(O heavens!)

Lindoro
(What do I see?)

Isabella
(Am I dreaming?)

Lindoro
(Have I gone mad? That's Isabella!)

Isabella
(That's Lindoro!)

Lindoro
(I'm turned to ice.)

Isabella
(My heart is pounding.)

Both
(Che mai sarà?
Amore, aiutami per carità.)

Mustafà
(Confusi e stupidi, incerti pendono;

non so comprendere tal novità.)

Isabella and Lindoro
(Oh, Dio, che fulmine!
Non so rispondere.
Amore, aiutami per carità.)

Taddeo
(Oh, Dio, che fremito! Oh, Dio,
che spasimo!
Che brutto muso fa Mustafà.)

Isabella
Dite: chi è quella femmina?

Mustafà
Fu sino ad or mia moglie.

Isabella
Ed or?...

Mustafà
Il nostro vincolo,
cara, per te si scioglie;
questi, che fu mio schiavo,
si dee con lei sposar.

Isabella
Col discacciar la moglie
Da me sperate amore?
questi costumi barbari
io vi farò cangiar.
resti con voi la sposa...

Mustafà
Ma questa non è cosa...

Isabella
Resti colui mio schiavo.

Both
(Whatever will happen?
Love, help me, for pity's sake!)

Mustafà
(Bewildered and astounded, they stand
      undecided;
I can't understand this new situation.)

Isabella and Lindoro
(O heavens, what a thunderbolt!
I don't know how to react.
Love, help me, for pity's sake!)

Taddeo
(Heavens, what agitation, what a shock!

What an ugly face Mustafà is making!)

Isabella
Tell me: who is this woman?

Mustafà
Until now she was my wife.

Isabella
And now?

Mustafà
Our bond, my dear,
is being dissolved for you;
this man, who was my slave,
is to marry her.

Isabella
You hope to gain my love
by discarding your wife?
I'll make you change
those barbarous customs.
let your wife remain with you...

Mustafà
But that's not what...

Isabella
And let that fellow remain as my slave.

Mustafà

Ma questo no può star.

Isabella

Andate dunque al diavolo.
Voi non sapete amar.

Mustafà

Ah! no . . . m'ascolta . . . acchetati . . .
(Ah! Costei mi fa impazzar.)

Elvira, Zulma, Lindoro (*laughing*)
(Ah! di leone in asino
lo fa costei cangiar.)

STRETTA
Taddeo, Mustfà, Elvira, Isabella,
   Zulma, Lindoro, Ali

Va sossopra il mio/suo cervello,
sbalordito in tanti imbrogli;
qual vascel fra l'onde e i scogli

Mustafà

But this is impossible.

Isabella

Then go to the devil.
You don't know how to make love.

Mustafà

Ah, no . . . listen to me . . . calm down . . .
(Ah! She's driving me crazy.)

Elvira, Zulma, Lindoro (*laughing*)
(Oh! She's changed him
from a lion to an ass!)

Taddeo, Mustfà, Elvira, Isabella,
   Zulma, Lindoro, Ali

My/his his brain is turning topsy-turvy,
stunned by such confusions;
like a ship caught between the waves and the
   rocks,

Io sto/Ei sta presso a naufragar.

Chorus

Va sossopra il mio cervello,
ei sta presso a naufragar.

Isabella and Zulma

La mia testa è un campanello
che suonando fa din din.

Lindoro and Ali

Nella testa un gran marello
mi percuote e fa tac tac.

Taddeo

Sono come una cornacchia
che spennata fra crà crà.

Mustafà

Come scoppio di cannone
la mia testa fa bum bum.

I am/he is about to be wrecked.

Chorus

My brain is turning topsy-turvy,
he is about to be wrecked.

Isabella and Zulma

My head's like a bell,
ringing out ding ding.

Lindoro and Ali

In my head a hammer is beating,
going bang bang.

Taddeo

I'm like a crow that's been plucked,
crying caw caw.

Mustafà

Like cannon fire
my head's going boom boom.

24

Gioachino Rossini (1792–1868)

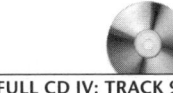

FULL CD IV: TRACK 9

Tancredi, Act I, Scene 5, "Oh patria! … Di tanti palpiti" (O homeland … So many heart throbs) (1813)

First performed in Venice in 1813, Rossini's *Tancredi* marked the beginning of Rossini's reputation as a leading composer of opera seria. The librettist, Gaetano Rossi (1774–1855), based the story on Voltaire's play *Tancrède*, which tells of a classic love triangle in Syracuse, Sicily, in the year 1005. To help seal a political alliance between two noble families, Amenaide, the daughter of one family, has been promised to Orbazzano, the head of the other. Although she agrees to the engagement under pressure, she is secretly in love with Tancredi, an exiled knight. Tancredi arrives in Syracuse in time to prevent her from going through with the marriage to Orbazzano, but complications make it impossible for Amenaide to declare her love for Tancredi, and he is led to suspect her of infidelity. Rossini's opera has two alternative endings: a happy ending, in which Tancredi learns of Amenaide's fidelity in the course of conquering the enemy and returns from battle unscathed to wed her; and a tragic one (composed for a second production at Ferrara), in which Tancredi learns of Amenaide's faithfulness only after he is mortally wounded in battle.

In the excerpt given here, Tancredi's boat delivers him to the grounds of the palace belonging to Amenaide's father. He disembarks and reflects first on his happiness at returning to his homeland and then on his excitement at the prospect of seeing his beloved Amenaide again.

"Di tanti palpiti" ("So many heart throbs) is the hero's "cavatina," here a designation meaning entrance aria. The aria is part of a "scena," or dramatic unit, that Rossini used frequently and that remained a staple for Italian opera through the middle of the nineteenth century. The dramatic unit comprises an accompanied recitative followed by a two-part aria consisting of a slow *cantabile* section leading to a showier, more animated concluding section referred to as the *cabaletta*. (The entire complex—recitative and two-part aria—is also known as a *scena ed aria* [scene and aria] or, in this case, *scena e cavatina* [scene and entrance aria], both of which are often simply referred to by the abbreviation *scena*.) "Di tanti palpiti" takes its name from the opening line of the cabaletta. As was frequently the case in early-nineteenth-century opera seria, the part of the romantic hero, Tancredi, is written for a *musico*, a female contralto dressed as a man ("in trousers"). The *castrati* (male singers with high voices due to castration before puberty) who would have taken this role a few decades earlier had largely disappeared by 1813, but their vocal register and style was still associated with serious opera.

In this case, the recitative-aria complex (*scena*) consists of five sections laid out in the following manner:

Measure Nos.	Section	Text	Keys	Comments
1–19	Orchestral introduction		C	Pastoral music to set the scene
20–51	Accompanied recitative	"Oh patria!"	C, F, B♭, F, d, B♭, F	
52–64	*Cantabile (moderato)*	"Tu che accendi questo core"	F ending on V	More declamatory and shorter than many cantabile sections
65–100	*Cabaletta*, strophe 1	"Di tanti palpiti"	F, A♭, f, [V/F]	Not significantly faster than the cantabile in this instance
101–142	*Cabaletta*, strophe 2	"sarà felice, il cor mel dice"	F	More embellished than first strophe

The orchestral introduction serves as the musical equivalent of the setting of the scene, the park around the palace. The music, in the pastoral meter of $\frac{6}{8}$, represents nature with pedal tones and bird sounds. The calm inspired by nature is soon disturbed by the hero's thoughts turning toward his beloved Amenaide. The orchestral accompaniment to the recitative closely mirrors Tancredi's changes of mood.

The final measures of this *cantabile*, which is more declamatory than many such sections, provide the singer with the first opportunity to display vocal virtuosity. In m. 62 the indications *a piacere* ("at pleasure," i.e., do whatever you want) in the vocal part and *colla parte* ("stay with the soloist") in the accompaniment call for vocal improvisation. The fermata in the next measure (m. 63) means "cadenza, please." Singers performed these passages as they pleased, sometimes embellishing the music to such an extent that the composer could hardly recognize his own work.

The F-major *cabaletta* that follows allows even more display of vocal pyrotechnics. But vocal virtuosity is not the only attractive feature of this *cabaletta*. One detail that contributes to the *cabaletta*'s effectiveness is the surprising modulation to the flat mediant (A♭ major) just where the first stanza seemed about to make its cadence (m. 89). The harmonic move functions as a tonal "far out point," requiring a modulation back to the tonic for the repetition of the opening line. The effect of departure and return (made all the more sweet by the cadenza implied by the fermata on the dominant chord in m. 100) plays on the meaning of the words, since the whole aria is about returning. For the French novelist Stendhal (1783–1842), Rossini's infectious "heart throbs" ("palpiti") meant a great liberating impetuosity that contrasted with what he considered the pompous and vapid spirituality touted in the Protestant north.

Tancredi	**Tancredi**
Oh patria! dolce, e ingrata patria!	O homeland, sweet and ungrateful homeland!
alfine a te ritorno! Io ti saluto,	finally I return to you! I salute you,
o cara terra degli avi miei: ti bacio.	O beloved soil of my ancestors: I kiss you.
È questo per me giorno sereno:	This is a happy day for me;
comincia il cor a respirarmi in seno.	my heart begins to beat again in my chest.
Amenaide! o mio pensier soave,	Amenaide! o my tender thought,
solo de' miei sospiri, de' voti miei	heavenly object of my sighs, and my prayers,
celeste oggetto, io venni alfin: io voglio,	I am coming at last: I want,
sfidando il mio destino, qualunque sia,	in defiance of my destiny, whatever it be,
meritarti, o perir, anima mia.	to be worthy of you, my soul, or to die.
Tu che accendi questo core,	You who set fire to this heart,
tu che desti il valor mio,	you who awaken my valor,
alma gloria, dolce amore,	glorious soul, sweet love,
secondate il bel desio,	join me in my noble desire,
cada un empio traditore,	hurl down an impious traitor,
coronate la mia fè.	and crown my steadfast faith.
Di tanti palpiti,	For so many heart throbs,
di tante pene,	for so many sorrows,
da te mio bene,	from you, my love,
spero mercè.	I hope for mercy.
Mi rivedrai . . .	You will see me again . . .
ti rivedrò . . .	I will see you . . .
ne' tuoi bei rai	in your sweet glances
mi pascerò.	I will revel.
deliri, sospiri . . .	ecstasies, sighs . . .
accenti, contenti!	murmurings, delights!
sarà felice, il cor mel dice,	I will be happy, my heart tells me,
il mio destino vicino a te.	My fate is to be near you.
Di tanti palpiti, etc.	For so many heart throbs, etc.

25

Vincenzo Bellini
(1801–35)

FULL CD IV: TRACK 10

Norma, "Casta diva" ("O pure goddess") (1831)

Bellini wrote *Norma* to a libretto by Felice Romani (1788–1865). By the time of its composition, Bellini was the highest-paid and most highly regarded Italian opera composer of his day. Although the work's premiere performance (Milan, 26 December 1831) was unsuccessful, *Norma* quickly became one of the most popular operas of the 1830s. The action takes place in ancient Gaul at the time of the Roman conquest. The native Druids are preparing their people for a revolt against the Roman occupiers. Their high priestess, Norma, is torn between her love for the Roman governor Pollione (to whom she has borne two children) and her duty to her people. At the end of the opera, Norma and Pollione perish on a sacrificial pyre in the Druids' temple in voluntary atonement for their sin.

The opera's most famous aria, "Casta diva," is part of a double-aria, *cantabile-cabaletta scena*, "Casta diva" being the opening text of the *cantabile*. Like virtually all such scenes it begins with an accompanied recitative (omitted in the excerpt in our anthology). The scene also includes a section known as *tempo di mezzo* (middle section) that provides a transition between the *cantabile* and *cabaletta*. Our excerpt begins with the *cantabile*, in which Norma leads the people in prayer during a ritual sacrifice to the moon goddess. Entranced, she cuts the sacred mistletoe from the holy oak and prays to the moon goddess to soothe her irate compatriots, preventing war with Pollione's troops.

The flute first plays the melody of the *cantabile*, its ecstatic third phrase (mm. 12ff) cut short at the end of its third measure (m. 14), enhancing expectations for the entrance of the voice. When Norma repeats the melody (mm. 16ff), she expands the third phrase and brings it to a full cadence (m. 30).

Despite its extraordinary length, the melody forms a coherent whole, achieved by a paradoxical trick. It is deliberately irregular in phrase structure, so it cannot be parsed entirely by successive binary divisions. The first two phrases (mm. 16–23) have "classical" regularity. The eight-measure whole comprises two equal and parallel four-measure phrases, and each of these in turn comprises a pair of two-measure units. Then follows a pair of parallel phrases (or, rather, a single phrase of one measure's duration and its embellished repetition at mm. 24–25).

These short gestures are followed by a five-measure phrase without any caesuras or internal repetitions (mm. 26–30). This last, longest, and least regular phrase encompasses a thrilling contour. It arches quickly up to the melody's highest note, preceded by a whole measure that does nothing but "stall" a half step below (m. 27). And then, over two luxuriant measures, the tension relaxes by degrees, with every beat sung to the same rhythm and the harmony zeroing in on the tonic along the circle of fifths (vi, ii, V, I). As the dynamics subside from the passionate *fortissimo* at the melodic peak to the *sotto voce* (in an undertone) on which the chorus will enter, the melody finally touches down on the low tonic G that has not been heard since the middle of the first phrase.

Bellini also keeps the melody afloat by constructing it with an increasing number of dissonances against the accompanying harmony. At first they are sparse, but every beat of m. 22 emphasizes the dissonant seventh or ninth of the dominant harmony, and the resolution to the tonic takes place against a chromatic appoggiatura to the third of the chord. The prize for melodic dissonances goes to the last two, ostensibly relaxing, measures (mm. 28–29), in which every single beat sounds a momentary discord.

Measure Nos.	Formal Designation	Text	Keys
1–60	*Cantabile* (begins with orchestral introduction)		G
16–30	*Cantabile* (stanza 1)	"Casta Diva, che inargenti"	G
30–40	Choral repetition of prayer	"Casta Diva, che inargenti"	G
41–60	*Cantabile* (stanza 2) (with chorus)	"Tempra, o Diva"	G
61–100	*Tempo di mezzo*, onstage band signals transition		E♭
71–86	Accompanied recitative, Norma	"Fine al rito"	E♭
86–94	Choral response	"Tuoni, e un sol del popol empio"	E♭ F/V
94–99	Norma's response	"Cadrà; punirlo io posso"	F
100–226	*Cabaletta* (begins with orchestral introduction)		F
109–129	*Cabaletta*, strophe 1	"Ah! bello a me ritorno"	F
130–141	Choral response	"Sei lento, si sei lento"	F
142–161	*Cabaletta*, strophe 2	"Ah, bello a me ritorno"	F
161–187	Choral response, joined by Norma	"Ma irato, si, il Dio t'affretta"	F
187–226	Orchestral conclusion		F

Norma's two *cantabile* stanzas are separated by the chorus's repetition of her prayer. After the second stanza of the *cantabile*, the onstage band (*banda*) signals the completion of the ritual and initiates the change of mood required between the *cantabile* and the *cabaletta*. In the elaborate accompanied recitative that precedes the *cabaletta*, Norma renews her vow to call her people into battle. But when the people declare that Pollione will be the first to be punished, Norma loses her composure and admits, in an aside, that she cannot kill the one she secretly loves. Her *cabaletta*, heard only by the audience, reflects her inner turmoil and, in dramatic irony, is contrasted with the martial fervor of her followers. Like virtually all *cabalettas* of the period, this one is set in a very regular form: aa′ba″. The light, dancing rhythm of Norma's melody expresses her fond memories of Pollione, while the syncopations and the sighs (falling chromatic scales mm. 118–120) register her agitation and sorrow. The burst of coloratura on "cielo" (heaven) that powers the fourth phrase and pushes it up to high C is hope, springing eternal. Norma is quickly brought back to reality by the entrance of the bloodthirsty chorus that leads back to the repeat of the *cabaletta*. The scene finishes with the cadential flourishes with which Italian opera composers and singers brought the audience to their feet. Formulaic as the scene's structure is, the juxtaposition of the *cantabile* and the *cabaletta* encapsulates Norma's characteristically operatic dilemma, the impossibility of at once satisfying private emotional needs and fulfilling public duty.

Norma
Casta Diva, che inargenti
Queste sacre antiche piante,
A noi volgi il bel sembiante
Senza nube e senza vel ...

Chorus
Casta Diva ..., etc.

Norma
Tempra, o Diva,
Tempra tu de' cori ardenti
Tempra ancora lo zelo audace,
Spargi in terra, ah, quella pace
Che regnar tu fai nel ciel.
Fine al rito: e il sacro bosco
Sia disgombro dai profani.
Quando il Nume irato e fosco,
Chiegga il sangue dei Romani,
Dal Druidico delubro
La mia voce tuonerà.

Norma
O pure goddess, who bathes in silver
These sacred ancient trees,
Turn your beautiful semblance on us
Unclouded and unveiled ...

Chorus
O pure goddess ..., etc.

Norma
Temper, O goddess,
These bold spirits,
Temper still their bold zeal,
Scatter on earth, oh, the peace
You cause to reign in heaven.
The rites are at an end: let the sacred wood
Be cleared of the uninitiated.
When the irate and gloomy God
Asks for the Romans' blood
My voice will thunder
From the Druidic temple.

Chorus
Tuoni, e un sol del popol empio

Non isfugga al giusto scempio,
E primier da noi percosso
Il Proconsole cadrà.

Norma
Cadrà; punirlo io posso.
(Ma, punirlo, il cor non sa.)
(Ah! bello a me ritorna
Del fido amor primiero;
E contro il mondo intiero
Difesa a te sarò.
Ah! bello a me ritorna
Del raggio tuo sereno;
E vita nel tuo seno,
E patria e cielo avrò.)

Chorus
Sei lento; sì, sei lento
O giorno di vendetta;
Ma irato il dio t'affretta
Che il Tebro condannò.

Norma
(Ah! bello a me ritorna, etc.)

Chorus
Ma irato, sì, il Dio t'affretta
Che il Tebro condannò
O giorno, il dio t'affretta
Che il Tebro condannò.

Norma
(Ah! riedi ancora qual eri allora,
Quando il cor ti diedi allora,
Ah, riedi a me.)

Chorus
Let it resound, and not one of the
wicked people
Will escape his just slaughter,
And, the first to be struck by us,
The Proconsul shall fall.

Norma
He will fall; I can punish him.
(But my heart is unable to do so.)
(Ah! Return to me the beauty
Of your first true love;
I'll defend you
Against the entire world.
Ah! Return to me the beauty
Of your serene gaze;
I'll have life, country
And heaven in your heart.)

Chorus
You may be slow; yes, you may be slow
O day of vengeance;
But the enraged god
Who has condemned Rome hastens
your coming.

Norma
(Ah! return to me, etc.)

Chorus
But enraged, yes, the god hastens you
Who has condemned Rome
O day, the god who has condemned Rome
Hastens your coming.

Norma
(Ah! return again as you were then,
When I gave you my heart then,
Ah, come back to me.)

26

Gaetano Donizetti
(1797–1848)

FULL CD IV: TRACK 11

Lucia di Lammermoor (Lucy of Lammermoor), Act III, Scene 2, "Mad Scene" (1835)

Measure Nos.	Formal Designation	Text	Keys
1–121	**Opening *parlante***	"Eccola!" "Oh giusto cielo"	c
7–33	Distorted fragments of Lucia's "Regnava nel silenzio" (Act I), in orchestra	"Il dolce suono . . ."	
44–51	Quotation of love duet "Verrano a te sull'aure" (Act I), in orchestra		E♭
99–118	Distorted fragments of wedding music (from Act II), in orchestra	"Ah! L'inno suona di nozze"	E♭
122–149	*Cantabile*, stanza 1	"Splendon le sacre faci"	E♭
150–162	*Cantabile*, stanza 2	"Del ciel clemente . . ."	
162–165	Cadenza and orchestral tag		
166–257	***Tempo di mezzo***	"S'avanza Enrico!"	C♭, a♭, G♭, V/e♭
258–336	*Cabaletta*, stanza 1	"Spargi d'amaro pianto"	E♭
337–426	*Cabaletta*, stanza 2	"Spargi d'amaro pianto"	E♭

Donizetti's *Lucia di Lammermoor* was premiered in Naples, 26 September 1835. The libretto by Salvadore Cammarano was based on Sir Walter Scott's novel *The Bride of Lammermoor*. The opera takes place in Scotland at the end of the seventeenth century. Lucia, daughter of the Lord of Lammermoor, is forced by her brother, Enrico, to marry Arturo. But Lucia is secretly engaged to the family's archenemy, Edgardo. Learning of the engagement, Enrico forges a letter in which he has Edgardo declare love for another woman. Misled by the forgery, Lucia agrees to marry Arturo, but during the wedding ceremony Edgardo appears and curses his unfaithful fiancée. The shock causes Lucia to lose her mind—after the wedding she kills her bridegroom and then dies herself of a broken heart. Hearing of Lucia's death, Edgardo stabs himself.

"Mad Scene"

The famous "mad scene" is based on the *cantabile/cabaletta* format now greatly expanded and including a *tempo di mezzo* (middle section) between the *cantabile* and the *cabaletta* (see chart).

The scene begins with the appearance of Lucia in her bloody wedding gown, having just killed Arturo. The shocked onlookers (members of the wedding party) react in horror, and she begins to sing against an extended flute solo. This constitutes an opening *parlante*, a section in which the orchestra carries the main melody while the voice declaims in a somewhat speech-like manner. What the flute plays is a distorted reprise of Lucia's first aria in Act 1, "Regnava nel silenzio" ([The night] reigned in the silence), in which she described a ghostly visitation of a long-slain Lammermoor lass who had been haunting the castle. The flute thus adds a multi-leveled commentary to the action, establishing itself as Lucia's demented inner voice. When Lucia sees the ghost again, standing between her and Edgardo, the flute and clarinet recall the *cabaletta* of their clandestine love duet in Act 1, "Verrano a te sull'aure" (My sighs shall be borne on the breeze), again somewhat deformed (mm. 44ff). The last reminiscence in this *parlante* is a poignantly elegant embellished reprise of music that accompanied Lucia's entrance to her

wedding in the finale of Act 2, now chromatically distorted in a way that at once boosts pathos and intensifies the portrayal of her derangement (mm. 99ff).

The *cantabile* part of the aria is marked *Larghetto* and is cast in aaba format (albeit somewhat deranged). The main melody of the *cantabile* begins in the flute while the voice continues *parlante*, thus disguising the beginning of the *cantabile* section. This blurring of boundaries between sections was likely intended as another representation of Lucia's disordered mind and was widely adopted thereafter as a "realistic" device. Lucia takes the melodic lead in the *cantabile* only in the "b" section ("Alfin son tua" [Finally I am yours], m. 133). When Lucia sings the closing phrase ("Del ciel clemente" [From merciful heaven], mm. 150ff) the tune is virtually buried in coloratura and crowned by a cadenza at m. 162. (The cadenza performed by Andrea Ros on the recording accompanying this anthology is a short improvised flourish for voice alone. The version of the cadenza heard most often in the twentieth century was an extensive duet for voice and flute introduced by soprano Nellie Melba [1861–1931] in a Paris Opera production in 1889.)

The *tempo di mezzo* (mm. 166ff) that provides the transition to the *cabaletta* is a lengthy *parlante* for several soloists and chorus, touched off by Enrico's arrival on the scene. He witnesses Lucia's delirium, in which she curses his cruelty in what seems at first like the start of the *cabaletta* (mm. 200ff). But the passage reaches a quick ensemble climax and then subsides, paving the way to the true *cabaletta*, in waltz time, marked *Moderato* ("Spargi d'amaro pianto" [Shed your bitter tears], mm. 258ff). Each of its two stanzas is followed by a response from a present, the second of them (mm. 382ff) including Lucia herself, who now imagines herself in heaven awaiting Edgardo's arrival.

The irony whereby Lucia's madness, a catastrophe to its observers, is a balm and solace to her is realized in the contrast between the musical style of the onlookers and the perfect harmony and beauty of Lucia's own contributions, especially in her duet with the flute, which only she can "hear." The beautiful harmony of voice and flute, conjuring up a better place than the one occupied by the sane characters, is a perfect metaphor for Romanticism's aspirations.

Raimondo
Eccola!

Chorus
(Oh giusto cielo! Par dalla tomba uscita!)

Lucia
Il dolce suono mi colpì di sua voce.
Ah! quella voce m'è qui nel cor discesa!
Edgardo! Io ti son resa, Edgardo mio,
Fuggita io son da' tuoi nemici.
Un gelo mi serpeggia nel sen!
Trema ogni fibra, vacilla il piè.
Presso la fonte, meco t'assidi alquanto!
Ohimè, sorge il tremendo fantasma,
e ne separa!
Qui ricovriamo, Edgardo, a piè dell'ara.
Sparsa è di rose! Un'armonia celeste
di', non ascolti?
Ah! L'inno suona di nozze!
Il rito per noi s'appresta!
Oh me felice!
Oh gioia che si sente, e non si dice!
Ardon gl'incensi.
Splendon le sacre faci, splendon intorno.

Ecco il ministro . . .
Porgimi la destra!
Oh lieto giorno!
Alfin son tua, alfin sei mio, a me ti
dona un Dio.

Raimondo
Here she is!

Chorus
(O heavens! She looks as if she had risen from the grave!)

Lucia
I hear the sweet sound of his voice.
Ah, that voice pierces my heart!
Edgar! I am restored to you, my Edgar,
I have escaped from your enemies.
A chill creeps into my breast!
Every nerve trembles; my steps waver.
Come sit with me by the fountain for a while!
Alas, that terrible specter is rising, and
separates us!
Let us take shelter, Edgar, at the foot of the altar.
It is strewn with roses! Don't you hear
the heavenly music?
Ah! It is the wedding hymn!
Our marriage ceremony is approaching!
Oh fortunate me!
Oh joy, felt but unspoken!
The incense burns.
The sacred torches shine brilliantly, shine, all
around.

Here is the minister . . .
Give me your right hand!
Oh happy day!
Finally I am yours, finally you are mine! God
gives you to me.

Normanno, Raimondo, Chorus
Abbi in sì crudo stato di lei
Signore, di lei pietà!

Lucia
Ogni piacer più grato mi fia con te diviso

Del ciel clemente un riso la vita a noi sarà.

Normanno, Raimondo
Pietà.

Raimondo
S'avanza Enrico!

SCENE 6
Enrico
Ditemi: vera è l'atroce scena?

Raimondo
Vera, pur troppo!

Enrico
Ah! perfida! Ne avrai condegna pena!

Chorus
T'arresta!

Raimondo
Oh ciel, non vedi lo stato suo?

Lucia
Che chiedi?
Ah me misera!

Enrico
Oh! qual pallor!

Raimondo
Ha la ragion smarrita.
Tremare, o barbaro,
Tu dei per la sua vita!

Lucia
Non mi guardar sì fiero,
Segnai quel foglio è vero:
Nell'ira sua terribile
Calpesta, oh Dio! l'anello,

Normanno, Raimondo, Chorus
What a terrible state she's in,
God have mercy on her!

Lucia
Every pleasure will be the sweeter shared with
you.
Life, for us, will be a smile from merciful heaven.

Normanno, Raimondo
Have mercy on her.

Raimondo
Henry is approaching!

SCENE 6
Enrico
Tell me: did the terrible event take place?

Raimondo
It is all too true!

Enrico
Ah! Treacherous girl! She will be punished!

Chorus
Stop!

Raimondo
Oh heaven, don't you see her condition?

Lucia
What do you want?
Ah, unhappy me!

Enrico
Oh! how pale she is!

Raimondo
She is bereft of reason.
Tremble, oh barbarous man,
You should fear for her life!

Lucia
Don't look at me so angrily,
I signed this paper, it is true:
In his terrible fury
He tramples—oh God!—the ring.

Mi maledice! Ah!
Vittima fui d'un crudel fratello,
ma ognor t'amai, e t'amo ancor
Edgardo mio, sì, te lo giurò.
t'amai, ah! E t'amo ancor!

He curses me! Ah!
I was the victim of a cruel brother,
but I loved you always, and still love you,
my Edgar, yes, I swear it,
I love you, oh! And still love you!

Enrico, Raimondo
Ah! di lei, Signor, pietà!

Enrico, Raimondo
Ah, God, have mercy on her!

Lucia
Chi mi nomasti? Arturo!
Ah! non fuggir,
Ah, per pietà! ah perdon!

Lucia
Who did you name to me? Arthur!*
Ah! don't run away,
Ah, for mercy's sake! ah, forgive me!

Enrico, Raimondo, Chorus
Infelice! Ah pieta, Signor, pietà!

Enrico, Raimondo, Chorus
Unhappy one! Oh mercy, Lord, [have] mercy
[on her]!

Raimondo, Chorus
Qual notte di terror.

Raimondo, Chorus
What a night of terror.

Lucia
Spargi d'amaro pianto
Il mio terrestre velo,
Mentre lassù nel cielo
Io pregherò per te.
Al giunger tuo soltanto
Fia bello il ciel per me!

Lucia
Shed your bitter tears
Where my earthly body will lie.
While above in heaven
I will pray for you.
But not until you come to me
Will heaven seem beautiful to me!

Enrico, Raimondo
Giorni d'amaro pianto
Serba il rimorso a me.

Enrico, Raimondo
Days of bitter tears,
Remain for me, in my remorse.

Chorus
Più raffrenare il pianto
Possible non è.

Chorus
It is not possible to
hold back the tears anymore.

Enrico, Raimondo
Ah! vita d'amaro pianto
Serba il ricanto a te.

Enrico, Raimondo
Oh life of bitter tears
Remain for me, in my remorse.

Lucia
Ah, ch'io spiri accanto a te,
Apresso a te.

Lucia
Ah, I will be near you
Next to you.

*Lucia is imagining a conversation with Arthur. The translation given here is literal, its unintelligibility a symptom of her madness. One can, however, construe the meaning behind the line as "With whom did you accuse me of being unfaithful? Arthur!"

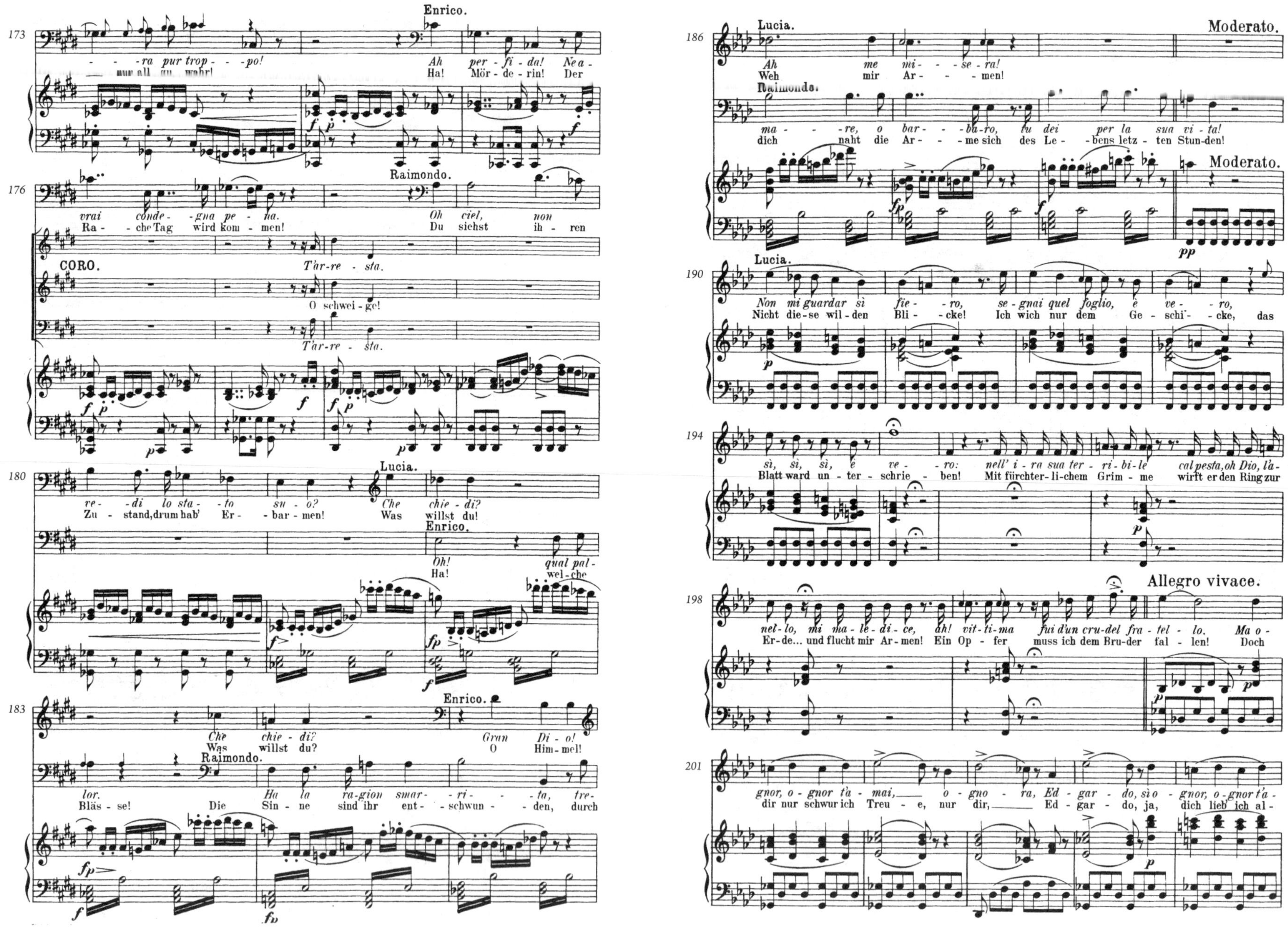
Enrico.
-ra pur trop- - -po! Ah per-fi-da! Nea-
nur all zu wahr! Ha! Mör-de-rin! Der
Raimondo.
vrai conde-gna pe-na. Oh ciel, non
Ra-che Tag wird kom-men! Du sichst ih-ren
CORO.
Tar-re-sta.
O schwei-ge!
Tar-re-sta.
Lucia.
re-di lo sta-to su-o? Che chie-di?
Zu-stand, drum hab' Er-bar-men! Was willst du!
Enrico.
Oh! qual pal-
Ha! wel-che
Enrico.
Che chie-di? Gran Di-o!
Was willst du? O Him-mel!
Raimondo.
lor. Ha la ragion smar-ri-ta, tre-
Bläs-se! Die Sin-ne sind ihr ent-schwun-den, durch
Lucia.
Moderato.
Ah me mi-se-ra!
Weh mir Ar-men!
Raimondo.
ma-re, o bar-ba-ro, tu dei per la sua vi-ta!
dich naht die Ar-me sich des Le-bens letz-ten Stun-den!
Moderato.
Lucia.
Non mi guardar si fie-ro, se-gnai quel foglio, è ve-ro,
Nicht die-se wil-den Bli-cke! Ich wich nur dem Ge-schi-cke, das
sì, sì, sì, è ve-ro: nell' i-ra sua ter-ri-bi-le calpesta, oh Dio, l'a-
Blatt ward un-ter-schrie-ben! Mit fürchter-li-chem Grim-me wirft er den Ring zur
Allegro vivace.
nel-lo, mi ma-le-di-ce, ah! vit-ti-ma fui d'un cru-del fra-tel-lo. Ma o-
Er-de... und flucht mir Ar-men! Ein Op-fer muss ich dem Bru-der fal-len! Doch
gnor, o-gnor t'a-mai, o-gno-ra, Ed-gar-do, sì o-gnor, o-gnor t'a-
dir nur schwur ich Treu-e, nur dir, Ed-gar-do, ja, dich lieb' ich al-

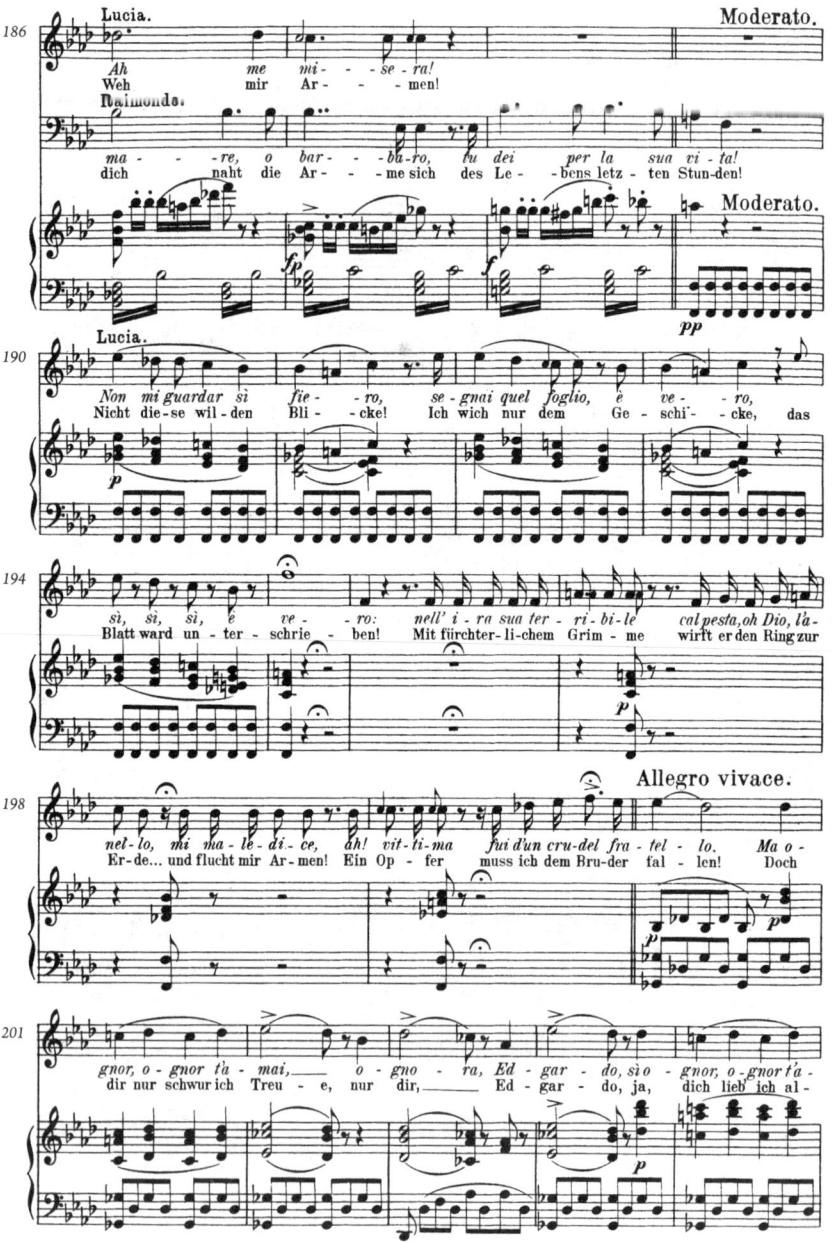

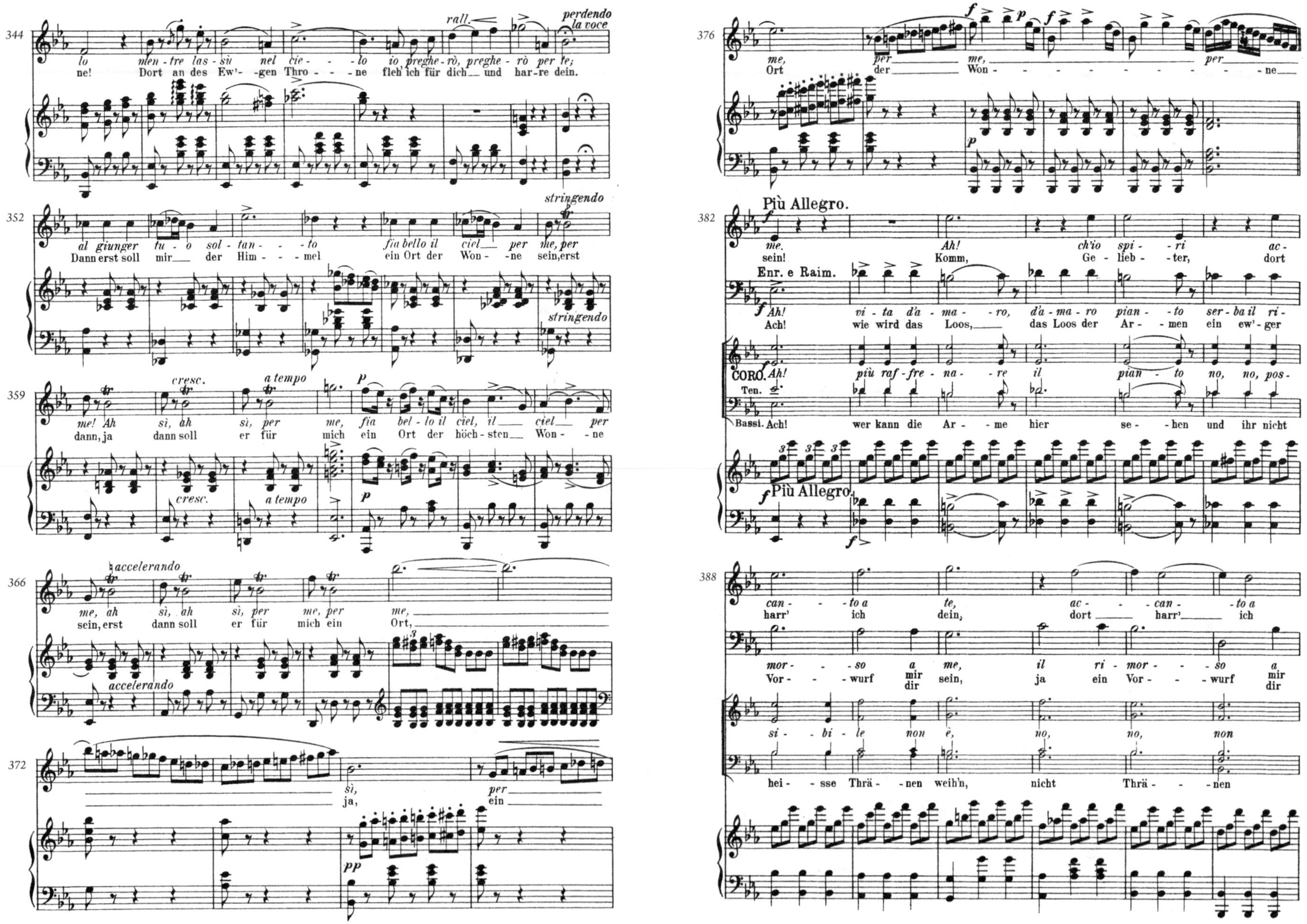
344
rall.
perdendo la voce
lo men - tre las - sù nel cie - - lo io preghe - rò, preghe - rò per te;
ne! Dort an des Ew'- gen Thro - - - ne fleh' ich für dich __ und har - re dein.
352
stringendo
al giunger tu - o sol - tan - - - to fia bello il ciel __ per me, per
Dann erst soll mir __ der Him - - - mel ein Ort der Won - - ne sein, erst
stringendo
359
cresc.
a tempo
p
me! Ah sì, ah sì, per me, fia bel - lo il ciel, il __ ciel __ per
dann, ja dann soll er für mich ein Ort der höch - sten __ Won - - ne
cresc.
a tempo
p
366
accelerando
me, ah sì, ah sì, per me, per me,
sein, erst dann soll er für mich ein Ort,
accelerando
372
sì, per
ja, ein
pp
376
me, per me, per
Ort der Won - - - ne
p
382
Più Allegro.
f
me. Ah! ch'io spi - ri ac -
sein! Komm, Ge - lieb - ter, dort
Enr. e Raim.
Ah! vi - ta d'a - ma - ro, d'a - ma - ro pian - to ser - ba il ri -
Ach! wie wird das Loos, das Loos der Ar - men ein ew'- ger
CORO. Ah! più raf - fre - na - re il pian - to no, no, pos -
Ten.
Bassi. Ach! wer kann die Ar - me hier se - hen und ihr nicht
Più Allegro.
388
can - - to a te, ac - - can - - to a
harr' ich dein, dort __ harr' __ ich
mor - - so a me, il ri - mor - - so a
Vor - - wurf mir dir sein, ja ein Vor - - wurf mir dir
si - bi - le non è, no, no, non
hei - sse Thrä - nen weih'n, nicht Thrä - - nen

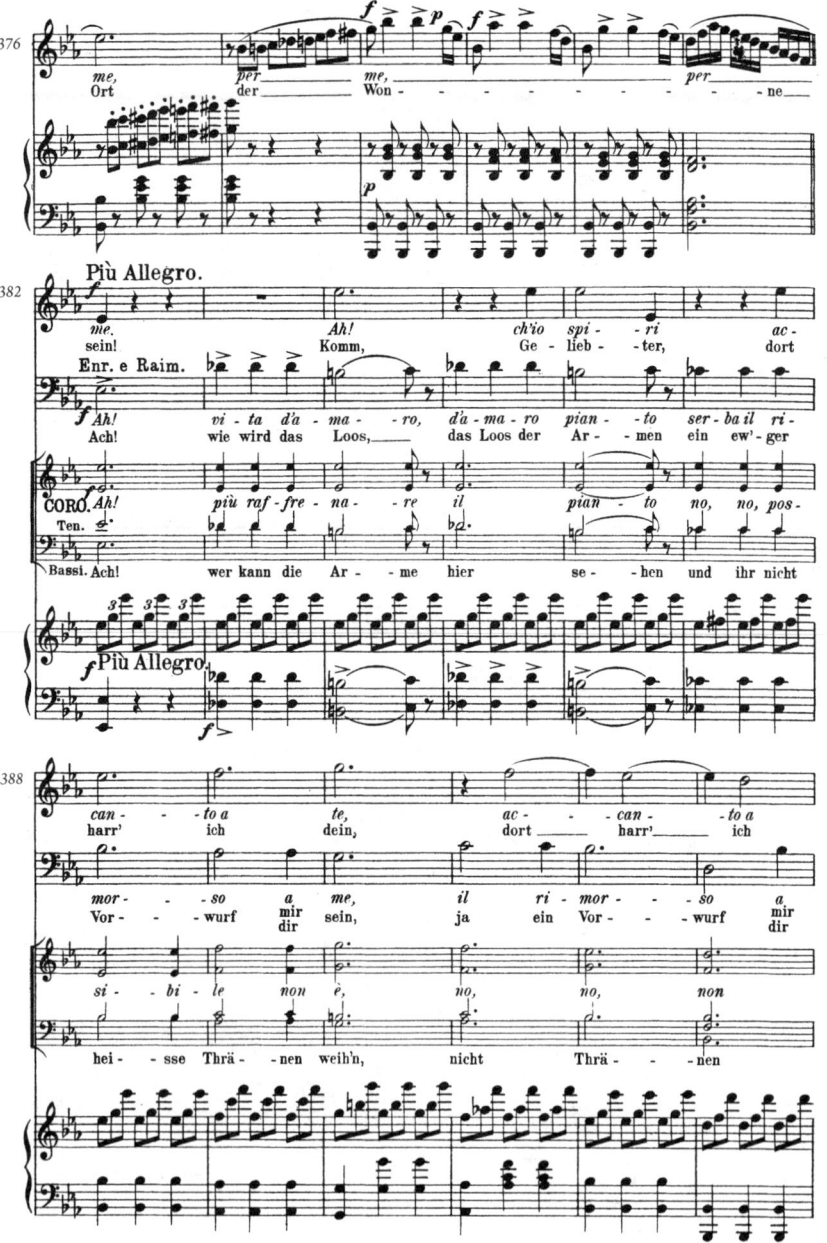

27

Carl Maria von Weber (1786–1826)

FULL CD IV: TRACKS 12–13

Der Freischütz (The Free Marksman) (1821)

Measure Nos.	Formal Designation	Sections	Keys	Comments
1–36	**Introduction**	*Adagio*	C	Horn theme, Samiel's f♯°⁷
37–159	**Exposition**	*Molto vivace*	c–E♭	
37–60		Primary theme	c	from Max's aria (Act 1)
61–92		Bridge		from Wolf's Glen scene
93–122		Secondary theme 1	E♭	from Max's aria (mm. 93–95 = introductory horn blasts)
123–145		Secondary theme 2	E♭	from Agathe's aria
145–159		Closing section		
159–218	**Development**			
159–190		Mainly from bridge	E♭	Wolf's Glen music
191–218		Mainly from secondary theme 2	G	Agathe's theme
219–342	**Recapitulation**			
219–232		Primary theme	c	
233–243		Bridge		
243–253		New transitional material		
253–278		Insertion	c	From introduction
279–287		Shift to C major	C	
288–311		Secondary theme 2 w/additional flourishes	C	
312–342		Closing section	C	With references to secondary theme 2

Weber's *Der Freischütz* premiered in 1821 in Berlin, the Prussian capital. Friedrich Kind's libretto is based on a ghost story from Johann August Apel and Friedrich Laun's *Gespensterbuch* (Ghost book, 1810). The title refers to a "free" (infallible) marksman who shoots with magic bullets. The story takes place in a forest in seventeenth-century Bohemia. Max, a forester, is having a long spell of bad luck. If he fails the shooting contest the following day, he will not be allowed to wed his beloved Agathe. A fellow forester, Caspar, thus convinces Max to join him in casting magic bullets. The bullets, however, come with a price—the one using them must serve the devil. Instead of the bloodbath that concludes the folktale, Weber provides his opera with a happy ending, achieved by the miraculous intervention of a saintly hermit.

a. Overture

Weber cast the overture to the opera in the customary sonata (or symphonic binary) form with a slow introduction and without a repeat of the exposition. Unlike Rossini, Weber includes a development section, and most of the themes he uses in the overture to *Der Freischütz* are taken from musical numbers in the opera.

In Weber's overture the introduction (*Adagio*) is in major while the following *Molto vivace,* forecasting the tragic turn of events in the opera, begins in minor. The *Adagio* contains the only important theme of the overture that will not appear in the opera (mm. 10ff). Yet this theme for four horns, called *Waldhörner* (forest horns) in German, is related to the opera's plot because, with its imitation of hunters' calls, it presents one of the opera's most important protagonists, the forest. The sound of the four horns was an unprecedented and electrifying effect that forever changed the nature of orchestral horn writing. Until Weber, horn parts had hardly differed from trumpet parts except in range. Now the horn became for German composers the *Naturlaut* (nature sound) par excellence. After Weber, four became the normal orchestral horn complement throughout Europe. What made Weber's horns sound particularly "German" was the close harmony, equivalent in range and "voicing" to the men's choruses of nationalistic singing societies popular in Germany. Weber's horn quartet thus effectively mediated between the human (vocal) and ghostly (forest) domains.

As soon as the horns finish (m. 25), the strings begin an eerie unmeasured tremolo, a device that was not yet commonplace in 1821. The tremolo makes the supernatural connotations of the forest-horn music even clearer; and in the very next measure harmonic color in the form of a diminished-seventh chord joins orchestral color to transport us to the sinister world of the devil (who is called Samiel in the opera). When the harmony returns to C in m. 30 it is to C minor, which forecasts the eerie atmosphere of the scene in which Caspar and Max cast magic bullets.

The *Molto vivace* begins with a theme borrowed from Max's first aria ("powers of darkness are weaving around me!"), in which he feels an inexplicable foreboding as Samiel steals across the stage behind him. The stormy bridge material (mm. 61–92) is drawn from the horror music that accompanies the casting of the magic bullets. The first secondary theme appears in the clarinet (mm. 96ff) and is taken from the same aria by Max ("No ray will shine upon my darkness"). The second, more flowing "secondary theme" (mm. 123ff) comes from the aria of Max's sweetheart, Agathe, in Act 2, in which, by contrast, she expresses her joyful hopes for the future ("All my pulses are beating, and my heart pants wildly, full of sweet enchantment at [Max's] approach!"). These quotations come from the most memorable, climactic sections of the arias. The development (mm. 159ff) starts with the bridge material (from the Wolf's Glen scene) and features the second "secondary theme," in G major (mm. 191ff).

The recapitulation includes an insertion section of the dark "forest music" from the slow introduction (mm. 253ff), which Weber contrasts with two bright C-major explosions (mm. 279ff). Agathe's optimism is now proclaimed from the rooftops in C major (mm. 288ff), telegraphing the joyous resolution of the drama. This pointed reference to Beethoven's rhetoric of contrasts in Weber's overture has many counterparts in the opera, in which time and again dark and light are strikingly juxtaposed.

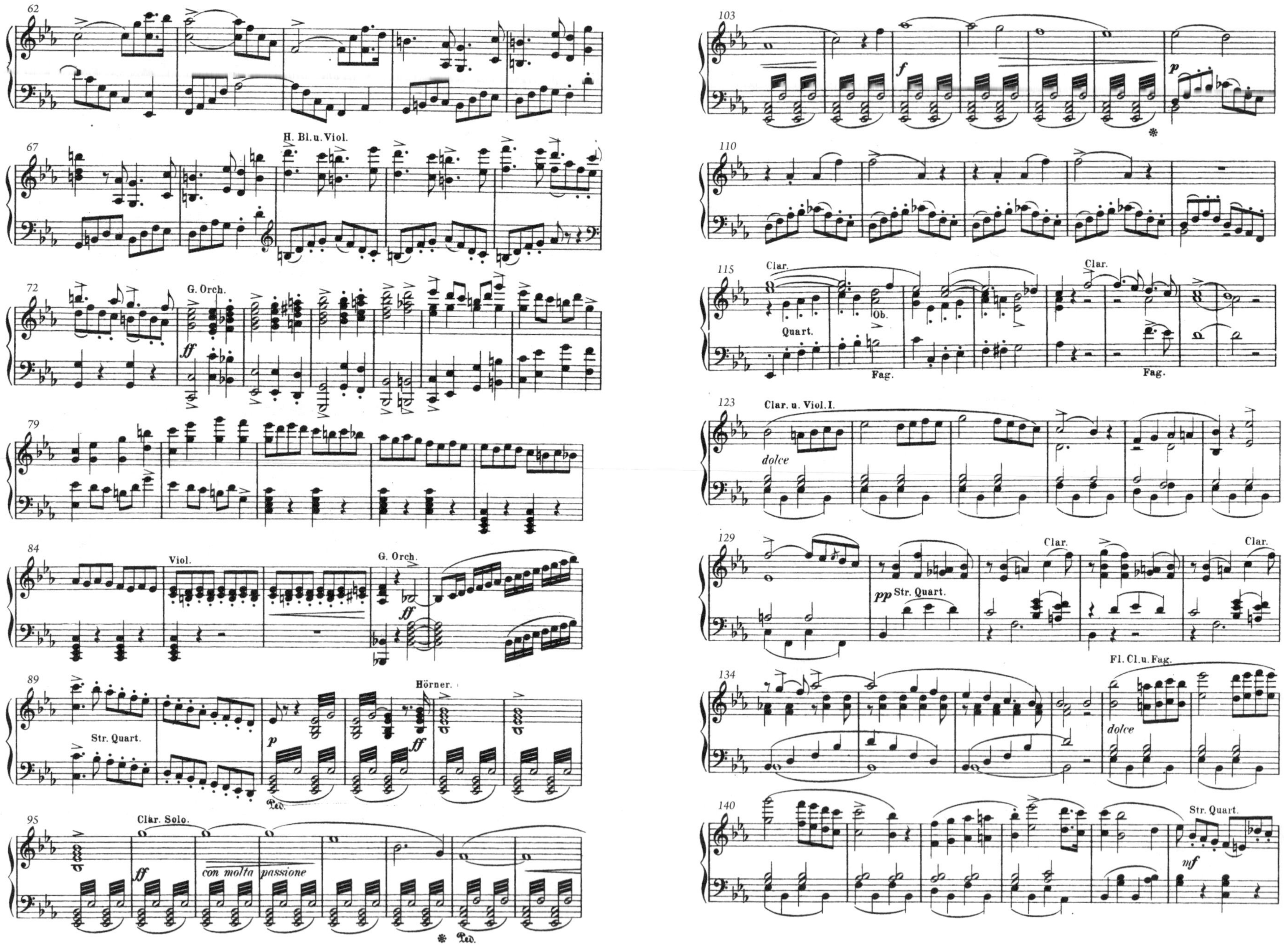
H. Bl. u. Viol.
G. Orch.
Viol.
G. Orch.
Str. Quart.
Hörner.
Clar. Solo.
con molta passione
Clar.
Quart.
Ob.
Fag.
Clar. u. Viol. I.
dolce
Str. Quart.
Fl. Cl. u. Fag.

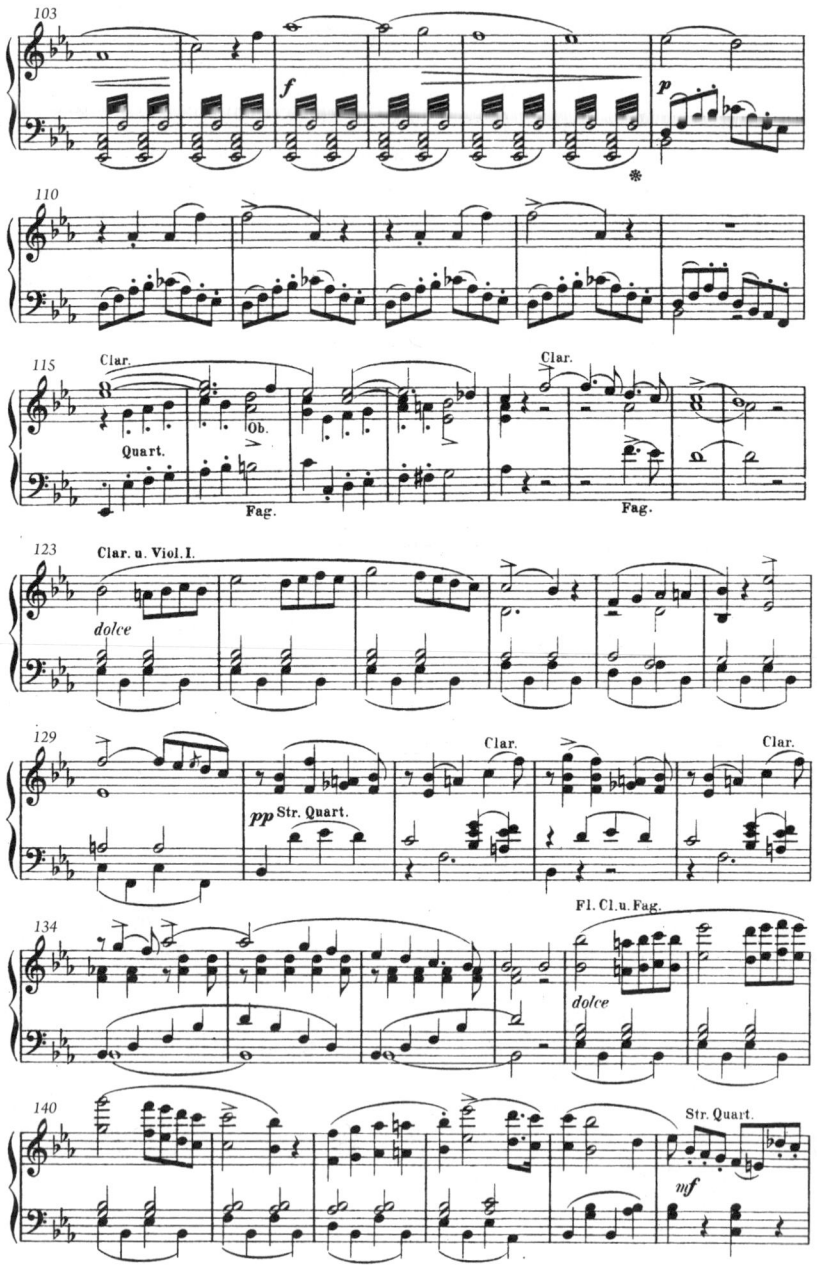

clarinets and tremolo strings, to which a soft trombone choir and bassoons are added—reinforces the mysterious mood onstage. When the unseen spirits wail and the harmony turns dissonant, the stage direction, in which an intermittently visible full moon "throws a lurid light over all," is matched by a pair of piccolos in octaves, adding their sinister shimmer to the unison woodwind choir. This music is exceptionally coloristic, and it continued to reverberate in the works of composers for the rest of the century.

The vocal writing effectively shifts between singing and melodrama (speech with musical accompaniment). As the most alien element on stage, Samiel never sings. We hear his speaking voice over tremolo strings and frightening timpani strokes. Max's first terrified outcry (m. 157) is preceded by an uncanny horn blast already heard in the Overture. The first ghostly vision is that of Max's mother in her grave (mm. 217ff); next comes Agathe, appearing to Max alone as a hallucination (her apparition is represented with agitated descending sixteenth notes in A minor, a key that should have warned Max that the hallucination has nothing to do with the pure, C-major key of the real Agathe [mm. 236ff]). When she seems about to plunge to her death in a waterfall, the orchestra sounds another reprise from the Overture (rushing strings at mm. 247ff).

When the casting of bullets begins, frightful apparitions, conjured by the orchestra, accompany the successful casting of all seven bullets, counted out by Caspar onstage and echoed offstage.

- At the shout of "One!" night birds with glowing eyes come flying out of the trees and flap their wings. Measured trills in the strings accompany glinting diminished-seventh chords (Samiel's harmony) in the winds (mm. 288ff).
- At "Two!" a black boar comes crashing through the bushes and darts across the stage. Tremolando strings accompany rumbling in the bass instruments with many diminished-seventh (Samiel) chords (mm. 291ff).
- At "Three!" a storm bends the tops of the forest trees. The music is clearly indebted to the Storm (fourth movement) in Beethoven's "Pastoral" Symphony (mm. 301ff).
- At "Four!" an invisible coach, of which only the supporting fiery wheels can be seen, rattles across the stage to precipitate triplets reminiscent of Schubert's *Erlkönig* (mm. 317ff).
- At "Five!" the "Wild Hunt," a ghostly mirage replete with horses and dogs, appears in midair. The phantasmic hunters urge their hounds on to the sound of the orchestral horns (mm. 329ff).
- At "Six!" volcanic eruptions break out, accompanied by a reprise of the whole madly squalling material of the bridge section in the Overture, but this time veering off into tonal regions (F♯ minor, A♭ minor) never even broached in the Overture's development section.
- At "Seven!" Samiel himself appears; Caspar and Max fall to the ground; the full orchestra negotiates an unprecedented juxtaposition of the keys of C minor and F♯ minor, with two reiterated diminished-seventh chords as the sole intermediary (mm. 395ff).

b. Wolf's Glen Scene, Act II, Finale

The Act II Finale is the eeriest part of the drama. It takes place at midnight in the "Wolf's Glen," where the evil ranger Caspar has lured his colleague Max to cast magic bullets with the help of the devil (Samiel). The scene consists of a succession of brief, strongly colored and contrasted episodes. It opens in the key of F♯ minor, as distant from the key of the Overture's C major/minor as a key can be. As soon as the "chorus of invisible spirits" intones its "Uhui! Uhui," however, the tonic chord is replaced with a diminished-seventh (C–E♭–F♯–A) tremolo that we have seen in the Overture. It functions as a mediator between C minor and F♯ minor. The whole scene will be an oscillation between these two keys a tritone apart. Weber was no doubt recalling the tritone's Medieval nickname of *diabolus in musica* (devil in music). But it is the mediator of the progression—the diminished-seventh chord—that is the scene's most characteristic harmony. It sounds whenever Samiel is invoked, and it is sustained for as many as eight measures at a stretch.

The scene takes shape through an ever-accelerating progression of ghostly images, with every component conspiring to project gloom. The orchestration—once again combining low

In the "Wolf's Glen" scene Weber creates a perfect synthesis between the aural and the visual effects of the theater. What Weber accomplishes with great success is painting with music. In so doing he contradicts Beethoven's precept, in describing the "Pastoral" Symphony, that music should aim at "more the expression of feeling than painting."

ACT II, NO. 10, FINALE

(*A terrible woodland glen with waterfall. Pale full moon. A thunderstorm approaches. In the front a tree, struck by lightning and withered, seems to glow. Crows and other woodland birds on other trees.*)

(*Caspar, without hat or overcoat but with hunting bag and knife, is busy laying out a circle with black stones. A skull lies in the center. A few paces away are a severed eagle's wing, a casting ladle, and a bullet mold.*)

Chorus of Invisible Spirits
Milch des Mondes fiel auf's Kraut! Uhui!!
Spinnweb' ist mit Blut bethaut! Uhui!
Eh' noch wieder Abend graut, Uhui!
Ist sie todt, die zarte Braut! Uhui!
Eh' noch wieder sinkt die Nacht,
Ist das Opfer dargebracht!
Uhui! Uhui! Uhui!

Chorus of Invisible Spirits
Milk of the moon fell on field! Uhui!
Spider's web is dewed with blood! Uhui!
Ere evening falls again—Uhui!
The gentle bride will be dead! Uhui!
Ere the next descent of night,
Will the sacrifice be made!
Uhui! Uhui! Uhui!

(*A clock strikes twelve in the distance. The circle of stones is complete. Caspar rips out his hunting knife and plunges it into the skull.*)

Caspar
Samiel! Samiel! erschein'!
Bei des Zaubrers Hirngebein!
Samiel! Samiel! erschein'!

Caspar
Samiel, Samiel, appear!
By the wizard's skull,
Samiel, Samiel, appear!

Samiel (*comes from a rock*)
Was rufst du mich?

Samiel (*comes from a rock*)
Why are you calling me?

Caspar (*bowing abjectly before him*)
Du weisst, dass meine Frist
Schier abgelaufen ist,

Caspar (*bowing abjectly before him*)
You know that my term
has almost run out.

Samiel
Morgen!

Samiel
Tomorrow!

Caspar
Verläng're sie noch einmal mir!

Caspar
If it might be extended once more!

Samiel
Nein!

Samiel
No!

Caspar
Ich bringe neue Opfer dir.

Caspar
I bring a new sacrifice to you.

Samiel
Welche?

Samiel
What?

Caspar
Mein Jagdgesell, er naht;
Er, der noch nie dein dunkles Reich betrat!

Caspar
My hunting companion, he is coming;
He, who has never entered your dark realm.

Samiel
Was sein Begehr?

Samiel
What does he want?

Caspar
Freikugeln sind's, auf die er Hoffnung baut.

Caspar
It is magic bullets on which he builds his hopes.

Samiel
Sechse treffen, Sieben äffen.

Samiel
Six will hit their mark, the seventh will mock him!

Caspar
Die siebente sei dein!
Aus seinem Rohr lenk' sie nach seiner Braut!
Dies wird ihn der Verzweiflung weih'n,
Ihn—und den Vater.

Caspar
The seventh shall be yours!
Steer it from his barrel to his bride!
This will make him despair,
Him—and her father.

Samiel
Noch hab' ich keinen Theil an ihr!

Samiel
I have no stake in her yet!

Caspar (*fearful*)
Genügt er dir allein?

Caspar (*fearful*)
Is he enough to satisfy you?

Samiel
Das findet sich!

Samiel
We shall see!

Caspar
Doch schenkst du Frist,
und wieder auf drei Jahr',
Bring ich ihn dir zur Beute dar!

Caspar
But you will set a term,
and in another three years' time,
I'll bring him to you as your prey!

Samiel
Es sei!—Bei den Pforten der Hölle!
Morgen er oder du!

Samiel
So be it—By the gates of hell!
Tomorrow he or you!

(*Disappears in a dull thunder.*)

(*The skull with the hunting knife has also disappeared; in its place a little fire with glowing coals comes up from below.*)

Caspar

Trefflich bedient!

Caspar

Excellent service!

(*He takes a draught from the hunting flask.*)

Gesegn'es, Samiel!
Er hat mir warm gemacht!
Aber wo bleibt Max?
Sollte er wortbrüchig werden? Samiel, hilf!

Bless it, Samiel!
He has made me warm!
But where is Max?
Could he break his word? Samiel, help!

(*He puts wood on the coals and blows on them. The owl and other birds raise their wings as if to kindle the fire. The fire smokes and crackles.*)

(*Max appears on the rocky peak above the waterfall, peering down into the glen.*)

Max

Ha!—Furchtbar gähnt
Der düstre Abgrund! Welch' ein Grau'n!
Das Auge wähnt
In einen Höllenpfuhl zu schau'n! -
Wie dort sich Wetterwolken ballen,
Der Mond verliert von seinem Schein!
Gespenst'ge Nebelbilder wallen,
Belebt ist das Gestein!
Und hier . . . husch, husch!
Fliegt Nachtgevögel auf im Busch!
Rotgraue, narb'ge Zweige strecken
Nach mir die Riesenfaust!
Nein! ob das Herz auch graust . . .
Ich muss . . . ich trotze allen Schrecken!

Max

Ha! Yawns frightfully
The gloomy abyss! What horror!
My eyes believe themselves to be
Gazing into a slough of hell!
How the storm clouds cluster there,
The moon loses its beams!
Ghostly mist-shapes waver,
The rock is alive!
And here . . . shoo, shoo!
Night birds fly into the bushes!
Branches, ruddy-grey and scarred, stretch
Out gigantic arms at me!
No! Though my heart dreads it . . .
I *must* . . . I defy all terrors!

(*He climbs down a few paces.*)

Caspar

Dank, Samiel! die Frist ist gewonnen!

Caspar

Thanks! Samiel. My term is achieved!

(*To Max*)

Kommst du endlich, Kamerad?
Ist das auch recht,
mich so allein zu lassen?
Siehst du nicht, wie mir's sauer wird?

Have you come at last, comrade?
Was it also right
to leave me so alone?
Can't you see how distasteful it is for me?

(*He has fanned the fire with the eagle's wing.*)

Max (*Staring at the eagle's wing with his hand on his brow*)

Ich schoss den Adler aus hoher Luft;
Ich kann nicht rückwärts—mein Schicksal ruft!

Max (*Staring at the eagle's wing with his hand on his brow*)

I shot the eagle out of the lofty air;
I cannot turn back—my destiny calls!

(*He climbs down a few paces, then stops again and gazes fixedly at the rocks on the other side.*)

Weh' mir!

Woe is me!

Caspar

So komm doch, die Zeit eilt!

Caspar

Come on already, time is passing!

Max

Ich kann nicht hinab!

Max

I can't get down!

Caspar

Hasenherz! Klimmst ja sonst wie eine Gemse!

Caspar

Coward! You usually climb like a mountain goat!

Max

Sieh' dort hin, sieh'!

Max

Look over there, look!

(*He points to the rock bathed in moonlight; a form veiled in white is seen raising its hands.*)

Was dort sich weist,
Ist meiner Mutter Geist.
So lag sie im Sarg, so ruht sie im Grab.
Sie fleht mit warnendem Blick,
Sie winkt mir zurück!

What shows itself there
Is my mother's ghost.
So she lay in her coffin, so she rests in her grave.
She looks, and weeps, and warns me.
She is waving me back!

Caspar (*to himself*)

Hilf, Samiel!

Caspar (*to himself*)

Help, Samiel!

(*aloud*)

Alberne Fratzen! Hahaha!
Sieh' noch einmal hin,
damit du die Folgen deiner
feigen Thorheit erkennst.

Ridiculous fancies! Haha!
Look again,
and you'll see what comes
of your cowardly stupidity.

(*Agathe's form is seen, with disheveled hair strangely adorned with leaves and straw. She is like a mad person and seems about to throw herself into the waterfall.*)

Max

Agathe! Sie springt in den Fluss!
Hinab! Hinab! ich muss!

Max

Agatha! She's jumping into the water!
Down! I must go down!

(*The moon grows dark. The image vanishes. Max climbs all the way down.*)

Caspar (*to himself, sarcastically*)
Ich denke wohl auch, dass du musst!

Max (*to Caspar, impetuously*)
Hier bin ich! Was hab' ich zu thun?

Caspar (*throwing him the hunting flask, which Max sets down*)
Zuerst trink! die Nachtluft ist kühl und feucht.
Willst du selbst giessen?

Max
Nein! das ist wider die Abrede.

Caspar
Nicht? So bleib ausser dem Kreise, sonst kostet's dein Leben!

Max
Was hab' ich zu tun, Hexenmeister?

Caspar
Fasse Mut! Was du auch hören und sehen magst,
verhalte dich ruhig.

(*With a peculiar furtive horror.*)

Käme vielleicht ein Unbekannter, uns zu helfen, was kümmert's dich?
Kommt was andres, was tut's?
So etwas sieht ein Gescheidter gar nicht!

Max
O, wie wird das enden!

Caspar
Umsonst ist der Tod! Nicht ohne Widerstand
schenken verborgene Naturen den Sterblichen ihre Schätze. Nur wenn du mich selbst, zittern siehst

---

Caspar (*to himself, sarcastically*)
I also think that you must!

Max (*to Caspar, impetuously*)
Here I am! What have I got to do?

Caspar (*throwing him the hunting flask, which Max sets down*)
First have a drink! The night air is cold and damp.
Will you do the casting yourself?

Max
No, that goes against the agreement.

Caspar
No? Stay outside of the circle, otherwise you pay with your life.

Max
What must I do, sorcerer?

Caspar
Take courage! Whatever you may see or hear,

keep quiet.

If someone unknown to you should come to help us, why worry?
If another should come, what does it matter?
A clever fellow wouldn't even notice such a thing!

Max
Oh, how will this end!

Caspar
Only death comes free! Not without resistance
does nature give its treasures to mortals.
Only if you see me tremble,

---

dann komm mir zu Hilfe und rufe, was ich rufen werde, sonst sind wir beide verloren.

(*Max makes a sign of objection.*)

Caspar
Still! Die Augenblicke sind kostbar!

(*The moonlight has dwindled to a tiny beam. Caspar takes the casting ladle.*)

Merk' auf, was ich hinein werfen werde, damit du die Kunst lernst.

(*He takes the ingredients out of his hunting bag and throws them in one after another.*)

Hier erst das Blei. Etwas gestossenes Glas von zerbrochenen Kirchenfenstern; das findet sich.
Etwas Quecksilber! Drei Kugeln, die schon einmal getroffen! Das rechte Auge eines Wiedehopfs, das linke eines Luchses!
Probatum est! Und nun den Kugelsegen!

(*Bowing to the earth in each of three pauses.*)

Schütze, der im Dunkeln wacht!
Samiel! Samiel! hab' Acht!
Steh mir bei in dieser Nacht,
Bis der Zauber ist vollbracht!
Salbe mir so Kraut, als Blei,
Segn' es sieben, neun und drei,
Dass die Kugel tüchtig sei!
Samiel! Samiel! herbei!

(*The mixture in the mortar begins to foment and bubble and gives out a green-white glow. A cloud passes over the moon so that the whole surroundings are only lit by the fire, the owl's eye and the rotten stump of the tree.*)

Caspar (*pours, lets the bullets fall out of their mold, and calls*)
Eins!

Echo (*repeats*)
Eins!

---

then come to help me and call out what I call, otherwise we'll both be lost.

Caspar
Quiet! Every moment is precious!

Observe what I throw in so that you learn the art.

First the lead. Some ground glass from broken church windows; that's easy to find.
Some mercury! Three bullets that have hit their mark, the right eye of a hoopoe bird, the left one of a lynx!
Probatum est! Now the blessing of the bullets!

Protect us, you who watch in darkness!
Samiel! Samiel! Pay *attention*!
Stand by me in this *night*
Till the spell is com*plete*!
Bless for me the herb and *lead*,
Bless them by seven, nine and *three*,
That the bullet useful *be*!
Samiel, Samiel, to *me*!

Caspar (*pours, lets the bullets fall out of their mold, and calls*)
One!

Echo (*repeats*)
One!

(Woodland birds fly down and settle around the fire.)

Caspar
Zwei!

Echo
Zwei!

(A black boar rushes past.)

Caspar (*seems to stop short and counts*)
Drei!

Echo
Drei!

(A storm arises.)

Caspar (*counting anxiously*)
Vier!

Echo
Vier!

(A rustling, the crack of whips and the trample of horses hooves are heard.)

Caspar (*counting, still more anxiously*)
Fünf!

Echo
Fünf!

(Barking of dogs and neighing; the wild hunt.)

Chorus of invisible spirits
*Durch Berg und Thal, durch Schlucht
und Schacht,*
*Durch Thau und Wolken, Sturm
    und Nacht!*

Durch Höhle, Sumpf und Erdenkluft,
Durch Feuer, Erde, See und Luft,
Joho! Wauwau! ho! ho!

Caspar
Sechs!

Echo
Sechs!

Caspar
Two!

Echo
Two!

Caspar (*seems to stop short and counts*)
Three!

Echo
Three!

Caspar (*counting anxiously*)
Four!

Echo
Four!

Caspar (*counting, still more anxiously*)
Five!

Echo
Five!

Chorus of invisible spirits
Over mountain and valley, through abyss
and pit,
Over dew and clouds, tempest and night!

Over cavern, bog and chasm,
Through fire, earth, sea and air,
Yahoo! Woof-woof, ho ho!

Caspar
Six!

Echo
Six!

(The whole sky turns black as night, the storms clash.)

Caspar
Samiel!—Samiel!—Samiel!
Hilf!—Sieben!—Samiel!

Echo
Sieben.

Caspar
Samiel!

Samiel (*appears*)
Hier bin ich!

Caspar
Samiel!—Samiel!—Samiel!
Help!—Seven!—Samiel!

Echo
Seven.

Caspar
Samiel!

Samiel (*appears*)
Here I am!

(Caspar falls to the ground.)

Max (*buffeted hither and thither by the storm, jumps out of the circle, seizes a branch of the rotten tree and calls out*)
Samiel!　　　　　　　　　　　Samiel!

(At this very moment the storm begins to calm down, and in the place of the rotten tree stands the black huntsman, reaching out for Max's hand.)

Samiel
Hier bin ich!

Samiel
Here I am!

(Max makes the sign of the cross and falls to the ground. The clock strikes one. Sudden silence. Samiel has disappeared. Caspar is still lying with his face to the ground. Max gets to his feet convulsively.)

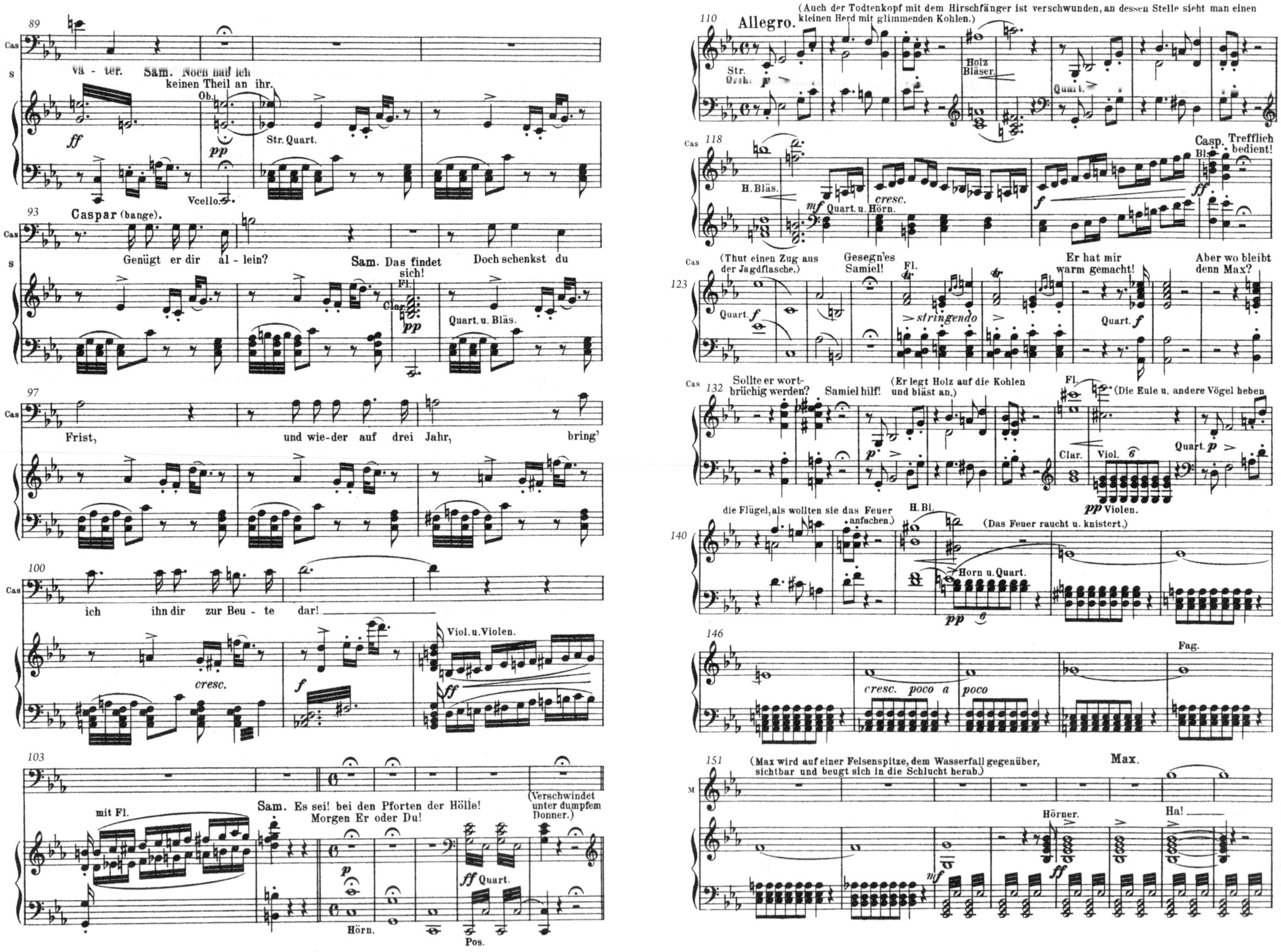
va - ter. Sam. Noch hab' ich keinen Theil an ihr.
Ob.
Str. Quart.
Vcello.
Caspar (bange).
Genügt er dir al - lein?
Sam. Das findet sich!
Doch schenkst du
Fl.
Clar.
Quart. u. Bläs.
Frist, und wie-der auf drei Jahr, bring'
ich ihn dir zur Beu - te dar!
cresc.
Viol. u. Violen.
mit Fl.
Sam. Es sei! bei den Pforten der Hölle! Morgen Er oder Du!
(Verschwindet unter dumpfem Donner.)
Quart.
Hörn.
Pos.
Allegro.
(Auch der Todtenkopf mit dem Hirschfänger ist verschwunden, an dessen Stelle sieht man einen kleinen Herd mit glimmenden Kohlen.)
Str.
Holz Bläser
Quart.
H. Bläs.
Quart. u. Hörn.
cresc.
Casp. Trefflich bedient!
Bl.
(Thut einen Zug aus der Jagdflasche.)
Gesegn'es Samiel!
Fl.
stringendo
Er hat mir warm gemacht!
Aber wo bleibt denn Max?
Quart.
Sollte er wort-brüchig werden?
Samiel hilf!
(Er legt Holz auf die Kohlen und bläst an.)
(Die Eule u. andere Vögel heben
Clar.
Viol.
Violen.
die Flügel, als wollten sie das Feuer anfachen.)
H. Bl.
(Das Feuer raucht u. knistert.)
Horn u. Quart.
Fag.
cresc. poco a poco
(Max wird auf einer Felsenspitze, dem Wasserfall gegenüber, sichtbar und beugt sich in die Schlucht herab.)
Max.
Hörner.
Ha!

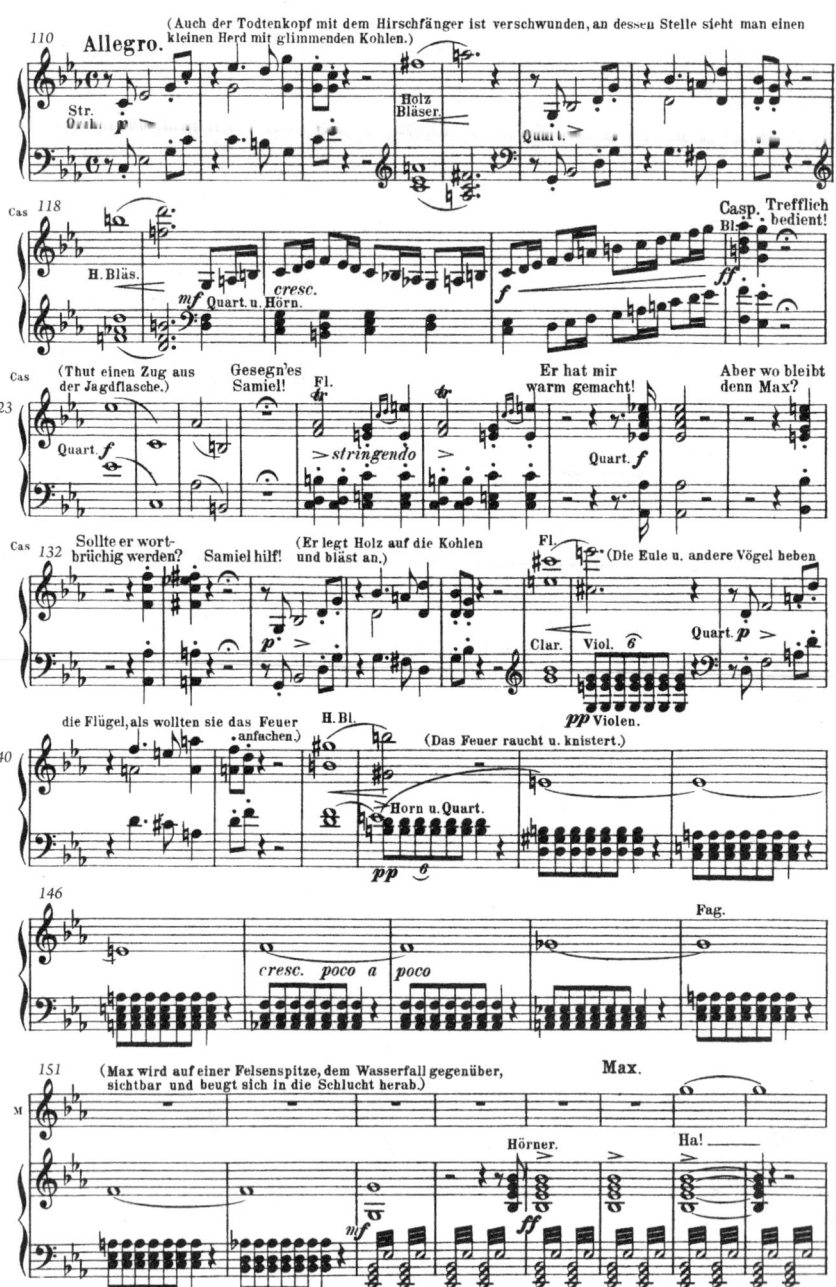

Caspar (wirft ihm die Jagdflasche zu, die Max weglegt). Zuerst trink' einmal! Die Nachtluft ist kühl und feucht. Willst du selbst giessen?

Max. Nein, das ist wider die Abrede.

[Caspar. Nicht? So bleib' ausser dem Kreise, sonst kostet's dein Leben!

Max. Was hab' ich zu thun, Hexenmeister?]

Caspar. Fasse Muth! Was du auch hören und sehen magst, verhalte dich ruhig. (Mit eigenem heimlichen Grausen.) Käme vielleicht ein Unbekannter, uns zu helfen, was kümmert's dich? Kommt was anders, was thut's?— So etwas sieht ein Gescheidter gar nicht!

Max. O, wie wird das enden!

Caspar. Umsonst ist der Tod! Nicht ohne Widerstand schenken verborgene Naturen den Sterblichen ihre Schätze. Nur wenn du mich selbst zittern siehst, dann komme mir zu Hülfe und rufe, was ich rufen werde, sonst sind wir beide verloren.

Max (macht eine Bewegung des Einwurfs).

Caspar. Still! Die Augenblicke sind kostbar! (Der Mond ist bis auf einen schmalen Streif verfinstert. Caspar nimmt die Giesskelle.) Merk' auf, [was ich hinein werfen werde,] damit du die Kunst lernst! (Er nimmt die Ingredienzen aus der Jagdtasche und wirft sie nach und nach hinein.)

Cas   Hier erst das Blei. Etwas gestossenes Glas von zerbroch'nen Kirchenfenstern, das findet sich. Etwas Quecksilber. Drei Kugeln, die schon einmal getroffen.

Cas   Das rechte Auge eines Wiedehopfs, das linke eines Luchses— *Probatum est!* Und nun den Kugelsegen!

(Die Masse in der Giesskelle fängt an zu gähren und zu zischen und giebt einen grünlich weissen Schein.
Eine Wolke läuft über den Mondreif, dass die ganze Gegend nur noch von dem Herdfeuer, den Augen der
Eule und dem faulen Holze des Baumes erleuchtet ist.)

Casp. Samiel!   Samiel!   Samiel!

Cas hilf!   Sieben!   Samiel! (Echo: Sieben) Samiel!   (Samiel erscheint.)
                                                                    Hier

Max (gleichfalls vom Sturme hin- und hergeschleudert, springt
aus dem Kreise, fasst einen Ast des verdorrten Baumes u. schreit):
Samiel! (In demselben Augenblicke fängt das Ungewitter an

Cas bin ich! (Caspar stürzt zu Boden.)

sich zu beruhigen, an der Stelle des

verdorrten Baumes steht der schwarze Jäger, nach Maxens Hand fassend.)

Samiel. Hier bin ich! (Max schlägt ein Kreuz und stürzt zu Boden.
Es schlägt Eins. Plötzliche Stille. — Samiel ist verschwunden. Caspar

liegt noch mit dem Gesicht zu Boden. Max richtet sich convulsivisch auf.)

pp Str. Quart. u. Pauke.

Ende des zweiten Aktes.

28

Franz Schubert (1787–1828)

Heidenröslein (Little Rose on the Heath) (1815)

Goethe's *Heidenröslein* (Little Rose on the Heath), a three-strophe poem with a refrain written in imitation of a folk-song text, is an example of a poetic genre that spread in Germany in the wake of Herder's promotion of the "folk" as a source of national pride. The subject of the poem, which tells of a boy picking a wild rose against its wishes, is a sustained metaphor for the deflowering of a maiden.

Schubert set the poem in 1815, at the age of eighteen. His song illustrates the strophic type of setting favored by Goethe: a single musical stanza that is repeated for each strophe of the poem. To match Goethe's asymmetrical five-line stanza (with a rhyme scheme abaab)—the least folk-like feature of Goethe's poem—Schubert constructs his stanza out of two melodic units of different lengths, a couplet (2+ 2) and a terzett (2 + 2 + 2).

In the first unit (mm. 1–4) each measure contains a single harmony, the whole describing a perfect cadence: The "artistic" challenge comes in the longer unit, where it becomes necessary to invent a three-stage harmonic design. Schubert makes a third phrase necessary, first by making m. 6 V⁷/V, a more restless harmony than the analogous second measure of the first unit, and next by ending the second phrase of the longer unit with a deceptive cadence (iii instead of V, the expected resolution in m. 8). Moreover, the five-line verse now ends with a half cadence, and it is left to the two-line refrain (mm. 11–14) to close things off with a full cadence. Thus the three cadences (couplet–terzett–refrain) together comprise a stable I–V–I progression, imparting a shapeliness and stability to the whole song despite the stanza's asymmetry.

But now take a closer look at the placement of the harmonies with respect to the words. In the second and the third stanzas, the tensest (most chromatic and dissonant) harmony—the "V⁷/V"—coincides with the promise and then the delivery of the rose's painful retaliation ("Ich steche dich," " . . . und stach" [I'll prick you . . . and pricked]). In *Heidenröslein*, despite the song's folksy character, formal strategy and poetic meaning are thoroughly combined as in only the most "artful" poems and songs. The eighteen-year-old Schubert was already a master of art-concealing art.

Sah ein Knab' ein Röslein stehn,
Röslein auf der Heiden,
War so jung und morgenschön,
Lief er schnell, es nah zu sehn,
Sah's mit vielen Freuden.
　Röslein, Röslein, Röslein rot,
　Röslein auf der Heiden.

Knabe sprach: Ich breche dich,
Röslein auf der Heiden!
Röslein sprach: Ich steche dich,
Dass du ewig denkst an mich,
Und ich will's nicht leiden.
　Röslein, etc.

Und der wilde Knabe brach
's Röslein auf der heiden;
Röslein wehrte sich und stach,
Half ihr doch kein Weh und Ach,
Musst' es eben leiden.
　Röslein, etc.

A boy saw a little rose growing,
A little rose upon the heath.
It was so young and morning-fresh,
He quickly ran to look at it up close.
He looked at it with much joy.
　Little rose, little rose, little red rose,
　Little rose upon the heath.

The boy said, I'll pluck you,
Little rose upon the heath!
The little rose said, I'll prick you,
So that you'll always think of me,
For I won't suffer it.
　Little rose, etc.

And the wild boy picked
The little rose upon the heath;
The little rose, defending itself, pricked away,
But no aches and pains helped it;
It had to suffer it all the same.
　Little rose, etc.

Sah ein Knab' ein Rös_lein_ stehn, Rös_lein auf der Hei _ den,
Kna_be sprach: ich bre _ che_ dich, Rös_lein auf der Hei _ den,
Und der wil _ de Kna _ be_ brach 'sRös_lein auf der Hei _ den;

war so jung und mor_genschön, lief er schnell es nah' zu sehn, sah's mit vie_len Freu_den.
Röslein sprach: ich ste_che dich, dass du e _ wig denkst an mich, und ich will's nicht lei _ den.
Röslein wehr_te sich und stach, half ihm doch kein Weh und Ach, musst' es e _ ben lei _ den.

Röslein, Röslein, Rös_lein roth, Röslein auf der Hei _ den.
Röslein, Röslein, Rös_lein roth, Röslein auf der Hei _ den.
Röslein, Röslein, Rös_lein roth, Röslein auf der Hei _ den.

29

Franz Schubert
(1787–1828)

FULL CD IV: TRACK 15
CONCISE CD II: TRACK 24

Erlkönig (The Elf King) (1815)

The most famous German ballad of its time, Goethe's "Erlkönig" (The Elf King) was originally written for the libretto of a Singspiel in 1782. It achieved fame when it was republished and set to music by Johann Friedrich Reichardt (1752–1814) in 1794.

Goethe modeled his poem on Herder's translation of a Danish folk ballad, in which a man riding at night meets with one of the Elf King's daughters. The topic is ancient, and it usually involves a supernatural female seductress and a mortal male victim. In Goethe's "Erlkönig" the seducer is the Elf King himself (mistranslated by Herder as Erl King), and his victim is a child in the agony of death. The sexual allure of the original is thus reoriented, and the story evokes another ancient subject, the temptation of death. Goethe contrasts the supernatural world with the rationality of the father who tries to protect his child, explaining away the nighttime visions as images and sounds of nature. He is powerless, however, against the spirits, who take the child in the end. Thus the Romantic themes of hidden reality, invisible truth, and the superiority of nature over culture are clothed in the imagery and diction of folklore.

Schubert's setting of "Erlkönig" went far beyond what Goethe considered appropriate for the musical settings of his poems. Schubert's music created both the natural imagery of a stormy night in the forest, measuring the passing of time and the approaching tragedy by the incessant hoof beats and the psychological drama inherent in the father's denial of his child's imminent death.

There are four "roles" in this narration, each characterized in relief against the unremitting gallop: the increasingly distraught child, the desperately consoling father, the grimly deadpan narrator who sets the scene and tells the outcome, and the sinister and beguiling title character. During the Elf King's lines the hoof beats fade into the background, the unremitting triplets turning into seductive dance figures (see the change in the accompaniment at mm. 56–69 and 84–93). Yet the sound of the hoof beats is transformed into sweet music only in the child's imagination, only he hears the Elf King. The moment the child calls out to his father, the sound of reality returns with double force, cruelly urging forward time, which seems to be suspended during the Elf King's sweet interludes. Reinforcing the spooky sweetness of the interludes, Schubert casts them in major keys, which contrast sharply with the minor-key nightmare music

that surrounds them. The Elf King appears first in the relative major (B♭, mm. 56ff), then in the subdominant major (C, mm. 84ff), and finally in the submediant (E♭, mm. 114ff). In the long horrific middle of the song (from the Elf King's first appeal to the child until his last) successive cadences are pitched hair-raisingly on ascending half steps. Using capital letters to represent major keys and lowercase for minor, the astonishing progression of tonics is B♭–b–C–c♯–d–E♭ (mm. 56, 79, 84, 103, 109, and 114).

Also perhaps unprecedented is the intensity of dissonance that underlines the boy's cries, "Mein Vater!" (my father!). At these points the harmony could be described as a dominant-ninth chord, with the root in the pianist's right hand. The voice has the ninth and the left hand has the seventh. The result is a series of virtual "tone clusters" (D against E♭ and C at m. 71; E against F and D at m. 95; and F against G♭ and E♭, at m. 123). The harmonic logic of these progressions, within the rules of composition Schubert was taught, can be demonstrated. That logic, however, is not what appeals so strongly to the listener's imagination; rather, it is the impression of wild abandon.

Perhaps the gloomiest aspect of Schubert's setting, however, is the cadences that initially underline the father's rational explanations but at the end, instead of consoling the frightened child, signal his death. The child's third and last outcry ends with a cadence in the original key of G minor (m. 128). The father, his authoritarian gestures of closure taken over by his dying child, speaks no more and the narrator finishes the story. The Elf King, a figment of the sick child's confused imagination, disappears with the child's death. Even the narrator, detached as he is from the story, reacts to the tragic death by abandoning melody in a slow recitative at the end (an operatic device Schubert also used in other ballad settings). In the last three measures the pounding of the piano stops, as if music had no power to express the father's grief.

Wer reitet so spät durch Nacht und Wind?	Who rides so late through night and wind?
Es ist der Vater mit seinem Kind:	It is the father with his child.
er hat den Knaben wohl in dem Arm,	He holds the boy in his arms,
er fasst ihn sicher, er hält ihn warm.	he clasps him firmly, he keeps him warm.
"Mein Sohn, was birgst du so bang dein Gesicht?"	"My son, why do you hide your face so fearfully?"
"Siehst, Vater, du den Erlkönig nicht?	"Father, don't you see the Elf King?
Den Erlenkönig mit Kron' und Schweif?"	The Elf King with his crown and train?"
"Mein Sohn, es ist ein Nebelstreif."	"My son, it is a patch of mist."
"Du liebes Kind, komm, geh mit mir!	"Come dear child, go with me!
Gar schöne Spiele spiel ich mit dir;	I will play beautiful games with you;
manch' bunte Blumen sind an dem Strand;	many are the bright flowers on the shore,
meine Mutter hat manch' gülden Gewand."	my mother has many robes of gold."

353

"Mein Vater, mein Vater, und hörest du nicht,	"My father, my father, and do you not hear
was Erlenkönig mir leise verspricht?"	what the Elf King softly promises me?"
"Sei ruhig, bleibe ruhig, mein Kind:	"Be calm, keep calm, my child:
in dürren Blättern säuselt der Wind."	in dry leaves the wind is rustling."
"Willst, feiner Knabe, du mit mir gehn?	"Will you go with me, brave boy?
Meine Töchter sollen dich warten schön;	My daughters shall tend you nicely.
meine Töchter führen den nächtlichen Reihn	My daughters will lead the dancing each night
und wiegen und tanzen und singen dich ein."	and will lull and dance and sing for you."
"Mein Vater, mein Vater, und siehst du nicht dort	"My father, my father, don't you see over there
Erlkönigs Töchter am düstern Ort?"	the Elf King's daughters in that deserted spot?"
"Mein Sohn, mein Sohn, ich seh es genau:	"My son, my son, I see it perfectly,
es scheinen die alten Weiden so grau."	the old willows look so gray."
"Ich liebe dich, mich reizt deine schöne Gestalt;	"I love you, I am charmed by your good looks,
und bist du nicht willig, so brauch ich Gewalt."	and if you are not willing, I shall have to use force."
"Mein Vater, mein Vater, jetzt fasst er mich an!	"My father, my father, he's clutching me now!
Erlkönig hat mir ein Leids getan!"	The Elf King has hurt me!"
Dem Vater grauset's, er reitet geschwind,	The father shudders, he rides apace;
er hält in den Armen das ächzende Kind,	in his arms he holds the groaning child.
erreicht den Hof mit Müh' und Not:	Sweating and straining he reaches the courtyard;
in seinen Armen das Kind war tot.	in his arms the child lay dead.

30

Franz Schubert (1787–1828)

FULL CD IV: TRACK 16
CONCISE CD II: TRACK 25

Moments musicaux (Musical moments), No. 6, D. 780 (1823–28)

Schubert's *Moments musicaux* (Musical moments) is a collection of short, self-contained piano pieces composed between 1823 and 1828 and published as a set in 1828. Simple in form, these pieces contain daring harmonic and tonal adventures as well as typically Schubertian enigmatic gestures. Although the descriptive title "musical moments" originated from the publisher, it captures the Romantic aspiration of Schubert's music by suggesting that the pieces draw the listener into a musical trance experienced outside of real time.

The sixth *Moment musical,* in A♭ major, is an enigmatic piece that expresses this uncanny sense of stopping time. Instead of following conventional circle-of-fifths progressions, Schubert's music wanders off into functionally perplexing flat submediant (♭VI) and Neapolitan (♭II) areas, transporting the listener into the realm of "the beyond." This odd tonal trajectory is cast in the old minuet-and-trio form. Here the enigmatic music of the first part surrounds a tonally clear trio.

The music preceding the first repeat sign constitutes a sixteen-measure period that encapsulates a "normal" binary procedure: eight measures out (I–V) and eight measures back (V–I). The music following the first repeat is far out of proportion with respect to the first section: sixty-one measures versus sixteen! The prolonged excursion to the key areas of ♭VI and ♭II so bloat its length. This section begins right off on the flat submediant (F♭), which initially functions as the bass of an augmented-sixth chord (a "German sixth"), which resolves to the minor form of the tonic (m. 18). At the change of key signature, however, F♭ (spelled enharmonically as E) is reinterpreted as a temporary tonic; thus the whole passage enclosed within the new key signature (mm. 29–39) is in fact a prolongation of ♭VI, a chord often associated with Romantic introspection.

With return of the original key signature (m. 40) Schubert respells E as F♭ and returns to the realm of A♭ major. But before Schubert brings the section to a close in the tonic key he makes yet another harmonically far-off excursion, again signaled by a change of key signature. Although the key signature has four sharps, all Ds are natural, so the key is A major, the

enharmonic equivalent of B♭♭ or the Neapolitan (♭II) in A♭. (Note that the chord that begins this section in m. 66 uses the same pitches—enharmonically respelled—as the augmented-sixth chord that launched the entire second section of the work in m. 17.)

Immediately after appearing in root position in m. 68, the A-major chord passes to its first inversion and progresses perfectly normally, in mm. 69–70, as a Neapolitan resolving to the dominant of the original key. Yet once again the composer postpones resolution with one more spin to the tonicized Neapolitan and one more repossession of A♭, this time in a resigned *pianissimo.*

The final resolution is not a chord at all, but a hollow doubled octave that leaves the mode unspecified. In a piece so rife with major–minor mixtures and sudden tonal shifts, an unambiguously major or minor concluding chord might have seemed too decisive a resolution. Beside the modal ambiguities, Schubert's transformation of chords and keys like the flat submediant and the Neapolitan into potentially stable, static moments lends Schubert's music the quintessentially Romantic quality of timelessness.

Allegretto D.C.

• dynamics fp — pp, p. (fortepiano)
   smaller venue
   subtle.

• rhythmic motive → short-long ($\frac{3}{4}$)

• organum m. 34

31

Franz Schubert
(1787–1828)

FULL CD IV: TRACK 17

Symphony No. 8 in B Minor ("Unfinished"),
D. 759, First movement (*Allegro moderato*) (1822)

Nobody knows why Schubert abandoned his Symphony in B Minor, two movements of which he finished in October 1822. The incompleteness of the symphony has, however, increased the fascination aroused by this dark work.

Schubert's choice of key, B minor, was almost completely unheard of as the key of a symphonic *Allegro* in Schubert's time. Also unusual for a symphony was Schubert's decision to begin the work with a "Preface theme." Although the first movement of the "Unfinished" Symphony adheres to the conventions of sonata form, its key structure is unusual: In the exposition the "second theme" appears in the key of the submediant (♭VI, G) as opposed to the relative major, the conventional secondary key area for works in minor; in the recapitulation this theme appears not in the customary tonic but in the relative major (III, D).

Starting the movement with a "Preface theme" in unison was not entirely new; it has precedent in Beethoven's oeuvre. But while in Beethoven this type of introduction is usually assertive, Schubert's unison theme, played *pianissimo* in the low registers of the cellos and double basses, creates a mysterious, mournful effect. (The register is so low that the double bass, which can normally reach down only to low E, needs an extension or an additional string to play the D and C♯.) Part of the enigma of the "Preface theme" is that it ends on a long F♯ ($\hat{5}$) arrived at in the sixth of its eight measures, which prevents it from feeling balanced or closed.

The primary theme and the murmuring in the violins that introduces it owe a debt to the first three notes of the "Preface" theme: the initial sixteenth-note accompanimental figures in the violins include this stepwise rising motive with the same pitches in the second violin (B–C♯–D, m. 9). The motive occurs transposed as A♯–B–C♯ in the first violin (m. 10), and this version of it also occurs in the oboe and clarinet's rendition of the primary theme (mm. 14, 16). Despite the regular length of its first part (8 mm.), the primary theme, like the "Preface theme," does not bring a sense of structural balance. Although it cadences in D major (m. 20), it then expands, as if transforming itself into a bridge section, only to cadence back in tonic B minor at

Measure Nos.	Formal Designation	Sections	Keys	Comments
1–111	**Exposition**		[b/G]	
1–8		"Preface theme"	b	Ends on F♯ (implying half cadence)
9–38		Primary theme	b	The theme proper begins after 4-measure introduction
26–38		False/nonmodulating bridge		May be considered part of the primary theme area because of cadence in tonic key
38–41		Bridge		
42–104		Secondary theme	G	In aba form with development-like middle section (mm. 63–93)
104–115		Transition		
115–218	**Development**	"Preface theme"	e, c♯, d, e, f♯, e	
219–328	**Recapitulation**			
219–253		Primary theme	b, f#	Cadences on f♯
253–257		Bridge		
257–329		Secondary theme	D	
329–369	**Coda**		b	Closure of "Preface theme"

m. 38. The real transition between the first and second themes occupies just four measures, of which only the last carries out the actual modulation (m. 41).

The secondary theme, in the Romantically charged submediant key, is reminiscent of Viennese piano music for domestic consumption. The theme is constructed a bit like these piano pieces in a miniature aba form, its b section constituting a development-like middle section (mm. 63–93) that breaks out of its domestic frame.

The real development section is based on the "Preface theme," fragmented and exquisitely reshaped to reach up instead of down (violin, mm. 123–26). The A♯ that ends this gesture in m. 126 creates an uncanny augmented-sixth chord, implying resolution through a B dominant chord to E minor, the development's point of departure at m. 115. But resolution to E minor is put off by deceptive resolutions and harmonic exploration all the way until m. 171, where the *fortissimo, tutti* appearance of the "Preface theme" has the rhetorical power of a recapitulation.

The real recapitulation occurs in an understated *pianissimo*-like the beginning of the movement but without the "Preface theme", which would have little novelty here due to its heavy use in the development. The recapitulation of the second theme occurs in the mediant (D major), a key that balances the theme's submediant key in the exposition. The coda (mm. 329ff) returns to the "Preface theme," its final F♯ now harmonized for the first time with a dominant-seventh chord (m. 336) that progresses to a full resolution.

Despite its adherence to symphonic traditions, Schubert's "Unfinished" Symphony creates a new symphonic tone in which passion and violence break through the placid surface at unexpected moments, in which third relations take precedence over tonal movement along the circle of fifths, and in which symmetrical phrase structure and tonal closure are the exception rather than the rule.

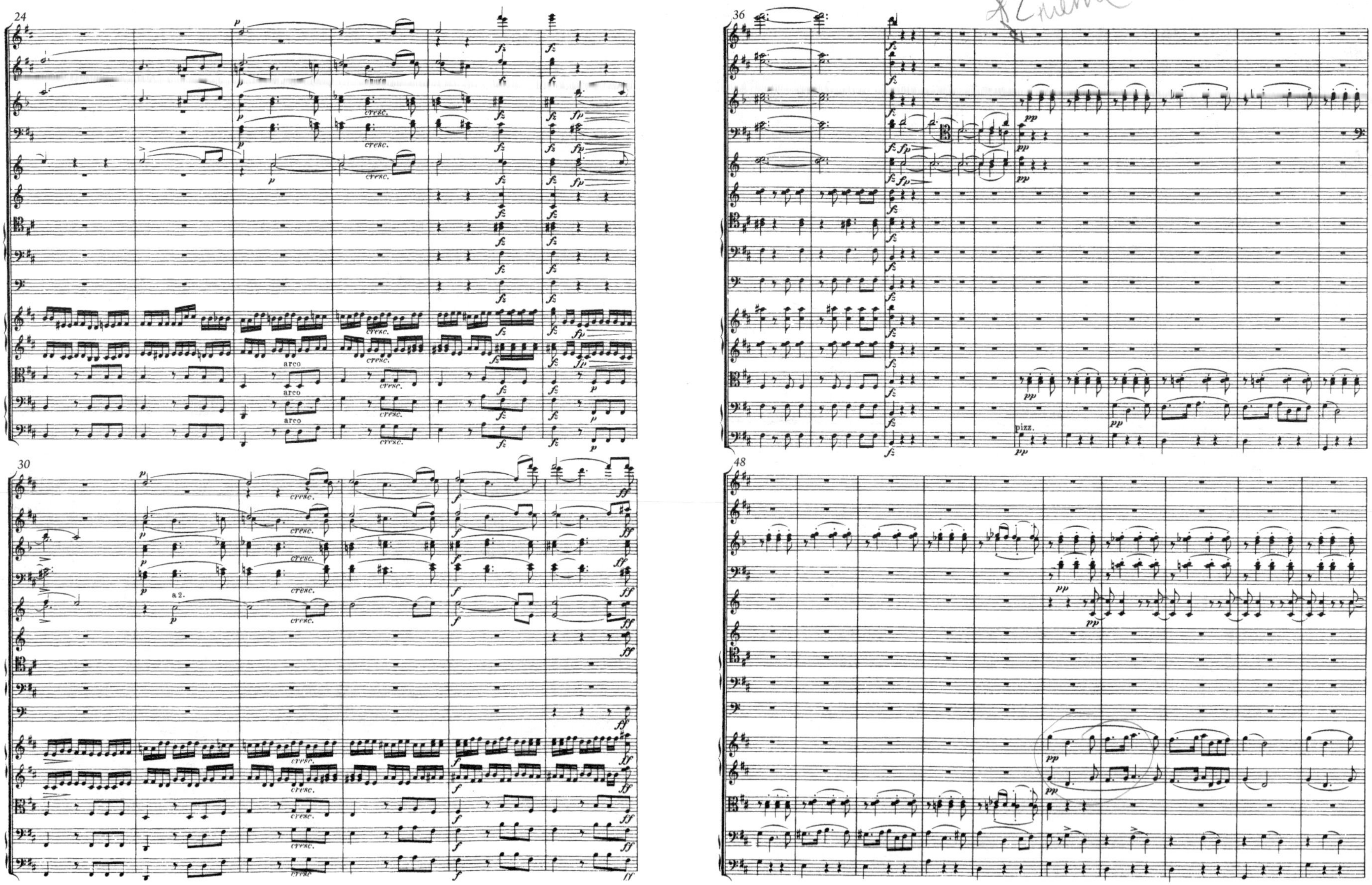
24
30
36
48
a 2.
arco
pizz.
cresc.

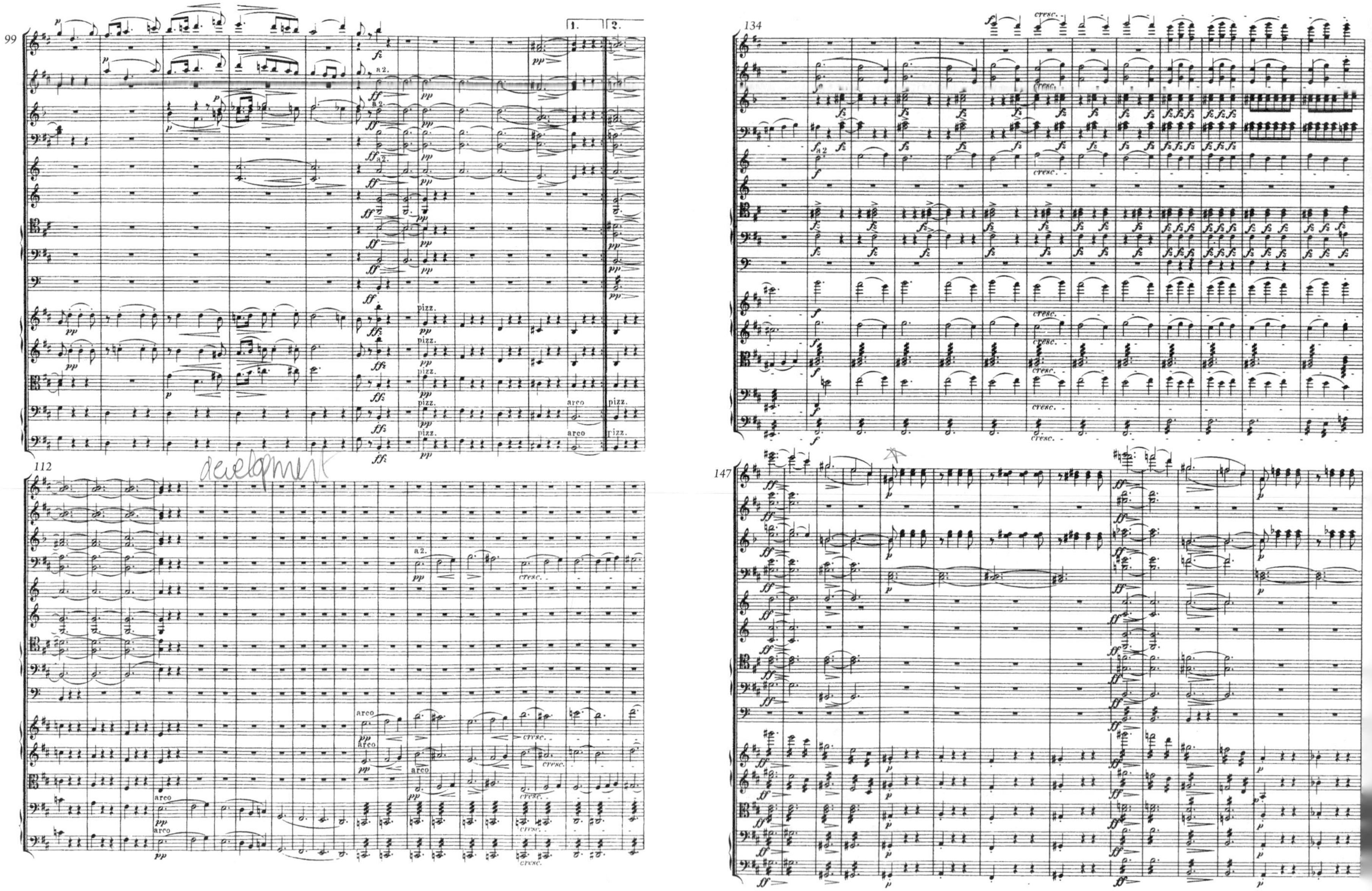
99
112
134
147
a 2.
pizz.
arco
cresc.
development

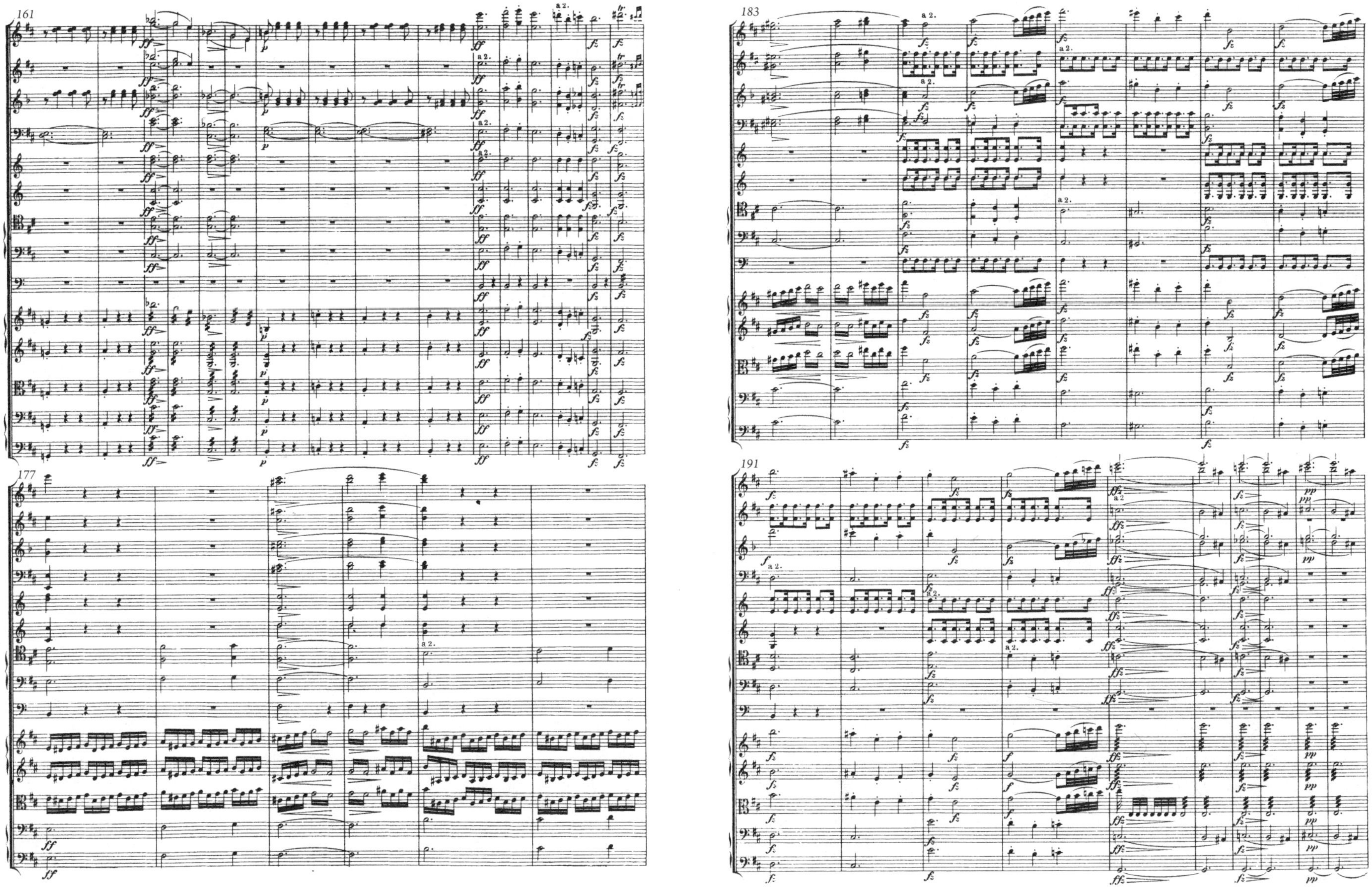
161
177
183
191

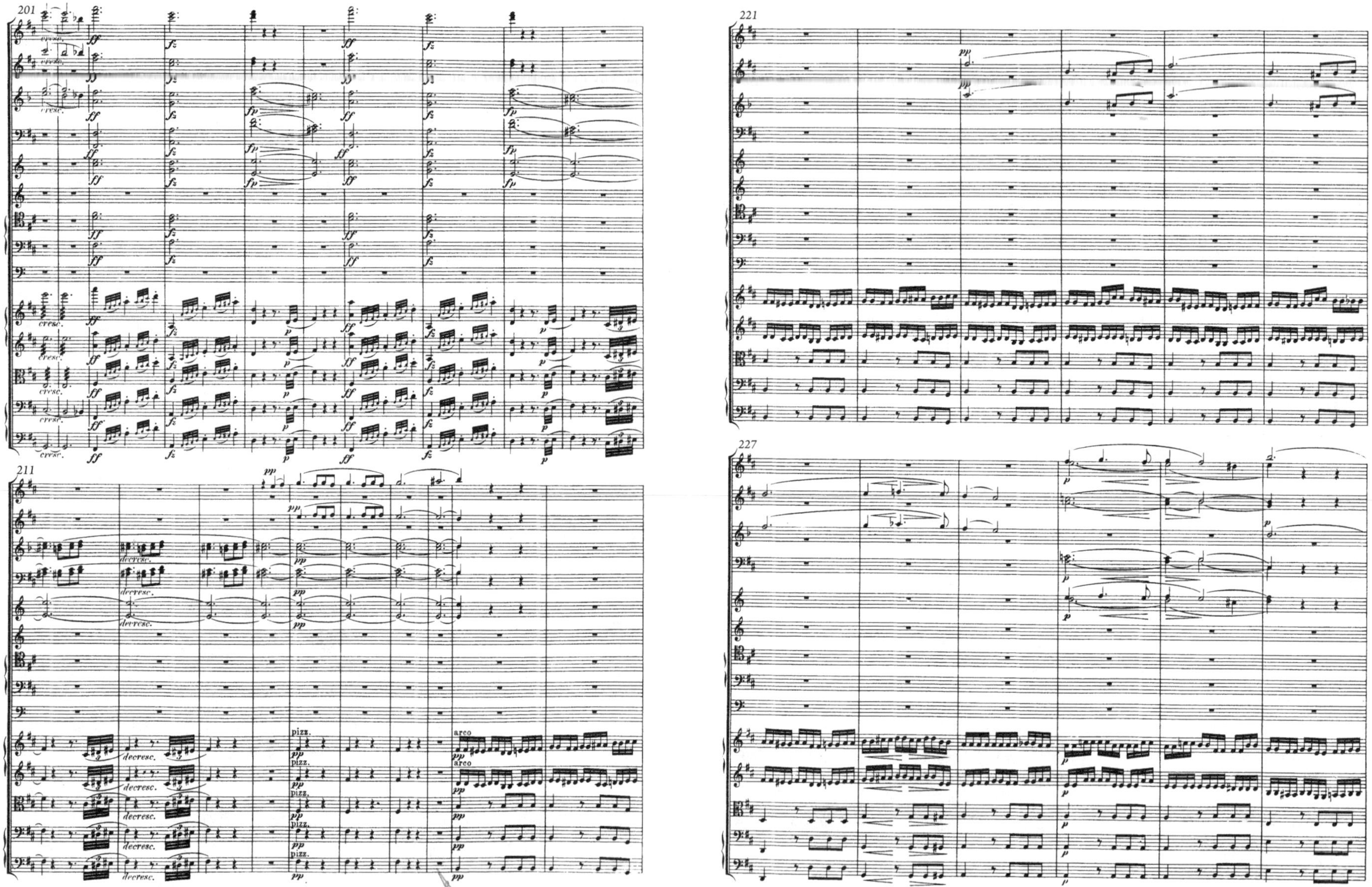
201
cresc.
ff
fz
fp
p
211
decresc.
pp
pizz.
arco
221
227

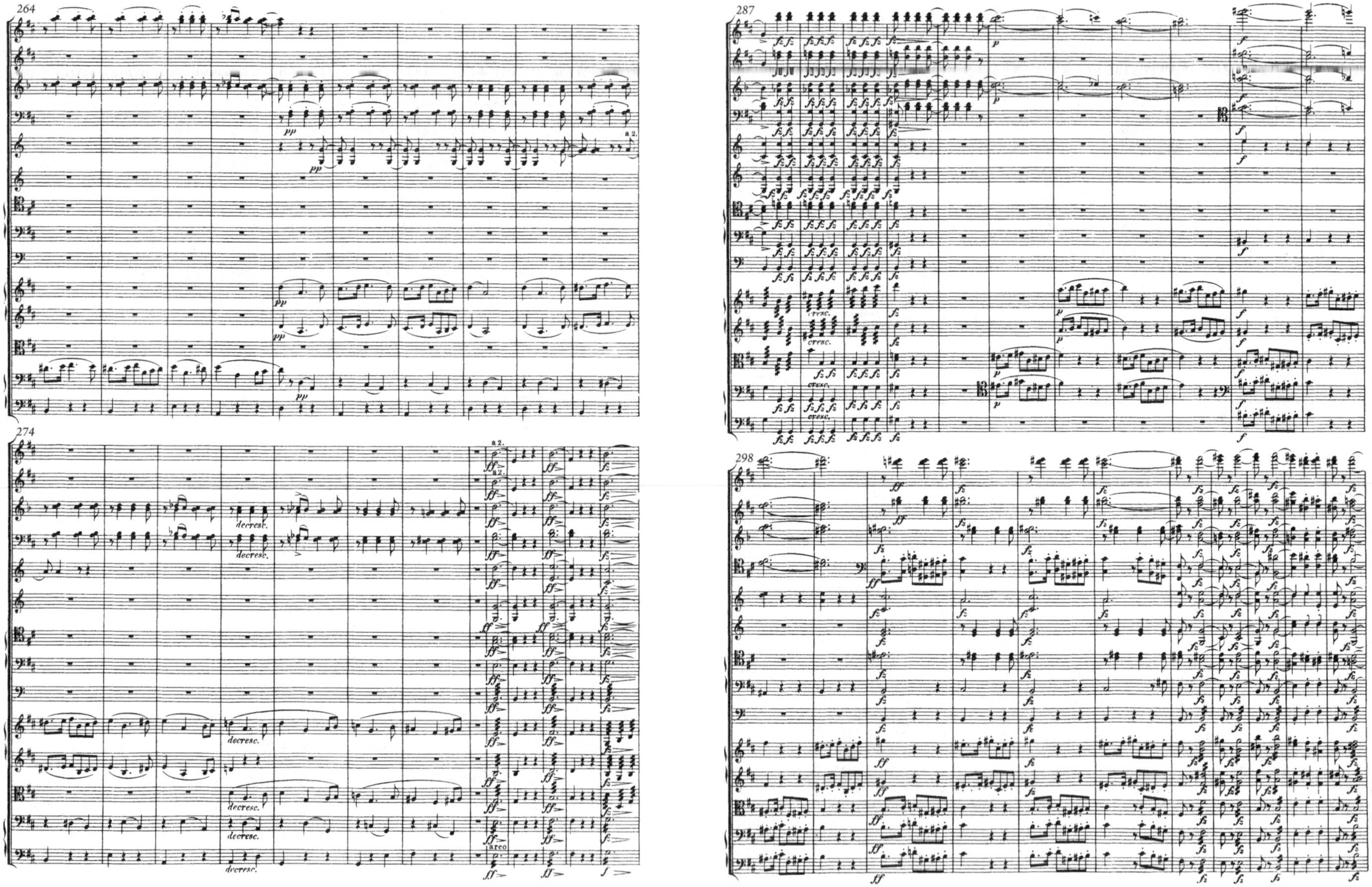
264
pp
a 2.
274
decresc.
a 2.
ff
arco
287
cresc.
298
ff

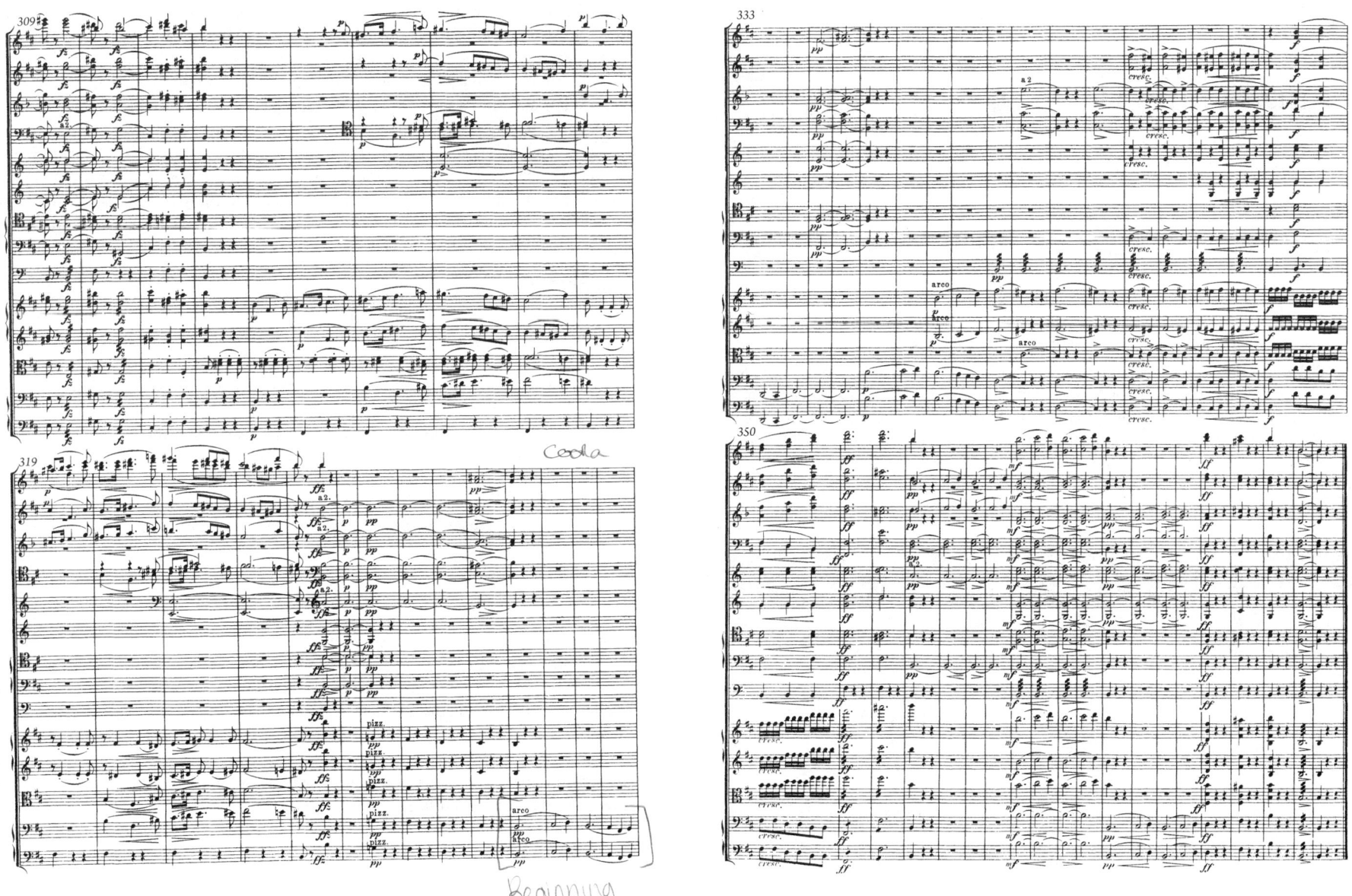

32

Franz Schubert
(1787–1828)

Piano Trio in E♭ Major, Op. 100, D. 929,
Second movement (*Andante con moto*) (1828)

Schubert began to compose his Trio in E♭ Major for violin, cello, and piano in late 1827 and completed it in 1828. It was first performed on 26 March 1828 at a concert Schubert gave on the first anniversary of Beethoven's death. The significance of the date is highlighted by Schubert's modeling the theme of the C-minor slow movement of the Trio on the theme of Beethoven's C-minor funeral march in the *Eroica* Symphony. There are even more references hidden in Schubert's theme. Its most striking melodic gestures, the descending figure in mm. 11–12, the octave leaps in mm. 15–16, and the upward-soaring tenths in mm. 17–19, are all borrowed from a Swedish song, "See, the Sun Is Setting."

Measure Nos.	Formal Designation	Sections	Keys	Comments
1–21	A	Main theme	c	Melody in cello, accompaniment in piano
21–41	A		c	Melody in piano, accompaniment in strings
41–84	B	Episode	E♭ (ends on V in c)	
84–104	A		c	
104–129	C	Development		Works with material of the main theme
129–195	B	Episode	C	
196–212	A	Main theme	c	Theme abbreviated

The second movement is a rondo in which Schubert uses the a particular episode twice, somewhat like a second theme in sonata form in that it appears first in the relative major and again in the tonic major after a development section.

In this simple framework Schubert focuses the listener's attention on intricate and exquisite musical details. The structure and the melodic gestures of the main theme are reminiscent of song. The dominant G and the tonic C in the melody seem to have a mesmerizing effect—the melody unfailingly gravitates toward these two notes. In contrast to the lyrical, free-flowing melody, the accompaniment proceeds with dry, staccato eighth notes in rigid march rhythm. The combination is reminiscent of the slow movement of Beethoven's Seventh Symphony, another haunting slow movement in minor.

The text of the Swedish song Schubert borrowed had the words "farewell, farewell" set to the descending leaping octaves of the theme—an appropriate expression of loss at a concert in memory of Beethoven. This leap, emphasized by echoes in the piano (mm. 14–16), becomes an important motive in both the bass and melody of the B section. The interval may change (in m. 17 it shrinks to a third, an interval that will become the building block of the thematic material starting in m. 57), but the descending gesture, with an accent on the first note entering off the beat, remains thematically significant. Thirds are also important on a tonal level. The main harmonic areas in the movement are C major/minor and E♭ major, with the "far out point" a minor third higher, spelled F♯ minor (mm. 116ff). After the recapitulation of the second theme in C major, the music has a short excursion to A major (mm. 158–163) and F major (mm. 164–166), thus exploring other third-related tonal areas.

Another detail that has long-range reverberations is Schubert's exploitation of bass motion by half step. The first such motion occurs in the deceptive resolution of the dominant G to A♭ in the course of the first theme (m. 19). Schubert later introduces the explosive development section with the same progression—locally a repetition of the deceptive progression in the main theme two measures earlier. Throughout the development, half-step motion in the bass is Schubert's main device for initiating modulation.

In the final, slowed-down appearance of the main theme in m. 198, only the first line of the melody returns, first in the piano, then unison in the strings. Both appearances contain distortions: The piano plays the melody with A natural (m. 200) instead of A♭, as if misremembering the original; the strings omit the leap to E♭, replacing it with C in m. 205 and with G in m. 207, while the bass engages in one last chromatic excursion. The movement closes with the strings' *pianissimo* octave leaps, as if repeating the "farewell" of the song on which the theme is based. These last measures sound as if they are emerging from the depths of memory, concluding the movement with a sense of nostalgia and loss. It is in these details that Schubert's music gains poetic meaning.

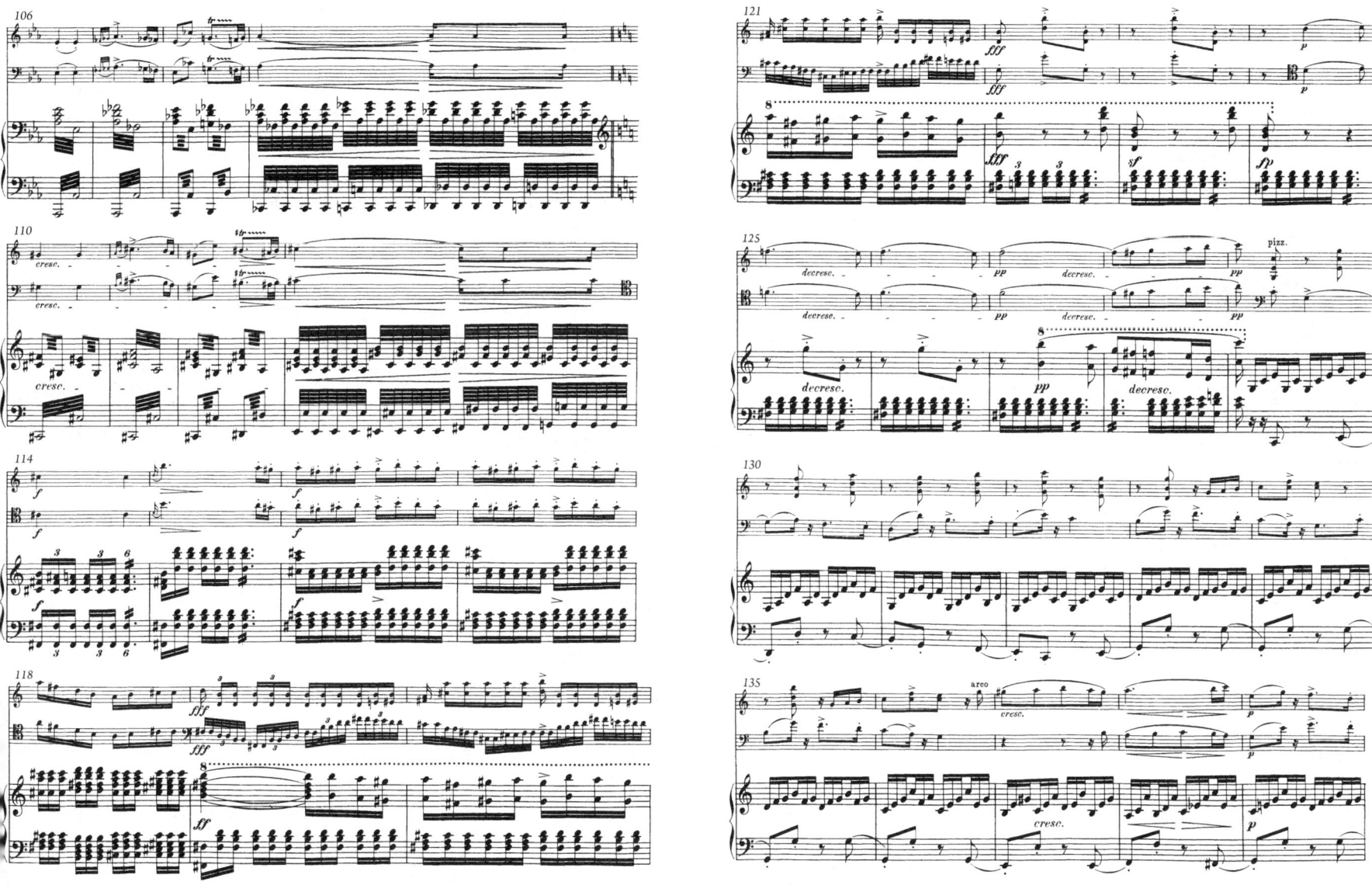

33

Franz Schubert (1787–1828)

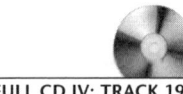

Der Doppelgänger (The Double) (1828)

One of Schubert's last masterpieces is *Der Doppelgänger*, from the posthumously published song cycle *Schwanengesang* (Swan song). Unlike in Schubert's earlier song cycles, the songs of *Schwanengesang* were not intended by Schubert to form a cycle, but were made into one by the composer's publisher. *Der Doppelgänger* is the most psychologically disturbing of the set. In it the poet confronts the Romantic subject of mental disintegration. The poem is from the collection *Buch der Lieder* (Songbook, 1827) by Heinrich Heine (1797–1856), Schubert's exact though longer-lived contemporary and a poet closely associated with the depiction of extreme or neurotic mental states triggered by thwarted desire. In *Doppelgänger* Heine addresses a subject that haunted Romantic artists as a metaphor for existential loneliness: the theme of dissociation, or "out of body" experience. The poem describes the protagonist's returning to the scene of his unhappy love and encountering his old self. There is no nature imagery, no folk-like simplicity—instead, urban alienation and its psychological consequences are presented with painfully bitter self-irony.

Schubert captures the poem's obsessional mood by building his song on a four-measure ostinato that runs through it like an incessant thought and provides a frame for the voice's breathless phrases in quasi-recitative. The melody of the ostinato is "harmonized" by a single note, an F♯ that provides a nearly constant pedal (it is omitted only in mm. 41, 48, 50–51, 59, and 61). There are two fixed and two variable notes in the ostinato. The B and D are unalterable, whereas A♯ and C♯ are often lowered by a half step, enhancing the effect of weirdness and abnormality.

The climax of the song occurs on one of the eerie alterations (C natural in the bass, m. 41) when, in response to recognizing his own horrifying image in the face of a stranger, the singer breaks through F♯ to G, his highest note. Harmonically the augmented-sixth chord supporting this climax does not provide an analogous escape but returns to the tonic, B minor (m. 43), the key dictated by the ostinato. Despite this momentary tonal return, the climax does briefly liberate the music from the ostinato and initiates a brief chromatic rise that culminates, at mm. 47–50, in an escape to D♯ minor.

At the end Schubert changes the last "chord" of the ostinato pattern by exchanging the F♯–C♯ open fifth of the original version with a C-major chord, the Neapolitan in B minor

(m. 59). Here as elsewhere the appearance of C points to possible relief. This C-major chord functions as ♭VI, leading to a B⁷ chord, the dominant of E minor. The song does not, however, end with an E-minor chord. The last chord we hear is a B-major triad, which can be interpreted both as the original tonic with a Picardi third or as a half cadence in E minor. Harmonic and tonal tensions accumulated in the song are thus not resolved, suggesting that in Heine and Schubert's world there is no conventional road leading out of a damaged psychological state.

Still ist die Nacht, es ruhen die Gassen,	The night is quiet; the streets are still;
in diesem Hause wohnte mein Schatz.	in this house lived my beloved.
Sie hat schon längst die Stadt verlassen	She left the town long ago,
doch steht noch das Haus auf demselben Platz.	but the house still stands in the same place.
Da steht auch ein Mensch, und starrt in die Höhe,	There, too, stands a man, and stares aloft,
und ringt die Hände vor Schmerzensgewalt;	and wrings his hands with the weight of his grief.
mir graut es, wenn ich sein Antlitz sehe,	I am filled with horror when I see his face;
der Mond zeigt mir meine eig'ne Gestalt.	the moon shows me my own features.
Du Doppelgänger, du bleicher Geselle!	You ghostly double, you pale companion!
Was äffst du nach mein Liebesleid,	Why do you ape my pain of love
das mich gequält auf dieser Stelle	that tortured me in this place,
so manche Nacht, in alter Zeit?	for many a night in time gone by?

34

Niccolò Paganini
(1782–1840)

Caprices, Op. 1, Nos. 17 and 24 (ca. 1805/1820)

Niccolò Paganini, the greatest violin virtuoso of the early nineteenth century, published only five pieces with opus numbers in his lifetime, all in 1820, although many of them were composed earlier. The scarcity of publications indicates Paganini's emphasis on performance as his main artistic expression; it also shows his fear of being copied and his belief that only he could play at the technical level required by his music.

In Paganini's day "caprice" and "capriccio" referred both to bravura cadenzas and to etudes. Paganini modeled his Caprices, Op. 1, on the free cadenzas (*capricci ad libitum*) in Pietro Locatelli's 1733 *L'arte del violino* (The Art of the Violin). Paganini's Caprices are also etudes, in the sense that they are studies in expanding the technical and expressive potential of the violin.

Caprice No. 17 demonstrates important technical innovations exploited by Paganini: downshifting on a single string, required by the rapid descending chromatic runs, and all manner of multiple stops (playing more than one note simultaneously on a string instrument), especially parallel octaves, which, because of the extreme speed, requires the rapid alternation of different pairs of fingers. (Paganini's adoption of a relatively flat bridge and his positioning the neck of his violin at a greater-than-usual angle aided the playing of multiple stops.) A simple formal structure provides the frame for the display of virtuosity. Four measures of slow introduction prepare the *Andante* section, which consists of two-measure units based on the almost mechanical alteration of textually and technically contrasting phrases: ascending and descending thirty-second-note runs in the high register complemented with ascending or descending eighth-note double stops (two-note chords) in the low register. Both the fast runs and the slower double stops have diatonic and chromatic versions. Although purposely simple, the structure of the first part follows conventional tonal procedures: the establishment of the tonic key, E♭ major, a longer stay on the dominant (mm. 7–11), a modulatory section that suggests the dominant of F minor (mm. 12–13) and then of E♭ minor (mm. 14–15). Continuous rapid runs, gradually shrinking and then expanding in range, lead us back to the return of the home key and the first tonic section (mm. 20–23). The contrasting middle section features parallel octaves in the relative minor. It leaves C minor for only two measures (mm. 32–33) to emphasize the dominant of the relative major.

The most well known of the Caprices is the last, No. 24. Its eleven variations are based on a 4 × 4-measure A-minor theme, the third section of which tonicizes D minor and then C major. In the variations the harmonic structure of the theme remains intact, while the melody is varied widely, each variation exhibiting a different virtuoso technique. The first variation is built on descending eighth-note triplets to be played *jeté*, that is, with a thrown bow stroke. Known also as *ricochet*, this bowing technique involves the player's throwing the bow on the string on a down-bow and allowing it to bounce so as to produce a series of rapid notes. The second, sixteenth-note variation is built on legato string crossings, in which the player rapidly switches between two strings. The third variation, like the middle section of No. 17, is written in Paganini's signature parallel octaves. Variation four shows chromatic downshifting, also familiar from No. 17. The special difficulty of the fifth variation is the extremely fast register changes combined with broken octaves. Variation six shows off parallel motion in thirds and in tenths, requiring maximum stretch of the fingers. The seventh variation, built on sixteenth-note triplets, displays quick register changes, asking for rapid string crossings between the lowest (G) and highest (E) strings. In the eighth variation Paganini uses triple stopping, which requires the violinist to play on three strings simultaneously. The technically most exciting variation is the ninth, which shows Paganini's famous left-hand pizzicato, in which notes are produced by plucking the string with the left hand (normally used for fingering) instead of the right hand, which holds the bow. The penultimate variation is played in an extremely high register, creating an eerie sound. The last variation, like Caprice No. 17, contrasts double-stopped passages with fast arpeggios. Paganini added a "Finale" to the last variation, expanding the previous technical idea so that it reaches maximum speed and maximum effect. These showpieces raise virtuosity to a level at which technique becomes a generating force.

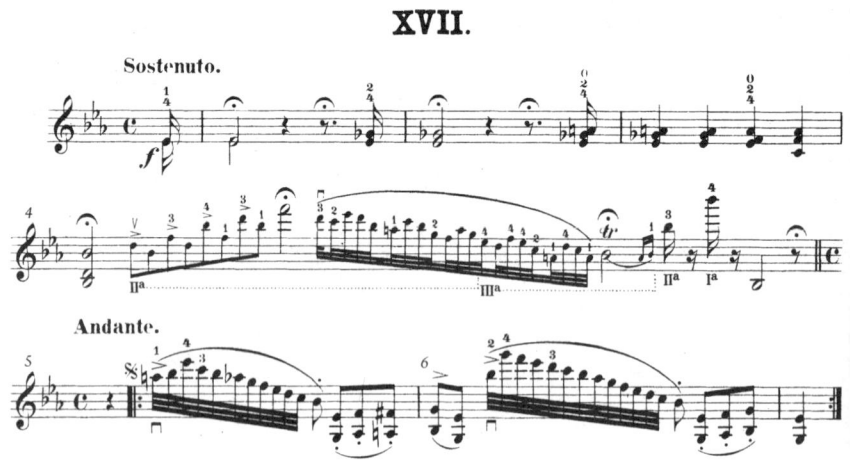

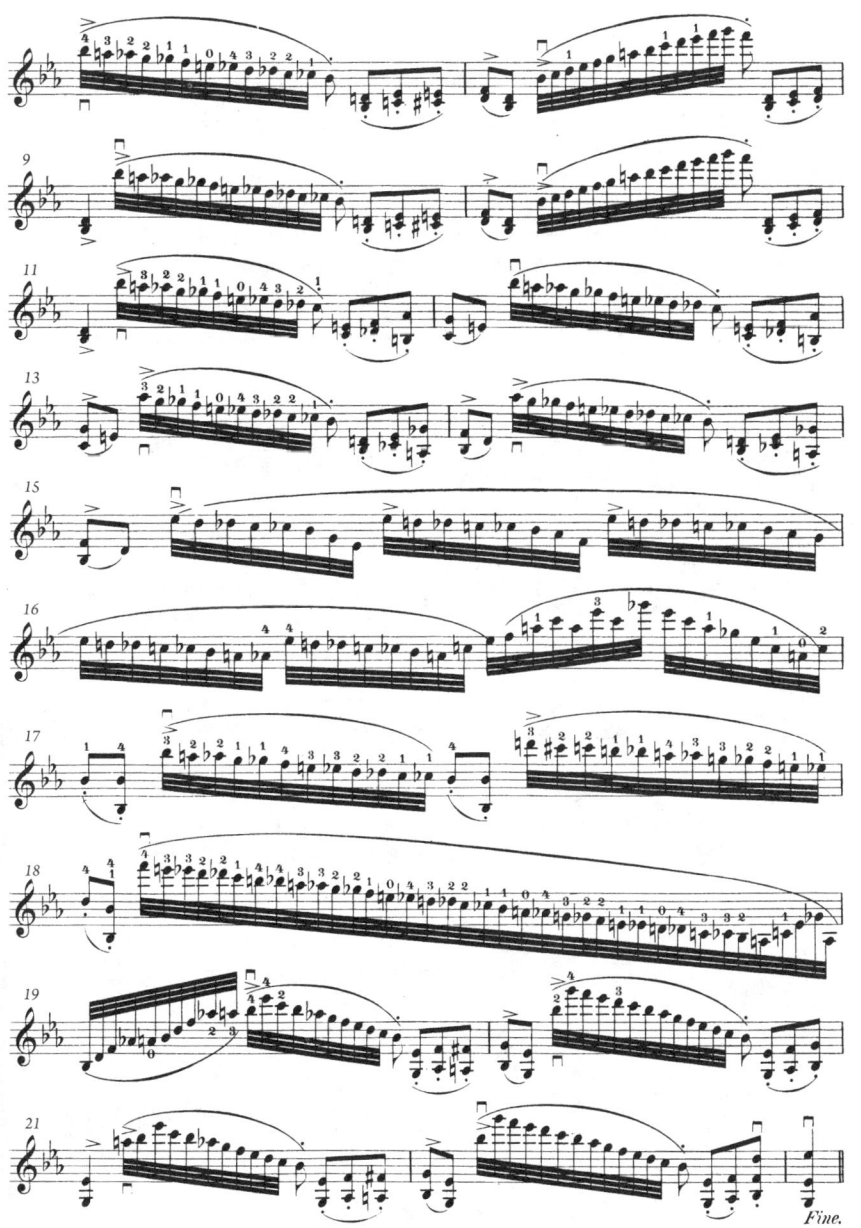

D. C. sino al Fine senza replica.

35

Franz Liszt
(1811–86)

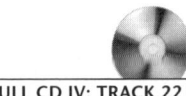

FULL CD IV: TRACK 22

Grandes Études d'après Paganini (Grand Studies after Paganini), No. 6 (1851)

In April 1832 the twenty-one-year old Liszt attended Paganini's concert at the Paris Opéra. Astonished by Paganini's superhuman virtuosity, Liszt decided to develop a new piano technique that could match Paganini's innovations on the violin. He shut himself up for many hours a day to experiment, as he wrote to a friend, with "thirds, sixths, octaves, tremolos, repetition of notes, cadenzas, etc." These experiments resulted in a revolution in keyboard playing. The first fruits of Liszt's new virtuosity were his planned *Vingt-quatres grandes études pour le piano* (Twenty-four grand studies for the piano, 1837–39), twelve of which were published in Vienna in 1839 and later became known as the *Études d'exécution transcendante* (Transcendental studies, 1851). More directly related to Paganini are Liszt's *Études d'exécution transcendante d'après Paganini* (Transcendental studies after Paganini, 1838–40), six grand etudes that Liszt derived from Paganini's Caprices. After performing them several times in public, Liszt published a revised version of his six etudes in 1851 under the title *Grandes études de Paganini* (Grand studies of Paganini), bringing them closer to Paganini's originals.

Although pianists other than Liszt originally considered the etudes almost unplayable, for him virtuosity was not simply a display of technical bravura. It was also a means for expanding the piano's expressive potential. Liszt's innovations involved developing fluency with unusual fingerings, leaps, and hand crossings that matched other pianists' command over more traditional techniques. To the dismay of piano teachers, his new approach required a major overhaul of earlier piano pedagogy.

Etude No. 6, the piano rendition of the twenty-fourth of Paganini's 24 Caprices (see the previous entry in this anthology), demonstrates many of the innovative techniques Liszt developed. Instead of simply transcribing Paganini's violin variations for the piano, Liszt translated the technical difficulties Paganini displayed in the Caprices into analogous technical challenges for the piano. In the first variation, for instance, he combines Paganini's descending arpeggios (played by the right hand) with the original theme (played by the left hand). The additions are even more challenging in the third variation. To Paganini's parallel octaves, now given to the

piano's left hand, Liszt adds a variation on the original theme in octave parallels in the right hand. Octave reinforcement seems to be the rule of thumb in many of the piano variations, although not all octave parallels have the same effect. In variation four, for example, Liszt uses a fingering that allows the chromatically descending parallel octaves to sound *legato*. Fingering was an important part of Liszt's new technique. The successive 2–4 fingerings for the left hand's parallel thirds in variation six help create a *martellato* (hammered) sound perhaps reminiscent of Paganini's cutting tone on the violin. In variation five Liszt re-creates the effect of Paganini's sudden register changes and translates the physical difficulties of Paganini's work to the keyboard by replacing the violin's broken octaves with tumults of parallel sixths. In variation ten Liszt achieves the eerie effect of the high register in Paganini's version by adding a continuous trill in the middle register.

But nothing compares to the difficulty of Liszt's last variation, which sounds as if played by more than one pianist. Liszt complements the left-hand parallel octaves with a third octave line that can be played only by the quick, precise leaps of the second finger of the left hand. The accompanying arpeggios in the right hand encompass a range of four octaves. Thus already in the first measure of this variation Liszt uses almost the entire keyboard, and he continues storming through it with arpeggios, triple-octave chromatic runs, or hair-raisingly risky leaps in both hands. In this concluding section, in which Liszt combined Paganini's last variation and Finale, the piano sounds like an orchestra of many instruments. There is no better example of how Liszt transformed components such as register, texture, color, and sheer pianistic technique into centrally important elements of composition.

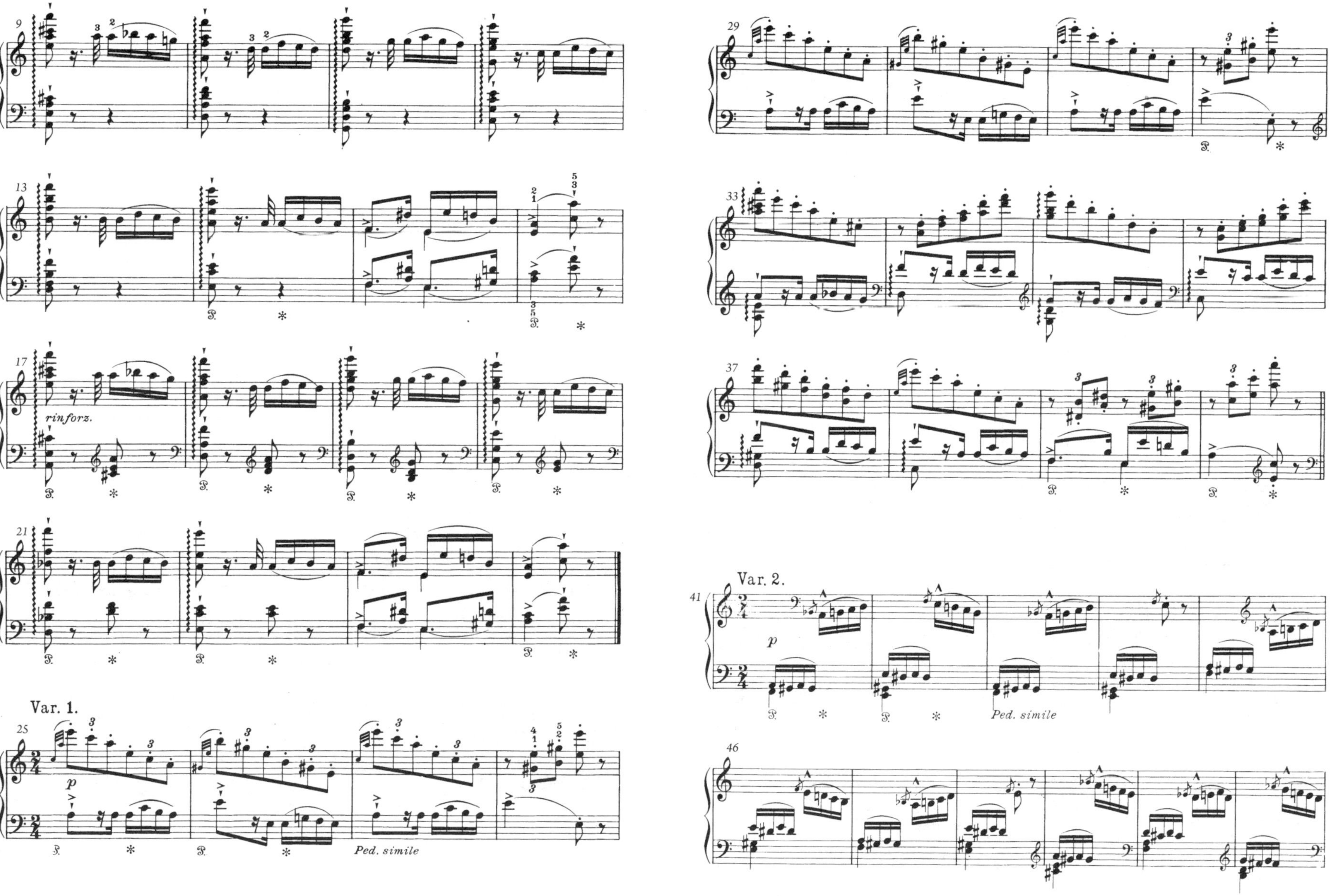
rinforz.
Var. 1.
p
Ped. simile
Var. 2.
p
Ped. simile

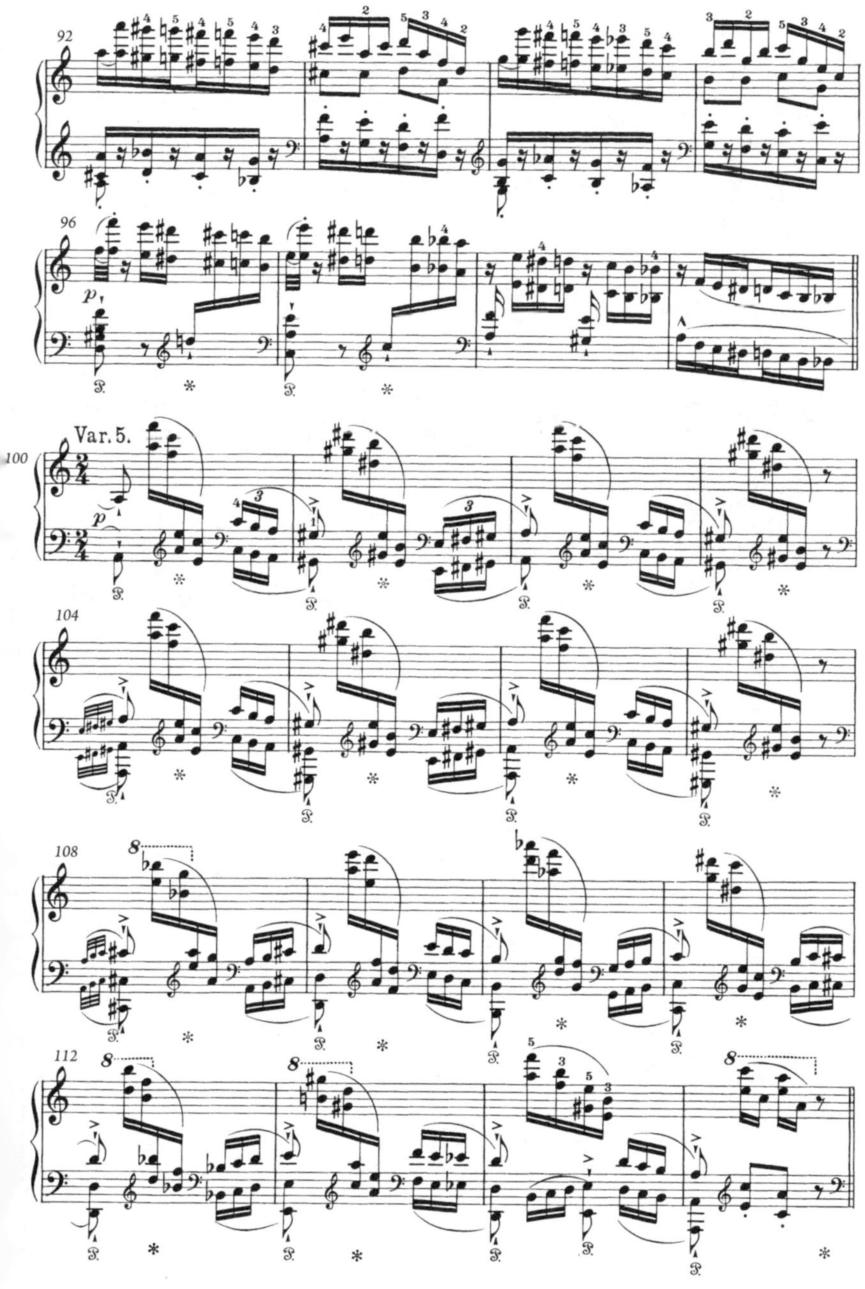
Var. 5.
p

Var. 6.
f con brio
rfz
rfz
Var. 7.
p scherzando
rfz
poco f
rinfz.

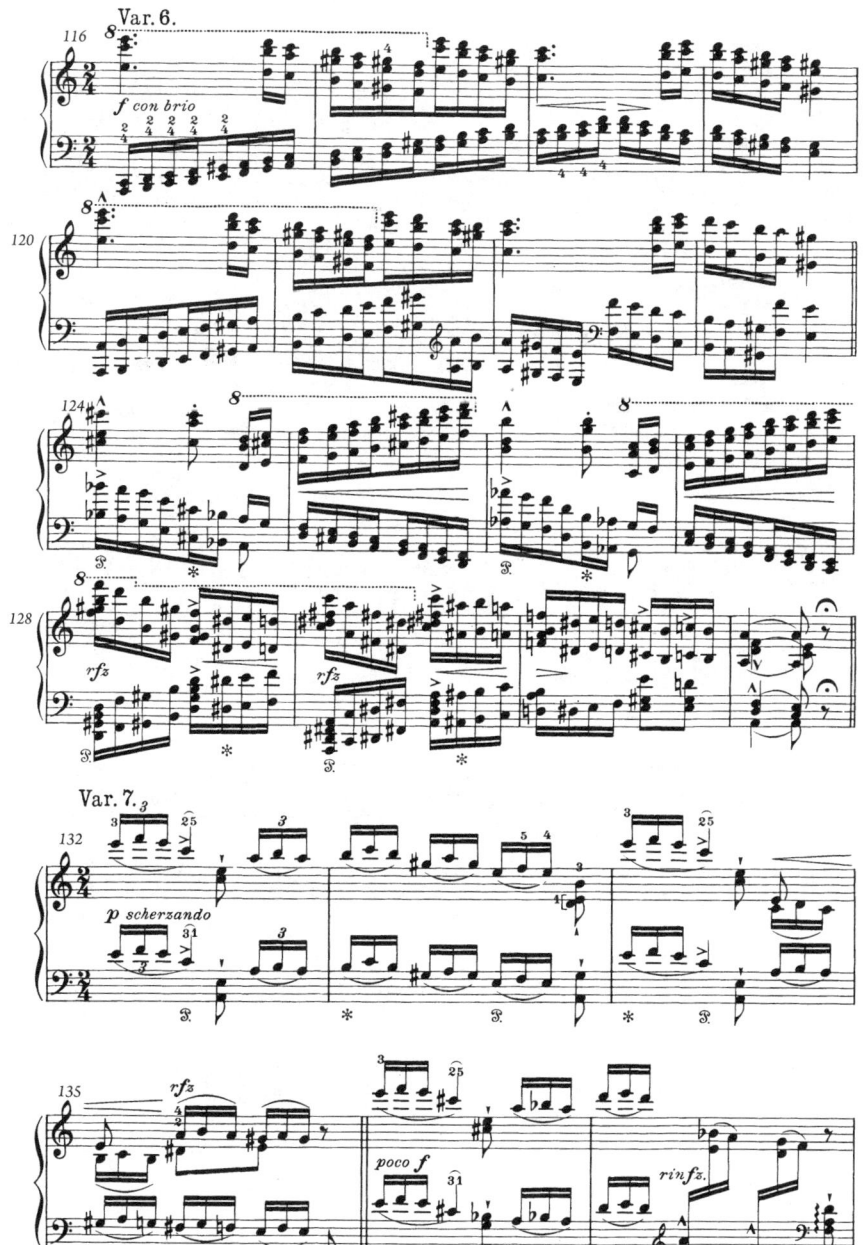

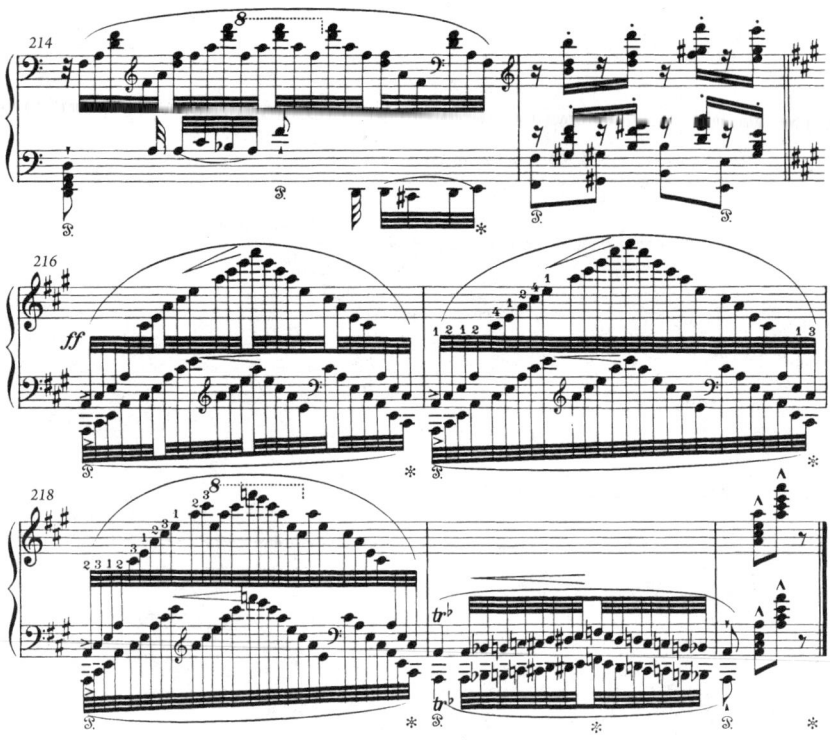

36

Franz Liszt (1811–1886)

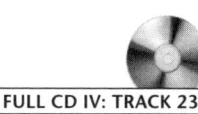

FULL CD IV: TRACK 23

Réminiscences de Don Juan (Don Juan Fantasy) (1841)

151–247	Variation 1	"Là ci darem la mano"	A
215	Cadenza ad libitum		
216–247	Variation continues	"Andiam, andiam mio bene . . ."	A
248–284	Variation 2	"Là ci darem la mano"	A
285–342	Interruption	"Tu m'invitasti a cena, il tuo dover or sai; rispondimi: verrai tu a cenar meco?" (*DG* II/15)	modulatory
343–622	*Presto* (Don Giovanni, pleasure)	"Fin ch'han dal vino" "Champagne" aria (*DG* I/15)	B♭
622–631	*Andante*	Return of statue's music (mm. 1–4) in B♭	B♭

Liszt's *Réminiscences de Don Juan* is one of the numerous operatic fantasies or paraphrases on popular opera tunes that were common virtuosic showpieces in the nineteenth century. Many of Liszt's paraphrases were not simple medleys of tunes but insightful musical commentaries on the operas on which they are based. His paraphrase of Mozart's *Don Giovanni* is also Liszt's self-portrait as Don Juan (for, like many champion performers, Liszt nurtured a reputation as a "Don Juan" himself).

The work contains five main sections:

Measure Nos.	Sections	*Don Giovanni* References	Keys
1–58	*Grave* (statue, death, hell)		
1–4		"Di rider finirai pria dell'aurora" (*DG* II/11)	a
5–9		"Ribaldo, audace! lascia a' morti la pace!"	Ends in G
10–13		Statue's entrance (*DG* II/17)	
14–40		Preceding materials combined	
41–58		"Non si pasce di cibo mortale, chi si pasce di cibo celeste!" (*DG* II/15)	modulatory
59–284	*Andantino* (love, seduction)	Duet "Là ci darem la mano" (*DG* I/9)	
59–68	Introduction	From end of duet, "Vieni, vieni . . ."	A
69–117	Theme	"Là ci darem la mano"	A
118–150	Allegretto	"Andiam, andiam mio bene . . ."	A

Liszt begins with the statue's terrifying speech in the graveyard: "Di rider finirai pria dell'aurora. . . . Ribaldo audace! Lascia a' morti la pace!" (You'll laugh your last laugh before daybreak. . . . Audacious rascal, leave the dead in peace!) (mm. 1–9). He makes the section more jarring than Mozart's original by leaving out the recitative that connects and harmonically joins these two lines in the opera. Next comes the wild diminished-seventh chord that brings the statue on stage for the final confrontation at the opera's finale (m. 10), and a repetition of the graveyard speech, now accompanied by the figuration (originally in the violin) that marked the statue's later appearance (mm. 14–23). Thus the two grimmest, most "diabolical" scenes in the opera are conflated in Liszt's first section. The section ends with a dramatic move from the statue's music for "Tu m'invitasti a cena" (You invited me to dinner, mm. 57–59) to Don Giovanni's lecherous invitation to Zerlina, "Vieni, vieni" (Come, come [with me], m. 60).

This is an ingenious juxtaposition, for "Vieni, vieni" is taken from the duet "Là ci darem la mano" (There I'll take your hand), in which the Don asks for the peasant Zerlina's hand as a token of his seduction, and the scene beginning with "Tu m'invitasti a cena" includes the statue's asking for the Don's hand as a token for the Don's agreement to follow him into the other world. By connecting these two scenes Liszt creates an interpretive link between love and death, between the erotic and the demonic, suggesting that the same force that drives his insatiable sexual desire also manufactures the Don's downfall.

This kind of intensifying conflation, the very opposite of the loose stringing together of tunes implied by designations such as "medley" and "potpourri," runs through the whole of Liszt's paraphrase. Later, the statue's creepy chromatic scales rumble sarcastically beneath the coda of the seduction duet (mm. 217, 219, 225, 227), where the Don sings to Zerlina, "Andiam, andiam, mio bene" (Let's go, my sweet), turning the line—provided we can recall the words when hearing the music—into the statue's leering summons to eternal damnation.

The irony is even more pointed when the statue's chromatic figures reappear within the grandiose bravura paraphrase of Don Giovanni's "Champagne" aria that finishes the paraphrase. As if the demon were already pursuing the Don, the tune flees timidly, trying to shake off the threatening shadow by frequently changing registers (mm. 344–373, 433–469). The statue's static lines, accompanied by thunderous eighth notes, interrupt the aria (mm. 469–518). One hears the Don's boisterous aria struggling to establish itself against the statue's music. In the return of the *Presto* (mm. 377ff) it seems that the Don's melody gains the upper hand; it finds its proper key, B♭ major (Liszt quotes all the melodies from the opera in their original key), and races along.

Significantly, the statue's music from the beginning of the paraphrase returns at the end (mm. 622ff) in the Don's key, in B♭ major. This can be interpreted either as the triumph of the statue over the Don or as the ultimate unification of the opera's erotic and demonic forces. This latter interpretation suggests that Liszt understood *Don Giovanni* in much the same way as his contemporary the Danish philosopher Søren Kierkegaard (1813–55), who considered Mozart's opera the perfect expression of the erotic and the demonic. The sheer physical force manifested in the diabolical virtuosity of Liszt's paraphrase, which can be seen as a metaphor for sexual dominance, adds a physical dimension to the eroticism of the work.

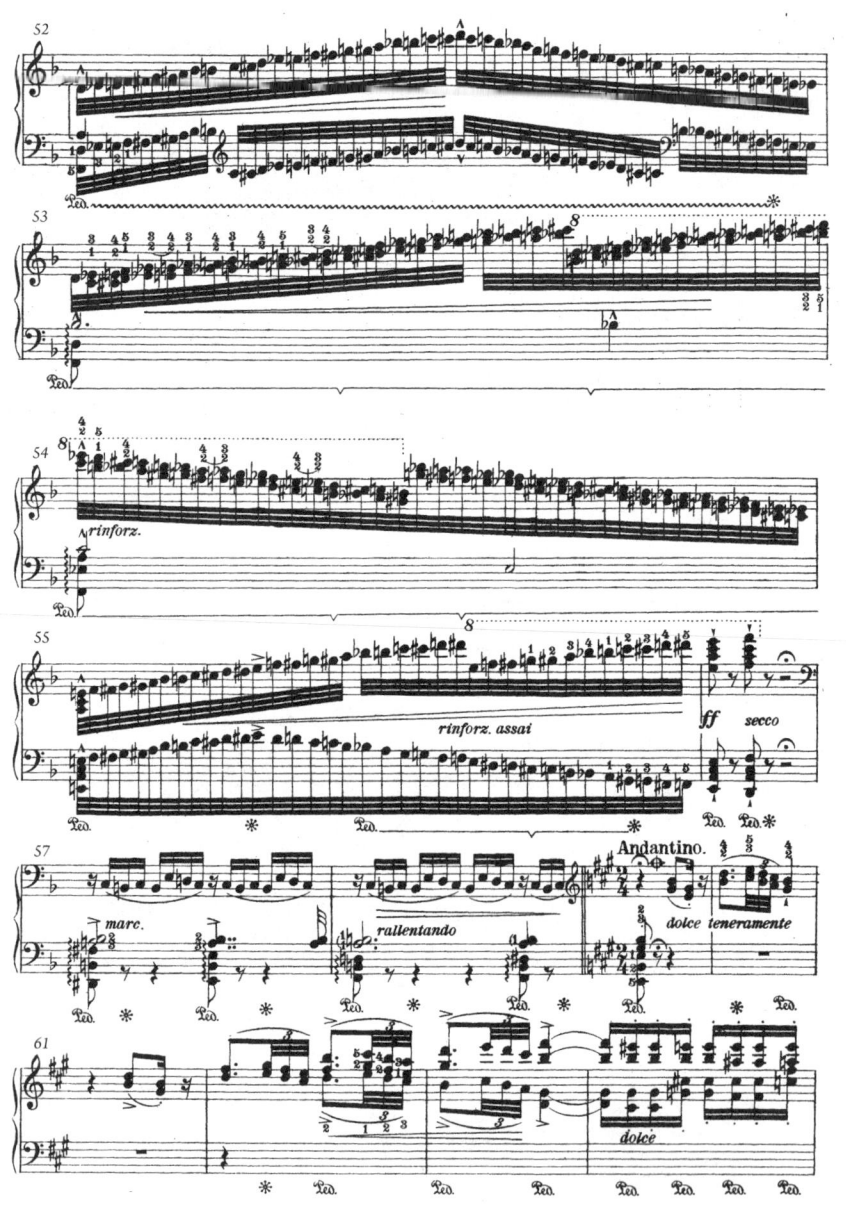

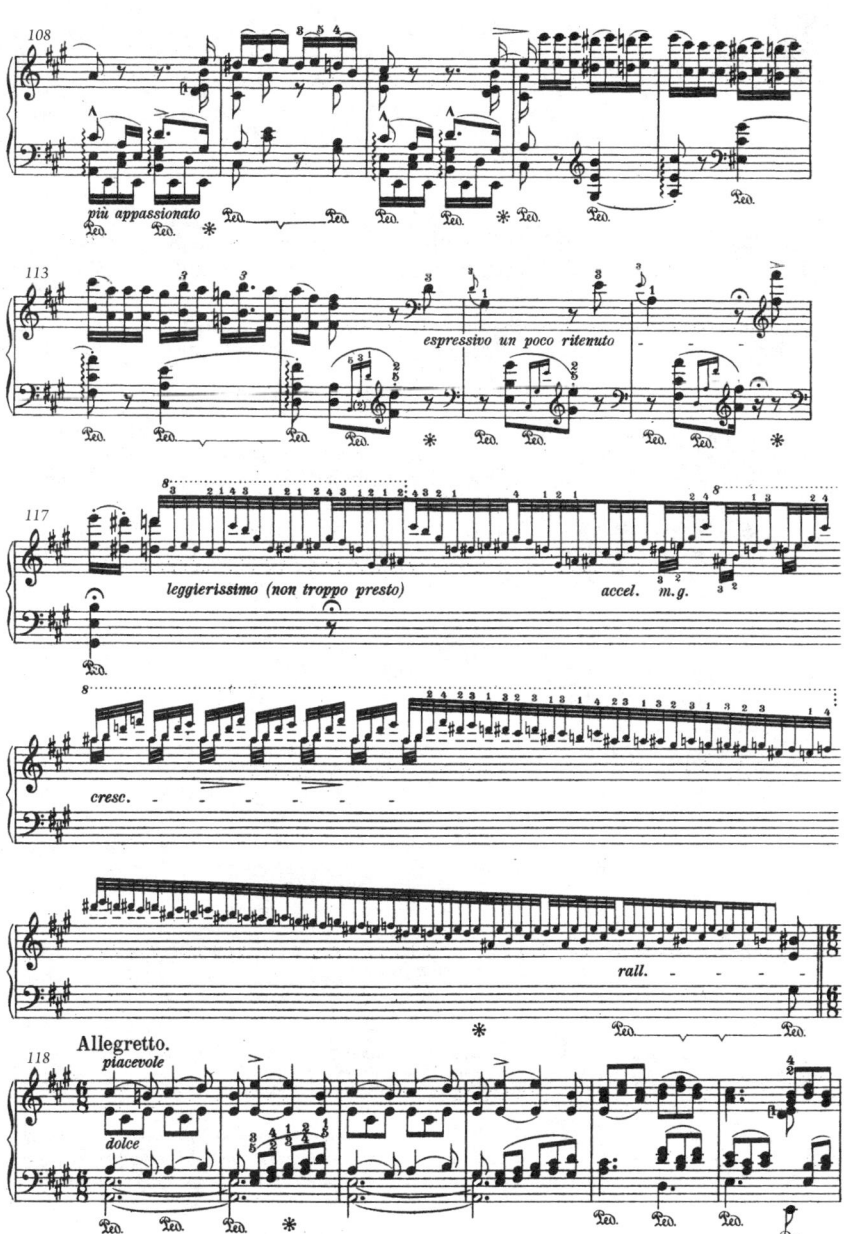

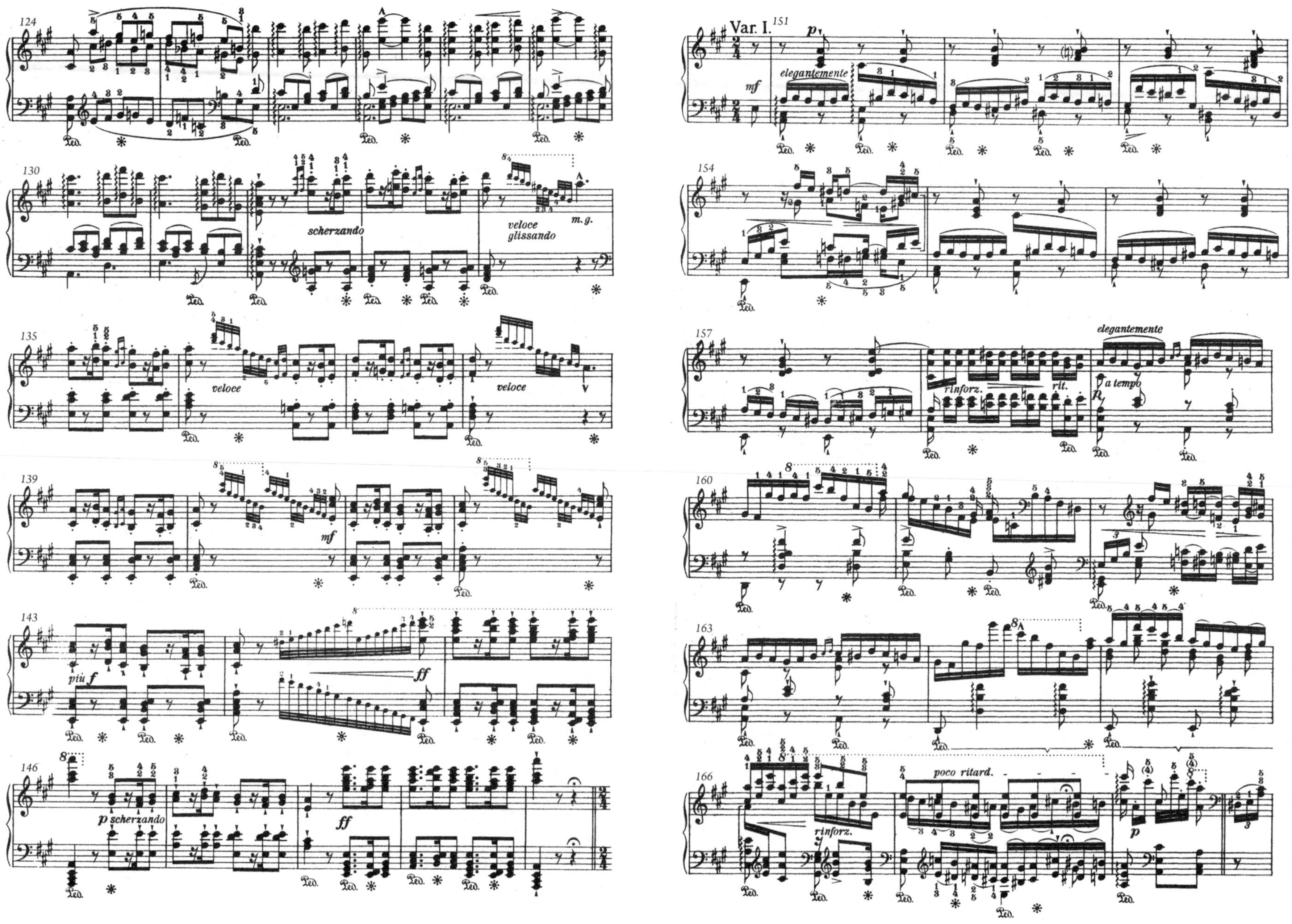
scherzando
veloce
glissando
m.g.
veloce
veloce
mf
più f
ff
p scherzando
ff
Var. I.
p
mf
elegantemente
rinforz.
rit.
a tempo
elegantemente
poco ritard.
rinforz.
p

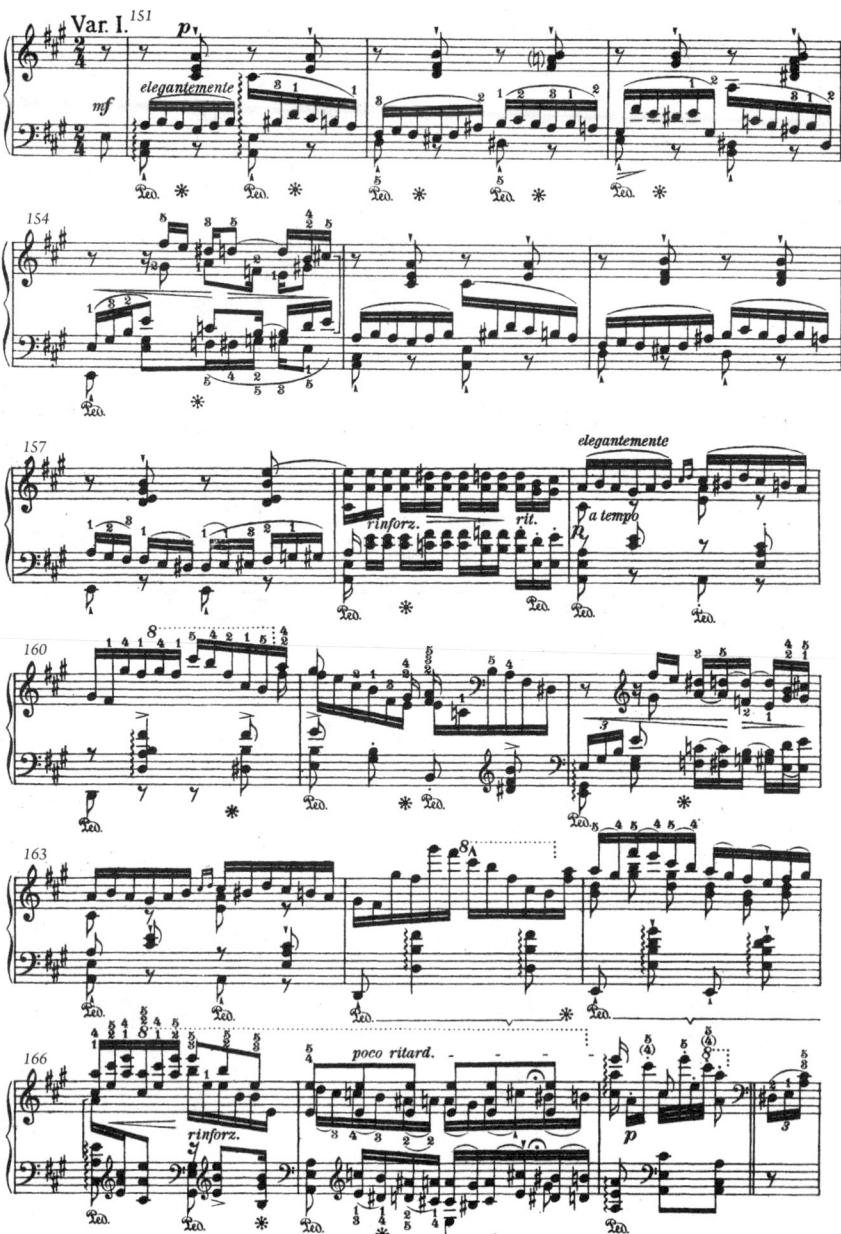

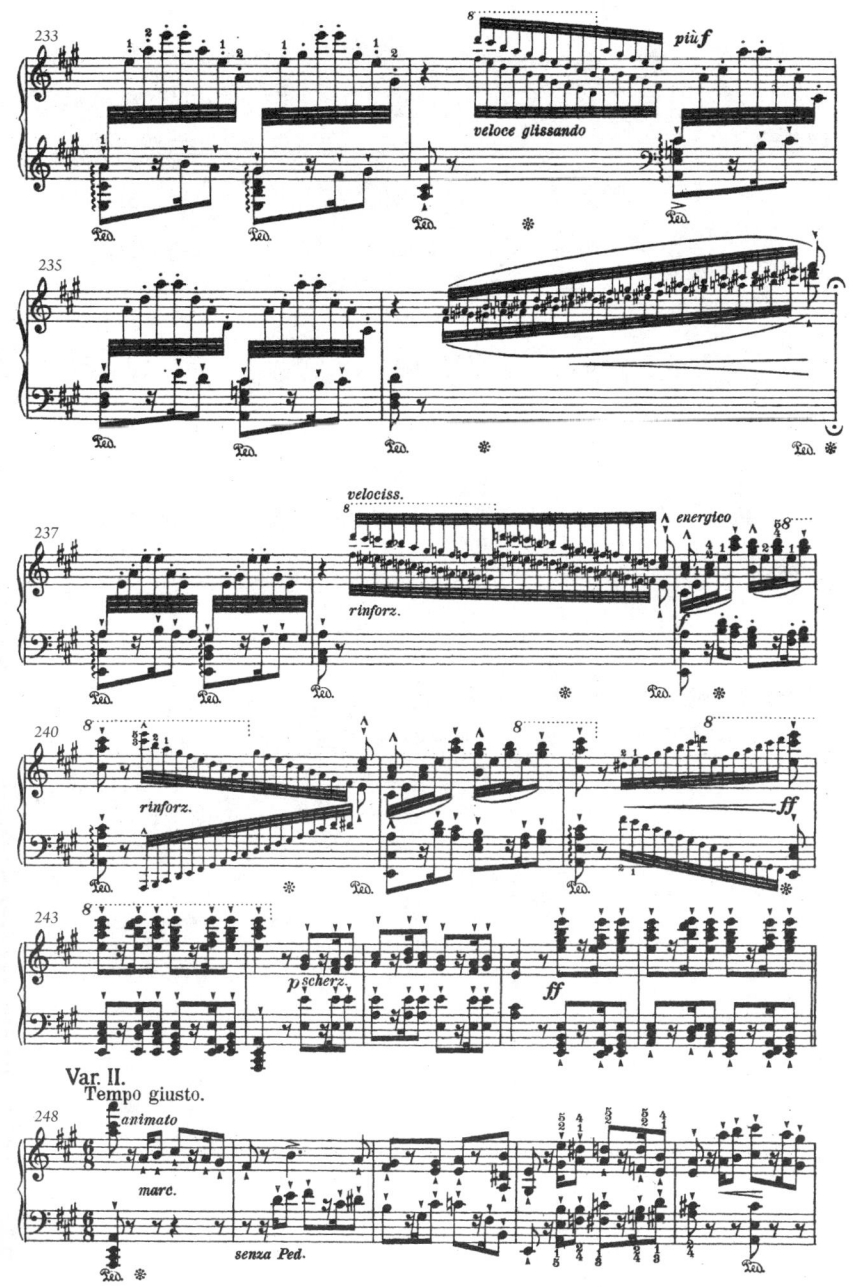

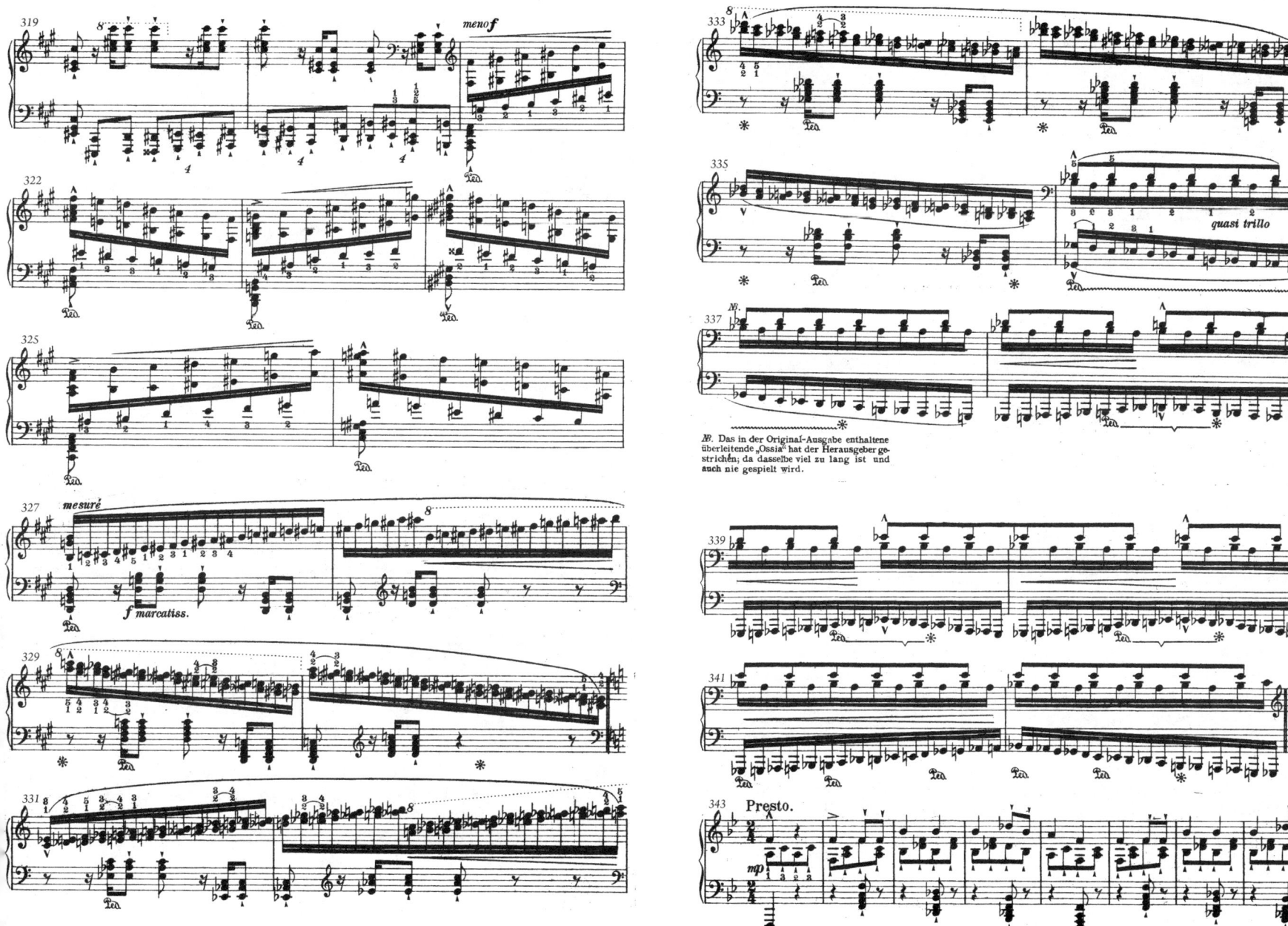

NB. Das in der Original-Ausgabe enthaltene
überleitende „Ossia" hat der Herausgeber ge-
strichen; da dasselbe viel zu lang ist und
auch nie gespielt wird.

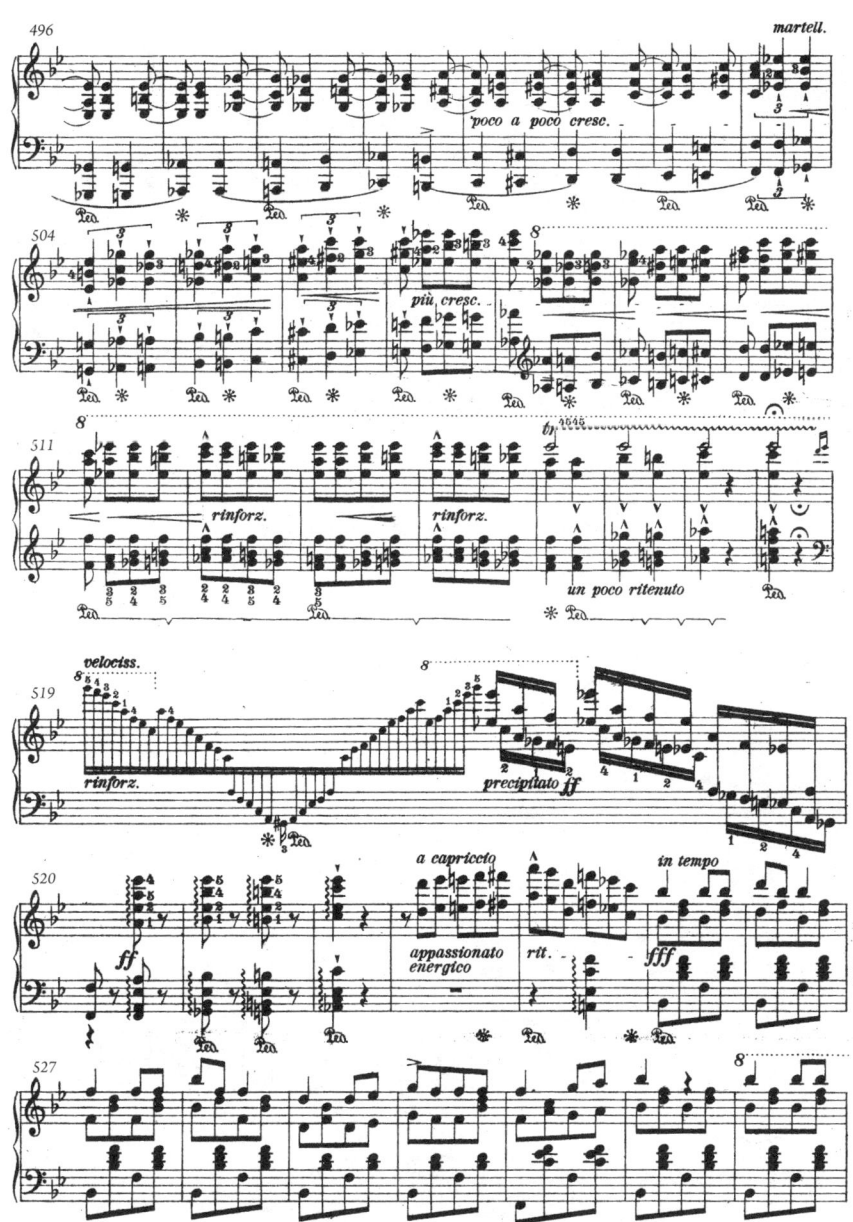

NB. Der Herausgeber empfiehlt folgende erprobten Kürzungen:
1. Von hier an Sprung bis zum Zeichen ⊕ auf nächster Seite unten und
2. Weglassung des *Andante* auf der letzten Seite vom Doppelstrich bis zum Zeichen ✕.

37

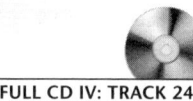

FULL CD IV: TRACK 24

Daniel-François-Esprit Auber (1782–1871)

La muette de Portici (The Mute Girl of Portici),
"Mieux vaut mourir" ("It is better to die") (1828)

Auber's *La muette de Portici* (The Mute Girl of Portici, also called *Masaniello* or *Fenella* after the main characters) was one of the most successful operas of the nineteenth century. Its success was due to its politically charged subject matter and careful coordination of spectacular sets, costumes, mass scenes, and ballets. The first, three-act version of the libretto, by Germain Delavigne (1790–1868), already contained the most important ingredients of the plot: the 1647 revolt led by the Neapolitan fisherman Masaniello against Spanish rule, and the role of his mute sister, Fenella, who, seduced and imprisoned by the Spanish Viceroy, is unable to express her feelings and hence becomes the perfect symbol of the politically oppressed. In its final version to a five-act libretto by Eugène Scribe (1791–1861), *La muette de Portici* contains all the characteristic elements of what came to be known as *grand opera:* historical (instead of mythological) plot, conflict of love and duty, prominent crowd scenes and ballets, a tragic ending, and an emphasis on special effects and spectacle (the opera ends with the spectacular eruption of Mount Vesuvius).

Premiered on 29 February 1828 in Paris's Théâtre de l'Academie Royale de Musique (later the Théâtre de l'Opéra), *La muette de Portici* fueled revolutionary sentiments in the atmosphere that preceded the 1830 July Revolution in France. Its performance in Belgium on 22 August 1830 gave the signal for the beginning of the Belgian revolution against Dutch rule. The opera's most incendiary number was the duet of Pietro (bass) and Masaniello (tenor), two would-be revolutionaries who, exasperated by Pietro's futile search for Fenella, express their desperation and hatred of Spanish rule.

The duet is cast as a military march, its rhythm reminiscent of *La Marseillaise*, the national anthem of the revolutionary years in France. The simple harmonies (often stuck for long stretches of time on the tonic or the dominant), light, virtuoso violin figurations, and the clear, formulaic structure of the duet show the influence of Rossini, whose *Il barbiere di Siviglia* took Paris by storm in 1819. The duet is set in a loose ABA′ form (mm. 1–99, 100–115, 115–186), with the "Amour sacré" section appearing first in the dominant (A major, mm. 48–99) and then in the tonic (D major, mm. 130–181) when it returns in A′. Two recitative-like passages serve as the direct stimulant for the patriotic outpourings: the first (mm. 23–36) falls between the first stanza sung by Masaniello and its reformulation sung by both characters (mm. 37–48); the second, in D minor, forms the short B section (mm. 101–115) that provides the bridge back to the tonic key. In the return to the "Amour sacré" section in A′ Auber redistributes the voice parts, the parallel thirds of its first statement now inverted to parallel sixths. Combined with the key change from dominant to tonic, this results in an even more brilliant part for the tenor, who now sings a step higher than he did in the first rendition.

Masaniello	**Masaniello**
Mieux vaut mourir que rester misérable!	It is better to die than to live in misery!
Pour un esclave est-il quelque danger?	Is there any danger for a slave?
Tombe le joug, qui nous accable,	The yoke that chokes us must fall,
Et sous nos coups périsse l'étranger!	And the foreigner perish under our blows!
Me suivras-tu?	Will you follow me?
Pietro	**Pietro**
Je m'attache à tes pas;	I will be at your side;
Je veux te suivre à la mort.	I want to follow you unto death.
Masaniello	**Masaniello**
À la gloire!	To glory!
Pietro	**Pietro**
Soyons unis par le même trépas.	We will be united by the same death.
Masaniello	**Masaniello**
Ou couronnés par la même victoire!	Or crowned by the same victory!
Pietro	**Pietro**
Oui, oui, partons, je suivrai tes pas.	Yes, yes, let's be off, I will follow you.
Masaniello, Pietro	**Masaniello, Pietro**
Mieux vaut mourir, etc.	It's better to die, etc.
Amour sacré de la patrie,	Sacred love of the fatherland,
Rends-nous l'audace et la fierté!	Give us back boldness and pride!
A mon pays je dois la vie,	I owe my life to my country,
Il me devra sa liberté.	It will owe me its freedom.
Pietro	**Pietro**
Songe au pouvoir dont l'abus	Think of the power whose abuse oppresses us!
nous opprime!	

Masaniello

Songe à la soeur arrachée à mes bras!

Pietro

*D'un séducteur peut-être elle est
la victime!*

Masaniello

Ah! quel qu'il soit, je jure son trépas!

Masaniello, Pietro

Mieux vaut mourir, etc.

Amour sacré de la patrie, etc.

Masaniello

Think of my sister torn from my arms!

Pietro

Perhaps she is the victim of some seducer!

Masaniello

Ah! whoever he be, I swear his death!

Masaniello, Pietro

It's better to die, etc.

Sacred love of the fatherland, etc.

38

Giacomo Meyerbeer (1791–1864)

FULL CD IV: TRACKS 25–27

Les Huguenots, "Bénédiction des poignards" (Blessing of the swords) and "Grand Duo" (1836)

Giacomo Meyerbeer's *Les Huguenots* (The Huguenots), which, like *La Muette de Portici*, is a grand opera to a libretto by Eugène Scribe, was first performed in the Paris Opéra on 29 February 1836. The plot concerns the horrendous historical events culminating in the St. Bartholomew's Day Massacre (24 August to 17 September 1572), during which French Catholics massacred thousands of Huguenots (French Calvinist Protestants). As in most of Scribe's libretti, the historical event serves as the background of a story of personal interest. In *Les Huguenots* the main story line concerns the love of Raoul de Nangis, a Huguenot, and Valentine, daughter of the Catholic Comte de Saint-Bris, leader of the massacre. The turning point in the complicated plot is the fourth act, during which Raoul overhears the Catholics' plot. Spurred by duty toward his brethren, he is about to go and warn the Huguenots of the coming danger, but he is stopped by Valentine, who, fearing for his life, attempts to keep him at her side by finally confessing her love to him.

The scene leading up to the great love duet is Scribe's most powerful "dramatic tableau," in which Saint-Bris leads a group of Catholic noblemen in plotting the massacre and the "Blessing of the Swords." The preparation for the blessing, with which our excerpt begins, is a moment of brutally degraded pomp, characterized musically by the dotted rhythms of the old French overture. The actual blessing is preceded by a chord progression that shows Meyerbeer to have been paying attention to the latest developments in Romantic harmony: the tonic, A♭, is shadowed by major thirds below (E major) and above (C major), completing an uncanny "thirds cycle" before the C-major chord resolves as a dominant to F (mm. 27–32).

After a curse has been pronounced on the Huguenots and an oath taken to spare no one, the stage erupts in a bloodthirsty *Allegro furioso* (mm. 104ff) that functions as a sort of choral *cabaletta*. Meyerbeer's virtuosity in the scoring of this sonorous explosion (still using "natural" brass instruments as opposed to those with valves) was widely admired and emulated. Even more impressive is the way in which the composer scales the sonority down by degrees to *pianissimo* as the conspirators disperse.

Here Scribe thought the act was over. And so it was when the opera went into rehearsal in June 1835, but Adolphe Nourrit (1802–39), the Opéra's leading tenor, playing Raoul, demanded that he and Valentine, played by Cornélie Falcon (1812–97), his protégé and mistress, be given a proper love scene. It was not an easy thing to rationalize in the narrative, and Scribe refused to supply it. Meyerbeer turned to a friend, Émile Deschamps, for the requisite text.

In the end, the "Grand Duo" went like this: Raoul emerges from hiding and immediately makes for the door so that he can warn his fellow Huguenots of the impending catastrophe. The desperate Valentine, losing her head and trying to detain him, blurts out that she loves him. Thunderstruck, Raoul asks to hear her say it again, over and over. This provides the cantabile portion of the duet (mm. 372ff), set in the remote key of G♭ major and marked *Andante amoroso*. Beautiful as this section of the duet is, it only highlights the painful contrast between moral duty and personal love. There is probably no other love duet during which the audience wishes more ardently the separation of the lovers and Raoul's quick departure to save his brethren. Finally, hearing the local church bells give out the fatal signal (mm. 432–450), Raoul tears himself away and runs to the Huguenots' aid, thus providing the pretext for a concluding "stretta," or fast finish, that can be heard as the duet's *cabaletta*.

What seemed to Scribe a contrived situation, improbable to the point of absurdity, became irresistible theater. The freezing of the action into "aria time" at this terribly fraught juncture of the plot—just long enough for the two doomed characters to catch a moment's "inward" bliss before being crushed by the inexorable march of external events—brought audiences to a frenzy of empathy. It was instantly the most successful number in the opera, chiefly responsible for the work's becoming the first grand opera to reach a thousand documented performances, in 1906. It has retained its reputation as a masterpiece even as Meyerbeer's music has fallen out of the active repertory.

BENEDICTION DES POIGNARDS

[A hall in the Parisian residence of Valentine's new husband, the Catholic Count of Nevers. The hall is populated by Catholic noblemen. Valentine has withdrawn to her room; Raoul has concealed himself behind a curtain.]

(The doors in the back are open; three monks advance slowly, carrying baskets of white scarves. Saint Bris reenters with them.)

Three Monks, Saint-Bris	**Three Monks, Saint-Bris**
Gloire, gloire au grand Dieu vengeur!	Glory, glory, to the avenging God!
Gloire au guerrier fidèle,	Glory to the true warrior
Dont le glaive étincelle	Whose blade shines
Pour servir le Seigneur!	To serve the Lord!

(The noblemen draw their swords and daggers; the monks bless the arms.)
(Saint-Bris and the monks stretch out their arms.)

Glaives pieux, saintes épées,
Qui dans un sang impur* serez
    bientôt trempées,
Vous par qui le Très-Haut frappe
    ses ennemis,
Glaives pieux, par nous soyez bénis!

Pious blades, holy swords,
That soon will bathe in impure blood,

You with whose edge the Most High smites his
    foes,
Pious blades, we bless you here!

**Three Monks, Saint-Bris, Chorus
  of Catholic Noblemen**
Oui, gloire au grand Dieu vengeur! etc.

**Three Monks, Saint-Bris, Chorus
  of Catholic Noblemen**
Yes, glory to the avenging God! etc.

Saint-Bris (*showing the cross and the
    white scarf that he carries to all*)
Que cette écharpe blanche et cette
    croix sans tache
Du ciel distinguent les élus!

Saint-Bris (*showing the cross and the
    white scarf that he carries to all*)
Let this white scarf and this spotless cross

Mark out the elect of heaven!

Three monks, Saint-Bris (*each
    addressing a group of noblemen*)
Ni grâce, ni pitié! Frappez tous
    sans relâche
L'ennemi qui s'enfuit, l'ennemi
qui se cache . . .

Three monks, Saint-Bris (*each
    addressing a group of noblemen*)
No mercy, nor pity! Strike them all,
    unflinchingly,
The foe that flees and the foe that seeks to
hide . . .

Chorus
Frappon, frappons, frappons!

Chorus
Strike, strike, strike!

Three Monks, Saint-Bris
Le guerrier suppliant à vos pieds abattu!

Three Monks, Saint-Bris
The warrior pleading at your feet!

Chorus
Frappon, frappons, frappons!

Chorus
Strike, strike, strike!

Three Monks, Saint-Bris
Ni grace, ni pitié! Que le fer et la flamme
Atteignent le vieillard, et l'enfant et
    la femme!
Anathème sur eux!

Three Monks, Saint-Bris
No mercy, nor pity! Let steel and fire
Strike down the elderly, children, and women!

Curse them!

Chorus
Anathème sur eux!

Chorus
Curse them!

Three Monks, Saint-Bris
Dieu ne les connaît pas!

Three Monks, Saint-Bris
God does not know them!

Three Monks, Saint-Bris

Three Monks, Saint-Bris

(*moving to the front of the stage, swinging their swords and daggers*)

Dieu le veut, Dieu l'ordonne!
Non! non! grâce à personne!
A ce prix il pardonne
Au pécheur repentant.
Que le glaive étincelle,
Que le sang ruisselle,
Et la palme immortelle
Dans le ciel vous attend! etc.
N'épargnons personne!

It is God's will, it is his command!
No, no mercy for anyone!
At such a price he will absolve
The penitent sinner.
Let the blade shine,
Let the blood stream,
And may the immortal palms
Await your brows in heaven! etc.
Let us spare no one!

Saint-Bris
Silence, mes amis!

Saint-Bris
Silence, my friends!

First Monk
Silence, mes amis!

First Monk
Silence, my friends!

Saint-Bris
Que rien ne nous trahisse!

Saint-Bris
May no one betray our plan!

First Monk
Que rien ne nous trahisse!

First Monk
May no one betray our plan!

(*The monks signal to all present to kneel, and they bless the different groups.*)

Saint-Bris, First Monk
Retirons-nous sans bruit!

Saint-Bris, First Monk
Let us withdraw without a sound!

Saint-Bris, First Monk, Chorus
  (*all rise*)
Pour cette cause sainte
J'obéirai sans crainte
À mon Dieu, à mon roi!
Comptez sur mon courage;
Entre vos mains j'engage
Mes serments et ma foi!
A minuit!

Saint-Bris, First Monk, Chorus (*all rise*)

For this holy cause
I'll obey without fear
My God, my king!
Count on my courage;
Into your hands I cast
My oaths and faith!
'Till midnight!

(*all leave slowly*)
Point de bruit!

Not a sound!

*"Un sang impur" is a reference to "La Marseillaise," the French national anthem, which contains the phrase
"Qu'un sang impur abreuve nos sillons!" (May their impure blood irrigate our fields!).

Que rien ne nous trahisse,
Et que de leur supplice
Rien ne les avertisse!
Retirons-nous!
Dieu le veut! Oui!
A minuit!

May nothing betray us
And no one warn them
Of their dreadful fate!
Let us withdraw!
It is God's will! Yes!
'Till midnight!

(*The crowd slips away in silence. Saint-Bris departs with them.*)

(*Raoul raises the curtain, assures himself that everybody has left, and darts toward the far door, but stops as he hears that outside they are bolting it. He moves toward the left door; at this moment Valentine leaves her room.*)

GRAND DUET

Valentine (*stopping Raoul*)
O ciel! Où courez-vous?
Raoul, répondez-moi!

Valentine (*stopping Raoul*)
Oh heavens! Where are you running?
Raoul, answer me!

Raoul (*in a broken voice, almost speaking*)
Où je vais? Secourir mes frères,
Dévoiler à leurs yeux ces complots sanguinaires,
Armer leurs bras, et, le fer à la main,
De nos vils ennemis prévenir le dessein!

Raoul (*in a broken voice, almost speaking*)
Where am I going? To assist my brethren,
To reveal these bloody plots

To arm them, and, bearing steel,
Confound the plans of our vile foe!

Valentine (*sweetly*)
Mais ces ennemis, c'est mon père,
C'est un époux qu'à present je révère!
Voudriez-vous les immoler?

Valentine (*sweetly*)
But the foe is my father,
This is a husband whom I now revere!
Would you then slay them too?

Raoul
Je dois punir des assassins!

Raoul
I must punish the murderers!

Valentine (*gravely*)
Armés au nom des cieux!

Armed in heaven's name!

Raoul (*with irony*)
Armés au nom des cieux!
Et voilà le Dieu que ton culte consacre,

Ce Dieu qui des Français ordonne le massacre!

Raoul (*with irony*)
Armed in heaven's name!
And this is the God you worship with your soul,

This God who commands the massacre of the French!

Valentine
Ah! ne blasphémez pas! C'est lui dont la pitié
Veut préserver vos jours, auxquels il s'intéresse!
Ne sortez pas!

Valentine
Oh, do not blaspheme! It is he whose pity

Would preserve your life, such is his care!

Do not leave!

Raoul
Je le dois!

Raoul
I must!

Valentine
C'est chercher la mort même!

Valentine
It is but to seek your death!

Raoul
Et rester, c'est trahir l'honneur et l'amitié.

Raoul
But if I stay, it is to betray my honor and my friends.

Jamais! jamais! Non!
Le danger presse et le temps vole;
Laisse-moi, laisse-moi partir!

Never, never, no!
Danger urges and time flies;
Let me, let me depart!

Valentine
Mais, sans défense, on vous immole!
Gardez-vous, ah! gardez-vous de fuir! Raoul!

Valentine
But defenseless, you'll be slain!
Do not, ah, do not flee! Raoul!

Raoul
Hélas!

Raoul
Alas!

Valentine
Toi, mon seul bien, toi mon idole!

Valentine
You are my only good, oh my idol!

Raoul
Ce sont mes frères qu'on immole!

Raoul
My brothers will be slain!

Et te laisser serait mourir!

To leave you is to die!

Raoul
Ah! laisse-moi, laisse moi partir!
L'honneur le veut, je dois te fuir.

Raoul
Oh, let me, let me go!
Honor commands, I must flee from you.

Valentine
Oui, je saurai te retenir!
Ah! par pitié,
Entends ma voix!

Valentine
Yes, I shall keep you here!
Oh! For pity's sake,
Hear my voice!

Toi, mon seul bien!
Non, par toi ce seuil redoubtable
Ne sera pas franchi!
Je m'attache à tes pas!

Raoul
En t'écoutant je suis coupable!

Valentine
En t'écoutant ne le suis-je donc pas?
Je le fais cependant; à cette heure
*   suprème,*
Je ne vois plus que toi, dont les jours
*   sont proscrits!*
Reste, Raoul; puisque tu me chéris,
Je t'implore enfin pour moi-même;
Car si tu meurs, je meurs aussi!
Reste! reste! je t'aime!

Raoul
Tu m'aimes?
Ah! quel éclair et quel transport!
Quel mot du ciel s'est fait entendre!
Ah! maintenant vienne la mort,
Puisqu'à tes pieds je puis l'attendre!

Valentine
O terreur! l'ai-je dit?

Raoul
Tu l'as dit! tu l'as dit!
Tu l'as dit: oui, tu m'aimes!
Dans ma nuit quelle étoile a brillé?
Je renais, c'est l'air pur des cieux mêmes!
Là, toujours, oubliant, oublié!
Tu l'as dit: oui, tu m'aimes!

Valentine
Qu'ai-je fait? Quel danger, ô mon
*   Dieu!*

Raoul
Parle encore, et prolonge

You, my only good!
No, this fearful threshold
You will not pass!
I am following your steps!

Raoul
In listening to you I am guilty!

Valentine
In listening to you, am I not guilty, too?
And yet I do; at this crucial hour,

I see no one else but you, whose life is
      condemned!
Stay, Raoul: since you love me,
At last I beg you for myself;
For if you die, I die also!
Stay, stay! I love you!

Raoul
You love me?
Oh! what light, what rapture!
What heavenly words did I hear!
Oh! let death come now,
If I can await it at your feet!

Valentine
Oh, what horror! Did I say it?

Raoul
You said it! You said it!
You said it! yes, you love me!
What star has shone upon my night!
I am reborn, it is heaven's purest air!
There, always, forgetting, forgotten!
You said it, yes, you love me!

Valentine
What have I done? What danger, oh, my God?

Raoul
Speak more, and thus prolong

De mon coeur l'ineffable sommeil!
Si l'extase ou je suis est un songe,
Que jamais je n'arrive au réveil!

Valentine
Qu'ai-je fait? Quel danger!

Raoul
Parle encore, etc.

Valentine
O mon Dieu!
Voiçi l'heure!
C'est la mort...
Il n'est plus d'avenir!

Valentine
Voici l'heure!
C'est la mort!
Il n'est plus d'avenir!
Nuit funeste!

Raoul
Tu l'as dit:
Oui, tu m'aimes!
Nuit d'amour!
Viens, fuyons!

Valentine
Non, non! Reste!

Raoul
Viens, fuyons! Ah! viens!

Raoul
Entends-tu ces sons funèbres?

Valentine
Ils me glacent de terreur!

Raoul
Du sein des noires ténèbres
S'élève un cri de fureur!
Où donc étais-je?

The ineffable slumber of my heart!
If my ecstasy is a dream,
May awakening never come!

Valentine
What have I done? What danger!

Raoul
Speak more, etc.

Valentine
O my God!
The time is here!
This is death...
There is no future!

Valentine
Now is the hour!
This is death!
There is no future!
Fateful night!

Raoul
You said it:
Yes, you love me!
A night of love!
Come, let's fly!

Valentine
No, no, remain!

Raoul
Come, let us fly! Oh, come!

Raoul
Do you hear those funereal sounds?

Valentine
They freeze my blood!

Raoul
From out of the depths of those black shades
A cry of fury arises!
Where was I, then?

Valentine (*tenderly*)
Près de moi, cher Raoul!

Raoul (*like a scream*)
Ah! souvenir fatal!
Du massacre de mes frères c'est
    l'horrible signal!
Non, non, non, non!
Plus d'amour! Plus d'ivresse!
O remords qui m'oppresse!
Je les vois, et sans cesse,
Égorger à mes yeux!
Mes amis vont m'attendre;
Je ne dois plus t'entendre;
Et je cours les défendre
Ou mourir avec eux!

Valentine
Quoi! Raoul, ma douleur
Ne peut donc toucher ton coeur?
Tu veux donc démentir et tes feux
    et ma foi?
T'échapper de mes bras,
Pour courir au trépas?
Tu le peux, en passant
Sur mon corps expirant!

Raoul
Plus d'amour! Plus d'ivresse!

Valentine
Eh! quoi! dans ton ivresse . . .

Raoul
O remords qui m'oppresse!

Valentine
Repousser ma tendresse? Hélas!
Et pourquoi repousser ma tendresse?
Le remords qui m'oppresse
Est-il donc moins affreux?
De l'amour le plus tendre
Tu ne peux te défendre!

Valentine (*tenderly*)
At my side, dearest Raoul!

Oh! Fatal memory!
This is the dreadful signal that marks the
    massacre of my brethren!
No, no, no, no!
No more love! No more rapture!
O remorse, you weigh me down!
I see them, ever and again,
As their throats are slit before my eyes!
My friends await me;
I should not listen to you;
I hasten to defend them
Or die with them!

Valentine
What! Raoul, my pain
No longer can affect your heart?
You want thus to deny your flame and all my
    trust?
To escape my arms
To hasten to your death?
You can do that, but only by passing
Over my dying corpse!

Raoul
No more love! No more delight!

Valentine
Eh, what! in your delight . . .

Raoul
O remorse, you weigh me down!

Valentine
You refuse my tenderness? Alas!
Why would you refuse my tenderness?
That remorse that weighs me down,
Isn't less dreadful than yours?
You cannot defend yourself
Against the most tender love!

Ah! Raoul, daigne entendre
Ou je meurs à tes pieds!

Raoul
Je les vois, et sans cesse
Égorger sous mes yeux!
Mes amis vont m'attendre;
Je ne dois plus t'entendre!
Plus d'ivresse! Plus d'amour!
Et je cours pour mourir avec eux!

Oh, Raoul, please listen
Or I will die at your feet!

Raoul
I see them, ever and again,
Slaughtered before my eyes!
My friends await for me;
I should not listen to you any more!
No more delight! No more love!
And I hasten to die with them!

(*Valentine draws Raoul to her breast to prevent his departure; he tries to free himself.*)

Raoul
C'en est fait; voici l'heure!
Le ciel veut que je meure!
Mes amis vont m'attendre!
Et je cours les défendre!
Vous m'arrêtez en vain!
Grand Dieu! Grand Dieu!
Soutiens mon courage!

Valentine
Non! Je ne vous quitte pas!
Frappez! Voilà mon sein!
Sois donc mon assassin!

Raoul
No more; the time has come!
It is heaven's will that I die!
My friends will await me!
I hasten to defend them!
You try to hold me back in vain!
Great God! Great God!
Strengthen my courage!

Valentine
No! I will not leave you!
Strike! Here is my breast!
You shall be my murderer!

(*Raoul draws Valentine to the window and shows her what is happening on the street.*)

Raoul
Tiens! vois, sur ce rivage,
vois ces cadavres sanglants!

Valentine
Ah! ma raison s'égare!
Ah! forfait exécrable!
Raoul! ils te tueront!

(*crying*)
Ah! pitié! je meurs!

(*she faints*)

Raoul (*almost speaking*)
Reviens à toi! Que faire?

Raoul
Hold! See, on the shore,
see all the bloody corpses!

Valentine
Oh! I'm losing my wits!
Oh! abominable crime!
Raoul! They'll kill you!

Oh! Have pity, I'm dying!

Raoul (*almost speaking*)
Revive yourself! What can I do?

O moment redoutable! Hélas!   Oh dreadful hour! Alas!

Pourrais-je encore résister à ses pleurs?   Could I withstand her tears for another

                                                                moment?

(He listens again to the bells.)

Non! fuyons! fuyons!   No, I must flee! I'll flee!

(looking at Valentine who starts to come to her senses)

Dieu, veille sur ses jours, Dieu secourable!   God, guard her days, merciful God!

(He rushes to the balcony and disappears. Valentine cries out and faints again.)

9209

9209

9209

9209.

9209

9209

9209

39

Hector Berlioz
(1803–69)

FULL CD IV: TRACK 28
CONCISE CD II: TRACK 28

Symphonie fantastique, Fifth movement (*A witches' sabbath*)
(1830)

Berlioz composed his *Symphonie fantastique* from January to April 1830 in the emotional tur-moil caused by his infatuation with the Irish actress Harriet Smithson, who played Ophelia in a Paris performance of Shakespeare's *Hamlet*. The score appeared with Berlioz's detailed program note in 1845. The program, which Berlioz compared to "the spoken text of an opera," involves "various situations in the life of an artist."

The most explicitly programmatic movement of the symphony was the fifth. The chart of the movement below contains the text of Berlioz's own program note for this movement. The first sentence sets up the scene. We have coordinated the remaining portions of Berlioz's text with the sections of the music that correspond to them most closely.

As Berlioz's program note attests, the movements of the symphony are tied together by the frequent appearance of the "beloved melody," which Berlioz called the *idée fixe* (literally "fixed idea" or obsession). In the course of the symphony this melody undergoes drastic transforma-tions and by the end turns into a grotesque distortion of what appeared first as the musical representation of ideal beauty.

Example 39–1

Idée fixe, original form (movement 1)

etc.

Idée fixe, grotesque form (movement 5)

etc.

Measure Nos.	Berlioz's Program	Sections	Comments
	Dream of a Witches' Sabbath. [The artist] sees himself at the Sabbath, in the midst of a frightful troop of ghosts, sorcerers, monsters of every kind, assembled for his funeral.		
1–20	Strange noises, groans, bursts of laughter, distant cries, which other cries seem to answer.	*Larghetto*	
21–28	The beloved melody appears again, but it has lost its character of nobility and shyness; it is no more than a dance tune, mean, trivial, and grotesque: it is [the beloved] coming to join the Sabbath.	*Allegro*	Distorted version of idée fixe in C clarinet, cut short by . . .
29–39	A roar of joy at her arrival.	*Allegro assai*	E♭ *fortissimo* explosion
40–101	She takes part in the devilish orgy.	*Allegro*	Distorted version of idée fixe in E♭ clarinet
102–126	Funeral knell.		Off-stage bells
127–240	Burlesque parody of the "Dies irae" ["Day of wrath," a chant sung at the Catholic Mass for the Dead].		"Dies irae" tune, first in bassoons and tubas, then in horns, then in woodwinds and high strings
241–413	Witches' round dance.		Begins with fugue, part of "Dies irae", mm. 348–362
414–524	The Witches' round dance and "Dies irae" combined.		

The fourth movement depicted the artist's drug-induced dream of being executed. In the fifth and last movement, the artist imagines his own funeral. The bizarre program serves to jus-tify outrageous musical effects. For example, the "unearthliness" of mm. 8–11 was due in part to the literally unheard-of timbre of the newly invented valve horn as well as to the octave glis-sandos, which, because of the instruments' limitations, have to be "faked." Timbre also plays a hitherto-unprecedented role in the transformation of the *idée fixe* into "an ignoble dance tune, trivial and grotesque," previewed at m. 21 and played in full at mm. 40ff. To depict his beloved taking part in the orgy Berlioz used the high, raucous E♭ clarinet, an instrument employed pre-viously only in military bands. The sudden *tutti* on E♭ that interrupts the C-major statement of the tune after its seventh measure (mm. 29–39) illustrates Berlioz's statement in the program, "a howl of joy greets her arrival." Without this programmatic justification, such a grotesque interruption would have been inexplicable.

For the most fantastic episode of the last movement (mm. 414ff), little verbal justification was necessary because Berlioz could rely on a musical symbolism that drew its referents from the Catholic Church. Berlioz's appropriation of the stern Medieval "Dies irae" (Day of wrath) melody and his burlesque treatment of it were a little risqué at a time when representations of religious services on the opera stage were subject to censorship.

Yet even here the device seems to have had its source not in real life but in literature. Goethe's *Faust*, a play all about diabolical havoc in which the "Dies irae" was employed as a stage effect, would seem to have furnished the pretext for Berlioz's strange use of the chant to symbolize not divine redemption (as in the liturgy) but devilish fun and games. The midnight chimes (mm. 102ff) that accompany the "Dies irae" device were also theatrical borrowings, making use of an instrument that had to be carted to the concert hall directly from the opera house. The most striking musical effect in the "Dies irae" section is the irregularity with which the eight-measure peal of the chimes (spaced now three, now five measures apart) impinges on the rhythmically regular "Dies irae" variations. That seemingly uncoordinated relationship was a naturalistic touch since the singers of chant and bell ringers would not be coordinated in a real ceremony.

The variations on the chant proceed in a curiously academic, even pedantic manner, by strict diminution. But that is only the first of Berlioz's ironic borrowings from conservatory routine. The *Ronde du sabbat* ("Witches' round dance," mm. 241ff) itself is introduced through an ungainly but altogether "correct" fugal exposition, and the climactic section, in which the round dance and the "Dies irae" are combined, is a cantus firmus exercise, such as counterpoint pupils are still forced to write (mm. 414ff).

All of these devices work together to make the latter part of the symphony's finale mock church music. The effect of the incongruity between the "learned," somewhat archaic compositional devices and the garish program (to say nothing of the orchestration, which reaches a peak of wildness with the *col legno* at m. 444, which requires the violinists and violists to strike the string with the wood of the bow), is a source of humor to those in the know. In *Symphonie Fantastique* Berlioz used a vast array of orchestral effects to illustrate his program with a vividness never before heard in the realm of concert music.

13
poco f
p
muta in G (Sol♮)
16
62
mf
dim.
I.
sf>pp
con sordino III.
pppp
f
pp
sf>p
div.
62

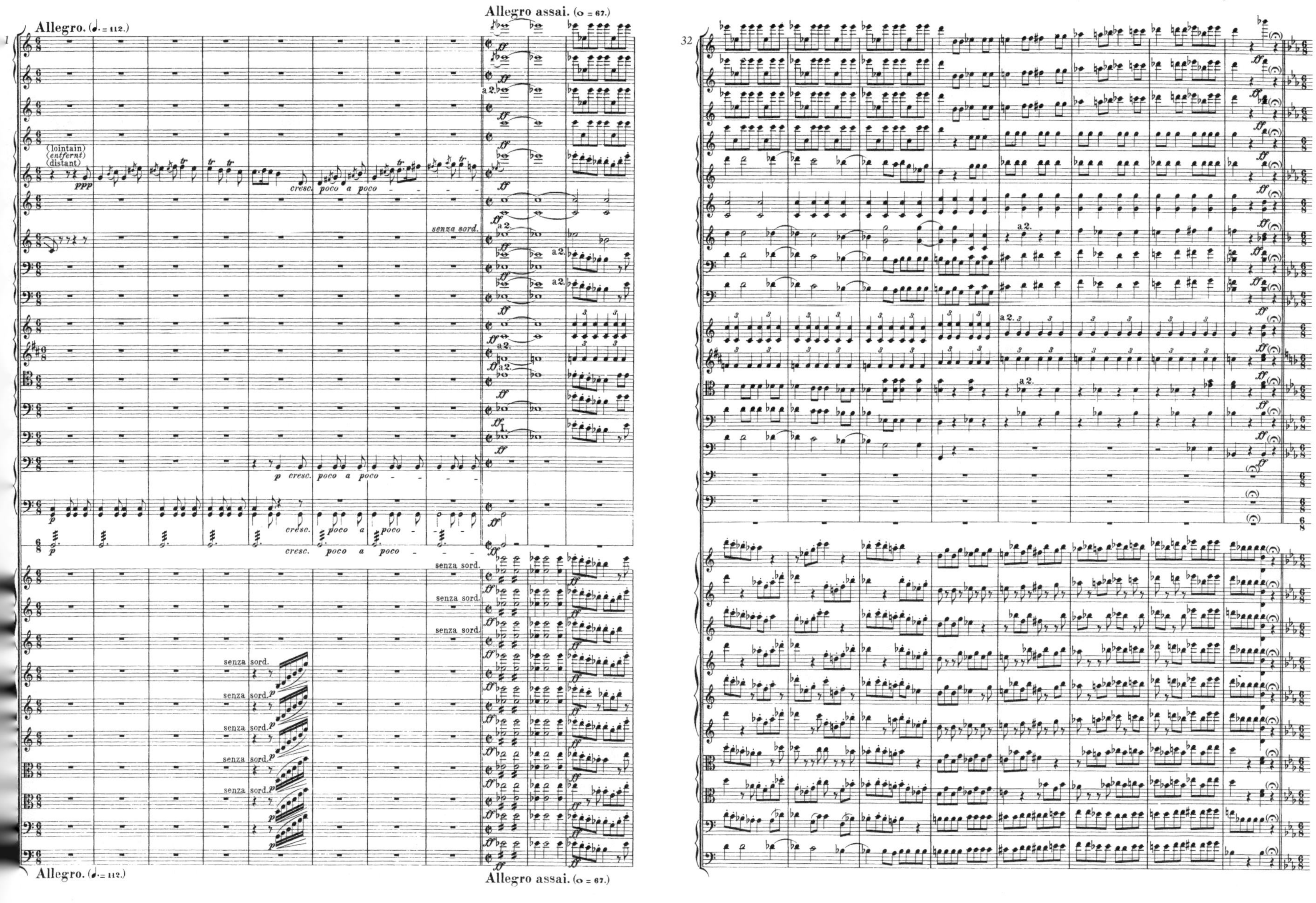
Allegro. (♩. = 112.)
Allegro assai. (𝅗 = 67.)
(lointain)
(entfernt)
(distant)
ppp
cresc. poco a poco
senza sord.
a 2.
p cresc. poco a poco
32

63
Allegro. (♩. = 104.)
40
Fl. picc.
Ob.
poco f
Clar. I in Es (Mib).
cresc.
Clar. II in C (Ut).
Fag.
a 4.
mf
Viol. I unis.
Viol. II unis.
Viola unis.
Vcllo.
C.B.
49
Clar.
Viol.
(sempre cresc.)
pp
55
Fl. I.
Fl. picc.
(mf cresc.)
a 2.
(f)
Cor.
(cresc.)
(mf)
64
61
Fl.
Fl. pic.
cresc.
(cresc. sempre)
ff

57
Fl. I.
Fl. picc.
Ob.
Clar.
Cor.
Fag.
a 4.
Tr.
Ctti
Tromb.
Tuba I.
Timp.
Viol.
a 2.
ff

74
a 2.
a 4.
ff
f

*) Die Herausgeber empfehlen, die folgenden Takte auf fünfsaitigen Contrabässen in der tiefen Octave zu spielen.
Les mesures suivantes se jouent une octave plus bas sur la contrebasse à 5 cordes. (Note des Éditeurs.)
The editor wishes the following bars to be played on a 5-stringed double-bass in the lower octave.

171
184
68
pizz.
pizz.
pizz.
arco
arco
arco
arco
arco
tenuto
tenuto
68

69
221
arco
arco
arco
a 2.
a 2.
69
231
70
Fl.
Fl. picc.
Ob.
a 2
Clar.
Cor.
Fag.
a 4.
Tr.
Ctti
a 2.
Tromb.
Tube.
Timp.
(Baguettes d'éponge.)
(Schwammschlägel.)
(Sponge-headed sticks.)
(Baguettes d'éponge.)
(Schwammschlägel.)
(Sponge-headed sticks.)
cresc.
Viol.
70

Hexenrundtanz.
Ronde du Sabbat.
Witches' round dance.
Poco meno mosso.*)

Poco meno mosso.

*) Le mouvement, qui a dû s'animer un peu, redevient ici comme au chiffre 63 Allegro (♩.=104)
Das Zeitmaass, welches sich etwas belebt hat, wird hier wieder wie bei Ziffer 63 Allegro (♩.=104)
The movement, which has animated itself, is here again as at number 63 Allegro (♩.=104)

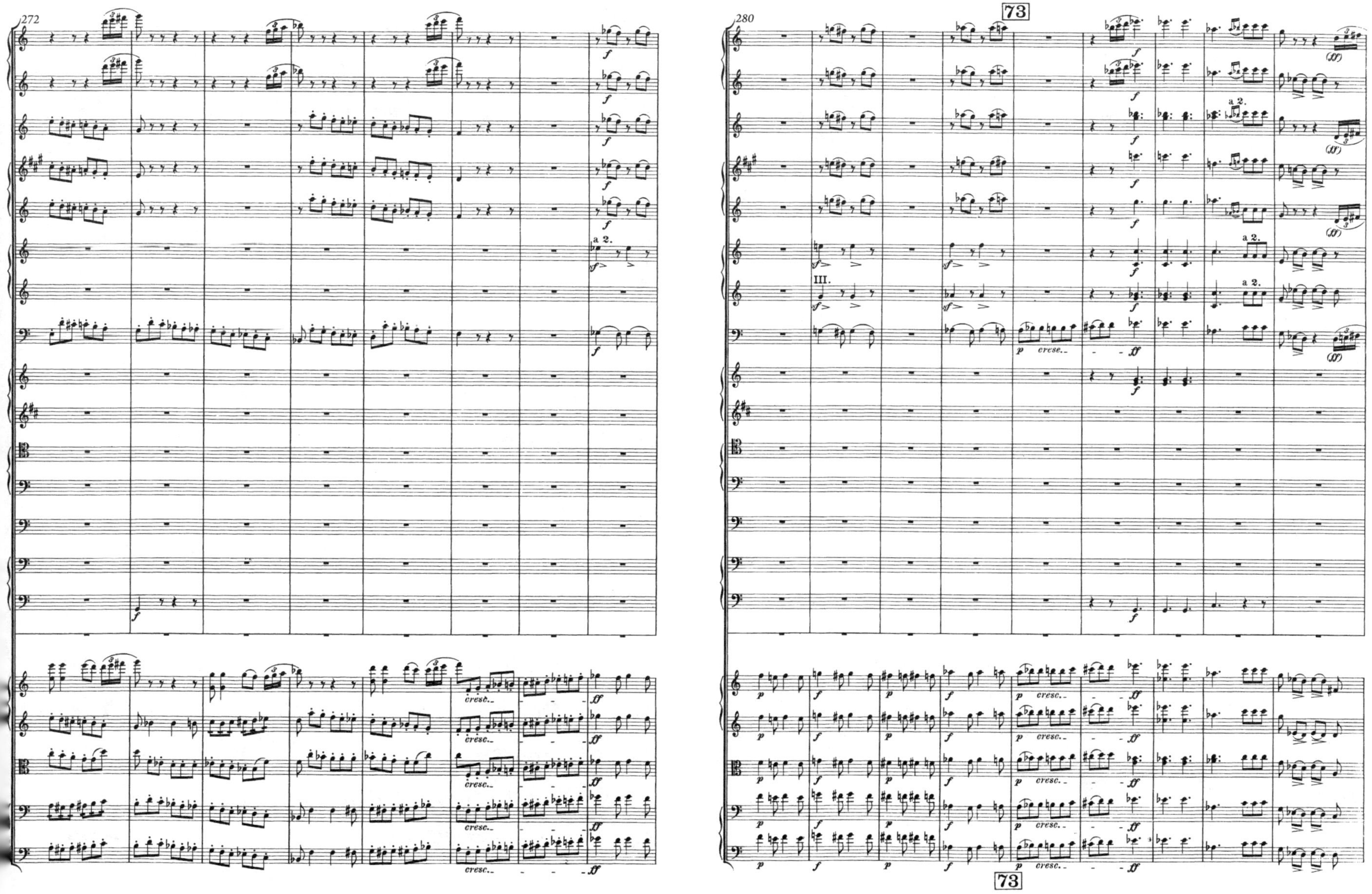
272
280
73
a 2.
III.
cresc.
73

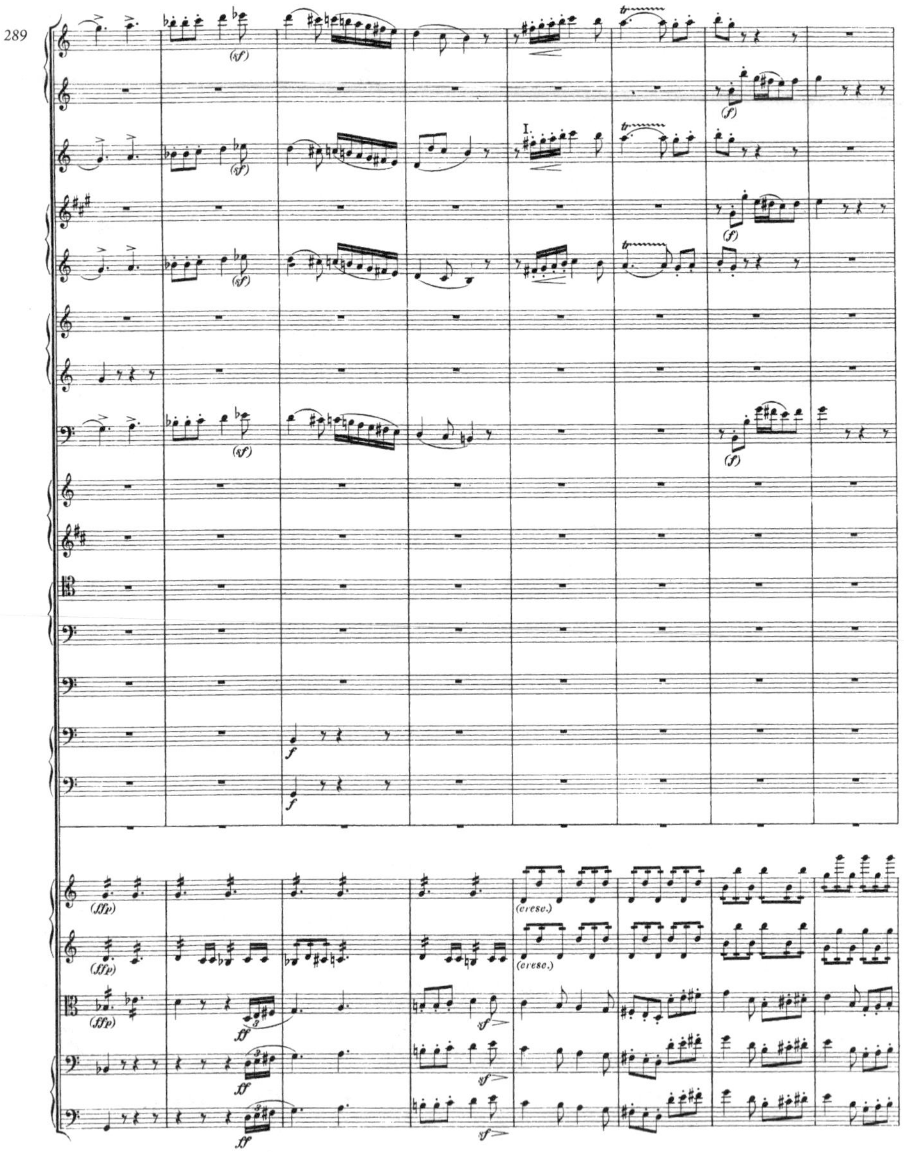
289
I.
(cresc.)

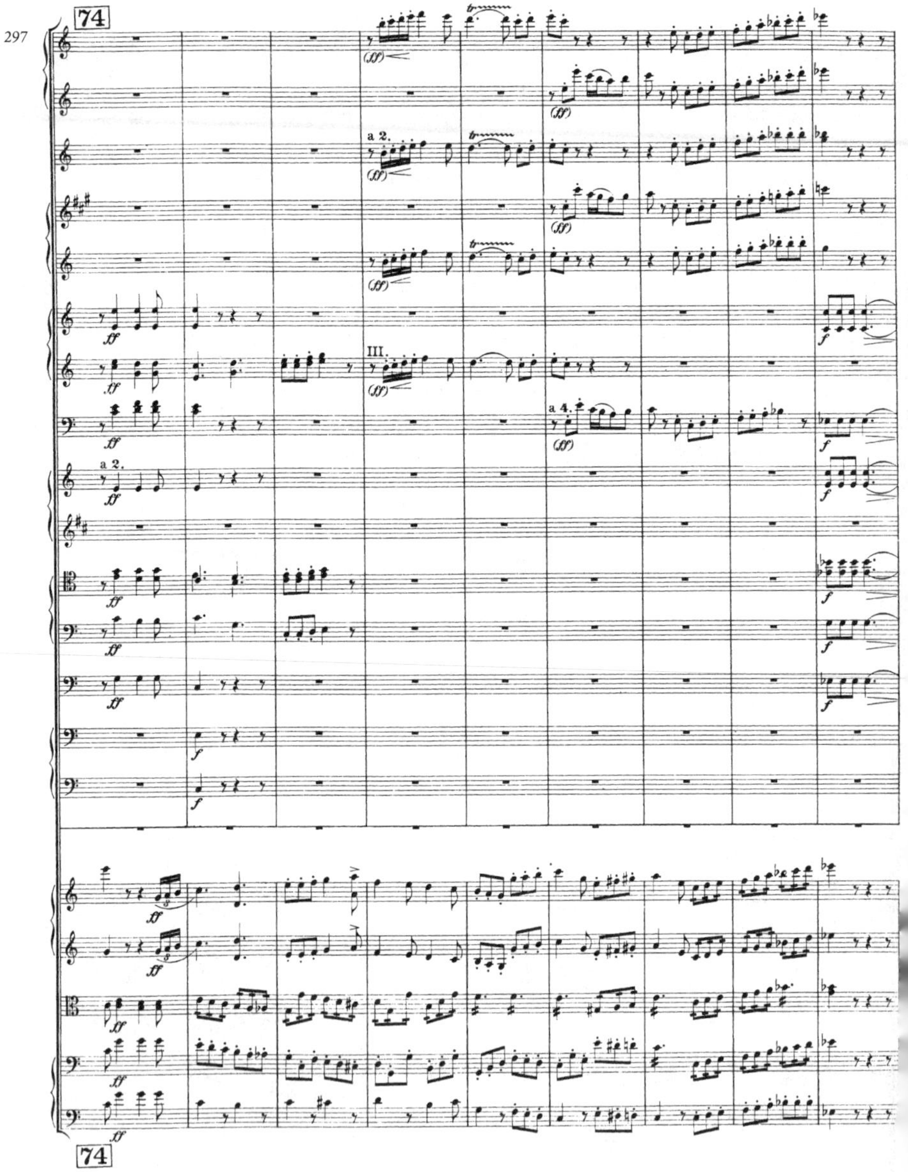
297
74
a 2.
III.
a 4.
74

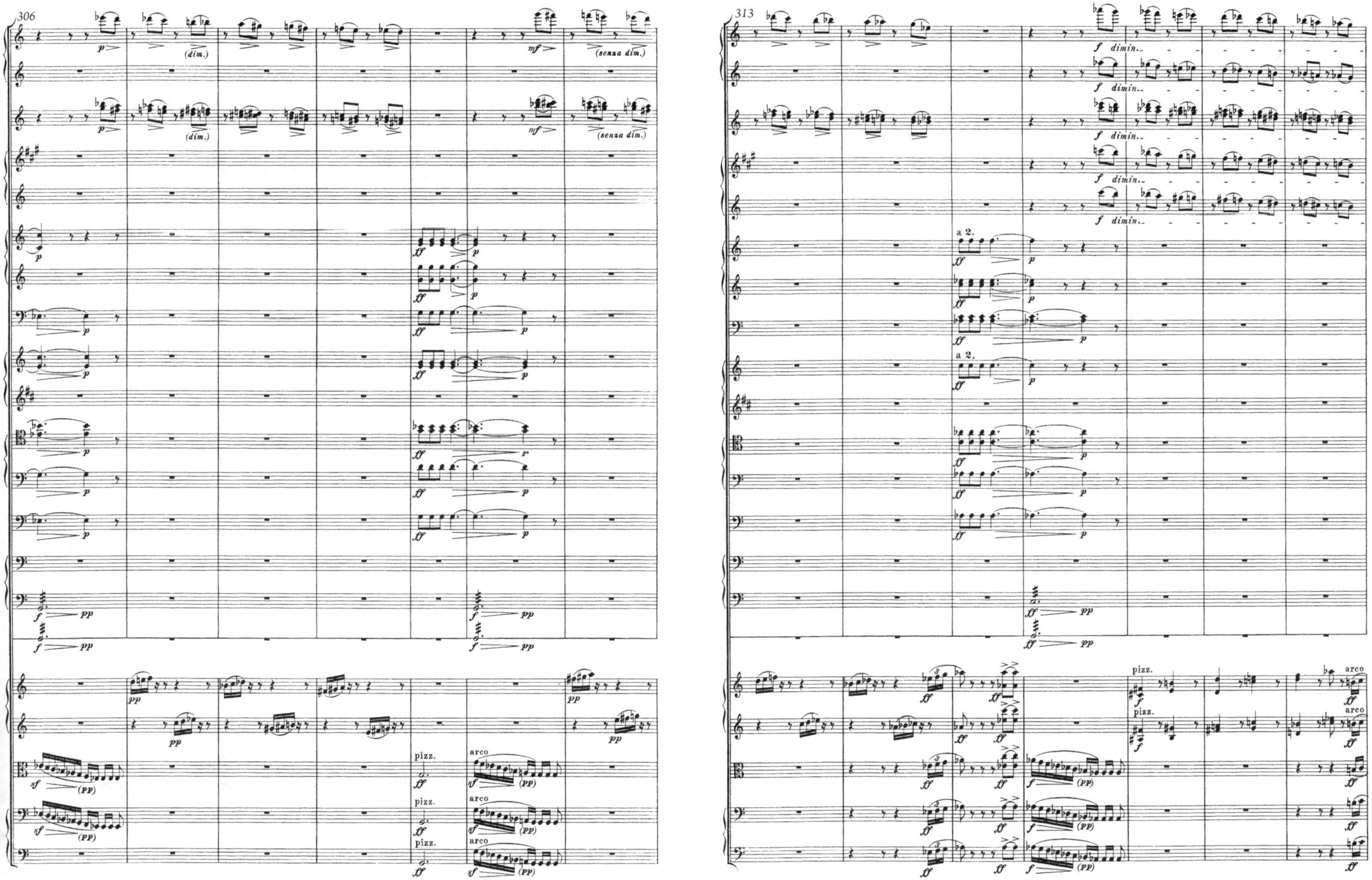
306
(dim.)
(senza dim.)
pizz.
arco
313
f dimin.
a 2.
pizz.
arco

75
320
f (senza dim.)
p (subito)
a 2.
a 4.
ff
mf
(p)
pp
pizz.
(ff sempre)
75
327
76
I.
III.
dim.
pp
sf
(poco f)
(pp)
arco
sf
sempre dim.
poco f
76

361
78
cresc. poco a poco
II.
con sord.
IV.
poco sf > p
Un Timbalier.
Ein Schläger.
One drummer.
pp
cresc. poco a poco
pp
pp
78
cresc. poco a poco
371
79
con sord.
II.
poco sf > p
Les deux Timbalier réunis.
Beide Schläger zusammen.
Both drummers together.
p cresc. poco a poco
p
p
79

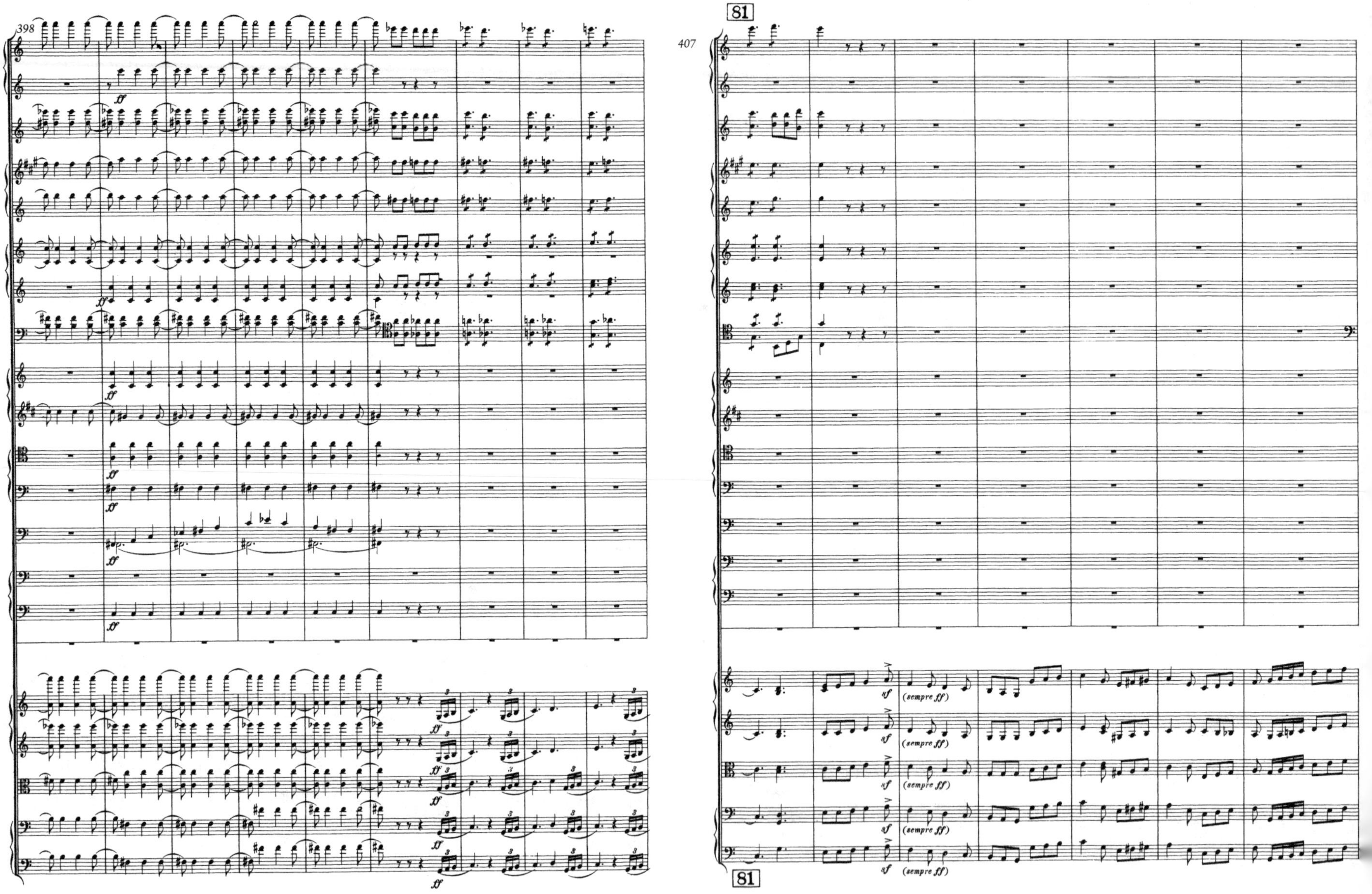
398
ff
81
407
sf
(sempre ff)
81

Dies irae et Ronde du Sabbat (ensemble).
Dies irae und Hexenrundtanz (zusammen).
Dies irae and witches' round dance (together).

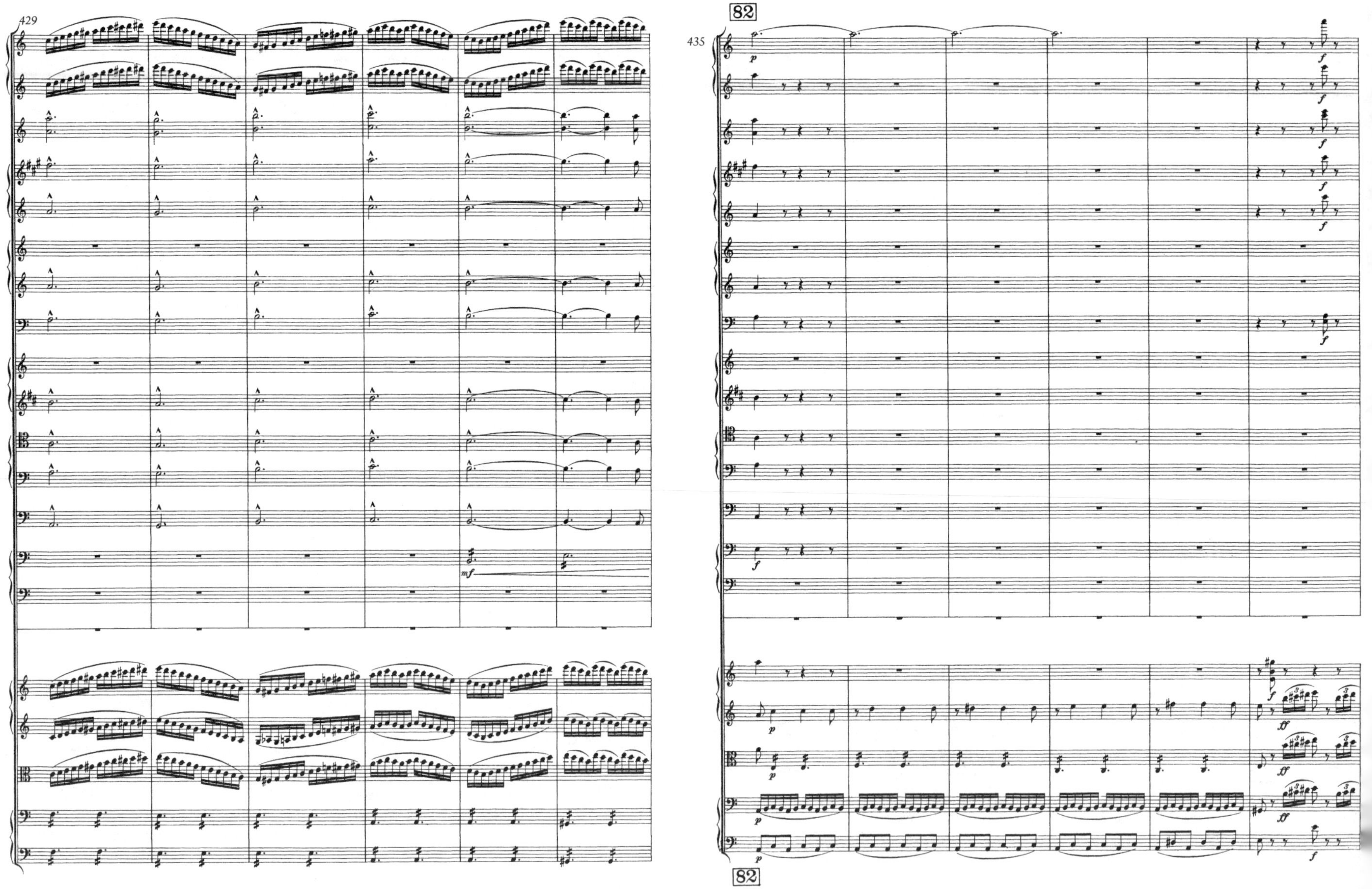
429
82
435
p
f
mf
ff
82

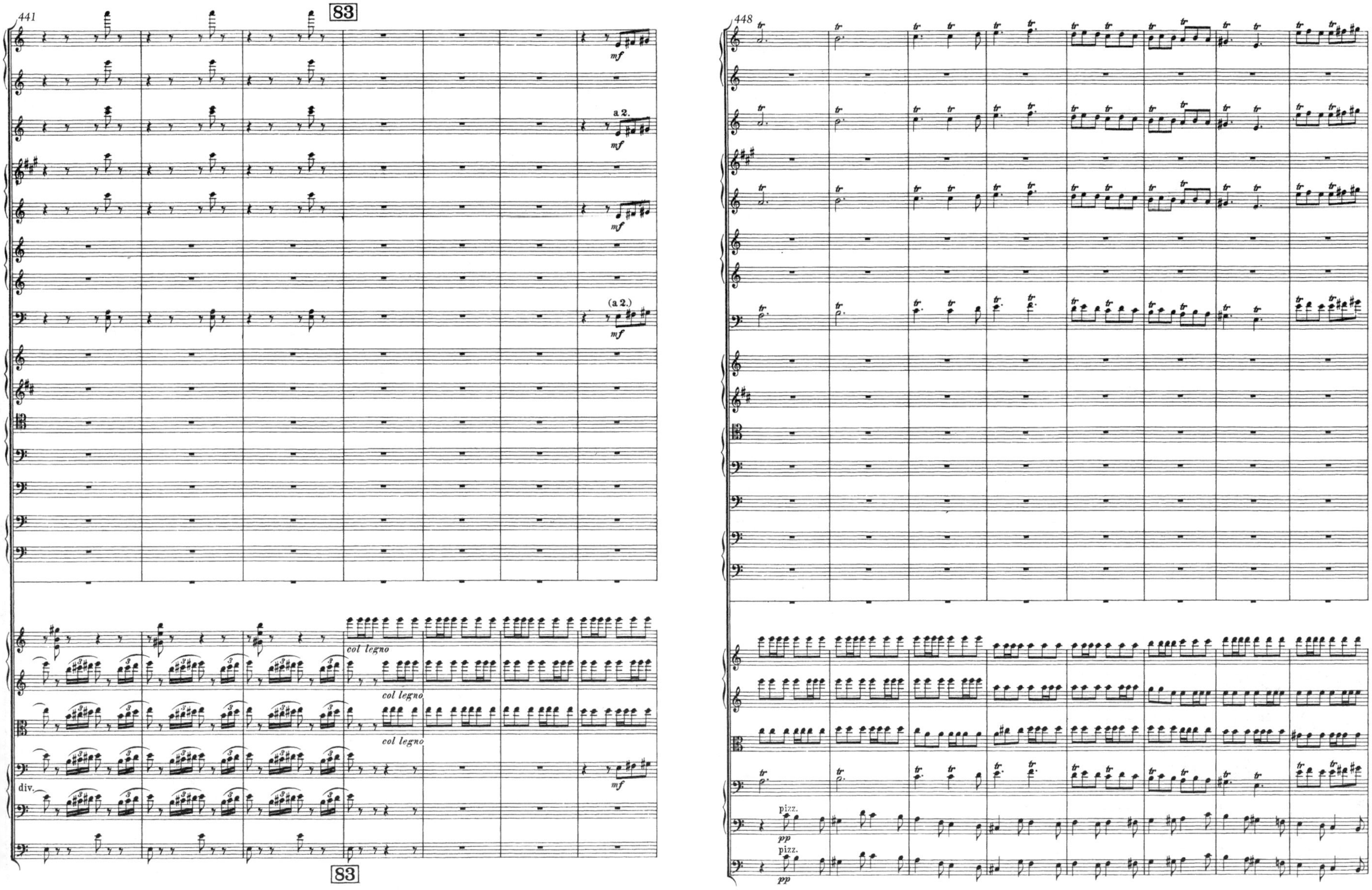
441
83
a 2.
mf
(a 2.)
col legno
div.
448
tr
pizz.
pp

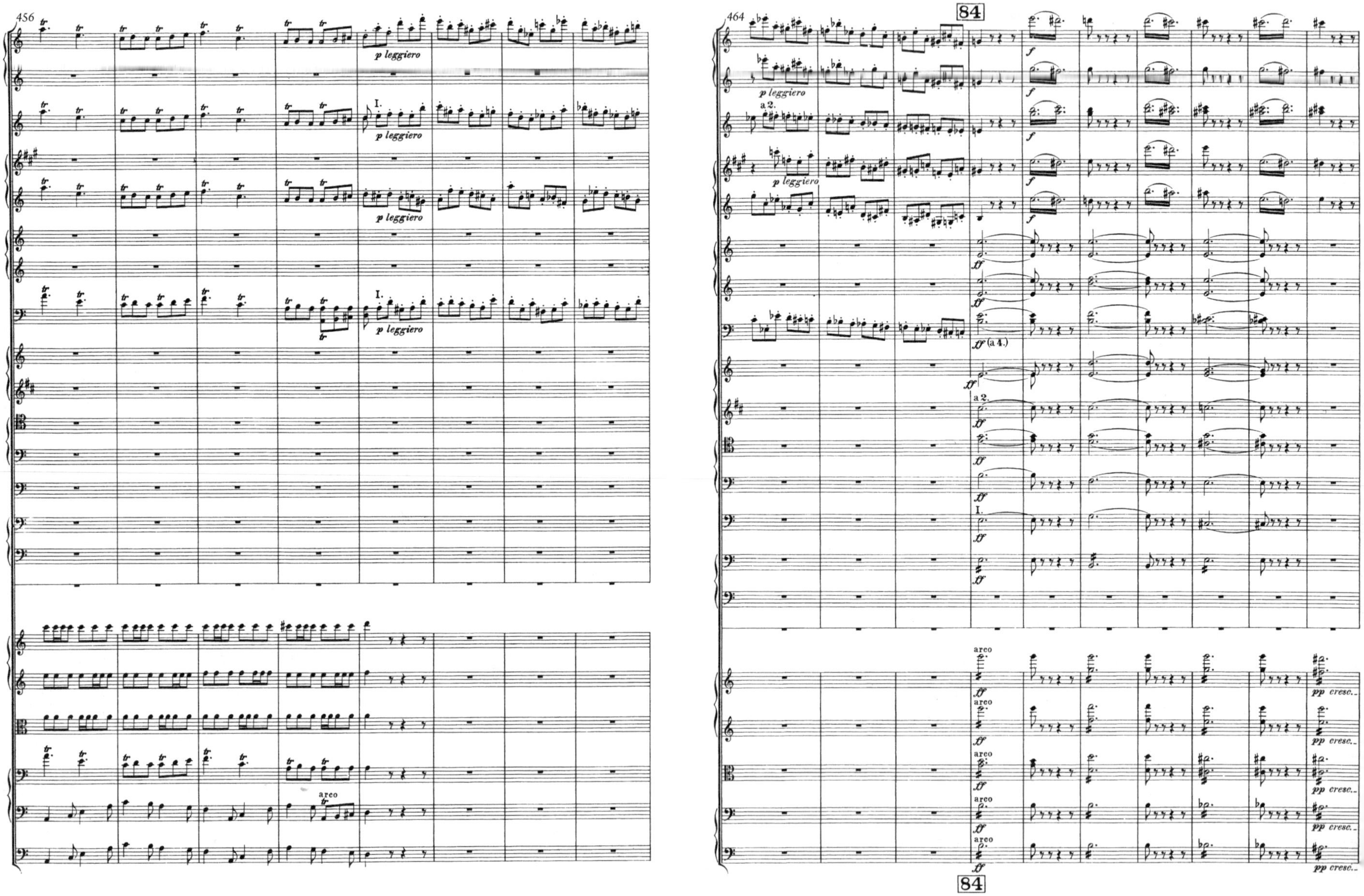
456
464
84
p leggiero
a 2.
I.
(a 4.)
arco
pp cresc.
84

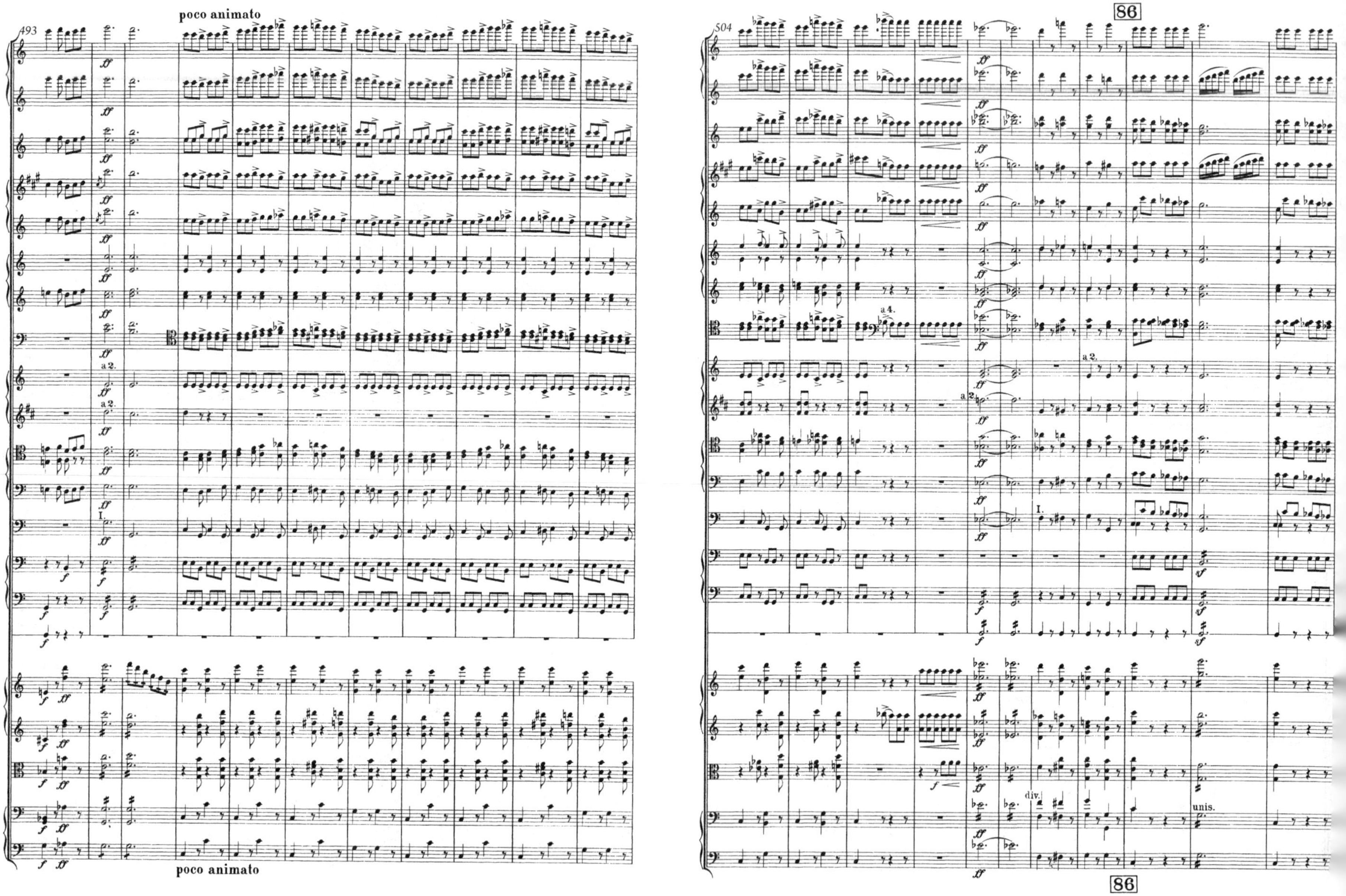
493
poco animato
a 2.
a 2.
I.
poco animato
504
86
a 4.
a 2.
a 2.
I.
div.
unis.
86

Coup frappé sur une Cymbale avec une baguette
couverte d'éponge ou un tampon.
Schlag auf ein Becken mit einem Schwamm-
schlägel oder Klöppel.
Struck on a cymbal with a sponge-headed
drum-stick.

Cinelli.

40

Felix Bartholdy Mendelssohn (1809–47)

Ein Sommernachtstraum (A Midsummer Night's Dream), Overture (piano reduction) (1826)

In 1826, at the age of seventeen, Mendelssohn composed his Overture to *A Midsummer Night's Dream* as a concert overture—an overture intended to be performed independently rather than serve as the introduction to a dramatic work. In 1843 he wrote additional musical numbers to go with an actual performance of Shakespeare's play. Mendelssohn was not the first to write concert overtures, but he gave the genre a specifically Romantic character by capturing the spirit of the literary work or landscape that served as a stimulus for composition.

From a structural perspective there is nothing particularly new in Mendelssohn's overture, which follows sonata principles (see chart).

More notable than his treatment of form is Mendelssohn's use of a descending tetrachord as the basis for much of the composition, a technique that anticipates the consistent thematic transformations of later composers. The tetrachord (E–D♯–C♯–B, with the D♯ and C♯ also appearing as D natural and C natural) is hidden in the bottom and middle voices of the opening chords; it serves as the main motive of the E-minor fairy theme and its E-major pair; and it appears in the bass of the dominant theme in m. 68 (B–A♯–G♯–F♯), the melody of which is also features descending scales.

Mendelssohn's originality here lies in the ingenious details he uses to convey the mood and characters of Shakespeare's play. The orchestration shows a highly developed sense for contrasting colors and textures. The stately opening chords, for instance, which Liszt compared to "slowly drooping and rising eyelids, between which is depicted a charming dream-world," are answered by the shimmering staccato flickering of the violins. This light, scurrying violin writing, which became a defining characteristic of Mendelssohn's style, served as a perfect depiction of Shakespeare's whimsical fairies—at the same time it sounded a new note of "fantastic Romanticism," four years before Berlioz's *Symphonie fantastique*.

What gives evocative power to the opening chords, which return at structurally significant places of the overture, is the combination of a rising triadic top line with a descending bass line and the magical chord change in m. 3 to an unexpected A-minor harmony that darkens the

Measure Nos.	Formal Designation	Sections	Keys	Comments
1–127	**Exposition**			
1–6		Opening chords		Mixture of major and minor chords introduces fairy realm
7–34		Primary theme 1	e	Fairy music (chromatic)
34–48		Primary theme 2	E	Majestic music (diatonic)
49–67		Bridge	Ends on V/B	
68–100		Secondary theme 1	B	"Love theme"
100–127		Secondary theme 2		Stomping, braying Bottom-as-ass
128–199	**Development**			
128–164		Primary theme	b, f♯, etc.	
165–199		Opening chords, fragmentation of secondary theme 2	Ends on c♯	End of development lacks traditional dominant pedal/retransition
200–314	**Recapitulation**			
200–206		Opening chords		
207–229		Primary theme 1	e	
230–262		Secondary theme 1	E	
262–298		Secondary theme 2	E	
298–307		Primary theme 2	E	Primary theme 2 used as closing theme
308–314				Bombastic E-major chords
315–350	**Coda**	Primary theme	e	
326–336				a♯°7 over B pedal
336–345		Primary theme 2		
346–350		Opening chords		

bright major of the preceding chords and at the same time allows the following E-major triad to be heard as a potential dominant. The E-major chord (mm. 4–5) does not, however, resolve like a dominant. Instead, Mendelssohn transforms it to E minor. When the emblematic chords return at the recapitulation, they again provide something surprising. In m. 200 the first interval (E–G♯) appears above a C♯ bass, thus giving a new tonal interpretation to the dyad E–G♯ (part of C♯ minor as opposed to E major). The reappearance of the opening chords at the end of the overture provides structural balance, but it also has programmatic significance. By bringing back the opening rhetorical gesture at the end Mendelssohn seems to recall the fairy Puck's farewell to the audience, in which he asks for forgiveness for his mischief and dismisses the previous events as part of a dream.

Other clear references to Shakespeare's play include the crude music following the secondary theme (mm. 101ff). The heavily stomping bass, the primitive melody, and especially the braying effects of the huge accented leaps at the end of phrases bring to life the Bottom-as-ass character, the object of the enchanted Fairy Queen Titania's misguided love. Two other themes in the exposition can also be related to Shakespeare. The two tonic themes, one in E minor and the other in E major, suggest the two main locations of the play: the Fairy King Oberon's forest, site of dreams and magic, and Duke Theseus's Athens, site of rational decisions and earthly celebrations. In contrast to the fairy's light, chromatically colored music in minor, Theseus's theme (mm. 34ff) is diatonic, majestic, and heavy. In the recapitulation Mendelssohn saves it for the end, using it as a celebratory closing gesture in mm. 298ff. The reordering of events in the recapitulation again points to the play, in which by daylight the fairy world disappears and rational human order is reestablished in Theseus's court, where wedding festivities take the place of the night's confused love affairs. The final return of Theseus's music in m. 336 is quiet, dreamy, and hesitant, as if the confident ruler of Athens had lost some of his rational security during the magical night of love.

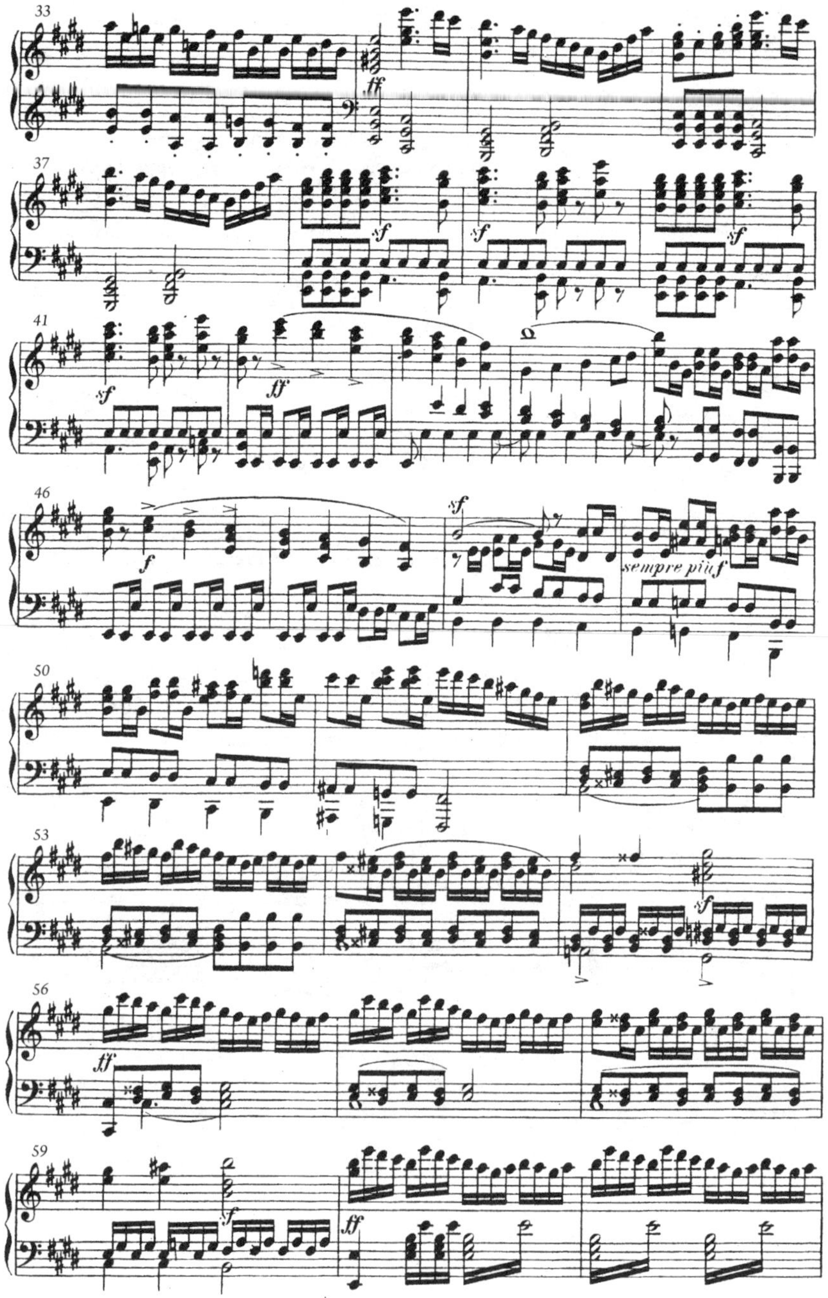
sempre più f

cresc.
cresc.
cresc.

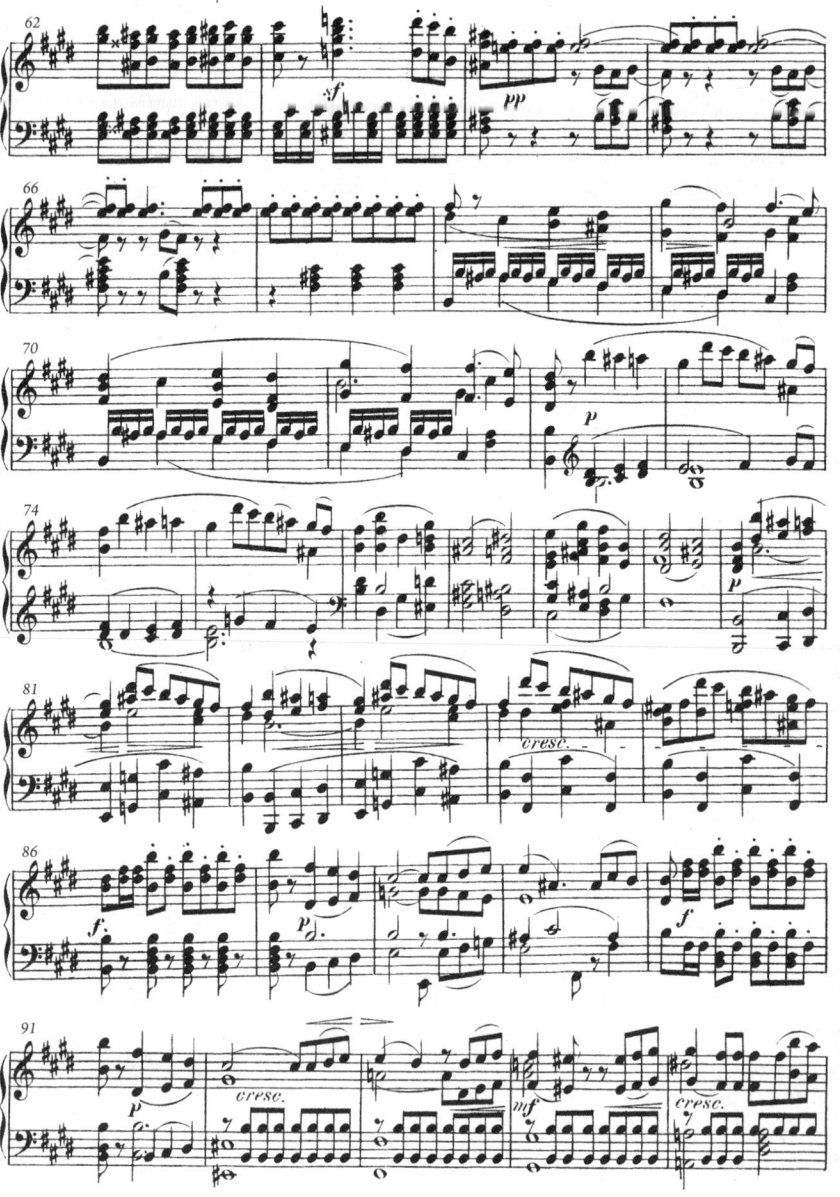

41

Felix Bartholdy Mendelssohn (1809–1847)

Paulus (St. Paul), Op. 36 (piano reduction) (1834–36)

Mendelssohn's *Paulus*, which premiered in 1836 at the Lower Rhine Music Festival in the Catholic city of Düsseldorf, was a milestone in the nineteenth-century oratorio revival. A renewed interest in oratorios in Germany was tied to the enthusiasm surrounding the revival of the music of Bach and Handel, a movement spearheaded by Mendelssohn's performance of Bach's *St. Matthew Passion* in 1828. Oratorios, which often involved hundreds of performers, were also well suited to expressing the new German national spirit awakened by the Napoleonic Wars.

Mendelssohn compiled the text of *Paulus* with the help of the Lutheran theologian Julius Schubring (1806–89), relying mainly on the "Acts of the Apostles" and St. Paul's letters to Christian communities. The oratorio enacts scenes from the life of Saul of Tarsus, an infamous Pharisee persecutor of Christians who, while travelling to Damascus, experienced a blinding vision of the resurrected Jesus that led to his conversion and baptism as Paul. The subject had biographical significance for Mendelssohn, whose father, Abraham, converted his Jewish family to the Protestant faith. The two-part oratorio contains six sections: the stoning of Stephen by a mob encouraged by Saul; Saul's journey to Damascus and his conversion; the restoration of his sight and his baptism; Paul and Barnabas's preaching to the Jews; their work among the Gentiles; and Paul's departure from the Ephesians.

a. Overture

Following Bach's example, Mendelssohn scattered chorales, emblems of Protestant worship, throughout his oratorio. The most important chorale Mendelssohn uses is "Wachet auf! ruft uns die Stimme" ([Sleepers] awake! the watchman's voice calls us). This chorale appears twice in the oratorio, first in the overture and then, following Saul's conversion in the first part, as a straightforward chorale setting.

Example 41–1

"Wa - chet auf," ruft uns die Stim - me,

The text of the chorale is based on the parable of the ten virgins in Matthew 25:1–13. Philipp Nicolai (1556–1608) adapted the melody from a tune by the famous minnesinger Hans Sachs (1494–1576).

> *"Wachet auf," ruft uns die Stimme*   "[Sleepers] awake!" the watchman's voice
> *Der Wächter sehr hoch auf der Zinne,*   Calls us from the highest tower,
> *"Wach auf du Stadt Jerusalem!*   "Awake, you city of Jerusalem!
> *Mitternacht heißt diese Stunde!"*   Midnight's solemn hour is tolling!"
> *Sie rufen uns mit hellem Munde:*   They call us with a bright voice:
> *"Wo seid ihr klugen Jungfrauen?*   "Where are you, clever virgins?
> *Wohlauf, der Bräutigam kommt,*   Awake, the bridegroom approaches,
> *Steht auf, die Lampen nehmt!*   Arise, take your lamps!
> *Halleluja!*   Hallelujah!
> *Macht euch bereit zur Hochzeitsfreud;*   Make yourself ready for wedding's joy;
> *Ihr müsset ihm entgegengehen!"*   You must go forth to meet him!"

The overture is set for a full symphonic orchestra, with festive brass instruments enhanced with trombones and a serpent (an S-shaped proto-tuba) and, at the end, the organ. The first part, in A major, uses the first three lines of the chorale in chiefly homophonic setting. The second part of the overture (*Con moto*) is a four-part fugue in A minor, the theme of which is a cleverly disguised variation of the first line of the chorale. Though the exposition of the fugue closely follows Bachian models, in the middle part (mm. 78ff) Mendelssohn updates the old genre by using its polyphonic texture as a basis for a development section with rapid modulations and motivic work based on the fragmented fugue theme and the original chorale. The first line of the chorale theme appears in E minor (m. 90), C major (m. 98), and D minor (m. 106); the fugue theme in D minor (m. 113), A minor (m. 117), and F major (m. 127) before the full three lines of the chorale theme are triumphantly restated in the tonic key of A major (mm. 156ff). The *fortissimo* A-major return, anticipated by long dominant preparation, has the effect of a true symphonic recapitulation.

Fugal

motives taken from chorale

Wachet auf! ruft uns die Stimme

b. No. 36, Chorus

The last chorale setting, by far the most significant both symbolically and musically, is placed in the scene of Paul's addressing the heathen, who have just mistaken him and his miracle-performing companion, Barnabas, for the gods Jupiter and Mercury. He rebukes them for their idolatry, preaching, "God does not reside in temples made by human hands." Instead, he exhorts them, "You yourselves are God's temple, and the Spirit of God dwells in you." These words are then given illustration by Mendelssohn in a remarkable exchange between St. Paul and the chorus. Paul sings, "Aber unser Gott ist im Himmel, er schaffet Alles was er will" (But our God is in heaven; he creates all according to his will). The melody to which the Apostle sings these words is not a chorale; rather, it is a folk-like tune of a type that can be plausibly transferred to a crowd of heathen "folk." When they take up the refrain, however, their counterpoint, doubled discreetly by the strings, becomes the background to a long-note chorale melody sung by the second sopranos. This is their first entrance in this chorus, illustrating the notion that their singing bodies, providing a "home" for the chorale melody, are indeed the dwelling place of God's spirit (mm. 49ff).

And what chorale melody do the second sopranos sing? None other than the tune to which Luther's translation of the Nicene Creed—"Wir glauben all' an einen Gott" (We all believe in one God)—had been sung since the earliest Lutheran hymnals. The second sopranos sing the whole first verse of the Lutheran creed, enshrined in an oratorio given its first performance before an audience made up largely of Düsseldorf Catholics, to consecrate an ideal of national religious union.

"ABER UNSER GOTT IST IM HIMMEL"

Aber unser Gott ist im Himmel,	But our God abides in Heaven,
er schaffet Alles was er will!	He creates all according to his will!
Wir glauben all an einem Gott,	We all believe in one God,
Schöpfer Himmels und der Erden,	Creator of Heaven and Earth,
der sich zum Vater geben hat,	who gave himself as the father
dass wir seine Kinder werden.	so that we would be his children.

42

Robert Schumann (1810–56)

FULL CD IV: TRACK 32
CONCISE CD II: TRACK 30

Fantasy, Op. 17, First movement (1836–38)

distant longing (handwritten)

Schumann completed his Fantasy for piano, Op. 17, in 1836, but he continued to revise it for two years, adding two movements and experimenting with various programmatic titles before settling on the unspecific Fantasy. Schumann also added a "motto" from Friedrich Schlegel's poem *Die Gebüsche* (The bushes) as an epigraph to the piece:

Durch alle Töne tönet	Through all the sounds
Im bunten Erdentraum	In the motley dream of earthly life
Ein leiser Ton gezogen	There sounds a soft, drawn-out sound
Für den der heimlich lauschet.	For the one who overhears in secret.

According to Schumann, the "soft, drawn-out sound" in the motto was a reference to his beloved Clara Wieck (1819–96), the daughter of Schumann's piano teacher, whom he would marry in 1840. The whole piece, in its original version, was conceived as "a deep lament" for Clara, whose father had sent her to Dresden in 1836 in one of his many attempts to break up her relationship with Schumann. In keeping with his programmatic conception of the piece as a lament for far-off Clara, Schumann quotes from the last song of Beethoven's famous song cycle *An die ferne Geliebte* (To the distant beloved) in the concluding *Adagio* section (mm. 295ff). Only at the end does the piece clearly articulate the tonic key with a full cadence.

The title Fantasy does not set up expectations of sonata form, although the recapitulation-like section of Schumann's work does bear a similarity to it. More characteristic of the work than its distant relationship to sonata form is its tonal instability. For example, instead of a tonally stable presentation of a first theme, Schumann launches the piece with a turbulent dominant-ninth chord in the left hand, "to be played," as Schumann instructs at the beginning of the score, "in an extravagant and passionate manner throughout." The melody, entering on the ninth of the chord, seems to begin not at the beginning, but in the middle of a process—as one might expect in a fragment torn off from some larger entity.

The opening material returns in m. 97. Some have called this a recapitulation, but the dominant pedal undermines the sense of tonic stability expected from a sonata recapitulation. A more likely candidate for recapitulation occurs in m. 225, which brings back almost one-third of the movement, with sonata-like transpositions of previous thematic materials to C or C-minor tonic. Despite this remnant of sonata principles, a lack of tonal stability and a seemingly extemporaneous introduction of new material mark this movement as a fantasy rather than a sonata.

A classic instance of the intrusion of new thematic material takes place about halfway through the movement (m. 129) with what can be described as a lengthy interpolated character

Measure Nos.	Thematic Fragments/Sections	Keys	Comments
1–128	**1st Part**		
1–33	Fragment 1	C, B♭	Fragment 1 begins in C over dominant pedal, but does not cadence in tonic
33–41	Fragment 2	c	Fragment 2 begins in middle voice
41–52	Fragments 3–4	d	Fragment 3 from m. 41, fragment 4 from 48
53–61	Transition		
61–73	Fragments 3–4	F	Fragment 3 at m. 61, fragment 4 at m. 69
73–77	Transition		
77–81	Fragment 5	d	*Adagio* section
82–97	Transition		
97–105	Fragment 1	C	No cadence in C, ends on V
106–119	Transition		Emphatic, based on fourths
119–128	Fragment 1	C	Over tonic pedal from m. 120, ends with out-of-time flourish
129–224	**Middle Section, Intrusion** ("Im Legendenton")	c	Uses fragment 2 as main thematic material, fragment 1 suggested in opening descending bass line. mm. 156–164, Beethoven fragment mm. 165–181, fragments of 2 mm. 181ff, fragments of 3
225–295	**Recapitulation-like section**	C or c	Repeats events from first part in tonic: 1 at m. 225, 2 at m. 229, 3 at m. 233, 4 at m. 241, 3 at 253, 4 at m. 261, 5 at m. 269 (*Adagio*)
274–286	Transition		Emphatic, based on fourths
286–295	1	C	
295–309	**Culmination**	C	*Adagio* quotation from *An die ferne Geliebte*, finally leading to full cadence in tonic.

tonal instability (handwritten)

Interruptions of new thematic material (handwritten)

481

piece in C minor. Schumann even delineates the section's new character with his marking "Im Legendenton" (<u>In the manner of a legend</u>). The theme of this new passage has some connection with the main body of the movement. But its quality of intrusion is strong and is confirmed at its conclusion, where the "main body" resumes just where it had been broken off by the intruder. If the whole "Im Legendenton" episode were omitted, unbroken continuity would be restored.

When the opening material recurs again at m. 286, it still has the character of an unconsummated gesture. Thus the concluding quotation from *An die ferne Geliebte* functions as the single consummation toward which the entire movement has been striving. Indeed, most of the main themes in the first movement of the Fantasy are related to the melody of the final song in *An die ferne Geliebte* (albeit not always to the part quoted in the Fantasy). Schumann constructs the most obvious connection between the fragmentary thematic material of the movement and the Beethoven motto by frequently providing closing phrases evocative of his borrowed melody (see mm. 15–19, 49–52, 69–72, 79–81, 261–264, 271–273 296–297). Understanding the whole movement in this light accords with the poetic "motto," which speaks of a tone sounding *throughout*. Thus the distinctive Beethoven reference at the end does not function simply as a quotation expressing Schumann's longing for his own "distant beloved," Clara, but as a consummation of desire painfully present in the movement, a tonal fulfillment and a thematic statement that synthesizes the fragments that preceded it.

43

Robert Schumann (1810–56)

FULL CD IV: TRACKS 33–34
CONCISE CD II: TRACKS 31–32

Dichterliebe (Poet's love), Op. 48 (1840)

Schumann composed his song cycle *Dichterliebe* on selections from Heinrich Heine's collection of poetry *Lyrisches Intermezzo* (Lyrical intermezzo) (1822–23). Like most of the songs he composed in 1840, his "year of song," *Dichterliebe* was written for his wife, Clara.

a. No. 1, "Im wunderschönen Monat Mai" ("In the lovely month of May")

The images in the text of the first song evoke springtime; the awakening of nature suggests the awakening of love. Schumann captures perfectly the tension in the painful longing expressed in Heine's poem with aching, drawn-out dissonances, sighing appoggiaturas, suspensions, and tonal instability. By ending on a dominant-seventh chord, Schumann suggests that this longing remains unfulfilled.

The tension that characterizes the song begins almost immediately when the piano's opening C♯ collides with the left hand's D. The C♯ serves as a dissonant suspension that resolves to B, thus forming a ii$_3^4$ chord in F♯ minor. The next measure brings a dominant-seventh chord; but instead of resolution to the tonic, F♯, the chord progression repeats unchanged. This drives the music to a cadence, but in the "wrong" key, A major (m. 6). Expectations for an F♯-minor resolution, built up so strongly in the introduction, are thus frustrated. Following the repetition of the A-major cadence (m. 8), the ensuing sequence further confuses the sense of a tonal center. A progression takes the song first to B minor (mm. 9–10), then to D major (mm. 11–12). Although the song is filled with authentic cadences, they all occur in the "wrong" keys (A, b, and D). The tonic, F♯ minor, is never stated, only implied through its dominant seventh.

Schumann combines the tonal uncertainty of the song with metric, rhythmic, and contrapuntal ambiguity. The incessantly flowing sixteenth notes, alternating between the right and left hands, weave a single melodic line, obscuring the meter. Our main guides to meter are the cadences that consistently fall on the strong beats. The relationship between the voice and the piano contributes to the ambiguity of the song. At times their melodies are one (the singer's

entrance sounds almost as if it grows directly out of the piano part), but at times slight differences between the two create expressive moments (see the right hand's clash with the voice in mm. 9 and 11).

The most important difference between the voice and the piano is their tonal preference. A major belongs to the voice, while F♯ minor seems to be the sole territory of the piano—F♯ minor is never alluded to when the voice is present. The final gesture, the dominant chord of F♯ minor, sounded on the piano without the voice, suggests that for Schumann infinite longing was best expressed when music was free of words and their specific meanings.

Im wunderschönen Monat Mai	In the lovely month of May,
als alle Knospen sprangen,	when all the buds were bursting,
da ist in meinem Herzen	then within my heart
die Liebe aufgegangen.	love broke forth.
Im wunderschönen Monat Mai	In the lovely month of May,
als alle Vögel sangen,	when all the birds were singing
da hab' ich ihr gestanden	then I confessed to her
mein Sehnen und Verlangen.	my longing and desire.

b. No. 2, "Aus meinen Tränen" ("From my tears")

The second song seems to promise the fulfillment of the dreams expressed in the first song. The buds become flowers in bloom, the birds are named as nightingales, and, although presented with the conditional "if," love appears to be a real possibility. The poem, the only one in the cycle in which the beloved is addressed as "little child," must have resonated strongly with Schumann, who got to know Clara when she was only twelve.

The sentimental tone of the poem finds its musical expression in Schumann's purposely simplified setting. Except for the third line (mm. 9–12), the song seems to consist of a series of authentic and plagal cadences. The tonic A is emphasized so strongly that one is tempted to see in it an ironic gesture of assurance. There is no doubt that the tonality is A major. Still, the shadow of F♯ from the previous song is not completely gone. The first sonority, following the V[7] of F♯ that ended "Im wunderschönen Monat Mai," consists of A–C♯, which can imply both F♯ minor and A major. As if remembering it from the previous song, the third line stops on the dominant of F♯ minor (m. 12). Although the piano repeatedly insists on A-major cadences, the voice stops on the dominant at the end of three lines out of four—the piano's hurried correction sounds almost like the hushing up of suppressed uncertainties and fears (mm. 4, 8, and 16). The piano's cadential gestures suggest either that the pianist does not hear the singer in these measures or that she or he purposely disregards the singer's preference for ending on a note of longing.

Aus meinen Tränen spriessen
viel blühende Blumen hervor,
und meine Seufzer werden
ein Nachtigallenchor.
Und wenn du mich lieb hast, Kindchen,
schenk' ich dir die Blumen all',
und vor deinem Fenster soll klingen
das Lied der Nachtigall.

From my tears spring up
many blooming flowers,
and my sighs become
a chorus of nightingales.
And if you love me, little child,
I'll give you all the flowers,
and before your window shall sound
the song of the nightingale.

44

Clara Schumann (1819–96)

FULL CD IV: TRACK 35
CONCISE CD II: TRACK 33

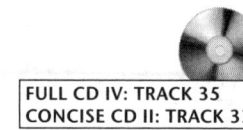

"Er ist gekommen in Sturm und Regen" ("He has come in storm and rain"), Op. 12, No. 2 (1840)

In 1840 Clara Schumann composed a few songs as a Christmas present for her husband, Robert, who had been encouraging her to try her hand at songs. Clara's present inspired Robert to propose a common project: a book of songs composed by Clara and himself. The result was a set of twelve songs on poems from Friedrich Rückert's *Liebesfrühling* (Love's Springtime), which the poet wrote while courting his future wife in 1821. In the original publication, which Robert rushed to press so that he could present it to Clara as a birthday present, the songs are not distinguished according to their composers—apparently Robert enjoyed critics' confusion about their authorship. "Er ist gekommen in Sturm und Regen" is the second in *Zwölf Lieder aus F. Rückert's* Liebesfrühling *für Gesang und Pianoforte von Robert und Clara Schumann* (Twelve songs from F. Rückert's *Love's Springtime* for voice and piano by Robert and Clara Schumann), designated in later editions as both Op. 37 (in Robert's oeuvre) and op. 12 (in Clara's oeuvre).

Rückert's poem describes the agitated excitement of a woman in love. The beloved man's coming "in storm and rain" suggests struggle and hardship that need to be overcome before the lovers can be united. The fast tempo, the key of F minor, "Leidenschaftlich" (passionate) expression, the piano's quickly rising and descending sixteenth-note figures, and the swelling dynamics depict both the storm that roars outside and the intensity of the emotion in the woman's heart. The rising melody and the rhythm of the first four measures of the vocal melody—each beginning with a rest, suggesting a quick breath—capture the protagonist's agitation.

Clara set the poem in a modified strophic form: The first two stanzas share the same music, while the last stanza charts new territory. Her alteration of the simple strophic form shows a sensitive reaction to the poem's structure. Rückert creates a parallel between the three stanzas by beginning each with the same line, but distinguishes the last stanza by replacing the subject "he" (er) with "love's springtime" (Frühlings Segen). Clara brings back the agitated first two melodic lines of the first stanza (sung to the text of the first line, mm. 18–23) before the change of mood beginning with the second line of the third stanza (mm. 24ff); she thus recalls the stormy, passionate F-minor passage before the arrival of the slower, calmer final section in A♭ major.

Clara creates the sudden calmness of the last three lines not only by slowing the tempo but also by the sudden drop in the dynamics, the elongation of note values in the first three measures of the melody (mm. 25–27), and a more continuous vocal line. Arpeggiation in the right hand gives way to block chords, and the texture simplifies further to a hymn-like homophonic chord progression at the repetition of the text at mm. 34–39. It is as if the protagonist, exhausted by the emotional upheaval, yields to quiet prayer. Only the recurring flat sixth scale degree (F♭), which lends a somewhat hesitant tone to the piano postlude, disturbs the sacred atmosphere.

Apart from the postlude, which sounds like a belated reflection on the previous music, the piano leads rather than follows the voice. In the introduction it forecasts the first two lines, in the transition to the second part of the strophe it acts as the agent of modulation to the parallel major (A♭ major), and at the end of the first and second strophes it leads back to F minor.

Clara confessed to Robert that she did not feel comfortable composing songs in which she had to "grasp fully the meaning of the words." A virtuoso pianist, she felt more at ease expressing herself without words on the piano, both as a composer and as a performer. Despite her initial misgivings about her ability to compose songs, the interplay between the voice's inability to express fully the feelings of the protagonist and the piano's unrestricted passion for saying what words could not describe captures both the meaning of "Er ist gekommen in Sturm und Regen" and the spirit of Romanticism.

Er ist gekommen in Sturm und Regen,	He has come in storm and rain,
ihm schlug beklommen mein	my anxious heart beats toward him.
Herz entgegen.	
Wie konnt' ich ahnen, dass seine Bahnen	How could I know that his paths
sich einen sollten meinen Wegen.	would unite with mine.
Er is gekommen in Sturm und Regen,	He has come in storm and rain,
er hat genommen mein Herz verwegen.	full of daring he has taken my heart.
Nahm er das meine? Nahm ich	Did he take mine? Did I take his?
das seine?	
Die beiden kamen sich entgegen.	Both drew nearer to one another.
Er is gekommen in Sturm und Regen!	He has come in storm and rain!
Nun ist gekommen des Frühlings Segen.	Now spring's blessings have come
Der Freund zieht weiter, ich seh' es heiter	My friend goes away, but I am happy,
denn er bleibt mein auf allen Wegen.	for he remains mine wherever we go.

Nature
longing
question

45

Frédéric Chopin (1810–49)

Préludes, Op. 28, Nos. 1–4 (1838–39)

Like J. S. Bach in the *Well-Tempered Clavier*, Chopin wrote a series of twenty-four preludes that move through all the major and minor keys. Instead of following Bach's ordering of keys—a rising sequence of semitones, with each major key followed by its parallel minor—Chopin arranged his preludes along the circle of fifths, with each major key followed by its relative minor (C major, A minor, G major, E minor, etc.). Chopin's ordering suggests that the set was intended not merely as a compendium but for performance as a set, for this arrangement of keys is much closer to the sequences found in actual harmonic practice than Bach's.

a. Prelude No. 1

The first prelude, in C major, the texture of which is indebted to Bach's C-major prelude, defines the genre as a Romantic fragment. The opening eight measures promise a balanced period. But the second phrase, instead of completing the first, soars aloft with chromatic alterations and only subsides harmonically in m. 25. Melodic resolution does not come until m. 29, with the sounding of the soprano C calculatedly withheld at m. 25.

When melodic resolution is finally granted in m. 29, harmonic motion is kept alive by placing the subdominant in the right hand over the root–fifth pedal in the left (a quintessentially Chopinesque touch). Full repose is not achieved until the final arpeggio, so the forthright eight-measure phrase of the beginning has now been answered by an asymmetrical twenty-five-measure continuation. Although the harmonic resolution makes for a very satisfying conclusion on one level, the resolution does not create a sense of completeness. Without the contrast and repetition (aba) needed to feel like an independent whole, the first prelude is paradoxically at once complete and incomplete.

b. Prelude No. 2

The second prelude, in A minor, is one of the most written-about pieces in the Romantic repertoire. Its attraction is the undeclared and withheld A minor tonality, which is clarified only at the very end of the prelude. The dissonant left-hand accompaniment, with its open fifths and chromatic middle-voice neighbors that frequently distort the effect of the chord tones, and the strangely awkward melody suggest a deliberately grotesque utterance. The monotony of the left-hand eighth notes, the slow tempo, and a middle voice that occasionally sounds the first four notes of the "Dies irae" hymn from the *Requiem* mass (see, for instance, the C–B–C–A in mm. 15–16) lend a dark tone to this prelude.

The piece begins, straightforwardly enough, as if in E minor, with the first melodic phrase ending on G, the ostensible relative major. The phrase, starting on a weak beat in m. 14, however, is famous for its functional ambiguity. Where it is leading is anyone's guess. Even the first three harmonies of the final cadence (mm. 21–22) suggest E major rather than A minor. When the final cadence is made on A minor, it seems arbitrarily tacked on—almost mockingly so, given the incongruous little chorale (marked *sostenuto*) that introduces it. There is little sense of inevitability about the harmonic trajectory of the piece; thus the final cadence does not fully release the tension of the strange dissonances and fragmented melody from earlier in the work.

c. Prelude No. 3

The third prelude is a light, virtuoso piece in G major, built on figuration in the left hand and playful nature sounds in the right. Unlike the ambiguous harmonic trajectory of the previous prelude, this one wears its simple, conventional tonal structure on the surface. It starts clearly in G major, tonicizes the dominant D major (m. 7), returns to G major (m. 10), and, like Bach's preludes, arrives to the final tonic cadence via the subdominant C major (mm. 16–21). The left-hand figuration accordingly is played from G, A, D or C, indicating either the tonic or the dominant function of a given key. Although technically demanding, this third prelude is free of the harmonic and melodic quirks that suggest intimate poetic messages in many of Chopin's preludes.

suspensions rather than a root progression by fifths was not a novel device—its origins lie in the ground basses of the sixteenth and seventeenth centuries. Precisely this old-fashioned quality made it esoteric and exotic and therefore striking. Although the texture of this prelude is that of melody and accompaniment, its strong contrapuntal backbone testifies to Chopin's thorough and conservative grounding in counterpoint.

d. Prelude No. 4

The next prelude, in E minor, provides both technical and emotional contrast to the preceding one. Despite its *espressivo* melancholy, this is actually one of the more gracious preludes. It has a formally straightforward binary design in which two parallel periods of equal duration (mm. 1–12 and mm. 13–25) proceed without detour first to a dominant half-close and then, more emphatically, to a full stop on the tonic.

The highly chromatic harmony has made this prelude popular. But its chromaticism, far from enigmatic or confusing like that of the second prelude, consists of a lucid, regular, and very intelligible application of chromatic passing tones to all three voices in a contrapuntally pristine though rhythmically wayward series of 7–6 suspensions. Harmony based on a chain of

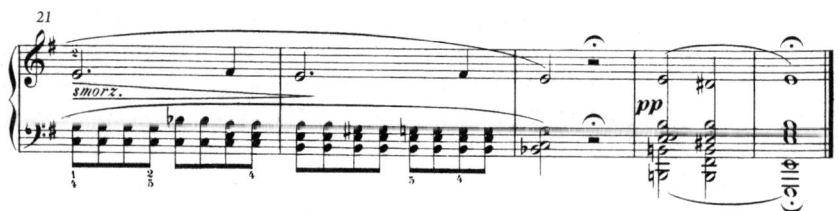

46

Frédéric Chopin (1810–49)

Mazurka, Op. 17, No. 4 (1833)

Indeed, Chopin's florid embellishments of melodic repetitions are most closely associated with another genre of character piece, the nocturne (see mm. 15, 31, and 55).

The end of this mazurka perfectly embodies the Romantic fascination with evocative incompletion. The idea is simplicity itself: a closing repetition of the mazurka's first four measures, which in their harmonic open-endedness had made an effective preface (or "prelude") to the dance. In a postlude, the same open-endedness is uncanny. Ending on an F major gives a sense that the piece has not ended but merely passed out of earshot (also implied by the marking *perdendosi*, "gradually dying away"). Nothing can follow such an ending without spoiling its special mood of enchantment. To do it justice, silence must hang palpably in the air.

The mazurka is a Polish folk dance from the Masovia region, characterized by triple meter with accents on the second and third beats (indicating stamping or heel-clicking leaps), and by the accompaniment of tonic or tonic-dominant drones (originally played on the Polish bagpipe). Mazurka rhythms appear in other dances of the Masovia region, such as the fast *oberek* or *obertas* and the moderate *kujawiak*. With their various tempi and rhythmic characteristics, Chopin's mazurkas rely alternately on these related Polish dances. Although he preserves some of the characteristic rhythms and accents of the original dances (♩ ♪ ♪), Chopin's mazurkas are highly stylized—reminiscences rather than re-creations of the musical flavors of Chopin's homeland.

Although Chopin composed a handful of the dances in Poland, he wrote his first collected sets of mazurkas (Opp. 6 and 7) in Vienna in 1830, the first year he spent away from home. By 1832 he was in Paris, an exile from his native land and a favorite of Parisian salons, where mazurkas were in high fashion. The four mazurkas of Op. 17 were written in Paris and, like those he composed in Vienna, marked Chopin's nostalgia for Poland.

In the first section of Op. 17, No. 4, hardly anything is left of the traditionally simple accompaniment or the oompah-pah that characterizes the left hand of the previous mazurkas in the series. Instead, Chopin uses a gradually descending, steady harmonic progression in the mid-register, *sotto voce* (in an undertone). The harmonic progression in mm. 5–12, which Chopin repeats eight times in the course of the piece, is a variant of the Chopinesque suspension chain we encountered in the E-Minor Prelude, even closer this time to the ancient lamenting ground bass, which descends mostly chromatically from I to V. The entire piece is built on the ground bass, with the exception of three sections: the rustic A-major middle section, which replaces the ground bass with steady open-fifth drones (mm. 61–92); an eight-measure transitory section on a dominant pedal (mm. 37–44); and the coda on a tonic pedal (mm. 109–132)—although in much of this section the bass's descending chromatic motion appears in the upper and middle voices.

As in conventional ground-bass variations, variety is provided by the lushly embellished melody. Grafting a basso ostinato onto a melody full of mazurka rhythms is a fantastic amalgam.

47

Frédéric Chopin (1810–49)

Ballade in G Minor, Op. 23 (1835)

The first instrumental work entitled ballade, Chopin's Ballade in G Minor for piano, Op. 23, may have been inspired by the literary ballads of the Polish Romantic poet Adam Mickiewicz (1798–1855), published in 1822. Chopin sketched the work soon after the Russians defeated the Polish uprising in 1831, which forced the Polish resistance into exile in France. The political significance of its inspiration has led many to hear Chopin's Ballade as an artistic expression of Polish revolutionary aspirations. The rhetorical progression of the piece, especially its catastrophic, stormy ending, supports such an interpretation. The violent scales on the last page, interrupted by what sounds like drum strokes heard from a distance, suggest a revolutionary narrative with a tragic ending. The final explosion of chromatic scales (mm. 258–262), the virtuosic fury of which seems to burn up all the motivic fragments scattered in the coda, reinforces the revolutionary implications. As Karol Berger has observed, the Ballade presents "a narrative which proceeds from a weak and open, soft and moderate beginning through successive waves of nervous intensification and acceleration, to an exceptionally strong and conclusive, frantic and fiery ending, with the final goal reached in an act of desperation." It also has similarities to sonata form (see chart).

Chopin's Ballade is filled with gestures that suggest the presence of a narrator as well as an untold story. One hears the narrator's voice at the beginning, in the *Largo* introduction, and at the very end of the work. The music of the introduction is vocal in style, comprising three phrases of "recitative," each one shorter, hence more urgent, than the last. It starts on an arpeggiated Neapolitan chord; the last phrase is left hanging in m. 7 on a remarkably evocative harmony containing three dissonances—two appoggiaturas (B♭ and E♭) and one suspension (G)—over a dominant root. This chord is so striking that an early biographer of Chopin called it "the emotional keynote of the work." Unheard throughout the main body of the Ballade, both of the two crucial harmonic events of the introduction—the Neapolitan sixth and the "keynote" chord—return in the coda. The Neapolitan sixth appears at the height of the *presto con fuoco* (m. 216), and the cadence it initiates is then repeated obsessively three more times. The

Measure Nos.	Formal Designation	Sections	Keys	Comments
1–7	Introduction		A♭ = ♭II = Neapolitan of g	Recitative-like. Arpeggio on the Neapolitan progresses to V/g, ends with a questioning phrase
8–90	"Exposition"			
8–36		Primary theme	g	Begins on C, like introduction; regular, song-like phrase structure, cadence at m. 33 interrupted with coloratura
36–44		Closing theme 1		Series of cadential gestures, cabaletta-like virtuosity
44–67		Bridge	Ends on V/B♭	"Horn calls" at the end, pastoral mood
68–82		Secondary theme	E♭	B♭, the expected key, turns out to be V of E♭, the actual key; long melody à la Bellini
82–90		Closing theme 2	E♭	
90–94	Transition			
94–194	Quasi-development			Previous themes juxtaposed
94–105		Primary theme	a	E pedal in bass
106–137		Secondary theme	A	
138–165		"Waltz episode"	E♭	
166–180	False recapitulation	Secondary theme	E♭	
180–194		Closing theme 2		
194–207	Recapitulation	Primary theme	g	(*sotto voce*, version from "development")
208–264	Coda	*Presto con fuoco*		Furious energy released, Neapolitan A♭ resolved to G in chromatic run at end

"keynote" chord, now arpeggiated, returns at m. 257 in the form of a passage in octaves that keenly recalls the rhetoric of the "narrator" of the introduction.

The vocal inspiration of the Ballade is evident not only in the recitative-like introduction. With its long, stretched-out melody, the lyrical section that follows recalls the vocal style of Vincenzo Bellini. The virtuoso passage in m. 33, which continues to delay the tonic cadence expected in m. 32, is reminiscent of operatic coloratura. The faster appendix that Chopin attaches to the first theme (mm. 36–44) recreates, on a small scale, the *cabaletta* section of the *cantabile-cabaletta* pair of nineteenth-century Italian opera arias. The second theme, starting in m. 68, is equally vocal in character, and it is also followed by a closing fast section (mm. 82–93).

Despite the presence of sonata principles, this is a peculiar adaptation of the form. In the bridge, for instance, modulation occurs not with a dramatic move but by a chromatic slide in the bass, from G in m. 58 to G♭ in m. 62, which leads to F, the dominant of the expected secondary key area (B♭). After intensive preparation on the dominant F, the new theme arrives not in the anticipated B♭ major but in the submediant E♭ major (m. 68). Stranger still, instead of a proper development there is a section in which themes are presented in their entirety without modulation. The section opens with the first theme over a dominant pedal in A minor in m. 94. Without transition, Chopin then segues to an explosive rendition of the second theme in A-major (m. 106), a tritone away from the theme's first statement.

The episode that follows next is sometimes called the "waltz episode," owing to the character of the accompaniment (mm. 138ff). Unlike typical episodes in developmental sections, it does not modulate; rather, it prepares the return of E♭ for the final statement of the second theme, which returns *fortissimo* with the rhetorical power of a recapitulation in m. 166. The double return of the tonic G minor and the first theme comes only in m. 194. This completes the Ballade's palindromic tonal plan: g (mm. 8ff)–E♭ (mm. 67ff)–A (A minor, m. 94; A major m. 108)–E♭ (mm. 138ff)–g (mm. 194ff).

Extra recurrences of the main themes, seemingly at odds with sonata procedures, are crucial to perceiving the Ballade as a ballad, that is, as a narrative unfolding in the stanzas of a strophic song. By synthesizing strophic and sonata principles, Chopin brilliantly solves the problem of capturing the relationship in a ballad between the recurrent tune and the ever-evolving narrative content. To pick the most obvious example, every time the first theme appears, its continuation is different. That is, on each appearance it is given a new narrative function, just as each repeated melodic stanza in a poetic ballad is invested with new words.

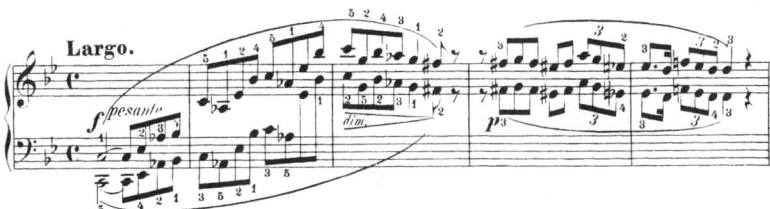

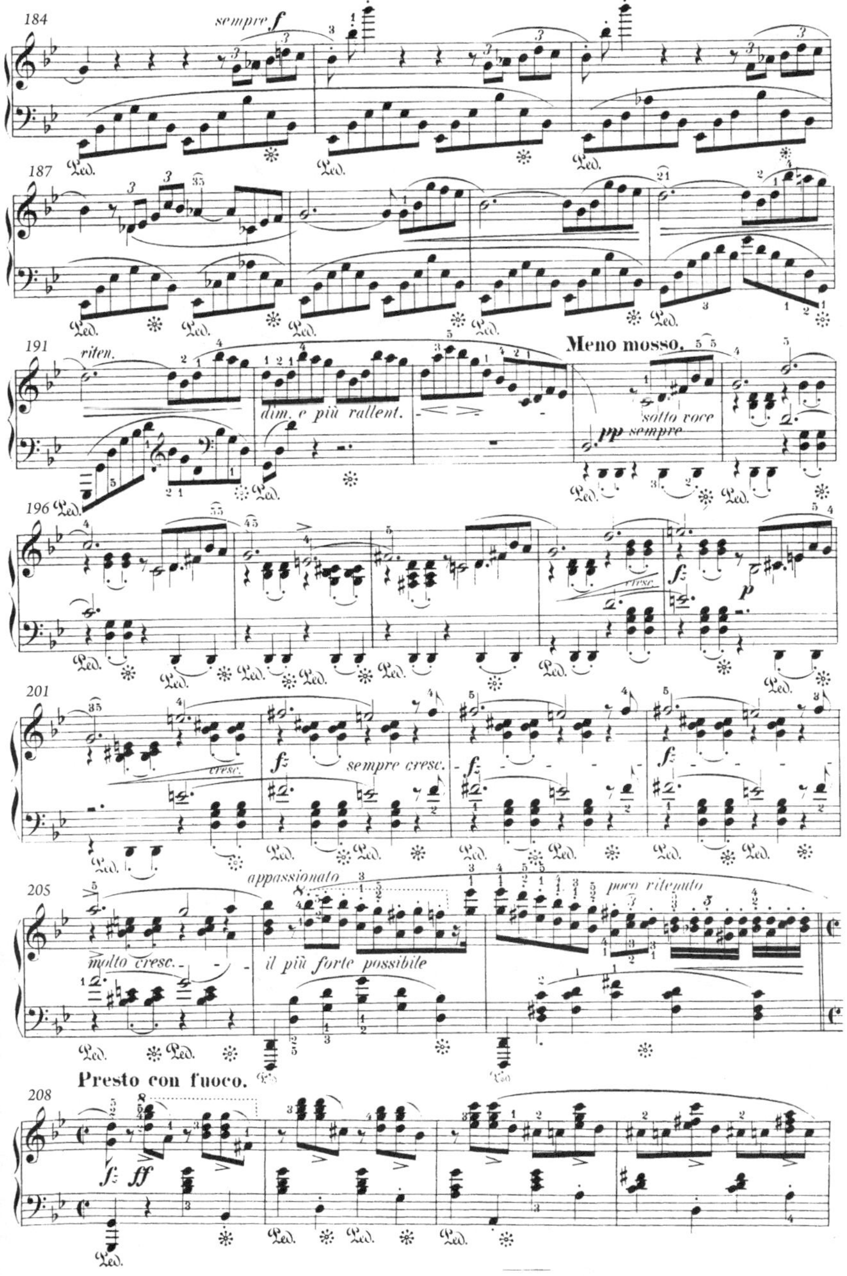
184
sempre f
187
191
riten.
dim. e più rallent.
Meno mosso.
sotto voce
pp sempre
196
cresc.
p
201
cresc.
sempre cresc.
205
appassionato
poco ritenuto
molto cresc.
il più forte possibile
Presto con fuoco.
208
ff

212
217
221
226
230
cresc.
234
ff
239
mf

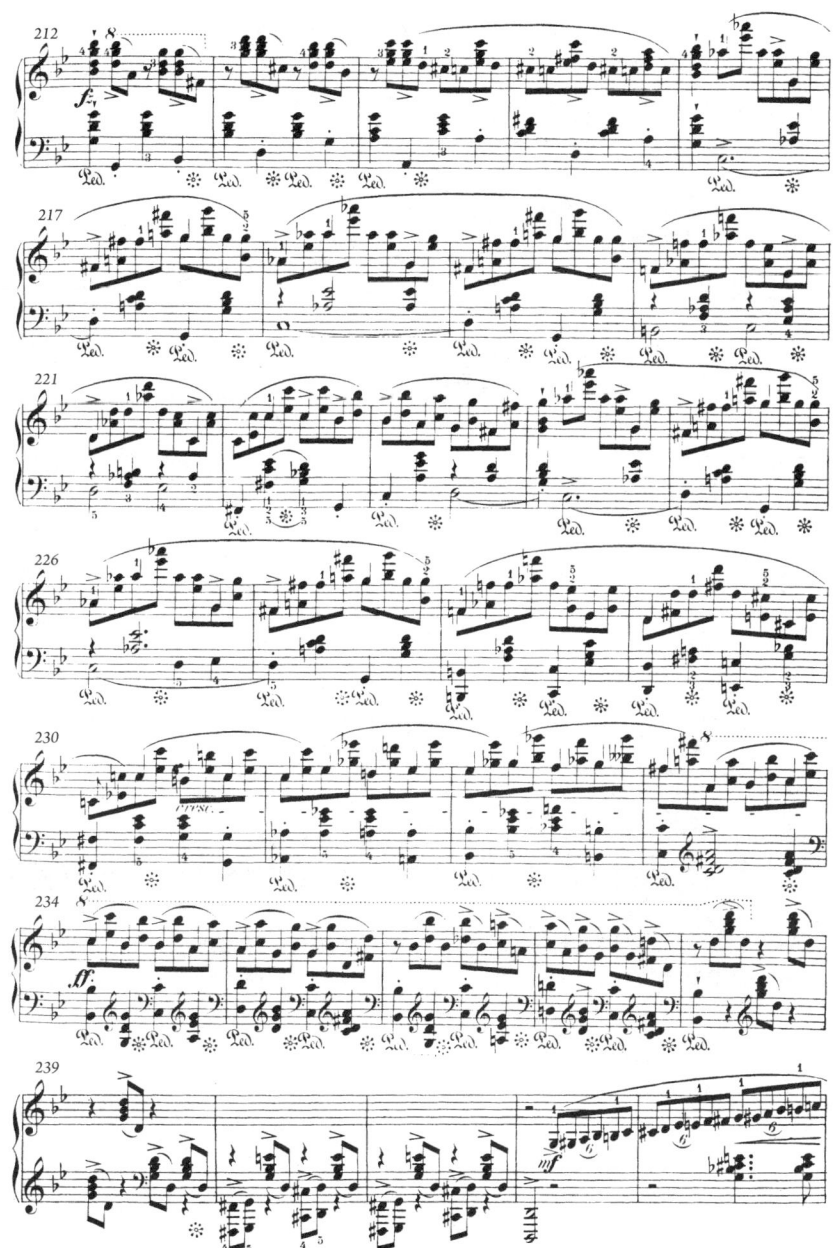

48

Louis Moreau Gottschalk (1829–69)

FULL CD V: TRACK 1
CONCISE CD II: TRACK 38

Bamboula, danse des nègres (Negro dance), Op. 2 (1844–45)

Bamboula refers both to a tambourine-like drum of African origin and to a dance for which this drum provides the accompaniment. The dance was frequently performed in New Orleans in the first half of the nineteenth century at Place Congo (now Congo Square in Louis Armstrong Park), where slaves gathered to sing, dance, and play music. These sounds and sights were part of Louis Moreau Gottschalk's childhood—from 1831 to 1833 his family lived on Rampart Street, just across from Place Congo. A work of early Americana, Gottschalk's *Bamboula* is a virtuosic showpiece that established the fifteen-year-old's reputation in Europe as a brilliant pianist and fashionably exotic American composer.

As a New Orleans–born pianist active in Paris, Gottschalk used his foreign origin as a marketing tool: on advertisements his name usually appeared with the qualification "de la Louisiane" (from Louisiana). Gottschalk's *Bamboula* is just the sort of exotic showpiece that was a nineteenth-century virtuoso's stock and trade—like Liszt's Hungarian rhapsodies or Chopin's mazurkas and polonaises. To Europeans Gottschalk's American piano pieces sounded even more exotic than the ethnically colored music of European virtuosos. As the enthusiastic Berlioz put it, the young American introduced his audience to "ingenious fantasies in which the nonchalant graces of tropical melody assuage so agreeably our restless and insatiable passion for novelty."

Some believe that in *Bamboula* Gottschalk used a Creole folk melody ("Quand patate la cuite na va mange li!" [When the sweet potato is cooked, we shall eat it!]). He may have heard West Indian songs from his grandmother or from the family's slave Sally, both born in St. Dominique. Whatever their source, the emphatic rhythms of the main theme of *Bamboula* conveyed to its audience a clear sense of primitivism—even before the main theme enters, the low D♭ "drum strokes" with which the piece begins announce the physicality of its topic, and the striking rhythm of m. 6 effects a violent off-kilter cadence that recurs throughout the work.

Bamboula consists of two sections of roughly equal length and a short concluding section that serves to round things off. Part 1 (mm. 1–146) is characterized by sharply articulated rhythms; part 2 (mm. 147–316) features a smoother, syncopated theme of a sentimental nature;

Measure Nos.	Parts	Sections/Themes	Keys	Comments
1–146	**Part 1**			**Rondo form: ABCABCA**
1–16		Introduction	D♭	Introduces violent "stomping" and prefigures theme A
17–48		Theme A	D♭	*Fortissimo*. Theme A serves to unify the piece since it also appears as the middle section of part 2 and in part 3
49–64		Theme B	D♭–f	Begins *piano*
65–83		Theme C	F♯	Begins *pianissimo*, uses same cadential rhythm as A
84–146		Themes A, B, C, A	D♭–F♯–D♭	Themes always appear in their original keys. Theme A shortened
147–316	**Part 2**			**Theme with two variations**
147–150		Introduction	b♭	
151–185		Theme D	b♭	
186–212		Theme D, Variation 1		Melody embedded in left hand
213–223		Theme D	b♭	
224–231		Theme A	D♭	
232–251		Interlude		Oasis of tranquility
252–316		Theme D, Variation 2	b♭	Melody embedded in arpeggios
317–356	**Part 3**			**Two themes from Part 1, now highly embellished**
317–335		Theme C	F♯	
336–356		Theme A	D♭	*Tutta la forza* (with as much force as possible)

part 3 (mm. 317–356) returns to material from part 1.* The frequent returns of the main theme, A, lend both the first part and the entire work something of a rondo structure. In its first, fullest version theme A consists of eight four-measure phrases. Four-measure phrase units continue as

*The *ossia*, or alternative, small-note version of the score, contains one measure not in the original (cf. mm. 334–335 in large print with music in small print above this passage). The measure numbers in our score follow the large-print original.

the building blocks throughout the piece. The almost exclusive reliance on four-measure units in $\frac{2}{4}$ and the prevalence of dotted rhythms and syncopations show *Bamboula* to be a precursor of ragtime.

Part 2 continues the four-measure phrase units and syncopations of part 1 but with a smoothness that reflects the air of urban European salons (especially their sentimental parlor-piano repertory) more than it reflects that of open-air slave dances in New Orleans. The main theme of part 2, D, is a thirty-two-measure theme in B♭ minor (mm. 151–182) on which Gottschalk writes two variations—conventional virtuoso treatment for a conventional theme. The two variations are separated by an interlude that includes a short return to an unadorned statement of theme D, the return of theme A from part 1, and a passage of bird-like trills and light (*leggiero*) chirpy arpeggios (mm. 232–251) that provide a textural contrast to the rest of the piece. In part 3, Gottschalk returns to themes C and A from part 1, now both in versions that rival and even surpass the virtuosity of the variations of part 2. The last two measures conclude with yet another repetition of the violent cadential gesture first heard in mm. 5–6, ending the piece with the same *fortississimo* drum-like pounding on the low octave D♭s with which it began.

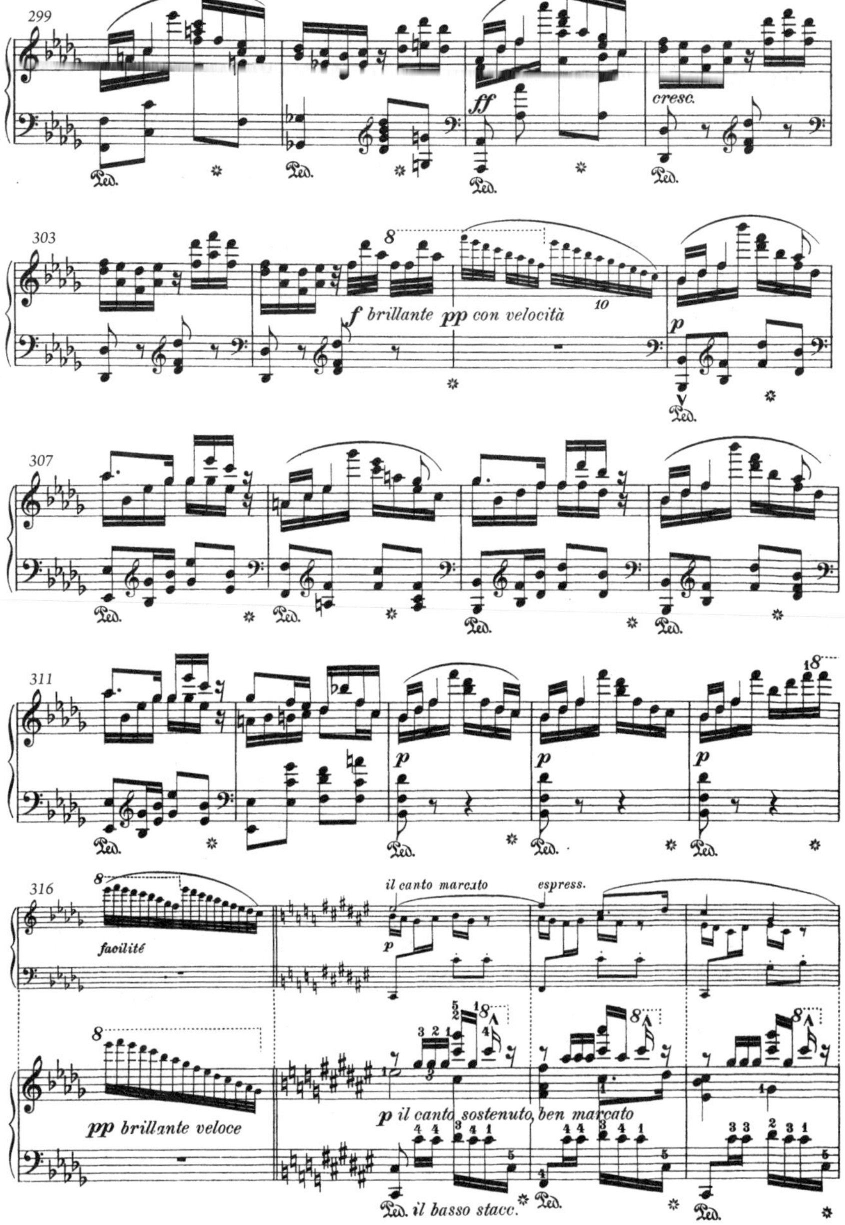
299
cresc.
303
f brillante pp con velocità
307
311
316
facilité
pp brillante veloce
il canto marcato
espress.
p il canto sostenuto, ben marcato
il basso stacc.

320
volante
p subito
324
329
p subito
cresc.

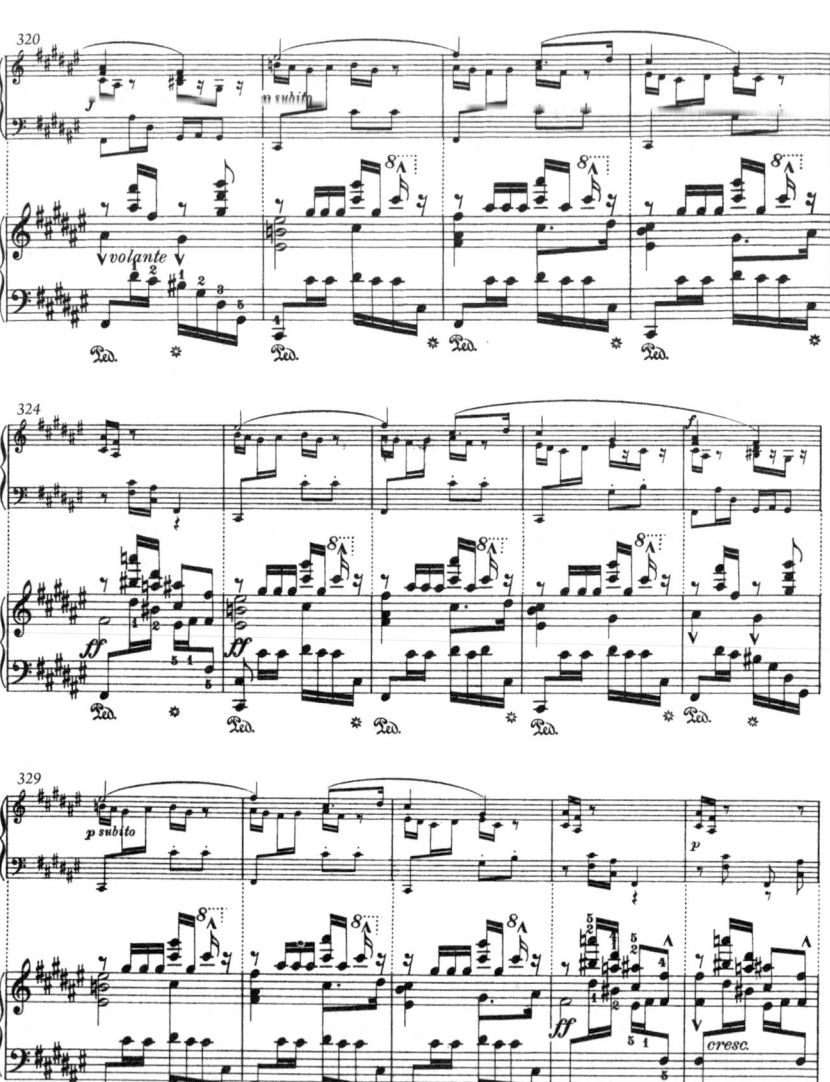

49

Mikhail Glinka
(1804–57)

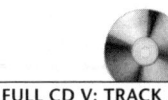

FULL CD V: TRACK 2

A Life for the Tsar, Finale from Epilogue, "Slav'sya, slav'sya" ("Glory, glory") (1836)

Glinka's first opera, *A Life for the Tsar*, concerns the heroic actions of the Russian peasant Ivan Susanin, who sacrificed his life for the first Romanov Tsar in 1613. (Susanin intentionally misleads a group of Poles and Lithuanians attempting to capture the new tsar. Realizing that Susanin has tricked them, the foreigners kill their cunning guide.) Glinka's mentor, Vasiliy Zhukovsky (1783–1852), suggested the topic and wrote the libretto for the opera's epilogue, a pageant in support of dynastic authority in Russia. Glinka's first opera was thus conceived in the spirit of the state-sponsored nationalism of the time, which required Russians to subscribe to the joint ideologies of orthodoxy, autocracy, and nationality. Glinka dedicated the opera to Tsar Nicholas I (ruled 1825–55), who returned the favor by giving the opera its title. Since its first performance in 1836, *A Life for the Tsar* has served as Russia's foremost national opera. Its status was due to Glinka's successful combination of an elevated, tragic tone with a recognizably Russian character. Even after the Bolshevik Revolution of 1917, Glinka's work remained an epitome of patriotism, although under communism the opera's title was changed to Glinka's original *Ivan Susanin*, and the score was revised to shift the focus from celebration of the Romanov dynasty to the peasant hero's self-sacrifice for his country.

With its versions of "slav'sya" and "slava" (glory or hail), the final chorus of the opera has served as the model for the numerous celebratory choruses in Russian music. Sycophantic "slava" choruses have been used variously to celebrate Russia and its tsars, Soviet power, the Communist Party, and Stalin. In Glinka's opera the cries of glory to the tsar remind us that in nineteenth-century Russia music was far from being an "autonomous" art. Opera served the state, without whose financial support it could not exist in Russia.

The first part of the chorus that concludes *A Life for the Tsar* is an example of Russian "changing background variations." Here the theme consists of four simple four-measure phrases (aabc) ending on the dominant (mm. 1–16), the accompaniment of which changes for each "variation": quarter-note triplets and occasional chromatic passages in the orchestra in variation 1 (mm. 17–32) and a second chorus singing long melismas on "slava" in variation 2

(mm. 33–48). In place of a third variation, the theme appears truncated and with its second line transposed to round off the first choral block on the tonic (*Più mosso*, mm. 49–59).

Respite from the full choral texture occurs in mm. 60–77 and 89–106, in which the basses address Susanin's children. These passages connect the impersonal celebratory chorus to the personal sentiments of Susanin's bereaved family. The basses' slow-moving melodic line gains momentum through an avalanche of third-related harmonies: the C-major chord that begins this section evolves into a C dominant-seventh chord in third inversion (mm. 66–69), which shifts to A♭ major (m. 70) instead of resolving according to the norms of functional harmony; the A♭-major chord then leaps down another major third to E major (m. 74) before completing a major-third cycle by moving back to C major for the repetition of the entire "Slava" section (mm. 78ff). (When Glinka repeats the bass section in mm. 99ff, he exchanges the A♭-major chord for an A-major harmony, which has a clearer functional relation to the subsequent E major.)

The last section of the chorus (*Ancora più mosso*, mm. 107ff) is built on a repeated four-measure phrase that starts deceptively as if it were the first theme. Like the previous section, it also contains adventurous harmonic progressions (for example, the climactic F-major chord in m. 120 is followed by E major, C minor, and then D major). This final section builds toward a climax by gradually speeding up motion in the chorus, culminating in long-held harmonies initiated by a sudden harmonic jolt: first on B major (mm. 143–146), which moves down a major third to G major in preparation for a resolution to C major; then, at its repetition (mm. 193ff) on B♭ major followed by ii$^4_3$ in C minor, before again zeroing in on an authentic cadence to C major. The euphoric hurrahs on the final, extended tonic chord are joined in the theater by the peal of bells, a particular Russian specialty. This final jubilation, which in the opera served to usher in 300 years of Romanov rule, became the mandatory tone for art addressing all rulers of Russia.

Moscow, Red Square. The scene is filled with jubilant people. In the foreground, Antonida, Sobinin, and Vanya [Susanin's daughter, son-in-law, and son]; next to them the leader of the detachment and the soldiers.

Chorus	**Chorus**
Slav'sya, slav'sya tï, nash Ruskiy Tsar'!	Glory, glory to our Russian Tsar!
Gospodom dannïy nam Tsar' Gosudar!	To our God-sent Tsar and Lord!
Da budet bezsmerten tvoy Tsarskiy rod!	May your royal line live forever!
Da im blagodenstvuyet Russkiy narod!	May the Russian nation prosper through it!

The leader and the soldiers   **The leader and the soldiers**

(to Susanin's children)

Uteshtes', vas Tsar' nagradit,	Take comfort, the Tsar will reward you
I narod vozglasit:	And the people will proclaim:
Pamyat' vovek, Susaninu!	May Susanin's memory live forever!

Slav'sya, slav'sya ti, nash Russkiy Tsar'! etc.	Glory, glory to our Russian Tsar! etc.

The leader and the soldiers

(to Susanin's children)

Vas Tsar' nagradit,	The Tsar will reward you,
I narod vozglasit:	And the people will proclaim:
Pamyat' vovek, Susaninu!	May Susanin's memory live forever!

Chorus

Vse blizhe Tsarskiy khod!	The royal procession is approaching!
Nash Tsar' idyot!	Our Tsar is coming!
Slava nashemu Tsaryu,	Glory to our Tsar,
Slava, slava Rusi svyatoy,	Glory, glory to holy Rus',*
Moskva, gremi, Moskva!	Rejoice, rejoice, Moscow!
Prazdnuy torzhestvennïy den' Gosudarya;	Celebrate the great day of our Lord;
Likuy, veselisya,	Rejoice, make merry,
Idyot nash Tsar'!	Our Tsar is coming!
Nash Tsar' idyot!	Our Tsar is coming!

(The leader and the soldiers join the basses of the chorus.)

Slava nashemu Tsaryu,	Glory to our Tsar,
Slava Rusi svyatoy!	Glory to holy Rus'!
Gremi, gremi Moskva!	Rejoice, rejoice, Moscow!
Ura! Ura! Ura! Ura! Ura!	Hurrah! Hurrah! Hurrah!

Rus' is the medieval name for Russia.

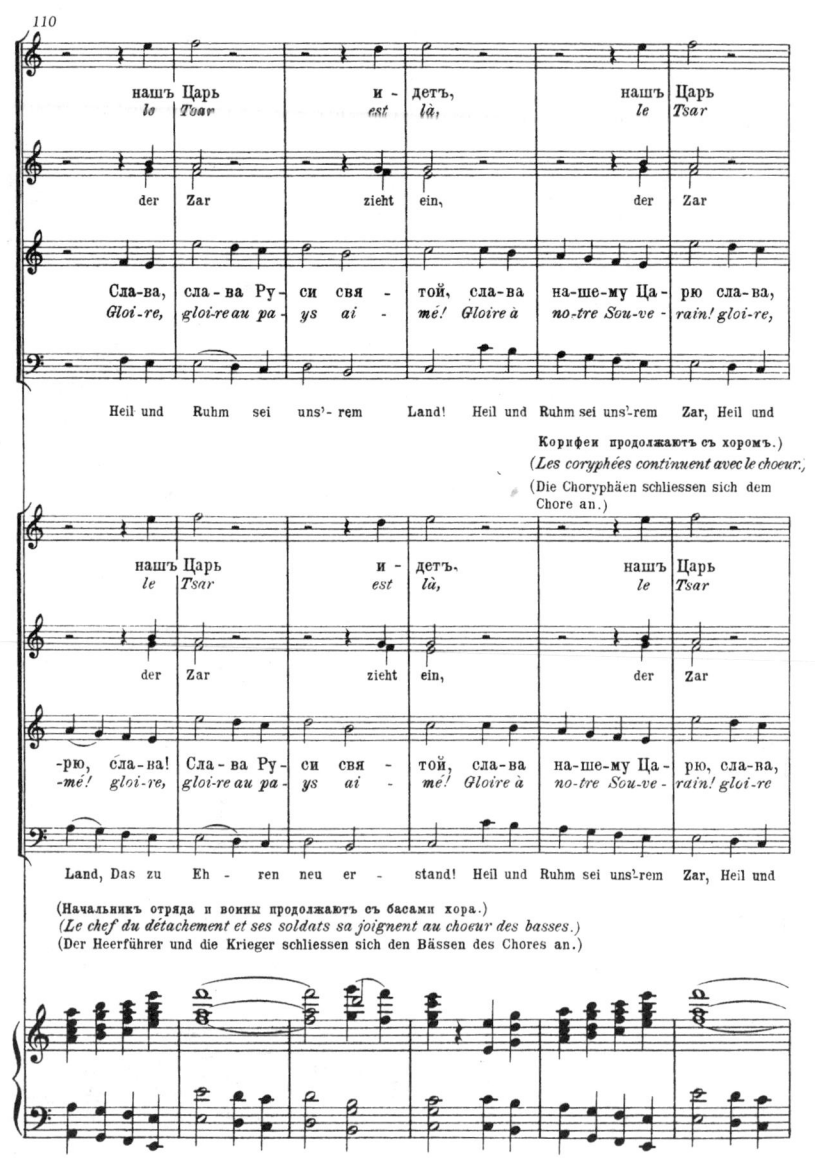

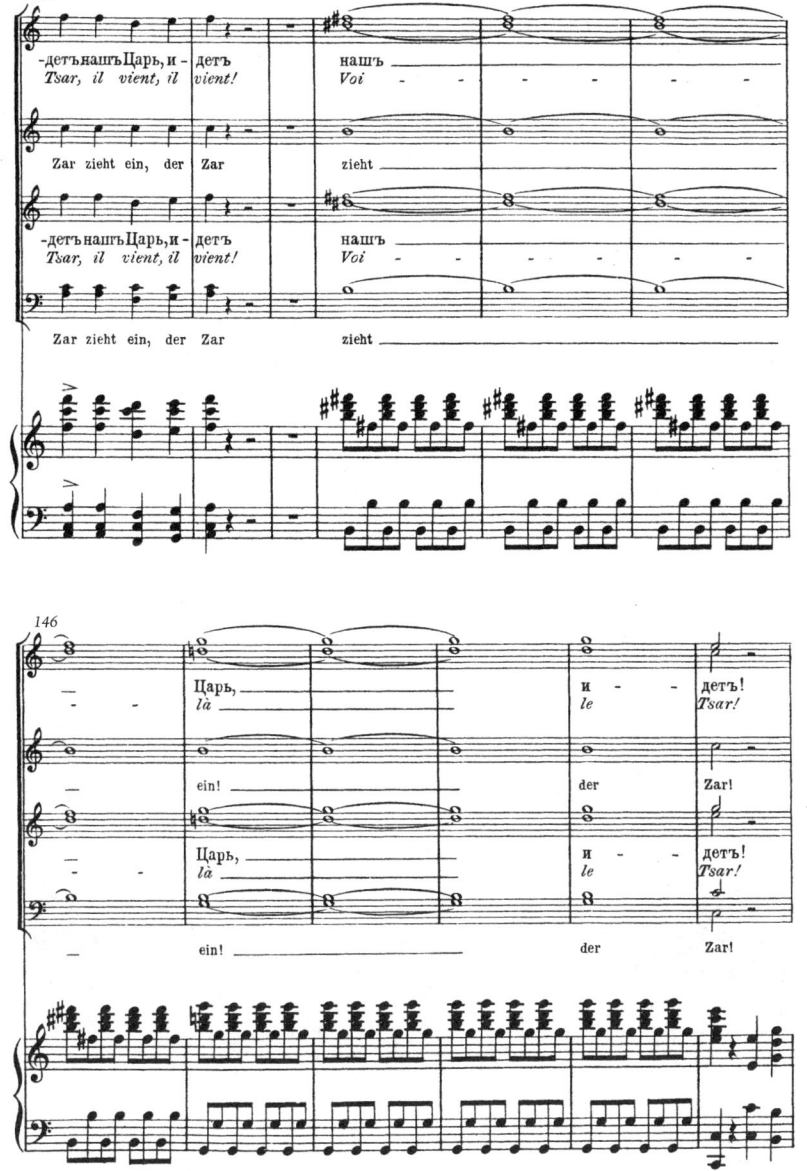

50

Mikhail Glinka (1804–57)

FULL CD V: TRACK 3

Kamarinskaya (1848)

Glinka composed his popular orchestral fantasy *Kamarinskaya*, originally titled "A Wedding Song and a Dance Song," during a stay in Warsaw in 1848. As the composer reported, he was inspired by his discovery of the melodic relationship between a wedding song, "Izza gor, gor vïsokikh gor" (From behind the mountains, the high mountains), which he heard in the country, and the well-known Russian dance tune "Kamarinskaya." The ingenious combination of the two melodies resulted in a piece that Chaikovsky called "the acorn from which the whole oak of Russian symphonic music grew." The chart on this page outlines the work's form.

The lyrical, slow-moving wedding song appears first after a brief introduction at m. 11, played unison by the strings. After four varied statements of the wedding song, a transition leads to the fast dance tune "Kamarinskaya" at m. 53. The subtle similarity between the two tunes can be detected if we compare the first five notes of the wedding song (F–A–B♭–A–G) with the structural notes of the dance melody ([D]–F♯–G–F♯–E).

Example 50–1

Glinka emphasizes the relationship by writing transitory sections in which one tune turns almost seamlessly into the other. The clearest example of this technique is at mm. 113–119, where the woodwinds, as if continuing the series of variations built on the dance tune, outline the

Measure Nos.	Section	Keys	Comments
1–10	Introduction	d–B♭	Based on motive from the wedding song (cf. mm. 13–14). Key somewhat unclear because of absence of V
11–34	Wedding song and variations	F	Six-measure wedding song played 4 times with varied orchestration and accompaniment
35–52	Transition	Ends on V/D	Based on the first motive of the wedding song and motive from the wedding song used in introduction
53–113	Dance tune and variations	D	Three-measure dance song ("Kamarinskaya") repeated ostinato with changing background
114–143	Transition	D–d–F	Notes from the dance song are emphasized so that their relationship to the wedding song becomes apparent
144–160	Wedding song and variations	F	Three statements of wedding song; the third is truncated
161–171	Transition		The last 3 notes of the truncated wedding song serve as a transition to the dance song
172–196	Dance tune and variations	B♭	Eight varied statements of the "Kamarinskaya" tune leading to . . .
197–208	Transition	B♭–d	Stalls on V⁷ over B♭ (mm. 197–203), the harmony turns to ii₃⁴ in d at m. 206
208–301	Dance tune and variations continued	D	"Kamarinskaya" tune resumes, with background variations
301–310	Coda	D	Includes fragments of "Kamarinskaya" tune

first motive of the wedding song. By the time the wedding song reappears in its original, slower tempo at m. 144, we hear it as derived from the dance tune. Less readily audible but no less motivically intricate are the other transitions between the two melodies in the piece. In the first transition, for instance, Glinka uses the first three notes (ascending) of the wedding song as the connecting motive (see mm. 35ff). After contrapuntally contrasting it with a descending motivic fragment, also taken from the wedding song, Glinka places the first motive (F–A–B♭)

in the bass (mm. 40–43), repeating it three times. The A that follows the motive in the original melody arrives at last via G in m. 45, creating yet another variant of the motive (F–A–B♭–A becomes F–A–B♭–G–A). In the context of the repeated F–A–B♭ motive in the bass, one hears the subsequent turns around the A's that set up the dance tune as a chromatic version of the motive ([F]–A–B♭–A becomes A–B♭–A–G♯–A). In a later transition leading from the slow to the fast tunes (mm. 160ff), Glinka singles out another motive from the wedding song to create the link between the two melodies. Here he breaks off the wedding song after the D–E–F of its fourth and fifth measures (mm. 159–160) and uses this motive to generate a turn figure around F that leads to the dance tune in B♭.

As these examples show, Glinka relies on intricate motivic work, familiar from the German symphonic tradition that Glinka's followers claimed to have rejected as foreign to Russian music. Also reminiscent of German symphonic music is the way in which a melodic detail relates to the tonal plan of the entire work. Melodically B♭ receives special emphasis by virtue of its being the first (and last) note of the introduction and the highest note of the wedding song (m. 11). It is hardly coincidental, then, that in addition to the tonic key of D minor (later D major) and its relative major (F), Glinka uses B♭ major prominently in the work's tonal scheme.

Despite the masterly motivic work and the coordinated interplay of melodic and harmonic events, the form that Glinka creates has little to do with German symphonic methods. *Kamarinskaya* is a double variation. The variations on the wedding song feature the melody in different registers, orchestrations, and contrapuntal textures. In the variations on the "Kamarinskaya" tune, Glinka repeats the three-measure-long melody as an ostinato, seemingly ad infinitum, without significant structural change. As in the previous excerpt, from *A Life for the Tsar*, what changes is the texture and instrumental colors of the tune and, more importantly, its background—the accompanying harmonies and countermelodies. This variation type came to be known as "Glinka variations" or "variations with changing backgrounds." It became a favorite of Russian composers, receiving both praise for being something genuinely Russian and scorn for being what some saw as a sign of laziness.

СВАДЕБНАЯ „Изъ за

горъ, горъ высокихъ.‟

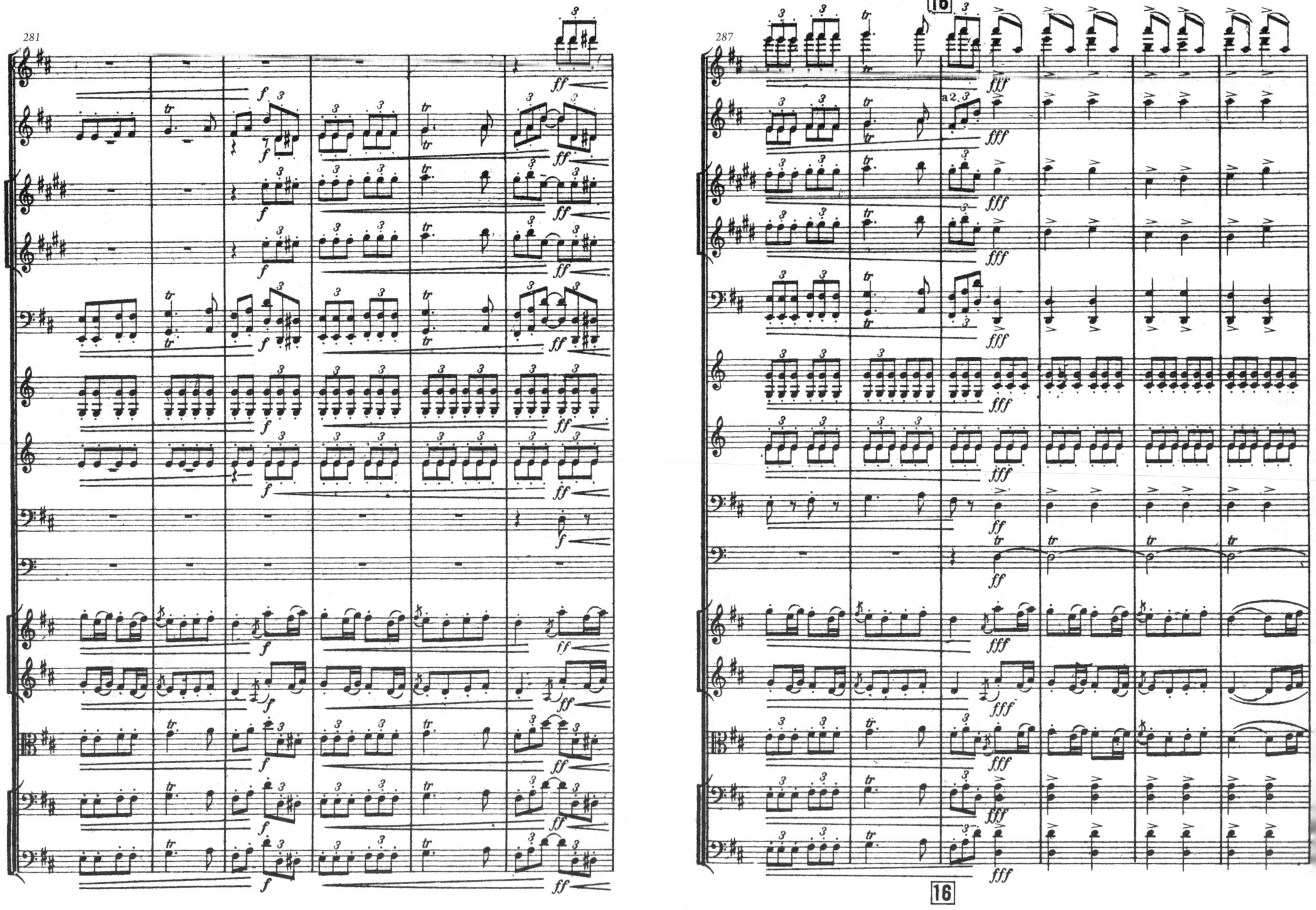
281
287
16
a 2.
16

51

Franz Liszt
(1811–86)

Les préludes (Preludes), Symphonic Poem No. 3
(piano reduction) (published 1856)

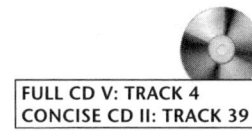

FULL CD V: TRACK 4
CONCISE CD II: TRACK 39

Les préludes is one of the twelve programmatic orchestral works Liszt composed between 1848 and 1858 and called "symphonic poem" (*symphonische Dichtung*). As the term indicates, Liszt had more than descriptive or illustrative music in mind; he aspired to express abstract, poetic ideas in music. The poems or paintings Liszt cites as the "programs" of these works serve only as inspirations. Their relationship to the music is usually loose, since Liszt rarely tried to re-create a precise narrative sequence that would correspond to the poem that gave the music its title.

The complex compositional history of *Les préludes* illustrates the flexibility of the programmatic content of Liszt's symphonic poems. The work's genesis can be traced to Liszt's 1844 choral setting of Joseph Autran's poem "Les Aquilons" (Floods). Later he added three more settings of Autran's poems (The Earth, The Stars, and The Wind) and combined them under the title *Les quatre éléments* (The Four Elements). Around 1849 he abandoned the choruses but reused some of their thematic material in a concert overture. In the early 1850s he reworked the overture, eventually calling it *Les préludes* after a poem by Alphonse de Lamartine (1790–1869). Since the original overture does not survive, we do not know how similar it was to the later symphonic poem.

At the work's premiere on 23 February 1854, instead of Lamartine's 375–line ode, Liszt circulated his own reflections on Lamartine's text:

> What else is our life but a series of preludes to that unknown Hymn, the first solemn note of which is intoned by Death?
>
> Love is the glowing dawn of all existence; but in whose fate are the first delights of happiness not interrupted by some storm, the mortal blast of which dissipates its fine illusions; the fatal lightning of which consumes its altar; and where is the cruelly wounded soul that, on issuing from one of these tempests, does not endeavor to rest his recollection in the calm serenity of life in the countryside? Nevertheless, man

hardly gives himself up for long to the enjoyment of the beneficent stillness that at first he has shared in Nature's bosom, and when "the trumpet sounds the alarm," he hastens to the dangerous post, whatever the war may be, which calls him to its ranks, in order to recover at last in combat the full consciousness of himself and the entire possession of his energy.

Although it contains elements completely missing from Lamartine's poem (the initial rhetorical question that suggests that life is a series of preludes to eternity has no equivalent in the poem), it describes the main topics of both the poem and the music: love, destiny, countryside, and warfare. Three of these four topics can easily be translated to the conventional musical topics of the lyrical, the pastoral, and the martial. The lyrical theme (mm. 47ff) serves as the representation of love. The "countryside" is recognizable in the *Allegretto pastorale* section (e.g., pedal tones, woodwind solos and the pentatonically inclined melodies [mm. 200ff]); the chromatic runs at mm. 109ff correspond to a storm section. The military character of the *Allegro marziale* suggests "warfare" with its march rhythms and predominant brass and percussion (mm. 346ff).

The novelty of *Les préludes* lies not in its topics and program, which adhere to the Beethovenian model of *Kampf und Sieg* (struggle and victory), but in Liszt's decision to let the entire movement grow organically out of one motivic cell. The organic construction of *Les préludes* has philosophical meaning: generating highly contrasting characters out of the same motive suggests that one essential element connects the different aspects of life. Liszt achieves this organic structure through thematic transformation. His unifying motive is a three-note figure, familiar from the last movement of Beethoven's String Quartet, Op. 135. In a jesting mood Beethoven attached a musical note to the movement, entitled "The Difficult Resolution," adding text to the three-note motive and its inversion: "Muss es sein?" (Must it be?), "Es muss sein!" (It must be!).

Example 51–1

Liszt first fashions a hesitant introduction (mm. 1–34) out of this three-note figure (m. 3), finding the tonic key and the first theme only in m. 35. The various themes in *Les préludes* are all related to this motive. The *Andante maestoso* theme (m. 35) starts with it, so does the first "love" theme on the violins and cellos (in the piano reduction notated in the upper part of the right hand, mm. 47–48), and the "storm" theme (mm. 109–110). Liszt's themes assume contrasting characters in various contexts. For example, the *Andante maestoso* theme that first appears in the "love" episode (mm. 70–71) becomes part of the military parade in mm. 374–375.

In the programmatic sections of *Les préludes* one can perceive remnants of both a conventional four-movement symphony and sonata form. Indeed, sonata form appears to lie behind the programmatically unmotivated repetition of the main "love theme" in tonic (mm. 296ff). This is the effective recapitulation, which begins with the lyrical theme, saving the more commanding main theme for the coda.

Measure Nos.	Sections Similar to 4-Movement Symphony	Elements Similar to Sonata Form	Keys	Possible "Poetic Content" & Comments
1–34	**Introduction**		C and modulatory	"Destiny" reiterating Beethoven's motive "Muss es sein?" (Must it be?)
35–46		"1st theme"	C	Key clearly established
47–108	**"Slow movement"**		C, E	"Love" (lyrical theme)
70–108		"2nd theme"	E	In key of mediant (Schubertian feature)
109–199	**"Scherzo" and . . .**	"Development"	Modulatory	"Storm" (with lyrical theme at end of section)
200–345	**"Trio"**		A	"Countryside" (pastoral topics), pastoral theme combined with 2nd theme, mm. 260ff
296–345		"Recapitulation"	C	"2nd theme" combined with pastoral theme
346–422	**Finale**		C and modulatory	"Warfare" (martial theme)
406–422		Coda	C	"1st theme"

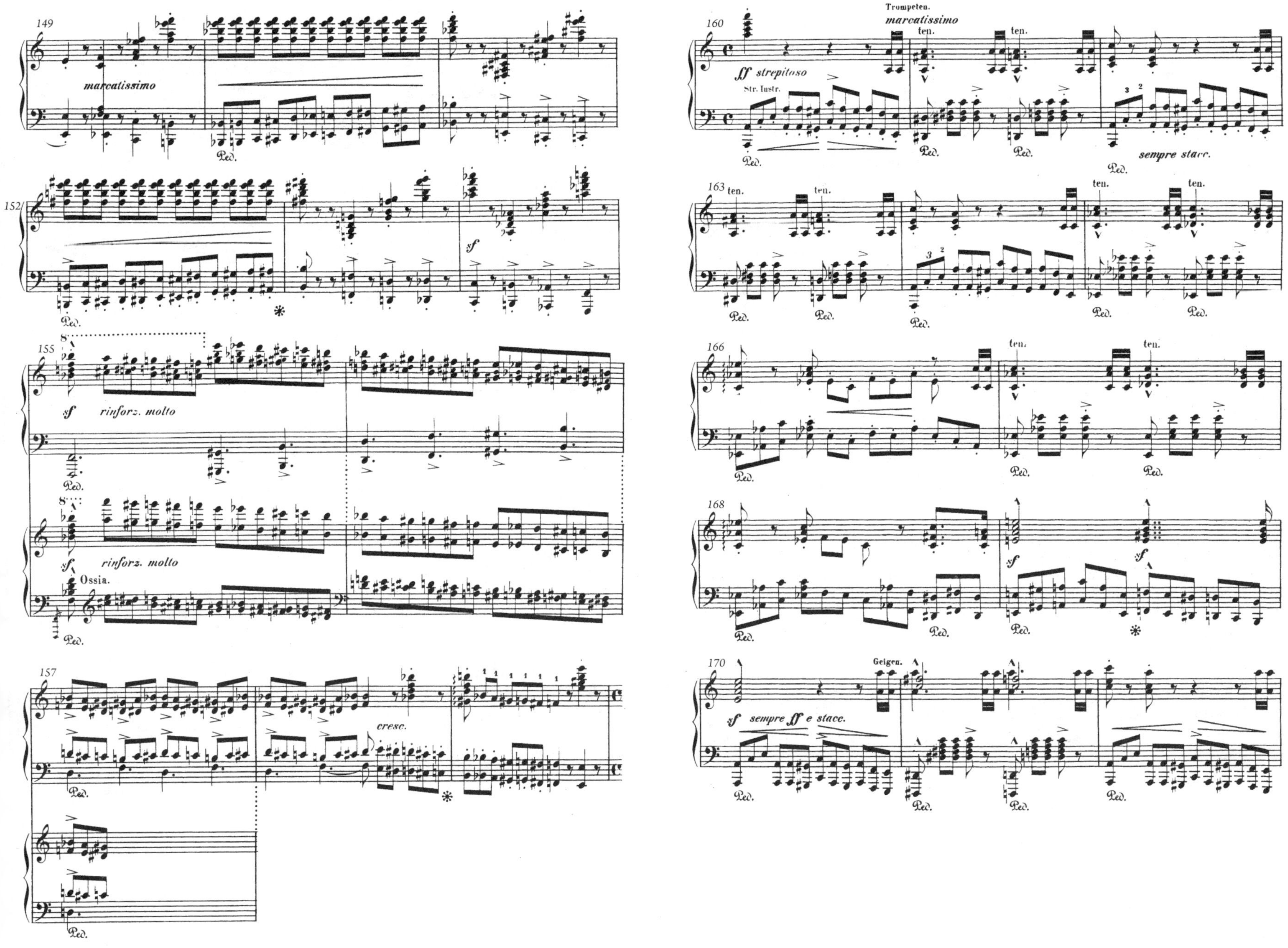
149
marcatissimo
Ped.
152
sf
Ped.
155
sf rinforz. molto
Ped.
sf rinforz. molto
Ossia.
Ped.
157
Ped.
cresc.
Ped.
160
Trompeten.
marcatissimo
ten.
ff strepitoso
Str. Instr.
Ped.
sempre stacc.
163
ten.
Ped.
166
ten.
Ped.
168
sf
Ped.
170
Geigen.
sf sempre ff e stacc.
Ped.

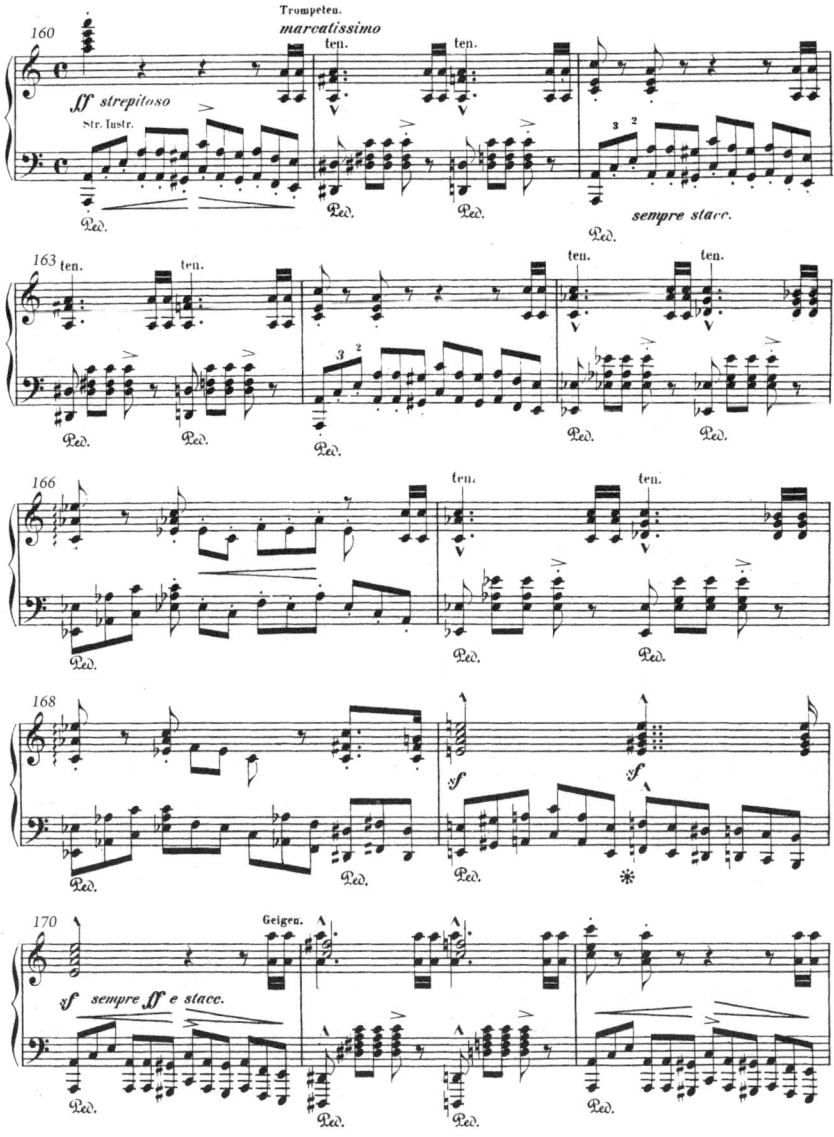

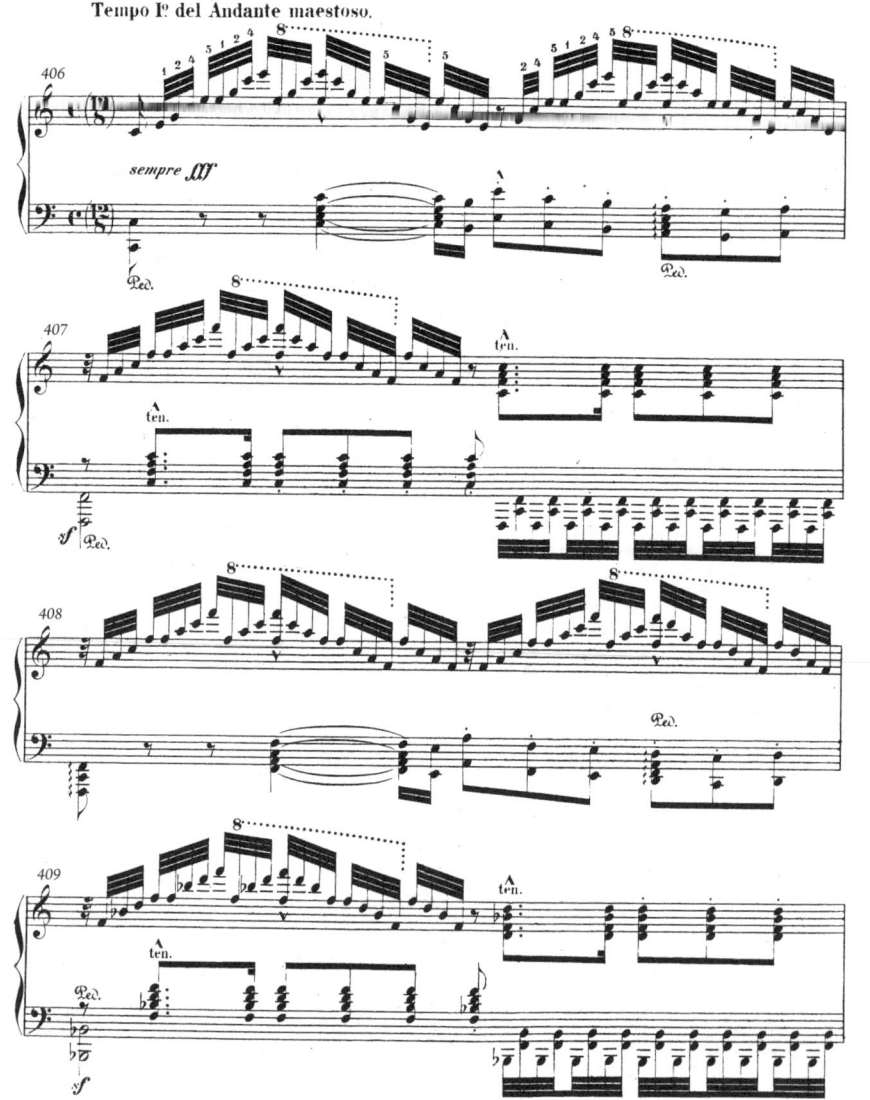

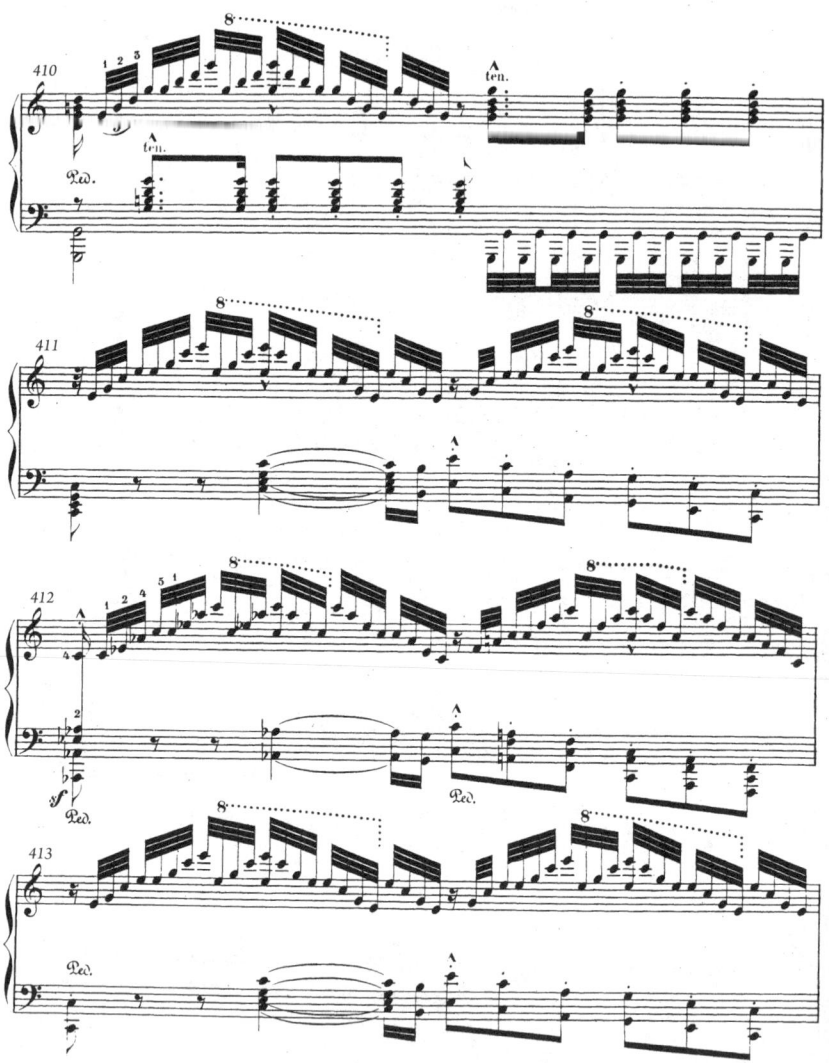

52

Felix Bartholdy Mendelssohn (1811–86)

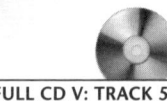

FULL CD V: TRACK 5

Violin Concerto in E Minor, Op. 64, First movement (*Allegro molto appassionato*) (1844)

Measure No.	Formal Designation	Section	Key	Comments
1–168	**Exposition**			
1–47		1st theme (Solo)	e	No "orchestral" exposition, violin begins 1st theme
47–72		1st theme (Tutti)	e	
72–131		Bridge (Solo/Tutti)		Bridge has its own theme
131–139		2nd theme (Tutti)	G	Theme in winds à la Beethoven's Violin Concerto
139–168		2nd theme (Solo)	G	
168–298	**Development**			
168–209		1st theme	G	
210–281		Further modulation		Built on fragments of primary theme and bridge theme
282–298		Retransition		Over dominant pedal
299–335	Solo cadenza			Incorporated into development as opposed to recapitulation
335–473	**Recapitulation**			
335–351		1st theme (Tutti)	e	Solo violin continues figuration from cadenza
351–377		Bridge		
377–418		2nd theme	E–e	Shifts to minor, m. 414
418–473		Closing section	e	Built on 1st theme
473–528	**Coda**		e	Built on bridge theme (last note holds into 2nd movement)

Mendelssohn wrote his Violin Concerto in E minor for Ferdinand David, concertmaster of the Gewandhaus Orchestra in Leipzig, with whom he premiered the work under the composer in 1845. It quickly became one of the most popular violin concertos of all time.

The innovation of Mendelssohn's Concerto lies in the conscious creation of a unified whole out of its distinct movements. Behind this striving for organic unity, which became a guiding principle in the nineteenth century, stood the influential idea that artistic form should imitate the forms of nature, first among which was the *Urpflanze,* the "primal plant," nature's microcosm, all of whose parts were interdependent. To minimize discontinuity, Mendelssohn connects the three movements without a break; allows the solo instrument to announce the principal theme in the first movement; and places the first-movement solo cadenza before the recapitulation, thus using the virtuoso passage to connect the development and recapitulation rather than as an interruption before the end of the movement.

Since the late eighteenth century, the first movements of most concertos combined ritornello and sonata forms in a manner that resulted in a "double exposition." Instead of following this convention, Mendelssohn merges the orchestral and solo expositions of the first movement into a more streamlined sonata form. The movement begins with the solo violin presenting the first theme, followed by the orchestra playing its own version of it before the combined forces of solo and orchestra build up a bridge to the dominant (mm. 72ff). The second theme appears first in the orchestra, but soon the solo instrument takes it over, creating its own rendition (mm. 131ff). The roles are reversed at the beginning of the recapitulation: the solo cadenza, which ends the development, concludes with virtuoso ricochet figures that continue while the orchestra quietly enters with the recapitulated first theme (mm. 335ff). Instead of the customarily dramatic double return, the recapitulation thus steals in *pianissimo* behind the solo violin's passagework. (The virtuosity of the arpeggiated figures keeps the solo instrument in the foreground during the recapitulation of the first theme.)

Because of the highly contrasting thematic materials, the sonata outline is easily recognizable in the first movement. In a Mozartean spirit Mendelssohn presents a related but distinct theme for the bridge section (mm. 72ff). The calm second theme, in G major, begins in the woodwinds, as does the second theme in Beethoven's Violin Concerto, which Mendelssoh[n] conducted while composing his own work. The division between the exposition and the deve[l]opment is not marked clearly, but by m. 210 we are definitely in the development, which is bui[lt] on the first theme and the first bridge. The development culminates in emphatic fragments [of] the first theme, in E major (mm. 255ff), before the retransitory dominant pedal settles in m[.] 282. As is customary, the recapitulation brings back the second theme in the tonic key of [E] major (mm. 377ff), although at the end of the second theme Mendelssohn shifts back to [E] minor (m. 414) for the remainder of the movement.

A large part of what makes Mendelssohn's Concerto so beloved is the attractive and exuberant personality of the solo instrument. Mendelssohn creates a voice for the violin that is highly individual and yet gentle in its relationship with the orchestra. Its first note, which seems to grow out of the timpani's strokes, already marks its register soaring high above the shimmering strings of the orchestra. Yet the theme, opening with an arpeggiation of the tonic triad, is closely related to its accompaniment. The first eight measures, ending on a half cadence, are balanced by a subsequent eight-measure phrase, ending on an authentic cadence in the orchestra. The violin, however, seems unable to stop and, after attempting to start the theme anew in m. 24, gives in to its virtuoso impulse and abandons the theme for brilliant passagework, reveling in the expansion of its range to more than three octaves. The solo violin behaves similarly in the bridge section, in which the theme dissolves into wide-register runs.

At the end of the bridge the violin makes a most extravagant decision: after climbing to b^3 in m. 127 it suddenly plunges down more than three octaves to the open G string, where it rests while the woodwinds present the second theme (mm. 131ff). The idea seems indebted to Beethoven's Violin Concerto, in which the sole accompaniment of the second theme is the solo violin's sustained trill on a high E. Despite its debts to Beethoven, however, Mendelssohn's work adheres to the spirit of Mozart in its thematic richness and light colors. Mendelssohn's violin does not struggle against the orchestra but graciously collaborates with it. Perhaps the last great nineteenth-century concerto in the Mozartean line, Mendelssohn's Concerto is beautiful without trying to fulfill the Romantic obligation of reaching the Beethovenian sublime.

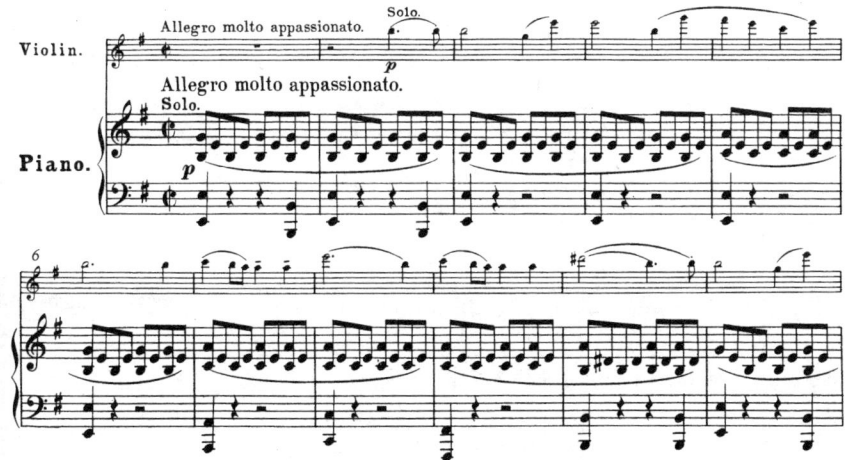

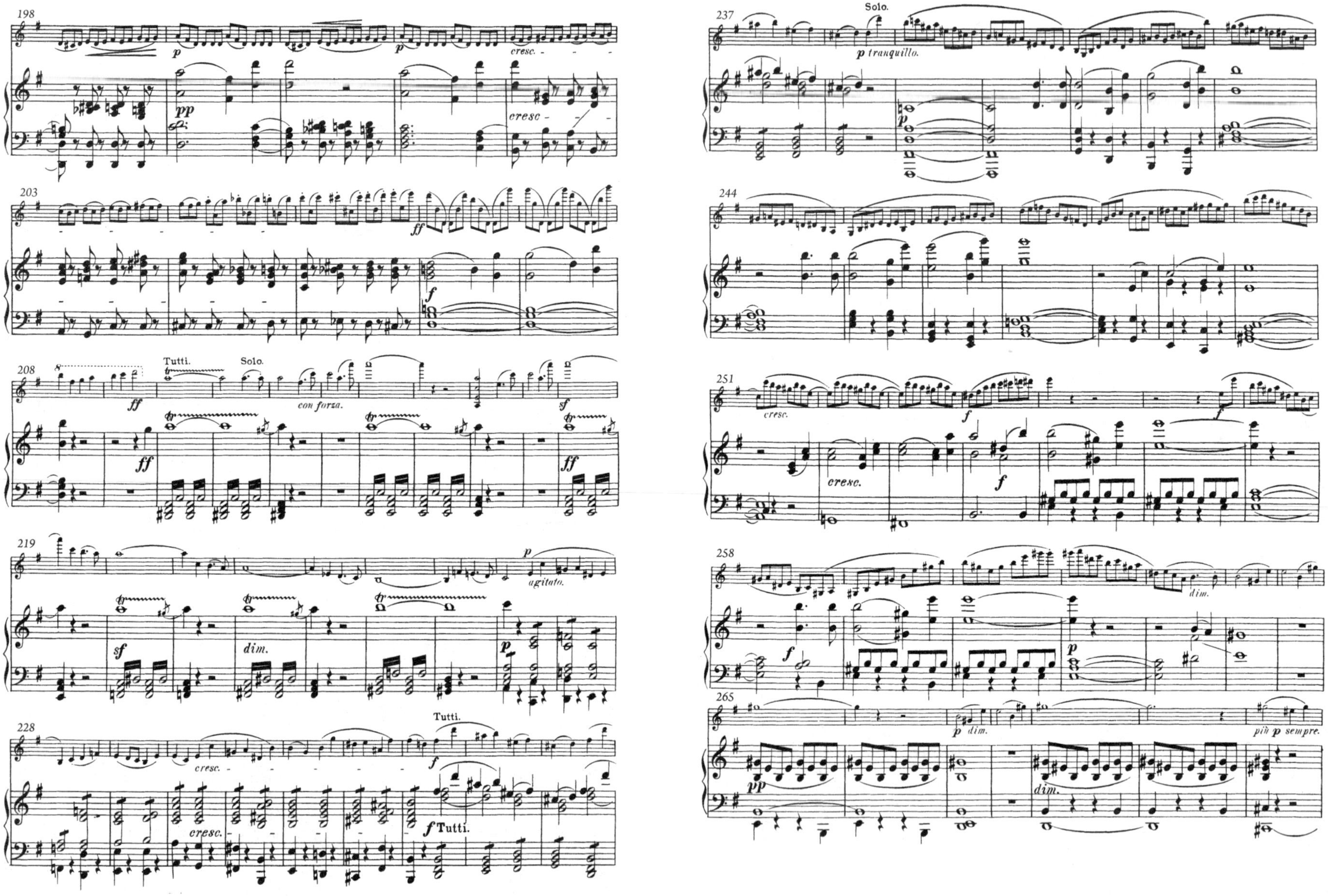
198
cresc.
203
208
Tutti.
Solo.
con forza.
219
agitato.
dim.
228
cresc.
Tutti.
f Tutti.
237
Solo.
p tranquillo.
244
251
cresc.
258
dim.
265
p dim.
più p sempre.

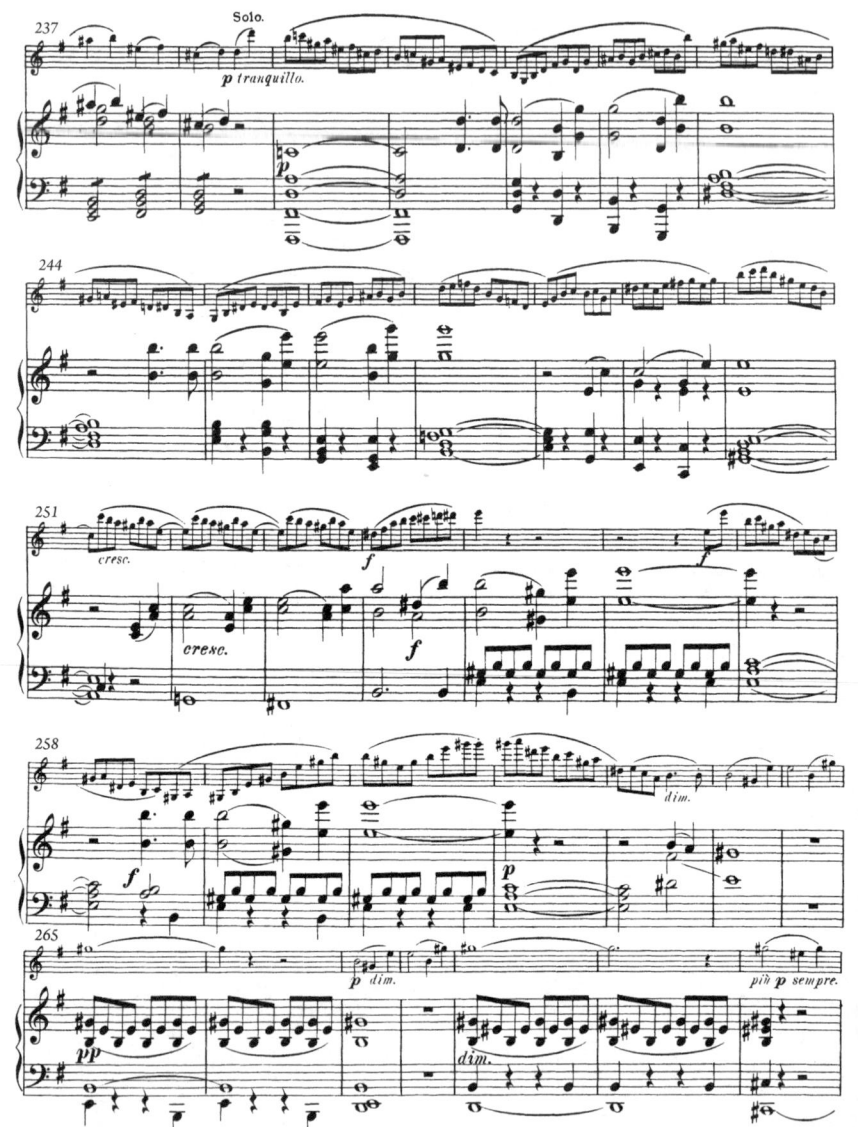

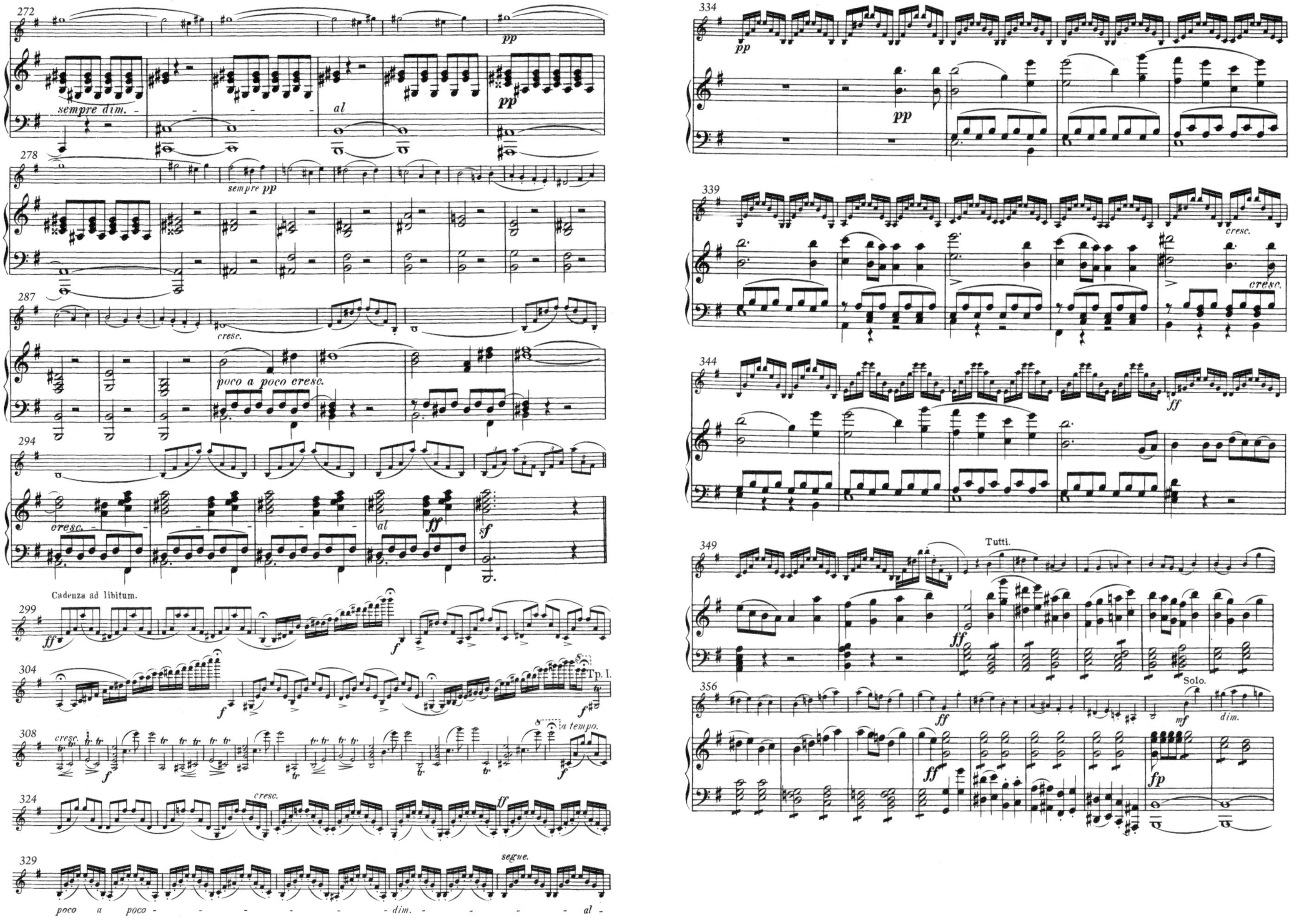
sempre dim.
al
sempre pp
cresc.
poco a poco cresc.
cresc.
al
Cadenza ad libitum.
Tp. I.
cresc.
a tempo.
cresc.
segue.
poco a poco - dim. - al -
cresc.
cresc.
Tutti.
Solo.
dim.

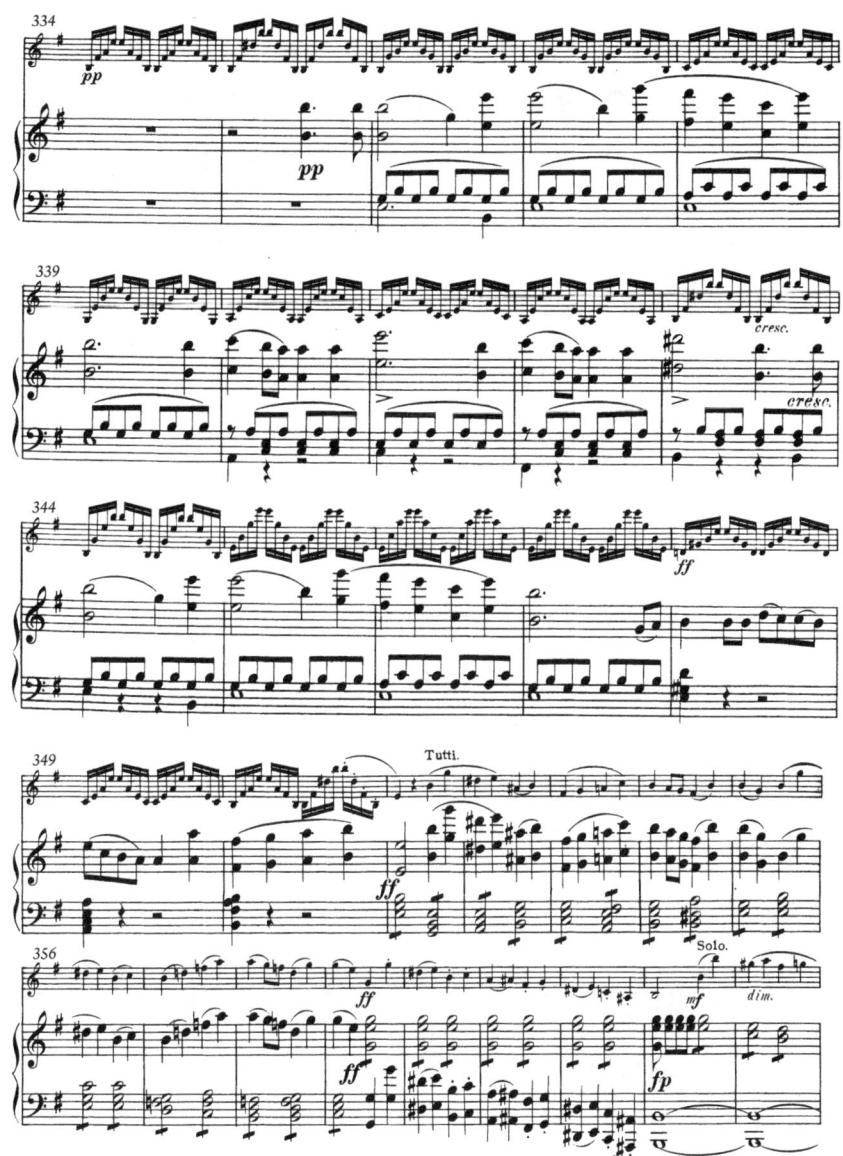

53

Richard Wagner
(1813–83)

FULL CD V: TRACKS 6–7
CONCISE CD II: TRACK 40

Tristan und Isolde (Tristan and Isolde) (1856–59)

Wagner's opera *Tristan und Isolde* premiered in Munich in 1865. While poor in plot (the first act is about Tristan and Isolde's fatal falling in love, the second act is about the illicit fulfillment of their love, and the third act is about their death), it is filled to the brim with what Wagner described as "yearning, yearning, unquenchable, ever-regenerated longing." This unquenchable desire is best expressed in the first three measures of the Prelude, the most commented-on phrase of music ever written.

a. Prelude

The dissonant first harmony is so distinctive that it has been christened the "Tristan-chord." Its quality as sheer aural sensation is much enhanced by the mixture of orchestral colors in which it is clothed. It is also the result both of its being the point of confluence between two characteristic motives (referred to as "leitmotifs" ["leading motives"] in writings about Wagner). These two leitmotifs later function independently: the rising sixth with its descending chromatic "recovery" in the cellos, and the rising chromatic tetrachord in the oboe.

The "Tristan-chord" first appears in A minor, a key hardly recognizable since there are no A-minor triads in the vicinity. Indeed, there is no simple triad of any kind until m. 17, and the triad that finally appears there is F major. In Wagner's musical language one expects keys not to be clearly asserted but to be implied through dominant chords, which carry the implicit promise of resolution to tonic. The end of the first phrase in the prelude is the dominant of A minor. The chord that the listener imagines during the ensuing silence is the unstated tonic of that key.

So the "Tristan-chord," which performs the function of a "predominant" in A minor, must be interpreted as having F as its root—an F that seeks resolution through descent by semitone to the dominant, since its degree function is VI. The spelling of the chord, in which F and D♯ coexist, implies an augmented-sixth chord. What makes the "Tristan-chord" unusual, then, is the fact that its "half-diminished" quality is the result of its containing a long, accented appoggiatura (G♯), which on its resolution to A clarifies the nature and function of the chord as a "French sixth" in A minor. In the first three measures all three downbeats are dominated melodically by

accented nonharmonic tones (the F on the first downbeat is an appoggiatura to E; the A♯ in m. 3 is a chromatic passing tone to B). Their restlessness contributes tellingly to the feeling of unfulfilled desire that is the subject of the opera.

The sense of restlessness is palpable in the unresolved dominant seventh in m. 3. It is made even more oppressively palpable in the sequential repetitions of the opening phrase. Each phrase of the continuation begins with cello notes drawn from the dominant harmony previously left hanging and proceeds through a "Tristan-chord" to a new dominant to be similarly left ringing, unconsummated, in the air. The tension in the third phrase is intensified and prolonged in a manner that may be fairly described as sadistic: its harmonized portion is repeated after a fermata that extends the agony of incompletion, and after another similarly agonizing fermata the last two melody notes are repeated—and repeated again at the octave to rub it in—then reharmonized with the hanging dominant from m. 3, only to resolve in a deceptive cadence supporting yet another accented appoggiatura. The ending chords in mm. 3, 7, and 11 are in turn the dominants of the root, third, and fifth of the governing A-minor tonic triad.

Thereafter, the Prelude is a voyage on the sea of harmony that may be thought of as analogizing the voyage of the ship transporting Tristan and Isolde from Ireland to Cornwall, aboard which the performance of Act 1 takes place. In its surges and swells, its climaxes on restless harmonies rather than on their resolutions, and its seemingly perpetual state of modulation, the Prelude to *Tristan*, which Wagner began sketching in 1856 after immersing himself in Schopenhauer's work, was an attempt to embody the motion of the sea, the very shape of desire.

The fluidity of Wagnerian phrase structure is every bit as original as the novel harmonic shadings and every bit as important in achieving the seamless, uncanny transitions to which Wagner gave the name "infinite melody." Upbeats and downbeats can be as ambiguous as harmonic pivots. The main theme of the Prelude, which seems to grow out of the great harmonic balk where the cadence to A major is thwarted by a deceptive resolution to F in m. 17, is the prime case in point. It arises, and mainly recurs, on the upbeat, but it is shifted imperceptibly to the downbeat in the turbulent middle of the piece (mm. 55–58). Effects like this are disorienting to the listener, for they produce something uncountable and ungraspable.

Most disorienting about the Prelude is the total lack of tonic resolution. After the almost unbearably tension-producing dominant built up in the middle of the Prelude, the last page brings back the initial motives, thinned down and accompanied by tremolo dominant pedals (mm. 84ff). The last "Tristan-chord" and the use of A♭, E♭, and B natural in the *pianissimo* unison melody in the last six measures indicate C minor, but the tonic harmony, like the A-minor harmony at the beginning, remains absent. After its long journey through numerous dominant preparations, the Prelude ends on another dominant, on pizzicato Gs. Only the very end of the opera brings resolution to the intense dominant tension built up in the Prelude.

b. Act III, Isolde's transfiguration

The last act of *Tristan* takes place in Tristan's castle in Brittany, where Tristan's faithful servant Kurvenal has taken his wounded master, who now waits for Isolde. When she finally arrives, Tristan, delirious, tears off his bandages and dies in Isolde's arms. Isolde sinks on his body and expires in love's complete fulfillment.

The music of what has come to be referred to as "Isolde's transfiguration" is the almost exact, abridged recapitulation of the ecstatic music of Tristan and Isolde's love duet from the second act, during which the lovers first speak of their desire to die together in a climactic act of love ("thus we die undivided"). Missing from the recapitulation is Isolde's maid Brangäne's song warning the lovers of the coming dawn and the great unison hymn to the night, "O ew'ge Nacht" (Oh eternal night). At the end of the opera Isolde "hears" the music sung by her and Tristan in the second act, but instead of the lovers' alternating and intertwining voices in the duet, here the orchestra carries their melody. Isolde's voice hovers over these wondrous sounds of memory, commenting on what she hears, tastes, feels, smells—in a word, the sensuous experience of her last physical ecstasy of love. Only from the line "Höre ich nur diese Weise die so wundervoll und leise . . ." (Do I alone hear this melody which, so wondrous and tender . . .) does Isolde sing her vocal line from the duet.

In the duet the appearance of the dominant F♯ pedal and the rising, swelling music that leads toward a climax is brutally interrupted—the dominant-seventh chord, this fundamental symbol of desire, is cut off by a *fortissimo* diminished seventh on G♯ as Kurvenal, followed by King Marke and his men, bursts in on the lovers. While nothing interrupts Isolde in her final ecstasy, at the end Wagner still manages to avoid the resolution of the dominant: the F♯-dominant pedal (mm. 54–60) never resolves directly to the tonic B. The tonic does arrive at the end, but not as a resolution of the dominant seventh that filled the entire opera with unquenchable desire, but within a plagal cadence to B major. The final resolution to B is part of a progression that begins in m. 75 with a repetition of the "Tristan chord." The F (spelled as E♯ in Wagner's full score) resolves to E, as it did at the beginning of the Prelude (mm. 2–3). Now, however, E is not the dominant, but the root of the subdominant E-minor chord. The chromatically rising line does not stop on the B as in the Prelude, but moves up to C♯ and D♯, which is the third of the new tonic, B major, which in this context can be heard as V of E minor. This plagal cadence thus sounds less like an ending than an opening to a new plane—a Schopenhauerian dissolution of the Self. In the context of the opera the dominant-seventh chord cannot resolve; it can only be transcended by giving up its desire for resolution.

Isolde	Isolde
Mild und leise	How gently and quietly
wie er lächelt,	he smiles,
wie die Auge	how sweetly
hold er öffnet—	he opens his eyes!
Seht ihr's, Freunde?	Do you see it, friends?
Seht ihr's nicht?	Do you not see it?
Immer lichter	How he shines

wie er leuchtet,	ever brighter,
stern-umstrahlt	soaring on high,
hoch sich hebt?	stars sparkling around him?
Seht ihr's nicht?	Do you not see it?
Wie das Herz ihm	How his heart
mutig schwillt,	proudly swells,
voll und hehr	and, noble and full,
im Busen ihm quillt?	it pulses in his breast?
Wie die Lippen,	How from his lips,
wonnig mild,	soft and gentle,
süsser Atem	sweet breath
sanft entweht—	flutters—
Freunde! Seht!	See, friends!
Fühlt und seht ihr's nicht?	Do you not feel and see it?
Höre ich nur	Do I alone
diese Wiese,	hear this melody,
die so wundervoll	which, so wondrous
und leise,	and tender
Wonne klagend,	in its blissful lament,
alles sagend,	all-revealing,
mild versohnend	gently pardoning,
aus ihm tönend,	sounding from him,
in mich dringet,	pierces me through,
auf sich schwinget,	rises above,
hold erhallend	blessedly echoing
um mich klinget?	and ringing round me?
Heller schallend,	Resounding yet more clearly,
mich umwallend,	wafting about me,
sind es Wellen	are they waves
sanfter Lüfte?	of gentle breezes?
Sind des Wogen	Are they billows
wonniger Düfte?	of heavenly fragrance?
Wie sie schwellen,	As they swell
mich umrauschen	and murmur round me,
soll ich atmen,	shall I breathe them,
soll ich lauschen?	shall I listen to them?
Soll ich schlürfen,	Shall I sip them,
unertauschen?	plunge beneath them,
Süss in Düften	to expire

mich verhauchen?	in sweet perfume?
In dem wogenden Schwall,	In the surging swell,
in dem tönenden Schall,	in the ringing sound,
in des Welt-Atems	in the vast wave
wehendem All—	of the world's breath—
ertrinken,	to drown,
versinken—	to sink
unbewusst—	unconscious—
höchste Lust!	supreme bliss!

(Isolde, as if transfigured, sinks in Brangäne's arms gently onto Tristan's body. Deep emotion and sense of exaltation among those present. Marke blesses the bodies.)

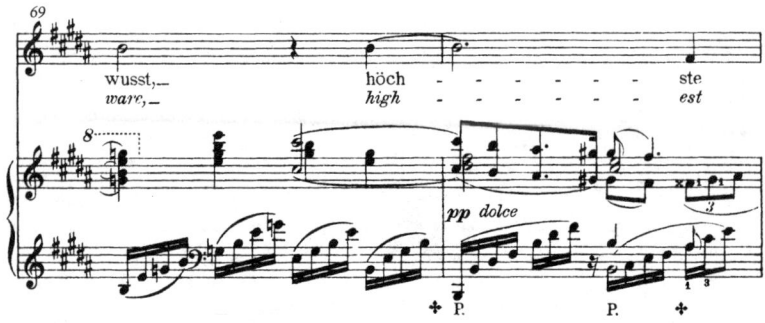

wusst,___   höch — — — — — ste
ware,___   high — — — — — est

pp dolce

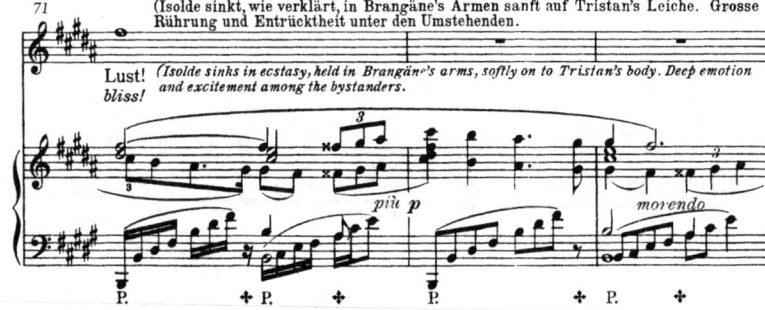

(Isolde sinkt, wie verklärt, in Brangäne's Armen sanft auf Tristan's Leiche. Grosse
Rührung und Entrücktheit unter den Umstehenden.

Lust!   *(Isolde sinks in ecstasy, held in Brangäne's arms, softly on to Tristan's body. Deep emotion*
bliss!   *and excitement among the bystanders.*

più p   *morendo*

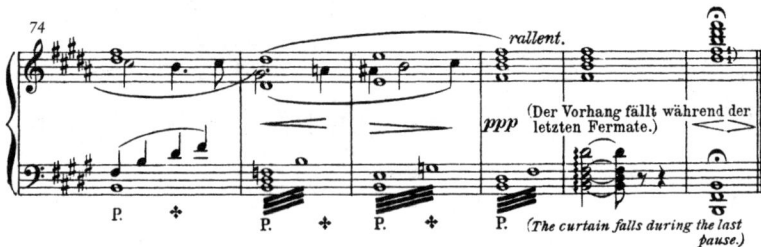

rallent.

(Der Vorhang fällt während der
ppp   letzten Fermate.)

*(The curtain falls during the last
pause.)*

54

Giuseppe Verdi (1813–1901)

FULL CD V: TRACKS 8–12
CONCISE CD II: TRACKS 41–45

Rigoletto, Act III, conclusion (1851)

Rigoletto was first performed in the Teatro La Fenice in Venice in 1851. Its libretto, by Francesco Maria Piave (1810–1876), author of ten libretti for Verdi, was based on Victor Hugo's 1832 play *Le Roi s'amuse* (The King amuses himself). To get around censorship Verdi and Piave turned the French king of the play into the Duke of Mantua. They also renamed the main character, the hunchback court jester Triboulet, Rigoletto, whose deformed body reflects his distorted morals. His tragedy is that he cannot ultimately separate his job of encouraging the Duke's vile behavior from his private responsibility for protecting his daughter, who becomes the target of the evil he himself endorses at the Duke's court.

The opening scene of the opera ends with a nobleman, whose daughter the duke seduced and who has endured the jester's merciless ridicule, putting a curse on Rigoletto. Rigoletto's own daughter, Gilda, then falls victim to the Duke. Rigoletto, bent on revenge, hires the assassin Sparafucile to kill the Duke. But Rigoletto also wants to cure Gilda of her love for the Duke and thus brings her to a ramshackle inn to witness the Duke's seduction of Sparafucile's sister, Maddalena.

The third act begins with the Duke, who arrives at Sparafucile's inn seeking Maddalena. His *canzone* (song), "La donna è mobile" (Women are fickle), is the opera's most famous number. Its cruelly ironic meaning and its dramatic significance can be understood only in the context of the whole act. The Quartet, where our musical example begins, is sung on a divided stage, showing the inside of the inn, with the Duke and Maddalena, and the outside, where Rigoletto and Gilda, spying through the cracks in the wall, witness the Duke's sordid affair.

The Duke begins the ensemble with an enticing vocal line that contrasts with Maddalena's cynical response and Gilda's shocked outcries. These forty-eight measures of furious *parlante* do not give way, as in earlier operas, to a single moment of shared reflection, but prepare for a cynical strophic song by the oblivious Duke (mm. 49ff) accompanied by three simultaneous commentaries from vastly differing perspectives. (The Duke's song, "Bella figlia dell'amore," is modeled on Donizetti's Sextet "Chi mi frena" from *Lucia di Lammermoor*.) Maddalena answers the Duke's first stanza with flirtatious simpering (m. 64), Gilda with a restrained outcry,

followed by Rigoletto's admonition to keep her voice down. The emotion of the two muffled outsiders, unable to find expression in sheer volume, finds an alternative outlet in harmony—the music briefly turns to the flat mediant (F♭ major) (mm. 68–70) before returning to the original D♭ major, which prepares the second stanza of the Duke's song (mm. 74ff).

The three other characters accompany the Duke's second stanza in actual counterpoint. Maddalena resumes her coarse flirting; Gilda resumes her long, lyrical sighs, descending from ever-greater heights; while Rigoletto gives his daughter moral (and harmonic) support. At the coda (mm. 81ff), the two women's voices come into the foreground, again in ironic contrast: Gilda, her voice breaking with grief, begins to sob on pairs of slurred sixteenth notes, while Maddalena laughs merrily in staccato sixteenths that fill the gap between Gilda's sobs. At the end of the Quartet, the contrast between the insiders and the outsiders becomes unbearably poignant: the Duke and Maddalena get ready to embrace, their voices mingling in the time-honored lovers' way, that is, with lyrical legato lines in well-lubricated parallel motion (mm. 97ff), Rigoletto and Gilda, their spirits pulverized by the sight of the other pair, sing correspondingly broken melodies, alternating sixteenth notes and rests. Next comes little clumps of dialogues between Gilda and Rigoletto, Rigoletto and Sparafucile (the latter above frighteningly hollow static harmonies), and finally between Sparafucile and Maddalena, played against a variety of picturesque musical backgrounds, to move the plot to the point from which the next dramatic ensemble is set to depart.

What gives the third act its special, gruesome color (or *tinta*) is the storm music, which consists of disjointed motives, depicting distant thunder (tremolo strings and timpani strokes), lightning (fast flute and piccolo figurations), moaning wind (wordless male chorus), and heavy rain (staccato woodwinds) (mm. 254ff). The musical climax is a two-stanza *terzetto* for Sparafucile and Maddalena, bickering on the inside about whether it is worth saving the life of the Duke, and Gilda on the outside, beside herself—at first with fear and then with frenzied resolve—to sacrifice herself for her undeserving lover (mm. 347ff). The ensemble follows not the Donizettian model of reflective stasis, but the older (Mozartean) one of evolving action that had its origin in comedy. At the moment of the murder, the orchestra bursts into violent sounds, reinforced, according to the original score, with the addition of a thunder machine behind the scene.

Two brief scenes remain. The first brings Rigoletto back onstage at the stroke of midnight to receive the Duke's body in a sack. Up to this point the scene is played entirely in recitative. The dramatic turn occurs when Rigoletto, ready to throw the sack into the river, hears the Duke carelessly repeating "La donna è mobile" in the distance as he strolls away from the house (mm. 591ff). Terrified, Rigoletto opens the sack and discovers that it contains his own daughter.

The final duet between the grieving Rigoletto and the dying Gilda might strike contemporary audiences as unrealistic. But the human emotions it portrays are realistic to the highest degree: Gilda, asking for forgiveness for both herself and her seducer, is leaving her physical body as the high strings elevate her soul to heaven, while Rigoletto remains alone with his failed revenge and terrible loss.

583

NO. 16, QUARTET

Duke

Un dì, se ben rammentomi,
o bella, t'incontrai
Mi piacque di te chiedere,
e intesi che qui stai.
Or sappi, che d'allora
sol te quest'alma adora!

Gilda

(Iniquo!)

Maddalena

Ah, ah, e vent'altre appresso
le scorda forse adesso?
Ha un'aria il signorino
da vero libertino . . .

Duke

Sì! . . . un mostro son . . .

(goes to embrace her)

Gilda

Ah padre mio!

Maddalena

Lasciatemi, stordito.

Duke

Ih che fracasso!

Maddalena

Stia saggio!

Duke

E tu sii[ES1] docile,
non fare tanto chiasso.
Ogni saggezza chiudesi
nel gaudio e nell'amore.

(takes her hand)

La bella mano candida!

Duke

One day, if I remember correctly,
my pretty one, I met you . . .
I was pleased and asked after you
and was told that you live here.
You should know that ever since
this heart has been yours alone.

Gilda

(How wicked!)

Maddalena

Ha! Ha! And later you seem
to forget them all?
I think my fine young man
is a real libertine . . .

Duke

Yes! . . . I'm a monster.

Gilda

Oh father!

Maddalena

Let me be, you scatterbrain!

Duke

Ho, what a fuss!

Maddalena

Be wise!

Duke

And you, be gentle,
don't make such a scene.
Every wise thought is closed off
in joy and in love.

Pretty white hand!

Maddalena

Scherzate voi, signore.

Duke

No, no

Maddalena

Son brutta.

Duke

Abbracciami.

Gilda

(Iniquo!)

Maddalena

Ebro!

Duke (*laughing*)

D'amore ardente.

Maddalena

Signor, l'indifferente,
vi piace canzonar?

Duke

No, no, ti vo' sposar.

Maddalena

Ne voglio la parola...

Duke (*ironically*)

Amabile figliuola!

Rigoletto (*to Gilda, who has seen and heard all*)

E non ti basta ancor?

Gilda

Iniquo traditor!

Maddalena

Ne voglio la parola.

Duke

Bella figlia dell'amore,
schiavo son de' vezzi tuoi;
con un detto sol tu puoi

Maddalena

You are joking, sir.

Duke

No, no.

Maddalena

I'm ugly.

Duke

Embrace me.

Gilda

(How wicked!)

Maddalena

You're drunk!

Duke (*laughing*)

With ardent love.

Maddalena

Sir, are you pleased to make fun,
of a fickle girl?

Duke

No, no. I want to marry you.

Maddalena

I want your word of honor.

Duke (*ironically*)

Amiable little maid!

Rigoletto (*to Gilda, who has seen and heard all*)

Haven't you seen enough?

Gilda

The wicked traitor!

Maddalena

I want your word of honor.

Duke

Fairest daughter of love,
I am a slave to your charms;
with but a single word you could

le mie pene consolar.
Vieni e senti del mio core
il frequente palpitar.

Maddalena
Ah! ah! rido ben di core,
chè tai baie costan poco;
Quanto valga il vostro gioco,
mel credete, sò apprezzar.
Son avvezza, bel signore,
ad un simile scherzar.

Gilda
Ah! così parlar d'amore
a me pur l'infame ho udito!
Infelice cor tradito,
per angoscia non scoppiar.

Rigoletto (*to Gilda*)
Taci, il piangere non vale;
Ch'ei mentiva sei sicura.
Taci, e mia sarà la cura
la vendetta d'affrettar.
Sì, pronta fia, sarà fatale,
io saprollo fulminar.

NO. 17, RECITATIVE
Rigoletto
M'odi! ritorna a casa,
oro prendi, un destriero,
una veste viril che t'apprestai,
e per Verona parti.
Sarovvi io pur doman.

Gilda
Or venite.

Rigoletto
Impossibil.

Gilda
Tremo.

relieve my every pain.
Come, touch my breast and feel
how my heart is racing.

Maddalena
Ha! Ha! That really makes me laugh;
banter like that costs nothing.
Believe me, I know exactly
what your game is worth!
I am quite accustomed, my fine sir,
to jokes like this.

Gilda
Ah, these are the loving words
the scoundrel spoke once to me!
O wretched heart betrayed,
do not break for sorrow.

Rigoletto (*to Gilda*)
Hush, weeping can do no good . . .
You are now convinced he was lying.
Hush, and let it be my part
to hasten our revenge.
It will be quick, it will be deadly,
I know how to strike him down.

Rigoletto
Listen to me, go home.
take some money and a horse,
put on the men's clothes I provided,
then leave at once for Verona.
I will meet you there tomorrow.

Gilda
Come with me now.

Rigoletto
It's impossible.

Gilda
I'm afraid.

Rigoletto
Va!

Rigoletto
Go!

(*The Duke and Maddalena continue to laugh and talk together as they drink. Gilda having left, Rigoletto goes behind the house and returns with Sparafucile, counting out money into the assassin's hands.*)

Rigoletto
Venti scudi hai tu detto?
Eccone dieci; e dopo l'pra il resto.

Ei qui rimane?

Rigoletto
Twenty *scudi*, you said?
Here are ten, and the rest when the deed is
done.
He is staying here?

Sparafucile
Sì.

Sparafucile
Yes.

Rigoletto
Alla mezzanotte ritornerò.

Rigoletto
At midnight I will return.

Sparafucile
Non cale.
A gettarlo nel fiume basto io solo.

Sparafucile
No point.
I can throw him into the river alone.

Rigoletto
No, no; il vo' far io stesso.

Rigoletto
No, no, I want to do it myself.

Sparafucile
Sia! Il suo nome?

Sparafucile
All right; his name?

Rigoletto
Vuoi sapere anche il mio?
Egli è Delitto, Punizion son io.

Rigoletto
Do you want to know mine as well?
He is *Crime*, I am *Punishment*.

(*He leaves. The sky darkens and it thunders.*)

Sparafucile
La tempesta è vicina!
più scura fia la notte.

Sparafucile
The storm is getting closer.
The night will be darker.

Duke (*trying to embrace her*)
Maddalena!

Duke (*trying to embrace her*)
Maddalena!

Maddalena (*pushing him away*)
Aspettate . . . mio fratello viene.

Maddalena (*pushing him away*)
Wait . . . my brother is coming.

Duke
Che importa?

Duke
Why does that matter?

Maddalena
Tuona!

Maddalena
Thunder!

Sparafucile (*entering the house*)
E pioverà fra poco.

Sparafucile (*entering the house*)
It's going to rain soon.

Duke
Tanto meglio!
(*to Sparafucile*)
Tu dormirai in scuderia . . .
all'inferno . . . ove vorrai!

Duke
So much the better.

You can sleep in the stable . . .
or in hell . . . wherever you like.

Sparafucile
Oh, grazie!

Sparafucile
Thank you.

Maddalena (*softly to the Duke*)
Ah no, partite.

Maddalena (*softly to the Duke*)
Oh no . . . you must leave.

Duke (*to Maddalena*)
Con tal tempo?

Duke (*to Maddalena*)
At a time like this?

Sparafucile (*softly to Maddalena*)
Son venti scudi d'oro.

Sparafucile (*softly to Maddalena*)
It means twenty gold scudi.

(*to the Duke*)

Ben felice
d'offrirvi una stanza.
se a voi piace
tosto a vederla andiamo.

I'll be glad
to offer you a room.
if you want to see it,
let's go up now.

(*Taking a lamp, he starts up the stairs.*)

Duke
Ebben! sono con te . . . presto, vediamo.

Duke
Good; I'll be with you in a moment.

(*He whispers to Maddalena, then follows Sparafucile.*)

Maddalena
Povero giovin! . . . grazioso tanto!
Dio, qual notte è questa!

Maddalena
Poor lad! He's so handsome!
God! What a night this is!

Duke (*upstairs, noticing that the loft is
open on one side*)
Si dorme all'aria aperta? Bene, bene.
Buona notte.

Duke (*upstairs, noticing that the loft is
open on one side*)
We sleep in the open, eh! Good enough!
Good night.

Sparafucile
Signor, vi guardi Iddio!

Sparafucile
Sir, may God protect you.

Duke
Breve sono dormiam . . . stanco son io.

Duke
We'll sleep a little . . . I'm tired.

(*He lays down his hat and sword and stretches out on the bed. Maddalena, meanwhile, has sat
down at the table below. Sparafucile drinks from the bottle, which the Duke left unfinished. Both
are silent for a moment, lost in their thoughts.*)

La donna è mobile,
qual piuma al vento,
muta d'accento
e di pensiero.

Women are fickle,
like a feather in the wind,
changeable of speech
and of thought.

(*He falls asleep.*)

Maddalena
È amabile invero cotal giovinotto!

Maddalena
He is really most attractive, this young man.

Sparafucile
Oh sì . . . venti scudi ne dà di prodotto.

Sparafucile
Oh, yes . . . to the tune of twenty scudi.

Maddalena
Sol venti? . . . son pochi!
valeva di più.

Maddalena
Only twenty? . . . That's not much!
He was worth more.

Sparafucile
La spada, s'ei dorme, va, portami giù.

Sparafucile
His sword, if he's asleep, bring it down to me.

(*Maddalena goes upstairs and stands looking at the sleeping Duke. Meanwhile Gilda appears
in the road wearing male attire, boots and spurs, and walks slowly toward the inn, where Sparafucile is drinking. Frequent thunder and lighting.*)

NO. 18, RECITATIVE, TRIO AND STORM

Gilda
Ah, più non ragiono!
Amor mi trascina . . .
Mio padre, perdono!

Gilda
Ah, my reason has left me!
Love draws me back . . .
Father, forgive me!

(*lightning*)

Qual notte d'orrore!
Gran Dio, che accadrà?

What a terrible night!
Great God, what will happen?

Maddalena (*returns and puts the Duke's
sword on the table*)
Fratello?

Gilda (*peeping through a crack*)
Chi parla?

Sparafucile (*rummaging in a cupboard*)
Al diavol ten va!

Maddalena
*Somiglia un Apollo, quell giovine . . .
io l'amo . . . ei ma'am . . . riposi . . .
nè più l'uccidiamo.*

Gilda (*listening*)
Oh cielo!

Sparafucile (*throwing her a sack*)
Rattoppa quell sacco!

Maddalena
Perché?

Sparafucile
*Entr'esso il tuo Apollo, sgozzato da me,
gettar dovrò al fiume.*

Gilda
L'inferno qui vedo!

Maddalena
*Eppure il danaro salvarti scommetto
serbandolo in vita.*

Sparafucile
Difficile il credo.

Maddalena
*M'ascolta . . . anzi facil ti svelo un
    progetto.
De' scudi già dieci dal gobbo ne avesti;
venire cogli altri più tardi il vedrai . . .
Uccidilo, e venti allora ne avrai,
così tutto il prezzo goder si potrà.*

Maddalena (*returns and puts the Duke's
sword on the table*)
Brother?

Gilda (*peeping through a crack*)
Who is speaking?

Sparafucile (*rummaging in a cupboard*)
Go to the devil!

Maddalena
He's an Apollo, that young man;
I love him, he loves me . . . let him be . . .
let's not kill him.

Gilda (*listening*)
Dear God!

Sparafucile (*throwing her a sack*)
Mend this sack!

Maddalena
Why?

Sparafucile
Because your Apollo, when I've cut his throat,
will wear it when I throw him in the river.

Gilda
I see hell itself here!

Maddalena
But I reckon I can save you the money
and save his life as well.

Sparafucile
Difficult, I think;

Maddalena
Listen . . . my plan is simple.

You've had ten scudi from the hunchback;
he's coming later with the rest . . .
Kill him, and you'll have your twenty,
so we lose nothing.

Gilda
Che sento! . . . mio padre!

Sparafucile
Uccider quel gobbo! . . . che diavol dicesti!

*Un ladro son forse? Son forse un bandito?
Qual altro cliente da me fu tradito?*

Mi paga quest' uomo . . . fedele m'avrà.

Maddalena
Ah, grazia per esso!

Sparafucile
È d'uopo ch'ei muoia.

Maddalena
Fuggire il fo adesso!

(*She runs towards the stairs.*)

Gilda
Oh, buona figliuola!

Sparafucile (*holding her back*)
Gli scudi perdiamo.

Maddalena
È ver!

Sparafucile
Lascia fare.

Maddalena
Salvarlo dobbiamo.

Sparafucile
*Se pria ch'abbia il mezzo la notte toccato
alcuno qui giunga, per esso morrà.*

Maddalena
*È buia la notte, il ciel troppo irato,
nessuno a quest'ora da qui passerà.*

Gilda
*Oh, qual tenazione! . . . morir per
    l'ingrato!*

Gilda
What do I hear? . . . My father!

Sparafucile
Kill the hunchback? What the devil are you
    saying?
Am I a thief? Am I a bandit?
What other client of mine has ever been
    betrayed?
This man pays me . . . he shall have my loyalty.

Maddalena
Ah, have mercy on him!

Sparafucile
He must die.

Maddalena
I'll see he escapes in time.

Gilda
Ah, merciful girl!

Sparafucile (*holding her back*)
We'd lose the money.

Maddalena
That's true!

Sparafucile
Don't interfere.

Maddalena
We must save him.

Sparafucile
If someone else comes here before midnight,
they shall die in his place.

Maddalena
The night is dark, the weather too stormy;
no one will pass by here at this late hour.

Gilda
Oh, what a temptation! To die for the ingrate!

Morire!... e mio padre!... Oh cielo,
pietà!

To die! And my father?... Oh, Heaven, have
mercy!

(*A distant clock chimes half-past eleven.*)

Sparafucile
Ancor c'è mezz'ora.

Sparafucile
There's still half an hour.

Maddalena (*weeping*)
Attendi, fratello...

Maddalena (*weeping*)
Wait, brother...

Gilda
Che! piange tal donna!...
Nè a lui darò aita!...
Ah, s'egli al mio amore divenne rubello,
io vo' per la sua gettar la mia vita.

Gilda
What! A woman like that weeps,
And I do nothing to help him!
Ah, even though he stole my love
I shall save his life with my own!

(*She knocks on the door to the inn.*)

Maddalena
Si picchia?

Maddalena
A knock at the door?

Sparafucile
Fu il vento.

Sparafucile
It was the wind.

(*Gilda knocks again.*)

Maddalena
Si picchia, ti dico.

Maddalena
Someone's knocking, I tell you.

Sparafucile
È strano!... Chi è?

Sparafucile
How strange! Who's there?

Gilda
Pietà d'un mendico;
asil per la notte a lui concedete.

Gilda
Have pity on a beggar;
grant him shelter for the night.

Maddalena
Fia lunga tal notte!

Maddalena
A long night will it be!

Sparafucile
Alquanto attendete.

Sparafucile
Wait a moment.

(*searching in the cupboard*)

Maddalena
Su, spicciati, presto, fa' l'opra compita:
anelo una vita con altra salvar.

Maddalena
Come on, get on with it, finish the job.
I am eager to save one life with another.

Sparafucile
Ebbene... son pronto; quel' uscio
*   dischiudi,*
più ch'altro gli scudi mi preme salvar.

Sparafucile
So, I'm ready; open the door;

all I want to save is the gold.

Gilda
Ah! presso alla morte, sì giovane sono!
Oh ciel, per quegl'empi ti chieggo
*   perdono!*
Perdona tu, o padre, a quest'infelice!
sia l'uomo felice ch'or vado a salvar.

Gilda
Ah, death is near, and I am so young!
Oh, Heaven, for these sinners I ask thy pardon.

Father, forgive your unhappy child!
May the man I am saving be happy.

Maddalena
Spicciati!

Maddalena
Get on with it!

Sparafucile
Apri!

Sparafucile
Open up!

Maddalena
Entrate...

Maddalena
Come in...

Gilda
Dio! loro perdonate!

Gilda
God! Forgive them!

Maddalena, Sparafucile
Entrate!

Maddalena, Sparafucile
Enter!

(*Dagger in hand, Sparafucile positions himself behind the door; Maddalena opens it, then runs to close the big door under the archway while Gilda enters. Sparafucile closes the door behind her and the rest is darkness and silence.*)

NO. 19, RECITATIVE
(*Rigoletto comes down the road alone, wrapped in his cloak. The violence of the storm has abated, now there is only the occasional thunderclap and flash of lightning.*)

Rigoletto
Della vendetta alfin giunge l'istante!
da trenta dì l'aspetto
di vivo sangue a lagrime piangendo,
sotto la larva del buffoon...

Rigoletto
At last the moment of vengeance is at hand!
For thirty days I have waited,
weeping tears of blood
behind my fool's mask...

(*lightning*)

Quest' uscio...

This door...

(*examining the house*)

È chiuso!... Ah, non è tempo ancor!
Is closed! Ah, it is not yet time!

S'attenda.
I shall wait.

Qual notte di mistero!
What a night of mystery!

Una tempesta in cielo!
A tempest above,

in terra un omicidio!
a murder below!

Oh come invero qui grande mi sento!
Oh, now I truly feel like a great man!

(*The clock chimes twelve.*)

Mezzanotte.
Midnight

(*He knocks at the door to the inn.*)

Sparafucile (*coming out of the inn*)   **Sparafucile** (*coming out of the inn*)

Chi è là?
Who's there?

Rigoletto (*about to enter*)   **Rigoletto** (*about to enter*)

Son io.
It is I.

Sparafucile   **Sparafucile**

Sostate.
Wait.

(*He goes into the house and returns with the sack.*)

È qua spento il vostro'uomo.
Here is your man, dead.

Rigoletto   **Rigoletto**

Oh gioia! Un lume!
Oh joy! A light!

Sparafucile   **Sparafucile**

Un lume? No, il danaro.
A light? No, the money!

(*Rigoletto gives him a purse.*)

Lesti all'onda il gettiam...
Let's throw him into the river quickly...

Rigoletto   **Rigoletto**

No, basto io solo.
No, I can do it alone.

Sparafucile   **Sparafucile**

Come vi piace... Qui men atto è il sito.
As you wish. This is not a good place.

più avanti à più profondo il gorgo.
Further on the stream is deeper.

Presto, che alcun non vi sorprenda.
Quick, so that no one surprises you.

Buona notte.
Good night.

(*He goes back into the house.*)

Rigoletto   **Rigoletto**

Egli è là! morto! oh sì!
He's in there!... Dead! Oh yes!

Vorrei vederlo!
I must see him!

ma che importa!... è ben desso!...
but what does it matter?... It's him all right!

Ecco i suoi sproni.
Here are his spurs.

Ora mi guarda, o mondo!
Now look upon me, O world!

Quest'è un buffone, ed un potente è questo!
Here is a buffoon, and this is a mighty prince!

Ei sta sotto i miei piedi! È desso!
He lies at my feet! It's him!

O gioia!
Oh joy!

È giunta alfine! la tua vendetta, o duolo!...
Your vengeance has come at last, O grief!

Sia l'onda a lui sepolcro, un sacco il suo lenzuolo!
Let the river be his tomb, a sack his shroud!

All'onda!
To the river!

(*He is about to drag the sack toward the river when he hears, to his amazement, the voice of the Duke in the distance.*)

Duke   **Duke**

La donna è mobile, ect.
Women are fickle, etc.

Rigoletto   **Rigoletto**

Qual voce!... Illusion notturna è questa!
His voice!... This is a trick of the darkness!

(*drawing back in terror*)

No!... No! egli è desso!
No!... No! This is he!...

Maledizione!
Damnation!

(*toward the house*)

Olà... dimon bandito!
Hola!... demon, bandit!

NO. 20, RECITATIVE AND FINAL DUET

Rigoletto   **Rigoletto**

Chi è mai, chi è qui in sua vece?
Who can this be, here in his place?

(*cuts open the sack.*)

Io tremo... È umano corpo!
I tremble... It's a human body!

(*lightning*)

Mia figlia!... Dio! Mia figlia!...
My daughter!... O God!... My daughter!

Ah no... è impossibil!...
Ah, no, it cannot be!

Per Verona è in via!	She has left for Verona!
Fu vision!	It was a vision!
(lightning)	
(kneeling)	
È dessa!	It is she!
O mia Gilda! fanciulla, a me rispondi!	Oh, my Gilda, child, answer me!
L'assassino mi svela . . . Olà? . . .	Tell me the murderer's name! . . . Who? . . .
(knocking desperately at the door to the inn)	
Nessuno? . . .	No one? . . .
Nessun! . . .	No one!
(returning to Gilda)	
Mia figlia? . . . mia Gilda? . . .	My daughter? My Gilda? . . .
Oh, mia figlia!	Oh, my daughter!

Gilda

Chi mi chiama?	Who calls me?

Rigoletto

Ella parla! . . . si muove! . . .	She speaks! . . . She moves! . . .
è viva! . . . Oh Dio!	She is alive! Oh, God!
Ah, mio ben solo in terra . . .	Ah, my only joy on earth . . .
Mi guarda . . . mi conosci . . .	Look at me . . . say who I am . . .

Gilda

Ah, padre mio!	Ah, my father!

Rigoletto

Qual mistero! . . . che fu? . . .	I'm mystified! . . . What happened? . . .
sei tu ferita? dimmi! . . .	Are you wounded? Tell me . . .

Gilda *(pointing to her heart)*

L'acciar qui mi piagò.	The dagger wounded me here.

Rigoletto

Chi t'ha colpita?	Who struck you?

Gilda

V'ho ingannato . . . coplevole fui . . .	I deceived you . . . I was guilty . . .
l'amai troppo . . . ora muoio per lui!	I loved him too much . . . now I die for him!

Rigoletto

(Dio tremendo! ella stessa fu colta dallo stral di mia giusta vendetta!)	(Ah God of dread! She was struck by the Bolt of my righteous vengeance!)
(to Gilda)	
Angiol caro, mi guarda, m'ascolta . . .	Beloved angel! Look at me, listen to me!
Parla . . . parlami, figlia diletta!	Speak . . . speak to me, dearest child!

Gilda

Ah, ch'io taccia . . . a me . . . a lui perdonate!	Let me be silent . . . For me . . . forgive him!
benedite alla figlia, o mio padre . . .	Bless your daughter, O my father—
Lassù in cielo, vicina alla madre . . .	in heaven above, near my mother,
in eterno per voi pregherò.	in eternity I will pray for you.
Non più . . . Addio!	No more . . . Farewell!

Rigoletto

Non morir, mio tesoro, pietade . . .	Do not die, my treasure, have pity!
Mia colomba, lasciarmi non dei!	My dove, you must not leave me!
Se t'involi, qui sol rimarrei.	If you fly away, I shall be alone!
Non morire, o ch'io teco morrò!	Do not die, or I shall die beside you!
Oh, mia figlia! Oh, mia Gilda!	Oh my daughter, my Gilda!

(Gilda dies.)

Gilda! mia Gilda! . . . È morta!	Gilda! my Gilda! . . . She is dead!
Ah, la maledizione!	Ah, the curse!

(Tearing his hair in anguish, he falls senseless upon his daughter's body.)

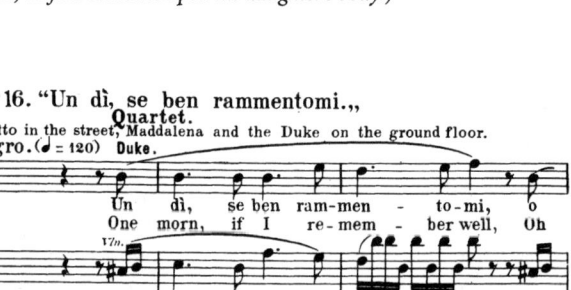

Nº 16. "Un dì, se ben rammentomi.,,
Quartet.
Gilda and Rigoletto in the street, Maddalena and the Duke on the ground floor.
Allegro. (♩ = 120) Duke.

Un dì, se ben ram-men - to-mi, o
One morn, if I re-mem - ber well, Oh

Nº 17. "M'odi!.. ritorna a casa.„
Recit.

Nº 18. "Somiglia un Apollo.„
Recitative, Trio and Storm.

(Enter at the back Gilda, in male attire, with boots and spurs. She comes slowly forward towards the inn, where Sparafucile is seated drinking.)

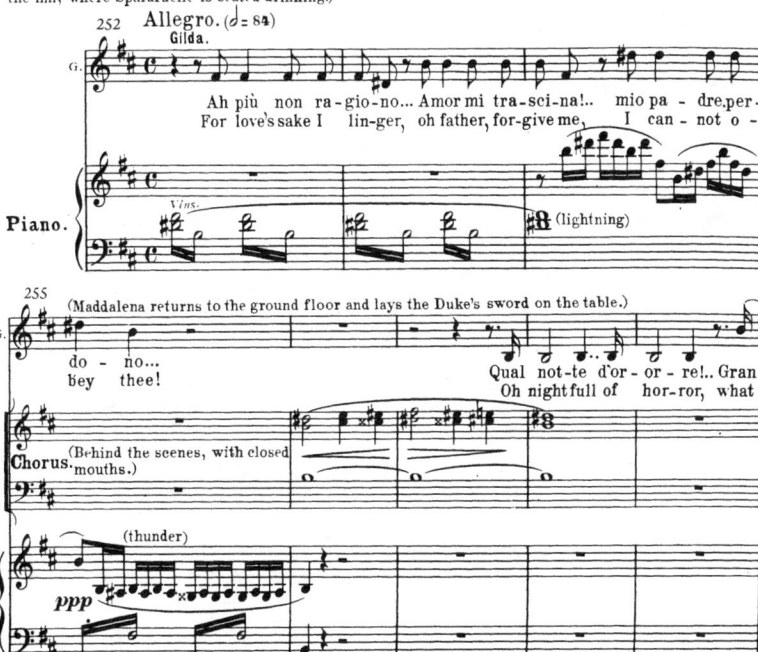

№ 19. "Della vendetta alfin giunge l'istante!"

Recitative.

Rigoletto alone, closely wrapped in his mantle, comes forward from the back of the stage. The violence of the storm gradually abates. There are still a few flashes of lightning, and thunder in the distance.

No. 20."V'ho ingannato... colpevole fui.,,

Recitative and Final Duet.

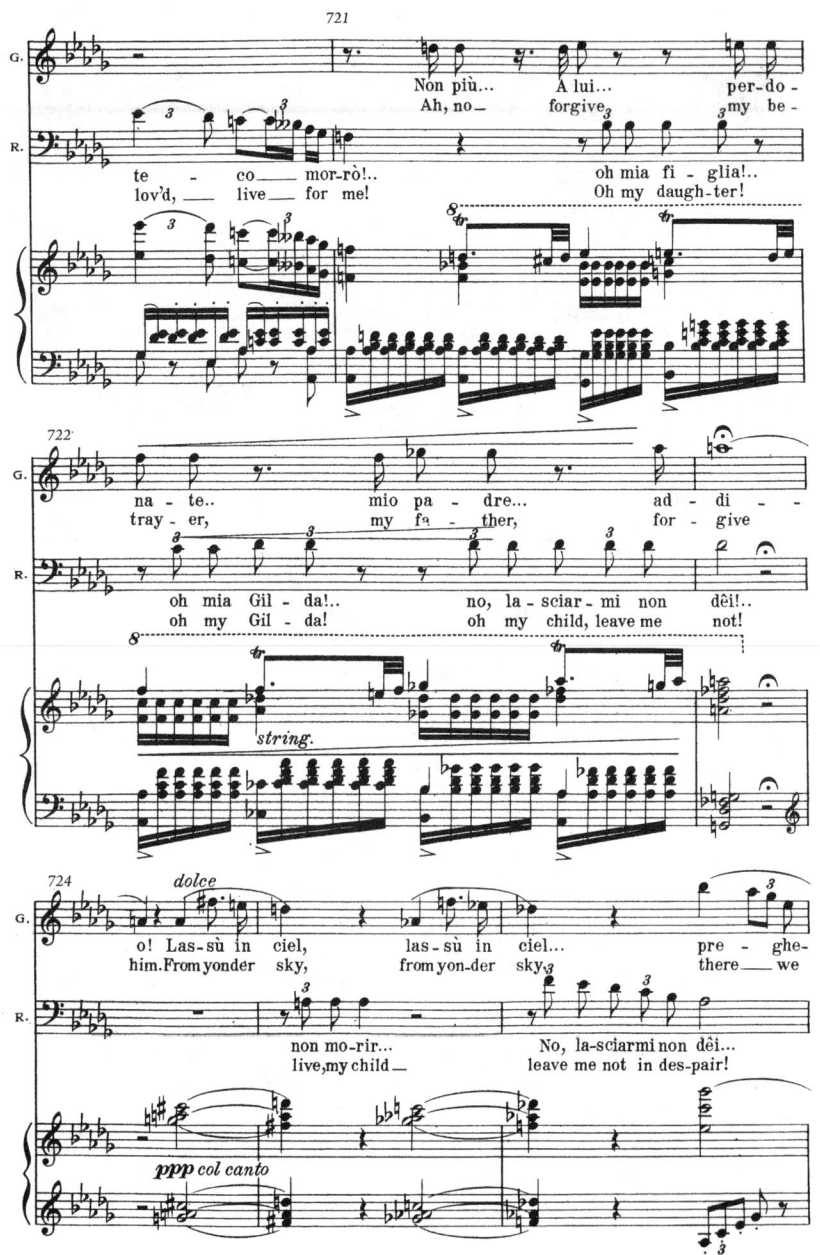

End of the Opera.

55

Bedřich Smetana
(1824–84)

FULL CD V: TRACK 13
CONCISE CD II: TRACK 46

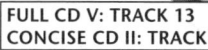

Má vlast (My Fatherland), *Vltava* (The Moldau or Vltava River) (1874)

Vltava is the most popular of the six symphonic poems that together make up Smetana's *Má vlast* (My Fatherland). Written in celebration of his Czech homeland, the composer dedicated the cycle to the city of Prague, where he had received his musical education and where he had been the principal conductor of the Royal Provincial Czech Theatre since 1866. Unlike the other pieces in *Má vlast,* in which Smetana evokes episodes from Czech history to celebrate the greatness of the Czech nation, *Vltava* is genuine nature music. In the composer's words:

> The composition depicts the course of the river [Vltava/Moldau], from its beginning where two brooks, one cold, the other warm, join a stream, running through forests and meadows and a lovely countryside where merry feasts are celebrated; water-sprites dance in the moonlight; on nearby rocks the outline of ruined castles can be seen, proudly soaring into the sky. Vltava swirls through the St. John Rapids and flows in a broad stream towards Prague. It passes Vyšehrad [castle] and disappears majestically into the distance, where it joins the Elbe.

Adding a few enumerations to the program printed in the score, one arrives at the following list of the work's musical sections:

Measure Nos.	Program	Keys	Comments
1–39	The river springs from its two sources, splashing gaily over rocks and glistening in the sunshine	e	
39–79	Main theme, the river broadens	e	Theme over running "water music"
80–117	Hunting horns ("Chase . . ." in score)	C	
118–173	Country dances ("Peasants wedding" in score)	G	Polka
174–231	Moonlight—("Dance of the Nymphs" in score)	A♭	
232–263	Reprise of main theme	e	Shifts to major, mm. 257–258
264–325	The rapids near St. John		Modulatory, developmental section
326–351	Main theme, then broadens again near Prague, where it is welcomed by . . .	E	Main theme in major (resembles Wagner's Rhine)
352–420	The old and venerable castle Vyšehrad	E	Opening I–vi–V–I progression from Smetana's *Vyšehrad*

The work opens with sixteenth-note runs in two alternating flutes representing the two sources of the river. The forests are depicted by hunting horns ("Chase in the forests," mm. 80ff), the meadows by the rustic dance of a "Peasants wedding" (mm. 118ff), which is contrasted with a dreamy section of "Moonlight, Dance of the Nymphs" (mm. 174ff) before the music of the first section returns in m. 232. To portray the river passing the St. John Rapids, Smetana makes the sixteenth-note "water music" more tumultuous (m. 264ff). Emerging from the rapids triumphant (m. 326ff), the river then salutes the rock at Prague's Vyšehrad castle (m. 352ff). (Here Smetana cites the harmonic progression I–vi–V–I he first used to represent the rock at Vyšehrad in the opening of the first symphonic poem, *Vyšehrad*, of *Má vlast*.)

Aside from the recapitulatory effect created by the reappearance of the first tune in its original key, E minor (m. 232), and the contrasting rustic theme in the relative major (m. 122), Smetana's form does not correspond to sonata models. Its key scheme—E-minor tonic counterbalanced by C major ("Chase . . .") and A♭ major ("Moonlight")—follows the symmetrical, major-third-related tonal trajectory characteristic of Liszt rather than conventional tonic–dominant relations. In one section, at the St. John rapids, Smetana builds the musical material on diminished harmonies, occasionally producing fragments of the octatonic scale (see the piano left hand upper part, mm. 288–289), a tone–semitone scale used by Liszt and exploited by Russian composers in musical depictions of supernatural forces in opera. The great apotheosis Smetana builds up at the climax of *Vltava* as he transforms the E-minor theme into a triumphant E major at m. 326 also owes something to Liszt. But it is not only Liszt whose influence is audible in Smetana's music. By the end of the piece the mythological river of the Czech people sounds much like the mythological river of the German nation. In its major, triumphant incarnation, Smetana's Vlatava seems to turn into Wagner's Rhine as it appears at the beginning of *Das Rheingold* (see Example 55–1).

In addition to depictions of the countryside and representation of national legends, the use of folk tunes is a common nineteenth-century technique for evoking national inspirations.

619

Example 55–1

(a) Wagner

(b) Smetana

In *Vltava* the rustic tune in the episode of the peasant wedding, with its first-beat accents and frequent syncopations, is a stylized Czech folk dance, although it has no specific model in folk music. The main tune of the piece is a melody borrowed from a non-Czech source, the Swedish melody "Akh Värmeland du sköna" (Ah Vermland you beautiful), which Smetana remembered from his years teaching in Sweden.

Today the tune is best known as adapted in the Israeli national anthem. It is unclear whether the arranger of the anthem, Samuel Cohen, knew the tune from Smetana's *Vltava* or from a collection of "Moldavian" (eastern Romanian) songs, in which it was published with the title "Carul cu boi" (Cart and oxen). Cohen fitted the words of Naftali Herz Imber's poem *Tikvatenu* (Our hope) to the tune. The resulting hymn, *Hatikvah* (The hope), became the official Zionist anthem in 1897 and later the national anthem of Israel. The history of this melody demonstrates that national significance is located not in musical properties but in historically accrued cultural associations.

The Moldau rises in the Bohemian woods, grows and soon becomes a wonderful stream.

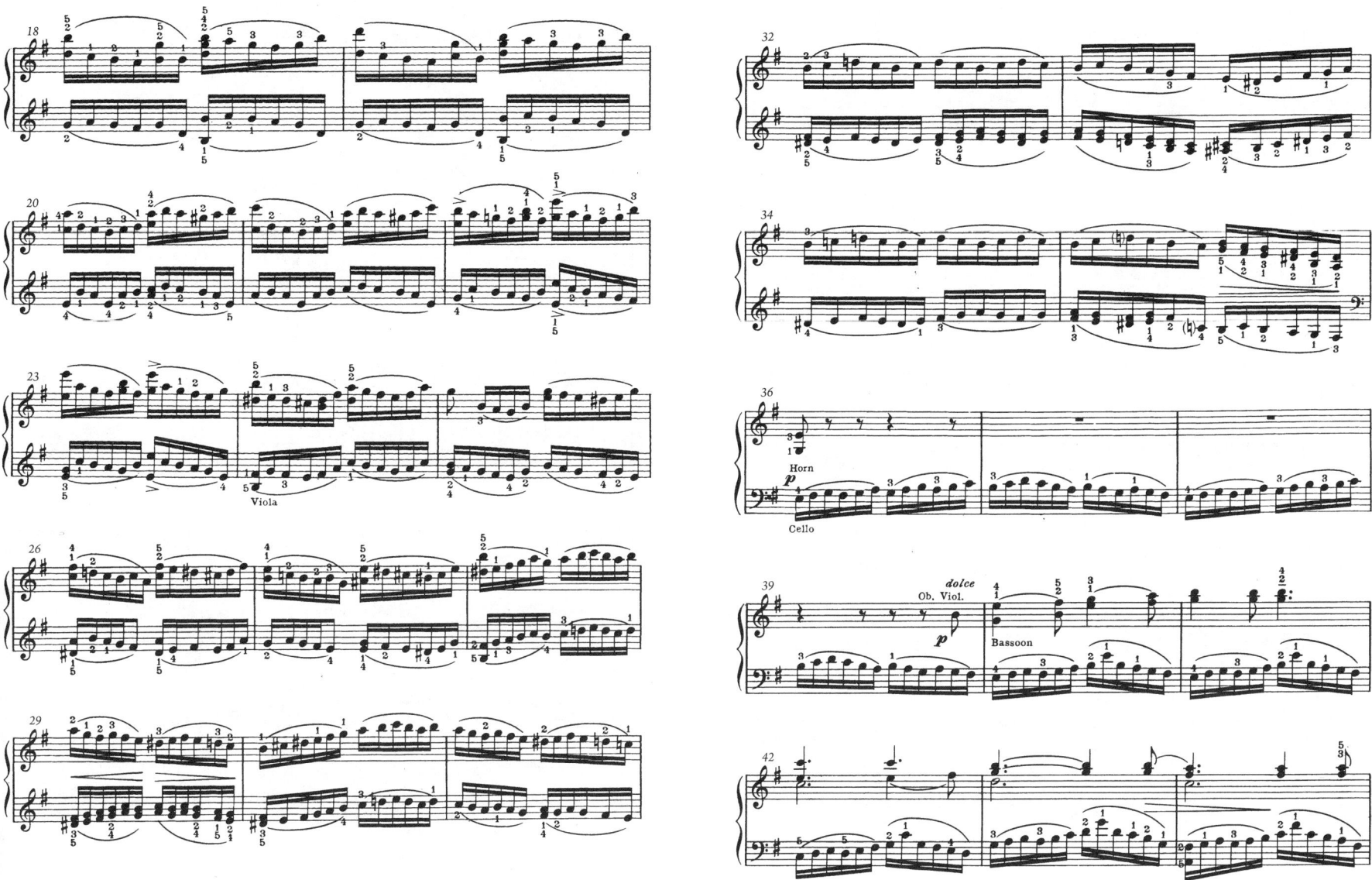

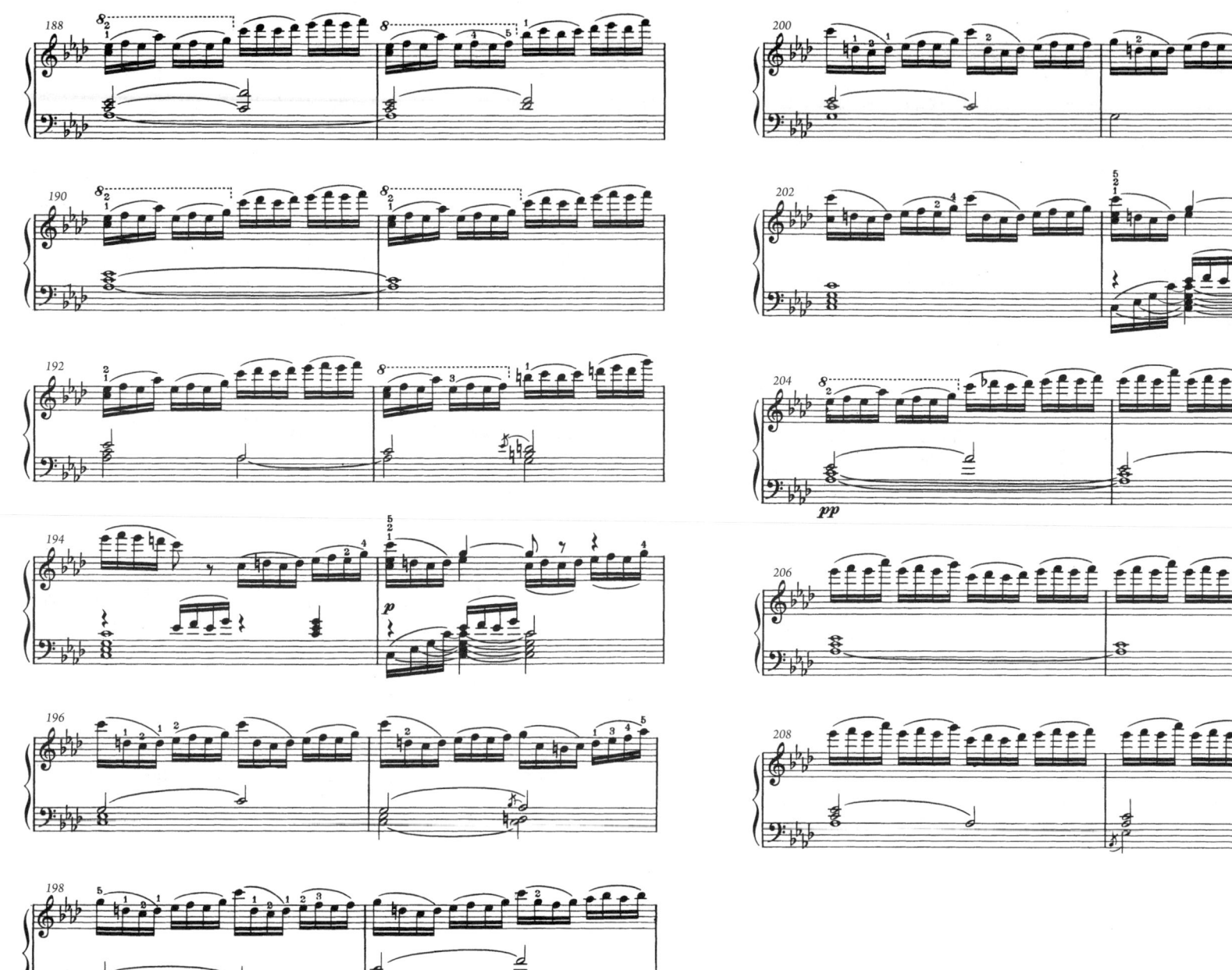

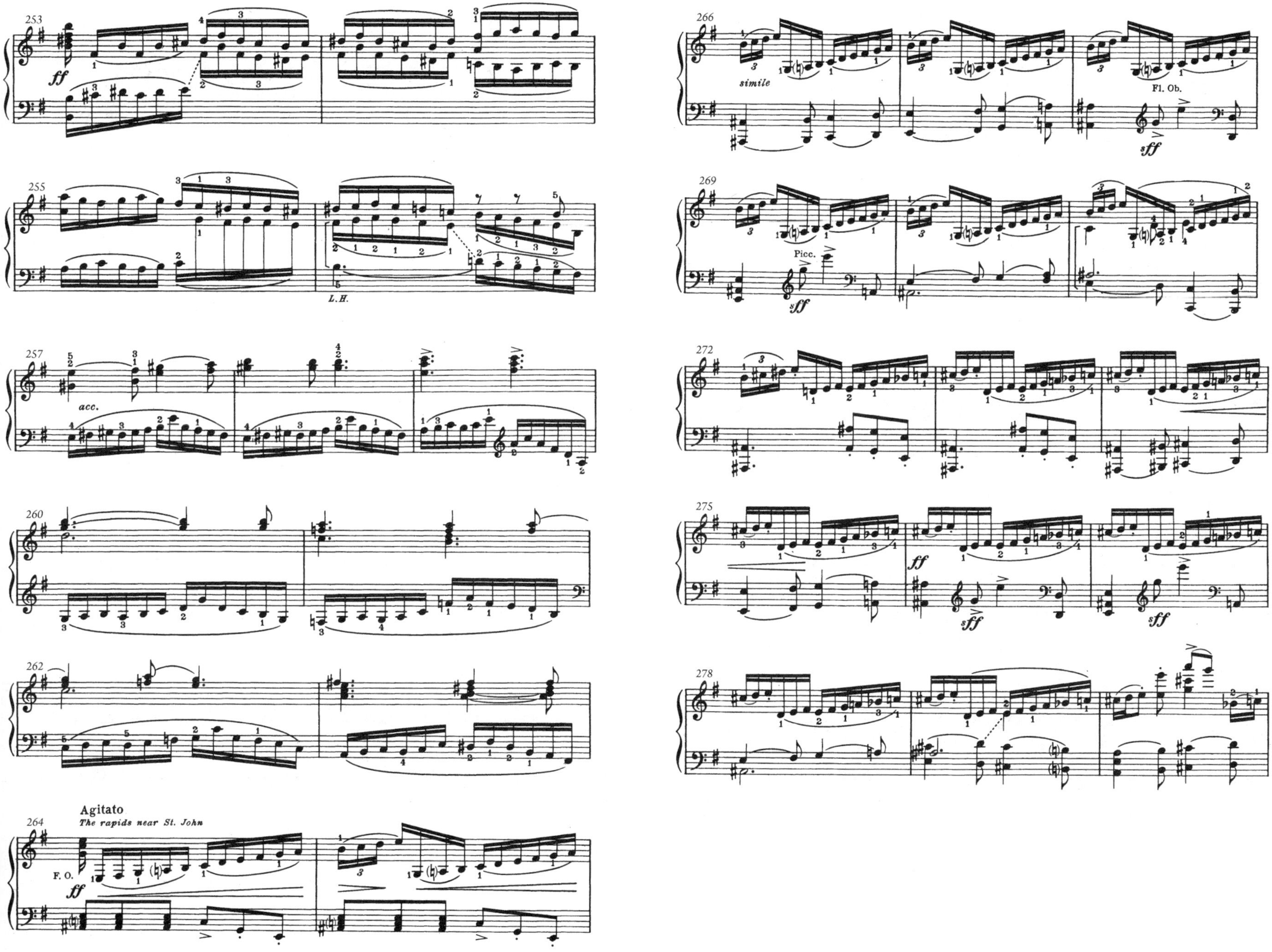
253
ff
255
L.H.
257
acc.
260
262
Agitato
The rapids near St. John
264
F. O.
ff
266
simile
Fl. Ob.
sff
269
Picc.
sff
272
275
ff
sff
sff
278

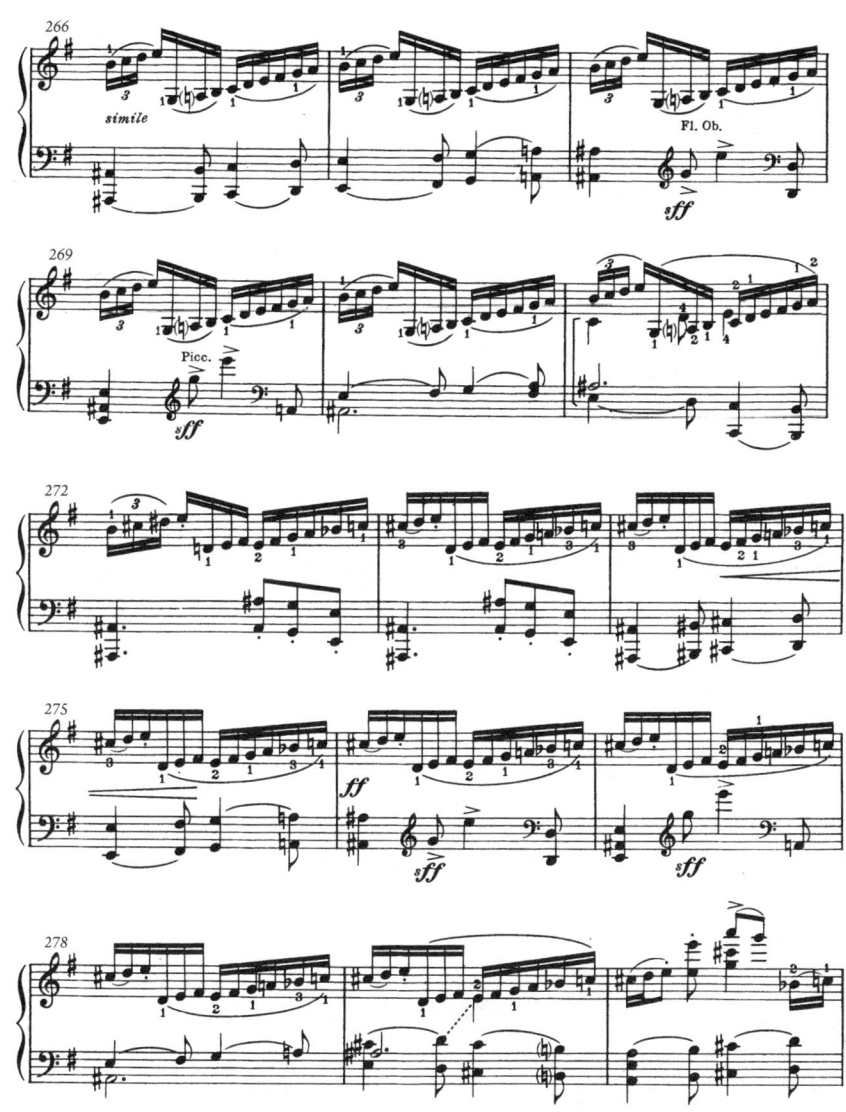

56

Modest Musorgsky (1839–81)

Boris Godunov, "Coronation Scene" (1869–72)

Based on Alexander Pushkin's 1825 play *Boris Godunov*, Musorgsky's opera of the same title recounts events surrounding the coronation and subsequent overthrowing of Boris Godunov, Tsar of Russia from 1598 to 1605. In order to gain power, Boris, brother-in-law of Fyodor who inherited the throne upon the death of his father, Ivan the Terrible, supposedly had Fyodor's stepbrother, Dmitri, killed in 1591. Musorgsky's opera depicts Boris as a tsar who, while intent on serving his people, is tortured by bad conscience and thus vulnerable to political intrigue. Boris dies before an impostor claming to be Dmitri reaches Moscow leading Polish troops and a revolutionary crowd.

Musorgsky finished the first version of his opera in 1869, the second in 1872 (first performed in 1874). Other versions have been created since Musorgsky's death, two by Nikolay Rimsky-Korsakov (1896, 1908), one by Dmitry Shostakovich (1939–1940), and another by Karol Rathaus (1952). The piano reduction in our anthology is from Rimsky-Korsakov's 1908 edition.

Emblematic of the opera is the second scene of the prologue, the so-called "Coronation Scene." Here Musorgsky's passion for realism manifests itself in the recreation of the sound of bells, the faithful reproduction of Russian declamation, and the use of an authentic folk tune as the musical expression of the crowd.

The most radically "realistic" harmonic effect in the opera is the one with which the scene opens. The stage direction specifies a "solemn peal of bells," and that is what the orchestral prelude depicts. It consists of just two chords, both of them describable in common-practice terms as dominant sevenths with roots on A♭ and D, respectively. This description is misleading, however, since neither of the chords resolves to its implied tonic (respectively D♭ and G). Nor, once their oscillation really gets going, do we expect them to do so, for the two chords share a tritone (C and F♯/G♭). The alternation of the two tritones, the one they share and the one between their roots (A♭ and D), neutralizes the chords' functional tendencies.

The alternation of these chords thus produces not forward motion but a stalemate. Musorgsky shapes the passage by rhythmic rather than harmonic means: at first by surface diminutions, then by doubling the harmonic rhythm, devices copied from actual bell-ringing techniques. At mm. 23ff the whole thing is repeated. Given that there is no possible functional cadence for this progression, all Musorgsky can do to bring the second passage to an end is to drown it out with heavy percussion.

For Musorgsky the most important aspect of realism was realistic declamation, here shown in Boris's central monologue (mm. 160–191). According to the composer's theory of music drama, realistic declamation was the very crux of dramatic truth. In this scene Boris's recitation uses a wider range, longer upbeats, and bolder melodic leaps than usually associated with recitative. These departures from the conversational norm elevate Boris's diction to the level of tragic eloquence; he assumes, as it were, the emotionally exalted tone that Russians traditionally adopt when reciting poetry. While still classifiable as recitative, the composer-critic César Cui (1835–1918) dubbed the style "melodic recitative," recognizing that each phrase has "song potential"; that is, one can easily imagine its development into an arioso.

During Boris's monologue Musorgsky uses modal harmonies that give the passage an archaic feel. At m. 181 the key signature is "cleared," and the tone centers become difficult to identify in terms of functional harmony. Is Boris's line starting at m. 182 centered on A? Then why does it end on B? Is the mode "Aeolian," as the minor V chord in the progression before Boris's entry seems to suggest? Then what is the status of the F♯? Part of an applied dominant to G? But what is the status of G? Or is the mode "Dorian"? Even within a resolutely diatonic idiom, Musorgsky makes radical departures from functional norms that evoke "otherness" (another time, another place than his own).

Boris's central monologue is set off by one of Musorgsky's few additions to Pushkin's script: a choral procession. Sung to the tune (and most of the words) of an old Russian folk song, it first appears in mm. 52–63. The song lends an authentic period flavor to a scene of public ritual. The tune Musorgsky used was famous—not least because Beethoven had used it in a quartet dedicated to Count Razumovsky, the Russian ambassador in Vienna, who had given Beethoven a folk-song anthology for the purpose. The original words—"As to Thee, God in heaven, there is glory, let there be glory to the Tsar"—recommend themselves as coronation fodder.

A square in the Moscow Kremlin. Facing the audience is the Red Staircase leading to the Tsar's apartments in the palace. Closer to the audience the crowd is kneeling between the Cathedral of the Assumption and the Cathedral of the Archangels (the porches of the cathedrals are visible).

Solemn pealing of bells.

A procession of boyars starts toward the cathedral.

Prince Shuyskiy   **Prince Shuyskiy**

(*on the porch of the Cathedral of the Assumption*)

Da zdravstvuyet tsar' Boris Feodorovich!   Long live Tsar Boris Feodorovich!

Crowd
Zhivi i zdravstvuy, tsar' nash batyushka!

Crowd
Long live the Tsar, our father!

Prince Shuyskiy
Slav'te!

Prince Shuyskiy
Praise him!

Crowd
*Uzh kak na nebe solntsu krasnomu
    slava, slava!
Uzh i slava na Rusi tsar'yu Borisu, slava!*

Crowd
As unto the beautiful sun in heaven, glory,
    glory!
So to Tsar Boris in Rus', glory!

(The Tsar's procession leaves the cathedral. The police officers organize the people in lines.)

*Zhivi i zdravstvuy! Tsar' nash batyushka,
Tsar' nash batyushka zhivi i zdravstvuy!
Raduysya, lyud! Raduysya, veselisya,
    lyud!
Pravoslavnïy lyud!
Velichay tsarya Borisa i slav'!*

Long live! Tsar our father,
Long live the Tsar our father!
People, rejoice! Rejoice and make merry,
    people!
People of the Orthodox faith!
Exalt and glorify Tsar Boris!

Boyars (*from the porch*)
Da zdravstvuyet tsar' Boris Feodorovich!

Boyars (*from the porch*)
Long live Tsar Boris Feodorovich!

Crowd (*bowing*)
Da zdravstvuyet!

Crowd (*bowing*)
Long live!

Boyars
Da zdravstvuyet tsar' Boris Feodorovich!

Boyars
Long live Tsar Boris Feodorovich!

Crowd
*Slava! Slava! Slava!
Tsar' tï batyushka nash!*

Crowd
Glory, glory, glory!
To you our Tsar and our father!

Boyars
Da zdravstvuyet tsar' Boris Feodorovich!

Boyars
Long live Tsar Boris Feodorovich!

(Boris appears and moves through the scene.)

Crowd
*Da zdravstvuyet!
Uzh kak na nebe solntsu krasnomu
    slava, slava!
Uzh i slava na Rusi tsar'yu Borisu, slava!
Slava tsaryu, slava, slava!*

Crowd
Long live!
As unto the beautiful sun in heaven, glory,
    glory!
So to Tsar Boris in Rus', glory!
Glory to the Tsar, glory, glory!

Boris
Skorbit dusha!

Boris
My soul is sad!

*Kakoy-to strakh nevol'nïy
zloveshchim predchuvstviyem skoval
    mne serdtse.
O, pravednik, o, moy otets derzhavnïy!
Vozzri s nebes na slyozï vernïkh slug*

Some unwanted fear
gripped my heart with ominous forebodings.

O Righteous One, o my almighty Father!
Look down from Heaven on your servant's
    tears

*i nisposhli tï mne svyashchennoye
na vlast' blagosloven'ye;
da budu blag i praveden, kak tï,
da v slave pravlyu svoy narod.
Teper' poklonimsya
pochiyushchim vlastitelyam Rusii,
A tam szïvat' narod na pir,
vsekh, ot boyar do nishchevo sleptsa,
vsem vol'nïy vkhod,
vse gosti dorogiye.*

and send down blessings
on my sovereign power;
May I be just and bountiful, like You,
may I rule my people in glory.
Now let us bow
before the deceased rulers of Russia,
and then call our people to feast,
all, from boyar to wretched beggar,
all can enter free,
all are our cherished guests.

(pealing of bells on stage)

(The procession advances toward the Cathedral of the Archangel.)

Crowd
*Slava! Slava! Slava!
Zhivi i zdravstvuy! Tsar' nash batyushka,*

Crowd
Glory! Glory! Glory!
Long live! Tsar our father,

(The police establish order. The people run toward the Cathedral of the Archangel.)

*Slava! Slava!
Tsar tï nash.*

Glory! Glory!
You are our Tsar.

Boyars
Da zdravstvuyet tsar' Boris Feodorovich!

Boyars
Long live Tsar Boris Feodorovich!

Crowd
*Da zdravstvuyet!
Uzh kak na nebe solntsu krasnomu
glory,   slava, slava!
Uzh i slava na Rusi tsar'yu Borisu, slava!
Slava i mnogaya leta!*

Crowd
Long live!
As unto the beautiful sun in heaven,
glory!
So to Tsar Boris in Rus', glory!
Glory and many years!

(Disturbance. The police officers struggle with the crowd.)

Slava! Slava! Slava!

Glory! Glory! Glory!

(Boris leaves the Cathedral and makes his way toward the apartments.)

57

Pyotr Ilyich Tchaikovsky
(1840–93)

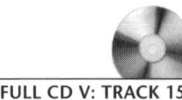

FULL CD V: TRACK 15

Yevgeny Onegin (Eugene Onegin), Act I, Scene 2
(Letter scene) (1878)

Measure Nos.	Sections	Keys	Comments
1–6	Introduction, part 1		Modulatory
7–15	Introduction, part 2	Db	Orchestra depicts Tatyana's agitation
15–33	**1st romance**	Db	AA′ form
34–46	Tatyana sits down to write		
46–98	**2nd romance**	d	ABA form, recitative-like B section (mm. 70–78)
99–101	Tatyana rises		
102–181	**3rd romance**	C	ABA form, slower B section in 2 parts: mm. 126–137 (prefigures main theme of 4th romance) and mm. 138–150
182–269	**4th romance**	Db	ABA form, faster B section (mm. 226–240)
269–290	Orchestral postlude	Db	Emotional climax
290–310	Tatyana rises and seals letter		Concluding lines

Tchaikovsky completed *Eugene Onegin* in 1878 to a libretto (written by the composer and Konstantin Shilovsky) based on Alexander Pushkin's 1833 novel in verse about a St. Petersburg dandy, Onegin, who involuntarily ignites a country girl's romantic passion. Defying convention, the girl, Tatyana, confesses her love in a letter to Onegin, which he receives coldly. The romance is thus thwarted. When years later Onegin again meets Tatyana, now married to a prince in St. Petersburg, he realizes that he threw away the possibility of true passion when he refused her; but it is too late to rekindle their love.

Romantic though the story is, Pushkin's novel in verse and Tchaikovsky's music render it realistic by mocking both Tatyana's naive passion (inspired by reading novels) and Onegin's cold cynicism (born of experience). Tchaikovsky's opera consists of a series of lyric scenes, played with the background of singing peasants, ballroom dances, and domestic songs. The most famous scene in the opera is the "letter scene" from Act I, Scene 2, in which Tatyana composes her confessional letter to Onegin. Tchaikovsky sets Pushkin's text (from the third chapter of the novel) almost in its entirety. He divides the seventy-nine lines into four separate parts, each reminiscent of a Russian romance, the genre of Russian song popular in the 1830s and 1840s for setting romantic poetry (see chart).

Used mainly as domestic entertainment, the romance was characterized by its lyricism and folk-song-like tone. The first romance in Tatyana's letter scene is quickly aborted by Tatyana's hesitation. In the more expansive second, third, and fourth romances, Tchaikovsky sets words of the actual letter and uses ABA form. For Tchaikovsky, setting Tatyana's letter scene as a series of romances served both as a realistic depiction of the young girl's domestic surrounding and as a historically accurate characterization of both Pushkin's and Tchaikovsky's time.

Although the tonality of the sections is rarely in question, Tchaikovsky's chromatic harmonic language is no less advanced than Wagner's was at the time. In the first four measures of the introduction, the ascending chromatic line in the second violins (B–B♯–C♯–C♯♯, in the left hand in the piano reduction) is countered by the descending motion of the bass, and it delineates harmonies reminiscent of the meticulously prepared but never resolved dominant harmonies in Wagner's *Tristan and Isolde*. The chromaticism in Tchaikovsky's music is also specifically Russian. Already in the introduction chromatic motion occurs between the fifth and sixth scale degrees (see the upper part of the left hand in m. 5 in the context of C♯ minor), a move that, when descending, marks the music of Russian composers such as Glinka, Balakirev, and Borodin with Eastern sensuousness. Tatyana's principal motive, heard at m. 34 in the violin, also contains descending chromaticism—it is in fact this descending chromatic turn that identifies other motives as related to Tatyana, making her, at least for short periods of time, akin to sexually irresistible, exotic opera heroines like Borodin's Polovtsian Konchakova in *Prince Igor* and Bizet's Gypsy Carmen.

Tchaikovsky, however, takes pains to preserve Tatyana's innocence. Her vocal part remains relatively simple, and its frequent use of the interval of the sixth, either as direct melodic leap or as melodic contour, invokes the Russian romance. The physical aspects of her passion are depicted not by her vocal line but by the orchestra. In the second romance, for instance, the woodwinds (especially the oboe) carry the sentimental, bittersweet melody, punctuated by solo flutes, horns, and harp (mm. 46ff). After Tatyana reaches a resolution in the fourth romance, the horn's heroic tone supports the heroine's determination (right hand at mm. 184–185). Even her climactic outburst in this section, "Voobrazi: ya zdes' odna!" (You cannot know: I'm so alone mm. 241–243), is subdued compared to the passionate explosion that follows in the orchestra at mm. 269ff, where the climactic melody is repeated *fortissimo* in the brass, accompanied by rushing strings and a chorus of woodwinds.

Keeping Tatyana somewhat removed even from her own passion, Tchaikovsky maintains a realistic approach to his subject. This realism differs from Musorgsky's. It manifests itself in the setting of an almost contemporary story with a Mozartean care for depicting physical sensation while keeping the music in the range of the beautiful through a reliance on the easily recognizable, popular idiom of the Russian romance.

Tatyana	Tatyana
Puskay pogribnu ya, no prezhde	Let me die, but first
ya v oslepitel'noy nadezhde	in blind hope, I summon
blazhenstvo temnoye zovu,	bliss however dangerous,
ya negu zhizni uznayu!	I will learn life's pleasure!
Ya p'yu volshebnïy yad zhelaniy	I drink the magic potion of desire,
menya presleduyut mechtï!	dreams haunt me!
Vezde, vezde peredo mnoy	I see me fatal tempter everywhere,
moy iskusitel' rokovoy,	he is everywhere
vezde on predo mnoyu!	before my eyes!

(She goes to the writing table, sits down, writes, then pauses.)

Net, vse ne to!	No, that's all wrong!
Nachnu snachala . . .	I'll begin again!

(She tears up the unfinished letter.)

Akh! Shto so mnoy! Ya vsya goryu . . .	Ah what's the matter with me! I'm all on fire . . .
Ne znayu, kak nachat'!	I don't know how to begin!

(She writes, then pauses and reads it over.)

Ya k vam pishu—chego zhe bole?	I'm writing you this declaration—
Shto ya mogu eshcho skazat'?	What more can I in candor say?
Teper', ya znayu, v vashey vole	It may be now your inclination
menya prezren'yem nakazat'!	To scorn me and to turn away;
No vï, k moyey neschastnoy dole	But if my hapless situation
khot' kaplyu zhalosti khranya,	Evokes some pity for my woe,
vï ne ostavite menya!	You won't abandon me I know.
Snachala ya molchat' khotela;	I first tried silence and evasion;
pover'te: moyego stïda	Believe me, you'd have never learned
vï ne uznali b nikogda!	My secret shame.

(She puts the letter aside.)

O da, klyalas' ya sokhranit' v dushe	O yes, I swore to lock within my breast
priznan'ye v strasti pïlkoy i bezumnoy!	this avowal of a mad and ardent passion!

Uvï! Ne v silakh ya vladet' svoyey	Alas, I have not the strength to subdue my
dushoy!	heart!
Pust' budet to, shto bït' dolzhno so mnoy!	Come what may, I am prepared!
Yemu priznayus' ya! Smeley,	I will confess all! Courage,
on vse uznayet!	he shall know all!

(She writes.)

Zachem, zachem vï posetili nas?	Why did you ever come to call?
V glushi zabïtogo selen'ya	In this forgotten country dwelling
ya b nikogda ne znala vas,	I'd not have known you then at all,
ne znala b gor'kogo muchen'ya.	Nor known this bitter heartache's swelling.
Dushi neopïtnoy volnen'ya	Perhaps, when time had helped in quelling,
smiriv, so vremenem (kak znat'?)	The girlish hopes on which I fed,
po serdtsu ya nashla bï druga,	I might have found (who knows?) another
bïla bï vernaya spruga	And been a faithful wife and mother,
i dobrodetel'naya mat'.	Contented with the life I led.

(She becomes lost in thought, then rises suddenly.)

Drugoy! Net, nikomu na svete	Another! No! On all creation
ne otdala bï serdtsa ya!	There's no one else whom I'd adore;
To v vïshnem suzhdeno sovete,	The heavens chose my destination,
volya neba: ya tvoya!	And made me thine for evermore!
Vsya zhizn' moya bïla zalogom	My life till now has been a token
svidan'ya vernogo s toboy;	In pledge of meeting you, my friend;
ya znayu: tï mne poslan bogom,	And in your coming, God has spoken,
do groba tï khranitel' moy!	You'll be my guardian till the end!
Tï v snoviden'yakh mne yavlyalsya,	You filled my dreams and sweetest trances;
nezrimïy, tï uzh bïl mne mil,	As yet unseen, and yet so dear,
tvoy chudnïy vzglyad menya tomil,	You stirred me with your wondrous glances,
v dushe tvoy golos razdavalsya!	Your voice within my soul rang clear!
Davno . . . net, eto bïl ne son!	And then the dream came true for me!
Tï chut' voshol, ya vmig uznala,	When you came in, I seemed to waken,
vsya obomlela, zapïlala,	I turned to flame, I felt all shaken,
i v mïslyakh molvila: vot on!	And in my heart I cried: It's he!
Ne pravda l'? Ya tebya slïkhala,	And was it you I heard replying
tï govoril so mnoy v tishi,	Amid the stillness of the night,
kogda ya bednïm pomogala,	Or when I helped the poor and dying,
ili molitnoy uslazhdala	Or turned to heaven, softly crying,
tosku dushi?	And said a prayer to soothe my plight?

I v eto samoye mgvoven'ye	And even now, my dearest vision,
ne tï li, miloye viden'ye,	Did I not see your apparition,
v prozrachnoy temnote mel'knul,	Flit softly through this lucent night?
priniknul tikho k izgolov'yu?	Was it not you who seemed to hover?
Ne tï l' s otradoy i lyubov'yu	Above my bed, a gentle lover,
slova nadezhdï mne shepnul?	To whisper hope and sweet delight?

(She returns to the table and sits down again to write.)

(With great feeling...)

Kto tï, moy angel li khranitel'	Are you my angel of salvation
ili kovarnïy iskusitel'?	Or hell's own demon of temptation?
Moi somnen'ya razreshi!	Be kind and send my doubts away;
Bït' mozhet, eto vse pustoye,	For this may all be mere illusion,
obman neopïtnoy dushi,	The things a simple girl would say,
i suzhdeno sovsem inoye?...	While Fate intends no grand conclusion...

(She rises again and paces pensively to and fro.)

No tak i bït'! sud'bu moyu	So be it then! Henceforth I place
otnïne ya tebe vruchayu,	My faith in you and your affection;
pered toboyu slezï l'yu,	I plead with tears upon my face,
tvoyey zashchitï umolyayu,	And beg you for your kind protection.
Voobrazi: ya zdes' odna!	You cannot know: I'm so alone,
Nikto menya ne ponimayet!	There's no one here to whom I've spoken,

(Approaching the proscenium, she becomes more and more animated.)

Rassudok moy iznemogayet,	My mind and will are almost broken,
i molcha gibnut' ya dolzhna!	And I must die without a moan.
Ya zhdu tebya, yedinïm slovom	I wait for you... and your decision:
nadezhdï serdtsa ozhivi	Revive my hopes with but a sign,
il' son tyazhelïy perervi,	Or halt this heavy dream of mine—
uvï, zasluzhennïm ukorom!	Alas, with well-deserved derision!

(She goes swiftly to the table, hurriedly finishes the letter and signs and seals it.)

Konchayu! Strashno perechest',	I close. I dare not now reread...
stïdom i strakhom zamirayu,	I shrink with shame and fear. But surely,
no mne porukoy vasha chest'	Your honor's all the pledge I need,
i smelo yey sebya vveryayu!	And I submit to it securely.

Lines by Pushkin are given in the translation by James E. Fallen, in Alexander Pushkin: Eugene Onegin
(Oxford: Oxford University Press, 1995), used by permission.

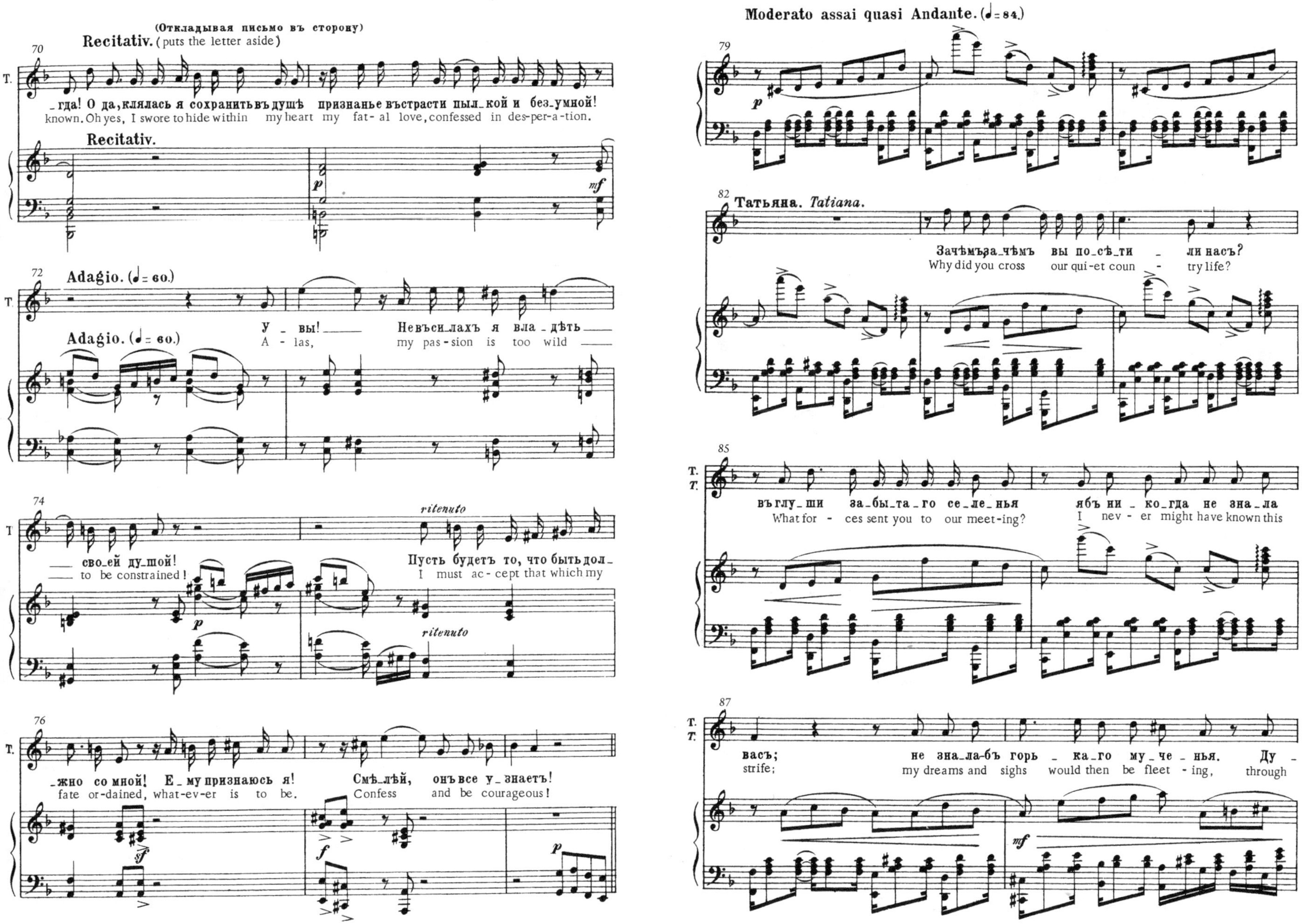
(Откладывая письмо въ сторону)
Recitativ. (puts the letter aside)
_гда! О да, клялась я сохранить въ душѣ признанье въ страсти пыл_кой и без_умной!
known. Oh yes, I swore to hide within my heart my fat- al love, confessed in des-per-a-tion.
Recitativ.
Adagio. (♩= 60.)
У _ вы! Невъ си_лахъ я вла_дѣть
A - las, my pas-sion is too wild
Adagio. (♩= 60.)
_ сво_ей ду_шой! Пусть будетъ то, что быть дол_
to be constrained! I must ac - cept that which my
ritenuto
_жно со мной! Е_му признаюсь я! Смѣ_лѣй, онъ все у_знаетъ!
fate or-dained, what-ev-er is to be. Confess and be courageous!
Moderato assai quasi Andante. (♩= 84.)
Татьяна. Tatiana.
Зачѣмъ, за_чѣмъ вы по_сѣ_ти _ ли насъ?
Why did you cross our qui-et coun - try life?
въ глу_ши за_бы_та_го се_ле_нья ябъ ни _ ко_гда не зна_ла
What for - ces sent you to our meet-ing? I nev - er might have known this
васъ; не зна_ла_бъ горь _ ка_го му_че _ нья. Ду _
strife; my dreams and sighs would then be fleet - ing, through

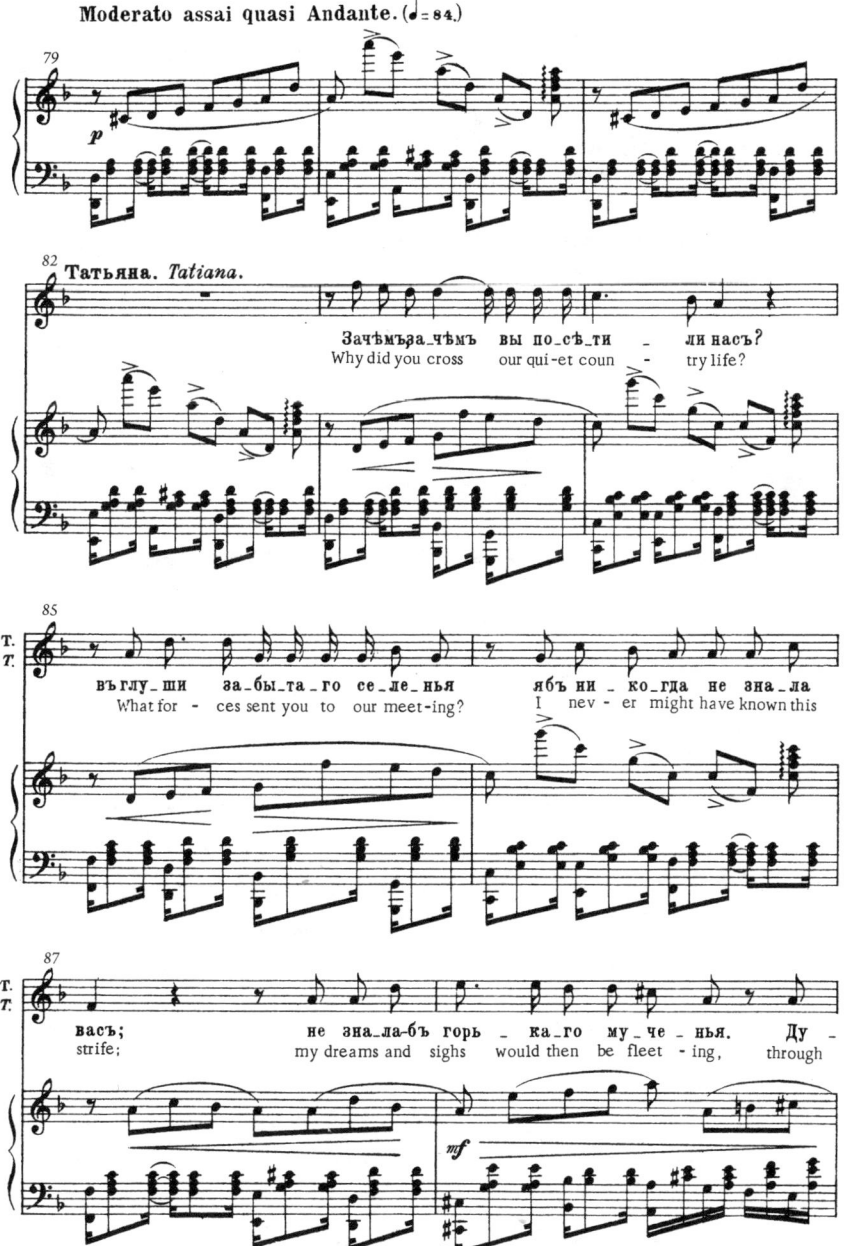

58

Pyotr Ilyich Tchaikovsky (1840–93)

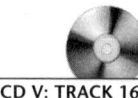

FULL CD V: TRACK 16

Symphony No. 4 in F Minor, Op. 36, First movement (1877)

Tchaikovsky's Fourth Symphony seemed to break with the whole symphonic tradition as viewed at the time of its composition. It lacks almost completely both the highly atomized motivic texture that Johannes Brahms (1833–97) had drawn from Beethoven and the "thematic transformation" employed by "Lisztian" symphonists like Camille Saint-Saëns (1835–1921) and Alexander Borodin (1833–87). Instead, Tchaikovsky's Fourth was something akin to a suite of giant character pieces: a "symphonic waltz" for a first movement; an *Andantino*, marked *in modo di canzone* ("in the manner of a ballad") for the second; an orchestrational tour de force of a scherzo for the third; and a finale consisting of variations on a famous Russian folk song. What seemed unprecedented was Tchaikovsky's constant, conspicuous reference to song and dance and his use of expansive melodies in place of tight motivic designs.

The first movement's main waltz theme, for example, is twenty-five broad $\frac{9}{8}$ measures in length (mm. 27–52), consisting of a regular eight-measure phrase to a dominant half cadence and an expertly extended answering phrase that, rather than leading to a bridge section, returns to a full cadence on the tonic. Even after this the theme continues, in expansive phrases, toward a climactic restatement in the tonic that reaches another full close before embarking on a modulatory transition (at mm. 104ff) that finally reveals the movement to be a symphonic binary, or "sonata-form," movement after all.

The symphony begins with earsplitting brass fanfares out of which the whole slow introduction is fashioned. Violence soon intrudes in the peremptory B-diminished seventh chord that cuts off the fanfares—virtually decapitates them—in unlucky m. 13. This has the dramatic force of program music; and the programmatic impression is confirmed when the fanfares begin acting like a Berliozian *idée fixe*, disrupting the movement at dramatically important moments (the beginning of the development, m. 193; the beginning of the coda, m. 355; and later at m. 389). The peak of violence occurs in the development section, when the fanfares suddenly return and make three collisions with the waltz theme (mm. 253, 263, and 278), each more terrible than the last. This is not merely "structure"; this is dramaturgy, which Tchaikovsky described as a program for the symphony. Although his written program may be regarded as a hasty verbal

paraphrase of ideas that Tchaikovsky formulated for the personal use of his patron, Nadezhda von Meck, it does correlate to the musical argument in the first movement:

The Introduction is the *kernel* of the whole symphony, without question its main idea: [here the fanfares are quoted]. This is Fate, the force of destiny, which ever prevents our pursuit of happiness from reaching its goal, which jealously stands watch lest our peace and well-being be full and cloudless, which hangs like the sword of Damocles over our heads and constantly, ceaselessly poisons our souls. It is invincible, inescapable. One can only resign oneself and lament fruitlessly: [Here the waltz theme is quoted].

This disconsolate and despairing feeling grows ever stronger and more intense. Would it not be better to turn away from reality and immerse oneself in dreams? [Here the second theme is quoted.] O joy! A sweet tender dream has appeared. A bright, beneficent human form flits by and beckons us on. [Here the end of the exposition is quoted.] How wonderful! How distant now is the sound of the implacable introductory theme! Dreams little by little have taken over the soul. All that is dark and bleak is forgotten. There it is, there it is—happiness!

But no! These are only dreams, and *Fate* awakens us from them. [Here the fanfares are quoted again as they appear at the beginning of the development section.] And thus, all life is the ceaseless alternation of bitter reality with evanescent visions and dreams of happiness. There is no refuge. We are buffeted about by this sea until it seizes us and pulls us down to the bottom.

One can explain the dramaturgical significance of the fanfares without relying on Tchaikovsky's private program. In the Fourth Symphony the composer relied, like Mozart before him, on codes of dance genres. The fanfares that Tchaikovsky described as the "Fate theme" are in the meter of a polonaise, a dance that had its origin in Polish court processionals and that remained the most socially elevated of all the ballroom dances of the nineteenth century. The polonaise was often associated with military parades, martial rhythms, and brass bands. The waltz, on the other hand, signaled lower social status. It is easy to see how the attributes of a polonaise could have attached themselves to Tchaikovsky's "Fate theme": its military associations, connoting aggression, hostility, and implacability; the idea of grandiosity and invincible power, derived from political or social awe; and finally, perhaps, the idea of impersonality, dwarfing individual concerns, as the idea of Fate frustrates the subject-persona of the Fourth Symphony (symbolized by the waltz theme) in pursuit of happiness. The submission of waltz to polonaise—of subject to fate—is palpably denoted in the coda, when the waltz theme is reprised for the last time in triple augmentation (mm. 402–411), that is, at the speed of the polonaise, each beat of the theme now stretched out to the length of one full measure, and therefore no longer a waltz at all. "Fate" or restricted social mores has thus succeeded in thwarting the possibility of individual happiness

Measure Nos.	Formal Designation	Sections	Keys	Comments
1–26	Introduction		f	Fanfares in polonaise rhythm
27–192	Exposition			
27–103		1st theme	f	"In movement of waltz"
104–115		Bridge		
116–133		2nd theme	a♭	
134–192		Closing theme	B	Fashioned out of the primary theme
193–277	Development			
193–252			B, f♯, etc.	Begins with fanfare
253–277				Collision of fanfare and waltz theme (mm. 253, 263, 278)
278–354	Recapitulation			
278–283		Fanfare		
284–292		1st theme	d	Over dominant pedal
292–293		Bridge		
295–312		2nd theme	d	
313–354		Closing theme	F	
355–422	Coda		f	Begins with fanfare; 1st theme in augmentation at m. 402

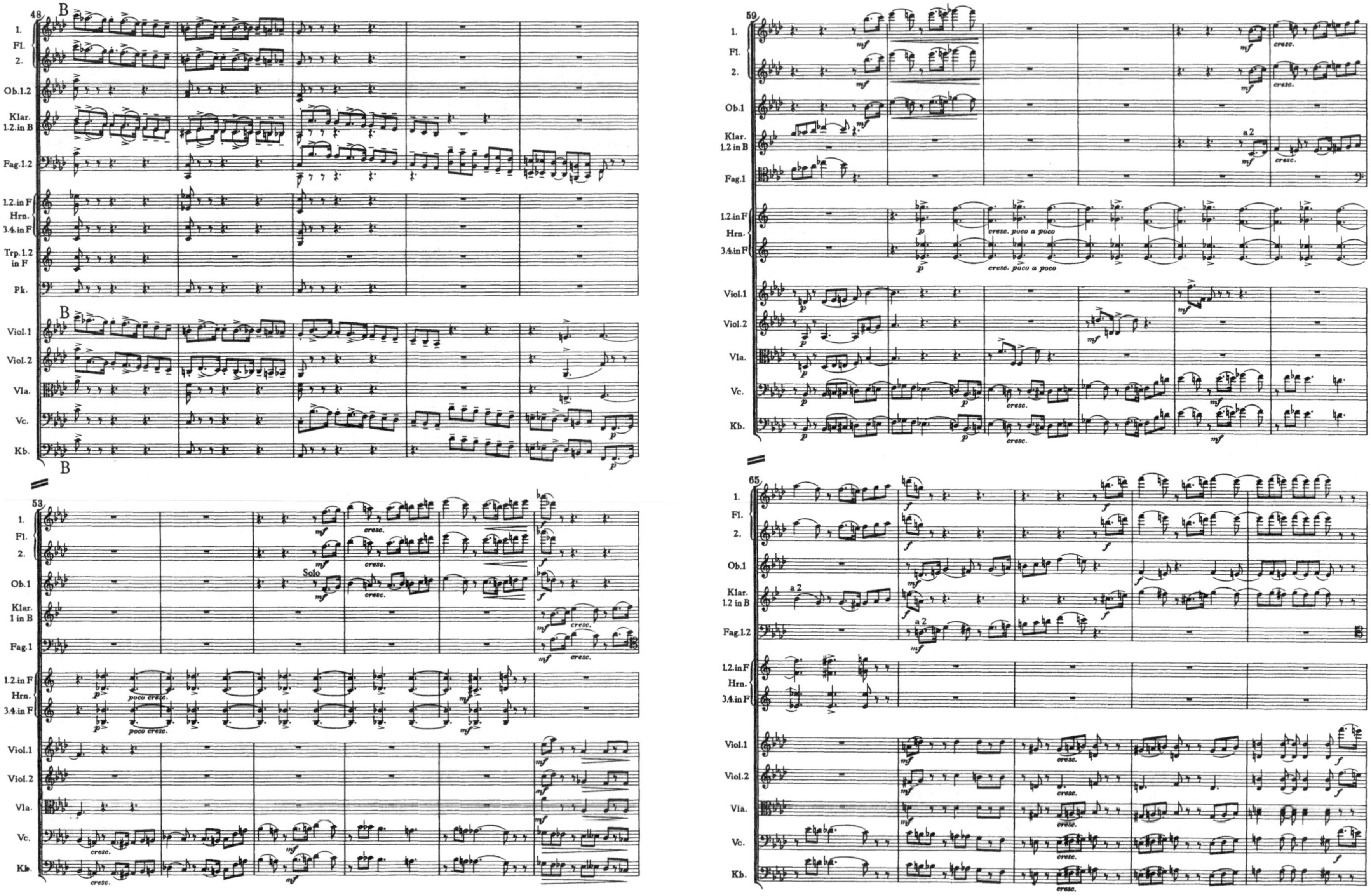
48
B
1. Fl. 2.
Ob.1.2
Klar. 1.2 in B
Fag.1.2
1.2 in F Hrn. 3.4 in F
Trp.1.2 in F
Pk.
Viol.1
Viol.2
Vla.
Vc.
Kb.
53
Ob.1
Klar. 1 in B
Fag.1
Solo
poco cresc.
cresc.
59
Klar. 1.2 in B
a 2
cresc. poco a poco
65

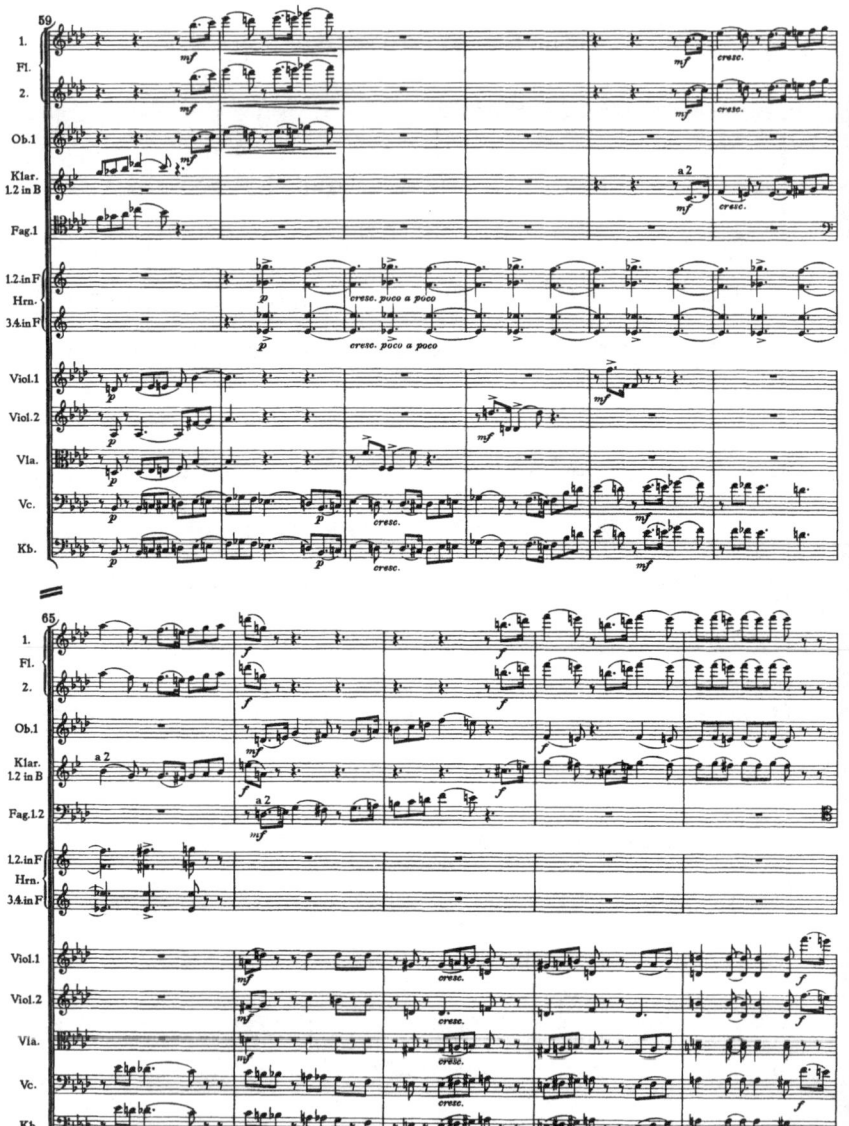

162
167
Fl.
Ob.1.2
Klar. 1.2 in B
Fag.1.2
1.2.in F
Hrn.
3.4.in F
Trp.1.2 in F
A.T.
Pos.
B.
Btb.
Pk.
Viol.1
Viol.2
Vla.
Vc.
Kb.
a 2
pizz.
arco

172
177
1.
Fl.
2.
Ob.1.2
Klar.
1.2 in B
Fag.1.2
1.2.in F
Hrn.
3.4.in F
Trp.1.2
in F
A.T.
Pos.
B.
Btb.
Pk.
Viol.1
Viol.2
Vla.
Vc.
Kb.
a 2
fff

182
1.
Fl.
2.
Ob.1.2
Klar.
1.2 in B
Fag.1.2
a 2
1.2.in F
Hrn.
3.4.in F
Trp.1.2
in F
A.T.
Pos.
B.
Btb.
Pk.
Viol.1
Viol.2
Vla.
Vc.
Kb.
187
K
Klar.
1.2 in F

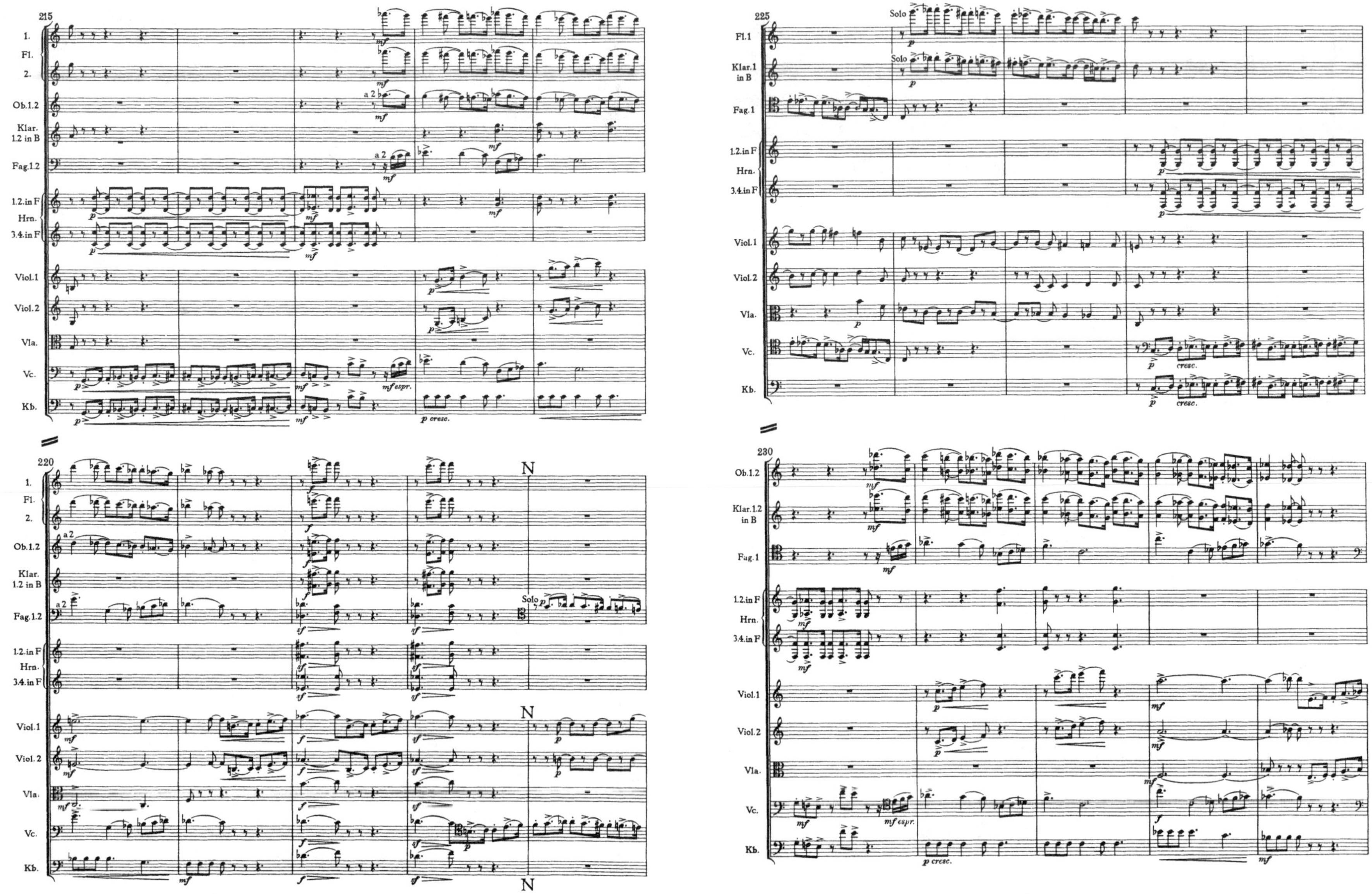
215
Fl. 1
Fl. 2
Ob. 1.2
Klar. 1.2 in B
Fag. 1.2
1.2. in F Hrn. 3.4. in F
Viol. 1
Viol. 2
Vla.
Vc.
Kb.
220
N
Solo
225
Fl. 1
Klar. 1 in B
Fag. 1
230
Klar. 1.2 in B
Fag. 1
mf espr.
p cresc.
cresc.
a 2

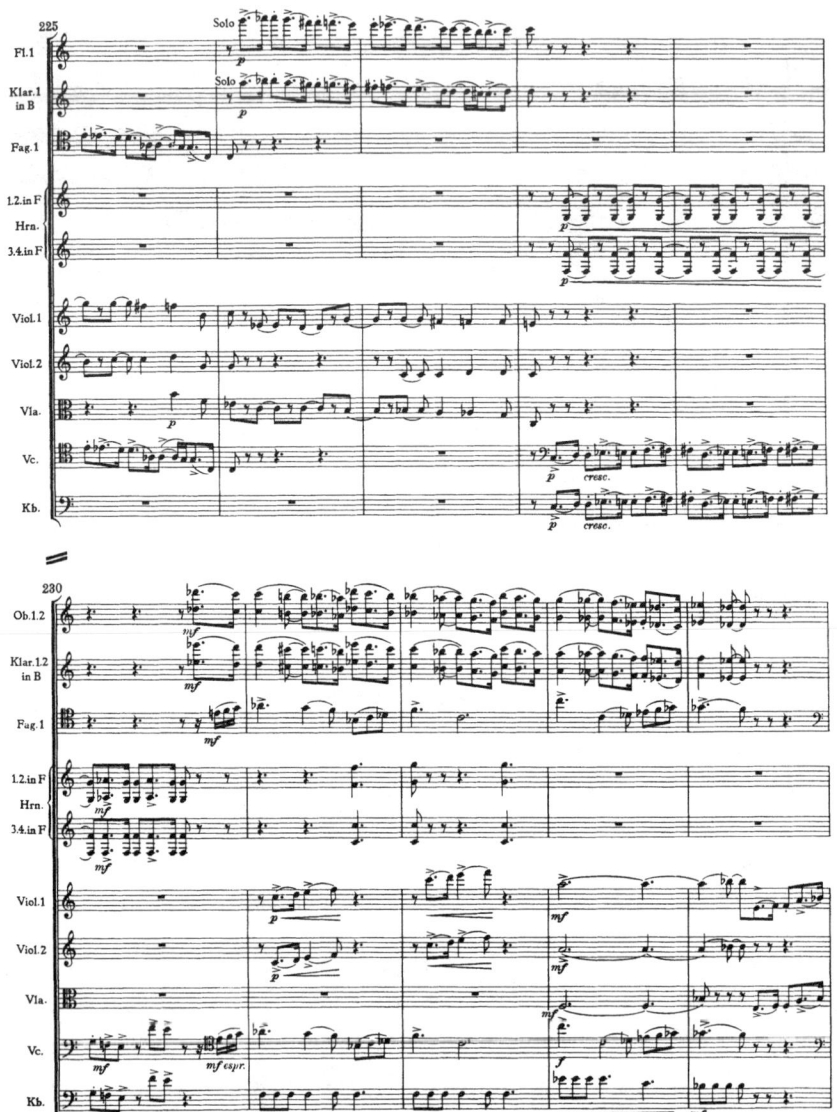

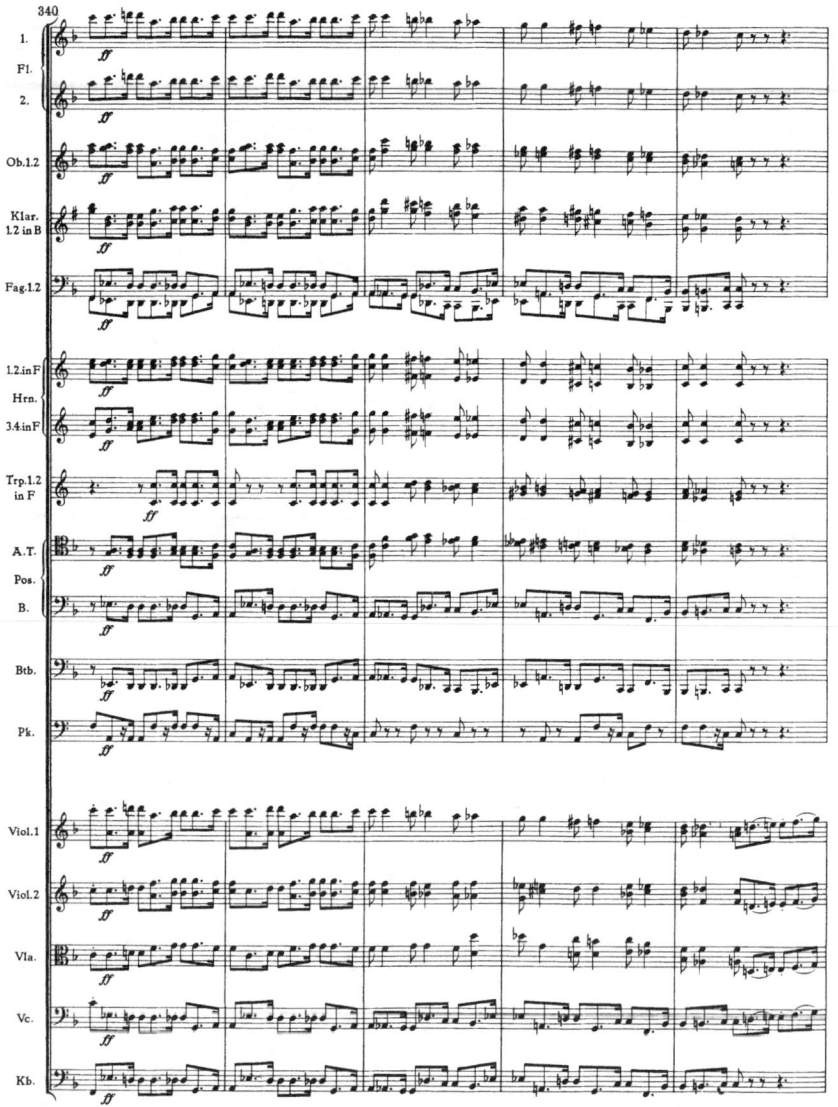

59

Johannes Brahms
(1833–97)

FULL CD V: TRACK 17
CONCISE CD II: TRACK 48

Piano Quartet in G Minor, Op. 25, Fourth movement (1861)

Measure Nos.	Formal Designation	Subsections	Keys
1–78	**Rondo theme (ABA)**		g
1–30	A	aabaa'	
31–60	B		
61–78	A	baa'	
80–115	**Episode 1 (CDC)**		
80–91	C		B♭
92–103	D		c, d
104–115	C		B♭
116–154	**Rondo theme (A)**	aabaa' and codetta	g
155–205	**Episode 2 (EF)**		
155–172	E	cdc'	G, g
173–205	F	ee'fe"	e
206–237	**Episode 1 (C)**		G
238–255	**Episode 2 (E)**	cdc'	G
256–293	**Rondo theme (BA)**		g
256–285	B		
286–292	A	b	
293	**Cadenza (piano)**		
294–362	**Episodes 2 and 1**		
294–302	Variation on F (strings)		g
303–312	Variation on C (piano)		e
313–334	Variation on E (strings)		F♯
335–362	C and E (piano and strings)		Dominant pedal
363–405	**Rondo theme (A)**	**aab and coda**	**g**

Brahms completed the Piano Quartet in G minor, Op. 25, his first work for the combination of piano, violin, viola, and cello, in Hamburg in 1861. The work was well received on Brahms's first trip to Vienna in 1862; in 1937 Arnold Schoenberg paid tribute to Brahms by arranging it for full orchestra.

The finale of the Quartet, subtitled Rondo alla Zingarese (Rondo in the Gypsy Style) is the first in Brahms's oeuvre relying on what in the eighteenth and nineteenth centuries was considered the Hungarian style. Until Béla Bartók's systematic ethnographic research, Hungarian music had generally been identified with popular music played by urban bands. This was the music that Liszt popularized in his Hungarian Rhapsodies. The Hungarian or "gypsy" style was used to evoke an exotic color. Hungarian music was especially fashionable in the Hamburg of Brahms's youth after Hungarian refugees appeared in the city following the failed Hungarian revolution of 1848. Brahms's experience with the style was deepened by his collaboration with Hungarian violinist Ede Reményi (1828–1898), with whom he toured Germany in 1852 improvising accompaniments to virtuoso showpieces in the Hungarian style. The chart summarizes the form of Brahms's rondo.

The rondo theme and the two episodes each consist of two thematic sections. The first episode is in the relative major (B♭); the second episode begins in the parallel major (G). Instead of a return to the rondo theme, after the second episode the C section of the first episode returns transposed to the tonic major as if it were a sonata recapitulation. Similarly, the E section of the second episode also returns in G. After the incomplete return of the rondo theme, things take an unexpected turn. Perhaps in mock tribute to the Hungarian Liszt, the piano surprises us with a short virtuoso cadenza, followed by variations on various sections of the two episodes in the strings and piano in alternation. The separation of the piano and strings ends with the recombination of forces and their previous thematic materials: above a dominant pedal Brahms combines materials from the two episodes. This twenty-eight-measure section serves as a gradual buildup to a climactic dominant chord that leads to the final, long-delayed, exuberant return of the A section of the rondo theme.

There are many musical features that contribute to the wild, fiery character of the movement, most of them common in the vocabulary of the Hungarian style. The minor mode with occasional augmented seconds (see C♯–B♭ in m. 18) that mark the music as exotic, the "crude" tonic pedal points, and pairs of accented quarter notes (evocative of stomping in Hungarian folk dances) are all common elements of the style. Another feature of the Hungarian style is Brahms's use of *short*-long dotted figures with the accent on the short first value, which corresponds to the speech pattern of the Hungarian language in which the first syllable is always

thematic sections

stressed. This *short*-long rhythm gives a dignified character to theme E in the second episode (see mm. 155–160).

Although folkish and rough, the movement also contains compositional intricacies. In most cases thematically contrasting sections are subtly linked by motives. The B section of the rondo theme, for instance, grows out of the stomping last two notes of the A section. The F♯–G pair is repeated in quarter notes at the beginning of the new section, and the same two notes initiate the sixteenth-note runs in the following measure. The F♯–G pair then moves sequentially to A–B♭, notes that will also provide the starting point of the subsequent runs. One can hear the F♯–G minor second lurking behind the minor seconds in the violin's accompaniment in the first episode (mm. 92ff) and in the sixteenth-note figurations initiated by minor seconds in the piano. The minor second also serves as the basis for the sequential development of the piano melody in the F section of the second episode (C–B–A♯–B, D–C♯–B♯–C♯, F–D♯–C♯♯–D♯, mm. 190–196).

Even in his popular Hungarian style, Brahms pays a great deal of attention to intricate motivic relationships. The sixteenth-note figurations in the B section of the rondo theme (mm. 31ff) provide the link to the sixteenth-note figures in the first episode (mm. 80ff). The triplets appearing in the E section of the second episode (mm. 161–166) prepare the triplets of the F section of the same episode (mm. 173ff). The relationship between the rondo theme and the second episode is less apparent. The embellished descending tetrachord in mm. 13–14 finds its major equivalent in the piano's descending tetrachord in mm. 156–157. The motivic intricacy of the movement betrays Brahms's deep roots in German tradition.

Rondo alla Zingarese

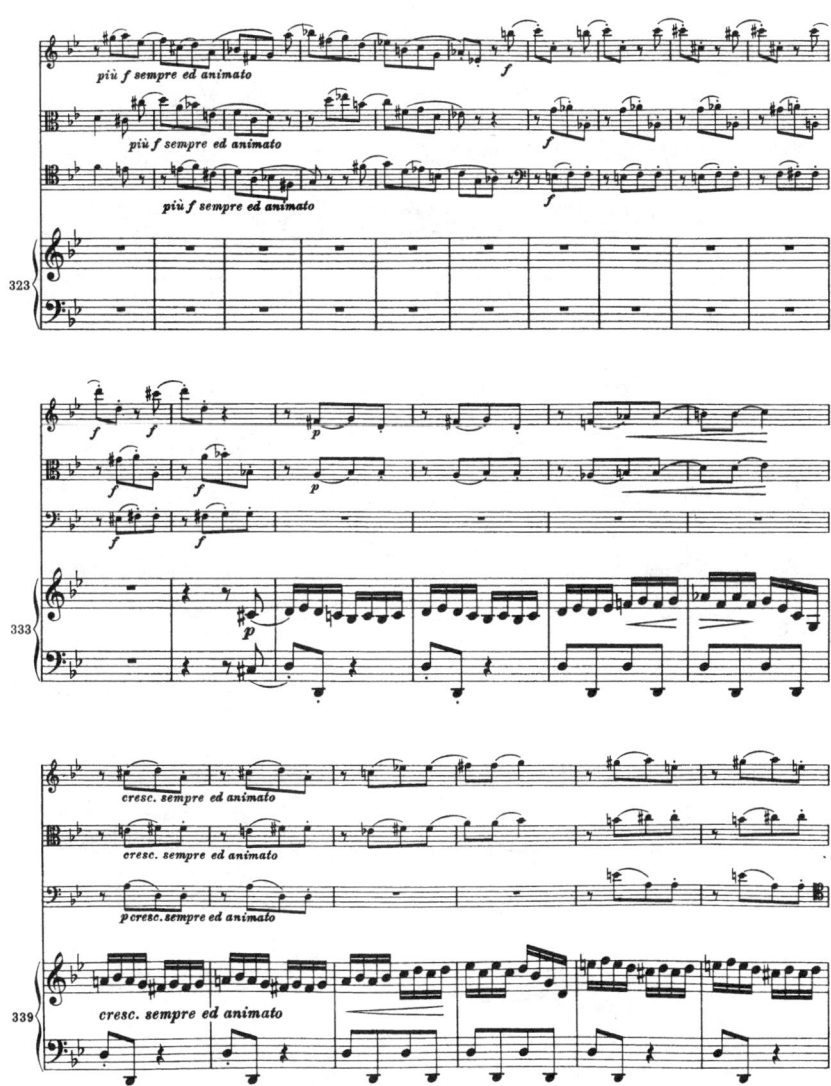

60

Johannes Brahms
(1833–97)

FULL CD V: TRACK 18
CONCISE CD III: TRACK 1

Symphony No. 1 in C Minor, Op. 68,
Fourth movement (1862–76)

After fourteen years of struggle, Brahms completed his Symphony No. 1 in C minor in 1876. The choice of C minor suggests that he was consciously modeling it on Beethoven's Fifth Symphony. Many believe that the difficulties Brahms faced in finishing his symphony came from the challenge posed by Beethoven, especially by Beethoven's decision to bring the human voice into a purely instrumental genre in the finale of his Ninth Symphony—a gesture that Wagner believed marked the end of the German symphonic tradition. In the shadow of Beethoven's Fifth and Ninth, Brahms rewrote Beethoven's quasi-narrative trajectory of a journey from darkness to light—struggle to victory.

Like the finale of Beethoven's Ninth, Brahms's final movement is difficult to define in conventional formal terms. It displays elements of sonata, rondo, and variations. The main structural points of a sonata exposition are easy enough to detect. Confusion begins at m. 186. Is the return of the main theme in the tonic key the beginning of the development or the recapitulation? If we consider it the development—an assumption supported by the ensuing developmental procedures at m. 220—we run into trouble with the recapitulation.

The structural ambiguities derive from the programmatic interaction of the highly diverse thematic materials of the movement. The slow introduction presents two important themes. The first is the "Alphorn theme" (mm. 30ff), which Brahms first notated on a postcard he sent from Switzerland to Clara Schumann and said he conceived as an imitation folk song. Brahms juxtaposes this "folk song" with a "chorale," here sounding on a choir of low brass and bassoons (mm. 47–51). The pastoral tone of the "Alphorn theme" and the religious connotation of the chorale-like theme evoke nature and community, two important tenets of nineteenth-century German national sentiment.

These two emblematic themes lead away from the agitated, dark C-minor section of the introduction and serve to introduce the symphony's main theme (mm. 62–78), which sounds like a wordless hymn. Its resemblance to the "Ode to Joy" theme from Beethoven's Ninth is so

Measure Nos.	Formal Designation	Sections	Keys	Comments
1–60	Slow introduction		c	Fragment of primary theme, mm. 2–3, 13–14
30–46		Alphorn theme	C	
47–51		"Chorale"		
52–61		Alphorn theme		
62–185	Exposition			
62–93		1st theme group		Cf. theme of finale of Beethoven's 9th
94–117		Bridge		Based on 1st theme
118–147		2nd theme group	G	Tiny variations over a four-note descending tetrachord ground bass
148–185		Closing group		
186–284	"Development"			Or recapitulation?
186–219		1st theme group	C, E♭, B	
220–284		Bridge		
285–366	"Recapitulation"			Real recapitulation?
285–301		Alphorn theme	C	
302–331		2nd theme group	C	
332–366		Closing group	E♭	
367–457	Coda			With developmental features
367–406			E♭, e, C	Fragments of 1st theme lead to expectation of triumphant return of 1st theme
407–416		"Chorale" theme		*Fortissimo*, triumphant
417–457		Coda continues		

apparent that it is easy to hear it not only as an homage to Beethoven but also as a challenge. The head motive of the theme is also related to a C-minor ground bass from J. S. Bach's Cantata (BWV 106) "Gottes Zeit is die allerbeste Zeit" (God's own time is the very best of times).

Sonata
Rondo
Variations

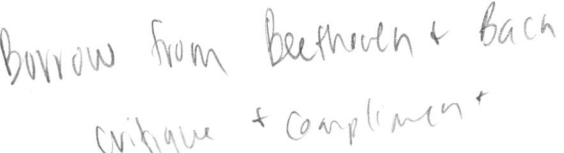

Borrow from Beethoven + Bach
Critique + compliment

Example 60–1 J. S. Bach, Cantata No. 106, ground bass

Example 60–2 J. S. Brahms, Symphony No. 1, finale, beginning of main theme

The references are likely juxtaposed here in order to forge a link between Brahms and the Germanic icons Beethoven and Bach.

The most significant aspect of Brahms's rewriting of the "Ode to Joy" theme is that it has no words, demonstrating that text was not needed to supplement the communicative power of instrumental music. The theme is thus both a tribute to Beethoven and a correction that can be seen as reasserting the purely instrumental symphony's status in the German musical canon.

Brahms's critique of Beethoven is also manifest in the fate of this hymn-like main theme. Its first appearance arouses expectation for its treatment in sonata form: that it will undergo development and return triumphantly restated in the tonic. The exposition fulfills the expectations of sonata form. After its first appearance, the full orchestra restates the main theme, first at m. 78, then *fortissimo* to initiate the bridge at m. 94. It is contrasted with a secondary theme, which arrives at m. 118, and turns out to be another Brahmsian reference to a historical musical procedure—a set of tiny variations over a four-note descending tetrachord ground bass. But the main theme fails to fulfill its most important function. The recapitulation contains no double return. Instead of the main theme, the "Alphorn theme" returns triumphantly in the tonic key at m. 285. We know that this is in fact the "official" tonal return because of the way in which the "second theme" follows the "Alphorn theme" in the tonic (mm. 302ff).

The main theme does return in the Beethovenesque coda with developmental features in a passage that alludes to the ascending chromatic sequence that begins the development section in the first movement of Beethoven's Third Symphony (see mm. 375–380, where the theme appears first in the bass). But only the Bach-derived head motive of the theme makes an appearance. The part of Brahms's theme that so strikingly recalled Beethoven's choral "Ode to Joy" is not restated. Brahms rejects a triumphant rendition of Beethoven's "vocal collectivity."

Yet Brahms does not reject every vocal collectivity. The fanfare-like *Più allegro* that begins at m. 391 makes a headlong dash to a rhetorical climax. When the climax comes, however, the main theme is once again preempted, this time by the chorale-like music unheard since the slow Introduction (mm. 407–416). With this exultant presentation of the "chorale" Brahms again reinforces his connection to a German musical tradition that goes back all the way to Bach—perhaps even to Luther.

By rejecting Beethoven's solution of a choral finale, Brahms pointed to a future for German music rooted in its past. It was not a return to the past, which is always impossible, but a

synthesis. Besides the evocation of "vocal collectivities," the new elements included old contrapuntal practices as well as overarching thematic reminiscences and mutations worthy of Wagner. These practices were, however, as thoroughly transformed by their inclusion in the genre of the symphony as the symphony, by including them, had been transformed.

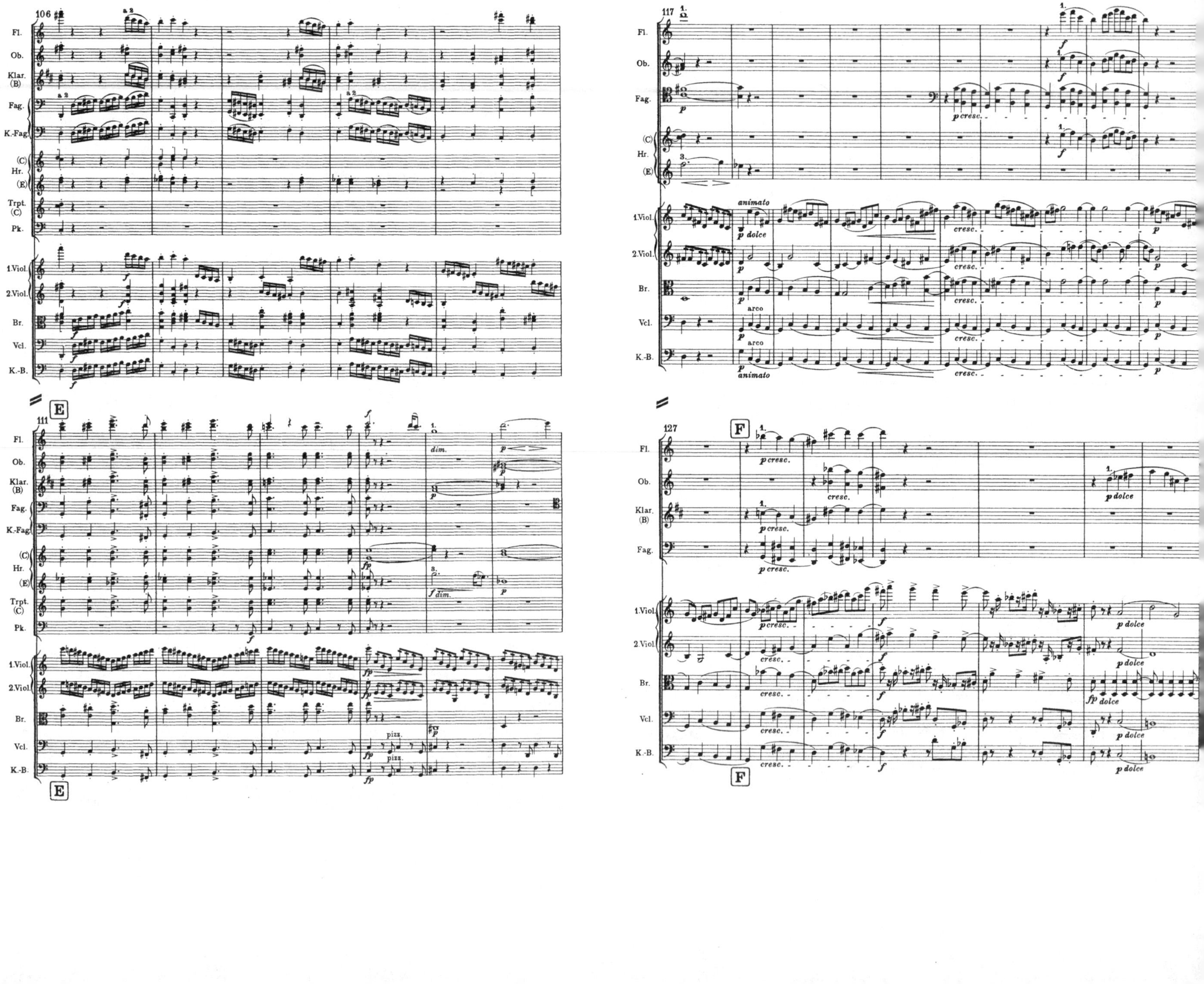
106
Fl.
Ob.
Klar. (B)
Fag.
K.-Fag.
(C) Hr. (E)
Trpt. (C)
Pk.
1.Viol.
2.Viol.
Br.
Vcl.
K.-B.
E
111
dim.
pizz.
117
animato
p dolce
arco
p cresc.
cresc.
F
127
p cresc.
p dolce
fp dolce

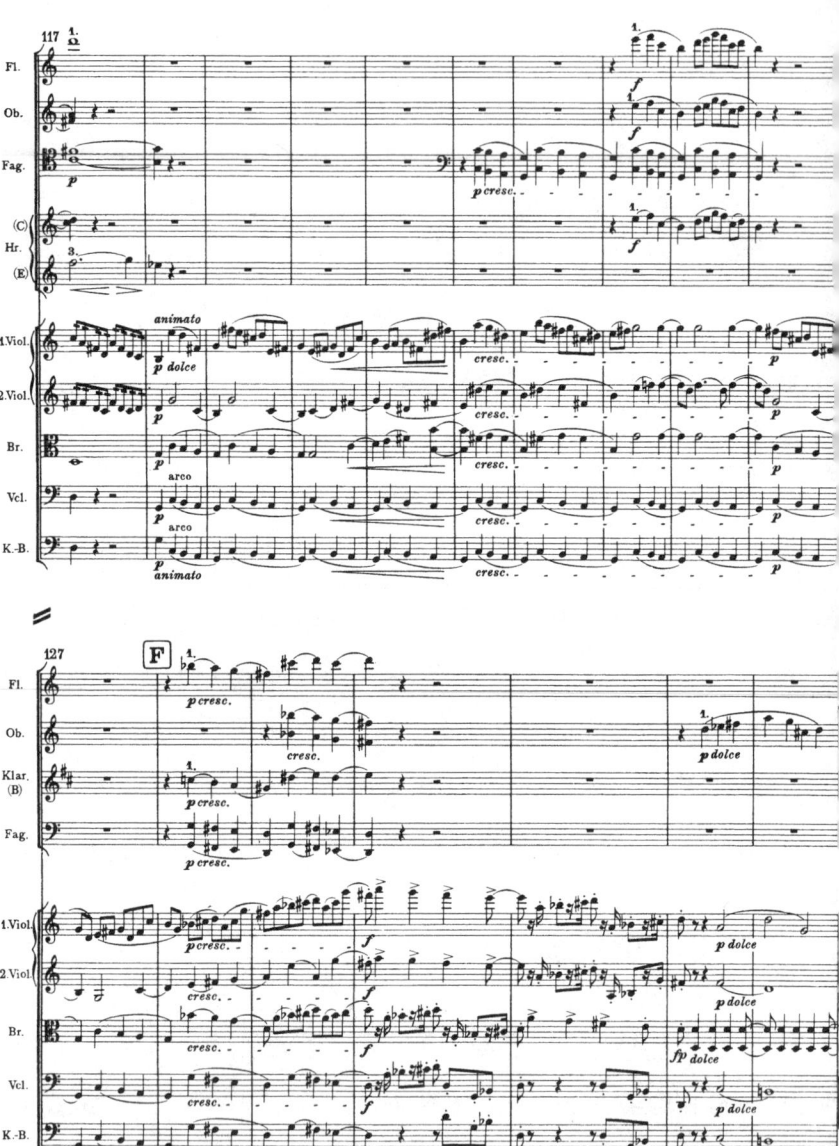

61

Antonín Dvořák
(1841–1904)

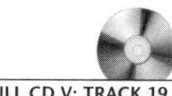

Piano Quintet in A Major, Op. 81, Second movement
("Dumka") (1887)

Dvořák's Piano Quintet in A major, Op. 81 was premiered in Prague on 6 January 1888. Dvořák modeled his work on the piano quintet by Robert Schumann, whose music was popular in Prague at the time.

Dvořák subtitled the second movement "Dumka," a designation that appears eleven times in his oeuvre. *Dumka* originally meant a slow western Ukrainian lyrical or lyric-epical song with melancholy character and usually in minor mode. More important for Dvořák, who never quoted an actual folk *dumka* in his music, the term also designates poetry and music composed in a "*dumka* mood," that is, with a reflective character. Dvořák seems to have added the "Dumka" title to the slow movement of his Piano Quintet as an afterthought; in the sketches no title appears, and the tempo of the movement is marked, similarly to the slow movement of Schumann's Quintet, "Tempo di marcia."

Two things shared by Dvořák's movements labeled *dumka* are a highly sectional structure and slow beginnings, usually in duple meter and in minor mode. The F#-minor "Dumka" of the Piano Quintet is a rondo with an ABACAB′A structure. The chart gives an overview of the structure and the tonal plan of the movement.

The tonally least stable section is C, a quasi-development in a fast tempo (*Vivace*), which is based on the piano's initial "motto" (four measures consisting mainly of an embellished arpeggiation of the tonic chord). The funeral-march character (indicated by the minor mode and the original "tempo di marcia" marking) is most conspicuous in the slow A sections, which contain passages in which steady chords obstinately marking the beats accompany dotted figures in the melody. The B section contrasts in character not only because of its slightly faster tempo, major key, and pastoral mood (evoked by pedal tones, trills and diatonic melodies) but also because it discontinues the march feel of the A section: the chords fall on the offbeats, while the piano and the low strings juxtapose triple and quadruple subdivisions of the beat. Although the "d" part of the B section returns to the minor mode (G minor, then B♭ minor), its rhythmic gestures avoid funeral-march associations.

Measure Nos.	Formal Designation	Sections and Comments	Keys
1–35	A	Motto (mm. 1–4); a (mm. 5–12); motto (mm. 12–15); b (mm. 16–23); motto (mm. 31–35)	f# (b section modulatory)
36–42	Transition		
43–88	B	c (mm. 43–62); d (mm. 63–88)	D (c section); d section in g and b♭
89–122	A (Variation 1)		f#
124–126	Transition		
127–185	C	Based on motto, developmental	Tonally unstable
185–190	Transition (based on motto)		
191–219	A (Variation 2)		f#
220–264	B′		F# (c section); d section in b and d
265–307	A		f#
308–324	Coda	Over tonic pedal	f#

Structural and tonal coherence, provided by the symmetrical arrangement of the episode and the recapitulation-like return of the B section in the major tonic key (m. 220), is further strengthened by the central role of the "motto." We hear the "motto" in three different tempo and in three different rhythmic proportions: most often in $\frac{2}{4}$ with a characteristic dotted-eighth note figure; in shorter note values in $\frac{2}{8}$ (mm. 185–190); and finally in augmented form in the coda (mm. 316–321). The thirty-second-note triplet figure that opens the "motto" frequently appears in others contexts and relates the main themes of the A section to the "motto" theme (for example, mm. 19, 23–24). The absence of the thirty-second-note triplet figure in the coda gives the "motto" its most ascetic form: stripped to its essentials, it is finally reduced to a falling minor third in the depths of the piano.

Although the movement adheres to the basic binary principle of moving away from and then back to the tonic, it conspicuously lacks a move to the relative major (A major). Neither do we encounter the dominant C# major or minor as a key area. Dvořák, like Schubert, favor the submediant (D major) over the dominant, and he uses it as the key of the first B section. The subdominant, B minor, also provides a frequent temporary tonal goal in the movement (mm. 87, 128, 143, 160). The central role of B minor can be explained not only by its subdominant function in the overall tonal plan of the movement but also as the tonic resolution of the

relative major

♯-major dominant chord, which occurs as the major version of the F♯-minor tonic chord at structurally significant places. For example, the F♯-major chord in m. 23, which resolves to B$^4_3$ that turns immediately into a B-minor seventh chord, serves as the first expressive climax in the movement. Subdominant relationships also play an important role in the B sections, in which the initial key is followed by its minor subdominant in the "d" part (D major by G minor in the first B section, and F♯ major by B minor in the second B section).

The "Slavic" sound of this movement owes a great deal to its modal ambiguity and avoidance of conventional tonal routes. Already the second measure of the "motto" is harmonized by a major IV chord; and the main theme has in its accompaniment major versions of IV, VII, and II chords (mm. 7 and 10), which obscure the tonal characteristics of F♯ minor. Sudden, effortless shifts between relative and parallel minor and major key areas, unexpected tonal progressions built on submediant relations, nondiatonic sequences of a whole step (mm. 16–19 and 20–23), and modal-sounding harmonic moves (especially the chorale-like transitions of mm. 36–38 and 123–125) make Dvořák's voice distinct from that of Brahms or Schumann, his two greatest predecessors in the genre of the piano quintet.

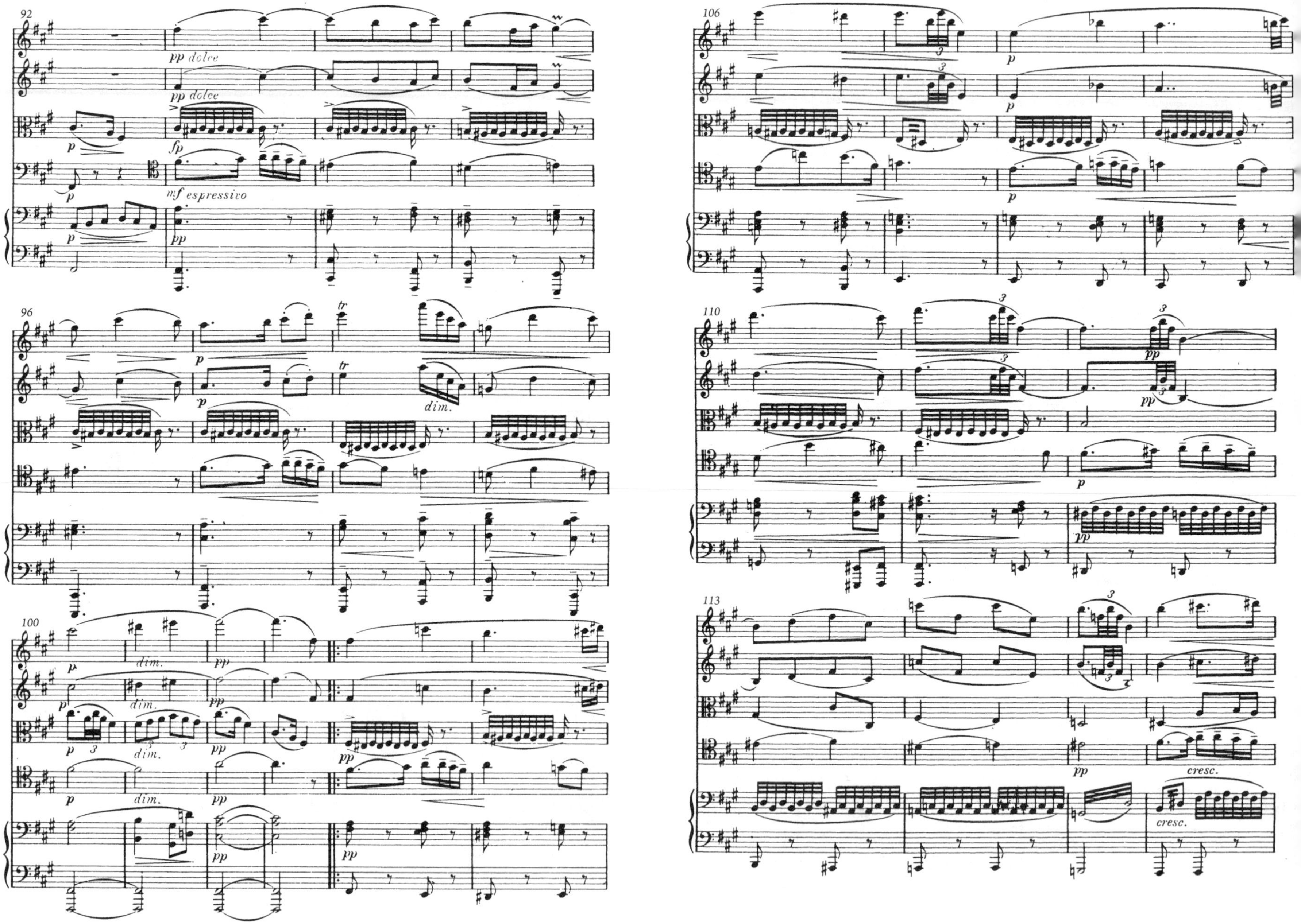
92
pp dolce
pp dolce
fp
mf espressivo
96
dim.
100
dim.
dim.
dim.
106
110
113
cresc.
cresc.

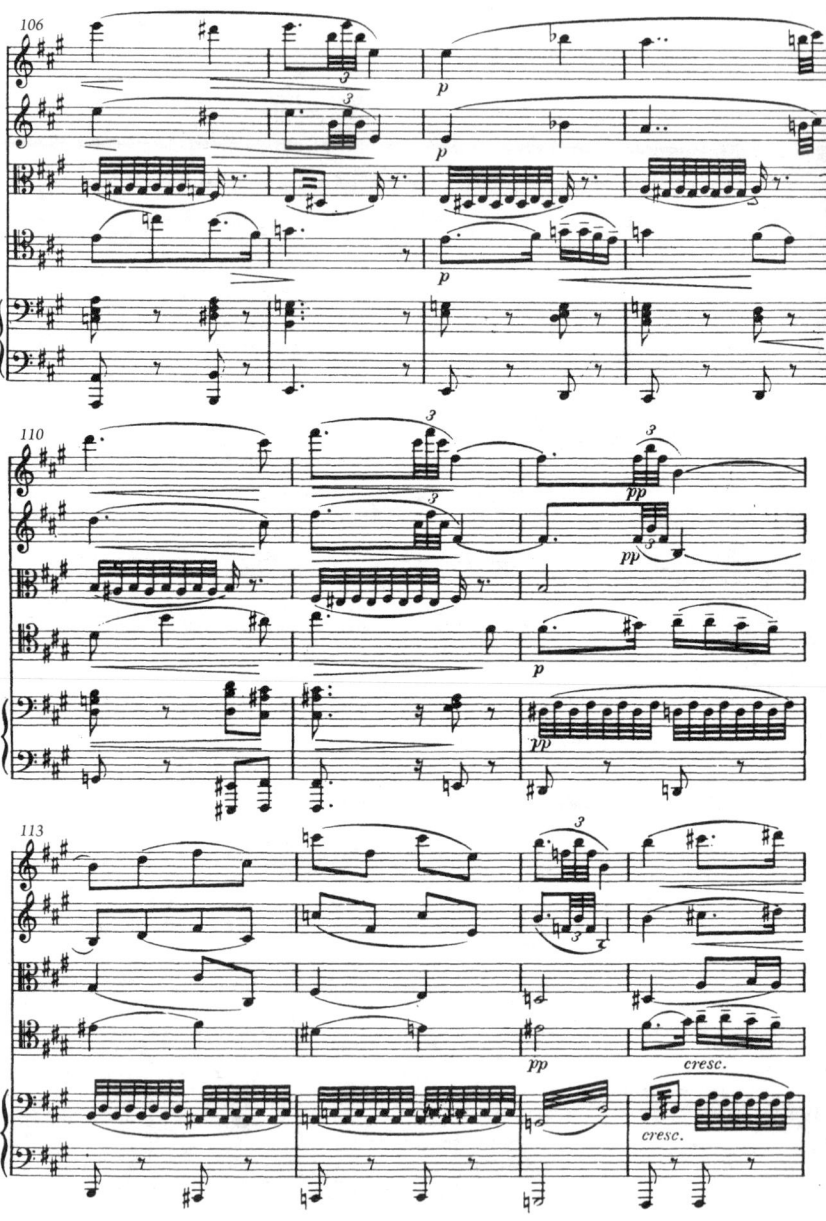

62

Antonín Dvořák (1841–1904)

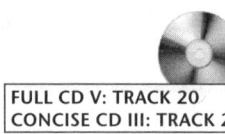

FULL CD V: TRACK 20
CONCISE CD III: TRACK 2

Symphony No. 9 in E Minor ("From the New World"), Second movement (1893)

Measure Nos.	Formal Designation	Episodes	Keys
1–45	**Section A**, *Largo*		D♭
1–6		"Chorale" motto	
7–21		English-horn theme (aba') (pentatonic "a" section)	
22–26		"Chorale" motto	
27–45		English-horn theme (b'a')	
46–100	**Section B**, *Un poco più mosso*		c♯/C♯
46–53		Theme with pentatonic inflections (c)	
54–63		Funeral-march theme (d)	
64–77		Theme with pentatonic inflections (c)	
78–86		Funeral-march theme (d)	
87–89		Theme with pentatonic inflections (c)	
90–95		"Bird" episode	C♯
96–100		Fragments from the first movement and from previous sections of the second movement	
101–127	**Section A'**, *Meno mosso*, Tempo I		D♭
101–119		English-horn theme (aba')	
120–127	**Coda**	"Chorale" motto	

Dvořák's Ninth Symphony, his last, was the first piece he composed during his three-year sojourn in the United States. Premiered at New York City's Carnegie Hall on 16 December 1893, the Symphony was a phenomenal success and has remained one of the most enduring pieces in the symphonic repertory. Its subtitle, "From the New World," which Dvořák scribbled on the score at the last minute, might have been a simple, postcard-like message, its meaning explained by Dvořák as "Impressions and greetings from the New World." It could have even been a joking reference to a speech given in Dvořák's honor by Thomas Wentworth Higginson (1823–1911), entitled "Two New Worlds: The New World of Columbus and the New World of Music." The audience and the critics, however, took the title as an indication that Dvořák intended to present them with a genuine "American" symphony.

Shortly after the Symphony's premiere, Dvořák mentioned that its two middle movements were inspired by Henry Wadsworth Longfellow's *The Song of Hiawatha* (1855), an epic poem based on legends of the Ojibway Indians. While Dvořák specified the poetic content of the third movement as depicting an Indian dance at the feast of Hiawatha, he remained unspecific about the connection between the poem and the slow movement. Guided in part by the writings of Dvořák's friend the American music critic Henry Krehbiel, musicologist Michael Beckerman has suggested that the first section of the slow movement reflects the landscape depicted during Hiawatha's homeward journey in the tenth chapter of the epic ("Pleasant was the journey homeward, / Through interminable forests, / Over meadow, over mountain.") and that the C♯-major episode (mm. 90ff), with its bird calls, represents the last thirty lines of the chapter ("All the birds sang loud and sweetly / Songs of happiness and heart's-ease"). According to Beckerman the dark C♯-minor episode (mm. 54ff) may be related to the part of the poem describing the forest funeral of Hiawatha's bride, Minnehaha, at the end of Chapter 20.

Even without specific references, the highly episodic structure of the movement inspires programmatic explanation. The following chart shows the episodes arranged within the overarching ABA' structure.

The prefatory, chorale-like chords beginning on E (the key of the symphony as a whole) and ending on D♭ (the key of this movement) may be interpreted as taking us from the real world to an alternate, mythical world. (In a sketchbook Dvořák labeled the second movement "Legend.") The main theme played by the English horn, an instrument with both pastoral and exotic connotations, could hardly be a more "finished" melody: twelve measures arranged by fours, in a symmetrical, aba' format (mm. 7–18). At the end of the section, muted horns echo the English horn's melody, adding a sense of distance to the scene (mm. 42–45).

The "middle section," in the parallel minor, at a slightly faster tempo, and in contrasting triplet rhythms, begins in m. 46. Like the first section, it features two alternating tunes. The pastoral mood created by the unison flute and oboe and occasional pentatonic turns of the melody suggest another nature image. Yet the accompanying tremolo in the strings and the dynamic swelling of the melody suggest the presence of human passion behind the depiction of nature. As a response to this short-lived passion, a new episode (mm. 54–63) brings contrast in the form of a stylized funeral march. (The pizzicato walking bass against the legato melody recalls the funeral march of the *Eroica* Symphony [mm. 117ff], one of several Beethoven references in the movement.)

At m. 90 the mood changes dramatically. The bird-like figuration in this section presents the most explicit nature imagery of the movement and recalls Beethoven's *Pastoral* Symphony. This nature episode leads to an eruptive climax at m. 96, which remains frozen on the fraught chord of the flat submediant (♭VI) for five measures. The passage is shot through with reminiscences: The trombones refer to the main theme of the first movement; the horns, violins, and woodwinds divide up motives from the first movement's second theme; and the trumpets play reverberations of the opening phrase from the slow movement's English-horn theme (employing rustic "horn fifths"). The whole passage occurs over a diminuendo, an apt way to represent the fading of a memory. Sharing of material between movements makes the symphony "cyclic" in form, typical of Dvořák's large-scale pieces. Following this climactic passage of recollection Dvořák returns to the main English-horn theme (m. 101). A reduced string section with mutes plays the "b" section of the theme (*pianissimo* and *sempre più diminuendo* [increasingly softer]) interrupted by rests, much like Beethoven's breaking up of the theme at the end of the funeral march of the *Eroica*. The coda ends the work symmetrically with material based on the introductory "chorale" (mm. 120–127).

Aside from "Swing Low, Sweet Chariot," which contemporary listeners recognized as related to the second theme of the first movement, no traditional melody has been identified in the New World Symphony. The English-horn theme of the second movement did, however, come to be regarded as a spiritual after Dvořák's student William Arms Fischer made a vocal arrangement of it in 1922 with the words "Goin' home, goin' home, I'm a-goin' home." Whatever Dvořák meant by attaching the subtitle "From the New World" to the work, it has become as much a part of musical Americana as other musical works in which American composers themselves attempted to give expression to a sense of national belonging.

110
Oboi
in B.
Solo.
molto cresc.
Tutti.
dimin.
118
ritard.
in tempo
Molto Adagio.
in E. a 2.
a 2.
dim.

63

Camille Saint-Saëns
(1835–1921)

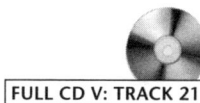

Samson et Dalila (Samson and Delilah), Bacchanale (1877)

Samson and Delilah premiered in 1877 in Weimar, where Liszt, a generous supporter of Saint-Saëns, was court composer. The opera enacts the biblical story of Samson (Judges: 13–16), to whom God gave enormous strength in order to deliver the Israelites from their Philistine oppressors. Samson was a Nazirite, a Jew consecrated to God by virtue of a vow prohibiting, among other things, cutting of his hair. Samson falls in love with a Philistine woman, Delilah, who, bribed by her countrymen, entices him to reveal the secret of his strength. She then has his hair cut and delivers him in his weakened state to the Philistines, who blind and imprison him. During the celebrations in the Temple of Dagon the Philistines bring out Samson, who, having regained his strength in captivity, pulls down the pillars of the temple, crushing thousands of Philistines.

In *Samson and Delilah* the seductive, orientalized enemy (the Philistines) is sharply contrasted with the righteous Hebrews, whom Saint-Saëns depicts as proto-Christians and thus representing Western values. Saint-Saëns's Hebrews sing melodies reminiscent of Gregorian chant, while the Philistines, their idol-worshipping opponents, revel in sensuous music, conventionally associated with Orientals in the West. The contrast in musical style signals both cultural and moral opposition between the two peoples. Delilah is the archetypal representative of the seductive (imagined) East. Irresistible and dangerous, her religion does not seem to distinguish between moral right and wrong; her love is paramount to hate; and her external beauty conceals her immoral soul.

However immoral its connotations, the music associated with Delilah and the Philistines proved irresistible. The most popular number of the opera, frequently played as an orchestral showpiece, is the Bacchanale from Act 3. The ballet takes place in the Temple of Dagon, where the Philistine chieftains have just enjoyed a night of love-filled revelry. Daybreak cannot bring them to stop the festivities, and thus they prolong their erotic dances. Originally a wild festival held in honor of Bacchus, the Roman god of wine and intoxication, "bacchanalia" generally refers to any drunken revelry. Saint-Saëns's Bacchanale may have been partially inspired by the Bacchanale in Wagner's *Tannhäuser*, a work he greatly admired. Like Wagner, Saint-Saëns focuses on the erotic aspect of the festivities in his Bacchanale, but instead of Wagner's chromatic music, which evokes painfully prolonged unfulfilled desire, Saint-Saëns writes genuine dance music with symmetrical phrases and rhythmic drive. The erotic connotations of Saint-Saëns's Bacchanale reside in its rhythms, exotic modes, and colorful instrumentation.

According to the key signature, the whole dance, except the contrasting middle section, is in D minor. But already the oboe's opening "snake charming" cadenza played above an A–E double pedal is more Phrygian than minor. It is an altered Phrygian on A created by raising the third and seventh degrees of the scale to create two augmented seconds (between scale degrees $\hat{2}$ and $\hat{3}$ and $\hat{6}$ and $\hat{7}$), an interval stereotypically used as a sign of Oriental music. Liszt and others often used a scale with two augmented seconds in Hungarian-style music. In Eastern European Jewish folk music the Phrygian scale with an augmented second between scale degrees $\hat{2}$ and $\hat{3}$ is called *Freygish*, in Biblical cantillation "ahavah-rabbah" mode, in Arabic music Hijaz mode. Whatever their origin, in Saint-Saëns's Bacchanale the augmented seconds unmistakably signal the Oriental character of the music. Using multiple leading tones allowed Saint-Saëns to move easily between keys: G♯ can shift the music to A minor (or E Phrygian), C♯ to D minor (or A Phrygian). The Neapolitan of D, E♭ can help move to C minor (or C major), the occasional augmented second (E♭–F♯) opens the way to G minor (or D Phrygian).

The metrically most exciting passage of the dance combines a symmetrically phrased melody (2 + 2 + 2 + 2) with an asymmetrical ostinato bass divided as 3 + 3 + 2 eighth notes (the ostinato begins at m. 107, the melody at m. 112). The same asymmetrical ostinato accompanies the C-major episode (at mm. 225–244) as a rhythmic pedal in the upper parts in diminished form. The languishing syncopated melody in the middle voice, often tied over bar lines, contrasts with the asymmetrical metric drive of the ostinato.

Formally the dance is a fairly straightforward ABA' (the order and tonal orientation of the subsections of A is somewhat rearranged in A'). The C-major melody of the B section provides respite from the surrounding orgy of exoticism. In the last two subsections the tempo gradually increases, ending the dance in a wild frenzy. The unbridled physicality of the music, expressed in the wild rhythms, incessant ostinati, and the sensuously coiling melodies replete with enticing augmented seconds, offers a voyeuristic journey through the consecrated pages of the Bible.

Note on the Score

Our example, excerpted from the opera score, ends immediately before the final note (D), which belongs to the next scene.

Measure Nos.	Main Sections	Subsections/Comments	Key/Mode
1–2	Introduction	Oboe cadenza	Altered Phrygian on A
3–224	A		
3–38		a (main theme)	d
38–56		b (crescendo theme)	d (over tonic pedal)
57–80		c (bass theme)	d and c
80–91		Transition	
91–107		d (ostinato theme)	d and a
107–149		e (melancholy theme w/ostinato)	Altered Phrygian on A
149–157		a, fragmentary	d and E♭
158–165		f (related to melody of introduction)	Altered Phrygian on G and A
165–173		a, fragmentary	a and B♭
174–180		f	Altered Phrygian on D and a
181–193		g (theme with dotted rhythm, related to introduction)	Altered Phrygian on D
194–224		e (dotted rhythms related to introduction, mm. 201–208)	Altered Phrygian on G
225–260	B		
225–245		h (lyrical syncopated theme with high-G ostinato)	C
245–260		f	Altered Phrygian on C and B♭
261–383	A′	Now almost entirely in tonic (d)	
261–277		b	In d over dominant pedal
278–293		c	d, c
293–309		a	d
309–319		c	d
320–328		Transition	d
328–364		e	Altered Phrygian on d
365–383		f	Altered Phrygian on d

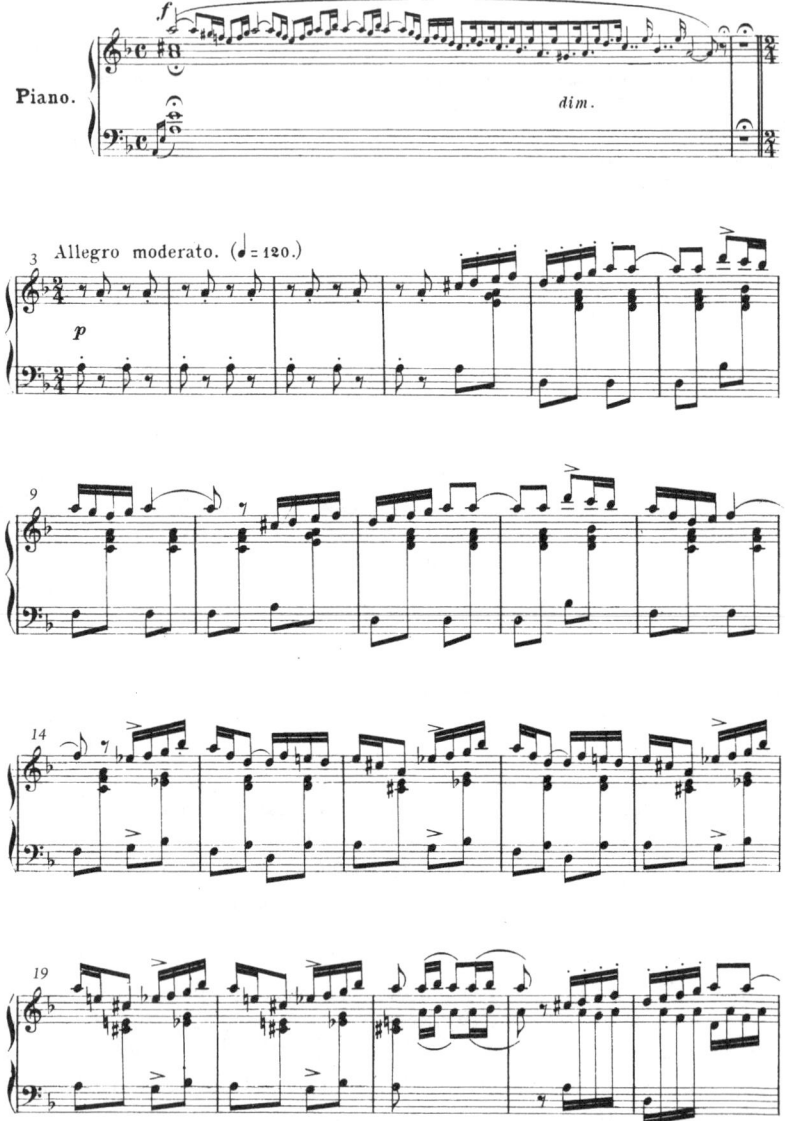

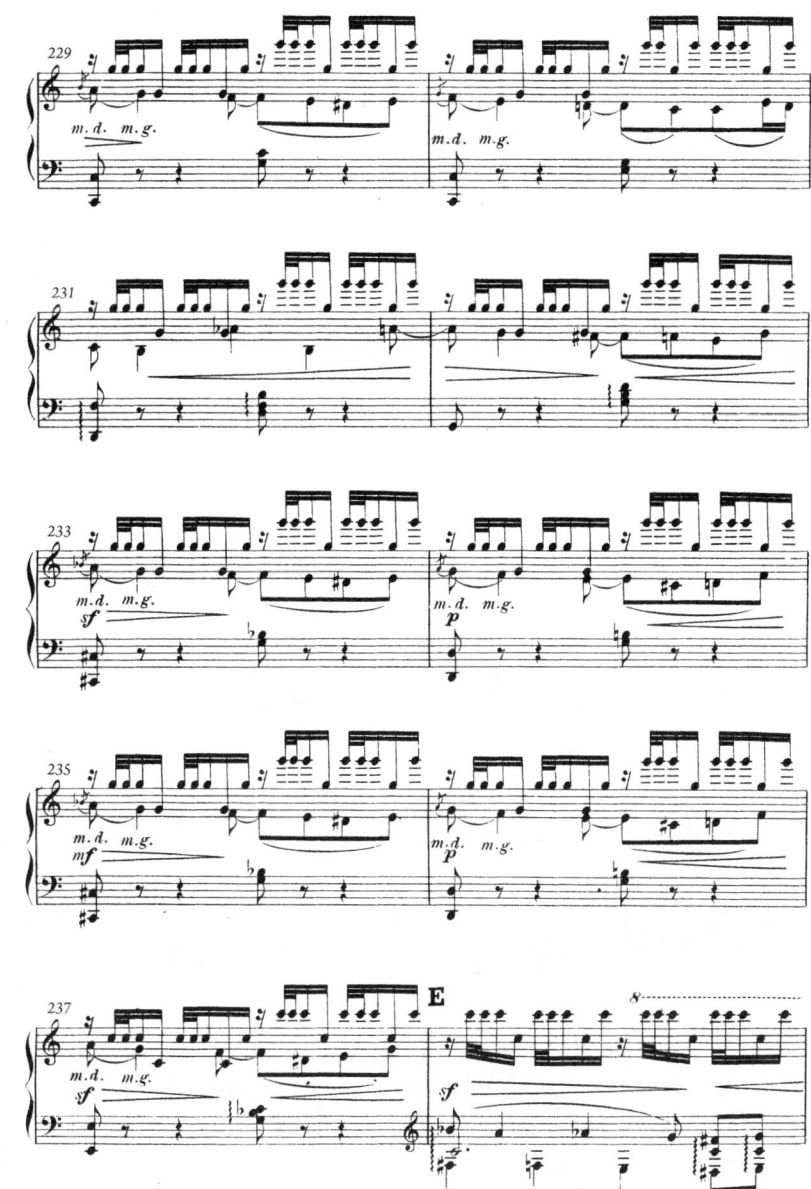

64

George Bizet
(1838–75)

FULL CD V: TRACK 22
CONCISE CD III: TRACK 3

Carmen, "L'amour est un oiseau rebelle"
("Love is a rebellious bird")/"Habanera" (1873–75)

Bizet and his librettists Henri Meilhac (1831–97) and Ludovic Halévy (1834–1908) wrote *Carmen* on commission for Paris's Opéra Comique. The plot, based on a novella of the same title by Prosper Mérimée (1803–70), involves the seductive Spanish gypsy Carmen, who is arrested for getting into a fight with a fellow worker in a cigarette factory in Seville. To avoid imprisonment she seduces her captor, Don José, a soldier who allows her to escape while escorting her to prison. Having gone to prison himself for letting Carmen escape, Don José deserts the army shortly after his release to join Carmen in the vagabond life of smugglers. Carmen, however, soon turns her affection to a famous bullfighter. Don José, who has given up everything for Carmen's love, cannot bear to lose her. Unable to win her back, he murders Carmen outside the bullfighting arena in Seville while the crowd within applauds the victory of Carmen's latest lover, the matador.

The premiere, on 3 March 1875, did not go well in the Opéra Comique, a theater designed mainly for family entertainment. The representation of the openly sexual Carmen, who seduces and drops her lovers without regard for social convention, was at least as scandalous as the brutal murder scene at the end. Carmen is an unusual female opera character: she is both victim and aggressor (her last act is to throw a ring Don José has given her into his face). Her sexuality, worn openly, is a destructive force that ruins Don José and ultimately causes her own downfall.

Bizet suggests Carmen's loose morals through her voice type (mezzo-soprano instead of soprano) and her exotically colored music. Carmen's signature aria, the famous Habanera in act 1, is her declaration of sexual independence. Bizet based the aria on the *canción habanera* "El arreglito" by Spanish composer Sebastián Iradier (1809–65), which Bizet mistook for a folk song. The name "habanera" derives from Havana, the Cuban capital where the dance became popular in the early 1800s. Its origins can be traced to the English contradance (country dance) that became widely popular in Europe in the eighteenth century. Afro-Cuban musicians added the dotted rhythms and syncopations that distinguish the habanera from other forms of the contradance. The descending chromatic line of the habanera melody is particularly interesting

as an Orientalist marker, because it is neither realistic sexual portraiture nor specifically "Oriental" in style. Nevertheless, it was a widely accepted convention used by composers all over Europe to signal exotic and dangerously alluring women characters.

Bizet changed the accompaniment of Iradier's original by harmonizing it in D minor (Iradier began his song in F major) and by turning the dotted habanera rhythm in the bass into a hypnotic ostinato. Bizet's setting emphasizes mesmerizing inertia: the first three measures of the melody are accompanied with an unchanging tonic chord, moving to a subdominant only at the end of the line. In the whole song Bizet uses only three harmonies: the tonic D (minor or major), the dominant, and the subdominant—all over a tonic pedal on the first beat of every measure. The formal structure is also purposely simplistic: The entire song consists of two themes, a D-minor chromatic melody and a D-major diatonic melody, repeated with slight variations and alternating with the chorus in a four-part structure of ABAB. This simplicity helps focus our attention on the sensuous aspects of the music: the rhythm, the voice, and the twirling vocal cadences that seem to imitate the seductive swaying of the body. The flexible triplets of the melody rub against the stubborn dotted figures, creating a sweet tension that enhances the sensuous effect.

Despite Bizet's inclusion of Spanish genres like the habanera and the seguidilla (a Spanish song or dance type in triple meter), *Carmen* exemplifies not the real Spain but its stereotyped vision, replete with gypsies, smugglers, bullfighters, fortune telling, singing, and dancing. A durable desire for such an unobtainable, exotic "other" makes *Carmen* one of the most popular operas of all time.

Carmen	Carmen
L'amour est un oiseau rebelle	Love is a rebellious bird
Que nul ne peut apprivoiser,	That nobody can tame,
Et c'est bien en vain qu'on l'appelle,	And it is quite in vain to call it,
S'il lui convient de refuser.	If it suits it to refuse.
Rien n'y fait, menace ou prière,	Nothing helps, neither threat nor prayer.
L'un parle bien, l'autre se tait;	One speaks nicely, the other one keeps silent;
Et c'est l'autre que je préfère.	And it's the other one that I prefer.
Il n'a rien dit; mais il me plaît.	He said nothing; but I like him.
L'amour! L'amour! L'amour! L'amour!	Love! Love! Love! Love!

Chorus	Chorus
L'amour est un oiseau rebelle, etc.	Love is a rebellious bird, etc.

Carmen	Carmen
L'amour est enfant de Bohême,	Love is a Bohemian child,
Il n'a jamais, jamais connu de loi,	It has never ever known any law,

Si tu ne m'aimes pas, je t'aime,
Si je t'aime, prend garde à toi!

Chorus

Prends garde à toi!
L'amour est enfant de Bohême, etc.

Carmen

Si tu ne m'aime pas, je t'aime, etc.
L'oiseau que tu croyais surprendre
Battit de l'aile et s'envola;
L'amour est loin, tu peux l'attendre;
Tu ne l'attend plus, il est là!
Tout autour de toi vite, vite,
Il vient, s'en va, puis il revient;
Tu crois le tenir, il t'évite;
Tu crois l'éviter, il te tient!
L'amour! L'amour! L'amour! L'amour!

Chorus

Tout autour de toi vite, vite, etc.

Carmen

L'amour est enfant de Bohême, etc.

Chorus

Prends garde a toi!
L'amour est enfant de Bohême, etc.

Carmen

Si tu ne m'aime pas, je t'aime, etc.

If you don't love me, I love you,
If I love you, be on your guard!

Chorus

Be on your guard!
Love is a Bohemian child, etc.

Carmen

If you don't love me, I love you, etc.
The bird you thought you would surprise
Beat its wings and flew away;
Love is distant, you can wait for it [in vain];
When you don't expect it, here it is!
All around you, swift so swift,
It comes, it goes, and then returns;
When you think you hold it, it escapes you,
When you think it escapes you, you have it!
Love! Love! Love! Love!

Chorus

All around you, etc.

Carmen

Love is a Bohemian child, etc.

Chorus

Be on your guard!
Love is a Bohemian child, etc.

Carmen

If you don't love me, I love you, etc.

65

Alexander Borodin
(1833–87)

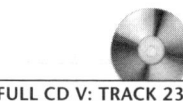

FULL CD V: TRACK 23

Prince Igor, "Polovtsian Dances," Act II, No. 17 (1869–87, 1890)

Measure Nos.	Tempo, Meter	Sections	Key
1–14	*Andantino,* $\frac{4}{4}$	Introduction	A
15–45	*Andantino,* $\frac{4}{4}$	(a) Gliding Dance of the Maidens	f♯/A
46–90	*Allegro vivo,* $\frac{4}{4}$	(b) Wild Dance of the Men	F
91–134	*Allegro,* $\frac{3}{4}$	(c) General Dance	D
135–179		(d) Dance of the Slave Girls	D
151–167		with Konchak's address	
171–232		General Dance	
233–266	*Presto,* $\frac{6}{8}$ . . .	(e) Dance of the Boys . . .	A Phrygian
267–320	and $\frac{2}{4}$, mm. 307ff	Dance of the Men . . .	D Phrygian and A Phrygian
321–344	$\frac{6}{8}$ . . .	Boys . . .	E Phrygian
345–368	and $\frac{2}{4}$	Men	E Phrygian
369–401	*Moderato alla breve,* $\frac{2}{2}$	(a) Gliding Dance of the Maidens . . .	A
401–432	$\frac{2}{2}$ combined with $\frac{12}{8}$	(a) combined with (e) Dance of the Boys	
433–468	*Presto,* $\frac{6}{8}$	(e) Boys . . .	A Phrygian
469–522	and $\frac{2}{4}$ (mm. 509ff)	Men . . .	D Phrygian
523–546	$\frac{6}{8}$ . . .	Boys . . .	D Phrygian
547–570	and $\frac{2}{4}$	Men . . .	D Phrygian (with B♭ pedal)
571–629	*Allegro con spirito,* $\frac{4}{4}$	General Dance consisting of (b) combined with the melody of the introduction (mm. 579ff)	A

Borodin wrote his opera *Prince Igor* to his own libretto based on a scenario by the influential nineteenth-century Russian music critic Vladimir Stasov. It tells the story of the 1185 campaign of Russian Prince Igor against the nomadic tribes of the Polovtsï (also called Cumans or Kipchaks). At the time of the opera's composition, the tale of hostilities between a Russian prince and the Polovtsï was virtually being played out in real life in the Russian wars of aggression in Central Asia.

A professional chemist of high repute, Borodin had little time to devote to the opera, and after eighteen years of sporadic work he left it unfinished. Completion fell to Nikolay Rimsky-Korsakov (1844–1908) and Alexander Glazunov (1865–1936). Their version was first performed in 1890 in St. Petersburg. The plot allows for one of the most essential features of nationalist opera: the contrasting representation of two groups, here the Russians and their enemies, the Polovtsï. The prologue and the first and last acts of the four-act work take place in Prince Igor's court, while the two middle acts are set in the camp of the Polovtsï, whose leader, Khan Konchak, has captured Igor and his son, Vladimir. In an effort to persuade them to join his campaign, Konchak entertains his noble prisoners with a sequence of dances, thus providing the dramatic motivation for a ballet. These dances constitute the opera's most popular number, performed frequently as an orchestral showpiece under the title "Polovtsian Dances" (the first of which was immortalized for Americans as "Stranger in Paradise," a pop standard from the 1953 Broadway musical *Kismet*).

There is nothing authentically "Polovtsian" or even Asian in the music. Yet for over a century this music has immediately signaled the East—both its imaginary feminized character, represented by the opening Gliding Dance of the Maidens, and its imaginary barbarity, represented by the Wild Dance of the Men. The series of dances begins and ends in A major, but it also moves through the third-related keys of F major and D major/minor and related modes. The following chart sums up the form.

The "Polovtsian Dances" display an entire arsenal of musical Orientalisms. Like Carmen's Habanera, they abound with pedal tones that insistently rub against the harmonies. While correct voice leading and intricacies of harmonic language are generally used to communicate Western sophistication, pedal tones often serve as signs of inertia, and are central to the representation of nature or "natural" people. In the "Polovtsian Dances" pedal tones are either tied, thus blurring metric sense, or articulated in repeated in rhythmic ostinatos. The unremitting syncopations of the second section (mm. 46ff) and the eighth-note drive of the fifth section (mm. 233ff) both gain energy from the metric rigidity of the underlying pedals. At the recapitulation of the Maidens' Dance (mm. 369ff) the melody is first presented with the syncopated ostinato of the Dance of the Men and then with the rapid eighth notes of the Dance of the

Boys, a brilliant stroke that imbues the melody with new energy. The music is not developmental but repetitive and accumulative, driving toward a climax both frightening and exhilarating in its unbound frenzy.

The melody also shows signs of unconstrained behavior. Chromaticism abounds, either sliding up and down for coloristic effect (e.g., mm. 159–166) or, even more typically, only descending (e.g., the melody at mm. 99–100 and the bass movement at mm. 607ff). In Russian music the chromatic pass from scale degree $\hat{6}$ to $\hat{5}$ or $\hat{5}$ to $\hat{6}$ became a frequent sign of what the Russians call *nega*, the bliss of gratified desire or the promise of it (as implied in the text of the first chorus: "the air is full of sweet bliss"). The musical depiction of *nega* originated in Glinka's opera *Ruslan and Lyudmila* (1842). In our excerpt it appears in the introduction (see the $\hat{6}$–$\flat\hat{6}$–$\hat{5}$ motion in the inner part in mm. 3, 8–9, and in the bass in mm. 22–24). In the introduction, other aspects of the Oriental soundscape as imagined by the West include pedal tones and throbbing ostinati, above which the melody undulates freely, and sensuous orchestration, replete with harps, English horn, and oboe. In 1909, when Borodin's "Polovtsian Dances" were brought to Paris by the Russian impresario Sergei Diaghilev (1872–1929), the audience understood the music as authentically Russian. From Paris it was Russia that represented "the East."

Slave men and women of the Polovtsi enter. Some of them carry tambourines and other musical instruments. Following them come the men of Konchak's retinue.

GLIDING DANCE OF THE MAIDENS

Chorus

Uletay na kril'yakh vetra
Ti v kray rodnoy, rodnaya pesnya nasha,
Tuda, gde mï tebya svobodno peli,
Gde bïlo tak privol'no nam s toboyu.
Tam, pod znoynïm nebom,
Negoy vozdukh polon,
Tam, pod govor morya,
Dremlyut gorï v oblakakh;
Tam tak yarko solntse svetit,
Rodnïye gorï svetom zalivaya,
V dolinakh pïshno rozï raztsvetayut
I solov'i poyut v lesakh zelenïkh;
I sladkiy vinograd rastet.
Tam tebe privol'ney pesnya,
Tï tuda i uletay.

Chorus

Fly away on the wings of the wind
To our homeland, O native song of ours,
There, where we sang you freely,
Where it was so free for us with you.
There under the hot sky
The air is full of sweet bliss,
There to the sound of the sea,
The mountains dream in the clouds.
There the sun shines so brightly,
Flooding the native mountains with light.
Magnificent roses blossom in the valleys,
And nightingales sing in the green forests,
And sweet grapes grow.
There you are free to sing,
Fly there!

WILD DANCE OF THE MEN
GENERAL DANCE

Chorus

Poyte pesni slavï khanu! Poy!
Slav'te silu doblest' khana! Slav'!

Slaven khan! Khan!
Slaven on, khan, nash!
Bleskom slavï
Solntsu raven khan!
Netu ravnïkh slavoy khanu
Net!

Chorus

Sing songs of praise to the Khan! Sing!
Praise the power and prowess of the Khan!
Praise it!

Praise the glorious Khan!
He is glorious, our Khan!
In the splendor of his glory,
The Khan is equal to the sun,
None is equal in glory to the Khan!
None!

DANCE OF THE SLAVE GIRLS

Chagi khana slavyat khana,
Khana svoyego.

The Khan's female slaves praise the Khan,
Their Khan!

Khan Konchak

Vidish' li plennits tï
S morya dal'nego,
Vidish' krasavits moikh
Iz-za Kaspiya.
O skazhi, drug,
Skazhi tol'ko slovo mne,
Khochesh',
Lyubuyu iz nih ya tebe podaryu.

Khan Konchak

Do you see the captives
From the distant sea;
Do you see the beauties,
From beyond the Caspian Sea.
Oh, tell me, friend,
Tell me just one word:
If you wish,
I give you any of them as a gift.

GENERAL DANCE

Chorus

Poyte pesni slavï khanu! Poy!
Slav'te shchedrost', slav'te milost'!
Slav'!
Dlya vragov khan grozen on,
Khan nash!
Kto-zhe slavoy raven khanu, kto?
Bleskom slavï
Solntsu raven, on!

Chorus

Sing songs of praise to the Khan! Sing!
Praise his generosity, praise his mercy!
Praise!
To his enemies the Khan is terrible—
Our Khan!
Who may equal the Khan in glory, who?
In the splendor of his glory
He is equal to the sun!

DANCE OF THE BOYS
DANCE OF THE MEN

Chorus	**Chorus**
Slavoy dedam raven khan nash,	Our Khan, Khan Konchak, is equal
Khan, khan Konchak!	To his forefathers in glory!
Slavoy dedam raven on,	He is equal to his forefathers,
Grozniy khan, khan Konchak.	The terrible Khan, Khan Konchak.

DANCE OF THE BOYS
DANCE OF THE MEN

Chorus	**Chorus**
Slaven khan, khan Konchak!	Glory to the Khan, Khan Konchak!

GLIDING DANCE OF THE MAIDENS

Uletay na kril'yakh vetra, etc.	Fly away on the wings of the wind, etc.

GLIDING DANCE OF THE MAIDENS AND

Tam tak yarko solntse svetit . . . etc.	There the sun shines so brightly . . . etc.

DANCE OF THE BOYS

Dance of the Men	**Dance of the Men**
Slavnoy dedam raven khan nash,	Our Khan, Khan Konchak, is equal
Khan, khan Konchak!	In glory to his forefathers!
Slavoy dedam raven on,	The terrible Khan, Khan Konchak, is equal
Grozniy khan, khan Konchak.	In glory to his forefathers!

DANCE OF THE BOYS

Dance of the Men	**Dance of the Men**
Slaven khan, khan Konchak!	Glory to the Khan, to Khan Konchak!
Khan Konchak!	Khan Konchak!

General Dance

General Dance	
Plyaskoy vashey tesh'te khana,	Dance to entertain the Khan,
Plyaskoy tesh'te khana, chagi,	Dance to entertain the Khan, slaves!
Khana svoyego.	Your Khan.
Plyaskoy vashey tesh'te khana,	Dance to entertain the Khan,
Plyaskoy tesh'te!	Dance to entertain!
Nash khan Konchak!	Our Khan Konchak!

66

Johann Strauss II (1825–99)

An der schönen, blauen Donau (On the Beautiful Blue Danube), Op. 314 (1867)

On the Beautiful Blue Danube was the most popular waltz of Johann Strauss II, the "Waltz King," whose dances ruled in the ballrooms of Vienna and all Europe (as far as St. Petersburg) in the second half of the nineteenth century. Like Strauss's other waltzes it was probably conceived as an instrumental piece, although the work was first performed in a vocal-orchestral version at a Carnival concert in February 1867. The original text was provided by chorus master Josef Weyl (1821–95) and included references to the Shrovetide festivities intended to console the Viennese public after the 1866 defeat of Austria by the Prussians. The title of the waltz was taken from "An der schönen blauen Donau," a melancholy poem by Karl Beck (1818–79). In 1890 Franz von Gernerth (1821–1900) supplied another text, more appropriate to the waltz that according to Viennese music critic Eduard Hanslick became the unofficial national anthem of the Habsburg Empire. The first lines of Gernerth's text make the connection between the title and Vienna explicit:

> Danube so blue, so bright and blue,
> Through vale and field you flow so calm,
> Our Vienna greets you, you silver stream . . .

Strauss premiered the instrumental version with his own orchestra in March 1867 and then took the piece to Paris, where it created a sensation at the concerts Strauss gave at the World Exposition in May. The "Blue Danube" instantly became a staple encore item, especially in Vienna, where it is played at every New Year's concert of the Vienna Philharmonic.

Like the minuet, the waltz has been an unusually enduring dance in Europe. A couples' dance in triple meter, it originated in eighteenth-century rustic dances of various names but generally designated as "Deutscher" (German dance). In the late eighteenth and early nineteenth centuries these dances increased in tempo and thus became more notable for gliding and spinning, which gave rise to the term *waltz* (from the German *walzen*, to turn about). The waltz spread rapidly in Europe despite suspicions that it was harmful to the health and morals of youth—the couples embraced tightly, and the spinning all too often caused women's skirts

to be raised high enough to reveal the ankle. (In 1797 a pamphlet was published under the title *Beweis dass das Walzen eine Hauptquelle der Schwäche des Körpers und des Geistes unserer Generation sey* [Proof that waltzing is a main source of the weakness of the body and mind of our generation].)

By the mid-nineteenth century Johann Strauss II solidified the form. His waltzes with titles are sets of dances, usually five, framed by an introduction and a coda. This structure had already been used by his father, Johann Strauss I, and first appeared in Carl Maria von Weber's 1819 piano rondo *Aufforderung zum Tanz* (Invitation to the dance), which included an introduction, a sequence of dances, and a coda that recalled waltzes heard earlier in the piece. With this form the waltz graduated from a genre intended primarily for dancing to one also capable of holding its own in the concert hall.

The "Blue Danube" is scored for a large orchestra, including full brass, harp, and percussion in addition to the usual woodwinds and strings. All of its five waltzes are in *da capo* form and have two sections, each consisting of two eight-measure phrases repeated (sometimes with repeat signs, sometimes written out with slight variation) to constitute thirty-two measures. The B sections of the first two are in keys contrasting with the tonic, D major (A and B♭, respectively). Together the keys of the dances and the coda display the tona variety required of concert music. The fourth and fifth dances begin with short introductions that modulate to the new key.

In this simple framework Strauss manages to give a contrasting character to each section with inventive rhythmic and melodic formulas. What lends special color to the first waltz is the harmonization of the sixth scale degree (B), which is treated either as the ninth of a dominant-ninth chord or as an added sixth to the tonic chord. The introduction is in fact a double introduction; its first part, a miniature tone painting that presents fragments of the first tune in the horns below tremolo strings in the dominant key, is a teaser that instead of introducing the waltz introduces another introduction, which comes as a "Tempo di Valse" in the tonic key and establishes the tempo, meter, and key of the section to come.

Strauss especially prized his codas, and they are the least formulaic part of his waltzes. Here the coda begins with thematic material from the third waltz, then recalls the A section of the second waltz in its original tonic key, and modulates first to D minor and then to F major in order to recall the A section of the fourth waltz, the end of which becomes a transition to the recapitulation in D of the first waltz. Strauss replaces the final cadence with a dramatic grand pause, which is followed by a codetta on a tonic pedal.

Of Strauss's some 500 waltzes, the "Blue Danube" has become the quintessential representative of both pleasure-seeking Vienna and Strauss's musical talent. At the concert at which his death was announced to the audience, the orchestra played the "Blue Danube," *pianissimo*, to great effect.

67

Arthur Sullivan (1842–1900)

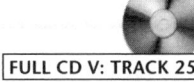

FULL CD V: TRACK 25

Ruddigore, "My eyes are fully open to my awful situation" ("Patter Trio") (1836–1911)

Ruddigore was the tenth collaboration of Arthur Sullivan and the librettist William S. Gilbert (1836–1911). Their "light operas," or operettas, are often referred to as Savoy Operas after the Savoy Theater that impresario Richard D'Oyly Carte had built in London in 1881 for their works. *Ruddigore*, like all the operettas on which the team collaborated, features an implausible, twisted plot that spoofs the conventions of opera and English high society. The improbable premise of *Ruddigore* is a witch's curse that forces all baronets of Ruddigore to commit a crime every day or die in agony. Consequently all subsequent baronets become villains, until Sir Ruthven Murgatroyd (who has tried to avoid the curse by disguising himself as the simple farmer Robin Oakapple) figures out that refusing to commit a crime under the curse is "tantamount to suicide," which, being a crime, fulfills his obligation as a villain.

The characters and situations on stage are almost all borrowed from the opera repertory: the heroic lover in disguise; the mad woman (whose aria "Cheerily carols the lark" spoofs Lucia's mad scene from Donizetti's *Lucia di Lammermoor*); the poor but virtuous maiden who at the end is rewarded by marrying the good baronet; and the ghosts of ancestors who take the place of the authoritarian father figure common in nineteenth-century opera and force the young to act against their will. The comic effect derives from parody: the noble lover turns bad (before he turns good again); the evil baronet becomes good; the mad woman is mad not because she is forced to marry against her will but because her husband turns out to be the bad baronet; and the virtuous maiden is able to fall in love "passionately, madly" at any time and with anyone.

"My eyes are fully open," commonly referred to as the "Patter Trio," is sung by Sir Ruthven (alias Robin Oakapple), Mad Margaret, and Sir Ruthven's brother, Sir Despard Murgatroyd. Following the discovery of Robin's true identity as Sir Ruthven, he is forced by his ancestors to commit a crime a day. In the action leading to up to the trio, Margaret and Sir Despard convince Sir Ruthven to renounce his life of crime. He declares that he will defy his ancestors and die rather than be a bad baronet. At this point the three sing the trio, giving voice, very rapidly and garrulously, to their opinions.

Patter songs, usually sung by basses or baritones, had been a staple of comic opera since the early eighteenth century. Originally they parodied the vocal virtuosity of opera seria, substituting an almost unutterable number of fast syllables for the almost unsingable number of notes in coloratura arias. The "Patter Trio" in *Ruddigore* parodies the comic convention by exaggerating the speed of the utterance of the syllables; by having three characters onstage compete to see who can sing his or her words more quickly; and by self-ironically admitting the futility of the exercise ("This particularly rapid unintelligible patter isn't generally heard and if it is it doesn't matter"). The Trio is thus at once a spoof of both comic and serious opera and as such the very embodiment of the carefree spirit of nineteenth-century operetta. The popularity of the "Patter Trio" has recently led to its incorporation into productions of Gilbert and Sullivan's *The Pirates of Penzance* (1879). In 2002, the music of the "Trio" was used for "The Speed Test" in the musical *Thoroughly Modern Millie*.

Robin (Sir Ruthven)

My eyes are fully open to my awful situation

I shall go to at once to Roderic and make him an oration,

I shall tell him I've recovered my forgotten moral senses,

And I don't care two-pence half penny for any consequences.

Now I do not want to perish by the sword or by the dagger,

But a martyr may indulge a little pardonable swagger,

And a word or two of compliment my vanity would flatter,

But I've got to die tomorrow, so it really doesn't matter!

Sir Despard and Margaret

So it really doesn't matter, matter, matter . . .

Margaret

If I were not a little mad and generally silly

I should give you advice upon the subject, willy-nilly;

I should show you in a moment how to grapple with the question,

And you'd really be astonished at the force of my suggestion.

On the subject I shall write you a most valuable letter,

Full of excellent suggestions, when I feel a little better,

But at present I'm afraid I am as mad as any hatter,

So I'll keep 'em to myself, for my opinion doesn't matter!

Sir Despard and Robin (Sir Ruthven)

Her opinion doesn't matter, matter, matter . . .

Sir Despard

If I had been so lucky as to have a steady brother

Who could talk to me as we are talking now to one another,

Who could give me good advice when he discovered I was erring,

(Which is just the very favour which on you I am conferring)

My existence would have made a rather interesting idyll,

And I might have lived and died a very decent indiwiddle.

This particularly rapid, unintelligible patter

Isn't generally heard, and if it is it doesn't matter!

Robin (Sir Ruthven) and Margaret

If it is it doesn't matter, matter, matter . . .

All

This particularly rapid, unintelligible patter

Isn't generally heard, and if it is it doesn't matter!

is it does-n't mat-ter, mat-ter, mat-ter, mat-ter, mat-ter,mat-ter, mat-ter, mat-ter, mat-ter, mat-ter, mat-ter!

is it does-n't mat-ter, mat-ter, mat-ter, mat-ter, mat-ter,mat-ter, mat-ter, mat-ter, mat-ter, mat-ter, mat-ter!

is it does-n't mat-ter, mat-ter, mat-ter, mat-ter, mat-ter,mat-ter, mat-ter, mat-ter, mat-ter, mat-ter, mat-ter!

68

Ruggero Leoncavallo
(1857–1919)

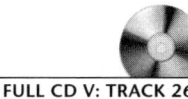

Pagliacci (Clowns or Players), "Vesti la giubba"
("Put on the costume") (1892)

The young Arturo Toscanini (1867–1957) conducted the first performance of Ruggero Leoncavallo's *Pagliacci* on 21 May 1892 at the Teatro Dal Verme in Milan. The work is one of the first operas to exemplify *verismo*, the late nineteenth-century fashion for realism in Italian opera. Operatic *verismo* stems from the Italian literary movement of the same name characterized by subject matter drawn from the life of lower classes and the use of local dialects. Inspired by French naturalism, *verismo* had its most influential representative in the Sicilian writer Giovanni Verga (1844–1922). Once on the opera stage—a highly unrealistic dramatic environment—it lost some of its realistic features, but preserved an emphasis on local color and characters from low social classes. Other characteristics of operatic *verismo* include a lack of *bel canto* singing, and passionate expression suited to intense vocal outbursts. The prototypical *verismo* opera was Pietro Mascagni's *Cavalleria rusticana* (Rustic Chivalry, 1890), a one-act work based on a short story by Verga. Leoncavallo modeled *Pagliacci* on Mascagni's opera and the two operas are regularly paired on a double bill familiarly referred to as "Cav and Pag."

Leoncavallo, who wrote his own libretto, claimed that *Pagliacci* was based on a real crime that he witnessed as a child during a theatrical performance. Whatever its source, the topic of murder committed by actors was popular at the time. *Pagliacci* is set between 1865 and 1870 on the outskirts of a small village in the southern Italian region of Calabria. A troupe of *commedia dell'arte* (improvised street theater) actors arrive to entertain the villagers. The group's leader, Canio, learns that his wife, Nedda, is having an affair. During the performance, which replicates their real-life conflict, the jealous Canio, who plays the clown Pagliaccio, kills Nedda, who plays the female lead, Columbina. He also kills her lover, the villager Silvio, who rushes on stage in an attempt to help her.

The opera's most famous number, Canio's "Vesti la giubba" ("Put on the costume") is the emotional climax and closing number of Act I. It exemplifies the fundamental dichotomy inherent in the story. His fellow actors tell Canio that he must prepare to perform in the play, despite the fact that he has just learned of his wife's infidelity and has just been prevented from killing

her. As he dresses for the performance Canio reflects on his profession, which forces him to act cheerfully in spite of his true state of mind.

"Vesti la giubba" is not a full-scale aria but an "arioso" introduced by an eleven-measure recitative ("Recitar!" [Act!]). At the end of the high A in the recitative ending the line "are you a man?" ("sei tu forse un uom?") Leoncavallo has the singer break into a bitter laugh. The gesture marks Canio as emotionally trapped in his profession as actor. In the arioso section his command to himself to laugh ("Ridi Pagliaccio"—"Laugh, clown!") is delivered as an excruciatingly emotional cry, the musical high point of the opera. He sings the line to a climactic motive (mm. 37–38) that acts as a veritable "hook." The rhythm and the melodic contour of this motive shapes the entire arioso. We hear its rhythm at the beginning of the arioso (m. 12) and again in mm. 14, 16, and 20. At m. 24 the rhythm appears together with the text "ridi Pagliaccio," but Leoncavallo saves the motive's catchiest melodic setting. The motive is absent for the next nine measures, but then Leoncavallo uses it twice in rapid succession (mm. 34 and 37). While the statement at m. 34 is confined to the orchestra, at m. 37 it is in the tenor's most powerful register and it resolves the wrenching dominant build-up of the previous three measures. The harmonic release is not, however, to the expected tonic chord, but down a step to a bitter-sweetly dissonant sub-dominant seventh (iv^7) (progressions down by whole step are characteristic of Leoncavallo's approach to striking dramatic moments, see also the progression in mm. 29–30).

In this short arioso, neither the harmonies, nor the phrase structure (which consists of 2 + 2, 4 + 4, and 8 + 8-measure phrases) are strikingly original. But there is an unabashed calculation of effect achieved by forecasting the climax while saving it to the end, and by backing it up with sensual harmonies. Whether we can call this representation of emotion "realist" is debatable. But with his ability to concentrate human emotion so powerfully in the climax of "Vesti la giubba," Leoncavallo proved to be a realist of the opera market. It is no accident that this arioso became an absolute must for all superstar tenors. The great tenor Enrico Caruso (1873–1921) recorded "Vesti la giubba" three times. His third recording, made in 1907, is generally claimed as the first recording to sell a million copies. The same year *Pagliacci* became the first opera to be recorded in its entirety.

Canio	Canio
Recitar! Mentre preso dal delirio,	To act! While in the grip of delirium
non so più quel che dico,	I no longer know what I say,
e quel che faccio!	or what I do!
Eppur è d'uopo, sforzati!	And yet it is necessary, force yourself!
Bah! (con ira) sei tu forse un uom?	Bah! (*angrily*) Are you, perhaps, a man?
(laughing bitterly with pain)	
Ah! Ah! Ah! Ah! Ah!	Ah! Ah! Ah! Ah! Ah!
Tu se' Pagliaccio!	You are a clown!

(pressing his head desperately between his hands)

Vesti la giubba,
e la faccia infarina.
La gente paga, e rider vuole qua.
E se Arlecchino t'invola Colombina,
ridi, Pagliaccio, e ognun applaudirà!
Tramuta in lazzi lo spasmo ed il pianto;
in una smorfia il singhiozzo il dolor, Ah!
Ridi, Pagliaccio,
sul tuo amore infranto!
Ridi del duol, che t'avvelena
(singhiozzando) il cor!

Put on the costume,
and powder your face.
The people pay, and want to laugh.
And if Harlequin steals Colombina
laugh, clown, and everyone will applaud!
Turn your anguish and tears into jest;
the moaning and pain into a grimace, Ah!
Laugh, clown,
at your broken love!
Laugh at the sorrow that poisons
(sobbing) your heart!

Slowly moves toward the little theater, crying; but reaching the curtain, which leads backstage, recoils from it violently as if he does not want to enter; then, gripped by a new attack of weeping, takes his head between his hands, hiding his face, takes another three or four steps toward the curtain, from which he had withdrawn enraged, and, [during the final chords of the orchestra], enters and disappears.

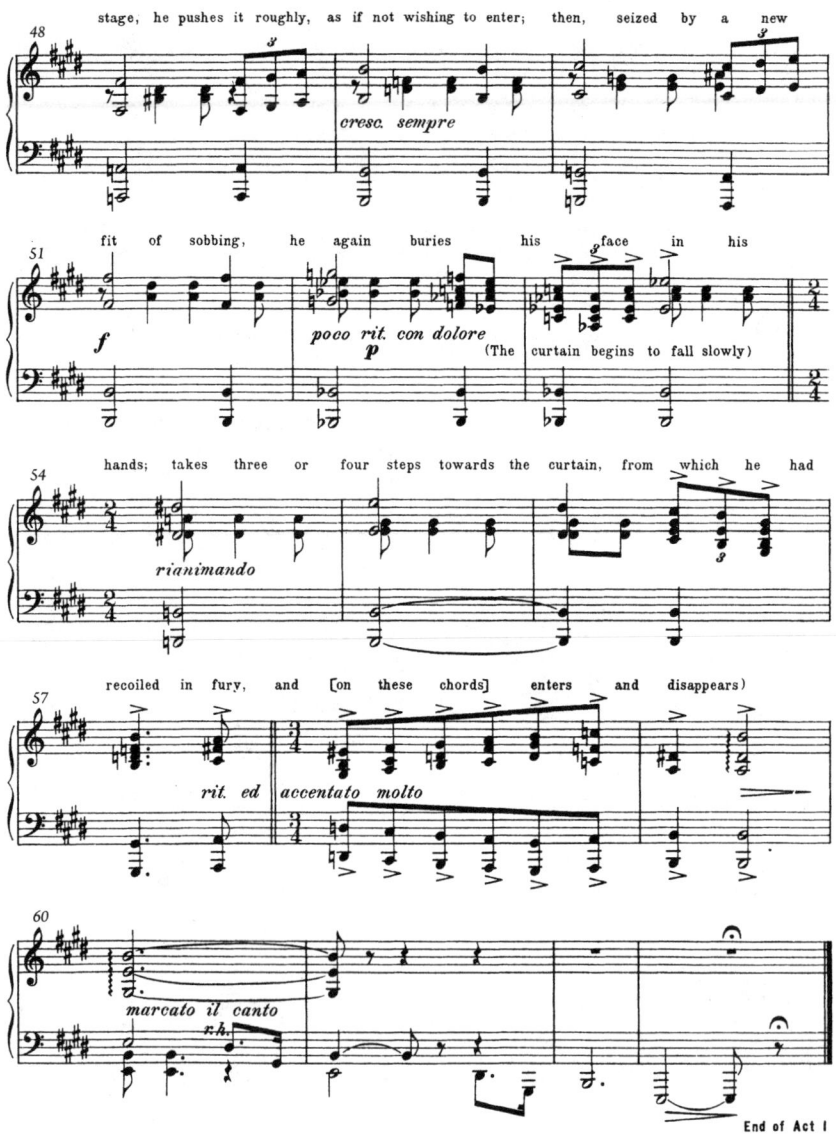

End of Act I

69

Giacomo Puccini
(1858–1924)

FULL CD V: TRACK 27
CONCISE CD III: TRACK 4

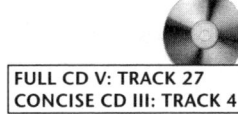

Madama Butterfly (Madam Butterfly), "Un bel dì, vedremo" ("One fine day we'll see") (1904, rev. 1904, 1905, 1906)

Puccini's fourth successful opera, *Madama Butterfly*, was premiered in Milan on 17 February 1904. The librettists, Giuseppe Giacosa and Luigi Illica, relied on David Belasco's one-act play *Madame Butterfly* (1900) and on a short story by John Luther Long (1897), itself the basis for Belasco's play. Long's story also has two sources: a true story reported by Long's sister who had lived in Nagasaki as the wife of a missionary, and Pierre Loti's *Madame Chrysanthème* (1893).

Since the seventeenth century the institution of temporary marriage existed for foreigners in Japan who could pay to obtain a Japanese "wife" for a limited period. *Madama Butterfly* tells the tragic story of one such arrangement between the American naval officer Benjamin Franklin Pinkerton and Cio-Cio-San (Butterfly), a fifteen-year-old girl from a once-respected family that has fallen into disgrace. Pinkerton deceives Butterfly by entering into a marriage he has no intention of making permanent and by falsely promising to return within a year. The young Butterfly devotes herself entirely to Pinkerton, converts to Christianity, and refuses to accept the offer of marriage by a Japanese prince, even when it becomes obvious that Pinkerton has misled her. When Pinkerton returns after three long years, he brings his American wife, who intends to adopt Cio-Cio-San's son, born in Pinkerton's absence. The shattered Cio-Cio-San agrees to give up her son on the condition that Pinkerton, who has been too ashamed to face her, return for the boy himself. Cio-Cio-San fatally stabs herself just before Pinkerton arrives. The last words of the opera are his anguished cries "Butterfly, Butterfly!"

Cio-Cio-San sings the aria "Un bel dì, vedremo" in Act 2. Three years have passed since Pinkerton's departure, and Cio-Cio-San's servant, Suzuki, expresses doubt that he will ever return. Cio-Cio-San harshly chastises Suzuki and goes on to describe in detail exactly how it will be when Pinkerton arrives.

The aria divides into six sections (mm. 1–8, mm. 9–18, mm. 19–37, mm. 38–48, mm. 49–56, and mm. 57–62) followed by an orchestral postlude. These sections correspond to the major divisions of the text, except the climactic return to the opening eight-measure melody (m. 49), which Puccini begins on "morire" (to die), the last word of the poetic line belonging to the previous section. Puccini's emphasis on "morire" creates highly effective melodrama—in the aria, Butterfly refers metaphorically to dying of pleasure at Pinkerton's return, whereas the

word foreshadows her death in an all-too-literal sense. The opening phrase and its climactic return both lack the grounding of a bass line, just as Butterfly's faith in Pinkerton's return lacks a rational foundation. The greatest emotional outpouring comes, however, not in the voice but in the orchestra, when, after an explosive coda in which the singer reaches her last and highest note (B♭), the orchestra repeats the main theme, now over a tonic pedal (mm. 62ff). This phrase from "Un bel dì" returns again later in the opera as a reference to Cio-Cio-San's unshakable belief in Pinkerton, which becomes more painfully illusory as the opera unfolds.

Throughout the opera Puccini wraps his tragic heroine in exotic musical garb. Pentatonic phrases, like the one beginning "Chi sarà" (Who can it be) (mm. 38–47), and Lydian-inflected passages (mm. 11, 15, and 34–37) mark Cio-Cio-San as an Easterner. Unlike many other exotic operatic heroines (e.g., Carmen, Delilah), Butterfly is no femme fatale. Cio-Cio-San's melody is diatonic; her lyrical outpourings often break and dissolve into recitative-like childish chattering. Her music thus depicts a character incapable of dominating through seduction—she presents no danger to the Westerner who marries her. On the contrary, the colonizing West seduces her and distorts her view, depriving her of her own cultural values and leaving her without support.

Over the course of her long wait for Pinkerton's return, her childlike devotion to him matures into adult passion. Thus the Japanese teahouse girl, whom Pinkerton's wife calls a "plaything" in Long's story, develops in Puccini's version into a genuine operatic heroine. Colonialist in its stereotypical depiction of the East, Puccini's *Madama Butterfly* also criticizes the exploitative nature of colonialism. The raw, elemental brutality with which Puccini destroys Cio-Cio-San combines the grit of *verismo* with the late-nineteenth- and early-twentieth-century fashion for exoticism.

Cio-Cio-San (*acting the scene as if it were taking place*)	**Cio-Cio-San** (*acting the scene as if it were taking place*)
Un bel dì, vedremo	One fine day we'll see
levarsi un fil di fumo	a thread of smoke arising
sull'estremo confin del mare.	over the far horizon of the sea.
E poi la nave appare.	And then the ship appears.
Poi la nave bianca	Then the white ship
Entra nel porto, romba	Enters the port thundering
il suo saluto. Vedi?	its salute. Do you see?
È venuto!	He has come!
Io non gli scendo incontro.	I do not go down to meet him.
Io no. Mi metto là	Not I. I remain there
sul ciglio del colle e aspetto,	on the brow of the hill and wait,
e aspetto gran tempo	and wait a long time
e non mi pesa,	and do not weary
la lunga attesa.	of the long wait.

E ... uscito dalla folla cittadina	And ... out of the crowd of townsfolk
un uomo, un picciol punto	a man, a tiny speck
s'avvia per la collina.	makes his way up the hill.
Chi sarà? chi sarà?	Who can it be? who can it be?
E come sarà giunto	And when he arrives
che dirà? che dirà?	what will he say? what will he say?
Chiamerà Butterfly	He will call, "Butterfly"
dalla lontana.	from the distance.
Io senza dar risposta	I without responding
me ne starò nascosta	will remain hidden
un po' per celia ...	partly to tease [him] ...
e un po' per non morire	and partly so as not to die
al primo incontro,	at the first meeting,
ed egli alquanto in pena	and he, a little worried,
chiamerà, chiamerà:	he will call, he will call:
"Piccina mogliettina	"Dear little wife
olezzo di verbena,"	fragrance of verbena,"
i nomi che mi dava	the names he used to call me
al suo venire	when he was here

(to Suzuki)

Tutto questo avverrà,	All this will happen,
te lo prometto.	I promise you.
Tienti la tua paura,	Hold back your fears,
io con sicura fede l'aspetto.	I wait for him with unshakable faith.

(*Butterfly and Suzuki embrace each other with emotion.*)

(*Butterfly dismisses Suzuki, who exits the door on the left, and Butterfly looks after her sadly.*)

Source Notes

1. Bach, Wilhelm Friedemann. Sonata in F Major. Nagels Musik-Archiv, 156, Book 3. Nagels Verlag Kassel. Ed. by Friedrich Blume. London: Bärenreiter Edition. pp. 20–25. Used by permission.

2. Bach, Carl Philipp Emanuel. Fantasia in C Minor, Wq 63/6/iii, reprinted from "*Probestücke*," "*Leichte*" *und* "*Damen*" *Sonatas*, ed. David Schulenberg, *Carl Philipp Emanuel Bach: The Complete Works*, Series I, Vol. 3, pp. 33–35 (Los Altos, California: The Packard Humanities Institute, 2005). Used by permission.

3. Bach, Johann Christian. Sonata in D Major, Op. 5, No. 2. Reprinted from *Johann Christian Bach: Drei Sonaten für Klavier*, ed. Franzpeter Goebels. Möseler Verlag: 1976. pp. 4–12. Used by permission.

4. Pergolesi, Giovanni Battista. *La serva padrona*. Score reset, based on the piano reduction published in Paris: Aux adresses ordinaires et chez l'editeur . . . ; Imprimé par Auguste de l'Orraine, 1752. Kindly provided by the North Texas State University Music Library.

5. Piccinni, Niccolò. *La buona figliuola*. Ed. by Giacomo Benvenuti. I Classici Musicali Italiani. Fondazione Eugenio Bravi. Vol. 7. Milan, Italy: I Classici Musicali Italiani, 1941. pp. 252–278.

6. Gluck, Christoph Willibald, *Orfeo ed Euridice*. Score reset, based on the piano reduction of Conradi and Brünbaum. Berlin: G. Bock, n.d.

7. Sammartini, Giovanni Battista. Symphony No. 13 in G Major. Reprinted by permission from *The Symphonies of G. Sammartini*, Vol. II, ed. Bathia Churgin, pp. 151–160, Cambridge, Mass.: Harvard University Press, Copyright © 1968 by the President and Fellows of Harvard College.

8. Bach, Johann Christian. Sinfonia in B♭ Major, Op. 18, No. 2. Copyright © 1925 by C. F. Peters Corporation. pp. 3–14. Used by permission. All Rights Reserved.

9. Haydn, Franz Joseph. Symphony No. 45 in F♯ Minor ("Farewell"). Leipzig: Breitkopf & Härtel, n.d.

10. Haydn, Franz Joseph. String Quartet in E♭ Major ("The Joke"), Op. 33, No. 2. Leipzig: Ernst Eulenburg, No. 52, n.d. pp. 1–18.

11. Haydn, Franz Joseph. Symphony No. 104 in D Major ("London"). London: Ernst Eulenburg, No. 409, n.d. pp. 1–74.

12. Haydn, Franz Joseph. *The Creation*. Ed. by A. Peter Brown. © Oxford University Press 1995. Extract reproduced by permission. All rights reserved.

13. Mozart, Wolfgang Amadeus. Symphony No. 40 in G Minor, K. 550. In *Wolfgang Amadeus Mozart's Werke*. Serie 8. Band 3. Ed. by J. Brahms and others. Leipzig: Breitkopf & Härtel, 1877–1905. pp. (181)1–(198)18.

14. Mozart, Wolfgang Amadeus. Symphony No. 41 in C Major ("Jupiter"), K. 551. *Wolfgang Amadeus Mozart's Werke*. Serie 8. Band 3. Ed. by J. Brahms and others. Leipzig: Breitkopf & Härtel, 1877–1905. pp. (264)36–(285)57.

15a. & b. Mozart, Wolfgang Amadeus. *Don Giovanni*. New York: G. Schirmer, Inc., 1900.

16. Mozart, Wolfgang Amadeus. Piano Concerto No. 17 in G Major, K. 453. In *Wolfgang Amadeus Mozart's Werke*. Serie 16. Band 3. Ed. by J. Brahms and others. Leipzig: Breitkopf & Härtel, 1877–1905. pp. 1–54.

17. Beethoven, Ludwig van. Sonata No. 8 in C Minor ("Pathétique"), Op. 13. In *Ludwig van Beethovens Werke: Vollständige kritisch durchgesehene überall berechtigte Ausgabe*. Serie 16. Leipzig: Breitkopf & Härtel, 1862–5. pp. (121)1–(127)7.

18. Beethoven, Ludwig van. Septet in E♭ Major, Op. 20. In *Ludwig van Beethovens Werke: Vollständige kritisch durchgesehene überall berechtigte Ausgabe*. Serie 5. Leipzig: Breitkopf & Härtel, 1862–5. pp. 21–31.

19. Beethoven, Ludwig van. Symphony No. 3 in E♭ Major, Op. 55. In *Ludwig van Beethovens Werke: Vollständige kritisch durchgesehene überall berechtigte Ausgabe*. Serie 1. Leipzig: Breitkopf & Härtel, 1862–5. pp. (113)3–(145)35.

20. Beethoven, Ludwig van. Symphony No. 5 in C Minor, Op. 67. In *Ludwig van Beethovens Werke: Vollständige kritisch durchgesehene überall berechtigte Ausgabe*. Serie 1. Leipzig: Breitkopf & Härtel, 1862–5. pp. 3–100.

21. Beethoven, Ludwig van. String Quartet in B♭ Major, Op. 130. In *Ludwig van Beethovens Werke: Vollständige kritisch durchgesehene überall berechtigte Ausgabe*. Serie 6. Leipzig: Breitkopf & Härtel, 1862–5. pp. (103)25–(105)27.

22. Rossini, Gioachino. *Il Barbiere di Siviglia*. G. Schirmer's Collection of Operas. New York: G. Schirmer, Inc., 1900. pp. 1–8.

23. Rossini, Gioachino. *L'Italiana in Algeri*. No score included.

24. Rossini, Gioachino. *Tancredi*. Score reset, based on copy kindly provided by the Sibley Music Library of the Eastman School of Music. Paris: Janet et Cotelle [c. 1827].

25. Bellini, Vincenzo. *Norma*. The Royal Edition, "Norma" (38). Ed. by Arthur Sullivan and J. Pittman. New York: Boosey & Hawkes, Inc., [187–?]. pp. 38–51.

26. Donizetti, Gaetano. *Lucia di Lammermoor*. Piano reduction by Gustav F. Kogel. Leipzig: C. F. Peters, 1890s. pp. 158–176.

27. Weber, Carl Maria von. *Der Freischütz*. Piano reduction by Gustav F. Kogel, Leipzig: C. F. Peters, 1893. pp. 3–10, 75–91.

28. Schubert, Franz. *Heidenröslein*. In *Franz Schubert's Werke, Kritisch durchgesehene Gesammtausgabe*, ed. E. Mandyczewski, J. Brahms and others. Serie 20. Lieder und Gesänge. Band 3. Leipzig: Verlag von Breitkopf & Härtel, Leipzig, 1884–97. p. 37.

29. Schubert, Franz. *Erlkönig*. In *Franz Schubert's Werke, Kritisch durchgesehene Gesammtausgabe*, ed. E. Mandyczewski, J. Brahms, and others. Serie 20. Lieder und Gesänge. Band 3. Leipzig: Verlag von Breitkopf & Härtel, Leipzig, 1884–97. pp. 202–207.

30. Schubert, Franz. *Moments musicaux*, No. 6, D. 780, In *Franz Schubert's Werke, Kritisch durchgesehene Gesammtausgabe*, ed. E. Mandyczewski, J. Brahms, and others. Serie 10, Sonaten für Pianoforte. Leipzig: Verlag von Breitkopf & Härtel, Leipzig, 1884–97. pp. 16–17.

31. Schubert, Franz. Symphony No. 8 in B Minor ("Unfinished"), D. 759. In *Franz Schubert's Werke, Kritisch durchgesehene Gesammtausgabe*, ed. E. Mandyczewski, J. Brahms, and others. Serie 1. Symphonien für Orchester. Band 1. Leipzig: Verlag von Breitkopf & Härtel, Leipzig, 1884–97. pp. 239–256.

32. Schubert, Franz. Piano Trio in E♭ Major, Op. 100. In *Franz Schubert's Werke, Kritisch durchgesehene Gesammtausgabe*, ed. E. Mandyczewski, J. Brahms, and others. Serie 7, Pianoforte-

Quintett,-Quartett und-Trios. Band 2. Leipzig: Verlag von Breitkopf & Härtel, Leipzig, 1884–97. pp. 23–31.

33. Schubert, Franz. *Der Doppelgänger*. In *Franz Schubert's Werke, Kritisch durchgesehene Ge-sammtausgabe*, ed. E. Mandyczewski, J. Brahms and others. Serie 20. Lieder und Gesänge. Band 9. Leipzig: Verlag von Breitkopf & Härtel, Leipzig, 1884–97. pp. 180–181.

34. Paganini, Niccolò. Caprices, Op. 1. Ed. by Jean Becker. Leipzig: C. F. Peters, 1890–1899. pp. 32–33, 43–45.

35. Liszt, Franz. *Grandes Etudes d'après Paganini*. In *Werke, Klavier zu 2 Händen, Franz Liszt*. Ed. by Emil von Sauer. Band 4. Etüden. Frankfurt, London, and New York: C. F. Peters, 1919, © renewed 1947. pp. 152–162.

36. Liszt, Franz. *Liszt-Mozart Don Juan-Phantasie*. Ed. by Ignaz Friedman. Vienna and Leipzig: Universal-Edition, 1917. pp. 2–27.

37. Auber, Daniel-Francois-Esprit. *La muette de Portici*. Ed. and trans. by Natalia MacFarren. Novello's Original Octavo Edition. London: Novello, Ewer and Co., and Simpkin, Marshall and Co., 1872. pp. 128–139.

38. Meyerbeer, Giacomo. *Les Huguenots*. Paris: Ph. Maquet, [1880–1889?]. pp. 364–404.

39. Berlioz, Hector. *Symphonie fantastique*. In *Hector Berlioz Werke. Serie I. Symphonien*. Abthei-lung I. Ed. by Felix Weingartner and Charles Malherbe. Brussels, London, and New York: Verlag von Breitkopf & Härtel in Leipzig, 1900. pp. 97–150.

40. Mendelssohn, Felix Bartholdy. *Ein Sommernachtstraum*. In *Felix Mendelssohn Bartholdy's Sämtliche Werke*. Ein Sommernachtstraum von Shakespeare. Klavierauszug zu 2 Händen. Leipzig: C. F. Peters, n.d. pp. 2–12.

41. Mendelssohn, Felix Bartholdy. *Paulus*, Oratorium von Felix Mendelssohn-Bartholdy, Op. 36. Klavierauszug mit Text. Ed. by Franz Abt. Collection Litolff. Braunschweig: Henry Lit-loff's Verlag, 1900–1909. pp. 3–7, 159–166.

42. Schumann, Robert. *Phantasie*, Op. 17. In *Robert Schumann's Werke. Serie VII. Band 3. Für Pianoforte zu zwei Händen*. Ed. by Clara Schumann. Leipzig: Verlag von Breitkopf & Härtel, 1879. pp. 2–12.

43. Schumann, Robert. *Dichterliebe*. In *Robert Schumann's Werke. Serie XIII. Band 3. Für eine Singstimme mit Begleitung des Pianoforte*. Ed. by Clara Schumann. Leipzig: Breitkopf & Härtel, 1885. pp. 2–3, 32–35.

44. Schumann, Clara. "Er ist gekommen in Sturm und Regen," Op. 12, No. 2. In Clara Schu-mann *Sämtliche Lieder für Singstimme und Klavier*. Ed. by Joachim Draheim and Brigitte Höft. Wiesbaden, Germany: Breitkopf & Härtel. pp. 10–13. Copyright © 1990 by Breitkopf & Härtel, Wiesbaden, Germany. Used by kind permission.

45. Chopin, Frédéric. *Préludes*, Op. 28. In *Fr. Chopin's Sämtliche Pianoforte-Werke*. Band 2. Ed. by Hermann Scholtz. Leipzig: C. F. Peters, [1870-79?]. pp. 489–492.

46. Chopin, Frédéric. *Mazurka*, Op. 17, No. 4. In *Fr. Chopin's Sämtliche Pianoforte-Werke*. Band 1. Ed. by Hermann Scholtz. Leipzig: C. F. Peters, [1870-79?]. pp. 20–22.

47. Chopin, Frédéric. *Ballade in G Minor*, Op. 23. In *Fr. Chopin's Sämtliche Pianoforte-Werke*. Band 2. Ed. by Hermann Scholtz. Leipzig: C. F. Peters, [1870-79?]. pp. 3–12.

48. Gottschalk, L. M. *Bamboula, danse des nègres*, Op. 2. Ed. by Arthur Hochman. New York: G. Schirmer, 1908. pp. 3–17.

49. Glinka, Mikhail. *A Life for the Tsar*. Piano reduction by A. Winkler, revised by N. Rimsky-Korsakov and A. Glazunov. Leipzig: M. P. Belaïeff, 1907. pp. 411–435.

50. Glinka, Mikhail. *Kamarinskaya*. Leipzig: M. P. Belaïeff, 1902. pp. 3–40.

51. Liszt, Franz. *Les preludes*. Piano reduction. Breitkopf & Hartel's Klavier-Bibliothek. Arranged by K. Klauser. Leipzig: Breitkopf & Härtel, n.d. pp. 3–29.

52. Mendelssohn, Felix Bartholdy. Violin Concerto in E Minor, Op. 64. Schirmer's Library of Musical Classics, Vol. 235, piano accompaniment by Schradieck. New York: G. Schirmer (Inc.), 1895, copyright renewed, 1923. pp. 1–13.

53. Wagner, Richard. *Tristan und Isolde*. Vocal score by Karl Klindworth. London: Schott & Co., 1906. pp. 1–4, 379–387.

54. Verdi, Giuseppe. *Rigoletto*. G. Schirmer's Collection of Operas. Trans. by Natalia MacFar-ren. New York: G. Schirmer, 1902. pp. 177–232.

55. Smetana, Bedřich. *Moldau*. Piano trans. by Felix Guenther. New York: Mercury Music Corporation, 1942. Used by permission of Carl Fischer.

56. Musorgsky, Modest. *Boris Godunov*. Ed. by Nikolai Rimsky-Korsakov. Paris: B. Bessel & Cie, editeurs, 1908. pp. 25–44.

57. Tchaikovsky, Pyotr Ilyich. *Yevgeny Onegin*. Kalmus Vocal Scores. Melville, N.Y.: Belwin Mills, Edwin E. Kalmus, 1969. pp. 68–85.

58. Tchaikovsky, Pyotr Ilyich. Symphony No. 4 in F Minor, Op. 36. Breitkopf & Härtels Partitur Bibliothek. Nr. 4984. Wiesbaden, Germany: Breitkopf & Härtel, 1900. pp. 3–62.

59. Brahms, Johannes. Piano Quartet in G Minor, Op. 25. In *Johannes Brahms Sämtliche Werke*, Band 8. Leipzig: Verlag von Breitkopf & Härtel, 1926. pp. 134–153. Used by kind permission.

60. Brahms, Johannes. Symphony No. 1 in C Minor, Op. 68. In *Johannes Brahms Sämtliche Werke*, Band 1. Leipzig: Verlag von Breitkopf & Härtel, 1926. pp. 46–86. Used by kind permission.

61. Dvořák, Antonín. Piano Quintet in A Major, Op. 81. Leipzig: N. Simrock; Leipzig: E. Euler-burg, 1900. pp. 33–53.

62. Dvořák, Antonín. Symphony No. 9 in E Minor, "From the New World." Berlin: N. Simrock, 1894, 28–37.

63. Saint-Saëns, Camille. *Samson et Dalila*. G. Schirmer's Collection of Operas. New York: G. Schirmer, 1892. pp. 166–181.

64. Bizet, George. *Carmen*. New York: G. Schirmer, 1895/1923. pp. 44–54.

65. Borodin, Alexander Porfir'yevich. *Prince Igor*. Leipzig: M. P. Belaïeff, n.d. (1888). pp. 197–229.

66. Strauss II, Johann. *An der schönen, blauen Donau*. New York: G. Schirmer, 1899. pp. 2–9.

67. Sullivan, Arthur and William S. Gilbert. *Ruddigore*. Arr. by George Lowell Tracy. New York: William. A. Pond & Co., London: Chappell & Co., n.d. [1887]. pp. 116–121.

68. Leoncavallo, Ruggero. *Pagliacci*. Trans. by Henry Grafton Chapman. Milan, Italy: Edoardo Sonzogno, 1893, assigned to G. Schirmer, 1906. pp. 129–133.

69. Puccini, Giacomo. *Madama Butterfly*. Arr. by Carlo Carignani. Milan, Italy: G. Ricordi, 1905. pp. 133–137.

Index of Names

Index of Terms

accompanied recitative (recitativo accompagnato), 5, 38, 307, 311, 312
ad libitum, 378, 389
Aeolian, 634
Alberti bass, 8, 9
Allegro (fast), 15
Allegro assai (very fast), 43, 49–62, 437
Allegro con brio, 227–43, 245
Allegro con spirito, 760
Allegro di molto, 8
allegro furioso, 411
Allegro ma non tanto, 43
Allegro marziale, 551
Allegro moderato, 5, 63
Allegro molto, 162–85
Allegro molto e vivace, 220–25
Allegro movements, 63, 74, 75, 114, 121, 186, 215, 216, 246, 360, 437
Allegro spiritoso, 75
Allegro vivace, 303
Allegro vivo, 760
andante amoroso, 411
Andante con moto, 245
Andante di molto, 9
andante maestoso, 551
Andante movements, 75, 187, 220–25
Andante sections, 121, 378, 389
andantino sections, 303, 389, 658, 760
piacere, 307
appoggiatura, 5, 311, 488, 500, 574
rioso, 5, 634, 789
augmented-sixth chord, 5, 9, 15, 245, 358, 360, 376, 574

allad, 41, 353, 500, 501, 658
allade, 500–506
anda, 312
asso continuo, 1, 43
asso ostinato, 497
bung, 5

bel canto, 789
binary form, 1, 9, 43, 49, 74, 75, 186, 246, 298, 332
binary procedure, 358
buffa, 18, 21, 121, 122, 133, 134, 173, 188, 298, 303

cabaletta, 307, 311, 320, 500
cadenza, 186, 187, 188, 220, 244, 245, 307, 320, 378, 382, 389, 566, 690, 743, 744
canon, 1, 174, 703
cantabile, 63, 298, 307, 311, 312, 320, 411, 501
cantus firmus, 438
canzone, 139, 583, 658
caprice, capriccio, 378–82
castrato, 38, 41, 307
cavatina, 296, 297, 307
changing background variation, 516, 530, 531
choral cabaletta, 411
chorale, 473, 476, 494, 702, 703, 725, 736, 737
chromaticism, 5, 43, 495, 646, 761
chromatic scale, 312, 389, 500, 703
clavichord, 5
coda, 8, 75, 76, 163, 173, 174, 187, 188, 215, 216, 220, 226, 227, 244, 245, 246, 296, 298, 360, 361, 389, 466, 497, 500, 530, 552, 566, 583, 658, 659, 690, 702, 703, 724, 736, 737, 779, 793
codetta, 245, 690
colla parte, 307
col legno, 438
coloratura, 21, 303, 312, 320, 500, 501, 784
concerto, 186–214, 244, 566–73
concert overture, 466, 551
continuo, 1, 5, 38, 43, 122
contradance, 753

counterpoint, 1, 74, 173, 174, 187, 438, 476, 495, 583

da capo aria, 18, 38, 187
da capo form, 15, 75, 779
Deutscher, 779
development, 8, 9, 43, 49, 50, 57, 58, 63, 74, 75, 76, 121, 162, 163, 173, 186, 187, 215, 216, 220, 226, 227, 244, 245, 246, 298, 332, 333, 337, 360, 361, 370, 411, 466, 473, 500, 501, 552, 566, 619, 634, 658, 659, 691, 702, 703, 724, 761
diabolus in musica, 337
Dies irae, 437, 438, 494
diminished-seventh chord, 1, 122, 133, 215, 227, 245, 332, 337, 389
divertimento, 63
double exposition, 566
double return, 1, 2, 8, 9, 43, 49, 57, 64, 75, 187, 227, 566, 703
double stops, 378
downshifting on a single string, 378
drama giocoso, 121
dramatic tableau, 411
dumka, 724–35

Eb clarinet, 437
elision, 74
empfindsamer Stil, 5
etude, 378, 382–88
exposition, 8, 9, 43, 49, 50, 58, 63, 74, 75, 76, 121, 163, 173, 186, 187, 215, 216, 226, 244, 245, 246, 298, 332, 360, 361, 438, 466, 467, 473, 500, 566, 658, 659, 702, 703

fantasy, 5, 8, 244, 389–403, 481–87, 530
"far out point," 1, 8, 9, 43, 57, 58, 63, 74, 75, 76, 162, 186, 187, 226, 244, 245, 298, 307, 370
fermata, 75, 138, 187, 188, 244, 245, 246, 307, 308, 574
French overture, 215, 411
"French-sixth chord" (augmented-sixth chord), 574. See also augmented-sixth chord

fugato, 227, 246
fugue, 134, 173, 296, 437, 473

galant, 1, 122, 173
gallop, 353
"German-sixth chord" (augmented-sixth chord), 358. See also augmented-sixth chord
gigue, 43
grand opera, 404, 411
ground bass, 495, 497, 702, 703

half cadence, 8, 57, 74, 134, 187, 351, 360, 376, 567, 658
Hatikvah, 620

idée fixe, 437, 658
imbroglio, 17, 18, 21, 122, 303, 306
"infinite melody," 574
intermezzo, 15, 21, 488
introduzione, 122, 134

jeté, 378
jig, 15, 21

Kampf und Sieg, 551

kujawiak, 497

left-hand pizzicato, 378
leggiero, 508
leitmotif, 574
libretto, 21, 49, 114, 121, 303, 311, 320, 332, 353, 404, 411, 516, 583, 645, 760, 789
"Lombard" rhythm, 1

"Mannheim rocket," 49, 50
martellato, 382
mazurka, 497–99, 507
medley (potpourri), 389
"melodic recitative," 634
melodrama, 337, 793
mezzo carattere, 121
minuet, 1, 9, 43, 63, 64, 75, 220, 303, 358, 779
minuet-trio form, 75
modal mixture, 358, 634, 725